Shop Floor Control Principles and Practices and Case Studies

Steven A. Melnyk, Ph.D., CPIM
Phillip L. Carter, Ph.D., CFPIM

This publication was prepared through a grant provided by the APICS Educational and Research Foundation.

International Standard Book Number: 0-935406-95-6
Library of Congress Catalog Number: 87-072180

Stock No. 08009, 5/90, 100

With contributions from:
David M. Dilts, associate professor, University of Waterloo, Waterloo, Ontario
David M. Lyth, assistant professor, University of Wisconsin, Eau Claire, Wisconsin

SHOP FLOOR CONTROL PRINCIPLES AND PRACTICES AND CASE STUDIES

Table of Contents

FOREWORD

The key to effective manufacturing lies in a thorough mastery of the basics of manufacturing and production and inventory control (PIC). No firm can hope to implement and use any new technology successfully without first having this mastery. This fact of manufacturing is one often forgotten by managers working under pressure to improve the operation of their production systems. The basics of manufacturing and PIC lie in the development, implementation, and use of a complete and integrated manufacturing system. The components of such a system are familiar to most readers and include the elements of production planning, master scheduling, material and priority planning, capacity planning, and shop floor control working in a closed-loop environment.

To be successful in manufacturing, we must have a thorough understanding of each component. We must be able to recognize and implement those principles and practices that govern each component.

Through the efforts of APICS, we have started to examine, in detail, each component of the manufacturing system and to identify the crucial principles and practices. We have looked at the master scheduling function and begun to understand it. We have also looked at MRP and capacity planning. As a result, we now have a better understanding of the planning side of the manufacturing system.

Today we have a new study -- one that deals with shop floor control. I'm impressed by this study because of the subject matter and the contributions made by the authors. Shop floor control is one area which has always frustrated both PIC managers and students. The idea of being able to identify principles and practices applicable to all shop floor control systems has always seemed to be an impossibility. After all, isn't everyone's shop floor different? But this is exactly what the authors of this study have done. They have looked at a number of firms representing a variety of industries and have identified a number of universal principles of shop floor control. The result is a study which tells other practitioners what shop floor control is (and is not), how it works, how it is linked closely not only with manufacturing planning but also with corporate strategy, what it looks like and what has to be done to make it work. In this study, the experiences of the various firms with shop floor control are covered in a level of detail never before published. The operation of these systems is presented not in isolation but as a part of both the entire manufacturing system and the corporate organization. After reading the individual cases that make up this study, we are shown repeatedly the importance of good control over the execution side of manufacturing. Good planning, no matter how well done, is never enough by itself. We are also shown how planning and execution are closely bonded activities -- each relying on the other.

Shop Floor Control Principles and Practices and Case Studies is a significant and welcome achievement. Coming at a time when our attention is being drawn more and more to the shop floor by such technological innovations as robotics, machine cells, bar coding, and flexible manufacturing systems, this study also represents a timely and needed addition to the body of knowledge. Its publication marks another step in the continuing development of a more complete mastery of the basics of manufacturing.

Great credit is due to APICS, the managers, and the companies that participated in the study, and the two educators who worked to publish this book. Each group has committed a great deal of time and effort to this study. The results are well worth the effort. Without exception, this study is currently the most thorough work on the practice of shop floor control. It is also the first serious study of shop floor control systems in action. This book deserves to have a place in the library and reading list of any serious PIC manager and student.

To the readers who have struggled with the question of how to improve their shop floor control systems, the only recommendation I can make is to read this study and find out.

William R. Wassweiler
President, MRM, Inc.
Brookfield, Wisconsin

PREFACE

...What makes effective shop floor control? How are effective shop floor control systems developed? What lessons can be learned from examining the experiences of effective shop floor control systems? Are there any principles or practices that are associated directly with effective shop floor control?

These and other questions were examined by representatives of thirteen firms in August 1983 at a conference held at Michigan State University, hosted by the American Production and Inventory Control Society (APICS) and the Department of Management of Michigan State University. These firms represented a wide diversity in terms of manufacturing processes, products, company size, nature of ownership, and manufacturing and marketing environment. They shared, however, one important characteristic -- they all had completed, or were in the process of developing effective shop floor control. The management of each firm had struggled with and successfully solved the problem of how to manage the execution side of the manufacturing process effectively and efficiently.

From August 29 to September 1, 1983, firm representatives discussed the development and use of effective shop floor control systems at their firms, the problems and obstacles encountered, and the benefits obtained once these systems were in place and operating. The conference was not to be "show and tell." Instead, it brought together the representatives to share their experiences, learn from each other, and, most importantly, identify principles and practices associated with effective shop floor control systems.

This conference was the culmination of the efforts of the thirteen participating members and a steering committee consisting of APICS members drawn evenly from industry and Michigan State University.

This book brings together the presentations of the thirteen participants and the general thoughts that came from the conference. The presentations found in this book differ from those given at the conference because they have been edited by the authors to ensure that the major features of each firm's shop floor control system can be understood clearly by someone unfamiliar with that system. They also have been edited to conform to a common structure that:

- o Emphasizes the relationship between the planning system and the shop floor control system
- o Focuses attention on the set of activities common to all shop floor control systems
- o Identifies clearly the lessons that can be learned from studying the development and operation of a specific shop floor control system.

This book is the result of a two-stage research project presented by the authors to the Education and Research Foundation of APICS in early 1982. The authors were interested in trying to provide some structure to a very unstructured area of manufacturing -- shop floor control.

A major objective of the first stage was to develop an integrative framework for shop floor control based on a thorough review and evaluation of the shop floor control literature. A second objective was to uncover recommended practices contained in the literature. On the basis of this review, initial expectations of a good shop floor control system were to be developed. A third objective was to develop a glossary of terms applicable to shop floor control. The result of this first phase was the book, Shop Floor Control.[1]

The second stage was concerned with identifying good shop floor control systems and sound principles and practices based on the experiences of those firms with well-developed or leading edge shop floor control systems. This book is the direct result of the second stage. It summarizes the experiences of these few leading edge firms.

The completion of both the book and the conference is due in large part to the efforts of the steering committee. The steering committee, made up of APICS members drawn from industry and Michigan State, was chosen to represent a broad base of opinion, management positions, and types of industry, as well as knowledge about firms actually doing effective shop floor control. The committee members were Ken Jorgensen (vice president, Aladdin Industries); Michael Hablewitz (materials manager, Twin Disc Corp.); Larry Barton and Jim Austhof (Steelcase, Inc.); the two contributors to this book, David Lyth and David Dilts; and the two authors. The steering committee

---

[1]S. A. Melnyk et al., Shop Floor Control (Homewood, Ill.: Dow Jones-Irwin, 1985).

designed the structure for the conference and the individual presentations, helped identify participating firms, and established the conference standards.

The authors acknowledge with appreciation the financial support and encouragement given by the Educational and Research Foundation of APICS under Grant 82-6.

Steven A. Melnyk
Phillip L. Carter

Department of Management
Graduate School of Business Administration
Michigan State University

ACKNOWLEDGMENTS

To my wife, Christine Ann Melnyk

To Gene Woolsey, who has taught me the importance of learning from those that do.

To Leigh Zunke and the members of the APICS Educational and Research Foundation for all their encouragement and patience.

Steven A. Melnyk

To my wife, Sue Ellen Carter

P. L. Carter

CHAPTER 1: THE NEED FOR A STUDY OF SHOP FLOOR CONTROL

INTRODUCTION

Every production manager knows that, even under the best conditions, managing the manufacturing process is not an easy task. There are many factors that must be considered, and there are many things that can go wrong. One fact of manufacturing never changes: Success in manufacturing, however measured (short lead times, high customer service levels, high quality levels), is only achieved when management is able to match good planning with effective implementation of these plans on the shop floor. One component by itself, no matter how well done, is never enough.

Over the past twenty years, most of the significant developments in manufacturing and, specifically, in the area of production and inventory control, have taken place on the planning side. Developments such as material requirements planning (MRP), capacity requirements planning (CRP), the closed-loop MRP system, and manufacturing resource planning have dealt primarily with the planning capabilities of the manufacturing system. These developments have tried to improve the speed and efficiency of the planning function. The benefits that result from the use of these new planning-oriented systems have been sizable and well documented. The development of a matching excellence in execution has been ignored until recently.

Managers are now aware of this execution side of the manufacturing system. In part, this awareness is due to the increasing use of such new manufacturing developments as just-in-time (JIT) manufacturing, computer-aided design/computer-aided manufacturing (CAD/CAM), computer-integrated manufacturing (CIM), group technology, flexible manufacturing systems (FMS), and automated identification (e.g., bar coding). The effects of these developments are most evident on the shop floor. Whatever the reason, the focus is now shifting to shop floor control, the manufacturing system responsible for the management of the shop floor.

Shop floor control is known under several different names: manufacturing activity planning, production activity control, or job shop control (Browne, Boon, and Davies 1981).[1] Regardless of the name, shop floor

---

[1] In this study, the terms manufacturing activity planning, production activity control, and job shop control are viewed as interchangeable. The term, shop floor control, is used throughout the report because it is believed that more people are familiar with this term than the others.

control plays an important part in any successful manufacturing system. It complements the activities of the manufacturing planning system (Figure 1-1) and is an integral element of a complete manufacturing system. Shop floor control uses information provided by the planning system to identify those orders for which action must be taken. The system is responsible for allocating resources (in the form of labor, tooling, material, and equipment) to the various orders on the shop floor, for preventive maintenance, and for the overall management of the flow of production orders and their attendant information flows. How important is shop floor control? Without an effective shop floor control system, management has no real control over costs, lead time, and quality. These dimensions are the ones on which most firms compete in today's marketplace.

In spite of its importance to manufacturing, shop floor control is a manufacturing mystery. While every firm must have a shop floor control system to control the shop floor, little is known about the total system. While there is a sizable body of knowledge dealing with the activities of shop floor control (e.g., dispatching, sequencing, monitoring, shop floor data collection),[2] there is little that looks at the structure. In short, shop floor control, as a concept and manufacturing subsystem, is a source of confusion, which is shared by the manufacturing manager and the researcher.

At the center of this confusion lies one inescapable fact: Shop floor control is not understood completely. Most manufacturing managers are able to identify some of the individual components and activities of shop floor control. Any manager knows that this system must assign operation priorities to orders, and that this system must collect data from the shop floor. Few, however, have been able to grasp the total concept. As a result, there appears to be very little agreement over the structure (components) of shop floor control. What is missing currently is an integrative and unifying framework and an extensive study describing the design and implementation of effective shop floor control systems. This study will fill those needs. Except for the occasional glimpse at an APICS conference or in literature, very little is known about which firms have

---

[2]This literature is reviewed in Appendix A of Melnyk, Carter, Dilts, and Lyth (1985). A copy of this report can be obtained from either Dow Jones-Irwin or the Educational and Research Foundation of APICS.

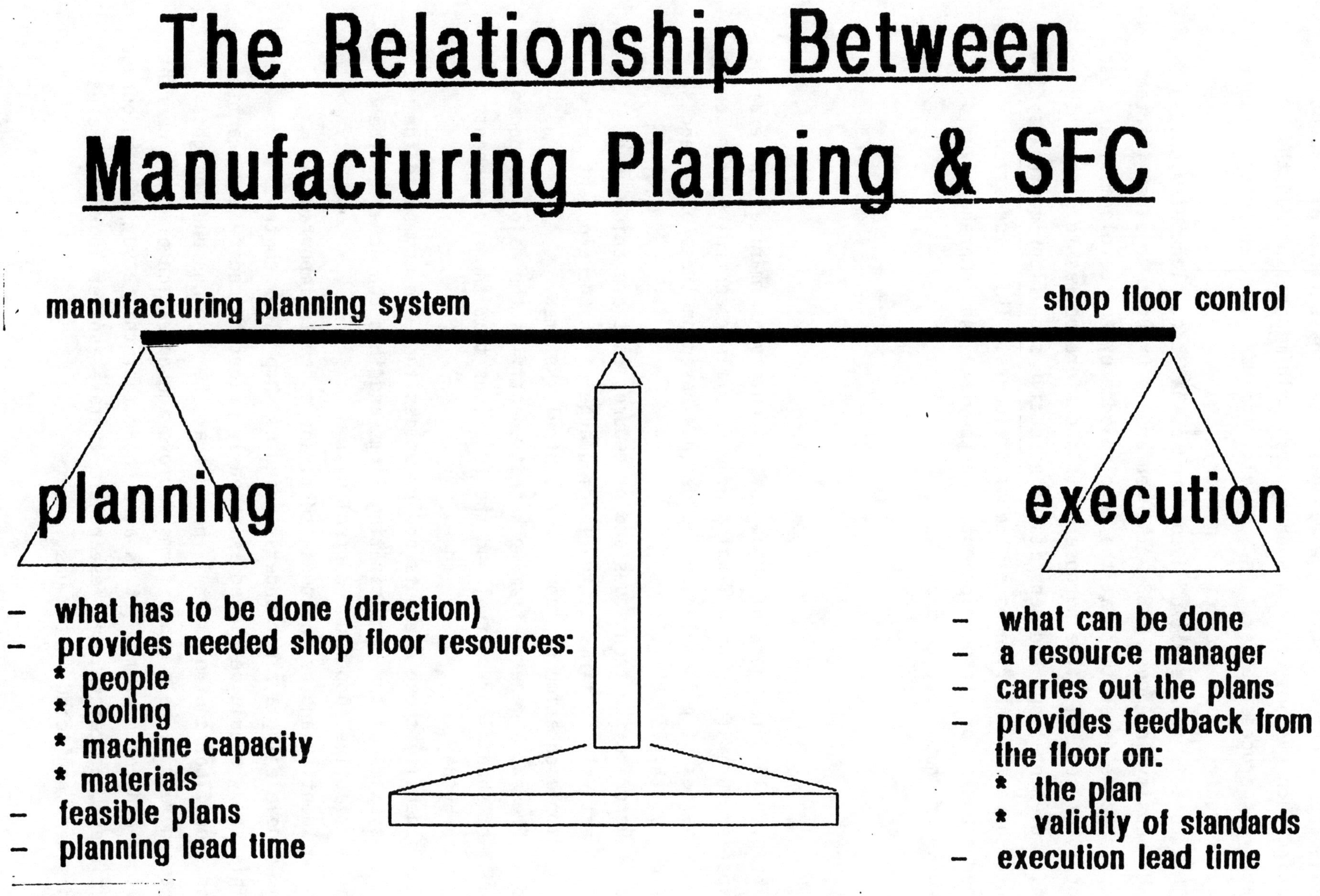
The Relationship Between
Manufacturing Planning & SFC
manufacturing planning system
shop floor control
planning
execution
– what has to be done (direction)
– provides needed shop floor resources:
* people
* tooling
* machine capacity
* materials
– feasible plans
– planning lead time
– what can be done
– a resource manager
– carries out the plans
– provides feedback from the floor on:
* the plan
* validity of standards
– execution lead time

Figure 1-1.

effective shop floor controls, how management in these firms went about developing such systems, or how such systems help management run the manufacturing process better. As a result, for many manufacturing managers, shop floor control is a production mystery.

This book is the result of a conference that took place at Michigan State University in August 1983. The conference brought together thirteen firms, each considered to be at the leading edge of the development and use of shop floor control. The purpose of this conference was to discuss the design, implementation, and benefits of effective shop floor control systems and to compare the experiences of the participants. This discussion provided a basis for the development of a complete and comprehensive framework for shop floor control.

OBJECTIVES

The overall intent of this book is to identify, summarize, and examine the experiences of firms with leading edge shop floor control systems and to develop a series of principles and guidelines based on these experiences. Specifically, this book will:

- Describe the techniques and procedures that are being used actively by firms at the leading edge of the development and implementation of shop floor control systems
- Present a general framework that identifies the major components of shop floor control and the functions that these components provide
- Identify those elements and practices that are common to the systems of the participating firms and that characterize the effective shop floor control system
- Identify and define those terms and concepts important in developing a clear understanding of shop floor control.

This study should be viewed as an early effort to codify the practices of good shop floor control. It is hoped that the findings and insights presented here will help other firms improve the operation of their current shop floor control systems. It is also hoped that this study will encourage practitioners, educators, and researchers to take another look at an area that has been neglected in the past.

FOCUS

The results reported in this book apply primarily to shop floor control systems developed for use in a job shop (i.e., discrete batch manufacturing). The decision to focus on one specific manufacturing setting reflects the view that it is impossible to cover comprehensively all information about shop floor control systems required for the major manufacturing settings.

Production can take place in a wide range of settings. These settings occupy a continuum that can be broken conveniently into the three major manufacturing categories of repetitive/continuous, job shop (discrete batch), and project. Each category has specific requirements and each needs a shop floor control system specifically tailored to these requirements. It is meaningful to identify and discuss principles and practices of effective shop floor control only as they pertain to each of these three categories. For most readers, the job shop setting is the one of greatest interest and, thus, the focus of this study.

APPROACH

This study was predicated on four major considerations. First, only operating shop floor control systems were to be studied, and only those firms considered to be in the forefront of the development and use of shop floor control were included. Second, knowledge of these systems and their operation would be obtained by having each firm prepare and present a detailed written presentation on its system. These presentations would summarize the most salient features of their systems and describe the factors affecting the development of the systems. These presentations would also serve as a starting point for discussions. Third, the firms examined would represent as much diversity as possible in terms of manufacturing processes, products, company size, nature of ownership, and manufacturing and marketing environments. This diversity would provide a base on which valid generalizations could be made. Fourth, when summarizing the firms' experiences, the presentations would all use the same format to emphasize structure similarities of the various shop floor control systems and to simplify the process of understanding these systems. All four considerations were achieved.

A PERSPECTIVE

This report represents the second stage of a comprehensive study dealing with the theory and practice of shop floor control. In the first part,[3] the shop floor control literature was reviewed and summarized. This first part also identified the major terms of shop floor control and presented an integrating framework.

The second stage, and the focus of this report, is concerned with identifying what constitutes a good shop floor control system and good principles and practices as observed in those firms identified as having well-developed or leading edge shop floor control systems. An important consideration of this second phase involves the degree to which the practices identified in the review of the literature coincide with the practices observed in the leading edge firms.

STUDY BACKGROUND

When examining shop floor control as it is carried out in those firms at the leading edge, the first step was to identify those firms that satisfied basic requirements. This information was obtained by soliciting the opinions of those persons considered to be familiar with the current state of shop floor control in industry. The persons contacted included industry consultants and selected practitioners who were asked to nominate any firms that they considered to have a good shop floor control system.

Next, the members of the research team contacted managers from each of the nominated firms. Each manager was asked to complete a questionnaire (included in Appendix B) about the firm's shop floor control system. In addition, each firm was asked to be a participant in a conference on shop floor control. Conditions for participation (in Appendix B) were presented and the invited firms agreed to meet these conditions. Thirteen firms agreed to attend the conference. The names of the participants from these firms are in Appendix C. This report summarizes the conference findings.

---

[3] S. A. Melnyk et al., Shop Floor Control (Homewood, Ill.: Dow Jones-Irwin, 1985).

ORGANIZATION OF THE REPORT

The principles and practices of effective shop floor control are presented in the eighteen chapters and four appendices of this book. These chapters and appendices are broken down into three parts:

- o Part One -- Shop Floor Control: Prelude
- o Part Two -- Shop Floor Control: Presentations
- o Part Three -- Shop Floor Control: Appendices

Part One, consisting of four chapters, is an overview of shop floor control. It also summarizes the major lessons that were learned while studying the experiences of the thirteen participating firms. The book begins with a description of the shop floor control framework and discusses the various components and functions of the system in Chapter 2. In Chapter 3, the general principles developed as a result of the conference are summarized. These principles are elements common to each of the participating firms. The major characteristics of the firms are summarized in Chapter 4.

Part Two looks at effective shop floor control systems in action. Chapters 5 through 17 describe the shop floor control system of each of the thirteen participating firms. Chapter 18 provides observations on shop floor control and the current state of the art. The references for this report are contained in Appendix A.

Because shop floor control consistently deals with a central set of terms and concepts, a glossary of these terms is presented in Appendix D. The purpose of this glossary is twofold. First, it aids the readers as they proceed through the various chapters. Second, it standardizes shop floor control terminology. Part Three consists of all four appendices.

For those readers who may not want to read the whole book, the following strategy is proposed. Readers must first understand the framework presented in Chapter 2 and be familiar with the associated functions and terminology. Next, it is important that readers become familiar with the key common techniques and principles that were found in the participating firms (Chapter 3). Readers can examine the descriptions of the shop floor control systems presented in the subsequent chapters and can select those firms most similar to their own companies by consulting the summarized characteristics contained in Chapter 4.

The reader is encouraged to review the descriptions of all the shop floor control systems. Much can be learned about the systems by studying the firms operating in different production environments. As is evident from Chapter 4, the diversity among the participating firms is extensive. However readers choose to approach the various shop floor control systems, they are asked to compare the systems described in Chapter 2 and the general principles of Chapter 3.

A Note on the Format of the Presentations

Each presentation follows the same format to help the reader develop a better understanding of each system and to focus on the similarities that are present among systems. The format is:

- o <u>General nature of the firm</u>. The first section identifies the firm and its general characteristics, such as location of the firm; product line; size (annual sales and number of employees); number of divisions; major customers; nature of ownership (private vs. public); nature of labor force (union or nonunion); the nature of business; and the key success factors for the firm. The last factor identifies how the firm competes and what it must do well if it intends to succeed in the market for the long term.
- o <u>Production process</u>. The second section describes the major characteristics of the production process. For example, the nature of production (e.g., assembly line vs. job shop); number of end items produced; average run sizes; average capacity utilization; composition of the manufacturing facilities; and key manufacturing considerations are discussed. This last factor consists of those characteristics of the production process that have an impact on the resulting shop floor control system.
- o <u>Production planning</u>. The third section describes the production planning system. This discussion is important because it looks at the links between the two major manufacturing subsystems: the planning system and the shop floor control system.
- o <u>Shop floor control -- an overview</u>. The general elements of each firm's shop floor control system are discussed. Among the factors examined are the background to the current system; degree to which the system is computerized; objectives for the current system; organizational features of the current system (i.e., which position in the firm is responsible for shop floor control, how much people are involved in the function); and the major tenets of

shop floor control. Every firm's system is built on certain beliefs or tenets that are evident in both the structure and operation of the system.

- o Stages of shop floor control. The fifth section describes how the firm goes about carrying out the various activities of shop floor control (as described in Chapter 2), and how the firm evaluates and views its current system. This section also identifies and discusses the benefits that have occurred at the firm as a direct result of its shop floor control system, and discusses the next stage for the current system.
- o Lessons to be learned. The final section examines those lessons that can be learned from studying each firm's shop floor control system. The lessons are those features of the current system that management feels have played an important role in the system's success.

SUMMARY

The development and implementation of an effective shop floor control system are not easy tasks. The tasks cannot be done successfully by any one group nor can they be done in isolation. The tasks involve the careful fitting together of many different elements. If successfully achieved, however, the benefits to the firm are substantial. Effective shop floor control offers management a method to differentiate its firm from competition in an increasingly competitive marketplace.

CHAPTER 2: THE FRAMEWORK OF SHOP FLOOR CONTROL

INTRODUCTION

This report examines those practices and principles of effective shop floor control systems, as observed in its leading practitioners. Before looking at these practices, a thorough understanding of what shop floor control is and what it does is necessary. This understanding is developed through an integrating framework.

The framework is developed in three parts. First, shop floor control is defined. This is critical because there is no real agreement among production managers or researchers.[1] This definition sets the stage for the shop floor control framework used in this study. This framework, presented in the second part, can be viewed as being nothing more than an expansion of the definition. Within this framework, the major activities of all shop floor control systems are identified. Third, the relationships that exist between these activities are examined. Finally, the chapter concludes with a discussion of two critical prerequisites to effective shop floor control:

- The effective, format manufacturing planning system
- The manufacturing database.

In leaving the discussion of these two elements until the end of this chapter, a natural bridge between this chapter and the next has been created. The principles and practices of effective shop floor control drawn from the experiences of the conference participants can be summarized and examined.

SHOP FLOOR CONTROL: DEFINING THE SYSTEM

Shop floor control, an integral element of any production and inventory control system, enables management to control the transformation process. The presence of a shop floor control system is crucial to the successful operation of any manufacturing system. It is as important to the firm as is

---

[1] S. A. Melnyk et al., Shop Floor Control (Homewood, Ill.: Dow Jones-Irwin, 1985).

the presence of a formal material and priority planning system (e.g., material requirements planning).

Shop floor control systems are as diverse as the companies that use them. At one extreme, there are very sophisticated computerized shop floor control systems that can track and record the progress of a job at every stage of the process. At the opposite extreme, there are very simple informal systems, completely manual in operation. This diversity in shop floor control systems is not surprising given the differences in production processes.

Production processes have numerous configurations, ranging from a project layout to the assembly line. Each configuration has different information requirements, and each type of process must manage different forms of resources and track various types of shop orders. The lead times for the different processes vary, thus affecting the speed of response and reaction required of the shop floor control system. As a result, each type of production configuration must be controlled differently. The observed variety in shop floor control systems partially reflects management's attempts to match the capabilities of the control system with requirements of the transformation process. In spite of these differences, all shop floor control systems, regardless of where they are found, are similar in what they do and how they do it. These similarities are reflected in the definition of shop floor control.

SHOP FLOOR CONTROL DEFINED

What does shop floor control mean? A broad definition is:

> Shop floor control is that group of activities directly responsible for managing the transformation of planned orders into a set of outputs. It governs the very short-term detailed planning, execution, and monitoring activities needed to control the flow of an order from the moment the order is released by the planning system for execution until the order is filled and its disposition completed. The shop floor control system is responsible for making the detailed and final allocation of labor, machine capacity, tooling, and materials to the various competing orders. It collects data on the activities taking place on the shop floor involving the progress of various orders and the status of resources and makes this information available to the planning system. Finally, the shop floor control system is responsible for ensuring that the shop orders released to the shop floor by the planning system are completed in a timely and cost-effective manner. (ibid., p. 35)

This definition views shop floor control as a subsystem within the entire manufacturing system that complements other planning systems such as MRP and CRP. Shop floor control closes the loop between the planning and execution phases of the manufacturing system by feeding back information from the shop floor to the planning systems.

ELEMENTS OF THE FRAMEWORK

The Shop Order

A focal point of any shop floor control system is the shop order. In the typical job shop, the individual order is the focus because the planning system releases individual orders to the shop floor. In continuous/repetitive manufacturing settings, however, the planning system releases schedules, which consist of groups of orders. In this setting, shop floor control deals with orders in aggregate. All of the activities undertaken by the shop floor control system are directed at ensuring the timely and efficient completion of the shop order, either individually or collectively. In this report, the individual shop order is considered.

The shop order is an authorization given by the planning system for the shop to produce a predetermined quantity of a particular item (as identified by its part number) to arrive in inventory at a prespecified time (i.e., the order due date). The shop order allows the shop floor control system personnel to allocate the physical resources (i.e., inventory, machines, labor, and tooling) against the order.

There are two flows accompanying the shop order that the shop floor control system must manage -- product flow, and the attendant physical allocation of resources, and information flow. As the shop order progresses through the various stages of processing, it generates information that is then used to monitor its progress. This flow of information, used by the planning system and the shop floor control system, allows the latter to close the loop initiated by the planning system.

Forms of the Shop Order

When first released by the planning system, the shop order is simply a statement of intent. It describes the requirements of the planning system in terms of quantity, part number, and order due date. As the order moves from operation to operation on the shop floor, it undergoes a series of physical changes. At each operation, the addition of material components, labor, tooling, and machining alters the order, bringing it closer to the desired finished form. After each operation is completed, a decision must be made about how to handle the order next. This decision is made by comparing the actual progress of the order with its planned progress.

If the actual quality progress of the order is within tolerance limits acceptable to management, the order is directed to the next operation (as specified in its routings). When the actual quality progress is not acceptable, some form of corrective action must be initiated by management. In some cases, correcting the problem may call for simply rescheduling the problem order. In most other cases, however, correcting the problem may require management to change the order, either in whole or in part, into one of three other forms: rework, salvage, or scrap. Each form requires different handling by the shop floor control system.

Rework

Rework refers to those items that can be brought up to the required quality levels by extra processing or special handling. Some parts may be unacceptable because of correctable processing defects (e.g., excessive or insufficient cutting, insufficient grinding). As a result, rework often requires a change in the standard routing to reflect these additional corrective actions. The lead time for rework items usually is longer than that of a normal or nonrework item. When these corrective actions are completed successfully, the rework portion of the order should meet the quality specifications.

Rework items require different handling and in many manufacturing systems, they are given their own identity by the system. The rest of the original order is adjusted to reflect the effect of the rework (the order quantity is reduced by the amount of rework) and a new order, with its own due date and order quantity (equal to the amount of the rework), is created. The new order due date may or may not be the same as the order due date of the original order, depending on the amount of additional lead time needed for rework. These two orders are now controlled separately by the planning system. By creating new order identities for rework items, planners recognize that rework cannot be controlled the same way as nonrework. The integrity of the system is maintained.

Rework is only a temporary form of shop order. If the rework operations are successful, the reworked parts, as a separate entity, disappear as soon as they have completed the rest of the route. Rework does not guarantee that the items will meet specifications. After rework, the items must be inspected either by an inspector or the operator. If the items do not meet specifications, they undergo a further transformation and become either salvage or scrap.

Salvage

Salvage describes that portion of a shop order that cannot be completed as initially planned and released. The items cannot be recovered by converting them into a rework order, but they still are useful to the system. This usefulness comes in one of two forms -- order salvage and component salvage.

In order salvage, the problem items can be processed and completed in a form that is different from that required by the planning system but still usable by the planning system. A classic example of order salvage involves a company that manufactures two types of cloth, a 60-inch bolt and a 48-inch bolt. The planning system has released a shop order for a quantity of cloth in 60-inch bolts. During process, a defect is discovered in the 12 inches. The order can no longer be completed as initially released, but it is still useful to the planning system. It can be recut into a 48-inch bolt. The cloth can now be completed and put into the inventory.

Component salvage, in contrast, involves recovering any components used in the manufacture of the affected items. For example, an inspector has failed a computer board because of defects in the connectors on the board. The board uses several expensive chips that socket into it. The board itself cannot be recovered, but the components (chips) can be. During salvage operations, these chips are removed by the worker and returned to component stores (where they increase the available on-hand balance).

Like rework, salvage must be treated as a separate entity by the planning system. Salvage can generate two different effects. If completed, salvage can result in an unplanned increase in inventory (either at the component or completed assembly levels). This increase may require that the planning system adjust its production schedule to reflect this unanticipated change in inventory. Second, if a shop order, either all or part, becomes salvage, then the order, as initially planned and released, can no longer be completed. The order quantity of the original order is now decremented by the amount of salvage. The planning system now has an unfilled need. As a result, the presence of salvage may require the release of another shop order that is primarily remedial (i.e., intended to fulfill the initial needs of the planning system).

Scrap

Scrap denotes an order that can no longer be completed into a part to be used by the system either as originally intended or as salvage. For all purposes, scrap is useless to the planning system. (This does not mean that scrap is useless to everyone. Often scrap may have high value when sold to an outside processor.) In the case of scrap, the shop floor control system must still account for the shop order and must supervise its disposal.

Scrap should never be confused with salvage. Scrap is not usable by the planning system; salvage has an item or component still usable by the system. A defective part that can be remelted into a metal ingot is salvage; a defective part that must be thrown out by the system is scrap.

The shop floor control system must recognize that any shop order, as it progresses through the various operations on the shop floor, can take on several different forms. The form taken can change for operation to operation. The system must always be able to control the movement of the shop order regardless of the form that it takes.

The Major Resources Controlled by Shop Floor Control

Shop floor control manages the flow of shop orders and allocates various quantities of four resources to the shop order. These resources are:

- Workers. This resource includes all of the personnel that the shop floor can draw on to execute the plans released to it. The personnel resource can take various forms such as overtime, workers transferred in from other locations, part-time help, and multiple shift operations. Work force includes both direct and indirect labor.
- Tooling. Tooling is all of the equipment and special fixtures that are used during the setup and operation of a machine or assembly operation.

- <u>Machine capacity</u>. This is the total amount of productive capacity offered by the equipment available.
- <u>Material</u>. Material is the total stock of components that can be used to complete shop orders.

The shop floor control system does not determine the level of each resource that can be drawn. That task is a primary responsibility of the planning system. The planning system determines the total amount of material available, and it also sets the number of work-hours that are available in any one period. In this sense, the planning system constrains the shop floor control system by placing an upper limit on the availability of these resources.

The shop floor control system is responsible for working within these constraints. It makes the detailed allocation of resources to the various shop orders and controls and monitors the use of these resources when they are assigned.

The Major Activities of Shop Floor Control

The activities governed by shop floor control can be divided into five groups -- order review/release, detailed assignment (the scheduling of orders and facilities), data collection/monitoring, feedback/corrective action, and order disposition. These activity groups encompass the entire process of transforming a planned order into a completed order that is available to support the further activities of the planning system. A schematic of this process and the position of these five groups are shown in Figure 2-1.

<u>Order Review/Release</u>

Order review/release includes those activities that must take place before an order can be released to the shop floor. These activities are necessary to control the flow of information and orders passing from the planning system to the execution system and to ensure that the released orders have a reasonable chance of being completed on time and in the quantity wanted. The first of the order review/release activities is order documentation.

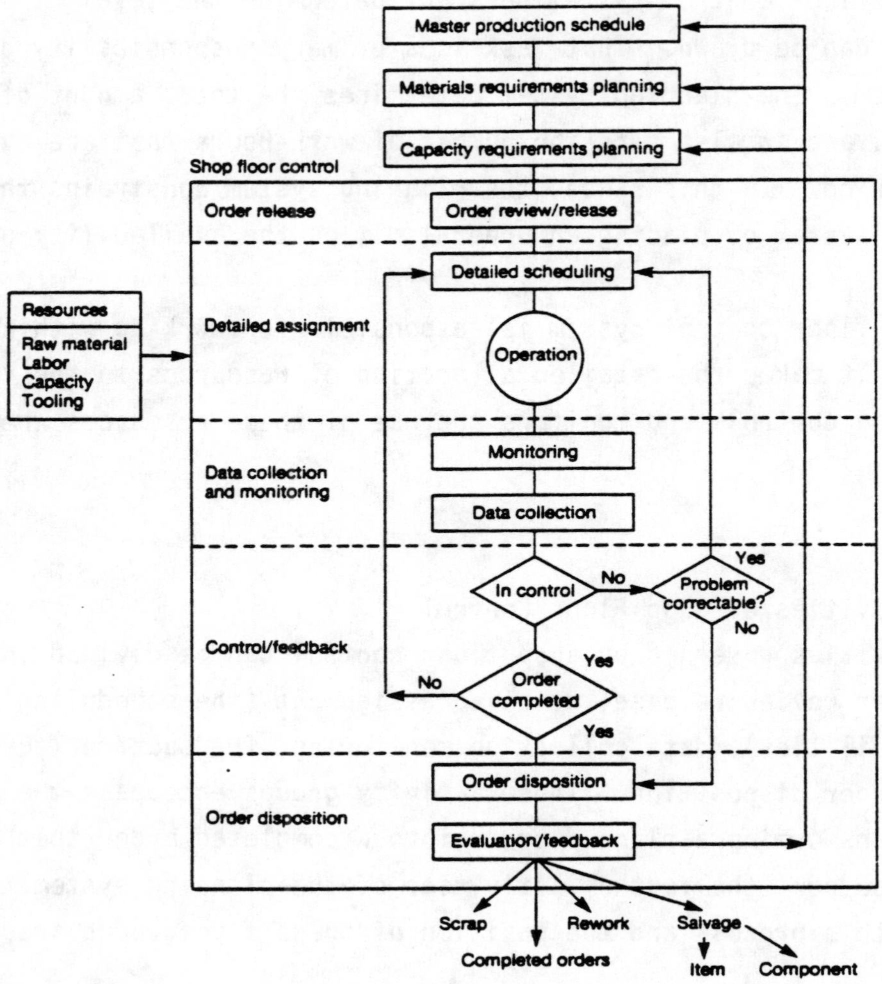

Figure 2-1. -- An Integrative Framework

Order documentation

An order, once it matures, can be regarded as an authorization to produce a specified quantity of a specified item by a specified time. The order documentation activities provide information not given by the planning system but needed by the shop floor. Typically, the following information is added to the order at this stage:

- o Order identification. The order is given a number or code that can be used to track the order on the floor and to retrieve necessary information about the order (e.g., the processing time or next operation). The order identification (which may be distinct from the part number) links the shop floor with the planning system.
- o Routings. The order is described in terms of the various operations through which it must pass. The routing also helps identify order's resource requirements.
- o Time standards. The order is described in terms of the resources (machine and labor) required at each stage in its transformation. Such information is important for activities such as order sequencing (dispatching), monitoring, and capacity management.
- o Material requirements. The order is described in terms of the raw material and components needed and the stage in the process at which these components are needed.
- o Tooling requirements. Orders, as they progress through their various stages, may require special tools. The tooling needed by the order and the stage at which this tooling is required must be identified and the information provided to the shop order. This information forms the basis for issuing the tool order.
- o Other. Other information provided at this stage may include report forms, operation due dates, and any special handling requirements.

Material checking

Another part of the order review/release activity is checking the inventory status of those components and raw materials required by the shop order to ensure that they will be available in sufficient quantity at the necessary time. By ensuring that orders released to the floor will have the necessary components, shop floor control keeps work-in-process (WIP) inventory low and avoids needlessly tying up shop capacity.

Capacity evaluation

Inventory availability, by itself, is a necessary but not a sufficient condition for the successful completion of a shop order. Another requirement is the availability of capacity. In the capacity evaluation activity, the capacity required by the shop order is compared against the capacity available in the system. If the capacity is not adequate, then the release of the order may be delayed until such capacity becomes available. By evaluating capacity, shop overload, with increased queues and lengthened lead times, is avoided.

Load leveling

The final activity assigned to order review/release is load leveling. The orders that are recommended for release by the planning system are not released immediately in most shop floor control systems. Instead, they are accumulated (backlogged) for a short time to level the load on the shop floor by controlling the rate at which orders are released to the floor. This activity seeks to ensure that capacity use is high by smoothing out the peaks and valleys of the load on work centers. This pool of backlogged orders effectively decouples the planning system from the shop floor system.

The various activities of order review/release are essentially short-term planning activities that occur before the other shop floor control activities. They also decouple the planning system from the shop floor and do not require that the resources required by the various matured orders actually be committed. Instead, the availability of these resources is evaluated to determine if there are sufficient resources to justify the release of the order. The actual commitment of shop floor resources to a given order is the major focus of the second set of shop floor control activities termed detailed assignment.

<u>Detailed Assignment</u>

The shop floor control system has to manage the allocation of the four major resources under its control -- material, labor (both direct and indirect), tooling, and machine capacity. These resources must be used to satisfy not only the demand of competing orders but also other activities required to continue the provision of these resources (e.g., scheduled preventive maintenance). The activities included in detailed assignment are responsible for formally matching (assigning) the supplies of shop floor resources with the competing demands being placed on these resources. When matching supply with demand, the assignment decisions made must be detailed enough to address the following concerns:

- Type of resources. The assignment of resources must identify the specific type of resource.
- Quantity of resources. The amount of the resource to be used must be identified in terms meaningful for the assignment. For example, the amount of labor to be used may be described in terms of standard labor-hours.
- Timing of assignment. The time at which the resource(s) is to be assigned must be identified, including the expected time the resource is to be assigned and the expected time the resource is to be released.
- Placement of resources. If the resource to be assigned is available in more than one location, then the assignment procedure should identify the location that is to be allocated to the given order.
- Priority of processing. The final aspect of the assignment process is determining the sequence in which competing orders are to be permitted access to the limited resources. The priority rules are used to manage the backlog of demand that may occur at each resource location (e.g., work center).

Three major activities make up detailed assignment. These are order sequencing/dispatching, scheduled maintenance, and other assignments.

Order sequencing/dispatching

Once a shop order is released to the shop floor, it must compete with other orders for access to resources. These orders are often differentiated by order due dates, amount of processing time required at the various operations, amount of slack remaining (order due date minus remaining processing time) until the order is needed, and the number of operations left until the order is done. The process of assigning resources to shop orders is called order sequencing/dispatching. For most shop floor control systems, this activity is one of the most visible. It is also one that has been the focus of much of the shop floor control literature.

In this study, order sequencing/dispatching is defined as:

> ...the process of determining by means of a prespecified set of rules, the sequence in which a facility is to process a number of different shop orders. When processing these orders, order sequencing/dispatching is also responsible for the corresponding assignment of workers, tooling, and material to selected jobs. The sequence of resource assignment is consistent with a predetermined set of goals that the shop floor control system attempts to satisfy (meeting due dates, reducing maximum lateness of orders, etc.). (ibid., p. 44)

The major task of order sequencing/dispatching is setting the order priorities that help determine the order competing jobs gain access to the capacity of a work center. A decision procedure referred to as either a dispatching rule or a priority rule can be used to determine order priority. Earliest due date, earliest operation due date, shortest processing time, and critical ratio are typical dispatching rules found under order sequencing/dispatching.

Scheduled maintenance

The second activity of the detailed assignment phase is scheduled maintenance -- the assignment of resources to preventive maintenance. Preventive maintenance can be defined as:

> ...maintenance work to be repeated at intervals. It includes both minor operations like lubrication and inspection, and major jobs like the overhaul of a press. (IBM COPICS, Vol. 1., 1972, p. 13)

Shop floor resources do not have infinite lives. They are subject to the wear and tear that day-to-day operations place on them. Periodically, machines break down and when they do, the production capabilities are lost temporarily. The longer the shop floor resources are operated without scheduled maintenance, the greater the chance of a breakdown. The intent of scheduled maintenance is to reduce and, if possible, eliminate the risk of such breakdowns.

Preventive maintenance involves occasionally withdrawing various shop floor resources such as machines, tools, and dies from shop use while they are worked on. The use of shop floor resources for preventive maintenance can be regarded as a nonproductive use of resources. That is, while preventive maintenance takes place, no additional units of output are produced. When a resource is scheduled for preventive maintenance, its availability for processing shop orders is reduced in the short run. Preventive maintenance prolongs or improves resource availability in the long run.

The management of preventive maintenance is considered part of the detailed assignment phase of shop floor control. The same detailed resource assignment decisions made for shop orders during order sequencing/dispatching must also be made for the preventive maintenance activities. In most facilities, these maintenance activities often compete with shop orders for access to resources.

Other assignments

Shop floor resources are also assigned to other activities such as scheduled downtime or indirect labor activities. Such activities may take place to level current capacity use (in the case of scheduled downtime) or to use capacity that is currently available but not required by the orders on the shop floor (in the case of the transfer of workers to indirect labor activities).

Data Collection/Monitoring

Information plays a very important role in shop floor control and is the link between the planning and execution systems. This information flow is bidirectional. The planning system keeps the shop floor informed of any changes in planned requirements (e.g., the cancellation/addition of orders, customer-requested changes in order due dates). In turn, the shop floor control system keeps the planning system aware of the progress of any and all open orders. It also informs the planning system of conditions on the shop floor (e.g., level of capacity utilization, status of various shop resources). The process of collecting and analyzing the information generated on the shop floor is the primary responsibility of the data collection/monitoring activity.

The first task of this activity involves the collection of information pertaining to the actual progress of an order as it moves through the shop. Information collected includes:

- Current location of the shop order
- Current state of completion
- Actual resources used at current operation
- Actual resources used at preceding operations
- Any unplanned delays encountered.

Data collection is an objective recording of information pertaining to any given order. No interpretation is added to the information provided. The information must be compared with a standard before management can react to it. The task of comparing the actual performance and progress of the shop order with its planned progress is called monitoring.

The standards used in monitoring can be based on engineering or accounting information, past performance (i.e., last year's performance), or management's expectations. Monitoring requires not only a set of standards but also a tolerance. Tolerances set the amount of deviation considered acceptable between actual and standard. The purpose of monitoring is to identify those orders that fall outside the tolerances. Such orders often require special management attention. Monitoring is done not only on shop orders but also on the status of shop resources. This evaluation is done either periodically (e.g., at the end of every shift or every week) or continuously (e.g., as each item comes out of the process). This special attention is the major responsibility of the fourth major activity in shop floor control -- control/feedback.

Control/Feedback

Corrective action by management is required any time the actual progress of a shop order exceeds some predefined margin of difference from its planned progress. Progress can be monitored along several different dimensions: stage of completion, costs, scrap produced, or nearness to due date. This margin of error, set by management, partially reflects such considerations as the relative costs of having late and early orders. The orders requiring management intervention may include orders that are ahead or behind their planned progress. There are two different forms of corrective action that management can take:

- o <u>Capacity control</u>. The short-term adjustment of the shop floor capacity to compensate for any difficulties being experienced.
- o <u>Feedback</u>. Information pertaining to the actual progress of orders on the shop floor is related from the shop floor control system to the planning system. Frequently, the information communicated involves orders experiencing difficulties that cannot be solved by the shop floor control system alone. At this stage, the planning system may choose to evaluate alternatives to correct the problems. Frequently, the corrective actions introduced at the planning

system affect either the demand on the shop floor or the demand for the problem orders themselves.

Capacity control refers to any corrective actions taken by management that attempt to correct the problems by short-term adjustments in the level of resources available on the shop floor. Examples of short-term shop adjustments are changes in work rate; use of overtime or part-time labor; use of safety capacity, alternate routings, and lot splitting; and subcontracting of excess work. In the preceding list, the flow of orders onto the shop floor largely is left unaltered. Instead, these adjustments alter the amount of capacity available on the shop floor in the short term.

Under certain conditions, the problem(s) with a shop order may not be addressed adequately by such capacity changes. In these instances, the shop floor control system may be required to inform the planning systems of the problems (via the feedback link). At this point, the planning system may examine how best to adjust those plans affected by the problem orders. The adjustments may involve changing the due date for the order, canceling the order, reducing the load coming into the shop (in order to free up capacity), or changing the quantity needed. These changes alter the demand of the planning system for the output of the production system and because of feedback, take place only after the shop floor control system has determined that the short-term changes in capacity are not sufficient.

A key element of control/feedback is exception reporting. Control/feedback produces information that requires some form of management action. Exception reporting serves to direct this information to the manager or managers who are responsible for taking the appropriate corrective actions.

Order Disposition

The final set of activities is order disposition, which is required to transfer an order out of the shop floor control system. This stage is responsible for both completed orders and scrap. Order disposition has two major objectives:

- To relieve the shop floor of responsibility for these items
- To provide the rest of the firm with ending information on which to evaluate the performance of the shop floor.

In the case of an acceptable completed order, order disposition relieves the shop floor by updating the inventory records and informs the planning system by changing the status of the orders from WIP to on hand.

Alternatively, in the case of scrap, order disposition transfers the items from WIP to one or more profit and loss accounts. For example, if there is no recoverable salvage value, the cost of the scrapped items is charged off to an expense account such as scrap expenses. If there is some recoverable salvage value, the scrapped items can be charged off to a combination of revenue and expense accounts. Regardless of how the order is treated, the items must be accounted for both in terms of unit quantities and cost.

As part of order disposition, the quantity received from the shop floor is recorded, and the performance of the shop floor system is evaluated. The performance evaluation involves recording the actual performance of the shop in completing the order. Performance measures collected may include:

- The number of labor-hours required
- The breakdown of labor-hours between regular time and overtime
- The materials required by the order
- The number of hours of setup time required
- The amount of tooling required
- Completion date of the order
- Amount of rework or scrap generated by the order
- The number of machine-hours required.

This information is made available for use by other departments in the firm and forms the basis for various cost-based reports. It also enables management to evaluate the shop floor control system by comparing actual performance with planned performance. Finally, the information collected during order disposition is used by management to identify and solve longer term problems involving the shop floor (e.g., the lack of demonstrated capacity) and to modify the cost and time standards used by the planning system.

Interactions Among the Major Activities of Shop Floor Control

The five major activities of the shop floor control framework are not independent of each other nor do they take place all at once. Instead, these activities are interrelated and ongoing. For example, consider the detailed assignment, data collection/monitoring, and control/feedback activities. At every stage of processing the order, shop floor personnel must decide whether the order is completed, ready to go on to the next stage, or in need of special or additional treatment. Determining the status of the order is a function of the data collection/monitoring and control/feedback activities. If the order is ready to go on to the next stage, the activities of detailed assignment will be invoked. The activity on the shop floor, as related by the data collection/monitoring and control/feedback activities, influences the order review/release and order disposition activities. It is these relationships that make shop floor control a system.

PREREQUISITES TO EFFECTIVE SHOP FLOOR CONTROL

All shop floor control systems must carry out the five major activities described in this chapter. These activities by themselves, however, do not ensure an effective shop floor control system. Effectiveness can be defined generally as the capacity of a shop floor control system to execute all plans released to the shop floor on time, efficiently, and cost effectively. The effectiveness of any shop floor control system depends on the presence of two essential elements:

- The existence of an effective, formal manufacturing planning system
- The existence of a manufacturing database containing all of the information needed by the shop floor control system.

These elements play such a critical role in the operation that they should be regarded as prerequisites to effective shop floor control. A system can operate in the absence of these two elements, but it cannot operate effectively. Without these elements, any success observed on the shop floor is more of a random than a planned event.

The Manufacturing Planning System

The importance of the manufacturing planning system comes from three major premises:

- It does not set plans. It carries out the plans and directions established by the planning system.
- It determines and controls operation priorities, not order priorities. The manufacturing system alone determines order priorities.
- It manages shop floor resources; it does not acquire them. It is the planning system that changes the levels of resources available by either acquiring more resources or by disposing of existing resources.

Shop floor control depends on the manufacturing planning system for direction, resources, and information on changes in areas such as order priorities. In short, shop floor control depends on the manufacturing system for answers to:

- What products shall we build?
- How many of the products to build?
- When is the product needed?
- What type of product are we building (e.g., for a customer or for the replenishment of safety stock)?

For the shop floor control system to be effective, the planning system must meet three minimum requirements:

- The planning system must be complete and integrated. The system must contain a production plan, a master production schedule, a material planning system, and a capacity planning system. MRP and CRP are examples. All components should be well integrated. The plans generated by the material planning system should be consistent with the capacity planning system plans. Both plans should be consistent with the production objectives set down in the master production schedule that should be a disaggregation of the production plan. Finally, the production plan should be a statement of what manufacturing has to do to satisfy corporate objectives. This first requirement ensures that the planning system can provide shop floor control with access to the necessary levels of resources and the required direction (in the form of the production plan and the master production schedule). These requirements are summarized in Figure 2-2.
- The planning system must be formal. All of the inputs used by the shop floor control system must be generated by the planning system alone.
- The planning system must generate valid and feasible plans for shop floor control. Shop floor control requires that all plans generated must be valid and feasible. That is, the plans must embody accurately the objectives the manufacturing system wants to accomplish (i.e., the plans must be valid). The plans must also be feasible because the system should have access to the necessary levels of resources required in each period to execute the plans. Shop floor control does not have the ability to acquire more resources should the current levels be insufficient.

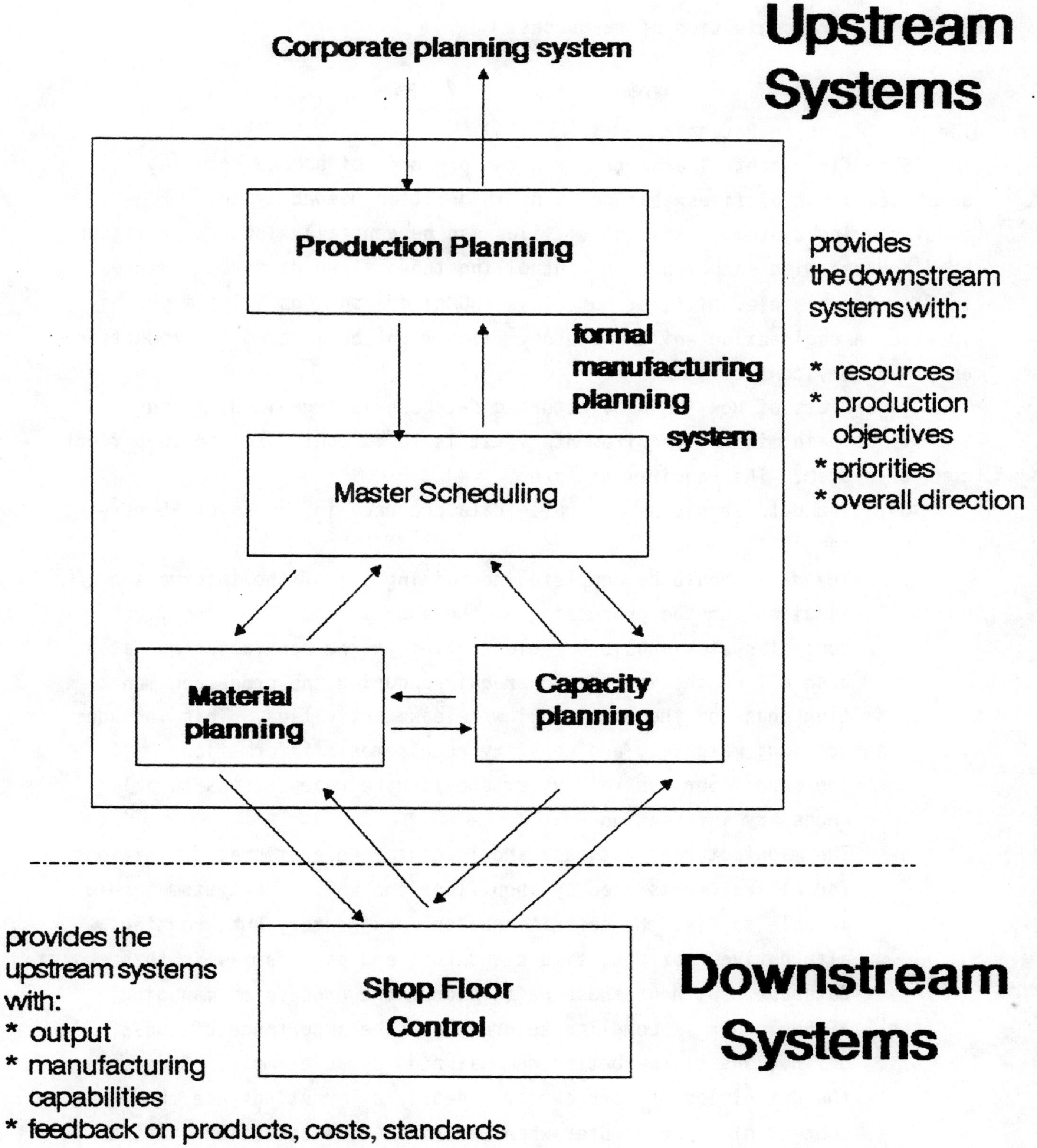

Figure 2-2. -- Major Components of the Manufacturing System Summarized

This capability belongs to the planning system alone. The function of shop floor control is to implement plans, not to plan for acquisition of resources.

The Manufacturing Database

Shop floor control also requires the presence of a manufacturing database, a set of files that contains information needed by the manufacturing system. This set of files can be centrally located or it can be dispersed with each function controlling those files of direct interest to it. For example, bills of materials (BOMs) or routings files might be located in engineering while inventory files might be located in production and inventory control.

Regardless of how the manufacturing database is organized, it must satisfy certain minimal requirements if it is to be useful to the shop floor control system. The requirements are:

- The data should be accurate (data accuracy in excess of 95 percent).
- The data should be complete, containing all of the information required for the processing of the shop order. The shop floor control system should be able to find in the manufacturing database all of the information required during the order documentation phase of the order review/release activities. This includes tooling, material, and capacity requirements information.
- The shop floor control system should have ready access to all necessary information.
- The manufacturing database should contain operational definitions for all key terms used by shop floor control. The system should be able to find the definitions for work center, BOM, routings, alternative routings, time standards, and part family in this database. Without these definitions, the process of managing a shop order is complicated greatly. The importance of these definitions can be better demonstrated by an example. Consider the definition of work center. Nearly all routings use the concept of a work center when describing the operations that an order must pass through. The definition is not always straightforward. In some settings, a work center is no more than a grouping of either identical or similar machines while elsewhere,

a work center consists of all machines working on either the same part or part family. In order for someone on the shop floor to process the order, the person must know how a work center is defined and must be able to identify which machines belong to a given work center.

SUMMARY

Shop floor control is complex. It is also a concept about which there is little agreement and much confusion. At times, the concept is like a jigsaw puzzle newly opened and dumped on the ground. There are many pieces that go to make up shop floor control that at a first glance seem to be scattered and unrelated. After the pieces are put together, it is easy to see both the big picture and the fit among the various pieces. It is always easier to understand the puzzle after it has been put together.

This chapter has attempted to put together the pieces of the shop floor control puzzle by defining the term and by presenting an integrative framework for the system. This framework has described a process that produces both a physical entity (the completed shop order) and information. It has also identified the major activities found in any shop floor control system and the links that exist among them. The framework has also identified those boundaries that separate it from the planning system. Finally, this chapter has examined two key prerequisites of effective shop floor control -- the planning system and the manufacturing database.

CHAPTER 3: PRINCIPLES OF EFFECTIVE SHOP FLOOR CONTROL

INTRODUCTION

Although leading edge shop floor control systems have been developed by the thirteen companies examined in this book, very different environments are represented. Each firm's experience in developing its own system has been unique. The casual reader of this book might question whether any general principles could be coaxed from these case studies. Nevertheless, an extensive study of the experiences of these thirteen leading edge systems has proved that there are several principles of good shop floor control that are common to most, if not all, of the companies. Principles that exist in successful shop floor control systems are summarized in this chapter and provide a checklist to be used not only when reviewing the experiences of the participating firms but also when evaluating any shop floor control system.

These principles are not exhaustive; they summarize early efforts to understand shop floor control. The principles are divided into two major categories -- design and operation of shop floor control systems. Within each main category, the principles are grouped into logical subcategories that follow the structure of the shop floor control framework presented in Chapter 2.

The principles are presented in two parts where possible. In the first part, each is discussed and its importance to the development of an effective shop floor control system is identified. In the second part, the principle is illustrated by examples from the experiences of one or two of the participating firms. It is not the intent of the authors to identify and discuss the experiences of every participating firm that illustrates the principle under discussion. Instead, the illustrations simply show the principle in action.

Overall Design Principles

Overall design principles are those that must be followed by anyone involved in the design, implementation, development, or modification of a shop floor control system regardless of the manufacturing process and its characteristics (i.e., job shop versus repetitive versus continuous process) and the marketing environment (make-to-order [MTO], make-to-stock [MTS], assemble-to-order [ATO], engineer-to-order [ETO]). These principles are basic to all effective shop floor control systems.

Only one such principle could be identified from the experiences of the thirteen participants. This principle, however, was so dominant that it was present in all of the systems examined. Nearly all of the participants identified this principle as the foundation block on which their systems were built and one of the major reasons for the continued success of their current system.

> Any effective shop floor control system should recognize the importance of people (especially shop floor personnel) to its operation and, as a result, it should be designed to make the best use of the capabilities offered by people.

In contrast to the other components of a typical manufacturing system (e.g., master scheduling, material planning, capacity planning, or production planning), shop floor control relies heavily on the knowledge possessed by its users (especially those on the shop floor). The information provided by users frequently is not available to the computer information systems used by shop floor control systems. Furthermore, these insights are in a form difficult for most computer systems to handle. As a result, an effective shop floor control system must be essentially a people system. The users must take information provided by the shop floor control system and combine these data with their own knowledge of the product and the shop floor to arrive at a decision for which they can be held accountable. The computerized systems found in shop floor control should never take action on their own. They should never release orders automatically even though the orders have been identified as mature by the planning system. They should not determine the next order to be processed for the user at the work center. Instead, these systems should identify conditions requiring user intervention and recommend action. It is then up to the user to act on these conditions because the user is the ultimate decision maker.

To rely on the users and their insights recognizes an important reality of shop floor control: No computer system can ever keep track of all the information required by shop floor personnel. There are numerous variables that must be taken into account when managing the order flow from the planning system to the shop floor and its various operations and back to the planning system on completion of the order. Much of this quantitative information can be managed by the shop floor control system. For example, the system can keep track of such information as the number of matured orders not yet released to the shop floor, order routings, setup requirements, tooling requirements, current location of released orders, and bottleneck operations. There are other variables that must be considered. These data, frequently qualitative and variable, form the hidden agenda with which many shop floor personnel are familiar. Items belonging to the hidden agenda are important because they are the source of efficiency observed on the shop floor.

For example, supervisors operating on the shop floor are able to assess the capacity of a work center because they know how to group orders to decrease lead time (and capacity demands) by taking advantage of similarities in either setups or components. They can identify those work centers and workers best suited for a given job. They can adjust order priorities and order flows on the shop floor to reflect considerations such as a worker going on vacation or a work center that has a new operator. Parts planners (those responsible for reviewing matured orders before releasing them to shop) use their familiarity with orders to assess how to respond to shorted orders (i.e., orders lacking adequate inventory of one or more component parts).

As a result, an effective shop floor control system should be structured to support the decision-making activities of the users and designed to encourage them to contribute their insights. This integration of the user into the formal system is achieved by using the following principles.

First, the users should understand the objectives of the shop floor control system. Second, there must be a distinction in the minds of the users between the role of the computer systems and the user's role on the floor. Third, both operating and management personnel must find the system simple to use and understand. Finally, the user must be supported by an on-line, highly computerized system.

Bently Nevada has developed a shop floor control system in which shop personnel decide what jobs to release to the shop floor, the order in which jobs at each work center are processed, and whether or not to bring work forward (i.e., release work in advance of its scheduled release date). People run the shop floor. Management encourages the dominant role of shop personnel. To improve the effectiveness of its personnel, Bently Nevada has developed an extensive computer system that provides the workers with information they need on time. As a result, the shop floor control system benefits from the experience of its work force.

Other illustrations of this principle can be found from reading the cases for the Vollrath Company, Steelcase, Moog, Miles Laboratories, Joy Manufacturing, and Consolidated Diesel.

External Design Principles

External design principles are those that govern the interrelationships that exist between the shop floor control system and the rest of the firm. Shop floor control does not exist in isolation, and it is an integral element of the manufacturing system. As a result, the rest of the manufacturing system must provide the shop floor control system with certain preconditions before it can be expected to operate effectively. Similarly, the system must fulfill certain obligations to the rest of the manufacturing system.

Effective shop floor control requires the presence of effective formal material and capacity planning systems.

Any shop floor control system is concerned primarily with successful implementation and completion of orders released to it by the planning system. As such, it is a short-range activity. For the system to complete its objectives, it must be assured of adequate material and capacity on a period-by-period basis. This requires that management evaluate, in advance, the material and capacity availability of any production schedule to be turned over to the shop floor control system. Any problems must be identified and resolved at this stage. If not, these problems will be passed down to the shop floor for resolution.

Passing these problems to the shop floor generates several adverse effects. First, because the shop floor control does not have the capability to increase the level of resources available to it (that capability belongs to the material and capacity planning elements of the manufacturing system alone), the result will be confusion and adjustments in the production schedule until the capacity and material demands of the schedule match up with the levels of available capacity and material. Second, frustration at all levels in the firm will increase. Those in the planning system will become frustrated with the constant inability of those on the shop floor to carry out apparently good plans. Shop floor personnel will become frustrated with the constant presence of infeasible plans. Finally, the credibility of the manufacturing plan will deteriorate and users will turn to the informal system.

Management can only evaluate and correct problems in available material and capacity if it has developed effective, formal planning systems. Of these two systems, the development of an effective capacity system is the more difficult and also the more important. It is not accidental that each of the participating firms in the conference had not only an effective capacity planning system but also an effective material planning system. Firms such as Steelcase and Twin Disc have long been known for classic implementations of MRP and CRP. To the managers of firms such as Joy Machinery Company, Steelcase, Twin Disc, Aladdin, Moog, Bently Nevada, Miles Laboratories, and the Vollrath Company, the real strength of their planning systems is the ability to generate plans that are always feasible from a material and capacity standpoint. To these managers, effective capacity and material planning are prerequisites to effective shop floor control. Middle and upper management alone are responsible for the effectiveness of this planning.

Steelcase, Inc., of Grand Rapids, Michigan, offers a good example of this principle. A key capacity plan is the sales operating plan (SOP). The SOP establishes quotas for each plant, which are essentially capacity quotas because they identify the number of standard hours available by plant by week. Once these quotas are identified and agreed to, they become capacity constraints. While there is some flexibility in capacity availability (production can accommodate an increase of up to 5 percent and a decrease of up to 2 percent), everyone in the firm recognizes that these constraints cannot be violated (except under extraordinary circumstances). Capacity on the shop floor is never overbooked. The formal capacity planning system has identified the amount of capacity needed by period and the amount of capacity available, and the system has helped resolve conflicts with top management.

The shop floor control system should be consistent with and linked to the other systems in the organization.

This is true for material planning, cost accounting, engineering, tool control, maintenance, personnel systems, purchasing, and so forth. These systems should be linked with the shop floor control system because they provide information, direction, and resources. In return, the systems receive information and products from the shop floor control system. For this interchange to be mutually beneficial, the ties between the systems should be formal, reliable, and ongoing.

The information generated by the systems outside shop floor control must be presented to the control system in a form that can be understood immediately by system users. Furthermore, the information generated must also be recorded in a form that is useful to other systems. This rapid exchange of information is encouraged by the use of similar operating definitions by both the planning and shop floor control systems. Reporting labor inputs by order is consistent with a job costing system; it is not consistent with a cost accounting system that reports all labor for a single department.

Consistency involves ensuring that the objectives and performance measures used on the shop floor support the objectives observed in the other systems in the organization. The consistency principle is illustrated by the shop floor control system used at the Vollrath Company. At Vollrath, success is defined by customer service (on-time delivery), cost control, and quality. Success on the shop floor is measured by the percentage of orders released to the shop within the lead time and the percentage of orders completed on time. The second measure reflects the basis on which Vollrath competes -- service to the customer. These measures also link the actions of the shop floor to corporate objectives. Similar examples can be found at Steelcase, Bently Nevada, Moog, and Miles Laboratories.

The development of an effective shop floor control system is enhanced by the presence of a common corporate database.

Information is the cement that binds the shop floor control system to the rest of the firm. The system depends on information generated by such functional areas as engineering, material planning, cost accounting, and quality assurance. To operate efficiently, shop floor control should be kept informed of any changes in order due dates (typically generated by a material planning system such as MRP), routings, or standard costs. In turn, the other functional areas depend on the shop floor control system to monitor the accuracy of their information. Any persistent discrepancies in routings or standards should be identified by the shop floor control system and communicated to the appropriate functional areas. This information exchange is helped greatly by a common database.

A common database describes a set of files accessible to every functional area in the firm and which contains all information, financial and operating, needed to manage the firm. It is the one set of numbers used by everyone in the firm. A common database enhances the operation of shop floor control by ensuring that the system is always aware of changes taking place in other functional areas. It also enables the system to provide the rest of the planning system with complete and immediate feedback. In short, a common database facilitates a constant flow of information between shop floor control and the rest of the firm. It also simplifies the development and maintenance of accurate data files.

The importance of a common, corporate database was recognized by the participating firms. Every one of these firms had either developed a common corporate database, or they were moving toward the establishment of one. The common database was used by Vollrath management to coordinate the shop floor control system and its activities with those of the rest of the firm. For Vollrath, a common database provided the entire system with complete and immediate feedback. Such feedback ensured that people were making their decisions based on the most current information and that they could identify all of the possible implications of their decisions.

Internal Design Principles

Internal design principles are those principles that govern the structure of the shop floor control system in isolation. These principles ignore the interrelationships between this system and the rest of the firm.

The shop floor control system requires the presence of a manufacturing database supplying prompt, complete, and accurate information.

At a minimum, an effective shop floor control system needs information on such topics as lead times (planned), routings, priorities (order need dates and order dues dates), tooling, components needed, on-hand quantities, lot-size quantities, substitute items, alternative routings, and expected scrap. For this information, provided by the manufacturing database, to be useful to the shop floor control system, it must be accurate, timely, and complete.

The data had to be error free. Nearly all of the participating firms viewed a 95 percent level of data accuracy as being barely acceptable. While it was recognized that it was difficult to maintain a 100 percent level of accuracy, nearly all viewed this level as a target toward which everyone should strive. Inaccurate information was seen as leading to the wrong decisions that affected the credibility of the shop floor control system.

Any information required by the shop floor control system also had to be made available rapidly when requested (timeliness). This was a major reason for emphasis of on-line systems. Nearly all of the participating firms used on-line inquiry systems because such systems provided users with instantaneous access to information. Firms such as Vollrath and Miles Laboratories combine on-line access with on-line updatings and data file revision. This merger maintains the accuracy of the manufacturing database moment to moment.

Finally, all of the information needed by the shop floor control system had to be present in the manufacturing database (completeness). Such information helped the shop floor personnel make the right decisions regarding orders.

<u>The shop floor control system should be computerized to offer a complete on-line capability and be designed to support the system user activities.</u>

Nearly all effective shop floor control systems are 100 percent computerized. The computer systems are designed to support the activities of system users by providing them with several distinct capabilities. The most significant of these capabilities is data entry/bookkeeping. The computer systems are used as the primary means for entering information about jobs or resource status. For example, a work center operator enters information about the number of pieces received, the number of good pieces completed, the number scrapped, the number that requires rework, the actual setup time needed, the actual processing time, and operator identification. Based on this information, the system updates the appropriate records in the manufacturing database. The computer system, not the operator, takes over the responsibility for system bookkeeping.

The second capability should be data inquiry. The computer system should provide information about the status of upstream workstations, on-hand inventory balances, status of tooling, and number of hours loaded and available at a given work center.

The third capability that should be offered is data validation/screening. Based on reported information, the computer system should compare such items as the ending order quantities from one operation with the beginning order quantities reported at the subsequent operation. Any discrepancies noted by the computer system should then be reported to the user for action. The action may involve correcting wrong data or forcing the system to accept the discrepancy. In addition, the computer system should compare the number actually scrapped (both cumulative and by operation) with predetermined management standards to identify situations potentially requiring management intervention. This computer capability is the basis of computer-triggered exception reporting.

The computer system should also suggest potential actions to be taken by the user (action recommendations). These actions can range from the ordering of jobs on the dispatch list to suggested corrective actions for dealing with identified shop problems. These are only suggestions made for the users' benefit and they are not obligated to follow the suggestions. (See Overall Design Principles.)

Finally, the computer system should offer a what-if situation or simulation capability. The user should be able to identify the potential implications of alternative actions by entering the actions into the computer system and having the system identify potential impacts. When simulating the potential impact, the underlying database is not disturbed. As a result, the user should be encouraged to evaluate alternative solutions on the computer before implementing any on the shop floor.

These capabilities should be offered on line (entered, updated, and retrieved). Such a capability is consistent with the need for the user to respond to conditions that are present currently on the shop floor.

These capabilities are important because they directly support the user. The user is free from such routine work as data entry/recording and is warned about potential problems. The user has the capability to experiment with potential solutions. The computerized system provides a comprehensive, rapid, and powerful tool for decision making.

Nearly all of the systems examined had developed or were in the process of implementing extensive on-line computerized systems. Most systems were 100 percent computerized and nearly all of them offered the capabilities described above. All of the firms admitted that this was an important area and one that was constantly undergoing refinement, improvement, and extension. One firm, the Vollrath Company, had developed a sophisticated computerized system. Availability of material and tooling is evaluated on line before the order is released to the shop floor (using a what-if capability). Assignments are entered and communicated by the on-line computer system, which evaluates the entered data and identifies any potentially misentered information. Computerized systems offering on-line capabilities are also available at Bently Nevada and Miles Laboratories.

<u>A good shop floor control system should track orders and monitor and report on the status of all shop floor resources.</u>

The shop floor control system should provide the users specifically and the firm as a whole with a window into the activities taking place on the shop floor. In addition to such activities as order dispatching, the shop floor control system should be able to identify the current location of orders and their status (busy, waiting in queue, on hold). This information should be made available to all those in the firm who have the need to find out where an order (or orders) is located currently. This capability makes the shop floor control transparent to others in the firm. They know that they can use the system to identify the status of a given order quickly and accurately.

In addition, shop floor control should not only monitor the progress of orders, it should also monitor the status of all shop floor resources (tooling, machinery, labor, etc.). The collected information should include data on availability (e.g., is the tool available for production or is it being reworked?), status (idle or being used), location, condition (i.e., how near the resource is to being replaced or overhauled), and performance. This information should be used when assigning work and scheduling preventive maintenance. The shop floor control system is responsible ultimately for all resources under its control. Monitoring the status of these resources is one way that control is maintained over time.

All of the participating firms offered extensive tracking and monitoring capabilities. The visibility of the shop floor to the rest of the firm (and the firm's customers) is best illustrated by the Vollrath Company. The tracking and monitoring capabilities are most extensive at Bently Nevada and Miles Laboratories. At both these firms, order tracking and monitoring were crucial for several reasons (one of which was the requirement for such tracking capabilities placed on the firms by government regulatory agencies).

Provide the needed information on time in a format that is understandable and that provides only the needed information to make the decision.

The shop floor control system should not overwhelm the user with information. Too much information, no matter how accurate or timely, is worse than not enough. Too much information leads to confusion (over what data to use and what data to omit) and poorer decision making (paralysis of analysis). Instead, the system should provide the user with the minimum amount of detail sufficient for problem solving. This information should be presented in such a form that it can be read and understood quickly. As a result, the key to the effective management of the information flows is not in making all of the information available but in making the right information available.

The participating firms were well aware of the importance of giving the users access to the right information. Several different tactics were observed that would achieve this objective. One commonly used tactic involved the use of limits on the size of the reports generated by the shop floor control system. Vollrath, for example, insisted that all of its exception reports not exceed an 8½-by-11-inch sheet of paper. Larger size reports were not allowed because they contained too much information for the user to interpret readily.

A second tactic involved providing information in layers of progressively more detail. This principle was best demonstrated by Bently Nevada. Most of the reports produced by this system were summaries intended to give the user an overview of the situation on the shop floor and to answer frequently posed questions. For example, during order review/release, capacity availability is evaluated using the summary load report. The summary load report is a one-page summary of all work-hours loaded into a given work center for six months. Questions raised in reviewing this report can be examined in the detailed load report, which is a detailed capacity audit of the work center provided when the summary load report is not enough.

A third tactic used was linked, focused reports. Each report dealt with one topic and summarized all of the relevant information about that topic in a single-page report. Users were then made aware of the other reports that could be used in conjunction with the focused report. Moog, for example, presented the information for work center scheduling in two reports. The first report, the work center daily queue list, summarized all of the job priorities scheduled for that work center. It broke jobs into completed operations, in-process operations, available-to-be-worked-on operations, and scheduled and not available operations. Information about incoming jobs was not allowed. This information could be found in the work center look ahead report.

Two comments should be made about this principle. First, most shop floor control systems will use the three tactics discussed in this section. Information that cannot be summarized easily must be broken down if it is to maintain its continued usefulness. Second, the reports generated by the shop floor control system are always undergoing reevaluation and revision. As users gain better familiarity with the operation of the shop floor control system and the reports generated by this system and their needs, the users will need modifications to these reports. The management task is to ensure that data processing modifies the reports to reflect the changing requirements of the users. Miles Laboratories provides an interesting example of how to maintain this link between the users and data processing successfully.

<u>The shop floor control system should reflect the production process and be consistent with its critical characteristics.</u>

All shop floor control systems, regardless of the settings in which they are found, must contain the five major activities discussed in Chapter 2. The timing and importance of these activities, however, are not uniform and should, instead, reflect and be consistent with the characteristics of the production process being controlled. For example, at Miles Laboratories, production is characterized by relatively large batches run over a straight line routing (starting with withdrawal and weighing and ending with the inventory of finished tablets). In such an environment, dispatching is not carried out at each work center. Instead, the order processing sequence is determined during the order review/release phase (when the weekly production and work force schedule is set). The shop floor is held responsible for the timely withdrawal of inventory and data collection/monitoring, an important component of the shop floor control system.

At Miles, production runs are large in quantity but short in time, thus problems become costly very quickly. Continuous data collection/monitoring is required to identify problems before they become worse.

In other systems, the shop floor control system must be structured differently to be effective. Bently Nevada has more of a traditional job shop manufacturing environment with dispatching at the various work centers a separate activity from that of order review/release. Dispatching is also important because there are orders waiting at the various work centers. The production supervisors identify the best grouping of these orders to improve efficiency by minimizing setup times (without compromising on-time delivery). This structure, while appropriate for Bently Nevada, would be inappropriate for Miles Laboratories.

<u>The shop floor control system should be valid and transparent</u>.

The shop floor control system, along with all of its reports and procedures, should be transparent so that it is easy to use and understand by both operation and management personnel. Transparency and validity encourage the continued use of the formal system. These traits also reduce the confusion and increased cost that accompany an informal control system.

All of the participating firms worked hard at developing systems with these characteristics. Management invested money in education and training programs. At Joy Machinery, management spent time and money publishing and distributing extensive procedure books to employees. These books included employee responsibilities, computer reports, and the meaning of the various elements of these reports. In many instances, shop floor personnel were involved directly in the design of the shop floor control system. Finally, management in all of the participating firms was involved in a refinement process. The refinements were often based on feedback received from users. For example, Twin Disc had decided to abandon the critical ratio rule (CRR) in favor of the earliest operation due date. The reason for this change was the complaint frequently heard from shop personnel that they could not understand the current rule. Earliest operation due date was preferred because shop personnel saw the rule as being simple to use with easily understood priorities. This change took place even though Twin Disc was often cited as a classic user of the CRR.

SHOP FLOOR CONTROL SYSTEMS -- OPERATING PRINCIPLES

Operating principles describe those practices that should be considered in the day-to-day operation of the shop floor control systems. The first category consists of those practices that affect all activities of shop floor control daily. The second category consists of those operating principles that are specific to one of the five major activities of shop floor control.

Broad Operating Principles

The shop load from period to period should be as level as possible.

The shop floor control system controls the load on the shop floor. Shop load consists of both incoming load and the load currently released to the shop floor and not yet completed. Whenever possible, the system should try to ensure that the load on the shop floor is level from period to period. In other words, the number of hours that the shop is expected to work should remain constant.

The ease with which the shop load can be maintained at a constant level is largely a function of the type of production process. In those settings where the shop floor consists primarily of general purpose machines that can be easily substituted, a constant load in the entire department should be maintained. In settings where specialized equipment is not substituted easily, maintaining a constant load in the shop requires leveling the shop load by each work center.

By maintaining a level load on the shop period by period, the operation of not only the shop floor but also the manufacturing system as a whole is enhanced. A level load generates several distinct benefits. First, by maintaining a level load on the shop floor, the shop floor control system simplifies the task of lead-time control. Lead-time control (the management of lead times with a view to reducing the average lead time as well as the variability of lead times) is synonymous in many firms with queue control. Queue times tend to account for between 90 to 95 percent of typical manufacturing lead times. By ensuring a level load from period to period, queue variability can be reduced because any variability in load is often reflected in the variability of the queue.

Second, a level load encourages the development of good planned lead times. Planned lead times (as well as planned or standard queue times) are used extensively by the material and capacity planning systems. They are used by the shop floor control system when dispatching is done using the earliest operation start or due date priority rule. The effectiveness of these estimates is greatest when there is close agreement between the planned and actual values. Lead time and queue variability resulting from uneven or fluctuating shop loads are a direct threat to the effectiveness of these planned values.

In addition, by ensuring the presence of a level load over time, management can decrease the dependency of workers on the security blanket provided by queues while also enhancing the credibility of the planning and shop floor control systems. A level load is a good way of assuring shop personnel that there will be the same amount of work from week to week and that the manufacturing planning system will work at maintaining this constancy of load.

A level load also simplifies the process of identifying potential problems on the shop floor quickly. With level loads over, workers begin to develop expectations based on experience of what the various queues should be. Shop personnel should be able to identify those queues that are growing larger than they should. These queues now become indicators of potential problems. A level load supports management's objective of providing level employment for the firm's personnel.

All of the firms were aware of the importance of maintaining a constant load on the shop over time and that this one principle generated significant benefits. To some, the lack of level loads constituted an important threat to the credibility and validity of the formal planning system as well as offering an incentive for returning to the informal system. The management at Steelcase, for example, had taken the position that the planning system should ensure the workers on the shop floor forty-five hours of work per week. Because of specialized equipment and long routings, the management at Moog spends considerable time ensuring that the work load is constant and balanced among workstations. A balanced load is one of the building blocks on which Moog's shop floor control system is built.

The problems met on the shop floor usually require the cooperation of different areas and are best resolved through joint problem solving.

Shop floor control depends on the users' knowledge. No one user, however, has access to all of the resources, information, and perspectives needed to resolve shop problems as they occur. Furthermore, no one person can identify all of the causes of a given shop problem. So the shop floor control system should bring people together to work on problem solving. It is only then that all of the resources, information, and perspectives needed are present and used to arrive at an effective solution.

In most of the firms examined in this study, the need for joint problem solving is best illustrated by the shop floor control triangle. This triangle typically consists of three people from the shop floor: the parts planner (with knowledge of the operation of the planning system and its requirements), the department foreman/supervisor (with knowledge of the capacities and capabilities of the department and the requirements placed on the department by the various orders), and the operator (with knowledge of machines and the production of the various orders processed through a machine). Whenever a major problem occurs on the shop floor, these three people must review the problem, its causes, and potential solutions. In some instances, the problem may be solved by using either overtime or an extra shift (a decision made by the supervisor with the agreement of the parts planner). In other instances, the solution may require a change in the order's due date with a compression of manufacturing lead times at the parent stages (in the case of a late order) or the release of a remedial order (in the case of excessive high scrap on an order).

Other functions that should be considered as part of the joint decision-making process are engineering (process and industrial), quality control, cost accounting, and marketing.

To encourage such joint decision making, shop floor control systems should help communication between the various parties. The parties should be able to see the implication of any problem or decision as it affects them and their tasks. For example, an operator, facing a difficult job that is falling behind schedule, should be able to show the parts planner the implications of this problem on the feasibility of the order due date.

The emphasis on joint decision making was not unique to any of the firms examined. Most recognized that no one had all of the answers and that the best answer was arrived at by having people work together. The experiences of companies such as Bently Nevada and the Vollrath Company provide particularly good examples of this principle.

At Bently Nevada, management spent a considerable amount of time developing a system that encouraged joint decision making. Management viewed joint decision making as one of the foundations on which its system was built. The reports generated by the shop floor control system were designed to encourage communication.

At the Vollrath Company, joint decision making is frequently applied to the management of out-of-control orders. The management at Vollrath has defined an out-of-control order as any order which was due yesterday but which has yet to be released to the shop floor. Such problems are solved by having shop floor personnel work together with plant management to decide the best possible date for the completion of the order. This process brings together the master scheduler with supervisors and shop operators.

Special procedures should be in place for controlling the flow of salvage, scrap, and rework.

Rework, salvage, and scrap are facts of life for nearly all manufacturing firms and represent special problems for the shop floor control system. They are also too important an area for the firm to ignore. Salvage and rework, for example, represent sources of recoverable work for the manufacturing system -- work that can be used subsequently by the planning system. Rework, salvage, and scrap also represent important sources of information. Any system, if it is to be successful in the long run, must be examined not only for its success but also for its problems. Rework, salvage, and scrap are physical indications of what the shop floor has experienced when completing an order (either total or in part) that meets the standards. An analysis of these orders and an identification of the reasons for their presence can help management correct persistent production problems. Rework, salvage, and scrap must also be accounted for because these items are often the difference between beginning (i.e., before processing) and ending order quantities (i.e., after processing). Rework, salvage, and scrap still require access to the various shop floor resources. Rework, for example, often requires additional operations, extra processing, and additional tooling. These requirements affect capacity availability.

These procedures should incorporate certain key features. First, they should recognize that rework, salvage, or scrap items should be separated from the rest of the order and treated as a separate order (specifically in the case of rework and salvage). As separate orders, these items should be given their own feasible due date, which may or may not reflect the original due date. Procedures should be in place for determining the sequence in which rework, salvage, and good orders are to be processed at a given work center. Rework, salvage, and scrap orders should be documented to identify the reasons for their presence. These orders should also be tracked, monitored, and reported.

Of the participating firms, Twin Disc reported the most advanced system for managing rework, salvage, and scrap items. Management developed an on-line salvage system that embodied an automated link with the total material and MRP system and with the total capacity and CRP systems. This link allows for instant monitoring of material status for either good or bad material. This link also enables management to evaluate the capacity effect of salvage. The resulting shop floor control system monitored and controlled rework, salvage, and scrap as tightly as it did good orders.

Most of the participating firms agreed that, with the increased use of JIT manufacturing principles and the increased costs of material, there was an increasing need for better control of rework, salvage, and scrap. Most were formalizing and improving current procedures.

Order Review/Release Principles

Order review/release is the first major shop floor control activity. It covers all of the activities that must take place from the time that a matured order is identified by the planning system until it is released to the shop floor. As such, order review/release controls the flow of orders on the shop floor, and it is a screening process by which potential problem orders are identified and kept off the shop floor until the underlying difficulties are solved. In general, order review/release is an important but often unappreciated stage in the effective shop floor control system. An effective order review/release process simplifies the operation of the rest of the shop floor control system.

Order review/release should be initiated by the formal planning system.

The shop floor control system is driven by the formal planning system, which identifies what part orders must be completed, when they are to be completed, and when they are considered matured. The planning system is also held responsible for maintaining the integrity and validity of the order due dates. As a result, nothing is done by the shop floor control system until a production schedule consisting of matured orders is released. The arrival of these matured orders into the shop floor control system initiates the first set of activities -- order review/release. Order review/release can only assess the feasibility of orders generated by the planning system and required by it. It cannot review any other order.

There are certain conditions under which this principle is "bent." These conditions involve out-of-control orders (i.e., orders that have been rejected by quality control or that have experienced too much scrap). Under these circumstances, a remedial order may be reviewed and released by order review/release. This order, however, can only be released in anticipation of an order release coming from the planning system.

Every one of the participating firms was driven by this principle. For each firm, the release of matured orders from the planning system marked the starting point from the order review/release activities. This strong tie is evident in firms such as FMC, Wright Line, Steelcase, Moog, Vollrath, Aladdin, and Twin Disc. One important result of this close link between the order review/release and the planning system was the requirement that the personnel involved in the order review/release stage had to be familiar with the operation of the planning system (in most cases, the MRP system) and the shop floor.

Only those orders with a good chance of being completed should be released to the shop floor.

Order review/release should be viewed as a screening device. The major purpose is to evaluate the feasibility of all orders waiting to be released to the shop floor. Only those orders that have a good chance of being completed on the shop floor should be released. These are orders for which there is adequate component inventory available (and noted as available), sufficient capacity, adequate tooling, proper work documentation, adequate planned lead-time allowances, and a credible due date. The personnel involved in order review/release should be prepared to evaluate every order to be released and accept responsibility for releasing orders on the shop floor.

Orders that do not pass through order review/release should be reviewed by personnel from planning, the shop floor, and the shop floor control system. If the problem order is being released within the minimum lead time, these people must determine whether the order can be completed by the time required. Otherwise, the order due date must be revised. If the problem order involves shorted material (i.e., not enough component on hand), these people must decide whether to release the order as is and expedite the needed component parts, release the order and take the component parts from other orders, or release part of the order. Any problem order must be reviewed and the appropriate corrective action taken before the order is allowed to proceed to the shop floor. The shop floor personnel should be allowed to concentrate on processing the orders, not correcting planning problems.

The importance of this principle was recognized by nearly every participating firm. In most systems, the people involved in the order review/release stage checked the feasibility of matured orders. In many instances, the primary focus was on capacity availability (e.g., Bently Nevada, Vollrath, Steelcase, and Miles) because capacity was viewed as the more important and more difficult resource to control. In these firms, material availability was assumed. At Moog, materials availability was checked explicitly. At Miles Laboratories, order review/release had to evaluate the feasibility of the order in light of an additional requirement. For the order to be released, the material required by the order had to be not only in stock but it also had to clear quality assurance. If the materials had not already cleared quality assurance, management had to ensure that the materials would clear by the time they were needed by the order on the shop floor.

<u>When smoothing load, work should be pulled forward whenever possible.</u>

In general, the work load should be smoothed at the planning stage. However, smoothing may not be enough. Changes often take place between the time the plans are formulated and the time the production schedule (based on these) must be implemented on the shop floor. Management on the shop floor can level work by either pulling work forward (i.e., releasing it earlier to the shop floor) or by pushing work back (i.e., delaying the release of the order). The preferred action is to pull work forward. Pushing work back can create potential problems for the manufacturing system by causing the rescheduling process to ripple through the customer order level. Pushing work back tends to create more problems than it solves.

Excessive pulling forward and early release of orders should be avoided. The need for frequent early releases indicates a problem with capacity and material planning and reduces the flexibility of the manufacturing system. If orders are not released to the shop floor until the last moment, they can be modified to reflect changes in either quantity or timing. After all, it is far easier to make changes to an order before it is released than afterwards.

Bently Nevada was one of the strongest advocates of this principle. The production controllers continuously review the planned orders and if faced by fluctuations in loading, they always react by pulling work forward. This principle was one of the major tenets on which Bently Nevada's shop floor control system was built.

The persons responsible for reviewing and releasing work should also monitor future work loads.

One of the major advantages offered by most modern material and capacity planning systems (especially MRP/CRP) is that they provide workers with visibility at all stages of the manufacturing system. This visibility is important to those involved in the order review/release stage. These people should not only concern themselves with the matured orders; they should also evaluate the incoming work load for the next two to four weeks (at a minimum). This analysis provides the shop floor with a warning. It also enables personnel from the shop floor control system to identify any capacity problems and to relay this information back to the planning system so such problems can be solved before the orders are released. If such problems are not identified until the orders are to be released, the reaction time is short and bad decisions might be made.

The future production schedules can be analyzed in several different ways. They can be assessed in terms of the loads they generate (i.e., how many hours of capacity are required by the production releases for a specific week) or projected loads (load in the shop plus additions to load). If there is a spike[1] in capacity requirements identified in the future, shop

---

[1]The term spike is used to indicate a sudden or large increase in capacity requirements occurring in one or more periods. For example, demand present four weeks from now goes from an average of 15,000 standard hours per week to 25,000 standard hours.

personnel can respond in several different ways. They can respond by pulling the work forward. They can also add extra capacity -- overtime or an extra shift. Because these demands are identified before they occur, shop personnel have the time to identify the best course of action and to communicate the decisions to the people involved. If the spike cannot be controlled by these actions, however, the problem should be passed back to the planning system for resolution (along with an explanation of the problem).

In all of the firms, monitoring the current and future loads was done continuously. Shop floor control personnel were aware of the need to identify and remove any problems before these problems passed to the shop floor.

Detailed Assignment/Dispatching Principles

In general, detailed assignment is the one activity of shop floor control that most people associate with this system. It involves the scheduling of shop orders and other shop activities (such as preventive maintenance) on the various shop resources. Scheduling orders involves assigning priorities. This assignment is not just a mechanical process in which a dispatching rule (such as the operation due date) identifies the order sequence and the operator implements this sequence. Instead, it is a process whereby the shop floor control system provides shop workers with access to all of the necessary information, and the shop workers determine the exact sequence in which the jobs are to be processed. Like the other activities of shop floor control, detailed assignment is primarily a people process.

Detailed loading should be done by the shop floor personnel.

The actual loading (i.e., the actual sequence in which orders are processed) of any work center or machine should be a human activity. Shop floor control, with the dispatch list and dispatching rules, identifies those jobs to be processed at a given work center and provides a recommended sequence (derived from the dispatching rules). These recommended priorities are only inputs into the dispatching process. No dispatching rule, however sophisticated, can consider adequately all of the relevant facts, such as sequence-dependent setups (a key concern for most of the participating firms); the need for certain operators, vacations, union work rules, potential engineering changes, high incidence of scrap, and first runs; and the status of upstream work centers. Shop personnel such as the dispatcher or the operator can consider these additional factors and modify the recommended sequence to reflect them. These modifications are the major source of shop efficiencies. The increase in efficiency cannot come at the expense of the schedule. All personnel should be made aware that they can work at improving efficiency provided that they are able to satisfy the major performance objectives for their centers. For most firms, the major objective is to process orders by their operation due date.

In Bently Nevada's system, the actual sequencing of orders is the responsibility of the production supervisor who is given the necessary latitude to improve efficiency by grouping orders to minimize setup time (as an example) provided that the schedule is met. At Steelcase, the dispatchers and operators are allowed to deviate from the dispatch list provided they can ensure that the load on the work center will be cleared on schedule. If they can, then they are allowed to regroup orders or to pull work forward from other work centers to improve efficiency by taking advantage of similarities in either setups or components. At FMC, the production control scheduler and the production team manager mutually decide on the daily production schedule. Their decision each morning takes into account tooling availability, equipment downtime, and work center backlog.

> Any acceptable dispatching rule should be simple and easy to under stand, should generate meaningful priorities promptly, and be consistent with the planning system.

The dispatching rule is an important element of the detailed assignment stage of shop floor control. Its purpose is not simply to determine job priorities but to help decision making by shop floor personnel. As such, a good rule was one that is simple to use, transparent and valid, and generates meaningful priorities. A rule that is simple to use is one that the user can learn quickly. The logic behind the rule being transparent and valid is so users can readily understand the advantages of employing it. A dispatching rule should generate priorities that can be interpreted readily. For many job shops, it is natural for dispatchers and operators to think in terms of either start dates or due dates. As a result, rules such as operation start date or operation due date are inherently attractive. These rules identify priorities in terms of how far behind or ahead of the start date or due date any order is. In contrast, the CRR suffers from a major shortcoming -- its priorities are stated in terms of fractions that are not as understandable.

The dispatching rule should ensure that priorities used on the shop floor reflect those found in the planning system. For most of the participating firms, MRP was the predominant method of planning material requirements and production scheduling. MRP is a due-date-driven system -- it identifies order due dates that must be met to maintain the overall feasibility of the generated plans. In such an environment, nondue-date rules, such as shortest processing time or first-in-first-out, should never be used because they are inconsistent with the due date orientation of MRP. Using such rules would convey the wrong message to those working on the shop floor. The use of a rule such as shortest processing time, which encourages the processing of the maximum number of jobs in a given period (regardless of due date), implies that processing the largest number of orders through a work center is more important than meeting due dates. This rule is in direct conflict with MRP objectives. Simple rules that were consistent with the planning system and that generated meaningful priorities were the most effective. All of the firms used a due date rule with the majority using either the operation start date or operation due date.

The Twin Disc experience was of interest. In the past, Twin Disc was recognized as being a successful user of the CRR. Recently, management decided to replace CRR with operation due date. The reason was that CRR, while it was effective, failed to satisfy two criteria identified in this principle. It was not seen as being valid and transparent, and it did not generate meaningful priorities. Foremen and operators did not understand this rule. Managers found themselves continually reexplaining the rule and its operation. Foremen and operators also had difficulty making sense of the priorities. They could understand operation due dates and start dates but the ratios generated by CRR were not understood as easily. The change to the operation due date rule was accepted readily by the shop personnel. One foreman remarked that he now knew what he was doing.

> The recommended priorities should be related to the operator by a dispatch list. At at minimum, the dipatch list should provide shop floor personnel with a set of feasible priorities and access to information concerning which jobs are expected into the work center in the near future, where the orders are to go on completion, and the status of the orders.

The major interface between the shop floor control system and the personnel involved in the dispatching process should be the dispatch list. To be effective, the dispatch list should satisfy certain conditions. First, it should provide the user with feasible priorities. That is, operators should be assured that if they process the jobs in the sequence found on the list, then they should be able to meet the due dates. The list should not be the efficient arrangement of jobs -- that condition comes from the intervention of the user. This condition is necessary if the shop floor control system is to maintain credibility with the users.

The priorities reported on the dispatch list should also be updated regularly (i.e., at least once a day). Without frequent updating, the validity of the priorities deteriorates, and the dispatch list loses much of its effectiveness. The dispatch list also should provide shop floor personnel with access (either on the dispatch list or by associated reports) to the following information:

- Order status. Not all the orders processed through a work center are the same. Some jobs, for example, are for customer orders while others are to replenish depleted safety stocks. The kind of order should be clear because this information provides the user with an indication of the true urgency of the order. Customer orders should always have priority over orders for inventory replenishment. If there is a conflict in priorities, it should always be resolved in favor of the customer.
- Capacity available and capacity required. The user should know how many hours of capacity (as measured in standard hours) and days of production available for the week, as well as the number of standard hours required by the jobs that have been assigned to the work center for that week. This information provides the user with an indication of the amount of flexibility available for order rearrangement. Flexibility decreases as the load approaches the level of available capacity.
- Work center look ahead/look back. The shop floor control system should provide the users with complete visibility over the shop load at a given work center. This visibility should cover upstream and downstream shop loads. Look ahead indicates the status of downstream work centers (i.e., those work centers scheduled to receive orders). Look back indicates those shop orders that have been released to the shop and are scheduled for a given work center

but are not yet available (i.e., upstream load). Based on the information provided by these two features, the users can help level the shop load. For example, jobs going to congested downstream work centers can be delayed in favor of those proceeding to relatively idle centers. Users can also identify those orders that can be pulled to the work center (especially if the work center needs work). Furthermore, this visibility provides the users with a warning. Hot (high priority) jobs can be identified in advance so the work center is ready to receive them. In short, the dispatch list should provide shop floor personnel with the detailed information needed to better manage the flow of work through a given center.

Most of these features are present in the shop floor control systems examined in this study. In some systems, such as at Joy Machinery, for example, all of the necessary information is provided on the dispatch list. Thus, visibility on capacity encompasses the current and upstream work centers. In other cases, such as Moog, the dispatch list (called the work center daily queue list) provides the users with the priorities for a given work center. The dispatch list is supplemented by other reports that are accessed by the users easily. For example, in the case of Moog, information about downstream work loads is provided through the work center look ahead report. In all the firms, management was concerned that the users have access to all of the information they needed and that the information encouraged improved efficiency.

As capacity use increases and approaches full use, due date dispatching rules increase in importance. Their priorities are followed much more closely by shop floor personnel.

The degree of flexibility the operator has in rearranging the recommended sequence is related to the level of capacity use. As the level approaches full use, the degree of deviation permissible from the recommended sequence decreases and disappears. As pointed out previously, the recommended sequence contained in the dispatch list is one that may not be the most efficient, but it does ensure on-time completion of jobs. At very high levels of capacity use, any rearranging of jobs involves delaying one or more jobs while other orders are brought forward. These delayed jobs then fall behind schedule. Furthermore, the work center does not have the slack (in the form of excessive capacity) to devote to these jobs. As a result, the operator has now created a problem for the shop floor control system, which must bring these delayed problems back on schedule.

Under conditions of high use, the major purpose of the shop floor control system should be to meet order due dates, not increase the efficiency of the shop floor. These two objectives are mutually exclusive when there is little or no spare capacity available.

Of the various participating firms, Twin Disc was the system in which the implementation of this principle was best demonstrated. Under normal conditions, the users determine the ultimate priorities. As capacity use increases, however, everyone in the system knows the schedule to meet. The priorities identified in the dispatch list are followed closely with the operator responsible for explaining the reasons for any deviation.

Monitoring/Data Collection

The major purpose of the third major stage of shop floor control is to collect data from the shop floor and to record the data in the manufacturing database. The database is also responsible for identifying potential problems on the shop floor by comparing actual performance with the standards. The quality of the information flows received from the shop floor is determined by this activity. Good information recorded on the shop floor contributes to good decisions made in the manufacturing system.

> All information should be collected from the floor on a transaction-by-transaction basis.

A major concern of the entire shop floor control system is the presence of timely information, which can only be provided when information is collected from the shop floor when a transaction (typically, a work center completing a job) has taken place. A transaction-by-transaction recording discipline offers several important advantages. First, the information about the job is still fresh in the mind of the operator. Data accuracy, as a result, tends to be higher. Second, anyone having access to this information knows where a job is at any moment. The user also knows what is happening to that job and why. These features make the shop floor control system more transparent to the rest of the firm. Finally, this discipline ensures that shop floor problems are identified and corrected at an early stage.

Transaction-by-transaction recording was practiced by all of the participating firms. The managers all agreed that this recording discipline was crucial to their successful operations. All emphasized that it was important to know what was happening from moment to moment on the shop floor. Without such timely information, the quality of the decisions deteriorated, and the costs of correcting shop floor problems increased. Vollrath, Miles Laboratories, Bently Nevada, and Joy Manufacturing provide examples of this principle.

<u>The data collection system should be adequate for recording quantitative and qualitative information.</u>

Recording quantitative information (such as the number of pieces completed at an operation, number of pieces scrapped, number of pieces removed for rework/salvage, the actual processing and setup time required, and the operator involved) may not always be adequate. Such information tells what has happened, not why. The answer to why can best be obtained by allowing the operator to enter comments into the database that explain what happened and what, if any, corrective actions were taken.

Such information should not be limited to explaining shop floor problems. Operators should be allowed to enter any comments pertaining to the order and its processing that they feel are important. For example, an operator might note that the steel being used is more brittle than usual. This information can be used by others. By combining quantitative with qualitative information, a clearer picture can be obtained of what is happening on the shop floor.

Vollrath and Joy Manufacturing provide examples of this principle in practice. Operators are allowed to make comments about an order. These comments are then linked to the shop order and become as accessible to the user as is information about routings or the number of pieces. Similar capabilities can be found at Moog, Bently Nevada, and Twin Disc.

<u>The shop floor control system should be responsible for the accuracy and validity of all information that it posts to the database</u>.

Personnel from the shop floor control system should be made responsible for the accuracy and validity of all information recorded from the shop floor because they are in the best position to ensure accuracy. Any data problems are best solved by having the persons who posted these data either correct the problem or explain their presence. For example, a discrepancy between the ending quantity recorded at one operation and the beginning quantity recorded at the subsequent operation should be resolved by the operators who entered the data.

The shop floor control system should have checks available on data validity. These checks should be present when the data are entered so that any data errors are flagged as soon as possible and resolved before they get into the database (where they can create much larger problems). These errors can be identified by either the on-line system or by edit and audit reports.

Generally, the shop floor control systems observed in the participating firms were held responsible for the accuracy of all information entered from the shop floor. These systems were supported by various verification rules that were used to identify potential data entry problems. For example, at Bently Nevada, the computer will flag any situation in which the quantity leaving the work center is not equal to the entering quantity (after adjusting for scrap). The computer will also trap any data in which there are major deviations in reported time as compared with the standard time. Using these reports, the supervisors are responsible for correcting any erroneous data entered that day.

Control/Feedback

Control/feedback deals with the problems of managing out-of-control situations and the maintenance of information flows from the shop floor control system to the rest of the firm. For most, the resolution of problem situations is a more important issue.

> <u>Management should identify, in advance, the conditions under which a situation is out of control.</u>

Before the shop floor control system can identify an out-of-control situation, management must lay out the conditions under which an order or a work center becomes out of control and requires management intervention. These conditions must be stated in terms of special activities (amount of scrap produced or machine downtime) or states (e.g., number of days behind schedule, order quality) that are critical to manufacturing. Once these conditions are identified and incorporated into the resulting computer system, the system can help the users by evaluating and flagging orders that violate these conditions.

All of the participating firms have identified, in advance, such conditions. Typically, these conditions dealt with order lateness, level of scrap, quality, and machine breakdowns.

<u>Expediting is an indicator of the performance of the shop floor control system.</u>

Expediting, or the chasing of production orders through the shop floor, is often a way to bring out-of-control orders back under control. Expediting, however, can be disruptive and should be used only as a last resort. It should be regarded as an indicator or barometer of the overall effectiveness of the shop floor control system. To rely on expediting indicates a major problem with the system because it is indicative of such problems as inadequate capacity, poor priority control, or inadequate order review/release. These underlying problems should be corrected rather than covered up by expediting.

Expediting should be avoided because it perpetuates the need for it rather than solving the conditions that gave rise to the need for expediting in the first place. Instead, the responsibility for expediting should be given to the operators, dispatchers, and planners. These people are familiar with the jobs and the equipment and know the reasons for the out-of-control situations.

Expediting should be a two-stage process. First, actions are taken to bring the out-of-control orders back under control. Second, the conditions that created the need for expediting must be identified and corrected.

Tight control over expediting and the general lack of expediters are characteristics common to all of the participating firms. Steelcase, for example, has one expediter who is responsible for expediting needed purchased parts. There are no expediters on the shop floor for manufacturing parts. Similar experiences were noted in the other firms. The management in some firms expressed an aversion to expediting in any form.

<u>Shop floor personnel should know in advance what options they can use and the order in which these options are to be used when resolving problems on the shop floor</u>.

Management should work with shop floor personnel to identify the options that can be used to remedy out-of-control situations, the conditions under which these options are to be applied, and the general sequence in which these options are to be used. This information should be available to anyone interested in the shop floor control system and its operation. By establishing these options in advance, management enhances the operation of the shop floor control system in several ways. First, the activities of shop personnel are simplified because they know in advance what they can and cannot do and when. Second, uncertainty involving the operation of the shop floor control system is reduced because everyone knows how shop personnel will respond to shop problems. This helps to develop credibility in the shop floor control system and its operation. Finally, in those cases where the due dates must be changed, the planners know what actions shop personnel have taken to correct the problems. The planners know that the orders cannot be completed by their original due dates and that they must be rescheduled.

The options considered should be order splitting, operation overlapping, rescheduling, overtime, subcontracting, or extra shifts.

Order Disposition

Order disposition is the last major activity of shop floor control. It is responsible for closing out shop orders and for relieving the system of final responsibility for completed orders, recovered salvage, and scrap.

> The order should be closed out quickly by the shop floor control system only after any unusual variances in the performance measures have been reconciled, and the reasons for these problems adequately accounted.

Given the constant tracking and monitoring that should follow an order as it proceeds through the various operations, order disposition should be a straightforward activity. In the case of a completed order, the order should be recorded as complete and its order quantity made available to the planning system. In the case of scrap, the number of pieces should be recorded. In either case, the order should be closed out as quickly as possible provided that all unusual variances have been accounted for adequately, and the reasons for all problems identified and properly recovered. Otherwise, the order should remain open. Management must know what happened and why. If the order is closed out without this information, then the data generated by that order are meaningless to the firm.

<u>The performance of the shop floor should be evaluated in terms of a limited number of well-understood and meaningful measures that indicate how well the plan was achieved.</u>

Effective systems are built on a small number of measures (no more than four) that are simple to evaluate and relate clearly to the basis on which the firm competes. By using only a few measures, the shop floor control system makes a clear statement of what is required. Using many performance measures, on the other hand, creates a situation where the persons being evaluated do not know which measures they have to do well. This confusion is aggravated by a tendency for these measures to conflict.

This principle is evident in the way Steelcase has structured its performance measures. Steelcase competes on dimensions of quality, on-time delivery, and service. Of these three dimensions, the first two are crucial. Each department at Steelcase is evaluated in terms of its ability to ship a quality product on time. This measurement involves taking the daily schedule for each shift and measuring the percentage of that schedule that was shipped to physical distribution that day that met or surpassed the quality standards. This measure is recorded every day and is posted in a prominent position in each department. Every work center in each department is evaluated in terms of its ability to relieve the standard hours booked for that week. Good performance for a work center means clearing out the booked standard hours and completing the load in less than standard time. Again, this measure emphasizes on-time performance.

As a result, there is no confusion about what each department (and each work center) has to do to succeed. Furthermore, the measures reflect corporate objectives and are effective because they are few and simple to measure and understand.

<u>The shop floor personnel should be monitored on a timely basis and should also track their own performance.</u>

In an effective shop floor control system, performance evaluation/feedback is not simply a periodic (e.g., once a month) review of shop personnel by management, on how closely the personnel have been able to achieve their objectives. Such an approach makes performance evaluation/feedback a punishment device. Instead, performance evaluation/feedback should provide personnel a way to monitor their performance and to correct any problems before the problems get worse. Ideally, the shop floor control system should provide the capability of monitoring performance shift by shift. That is, at the end of every shift, foremen can review how they did in terms of cost variances, on-time delivery, and material and labor variances. Any problems can be corrected easily because the events underlying the current level of performance are still fresh. As a result, this principle allows the shop floor control system to become self-regulating.

A good example of this principle can be found in the system developed and used at the Consumer Health Care Division of Miles Laboratories. The foremen are held responsible for the successful implementation of all plans released to them. Their performance is evaluated using the daily results provided by the production and labor report. The foremen are held responsible for all variances on this report. Because these reports are produced daily, the workers know how they are doing from day to day. Furthermore, they can call up this information on line.

Using this report, the foremen have an early warning device. The presence of unfavorable variances indicates the need for either corrective action or an explanation of the variances. The foremen can take any action they feel is necessary to correct the problem. As a result, the production and labor report is seen as a corrective device instead of a way to identify and punish poor performance.

Finally, by allowing prompt feedback to the shop personnel, there is never any uncertainty or confusion about how anyone is doing. Everyone knows what they have to do well.

THE KEYS TO EFFECTIVE SHOP FLOOR CONTROL SUMMARIZED

At first glance, the various principles and practices of effective shop floor control identified in this chapter seem to be too numerous to remember. As shown by Figure 3-1, these principles seem to point to a shop floor control jigsaw puzzle. There are seemingly so many pieces that management must carefully fit together to construct an effective system. However, these various principles are not as overwhelming as they seem at first glance. They can be summarized into four major keys:

- <u>People</u>. Shop floor control systems should always be computer systems designed to be used by people. The success of this system depends extensively on the human. It is the human who makes the

THE SHOP FLOOR CONTROL JIGSAW PUZZLE

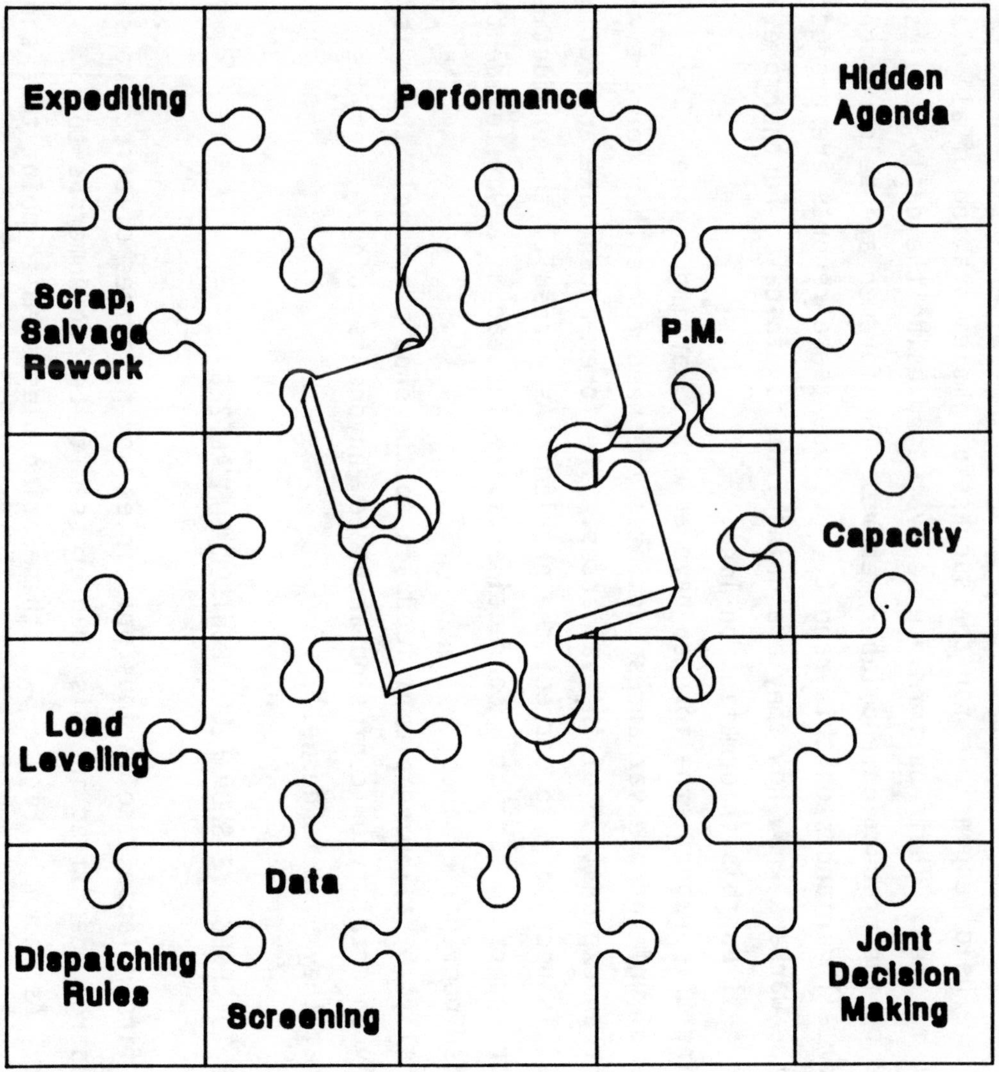

Figure 3-1. -- Shop Floor Control Jigsaw Puzzle

system work; it is also the human who brings much of the needed operating detail not available to the computer system.

- Accountability. For every action taken in the shop floor control system, someone must be held accountable. Accountability ensures that all shop floor control personnel take responsibilities seriously. It also ensures that they view any actions suggested by the computer system as only recommendations.
- Capacity. The shop floor control system is a resource manager. It is responsible for efficiency, not for feasibility. The planning system must provide the shop floor control system with access to adequate levels of resources.
- Systems. Effective shop floor control systems give the users the support they need. This support must come from the computer systems found in a shop floor control system. These systems relieve the users of the need for doing repetitive tasks, flag potential problems, inform the users, and recommend potential solutions. In short, the systems provide the users with necessary tools.

The summary of these four keys is found in Figure 3-2.

SHOP FLOOR VISIBILITY: THE ULTIMATE GOAL OF AN EFFECTIVE SHOP FLOOR SYSTEM

For many firms, the shop floor and shop floor control system can be best described as a black box. Orders are entered by marketing at one end of this box, and output is received at the other end. The problem with this black box is that no one within the firm seems to understand what takes place within the box. Problems are identified only after the time that the order was to be received. Customer inquiries must be passed on to someone who is familiar with the operation of the shop floor. The relationship between the actions of the planning system and the day-to-day activities on the shop floor is not understood.

This confusion and lack of understanding surrounding the shop floor and its activities extend to both top management and many of the people directly involved in the day-to-day activities of the shop floor. Shop floor control is seen as primarily tactical to top management. That is, shop floor control is required to carry out the plans assigned to it by the planning system. That shop floor control can be strategic is an unheard of

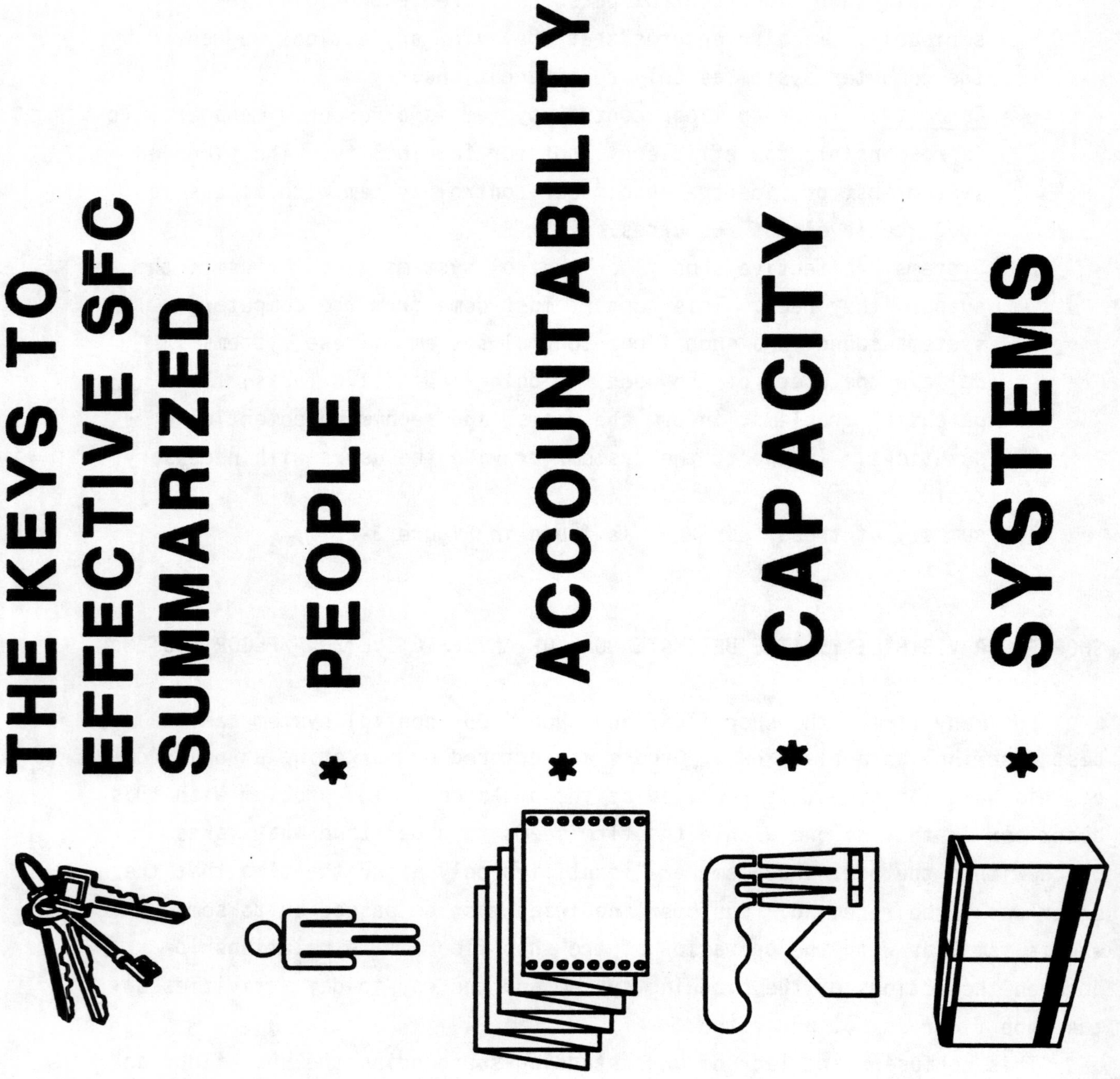
THE KEYS TO
EFFECTIVE SFC
SUMMARIZED
* PEOPLE
* ACCOUNTABILITY
* CAPACITY
* SYSTEMS

Figure 3-2. -- The Keys to Effective Shop Floor Control

proposition. To many of the people working on the shop floor, shop floor control involves the setting of unrealistic expectations. Work that should not have been released is released; priorities that shop floor personnel know cannot be met on time are set.

The firms examined in this study are distinguished from those described in the preceding paragraphs because they have been able to free their systems of the black box image. They have been able to make their shop floor control systems visible (transparent) to everyone in the firm. They have done this by using the principles discussed in this chapter.

These various principles, when combined, help create shop floor transparency by attacking and removing those elements that contribute to the black box image. For example, the presence of a common corporate database provides those working outside of the shop floor with an important window into the operation of the shop floor and the shop floor control system. This window's effectiveness is enhanced considerably by a computerized on-line system. By tracking orders on an ongoing basis, the shop floor control system provides others within the firm with the ability to identify the status of any given order quickly and accurately. This capability, when combined with the common corporate database and on-line reporting, enables a person from a department such as marketing to be able to track an order without having to rely on production people. Both sides benefit from this capability. Marketing benefits because the lead time required to process an order status request has been reduced greatly; manufacturing benefits because its personnel do not have to take time away from their tasks to process this request.

In addition, these principles also clearly demonstrate the responsibilities of both the planning and the execution system. The planning system provides the shop floor with access to adequate resources (in the form of personnel, material, tooling, and machine capacity); the shop floor control system carries out the plans on time and efficiently. Confusion that accompanies the system is reduced. By emphasizing the validity and the simplicity of the procedures on the shop floor level, the principles help to eliminate any confusion still remaining on the shop floor.

Shop floor visibility brings with it many benefits -- most important is the ability of management to ensure that good planning is complemented by good execution.

SUMMARY

This chapter has identified a set of general principles associated with effective shop floor control systems. These principles provide guidelines that can be used by managers interested in the development of an effective shop floor control system.

The authors have identified another set of guidelines associated with an effective shop floor control system in Melnyk, Carter, Dilts, and Lyth, Shop Floor Control. Unlike the guidelines discussed in this chapter, these prior guidelines were based on an exhaustive review of the literature related to shop floor control. It is interesting to note that many of these literature-based principles are supported by the empirically based principles of this chapter. To a large extent, the principles in this chapter are illustrated with actual company examples found in the thirteen presentations in this book.

CHAPTER 4: THE PARTICIPATING FIRMS

INTRODUCTION

The general principles described in Chapter 3 represent the most significant lessons that can be learned from the experiences of the thirteen participating firms. Any firm dealing with job shop operations and devoted to the development, implementation, and operation of an effective shop floor control system should make use of these principles. The lessons in Chapter 3 can be generalized because they are drawn from firms that, while similar in one major dimension (they all have discrete batch manufacturing facilities), are diverse in terms of market segment served, product lines offered, company ownership (private versus public), firm size (dollar sales and number of employees), and extent of government involvement. This diversity is not coincidental; it is a major feature of the study.

This chapter describes the process by which the thirteen firms were identified and selected. It then discusses the major features of the conference on which this book is based. Third, an overview of the participating firms is provided, highlighting the major corporate and manufacturing characteristics of each firm, and noteworthy features of each firm's shop floor control system are identified. These summaries, not intended to substitute for the case studies in the following chapters, are to guide the reader to those systems of greatest interest.

SELECTION OF THE COMPANIES

It became evident early in the project that a procedure had to be developed to identify firms considered to be at the leading edge of the development and use of shop floor control. Because it was impossible to bring together all of the firms considered to be leading edge, this procedure had to enable the authors to draw an appropriate sample from these firms.

The firms had to represent as much diversity as possible for this study. Without diversity, it would be impossible to claim that the principles derived from the conference can be generalized.

From the start of the project, the authors recognized that shop floor control systems could be divided into two major categories: those developed for job shop settings (discrete batch manufacturing) and those developed for repetitive/continuous manufacturing systems. These two types of shop floor control systems, while dealing with the same set of activities, were viewed as being too different to be compared productively. The authors decided to limit the focus of the study to shop floor control systems developed for job shops. Within this production setting, typical batch sizes would be allowed to vary (ranging from systems that produce batches of one or two items to firms producing millions of items).

Population Identification

The first task was to identify all the firms (population) that could be considered the leading edge users. To accomplish this task, the authors drew on three sources: literature related to shop floor control, expert opinion, and the steering committee. Each source provided the authors with a set of potential candidate firms, and each source validated the integrity of the nominated firms. The firms nominated by more than one source were viewed as likely having a true leading edge shop floor control system.

Literature Related to Shop Floor Control

As previously noted, this report is the second phase in a much larger project dealing with shop floor control. In the first phase, the authors undertook an extensive review of the literature regarding shop floor control to develop an integrating framework for shop floor control and to identify recommended shop floor control practices. A list of firms identified in the literature as having well-developed shop floor control systems was compiled. These firms were contacted during the first phase of the procedure.

Expert Opinion

The opinions of industry consultants, practitioners, and educators familiar with both shop floor control and its industrial applications were solicited. These people were asked to nominate those firms that they considered to have good shop floor control systems that they could recommend as models. They were also asked to explain why they regarded these firms as having good systems.

The experts had difficulty identifying good users of shop floor control. For most experts, the concept of a good shop floor control system was vague. They felt that while many manufacturing systems could do MRP well, few had effective shop floor control systems. The presence of a Class A MRP system did not necessarily indicate the presence of an effective shop floor control system.

The Steering Committee

A steering committee was formed early in the project. Steven A. Melnyk, Phillip L. Carter, David M. Dilts, and Dave Lyth represented the academic community. The members from industry were drawn not only from different types of manufacturing concerns but also from different levels in the firms. For example, one member (Ken Jorgensen) was a corporate vice president (see Appendix C). All committee members were APICS members who were knowledgeable in shop floor control.

The steering committee played a prominent role during the selection of the firms. The members identified the specific attributes that should be considered when selecting the companies. They also identified companies that they felt were at the forefront of shop floor control. In several instances, committee members were instrumental in securing the participation of such leading edge firms.

Thirty-five firms were identified as leading edge users of shop floor control. Each firm was contacted and thirty-two firms proceeded into the next stage of the selection process.

Information Gathering

In the second stage, information about these thirty-two firms and their shop floor control systems was collected by questionnaire. Areas covered by the questionnaire were:

- o Demographics
- o Characteristics of the production planning system
- o History of the production planning system
- o History of the shop floor control system
- o Organization of the shop floor control system

- o Information on how shop floor control is used and how the various activities of this system are carried out
- o An evaluation on the costs and benefits of shop floor control
- o Opinions on the next stages for their shop floor control system.

After being reviewed by the steering committee, the questionnaire was field tested, revised, and retested for effectiveness. The questionnaire was sixteen pages in its final form. A copy of the questionnaire can be found in Appendix B.

The thirty-two firms were contacted by telephone before they received the questionnaire. A follow-up telephone contact was made four weeks after the questionnaires were sent out to increase the response rate. Twenty-four firms completed and returned their questionnaires. The completion of the questionnaire was a necessary condition for continued participation in the study.

Screening and Selection

All of the responding firms were invited to attend the conference in August 1983 at Michigan State University. As a condition of participation, all were asked to complete detailed case descriptions of their shop floor control system for inclusion in the conference proceedings. No firm could attend unless it submitted a case in advance.

Of the twenty-four responding firms, thirteen were ultimately invited to participate in the conference. These firms substantially satisfied the requirements laid down at the beginning of the study.

The steering committee realized that not all of these firms could do an oral presentation on their system within the time allocated for the conference, so ten firms were invited to do presentations. These ten firms were chosen by reviewing the questionnaires.

The responses were analyzed using descriptive statistics, and a brief summary was compiled that identified several major attributes of each firm (e.g., what percentage of the production was MTO, MTS, ETO, or ATO; type of material planning system; and length of experience with shop floor control). The summary also identified the unique features of each firm's shop floor control system. On the basis of both the analysis and the summary, the steering committee chose those firms that would be of greatest interest to the APICS membership.

CONFERENCE OVERVIEW

The conference was held August 28 to 31, 1983. Ten company presentations were given. The participants also attended sessions at which they evaluated proposed shop floor control frameworks and discussed trends in shop floor control and its importance to the overall success of a firm. The shop floor control framework presented in Chapter 2 and the principles and practices discussed in Chapter 3 are the culmination of work begun in these sessions.

AN OVERVIEW OF THE PARTICIPATING FIRMS

The general company and manufacturing system descriptions that follow use a classification scheme similar to that developed by Berry, Vollmann, and Whybark.[1] The following are some of the major characteristics used to describe the significant company and manufacturing traits of the participating firms:

- Focus. Each presentation is based on a shop floor control system that is used by either the entire firm, a division within the firm, or a specific plant. This term identifies the extent of the system being discussed.
- Orientation of the manufacturing organization. This refers to the percentage division of production among MTO, MTS, ATO, and ETO.
- Major product lines. This is a generic description of the principal product lines manufactured and sold by the firm.
- Major markets. This variable identifies the major customers and the channels by which they are served.
- Principal process characteristics. Two variables are included under this attribute. The first is the production lot size for end items (as measured in terms of the average quantity and variability). The second identifies any unique features of that firm's production process. For example, Ingersoll Milling is an extensive user of CAD/CAM and FMS.

---

[1] W. L. Berry, T. E. Vollmann, and D. Clay Whybark. Master Production Scheduling: Principles and Practice (Washington, D.C.: American Production and Inventory Control Society, 1979), Chapter 4.

- Firm size. This attribute is described using two variables. The first variable is the number of employees at the location of the shop floor control system. The second variable is the level of annual sales for that location.
- Miscellaneous. If the presence of a union, the nature of ownership (private or public), government regulation, and so on, are thought to be relevant, they are noted under this attribute.

The second set of attributes focuses on the special features of each firm's shop floor control system. Among the features considered under this classification scheme are:

- Objectives for the shop floor control system. What is shop floor control expected to do for management?
- Shop floor control logic. This consists of two variables: software (packaged software, software developed in house, and packaged software modified in house) and extent of computerization.
- Shop floor control activities. This attribute looks at how the firm carries out the major activities of shop floor control as described in Chapter 2. Any unique features are also identified.
- Shop floor control interface to the planning system. The links between the planning and execution system are summarized.
- Shop floor control -- performance evaluation/feedback.

Major attributes of the thirteen firms are summarized in Figure 4-1. As can be seen from Figure 4-2, the firms participating in this study represented not only a great diversity in terms of their manufacturing characteristics but also a great deal of geographic diversity.

SUMMARY

This chapter has focused on the major features of each participating firm and its shop floor control system. The summaries or abstracts contained in Figure 4-1 are not intended to be exhaustive; they highlight what is unique about each firm. All repetition of features has been avoided. The summaries are intended to make the reader aware of what features to recognize when reading each presentation. To really learn about each system and those factors that make that system effective, the reader must study the detailed presentations found in the next thirteen chapters.

Company Name	Production Characteristics	Key Shop Floor Control (SFC) Features
Bently Nevada Minden, Nevada	o Relatively small (350 employees) o Manufacturer of high precision instrumentation and transducers o Vertically integrated o Extreme diversity in run sizes	Good integration of capacity planning and control with SFC Extreme integration of the human with the operation of the SFC systems Unusually complete reporting system
Steelcase, Inc. (Seating Division) Grand Rapids, Michigan	o Extensive fabrication and assembly facility o Traditional job shop structure o Well-known Class A MRP II system	SFC well integrated into the operation of the MRP II system Good example of effective SFC under MRP Detailed scheduling by operator Complete capacity planning and its link to SFC
Twin Disc, Inc. Racine, Wisconsin	o Primarily MTO and ATO environment o Large number of active part numbers and operations o Complete MRP II system	On-line, real-time system Comprehensive system for managing scrap, salvage, and rework in a real-time setting Procedures for managing the different types of orders (safety versus customer) Integration of capacity planning
The Vollrath Company Sheboygan, Wisconsin	o Mixture of ATO, MTS, and MTO demands o Unionized work force o Unique equipment o Presence of reserved capacity o Extensive revision of released orders o Complete MRP II system	On-line, real-time SFC system Electrically driven SFC system Joint problem solving on the shop floor Feasibility tests for orders and changes on the shop floor Direct user accountability
Moog, Inc. East Aurora, New York	o High percentage of ETO and MTO orders o Primary subcontractor to companies such as Grumman o Specialized work centers o Long routings o Significant scrap and rework problems	Extensive integration of engineering Role of the shop floor user well illustrated Importance of look-ahead/look-back reports in dispatching Role of layered reports demonstrated

Figure 4-1. Participating Firms: Key Company Attributes and Features

Miles Laboratories (Consumer Healthcare Division) Elkhart, Indiana	o High-volume batch production o Highly regulated o Need for complete documentation o High variable demand (due to promotions and seasonal nature of products)	Strong overlap between SFC and planning (especially in the area of order review/release and dispatching) Extensive integration of SFC with quality assurance Strong integration between SFC and cost accounting function Need for continuous fine-tuning of computer reports and role of management information system (MIS) in the process
General Electric (Control Manufacturing, Locomotive Division) Erie, Pennsylvania	o Revitalization of an old facility o Unionized work force o Highly volatile product mix o Strong replacement/repair market o Extensive product line o Fluctuating capacity requirements	Computer-supported reporting system Positioning of input devices to increase use by shop floor personnel Comprehensive scrap, salvage, and rework control system with material review board in operation Successful implementation of an effective SFC system demonstrated
Ingersoll Milling Machine Company Rockford, Illinois	o Classic CIM system o Extensive use of FMS o Extremely small production batches (1-2 units) o Little repetition of parts production (every part is unique) o Almost 100 percent ETO o Dominance of engineering o LEAD award winner (1982)	SFC under CIM Strong integration of engineering, manufacturing engineering, and SFC Comprehensive scrap, salvage, and rework control system Management of order review/release mechanism Applying SFC systems to a manufacturing system that is using FMS
Consolidated Diesel Company Whitakers, North Carolina	o JIT manufacturing o Team approach to the day-to-day management of the shop floor o Continuous low-batch production o Extensive commonality in engines/high option flexibility o Limited storage o 100 percent MTO o Extensive use of CIM	Effective control/feedback activities under JIT Importance of people in a JIT setting Effects of JIT on SFC system SFC as a mechanism for formally enhancing the operation of the shop floor Managing the joint introduction of new organizational structure, new production processes, and a new approach to production (JIT) and the effect of these moves on SFC Making the best use of the human in the system

Figure 4-1. Participating Firms: Key Company Attributes and Features (con't.)

Joy Machine Company (Division of Joy Manufacturing Company) Franklin, Pennsylvania	o Primarily ATO o Unionized work force o MRP II system o Extensive emphasis on capacity in the planning process	Extensive documentation of the SFC system On-line, real-time SFC Centralized dispatching Input/output reporting Links with industrial engineering Extensive use of computer-stored free format communication
FMC (Ordnance Division) Aiken, South Carolina	o Designer and manufacturer of defense equipment o Primarily subcontractor of component parts o Extensive use of computer numerical control o Participative management o Shallow bill of materials (2-3 levels) o Short lead times (3 weeks)	On-line, real-time system Extensive involvement of the operator in the detailed assignment process
Wright Lines Worchester Massachusetts	o Sheet metal fabrication and assembly facility o MRP II facility	A SFC system undergoing development and revision Identification of the issues to be addressed when revising an existing SFC system Structure of SFC implementation process discussed
Aladdin Industries, Inc. Nashville, Tennessee	o High-volume, high-speed, large-batch production (very close in the production characteristics of a repetitive manufacturing system) o Primarily MTO o Extensive mix of manufacturing processes (metal forming, welding, plastic injection molding, plastic extrusion, glass forming, and plastic decorating)	SFC in a high-volume production system Impact of highly seasonal demand on SFC Focusing of SFC activities on critical resources (injection molding areas) Detailed assignment in a high-volume production setting

Figure 4-1. Participating Firms: Key Company Attributes and Features (con't.)

LOCATION OF PARTICIPATING COMPANIES

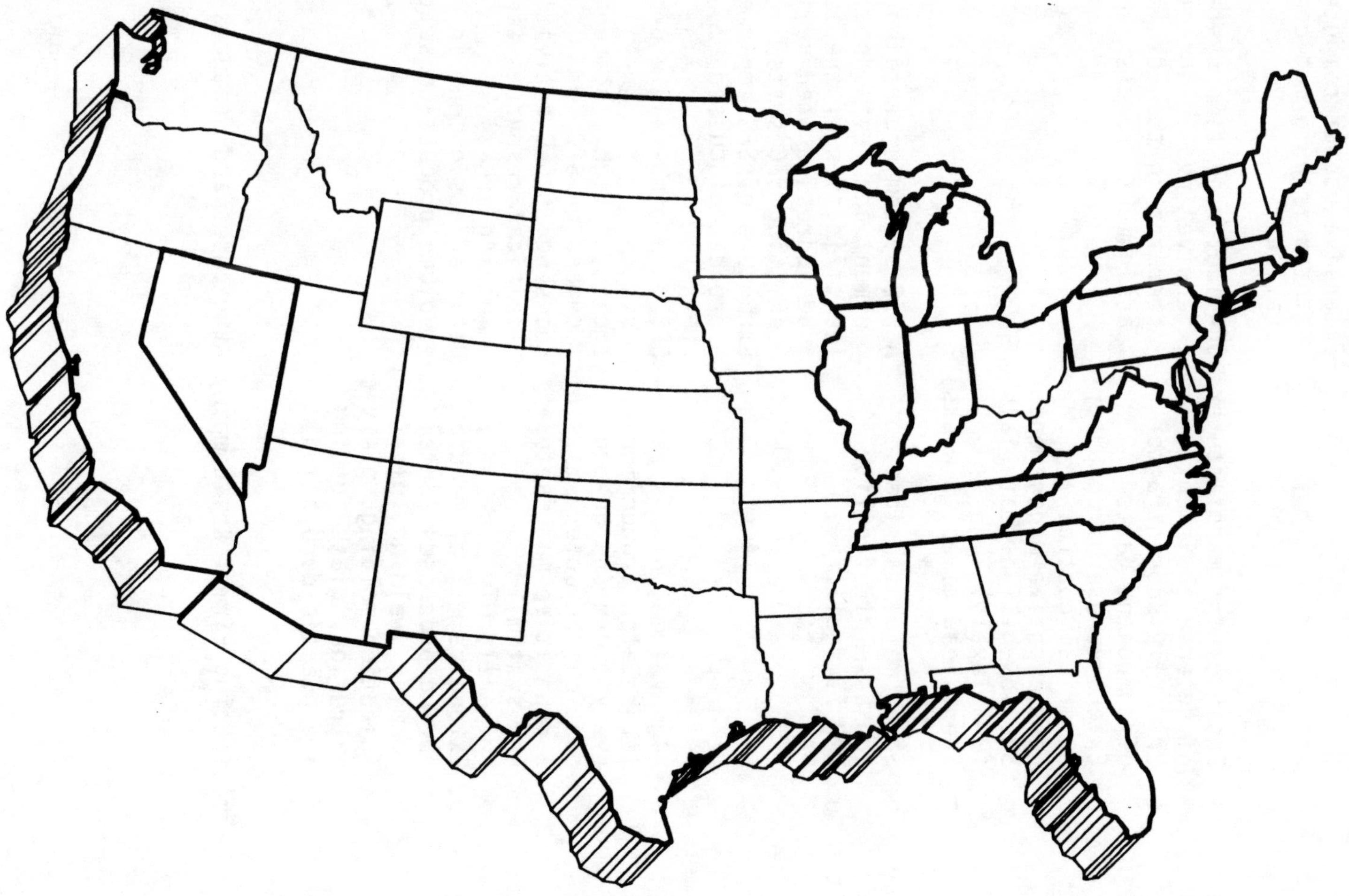

Figure 4-2. -- Location of Participating Companies

General Nature of the Firm

The Bently Nevada Corporation, headquartered in Minden, Nevada, is a privately held firm. Incorporated in the early 1960s by Donald E. Bently, the owner and current operator, Bently Nevada is a major manufacturer of instrumentation and transducers used to gather information on the operation of rotating machinery. The information gathered is used for predictive maintenance, quality assurance of machinery, and machinery problem identification. Bently Nevada offers a comprehensive line of products, ranging from simple, relatively inexpensive mechanical transducers to expensive computerized information systems that provide digital feedback. In addition, Bently Nevada also offers field maintenance, engineering, and turnkey services. For a fee, the manufacturer or buyer can have Bently Nevada engineers take over the responsibility of installing and testing the monitoring equipment. Major customers come from the petrochemical and energy transmission fields and include such firms as Exxon, Monsanto, Texaco, Esso, Pacific Gas and Electric, and Consolidated Edison. Currently, annual sales are approximately $50 million and are divided evenly between domestic and foreign markets.

Bently Nevada's production facilities consist of three plants (one located in Carson City, Nevada, and two plants in Minden) employing 340 people. Consistent with the corporate philosophy of remaining as vertically integrated as possible, the production facilities include a machine shop, a sheet metal shop, a printed circuit board fabrication unit, an electromechanical assembly unit, a final assembly operation, and a final test operation. The company operates under a no layoff policy.

Bently Nevada competes on the basis of several important production practices. These are:

- High quality and reliability. Because of the requirements placed on Bently Nevada products, the items must work the first time out. Because transducers are often buried in the machinery, repairing defects is often expensive and time consuming. To date, Bently Nevada has been successful in building reliable and accurate instrumentation. It is the only manufacturer that offers a ten-year warranty on most of the products.

- Product delivery in relatively short lead times. Bently Nevada's customers are now asking for delivery of products in less than six to eight weeks from the time that the order is placed. The cumulative lead time for typical Bently Nevada products is approximately twenty-six weeks.
- Products must be delivered on time. Bently Nevada products are often incorporated directly into the machinery during construction. As a result, these products must be on hand when they are to be built in. Otherwise, the completion of the machinery must be delayed until the part is received. For most manufacturers, such delays are expensive.
- Provide the customer with high levels of customer service. To Bently Nevada, customer service consists of two major activities: helping the customer during installation and providing quick repair service once the product is in the field. As part of the first activity, Bently Nevada provides engineering assistance to customers during installation. It can even take over the task of installing the transducers if the customer wishes. Because downtime due to transducer malfunctions is expensive, Bently Nevada has field offices located throughout the world. These offices provide its customers with repair services twenty-four hours a day, regardless of where the customer is located.
- Cost control. Bently Nevada's customers are becoming increasingly sensitive to product cost. As a result, since 1979, cost control and reduction have become increasingly more important as a basis of competition.

Bently Nevada is involved in all four major forms of production, with 10 percent of its average production ETO, 50 percent ATO, 10 percent MTO, and 30 percent MTS.

Characteristics of Bently Nevada

The production planning system described in this case is used by all of the Bently Nevada plants. There are forty product families, 600 master scheduled items, 5,000 purchased parts, and 6,000 fabricated or assembled parts in the production system. The typical BOMs consists of four levels. Consistent with the variability in the type of production (i.e., MTO, MTS, ETO, and ATO), end-item lot sizes vary considerably. At one extreme, 20 percent of production (primarily ETO) consists of one or two unit runs. At the other extreme, 30 percent of the runs are relatively large (1,000 to 2,000 units). These latter runs are primarily MTS. The remaining items (mainly ATO and MTO) are manufactured in intermediate run sizes of approximately 1,000 items. The typical end-item cycle time (i.e., cumulative lead time) is approximately fifteen weeks. Bently Nevada runs one shift operating typically at 70 percent capacity. The manufacturing system uses a variety of machines: general purpose machines (20 percent of capacity), numerical control machines (10 percent of capacity), direct numerical control machines (10 percent of capacity), and computer numerical control machines (60 percent). All of its workers are nonunion and are paid for a minimum of forty hours per week (regardless of whether they are actually working or not). This again reflects the no layoff policy.

The Production Process

Because of product variability, it is difficult to describe a typical product routing. Each product tends to use each of the production facilities previously noted. Within each facility, orders go through an average of eleven operations.

Capacity is measured by work center. At each work center, capacity is stated in terms of that center's critical resource. This resource can be either labor or machine.

Production Planning at Bently Nevada

The current production planning system is a direct result of a crisis. In 1976, a fire destroyed about 60 percent of the manufacturing facilities, and the company had a difficult time reestablishing a positive cash flow. After analyzing the situation, Mr. Bently decided that a large part of the prior production problems was due to the informal planning system. As a result, he established the goal of implementing a credible and effective formal planning system in the form of MRP. In implementing MRP, the intent was to give manufacturing a good management tool. Subsequently, MRP became a good management tool for the entire company.

The MRP effort was started in 1977. Since then, manufacturing's MRP has evolved into Bently Nevada's MRP II system. Most of the modules for MRP II are now in place. For example, planning starts with top management, and the financial and operating systems are integrated fully with both using the same database. The planning system consists of the production plan, master production schedule, material requirements plan, capacity requirements plan, and shop floor control. Capacity planning is considered a part of shop floor control along with the dispatch list, input/output reports, and shop floor activity reports.

The production planning and execution process is iterative and begins with the production plan. Every four weeks, the department heads meet with the general manager to review the production plan and make any required changes. During this review, marketing presents forecast changes and the actual demand (backlog) as indications of what is happening in the marketplace. Manufacturing presents the inventory levels and production capacity to show how the company can respond to the marketplace. Using these data, the department heads negotiate the best future production rate for each product family. In the case of disagreement, the general manager arbitrates a final solution.

Next, the master scheduler determines which of the master scheduled items should be changed to bring the aggregate master schedule quantities into conformance with the production plan. The detailed item forecasts, inventory levels, and actual demand are used to make these decisions. It is important to note that no capacity planning occurs during the formulation of the master production schedule. At this point, only the rough-cut capacity planning done during the production planning process controls the shop load.

The detailed material plan can now be calculated. The computer that before this stage had been used primarily for record keeping is now used extensively for calculations. The quantities that are on hand in the storeroom, bills of material, open work orders, planned lead times, and lot sizes are used to calculate the time-phased material plan. This plan is used by the production control department to determine which work orders should be opened. It is important to note that the computer is not allowed to open, close, or reschedule orders automatically. Such actions are left to a production control person. The person must determine whether such changes can be accommodated adequately by the system. After all, it is the person, not the computer, who is ultimately accountable.

The production control people check material availability to be sure that the work can be released to the shop.

The last plan to be generated is the detailed capacity requirements plan. Open order status, routings, and projected future work orders are used to generate a time-phased load projection for each work center. This plan converts quantities, part numbers, and order due dates into load hours, work centers, and operation due dates and will be discussed as part of the shop floor control system. The master production schedule, material requirements plan, and the capacity requirements plan are regenerated once a week over the weekend.

When Monday morning arrives, everyone begins to execute the plan and problems begin to occur -- customers order items that were not forecasted; vendors fail to deliver on time; engineering change orders occur; and machines and tools break. As these and other problems occur, the supervisors, production control people, and others begin to solve the problems jointly. The system is used primarily as a communication tool when solving problems. A major tenet at Bently Nevada is that while the computer is a good communication tool, only people can solve problems.

Shop Floor Control

The current shop floor control system has been in place since 1978. It is computerized completely with the computer used to collect and communicate all information to the users. The software in use was developed by taking a standard package (IPICS, acquired in 1976) and then extensively modifying it in house. The system is used primarily to:

- o Track orders through the shop
- o Monitor the progress of orders against the plan
- o Sequence and dispatch orders
- o Feed back information to the planning system
- o Report labor and machine efficiency
- o Check material availability
- o Facilitate communication between people for problem identification.

Shop floor control at Bently Nevada is an integral part of the formal planning system. It closes the planning loop by providing rapid and prompt feedback to the master production schedule. Responsibility for shop floor control is the joint responsibility of two groups (Figure 5-1). The pro-

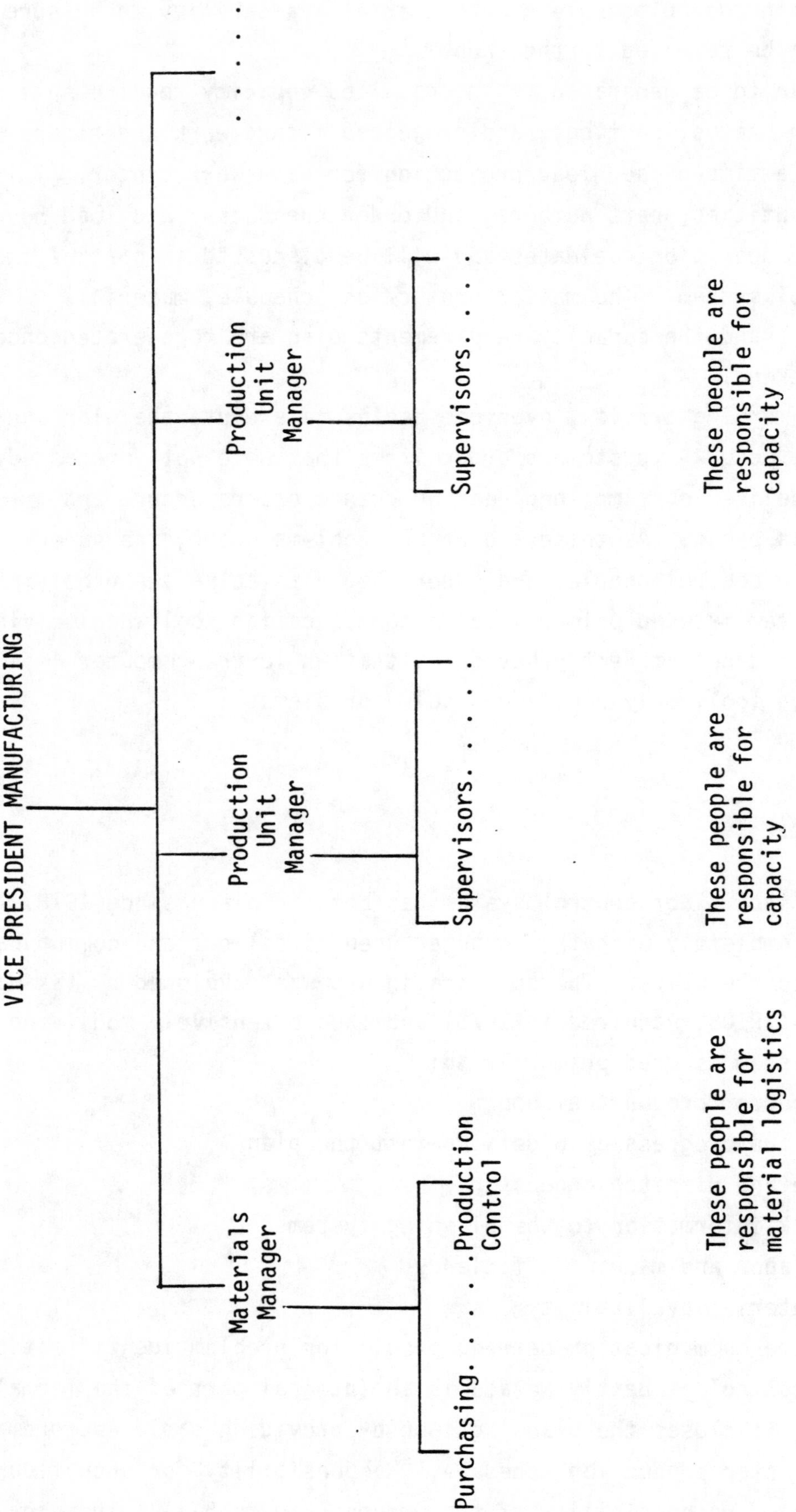

Figure 5-1. -- Shop Floor Control Responsibility

duction control people are responsible for material logistics, and supervisors and production unit managers are responsible for capacity. Production control does not batch work orders short of material or release more than a certain percentage of the work orders with a short lead time. Supervisors and production unit managers can do the jobs in any order they want, but they must complete the work on time or feed back to production control when problems occur.

One of the most interesting aspects of Bently Nevada's shop floor control system is that it operates in real time with a very short time delay (one hour or less) between the time that an operator submits information to the keypuncher for entry and the time that information becomes part of the database. Once information enters the database, it becomes a shared resource of the firm. People who need this information are given on-line access to it. It is this information combined with the computer that greatly helps communication and joint decision making.

The Stages of Shop Floor Control at Bently Nevada

Shop floor control at Bently Nevada is built on six key manufacturing tenets, which have affected significantly the structure, organization, and operation of the shop floor control system. It is useful to first identify and discuss these tenets before examining how Bently Nevada manages the various shop floor control activities.

- <u>People, not computers, are crucial to the operation of any execution system</u>. At Bently Nevada, management strongly believes that computer-based procedures such as linear programming cannot be relied on to solve capacity problems. There are too many essential variables that have to be taken into account to have the computer help production control load capacity into the various work centers. Instead, management feels that supervisors are more knowledgeable than production control people when it comes to assessing the capacity realities of a work center. Supervisors know what is happening on the shop floor from moment to moment. They also know how to make the shop run more efficiently. Supervisors know how to group parts for setups, what machines are best for specific jobs, who is sick, who is on vacation, who is the best worker in general, who is the best worker for a particular type of job, and so on. Such information is critical to the successful operation of the system. Such information is also difficult to quantify. People can work with qualitative information and computers cannot. To be successful, the shop floor control system must make the greatest possible use of the capabilities offered by people such as the supervisors. This tenet is best summarized in Bently Nevada's "Manufacturing Philosophy Statement" (found at the end of this case).

- Pulling work forward is the best way to level the work load. Management can level the load by either pulling work forward (i.e., releasing it earlier to the shop floor) or by pushing it back (delaying the release of the order). At Bently Nevada, the preferred option is pulling work forward. Pushing work back can cause the rescheduling process to ripple up to the customer order level, and generally it tends to create more problems than it solves.
- The causes of plan changes must be determined before these changes are executed on the shop floor. If the plan change is traced to a keypunch error, then the error can be corrected so that the resulting impact on the shop floor is minimal. If the keypunch error is not caught and the resulting plan changes are accepted and implemented on the shop floor, then the resulting impact is significant and expensive to correct. The keypunch error is an example of internal problems. Such problems can cause instabilities on the shop floor. While instability caused by the marketplace is unavoidable, internal problems are not. They must always be controlled.
- Allow feedback when making the appropriate corrective actions. Quite often when the realities of production are presented, they are not liked. Wishing that they would go away doesn't help. An analogy is driving a car on an icy road. If you receive feedback from your senses that the car is beginning to skid, you cannot respond simply by wishing the skid away. Instead, to stay in control, you must steer into the skid, even if you don't like that direction, and then make direction corrections as fast as possible without skidding again. The same perspective holds true on the shop floor.
- Joint problem solving is emphasized. At Bently Nevada, the shop floor control system is structured to encourage joint problem solving. No one person in the company has access to all of the

resources needed to solve a shop problem. Furthermore, no one person can identify all of the causes of a given problem. Encouraging people to work together brings together all of the resources and perspectives needed to arrive at effective solutions. This orientation is consistent with management's belief that people must attack problems not other people. If Bently Nevada is to compete with its market competitors, then people within the firm must work together to solve problems.

- Capacity must be ensured and never assumed to exist. At Bently Nevada, work orders are released according to the master schedule, and it is the supervisor's responsibility to ensure that the work load is matched to the available capacity. Supervisors use the future load summary and detail report to determine the work orders that will be released, and they have the authority to reschedule work to level the load. The shop floor control system is expected to manage capacity, not to plan it.

These tenets are emphasized in Bently Nevada's statement of its manufacturing philosophy, which is distributed to all employees.

Order Review/Release

The order review/release activity of shop floor control begins with the open work order released by the MRP system. At this point, a routing for the order is generated, which can be either standard or one of a kind (depending on whether the order is MTS or ETO primarily). This information is recorded in two forms -- in the corporate database and in hard copy (i.e., traveler), which is passed to the shop floor and accompanies the order through its various stages.

The typical routing consists of approximately eleven actual operations. To these operations, the shop floor control system at Bently Nevada adds two additional planning operations: planning and stores. The planning stage is a check introduced to ensure that the orders released to the shop floor can be completed to meet the schedule. The first area checked is material availability.

A pick list is generated during this stage. The production controllers use this list to check reported material inventories against order requirements before turning the order over to shop floor personnel. As a rule, whenever an order is found that cannot be filled with current inventories, it is not released to the shop floor. There are certain instances in which orders are released with short material, but these instances are rare (i.e., less than 1 percent of all work orders released).

The second area checked is reasonableness. The production controllers review the order and its characteristics (i.e., order quantities, routings, and so on) to determine if there is anything about the order that would prevent it from being completed in time to meet the schedule. If any order passes through this stage successfully, it then enters the stores stage.

During stores, the inventory required by the order is pulled physically. The order is then turned over to shop floor personnel. Both of these stages have planned lead times of one day.

The availability of tooling is not checked during order review/release. In general, the products manufactured by Bently Nevada require fairly simple and standard tooling so tooling availability is not an issue.

Central to order review/release is an ongoing concern with capacity and its availability, which begins during the rough-cut capacity planning that occurs during the production planning process. The objective of the rough-cut capacity plan is to keep the average shop load in balance with the available capacity in the critical work centers. The next stage is detailed capacity planning, in the form of CRP, which is done at every work center.

The objectives of detailed capacity planning are to determine if there are peak loads that are going to cause problems in the future and to level the work load. The evaluation of capacity is done using the summary load, the detailed load, and the input/output summary reports. Examples of these reports are found in Figures 5-2 to 5-4.

The summary load report (Figure 5-2) is a one-page summary of all work-hours loaded into a given work center for six months. It indicates the general match between capacity availability and capacity requirements. It is also used as a warning system by the production supervisors. For example, if a report indicates that in the near future there will be a high level of capacity requirements, the supervisors can use this information to bring orders forward to work out this load imbalance before it takes place. Even if the report covers six months, the supervisors use only the first six to eight weeks.

The detailed load report (Figure 5-3) is a capacity audit of the work center. Typically consisting of many pages, the report breaks down each work center's load by period and by part number. It is used when the summary load profile indicates a capacity problem. Using this report, the

CP220 W/C 00004 CHUCKER WORK CENTER LOAD REPORT DATED 28/04/84

CAPACITY PER WK 180

	---OPEN ORDERS---			---PLANNED ORDERS---			ACCUM	ACCUM	PERCENT CUMULATIVE LOAD TO CAPACITY
	SETUP	RUN	TOTAL	SETUP	RUN	TOTAL	CAP %	LOAD	. . . . .50. . . . .100. . . . .150. . . . .200. 250
LATE	0	0	0	0	0	0	0	0	
84124	19	94	113	8	43	51	91	164	0000000000000XXXXX
84129	5	14	19	26	173	199	106	382	0000000XXXXXXXXXXXXXX
84134	0	0	0	18	157	175	103	557	00000XXXXXXXXXXXXXXXX
84139	0	0	0	30	170	200	105	757	0000XXXXXXXXXXXXXXXXX
84144	0	0	0	5	20	25	87	782	000XXXXXXXXXXXXXX
84148	1	1	2	35	238	273	98	1057	00XXXXXXXXXXXXXXXXXX
84153	0	0	0	15	99	114	93	1171	00XXXXXXXXXXXXXXXXX
84158	0	0	0	29	161	190	95	1361	00XXXXXXXXXXXXXXXXX
84163	2	100	102	42	207	249	106	1712	000XXXXXXXXXXXXXXXXXX
84168	0	0	0	2	8	10	96	1722	000XXXXXXXXXXXXXXXX
84172	1	7	8	11	84	95	92	1825	00XXXXXXXXXXXXXXXX
84177	0	0	0	8	38	46	87	1871	00XXXXXXXXXXXXXXX
84182	0	0	0	32	210	242	90	2113	00XXXXXXXXXXXXXXXX
84187-84206	0	0	0	111	585	696	92	2809	00XXXXXXXXXXXXXXXX
84207-84225	0	0	0	91	615	706	93	3515	0XXXXXXXXXXXXXXXXXX
84226-84245	0	0	0	123	670	793	96	4308	0XXXXXXXXXXXXXXXXXX

Figure 5-2. -- Summary Load Report

CP210 CRP WORK CENTER LOAD DETAIL REPORT DATE [illegible]

	WK#	TYPE	DUE	PART NUMBER	ORDER#	OP#	SETUP	RUN HRS	ORDER QTY	PLNR CODE
W/C 00004 CHUCKER	01	O	84125	21515-00-16	0059520	0015	.88	10.20	200	12
	01	O	84125	21515-00-28	0061181	0015	.49	6.40	200	12
	01	O	84125	44238-01	0061324	0040	.81	6.00	100	16
	01	O	84125	20020-00-05	2100967	0015	1.00	4.05	50	12
	01	O	84126	16474-01	0061156	0030	.59	1.13	25	16
	01	O	84126	21513-00-20	0061180	0015	1.20	6.70	100	10
	01	O	84126	39511-01	0061269	0025	1.55	10.80	200	12
	01	O	84126	40963-01	0061298	0020	1.22	1.65	50	12
	01	O	84126	20012-00-24	2100969	0012	.50	10.00	50	12
	01	O	84126	20300-03	2100972	0014	1.50	7.50	30	12
	01	O	84126	21515-00-12	2702493	0015	.49	2.08	65	10
	01	O	84126	PROBE CASE	2702537	0015	.90	.94	4	14
	01	O	84127	40469-01	0061282	0020	2.00	13.30	100	16
	01	O	84127	44810-01	0061372	0020	.25	2.50	100	15
	01	O	84127	20038-00-37	2100963	0015	.61	.67	10	12
	01	O	84127	20091-01	2100970	0030	2.00	5.00	50	12
	01	O	84127	21519-00-96	2702494	0015	.85	2.71	41	10
	01	O	84127	PROBE CASE	2702527	0015	.90	.47	2	14
	01	O	84127	PROBE CASE	2702545	0015	.90	.71	3	14
	01	O	84128	4015-11	0061274	0008	.75	1.20	200	16
	01	P	84124	20806-01		0015	.50	8.00	50	11
	01	P	84124	20877-02		0015	1.50	10.80	200	12
	01	P	84124	27410-01		0020	1.03	1.63	16	11
	01	P	84124	42627-01		0020	1.00	14.61	250	16
	01	P	84124	44084-01		0010	1.31	.54	16	16
	01	P	84124	44238-01		0040	.81	3.00	50	16
	01	P	84124	46336-01		0020	1.00	.25	3	15
	01	P	84128	37550-01		0030	.83	1.18	10	11
	01	P	84128	44810-01		0020	.25	2.50	100	15
	***	TOTALS FOR WEEK 01 ***					27.62	136.52	2,275	
	02	O	84129	19023-00-20	2100973	0015	.50	.26	20	12
	02	O	84129	PROBE CASE	2702527	0018	.32	.14	2	14
	02	O	84129	PROBE CASE	2702548	0015	.90	.71	3	14
	02	O	84129	PROBE CASE	2702549	0015	.90	.24	1	14
	02	O	84130	9244-01	0057662	0030	.00	2.40	300	16
	02	O	84130	20012-00-24	2100969	0025	.20	6.00	50	12
	02	O	84130	PROBE CASE	2702537	0018	.32	.29	4	14
	02	O	84131	20091-01	2100970	0034	1.00	3.30	50	12
	02	O	84131	PROBE CASE	2702545	0018	.32	.22	3	14
	02	O	84133	PROBE CASE	2702548	0018	.32	.22	3	14
	02	O	84133	PROBE CASE	2702549	0018	.32	.07	1	14
	02	P	84129	19453-01		0015	.85	6.68	40	11
	02	P	84129	20040-02-12		0015	1.50	13.20	150	12
	02	P	84129	20763-02		0015	1.50	6.33	30	10
	02	P	84129	20763-05		0015	1.50	5.37	30	10

Figure 5-3. -- Detailed Load Report

CP210 CRP WORK CENTER LOAD DETAIL REPORT DATED [illegible]

		WK#	TYPE	DUE	PART NUMBER	ORDER#	OP#	SETUP	RUN HRS	ORDER QTY	PLNR COD
W/C 00004	CHUCKER	02	P	84129	44333-01		0020	1.00	13.35	150	16
		02	P	84129	45653-01		0015	.30	.50	30	15
		02	P	84129	6210-62		0020	.86	16.40	400	11
		02	P	84129	7262-01		0010	.50	.60	50	11
		02	P	84129	72771-01		0010	1.31	3.40	100	11
		02	P	84129	9559-01		0014	1.65	24.00	750	11
		02	P	84129	9802-01		0012	1.18	2.80	100	11
		02	P	84130	23311-01		0015	.50	4.40	50	11
		02	P	84133	10479-01		0010	.75	2.50	50	11
		02	P	84133	14725-03		0008	.66	3.90	150	12
			***	TOTALS FOR WEEK 02	***			30.92	187.31	3,902	
		03	P	84134	19312-01		0025	1.75	5.00	10	11
		03	P	84134	19350-01		0020	.83	2.18	10	11
		03	P	84134	20037-00-07		0015	.65	21.00	600	12
		03	P	84134	21515-00-00		0012	.88	30.60	600	12
		03	P	84134	23286-01		0015	1.25	2.70	300	12
		03	P	84134	26879-01		0025	2.00	6.50	50	11
		03	P	84134	26885-01		0020	.50	2.00	25	11
		03	P	84134	26886-01		0020	.50	1.00	50	11
		03	P	84138	14725-05		0008	.66	3.90	150	12
		03	P	84138	20784-01		0015	.09	24.00	3,000	12
		03	P	84138	20843-01		0015	.45	4.00	500	12
		03	P	84138	21519-00-28		0015	.85	2.71	41	10
		03	P	84138	21519-00-60		0015	.85	2.71	41	10
		03	P	84138	23063-01		0018	2.00	20.04	120	16
		03	P	84138	28159-02		0008	1.50	5.55	50	11
		03	P	84138	6894-01		0015	2.40	22.60	200	11
		03	P	84138	19315-04	0007722	0030	.50	.25	1	11
			***	TOTALS FOR WEEK 03	***			17.66	156.74	5,748	
		04	P	84139	40165-01		0030	.50	15.05	35	11
		04	P	84141	19315-04	0007722	0040	.01	.03	1	11
		04	P	84142	44810-01		0020	.25	2.50	100	15
		04	P	84143	14229-01		0015	.50	1.40	25	16
		04	P	84143	19066-00-50		0030	1.31	3.20	25	10
		04	P	84143	20024-00-08		0015	1.50	1.80	30	12
		04	P	84143	20027-00-05		0015	1.00	4.15	50	12
		04	P	84143	20091-04		0030	.50	3.00	30	12
		04	P	84143	20210-01		0120	.50	5.64	40	11
		04	P	84143	20517-01		0015	1.13	5.18	25	16
		04	P	84143	20763-02		0015	1.50	6.33	30	10
		04	P	84143	20763-05		0015	1.50	5.37	30	10
		04	P	84143	20842-01		0015	.35	9.00	1,000	12
		04	P	84143	20843-01		0015	.45	8.00	1,000	12
		04	P	84143	20850-01		0015	.97	1.50	50	11
		04	P	84143	20861-02		0020	.25	1.80	100	11
		04	P	84143	21513-00-08		0015	1.20	20.10	300	12

Figure 5-3. -- Detailed Load Report (continued)

CP210 CRP WORK CENTER LOAD DETAIL REPORT [illegible] 28/04/84

W/C	WK#	TYPE	DUE	PART NUMBER	ORDER#	OP#	SETUP	RUN HRS	ORDER QTY	PLNR C
W/C 00004 CHUCKER	04	P	84143	44239-01		0020	.69	6.60	200	16
	04	P	84143	44957-01		0020	.25	.55	69	11
	04	P	84143	44957-02		0020	.25	.80	100	11
	04	P	84143	46336-01		0020	1.00	3.33	40	15
	04	P	84143	50021-01		0020	1.16	2.74	10	11
	04	P	84143	6210-44		0020	.86	1.03	25	11
	04	P	84143	6210-52		0020	.86	4.10	100	11
	04	P	84143	6893-01		0015	1.25	2.45	50	11
	04	P	84143	6898-01		0015	1.20	12.25	175	11
	***	TOTALS FOR WEEK 04 ***					30.31	170.34	4,491	
	05	P	84144	16474-01		0030	.59	2.03	45	16
	05	P	84144	39511-01		0025	1.55	5.40	100	12
	05	P	84146	27804-01		0020	1.20	7.58	75	12
	05	P	84147	20091-04		0034	.50	2.50	30	12
	05	P	84147	37550-01		0030	.83	2.36	20	11
	***	TOTALS FOR WEEK 05 ***					4.67	19.87	270	
	06	O	84152	4015-31	0054541	0008	.75	1.20	200	16
	06	P	84148	14706-01		0012	.50	2.00	100	16
	06	P	84148	14725-01		0008	1.50	6.90	150	12
	06	P	84148	19091-01		0015	1.20	1.76	45	11
	06	P	84148	20010-00-50		0012	.85	2.20	50	10
	06	P	84148	20010-00-60		0012	.85	2.64	60	10
	06	P	84148	20011-00-35		0012	1.35	3.45	50	10
	06	P	84148	20026-00-05		0015	1.00	2.65	50	12
	06	P	84148	20026-00-08		0015	1.00	2.65	50	12
	06	P	84148	20037-00-15		0022	.65	3.50	100	10
	06	P	84148	20039-01-09		0015	.50	7.50	30	12
	06	P	84148	20090-01		0020	1.80	7.20	100	12
	06	P	84148	20169-01		0030	1.00	8.00	50	12
	06	P	84148	20762-03		0015	1.30	10.00	50	10
	06	P	84148	21166-01		0017	.68	2.15	50	11
	06	P	84148	21513-00-20		0015	1.20	6.70	100	10
	06	P	84148	21513-00-40		0015	1.20	5.03	75	10
	06	P	84148	21519-00-08		0012	.85	2.71	41	10
	06	P	84148	21519-00-20		0015	.85	2.71	41	10
	06	P	84148	21519-00-28		0015	.85	3.30	50	10
	06	P	84148	21519-00-40		0012	.85	2.71	41	10
	06	P	84148	21520-02-12		0015	1.00	60.00	200	12
	06	P	84148	26267-01		0015	1.20	6.50	50	11
	06	P	84148	28360-02		0030	1.03	9.10	100	12
	06	P	84148	40593-01		0020	1.50	2.90	50	11
	06	P	84148	42627-01		0020	1.00	14.61	250	16
	06	P	84148	44084-01		0010	1.31	.20	6	16
	06	P	84148	44739-01		0020	.75	.87	26	15
	06	P	84148	45143-01		0020	.50	7.50	150	11
	06	P	84148	6210-42		0008	.86	4.10	100	11
	06	P	84148	72772-01		0014	1.93	6.70	100	11
	06	P	84148	9802-01		0012	1.18	6.44	230	11
	06	P	84149	20026-00-15		0015	1.50	5.00	50	12
	06	P	84149	38496-01		0025	1.50	20.00	1,000	11
	***	TOTALS FOR WEEK 06 ***					35.99	238.08	3,795	
	***	TOTALS FOR WEEK 07 ***					14.62	99.41	3,699	
	***	TOTALS FOR WEEK 08 ***					29.22	160.59	5,150	
	***	TOTALS FOR WEEK 09 ***					43.42	307.44	12,278	

Figure 5-3. -- Detailed Load Report (continued)

CP210

CRP WORK CENTER LOAD DETAIL REPORT [illegible]

WK# TYPE DUE PART NUMBER	ORDER#	OP#	SETUP	RUN HRS	ORDER QTY	PLNR CODE
*** TOTALS FOR WEEK 10 ***			1.80	7.90	200	
*** TOTALS FOR WEEK 11 ***			11.43	90.82	3,395	
*** TOTALS FOR WEEK 12 ***			8.24	38.14	1,591	
*** TOTALS FOR WEEK 13 ***			32.38	209.54	8,725	
*** TOTALS FOR WEEK 14 ***			47.90	211.26	5,590	
*** TOTALS FOR WEEK 15 ***			15.52	77.57	2,871	
*** TOTALS FOR WEEK 16 ***			10.42	71.09	3,770	
*** TOTALS FOR WEEK 17 ***			36.99	225.17	6,346	
*** TOTALS FOR WEEK 18 ***			43.03	368.74	11,499	
*** TOTALS FOR WEEK 19 ***			.25	5.50	200	
*** TOTALS FOR WEEK 20 ***			9.43	58.32	2,455	
*** TOTALS FOR WEEK 21 ***			39.33	182.07	4,540	
*** TOTALS FOR WEEK 22 ***			42.01	208.71	7,281	
*** TOTALS FOR WEEK 23 ***			16.56	128.06	7,261	
*** TOTALS FOR WEEK 24 ***			17.95	97.65	3,806	
*** TOTALS FOR WEEK 25 ***			45.66	234.58	5,869	

Figure 5-3. -- Detailed Load Report (continued)

supervisors can determine whether the observed capacity problem is a one-time issue or a persistent problem. It is also used to identify which order hours are to be worked by period.

The input/output summary reports (Figure 5-4) help establish the demonstrated capacity by work center and is a measure of how well the plan is being executed.

These reports, done in advance of order review/release, provide the supervisors with a way to ensure that there is also adequate capacity available on the shop floor. Each report is regenerated every weekend and reflects all changes in either the master production schedule or the production plan.

The concern with capacity does not end at this point. Each production supervisor is required to monitor capacity regularly. If there is a problem (e.g., the supervisor is having difficulty clearing out the load for a given week because of unexpected machine breakdowns), then the supervisors can approach the production controllers and together these people can identify an acceptable solution. Problems are resolved face-to-face.

Detailed Assignment

At Bently Nevada, the detailed assignment activities of shop floor control are concerned primarily with scheduling and dispatching work orders. Detailed assignment is structured to enhance the capabilities and effectiveness of the production supervisor.

Initially, the priorities of all orders waiting at each work center are determined using the operation due date dispatching rule. These priorities are communicated to the shop floor by the dispatch list (Figure 5-5). This list is generated every day, and it communicates to the shop floor personnel the orders waiting at each work center and the dates by which these orders have to be completed. Access to the dispatch list is provided through one of the cathode ray tubes (CRTs) located on the shop floor or by the hard copy of the dispatch list that is distributed by 7:00 a.m. each morning.

The priorities identified in the dispatch list are guidelines only. The actual sequencing of orders is the responsibility of the production supervisor who is the best judge of how to use machines and people efficiently. At Bently Nevada, the supervisor is given the necessary latitude

PC420 PRODUCTION CONTROL WORK CENTER PERFORMANCE ANALYSIS BY WORK CENTER AS OF 27 APR 84 H-34123 PAGE 5

WORK CENTER 00004 CHUCKER PLANNED QUEUE - 160 ACTUAL QUEUE - 83.61

DATE - / M-DAY -	CURR WEEK 4-05	****** FUTURE WEEKS 11-05	18-05	25-05	1-06	8-06	15-06	22-06	29-06	6-07	13-07	20-07	27-07
FUTURE PLND INPUT	140	140	140	140	140	140	140	140	140	140	140	140	140
FUTURE PLND OUTPUT	180	180	180	180	180	180	180	180	180	180	180	180	180

DATE -	TOTAL	AVG.	4WK.AVG.	3-02	10-02	17-02	24-02	2-03	9-03	16-03	23-03	30-03	6-04	13-04	20-04	27-04
PRIOR PLND INPUT	1820	140	140	140	140	140	140	140	140	140	140	140	140	140	140	140
ACTUAL INPUT	2811	216	235	255	232	331	177	158	115	251	206	145	350	242	191	158
CUMULATIVE VARIA	7496	576	927	115	207	398	435	453	428	539	605	610	820	922	973	991
PRIOR PLND OUTPU	2340	180	180	180	180	180	180	180	180	180	180	180	180	180	180	180
ACTUAL OUTPUT	2695	207	228	223	238	259	249	136	160	128	183	206	214	214	311	174
CUMULATIVE VARIA	2536	195	286	43	101	180	249	205	185	133	136	162	196	230	361	355
UNITS COMPLETE	71863	5527	7089	7758	5391	3698	9203	5191	3288	2066	2732	4182	7084	7101	9353	4816
UNITS SCRAPPED	25	3	2						19	3					3	
UNITS SPLIT																
UNITS REWORKED	56	8								4	52					
OPERATIONS COMP.	492	37	38	40	45	50	39	21	29	37	39	39	39	27	51	36
ANTICIPATED DLYS	15	1	1	2	2			2			1	4		4		
REPORTED HOURS	2562.6	197.1	230.6	185.9	224.8	208.6	183.6	168.9	150.3	156.5	172.7	188.9	232.8	245.5	257.0	187.1
DEMO. STD. HOURS	2707.4	208.2	224.4	258.7	236.1	276.2	245.9	145.9	149.5	143.1	179.5	174.8	200.3	218.5	304.7	174.2
% STD. VS. ACT.		106.0	97.0	139.2	105.0	132.4	133.9	86.4	99.5	91.4	103.9	92.5	86.0	89.0	118.6	93.1
REPORTED REWORK	9.7	1.3								2.0	7.7					
REPORTED TOTAL	2572.3	197.8	230.6	185.9	224.8	208.6	183.6	168.9	150.3	158.5	180.4	188.9	232.8	245.5	257.0	187.1
REPORTED LABOR	2529.5	194.5	231.5	180.9	224.8	174.1	191.0	165.2	150.3	160.1	172.9	184.4	239.0	240.2	268.7	177.9
% RPT. VS. LAB.		102.0	100.1	102.8	100.0	119.8	96.1	102.2	100.0	99.0	104.3	102.4	97.4	102.2	95.6	105.2
TIMLINESS %		99.2	100.0	100.0	100.0	98.0	97.4	100.0	100.0	97.3	100.0	97.4	100.0	100.0	100.0	100.0
DOWN TIME	102.5	7.8	16.0	4.5	1.5	3.0	1.5	2.3	5.5	2.0	5.3	13.0	54.0	3.1	2.8	4.0

Figure 5-4. -- Input/output Summary Report

PC280

WORK CENTER 00207 SMART MONITOR ASSY

WORK CENTER DISPATCH LIST BY DUE DATE ON 6/05/85 M-85133 PAGE 59

LOCATION 557

ORDER	ITEM NUMBER	DESCRIPTION	ORG QTY	CUR QTY	- - OPERATION NO	DESCRIPTION - - - - -	WC DUE	WO DUE	OD	RUN TIME	SETUP	PREV WC	NEXT WC	PL	SALES ORDER #
7070761	SMART BEZEL	SMART BEZEL RTG	1	1	9999	ROUTE TO W/C 207	85132	85132	**			00923		TAK	10707600
7089374	SMUX	SMUX ROUTING	3	3	0020	ASSEMBLE & INSPEC	85133	85147		4.950		00276	00530	TAK	10893700
7089371	SMART SPARES	SPARES RTG FOR SMART	8	8	0025	OPTIONING/SOFTWAR	85134	85147		6.000		00276	00512	TAK	10893700
6172570	9000 MANUAL	SPARE MANUAL RTG	6	6	0025	PROGRAM & INSTALL	85140	85142		1.500		00277	00998	BAB	10772500

PC280

WORK CENTER 00208 9000 ASSEMBLY

WORK CENTER DISPATCH LIST BY DUE DATE ON 6/05/85 M-85133 PAGE 60

LOCATION 559

ORDER	ITEM NUMBER	DESCRIPTION	ORG QTY	CUR QTY	- - OPERATION NO	DESCRIPTION - - - - -	WC DUE	WO DUE	OD	RUN TIME	SETUP	PREV WC	NEXT WC	PL	SALES ORDER #
6118723	9000 SP MON	NON MRP PART	1	1	0030	FINAL ASSY & INSP	85133	85138		.250	.12	00209	00528	BAB	10872300
6162901	9000 SP MON	NON MRP PART	5	5	0030	FINAL ASSY & INSP	85133	85138		1.250	.12	00209	00528	BAB	10906200
6119211	9000/04-MON	9000 SYS RTG	1	1	0020	ASSEMBLE	85134	85140		9.500		00277	00209	BAB	10919200
6133291	9000/13-MON	9000 SYS RTG	1	1	0020	ASSEMBLE	85134	85142		17.900		00277	00209	BAB	10923300
6153542	9000/02-MON	9000 SYS RTG	1	1	0045	FINAL ASSY & INSP	85134	85138		1.000	.10	00209	00530	BAB	3401535
6153544	9000/02-MON	9000 SYS RTG	1	1	0045	FINAL ASSY & INSP	85134	85138		1.000	.10	00209	00530	BAB	3401535
6158541	9000/02-MON	9000 SYS RTG	1	1	0045	FINAL ASSY & INSP	85134	85138		1.000	.10	00209	00530	BAB	3401558
6158542	9000/02-MON	9000 SYS RTG	1	1	0045	FINAL ASSY & INSP	85134	85138		1.000	.10	00209	00530	BAB	3401558
6158543	9000/02-MON	9000 SYS RTG	1	1	0045	FINAL ASSY & INSP	85134	85138		1.000	.10	00209	00530	BAB	3401558
8593771	9000 SP MON	NON MRP PART	19	19	0030	FINAL ASSY & INSP	85134	85138		4.750	.12	00209	00528	BAB	10193700
6131591	9000 SP MON	NON MRP PART	2	2	0020	ASSEMBLE	85135	85142		2.644		00277	00209	BAB	10931500
6177251	9000 SP MON	NON MRP PART	6	6	0020	ASSEMBLE	85135	85142		7.932		00277	00209	BAB	10772500
6181621	9000 SP MON	NON MRP PART	1	1	0020	ASSEMBLE	85135	85142		1.322		00277	00209	BAB	10928100
6118278	9000/04-MON	9000 SYS RTG	1	1	0045	FINAL ASSY & INSP	85137	85142		1.000	.10	00209	00530	BAB	10827800

Figure 5-5. -- Dispatch List

PC280 WORK CENTER DISPATCH LIST BY DUE DATE ON 6/05/85 M-85133 PAGE 54

WORK CENTER 00176 ASSEMBLY NON-MRP LOCATION 559

ORDER	ITEM NUMBER	DESCRIPTION	ORG QTY	CUR QTY	OPERATION NO	OPERATION DESCRIPTION	WC DUE	WO DUE	OD	RUN TIME	SETUP	PREV WC	NEXT WC	PL	SALES ORDER #
9510233	5000 SPARE MON	NON MRP PART 5000	1	1	0025	ASSEMBLE	85130	85140	*	6.500	.04	00176	00504	FVR	10735500
9510365	1700 WITH HSG	1700 WITH HSG	3	3	0086	INSTALL IN HOUSIN	85133	85139		2.490	.10	00527	00530	FVR	10638800
9510621	37506AF	DIG TACH RTG	3	3	0047	INSTALL IN HSG	85133	85137		.300	.10	00529	00528	FVR	10560300
9510627	5000 SPARE MON	NON MRP PART 5000	2	2	0012	OPTION BOARDS PER	85133	85149		.620		00276	00504	FVR	10117900
9510854	1700	1700	1	1	0015	ASSEMBLE	85133	85140		.500	.05	00209	00504	FVR	10913600
9509190	5000 SPARE MON	NON MRP PART 5000	3	3	0025	ASSEMBLE	85134	85141		19.500	.04	00176	00504	FVR	10326000
9510357	1700 WITH HSG	1700 WITH HSG	5	5	0020	ASSEMBLE BOARDS	85134	85147		5.605	.01	00276	00504	FVR	10601900
9510363	1700 WITH HSG	1700 WITH HSG	1	1	0060	ASSEMBLE MONITOR	85134	85144		.560	.05	00209	00504	FVR	10686100
9510389	1700	1700	1	1	0015	ASSEMBLE	85134	85142		.500	.05	00209	00504	FVR	10769200
9510359	5000 SPARE MON	NON MRP PART 5000	2	2	0020	ASSEMBLE MONITOR	85135	85146		5.820	.14	00209	00176	FVR	10182901
9510360	5000 SPARE MON	NON MRP PART 5000	7	7	0020	ASSEMBLE MONITOR	85135	85146		20.370	.14	00209	00176	FVR	10142900
9510728	1700	1700	1	1	0007	ASSEMBLE BOARDS	85135	85149		1.000		00276	00504	FVR	10829700
9510358	5000 SPARE MON	NON MRP PART 5000	1	1	0020	ASSEMBLE MONITOR	85136	85147		2.910	.14	00209	00176	FVR	10551000
9510361	5000 SPARE MON	NON MRP PART 5000	1	1	0025	ASSEMBLE	85136	85144		6.500	.04	00176	00504	FVR	10730200
9510390	RMT READ OUT	RMT RDOT ROUTING	1	1	0020	ASSEMBLE PER PRIN	85137	85142		1.500	.04	00276	00504	FVR	10769200
9510364	RMT READ OUT	RMT RDOT ROUTING	1	1	0020	ASSEMBLE PER PRIN	85139	85144		1.500	.04	00276	00504	FVR	10686100
9510391	5000 SPARE MON	NON MRP PART 5000	2	2	0025	ASSEMBLE	85139	85147		13.000	.04	00176	00504	FVR	10769600
9510628	1700	1700	2	2	0015	ASSEMBLE	85141	85149		1.000	.05	00209	00504	FVR	10117900
2004197	PWAS	PWA,NON-MRP SPARE	6	6	0020	ASSEMBLE PER PRIN	85143	85154		1.380	.02	00276	00504	FVR	10635600
2004232	PWAS	PWA,NON-MRP SPARE	2	2	0020	ASSEMBLE PER PRIN	85168	85177		.460	.02	00276	00504	FVR	10799800

Figure 5-5. -- Dispatch List (continued)

to improve efficiency by grouping orders to minimize setup times (as an example). The only restriction on this freedom is that the schedule must be met.

At present, the preventive maintenance program is not a part of the shop floor control system. It is a responsibility of the manufacturing engineers.

Finally, scrap and rework are managed no differently from other work orders. In the future, Bently Nevada intends to handle scrap and rework separately so that a summary of these activities can be used to measure the quality control program.

Data Collection/Monitoring

As work orders are processed through the various work centers, information on their progress is filled in on a standard form and delivered to a central keypunch area. A keypunch operator enters the information into the corporate database. As a rule, there is no more than a one-hour delay from the time that the data are submitted until they become part of the database. Once in the database, the information can be accessed on line by Bently Nevada personnel through one of the thirteen CRTs located on the shop floor or one of the eleven CRTs located in the planning office. At this point, there is no assurance that the data have been entered correctly. Data verification and trapping potential data entry problems are done at the end of the shift.

Edit and audit reports are produced during the night and are given to the supervisors the next morning. These reports identify potential data entry problems by using certain verification rules. For example, the computer will flag any situation in which the quantity leaving the work center is not equal to the entering quantity (after adjusting for scrap). The computer will also trap any data in which there are major deviations in reported time as compared with standard time. Using these reports, the supervisors are responsible for correcting any erroneous data entered that day.

The progress of work orders is recorded in terms of:

- Unit quantity of an item completed
- Unit quantity scrapped
- Reason for scrap (this information is related by means of a defect code)

- Setup time used
- Run time used
- Date the work order was completed in the work center.

In addition, all of the time spent by an employee is charged against a job or an overhead account (e.g., when the employee is not working on a job).

One of the major features of information collection at Bently Nevada is the presence of a common corporate database. These data integrate shop floor control with quality control, cost accounting, maintenance, engineering, scrap control, personnel, and marketing/sales. The only exception is payroll. The payroll system is separated from this reporting system because workers manually fill in time cards that are then used to determine how much to pay the individuals. This separation has been introduced deliberately by top management to prevent the worker from contaminating the entered data to make the costs for that work center come out "right." A high level of accuracy is critical to the successful operation of this reporting system. Currently, accuracy exceeds 95 percent.

The documentation generated by Bently Nevada's system is extensive. It is regarded highly by many agencies with which Bently Nevada must work. The Nuclear Regulatory Commission, for example, has accepted this documentation as being sufficient for its purposes.

Control/Feedback

The control of out-of-control orders depends on the production supervisors. There are no expediters in Bently Nevada's shop floor control system, which reflects management's belief that such persons are ineffective and cause more problems than they solve. Expediters treat shop floor symptoms, not the causes of shop floor problems.

Each production supervisor is responsible for ensuring that the work orders are completed by their operation due date. If supervisors feel that an order will not be completed in time, they communicate this information to the schedulers in the form of an "anticipated delay." The supervisor, working with the scheduler, now reschedules the problem order. By rescheduling the order, the supervisors keep all of the production priorities valid. Priority validity is a key concern of the shop floor control system.

Order Disposition

Because the progress of the order has been tracked and reported constantly by the shop floor control system, the process of closing out the shop order is straightforward. When an order has completed its routing, it is closed out to the stockroom. This involves canceling the open order in the work order file and increasing the on-hand inventory levels in the stockroom. However, all of the data associated with the order are not frozen immediately on completion of the order. Instead, the records are left open for two weeks so that the record can be adjusted for such problems as a dropped work ticket. The labor content is frozen every Monday for all orders completed during the preceding week. At the end of the two weeks, the information is frozen into the records. With this, the order is completed.

Performance Evaluation/Feedback

At Bently Nevada, the performance of the shop floor control system is evaluated in terms of anticipated delays, timeliness, and conformance to budget. These items not only measure performance, but are also an important and integral element of the control/feedback activities of the shop floor control system.

Anticipated delays are summarized on a regular basis by work center and supervisor. This is done as a check and to identify either those work centers or those supervisors who regularly experience difficulties in meeting due dates.

A second measure related to anticipated delays is timeliness. At Bently Nevada, timeliness compares actual order completion time at a given work center with its standard completion time. Timeliness corrects for the potential distortions in work center reporting introduced by anticipated delays. That is, a work center that is able to complete the order in less than its standard lead time is not penalized for the failure of other work centers to deliver the order to it on time. Its good performance is reflected in the timeliness measure.

Like anticipated delay, timeliness is summarized regularly by work center and supervisor. It is expected that each supervisor will maintain a minimum timeliness level of 95 percent per week. The actions taken when this measure falls below 95 percent depend on the persistence and nature of the underlying problems. If the problem is short term (i.e., one week or less) and the causes equally short term (e.g., a machine breakdown that has been repaired), then the reduced timeliness measure is accepted. However, if the problem and its underlying causes are long term, then management works with the production supervisor to identify the most appropriate solution. As in all problem-solving endeavors at Bently Nevada, the solution is arrived at by a face-to-face meeting of the involved parties.

The third measure is conformance to budget. At the beginning of every year, the production supervisors are required to commit themselves to a financial budget. They are then evaluated on their ability to work within the limits set by the budget. When significant changes are made to the production plan, modifications are also made to the budget.

Evaluating Bently Nevada's Shop Floor Control System -- Benefits

The shop floor control system is an integral element of Bently Nevada's production planning system. As such, it is difficult to identify those quantitative benefits attributable to the shop floor control system alone. However, the current system has contributed to the following improvements:

- Significant decrease in WIP levels. The level of WIP inventory has fallen by over 25 percent.
- Significant reduction in subassembly lead times.
- Reduction in the percentage of orders released shorted. Before the implementation of the current system, orders generally were released with insufficient materials. This created problems that had to be solved on the shop floor by expediting, rush orders, and overtime. This problem has been eliminated; only 1 percent of the orders are now released shorted. Planners are now responsible for ensuring adequate material availability.
- Improved on-time delivery performance. Before 1976, with less than 10 percent of the orders being completed by their due dates, on-time delivery was the exception rather than the rule. At present, over 90 percent of the orders are completed by their due dates.

For Bently Nevada, the major benefits offered by the current shop floor control system are qualitative not quantitative. The most significant of these benefits include:

- Problems are now evident. The current system makes shop floor problems evident. It is now impossible to hide problems.

- <u>Bad managers are identified quickly</u>. Bently Nevada's system requires that its managers (production supervisors and production controllers) identify the shop floor problems before they occur. Identifying such problems requires using the visibility provided by the data. Managers who fail to make proper use of information and who consistently perform poorly in terms of the anticipated delay and timeliness measurements are identified. These are the managers Bently Nevada wants to retrain or remove.
- <u>Significant improvement in the working environment</u>. One area that has benefited greatly from the presence of the current shop floor control has been the working environment. Before the implementation of the system, there was a great deal of tension. The question of who was to blame for shop floor problems was a major concern. Supervisors usually worked long hours (in one case, from 6:30 a.m. until 7:00 p.m.). This has changed with the implementation of the current system. Placing blame is no longer the major issue. Instead, the emphasis is on joint problem solving and honesty of relationships among people. Furthermore, many of the problems previously encountered have been eliminated. Most of the supervisors now work regular hours. There is a general feeling that it is fun to work at Bently Nevada.

In short, the shop floor control system has played a significant role in the creation and maintenance of a credible and viable manufacturing planning system. It has also helped to enhance Bently Nevada's credibility both to its workers and to its customers. Finally, the shop floor control system is an important element in maintaining the firm's competitive position.

Shop Floor Control -- The Next Stage

Currently, there is only one major change being considered for the shop floor control system. This change involves providing a what-if inquiry capability for people to use to solve problems. Bently Nevada will also work on user education. The intent is to ensure that people in the firm can make the best use of the capabilities offered by the system.

In operation, the shop floor control system has shown itself to be effective and efficient. Its success is not accidental, but the result of incorporating into the shop floor control system certain lessons that have been learned at Bently Nevada. These lessons are:

- Identify those people on the shop floor best able to operate the system and organize the system around these people. At Bently Nevada, it has long been recognized that the production supervisors are crucial to the successful operation of the shop floor. As a result, the shop floor control system is organized around these people. The system provides the production supervisors with the tools that they need to make decisions. In many instances, these tools consist of providing them with the appropriate information. For example, supervisors are given the visibility over future loads. This information is used to determine whether or not future loads are to be pulled forward.

  Furthermore, the shop floor control system also allows the supervisors to control certain shop floor control activities. For example, an order is released only after the production supervisor is sure that there is adequate capacity available. By supporting and simplifying the work of the supervisors, the shop floor control system has become indispensable.
- Make the shop floor control system simple to use and understand. It is not enough to simply provide the user with the necessary tools. To be used on an ongoing basis, the system must be simple to use and understand. This lesson is evident in Bently Nevada's shop floor control system. All information is presented in a straightforward fashion with only the necessary data noted. For example, the summary load reports are used by supervisors to identify if and where there are potential problems. The information is summarized in both a numerical and graphic format to facilitate its use (people understand graphs more readily than the numbers that generated these graphs). Furthermore, the amount of paper on the floor is kept to a minimum. Finally, all supervisors know that they are evaluated primarily on three measures.

- The planning system must provide the shop floor control system with adequate capacity; the shop floor control system must then manage this capacity. The shop floor control system should never be placed in the position of having to plan capacity. This is not its responsibility. If the system is to be successful, then the availability of adequate capacity becomes a necessary condition for order review/release.
- The computer supports the actions of the shop floor personnel. The computer greatly simplifies the operation of the shop floor control system. It summarizes information, identifies possible error conditions, and helps to identify possible solutions. The computer, however, cannot solve problems, nor can it completely evaluate alternatives. These tasks are left up to such shop floor personnel as the production supervisor. By making a clear distinction between responsibilities, a lot of confusion and needless frustration is avoided.
- Accountability is essential to success. Production supervisors are given a great deal of freedom in the shop floor control system. In return, the supervisor's actions are evaluated on an ongoing basis. They must always be able to account for all of their actions. Accountability forces the supervisors to consider their actions carefully and to use the power given them by the shop floor control system judiciously.

Bently Nevada has been successful because it has been able to match good planning with good execution. The execution success is mainly due to its shop floor control system.

MANUFACTURING PHILOSOPHY STATEMENT

As the company grows, it becomes more difficult to communicate, in person, the basic beliefs and philosophies of the manufacturing organization. The Manufacturing Philosophy Statement is to help communicate the more important concepts of how the manufacturing organization should conduct business.

Resolving Conflicts Between Major Strategic Issues

Situations where strategic issues are in conflict will arise. When a decision must be made, which enhances one issue at the expense of another, a certain priority should be observed. The priority of the major issue is:

o	Safety	(our people)
o	Quality	(existing customers)
o	Dependable Delivery	
o	New Product Introduction	(future customers)
o	Cost	(dollars)

- Safety -- Quality, delivery, new product introduction, and cost cannot justify the relaxation of safety standards. Ideas which cannot be safely implemented are to be modified or discarded. Safety is the responsibility of each individual, and each person is encouraged to actively work on solving and preventing safety hazards. Safety rules and procedures must be followed, because improper use or handling of some materials will result in hazardous conditions. Supervisors must enforce safety rules and procedures without exception.

- Quality -- The quality of our products has a significant influence on a customer's future purchases. Customers use our products to protect life and equipment on a 24-hour, 7 day a week, year after year basis. We want to build and supply products which instill customer confidence. We do not want to improve delivery, lower cost, or introduce new products at the expense of quality.

  Quality must be built into the product. Quality cannot be inspected or tested into the product. Inspection and Quality Assurance are to provide information to the line functions, and the line functions are to fix existing problems and prevent future problems. Inspection and Quality Assurance are to avoid the role of separating good from bad hardware, and are to place emphasis on helping the line functions to build products right the first time. The line functions are responsible for quality. Manufacturing must take the initiative in interactions with Engineering, Marketing, Sales, and other departments when design, documentation, or other facets of a product compromise quality.

- Dependable Delivery -- Our customers depend on a known delivery date to schedule the installation of our equipment. Quite often, the installation cost can equal the sales price of our products. A missed delivery date can disrupt the customer's schedule, and cause the loss of thousands of dollars. We do not want to commit to delivery dates that will not be honored, but we do not want to pad delivery dates to be on the safe side. We expect realistic, aggressive delivery date commitments, and want everyone to do everything reasonable to honor the ship date. As a rule of thumb, our dates will be reasonable enough to ship 9 out of 10 jobs on time, and aggressive enough that we will miss 1 out of 10 by a small amount of time. Subquality hardware will not be shipped just to make the delivery date on an order. We will not sacrifice dependable deliveries to reduce cost or introduce a new product.

  MRP II concepts will be used to do forward looking planning so that delivery schedules are met. Shortage expediting, hot lists, and other ineffective activities will not be used.

- New Product Introduction -- New technology and knowledge of rotating machinery will make our existing products obsolete. New products will be required to secure our future. The introduction of new products is a painful process, and many problems will arise. We want the problems focused and solved in a timely manner, but do not want time and energy spent in finger pointing activities. We want all problems objectively highlighted, and we expect Manufacturing to positively and aggressively work with Engineering and Marketing. The introduction of a new product will cause temporary expenditures that are above the norm, but we do not want to block the new product on the basis of these costs. Manufacturing will aid in the timely introduction of new products by starting the production cycle before all testing and product verification is complete. This will result in in-process modification of circuit boards, sheet metal, etc. These modifications are part of the price which must be paid to remain competitive by quickly introducing new products.

- Cost -- A major factor in our ability to market our product is the value of the product versus its cost. We will strive to lower our costs, as long as we are not compromising safety, quality, delivery, or new product introduction. A person in Manufacturing cannot be an above average performer unless they are actively involved in cost reduction activities. Cost improvement ideas originate from all people in Manufacturing. There should be more ideas than can be acted on, and those which have the most potential benefits should be implemented first. It is harder to implement an idea than it is to think of the idea. Ideas are many; people who can implement ideas are few. Working smarter, not harder, will be the theme of reducing the labor content of our products.

Conduct of Personal Interaction

The manufacturing environment has many adversities. Many problems, disagreements, and aggravating situations do occur. These events cannot be avoided, and we expect people to conduct themselves in a manner that promotes teamwork, forward progress, and solves the problem at hand.

People must treat everyone with respect. Disagreement is necessary, but it is unacceptable for disagreements to result in disrespectful actions. As problems occur, attack the problems, not the people involved.

People must use objectivity, honesty, and sincerity in their communication. Personal views must be presented as personal views, not as fact. Facts must be presented in an unbiased manner.

People must be persistent. Most things worth accomplishing will not happen easily. "Nothing in the world can take the place of persistence. Talent will not; nothing is more common than unsuccessful men with talent. Genius will not; unrewarded genius is almost a proverb. Education will not; the world is full of educated derelicts. Persistence and determination alone are omnipotent."

People must be helpful. As problems arise, we expect all people to lend a hand. Even though an individual may not directly benefit from these efforts, as the company benefits, we all benefit.

CHAPTER 6: STEELCASE, INCORPORATED

General Nature of the Firm

Steelcase is a privately held corporation headquartered in Grand Rapids, Michigan. Established in 1912 to manufacture fireproof safes, Steelcase has grown to be the world's leading manufacturer and designer of office furniture. With current annual sales of over $1 billion, Steelcase (along with its two nearest competitors) accounts for approximately 33 percent of sales in a $5.8 billion industry.

Major product lines are panels, desks, files, chairs, task lights, tables, video display terminal (VDT) stands, and systems furniture for the open office. Worldwide, Steelcase and its joint venture operations have a work force of more than 14,000, more than 700 independent dealers, sales offices or dealerships in fifty-eight countries, 15 million-square-feet of manufacturing or assembly facilities in nine countries, and twenty-one manufacturing/assembly sites. Of these twenty-one sites, seven are in the United States, six in France, four in Africa, two in Canada, and one each in West Germany and Japan. The primary production location is in the Grand Rapids area.

Steelcase is engaged primarily in the production of MTO office furniture. The MTO component accounts for approximately 95 percent of all business. The remaining 5 percent is MTS and consists of a line of basic office furniture. The demand for products is not seasonal and is linked closely to other economic trends. Steelcase sells to a variety of customers, ranging from the small local insurance office to large corporations.

Regardless of the customer, Steelcase management believes that success results from satisfying three criteria: provide a quality product, deliver it on time, and give the best service. Of these three, the second bears further comment. In many instances, Steelcase is provided with a due date that is part of an overall construction schedule. Failure to deliver on time may delay the opening of the customer's office. Thus, Steelcase always strives to ensure on-time delivery of a quality product, regardless of cost.

Steelcase -- The Seating Division

The production facilities located in Grand Rapids consist of six plants totaling 7.6 million square feet. These plants employ approximately 7,000 nonunion people. Each plant is responsible for one major product line (e.g., chairs, panels, or system furniture) and is autonomous with its own plant manager. These plants, however, are linked by the production planning system and a completely integrated database. The material and production requirements for all plants are planned with one system. The database is used by everyone in the firm. This report focuses on the operation of one of those plants -- the chair plant.[1]

The chair plant is housed in a two-story, 1.2 million-square-foot plant. The plant houses the production facilities of the seating division and a ten-aisle Triax/Webb high-rise automated storage and retrieval system located in the middle of the plant. Currently, 1,225 hourly workers are employed at this facility.

The chair plant is responsible for 2,200 raw material part numbers, 5,500 fabricated piece parts and assemblies, and 7,177 distinctive and database-supported models. There is a high degree of commonality among the models so the various models break down into roughly two dozen chair lines. The typical bill of material for the seating division has between six and seven levels.

A large percentage of the raw materials is purchased parts for this plant. All of the chrome plating work for Steelcase is done by outside vendors. To better control the chrome vendors, management has developed the chrome vendor order detail system. Under this system, the vendors are incorporated directly into the production planning and control system. The chrome requirements are generated directly by the system. The chroming lead time is used to time-phase vendor production. The parts released to the chrome vendors are managed by decreasing on-hand inventory at Steelcase and increasing vendor on-hand inventory. The process is reversed as parts are received from the vendors. This system significantly improved the ability of Steelcase management to track and monitor vendor performance. It also has contributed to a significant reduction in vendor lead times and chrome WIP inventory.

The internal manufacturing lead time for chairs is twenty-eight working days. The chair plant is generally a two-shift operation with an average weekly output of approximately 25,000 chairs. The typical shift covers forty-five hours per week.

---

[1]The terms "chair plant" and "seating division" are used frequently in this discussion. They refer to the same plant and are used interchangeably.

The Production Process

The production process for the seating division, illustrated in Figure 6-1, is basically machine, weld, paint or plate, cut and sew, upholster, and assemble. The process can be broken down into two major levels, each with its own scheduling process.

The first level consists of machine and weld. Production is run using varying lot sizes. For example, "A" items are produced in lots of one week's usage, while the lot sizes for "D" items cover about six months' usage. Changes to released orders in the basic areas are infrequent; inventory corrections and changes in subsidiary demands are the major reasons for the variances.

The second or final level consists of paint, weld-finish, cut-sew-upholstery, and assembly. At this stage the chair is built to customer requirements. Changes by the customer may change the schedule, but this is not usually a problem because these areas run on a daily schedule starting five days ahead of shipping. Lot sizing is done lot for lot at this level.

Seating division capacity consists mainly of work force and equipment. It is tracked and measured by CRP, CRP simulations, machine use, and measurements against historical norms. The need to increase capacity at Steelcase is evaluated by the shift and one-half principle. That is, on most equipment, capacity is increased whenever the equipment is being used for at least one and one-half shifts. On the more expensive equipment, new capacity is added whenever the machine is used for at least one and three-quarters shifts.

The seating division operations are noteworthy for several other reasons. First, the work force is paid by piecework. Second, the seating division is responsible for the manufacture of all tubing in various shapes for all of the plants in Grand Rapids and all subsidiaries. Third, lead-time reduction is a way of life for Steelcase management. Lead times are reduced yearly. As a result, upholstery is now half a day in front of trim whereas previously it was one day. Also, the practice was to weld three days in front of chair assembly, now it is only one day in front. The compression of lead times has not only reduced inventory but also yielded significant benefits for the operation of the shop floor control system.

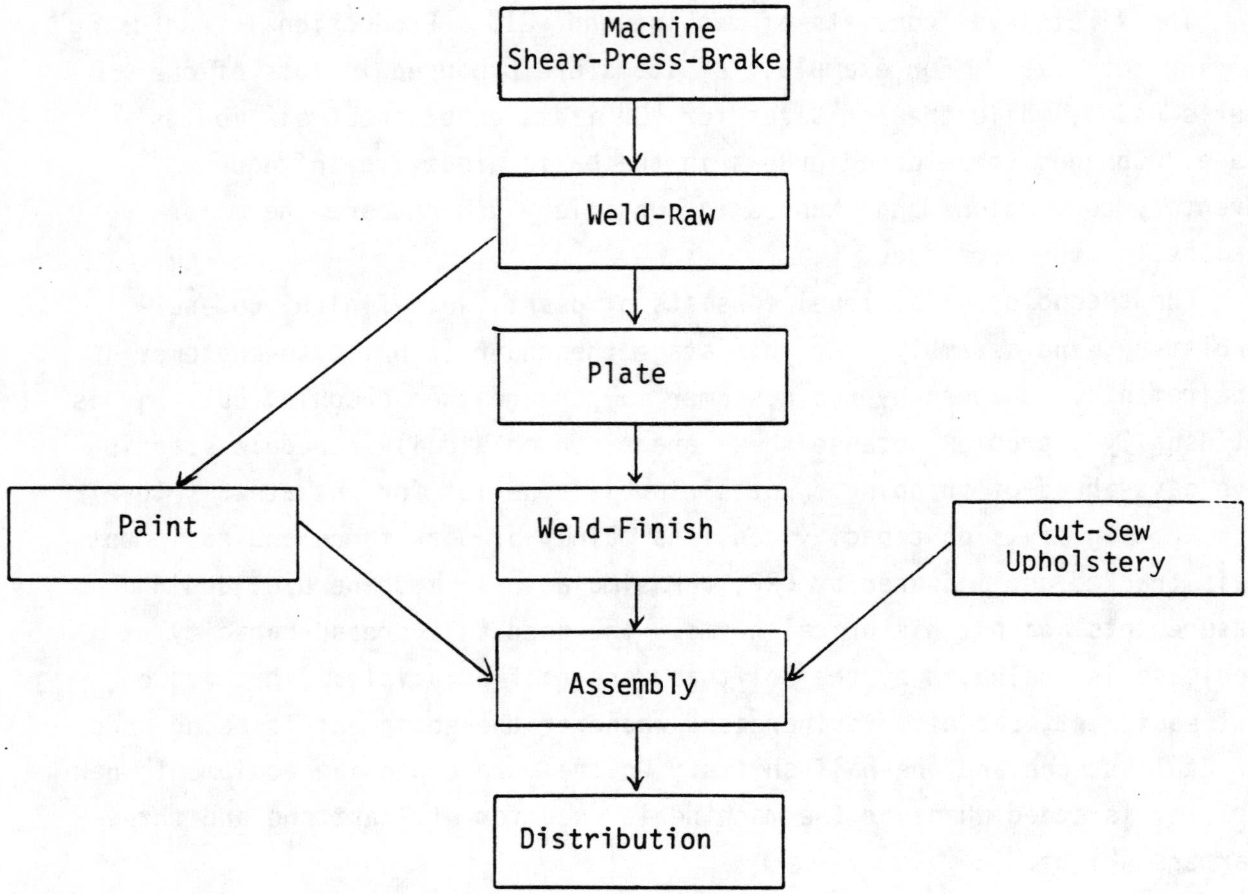

Figure 6-1. -- Production Process for Seating Division

Production Planning at Steelcase

The major steps in the production planning system used at Steelcase are illustrated in Figure 6-2. The current system is the latest stage in the evolution of a system first implemented in 1968. The SOP and the master production schedule (MPS) are central to this process. These plans form a two-level MPS with the SOP driving the MPS. The SOP is the first plan formulated, and it is crucial at this level that top management reaches agreement on how capacity at Steelcase is to be used.

The starting point for the SOP is sales forecasts, which are created in a meeting with the director of production and inventory control, representatives from business research, and marketing representatives. These forecasts form the annual plan, are used in budget planning, and are a major input into the SOP.

The SOP is a monthly plan that breaks down production for the thirteen weeks by week, by product group, and by plant. It is established by a committee consisting of the vice presidents of operations, marketing administration, and manufacturing, and the directors of production and inventory control and marketing administration. The committee meets monthly and reviews changes to the previous SOP and other additions.

The SOP is one of the most important production plans at Steelcase. It links and coordinates corporate strategy and the operation of the other functional areas. More importantly, however, the SOP is the rough-cut capacity plan for the entire firm.

The SOP establishes the output quotas for each plant. These quotas are stated in terms of model unit count (MUC). The MUC, a unit used by every area in the firm, is related to standard hours of direct labor. In the SOP committee meeting, marketing information that pertains to the quantity and mix of product sales is converted first into the number of MUCs required to support these sales by time period. Next, the capacity availability, measured in MUCs, of the various plants is examined. The SOP allocates the available capacity to these various sales. The committee loads each plant to maintain the desired level of manufacturing backlog.

Once the output quotas for the plants are set and agreed to by the SOP committee members, limits are placed around these quotas. These limits identify clearly the amount of production flexibility present. In general, the maximum production increase that can be accommodated is 5 percent, while the maximum decrease is 2 percent. As a result, the obligation of marketing

PLANNING LEVELS

Forecast

Sales Operation Plan

Master Schedule

Material Requirements Planning

Capacity Requirements Planning

Production Activity Control

Figure 6-2. -- Production Planning System

and production is set forth clearly. This plan is firm for the next four weeks with a flexible plan for the next two four-week periods. The production levels agreed upon in the SOP are then entered into the order entry report (or high-level master schedule).

Concern over capacity is one of the hallmarks of the Steelcase production planning system. It also plays an extremely important role in the operation of the shop floor control system.

Marketing administration is responsible for the master schedule, which is driven by numbers taken from the SOP. The master schedule maintains the customer backlog and uses this backlog to smooth out production. It is also a more detailed restatement of the SOP because it breaks down the numbers present in the SOP and restates them by plant and individual lines (grouped by commodity or product group). It is stated in enough detail to be used to drive the detailed material and capacity planning systems.

The master schedule drives the component planning or MRP system. Capacity is then checked with CRP, which evaluates capacity based on a look at all open and planned orders. MRP and CRP are done weekly. The MRP system used at Steelcase is regenerative. The machine and weld departments are scheduled to a standard hour goal that is determined from the CRP tracking. Currently, Steelcase is considered a Class A MRP user.

After the plans have passed through these stages, they are given to the shop floor control (called production activity control at Steelcase) personnel. These persons work with the material and capacity information generated by MRP and CRP. They are responsible for not only implementing these plans but for also providing the various types of feedback.

The software of the entire production planning system was purchased initially. The main component, the MRP system, was obtained from IBM. Since then, the software has been modified extensively in house to better satisfy Steelcase's requirements.

Shop Floor Control

Organizationally, shop floor control is part of production and inventory control (PIC). The PIC director reports directly to the vice president of operations. In addition to shop floor control, the PIC director is responsible for all production planning, material control, and warehousing. The director assists and guides all subsidiaries and outlying plants.

There is a PIC manager in each plant who has two reporting relationships. The manager reports directly to the PIC director and also has a dotted-line relationship to the individual plant manager (Figure 6-3).

In the chair plant, the PIC manager controls approximately seventy hourly and fourteen salaried people. These people are responsible for the warehouse, material handling, and dispatching. The PIC manager relies on five foremen (Figure 6-4). Two of these foremen are production activity control supervisors, one is assigned to the basic area and the other to the final area. The production activity control foremen are responsible for priority control and capacity control. The major responsibilities of the production activity control system are maintaining accurate inventory numbers, accurate reporting of schedule status, and priority control. The four major components of the production activity control system are receiving, material handling, warehousing, and dispatching. Warehousing, operational reporting, and completion reporting are all done on line in real time.

The production activity control system is generally an on-line system with batched hard-copy printouts that make use of two IBM 3081 computers. These computers are used to maintain warehouse records; order from the warehouses; do on-line operational posting, on-line order completion, automated input/output reporting, and database inquiries; and make order status inquiries. Access to these computers is through one of twenty-four VDTs used by PIC personnel. The entire production activity control system was developed completely in house.

The Stages of Shop Floor Control at Steelcase

The chair plant's shop floor control system reflects several of the key management philosophies of Steelcase. Understanding this philosophy should clarify many of the practices noted in each of the phases of shop floor control. These philosophies include:

- Commitment to the master schedule. The master schedule must be met at all costs. For all purposes, the master schedule is treated as if it were fixed. The extent of this commitment to the master schedule is indicated in the sign reproduced in Figure 6-5. This sign is posted everywhere on the shop floor and is the closest to a company motto that Steelcase has. The only instances in which a

- **Senior Vice-President, Operations**
  J. STEGMIER
  - **Vice-President, Manufacturing**
    G. J. HEKKER
    - Director, Plant/Facilities/ Env./ Engineering
      A. DYKHOUSE
      - Superintendents, Maintenance
        R. FABIAN
        F. SCHMIDT
        J. EINIG
      - Manager, Kentwood Facilities and Construction
        J. DeRUYTER
      - Manager, Grand Rapids Facilities & Energy
        D. DORNBOS
      - Manager, Natural Resources Protection
        G. EGLESTON
      - Manager, Plant/Engineering Maintenance Controls
        L. LUBBERS
      - Manager, Finishing Technology
        C. SMITH, Jr.
    - Plant Manager, Desk Division
      J. GRUIZENGA
      - Superintendents, Desk Plant
        R. MARTENS
        R. BIERSCHBACH
        R. DEVOOGD
    - Plant Manager, Chair Division
      H.G. NIEMI
      - Assistant Plant Manager,
        R. NEASON
      - Superintendents, Chair Plant
        C. KELLEY, Jr.
        L. HENSON
        J. BESSELSEN
        D. TERPSTRA
        R. BAAR
    - Plant Manager, Panel Division
      J. WAYBRIGHT
      - Superintendents, Panel Plant
        R. BOORSMA
        M. HITCHCOCK
        G. NELSON
        H. KUIPER
    - Plant Manager, Systems Division I
      L. CLARK
      - Superintendents, Systems Plant I
        H. BERRIER
        J. McDOWELL
        L. SELIG
        R. BONZHEIM
    - Plant Manager, Systems Division II
      H. RINGERWOLE
      - Superintendents, Systems Plant II
        J. VanENK
        G. COX
        J. WORMMEESTER
        L. SNYDER
    - Plant Manager, File Division
      G. VREDENBURG
      - Superintendents, File Plant
        J. LAURIA
        R. VanWINGEN
        R. BEETHAM
        K. MARQUARD
    - Plant Manager, Computer Furniture Division
      R. HOOGTERP
      - Superintendents, Computer Furniture Plant
        A. AGIN
        D. STINGER
        C.T. BENEDICT
        R. BURCH

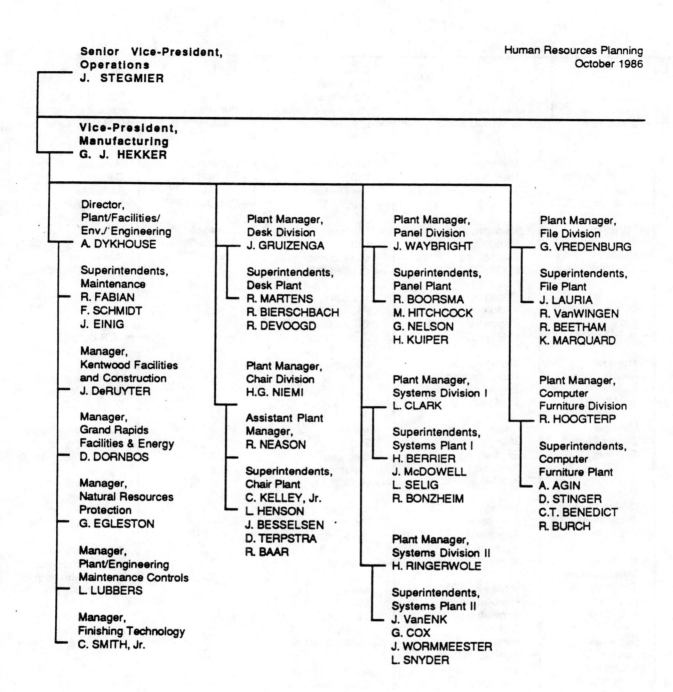

Figure 6-3. -- Operations

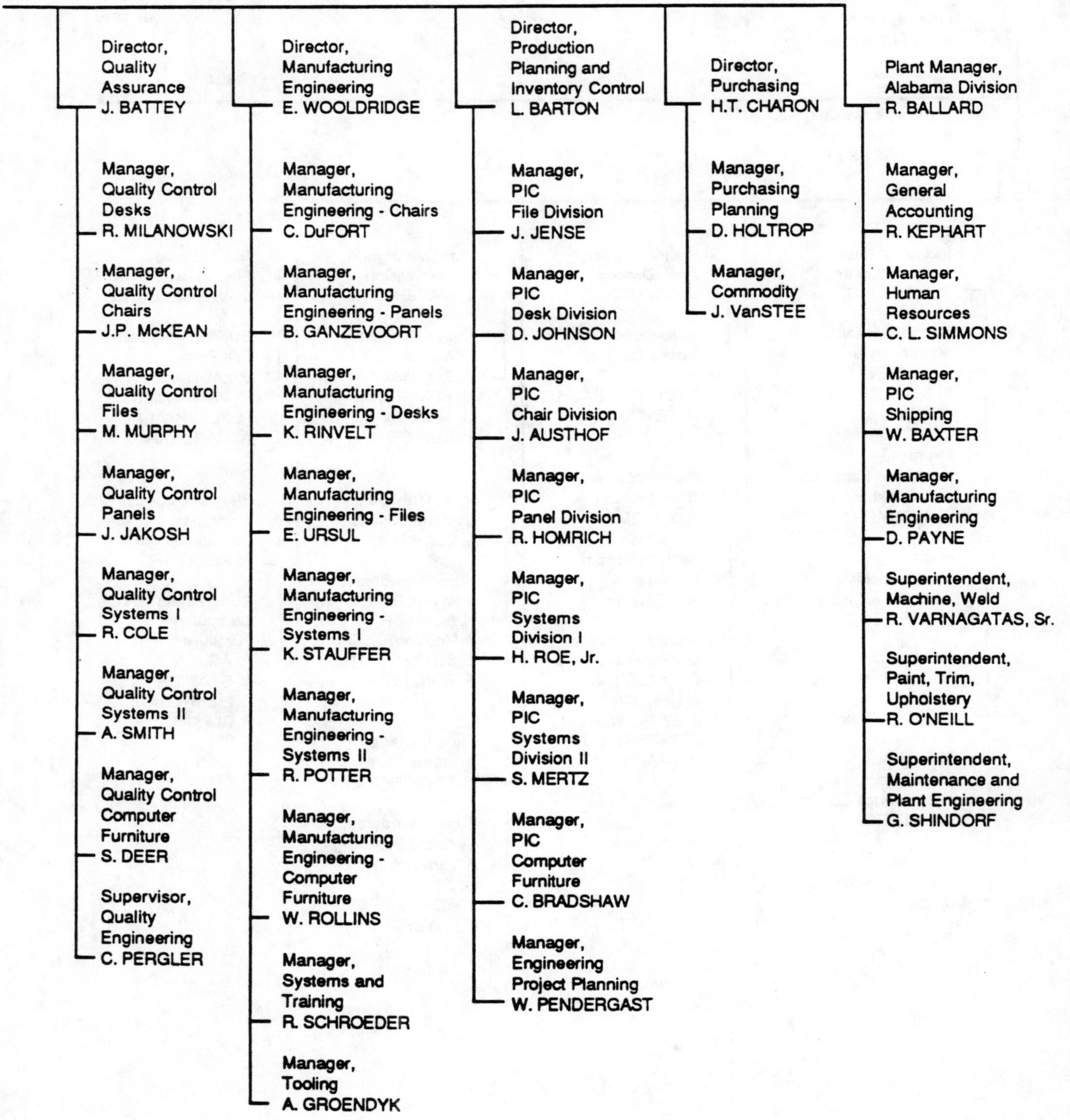

Figure 6-3. -- Operations (continued)

CHAIR PIC ORGANIZATION

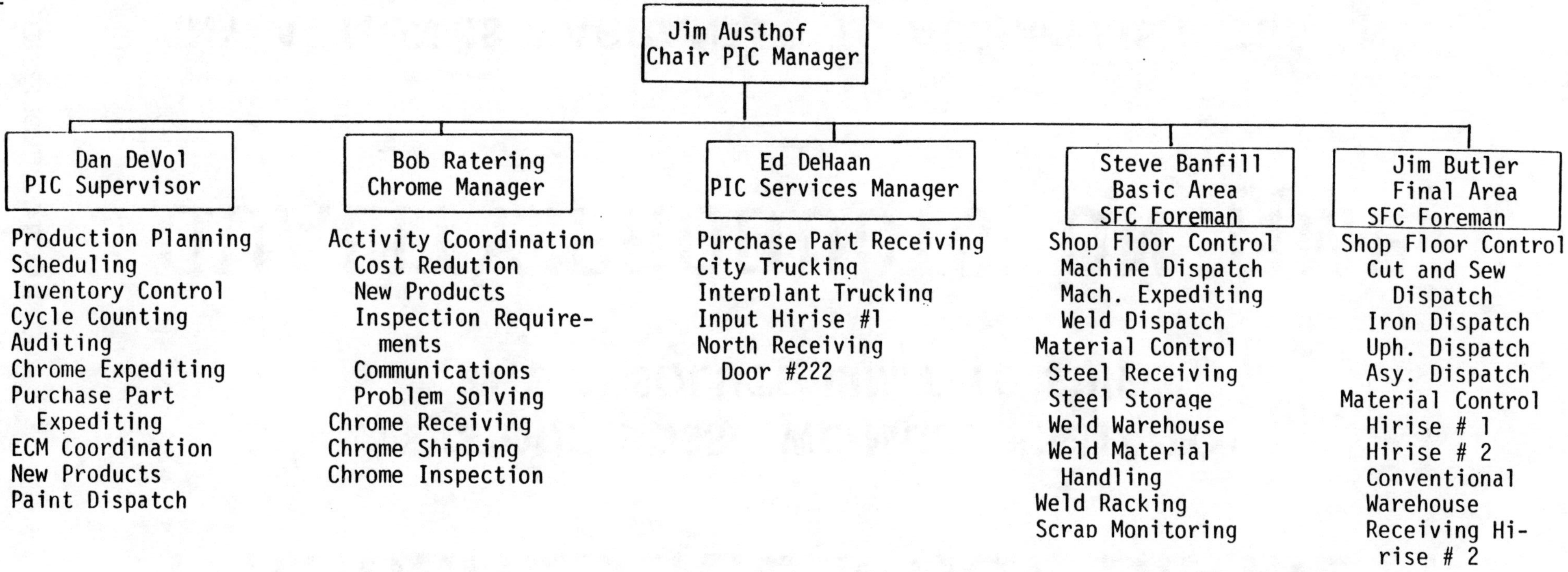

Jim Austhof
Chair PIC Manager
Dan DeVol
PIC Supervisor
Production Planning
Scheduling
Inventory Control
Cycle Counting
Auditing
Chrome Expediting
Purchase Part Expediting
ECM Coordination
New Products
Paint Dispatch
Bob Ratering
Chrome Manager
Activity Coordination
Cost Redution
New Products
Inspection Requirements
Communications
Problem Solving
Chrome Receiving
Chrome Shipping
Chrome Inspection
Ed DeHaan
PIC Services Manager
Purchase Part Receiving
City Trucking
Interplant Trucking
Input Hirise #1
North Receiving
Door #222
Steve Banfill
Basic Area
SFC Foreman
Shop Floor Control
Machine Dispatch
Mach. Expediting
Weld Dispatch
Material Control
Steel Receiving
Steel Storage
Weld Warehouse
Weld Material Handling
Weld Racking
Scrap Monitoring
Jim Butler
Final Area
SFC Foreman
Shop Floor Control
Cut and Sew Dispatch
Iron Dispatch
Uph. Dispatch
Asy. Dispatch
Material Control
Hirise # 1
Hirise # 2
Conventional
Warehouse
Receiving Hi-rise # 2

Figure 6-4. -- Organization Structure

THE SCHEDULE MUST BE MET!

IT IS OUR BOSS! WE MUST FIGHT TO THE ABSOLUTE LIMIT TO SHIP

QUALITY PRODUCTS, ON TIME.

ANY ACTION IS WARRANTED TO ACCOMPLISH THIS END.

Figure 6-5. -- Sign Depicts Commitment to Schedule

reschedule of a customer order is permitted are those due to vendor fall down from which it would take more than two weeks to recover.

- Flexibility through employee involvement development. The management of Steelcase views its work force as extremely important to the success of the firm. One of the benefits that workers contribute is familiarity with the various product characteristics. This familiarity is far too detailed to be built into any computer-based planning system. As a result, management believes that the employee should have much say in plan execution. In the case of shop floor control, management has developed a system in which the planning system determines the objectives that must be met promptly while the employees (e.g., dispatchers and MRP planners) determine the exact method of carrying out these objectives. The employees are free to use any product information.
- Capacity. Management sees itself as responsible for ensuring that there is sufficient capacity with which to implement the SOP. Without adequate capacity, the validity of any given production plan is compromised severely. Furthermore, it is not acceptable to expect the shop floor to compensate for planning-related problems.

Order Review/Release

Order review/release starts with the reports produced by the weekly regenerated MRP. The basic area MRP planner reviews and firms up planned orders that are released automatically by the MRP system. Because orders jump inside the time frame for auto-release, all records are looked at on the planning day.

In releasing the orders to the shop, a number of data transactions must be completed. These include printing the process/routing sheet, generating the operator and locator cards, updating the posting file, and printing the standard hour load report and machine schedule. These reports are then passed on to the dispatcher.

All communications with the computer regarding order review/release are done on line. Orders are then released to the basic area once a week, twice a week in the final area. The schedule closing for the corporation is weekly and two weeks ahead of the actual build week. Therefore, in the final area, a three-day and a two-day block (referred to as "A" and "B" blocks, respectively) can be released and broken down into individual days

(Figure 6-6). The information passed from the planning system regarding the release order includes quantity needed, due data, amount of standard hours for the operation, and the raw material requirements. When preparing orders for release to the factory, certain standard hour and number of unit goals must be met. For example, CRP indicates the number of standard hours that should be scheduled in the machine room. This practice provides needed stability in capacity use on the shop floor. If changes are required in the goal, they are negotiated with the machine superintendent who, with foremen, is responsible for meeting the resulting schedules. They have the final say on whether to accept or reject the proposed changes. In the final area, the constraints are built into the high-level master schedule, which, in turn, is constrained by the plant output quotas set by the SOP committee.

Material availability, assumed in most cases, is made possible by MRP and the use of a common set of numbers by all planning functions. Also, material availability can be checked just before machine setup because the whole warehousing system is on line and available for viewing by the various dispatchers on their VDT units.

Labor availability is checked by the plant manager each time the SOP level changes. Capacity is changed to accommodate these changes. In some instances, people are added when necessary and at other times, personnel are moved from one plant to another as required. For day-to-day and week-to-week situations, overtime is used commonly as a quick fix for a lack of workers.

Tooling availability is mainly a manufacturing responsibility.

Detailed Assignment

The detailed assignment of orders to work centers is handled by dispatchers at Steelcase. The dispatchers can serve anywhere from one to three departments within a division. Priority control is a function of the scheduled due date set by the planning group. Thus, the overriding priority is order due date. The dispatcher must ultimately rely on the foremen and the superintendents to meet these due dates. As a result, the dispatcher must communicate clearly and accurately the production priorities to the shop floor.

The dispatcher divides the weekly schedule into work for the various work centers and then dispatches according to priority. The gateway work centers are due out two days before the other work centers. Dispatchers can

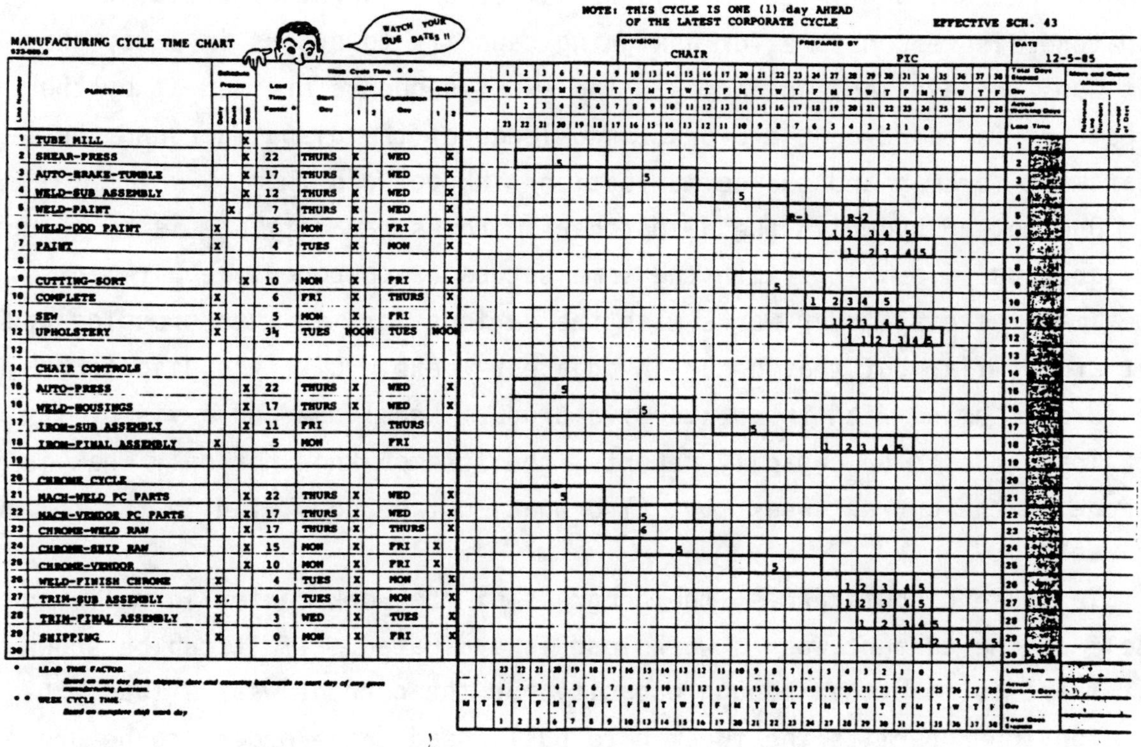

MANUFACTURING CYCLE TIME CHART
WATCH YOUR DUE DATES !!
NOTE: THIS CYCLE IS ONE (1) day AHEAD OF THE LATEST CORPORATE CYCLE
EFFECTIVE SCH. 43
CHAIR
PIC
12-5-85
1 TUBE MILL X
2 SHEAR-PRESS X 22 THURS X WED X
3 AUTO-BRAKE-TUMBLE X 17 THURS X WED X
4 WELD-SUB ASSEMBLY X 12 THURS X WED X
5 WELD-PAINT X 7 THURS X WED X
6 WELD-DOD PAINT X 5 MON X FRI X
7 PAINT X 4 TUES X MON X
9 CUTTING-SORT X 10 MON X FRI X
10 COMPLETE X 6 FRI X THURS X
11 SEW X 5 MON X FRI X
12 UPHOLSTERY X 3½ TUES NOON TUES NOON
14 CHAIR CONTROLS
15 AUTO-PRESS X 22 THURS X WED X
16 WELD-HOUSINGS X 17 THURS X WED X
17 IRON-SUB ASSEMBLY X 11 FRI THURS
18 IRON-FINAL ASSEMBLY X 5 MON FRI
20 CHROME CYCLE
21 MACH-WELD PC PARTS X 22 THURS X WED X
22 MACH-VENDOR PC PARTS X 17 THURS X WED X
23 CHROME-WELD RAW X 17 THURS X THURS X
24 CHROME-SHIP RAW X 15 MON X FRI X
25 CHROME-VENDOR X 10 MON X FRI X
26 WELD-FINISH CHROME X 4 TUES X MON X
27 TRIM-SUB ASSEMBLY X 4 TUES X MON X
28 TRIM-FINAL ASSEMBLY X 3 WED X TUES X
29 SHIPPING X 0 MON X FRI X
* LEAD TIME FACTOR
* * WEEK CYCLE TIME

Figure 6-6. -- Manufacturing Cycle-time Chart

consult a standard hour load by work center. The effect of priorities on short-term capacity is controlled by having the planning delay an equal amount of orders as those ranked. Departments are loaded starting with the standard hours on the low side to allow room for adds and priorities.

Dispatching at Steelcase is simplified by the availability of adequate capacity. The dispatcher knows there is always adequate capacity with which to complete the current week's production and is never placed in the position of "rationing" finite to a large number of orders. Instead, the dispatcher is responsible for assigning capacity to orders in a way that best uses the available capacity. The exact sequence arrived at by the dispatcher is based on the product knowledge of the dispatcher and the department foreman and the communication link between them.

One method by which the dispatcher improves capacity use is by grouping similar jobs (i.e., jobs with the same setups or component requirements). Sometimes the dispatcher works with the various foremen when grouping orders that are similar but that occur in adjacent weeks. Like the dispatchers, the foremen bring with them extensive product knowledge and a visibility on work load. Based on capacity reports, the foremen know not only what is to be done in the current week, but also what must be completed in the following week.

In these circumstances, the progress of the work center in relieving itself of the current week's work load is evaluated. If it can be shown that there is more than enough capacity for the current week's load, then the dispatcher permits the foreman to pull ahead those orders to be grouped. The overriding concern, however, is meeting the order due dates.

As is evident from this discussion, the order due date is an important element when determining order priority. It is not, however, the only element considered. By allowing the foremen and dispatchers to adjust order priorities to reflect such other factors as job similarity, management has recognized that there are many dimensions that must be considered when sequencing orders.

In addition to dispatching orders, the dispatchers serve as coordinators for all rescheduling and priority sequencing done in their respective departments.

As previously noted, Steelcase typically runs on a two-shift basis. To prevent conflicts involving shop floor control between the two shifts, the day shift dispatcher determines the orders to be processed on the night shift.

Preventive maintenance is an important part of the detailed assignment process at Steelcase. There is a roving preventive maintenance crew that schedules its work by presenting the department foreman with notice a month in advance of any needed preventive maintenance work. The department foreman sends this notice back to maintenance to acknowledge that the time and date are acceptable. It is the foreman's responsibility to communicate this information to the dispatcher so that the proper accommodations can be made when assigning orders to the various work centers.

Data Collection/Monitoring

The shop floor control system at Steelcase collects information pertaining to the progress of shop orders and to capacity use. This information is used extensively.

- o <u>Data collection -- shop orders</u>. The dispatchers assign work to operators and are responsible for collecting and entering the data on which Steelcase's various shop floor control reports are based. Specifically, dispatchers prepare operational time cards, post production to the records, provide schedule status reports, and input order completion to inventory. The dispatcher is responsible for ensuring that every operator turns in the time card immediately upon job completion. This information is then entered on line into the WIP database.

  Order status is updated constantly during the course of the production day. Whenever an operator completes an operation or job, the card is turned in. Shop floor control information is fed back on line in real time; MRP replanning is assimilated weekly by the planning system because of the weekly MRP regeneration. The information collected pertains mainly to part order status. Quantity completed, scrap or rejects run, and parts shortages are included.

- o <u>Data collection -- capacity use</u>. The foremen in each department are responsible for collecting information that pertains to capacity use. This information is first collected by work center and subsequently reaggregated. The information collected includes:
  - Actual hours worked in the work center
  - Standard hours relieved (completed) in the work center

  - Number of hours of increased load added to the work center in that day
  - The load factor (the comparison of actual to standard hours)
  - The balance (the number of standard hours remaining at the end of the day so that the work center can meet its standard hours load for the week).

The information collected is important because it enables the department foremen to evaluate immediately the progress of the work centers under their control.

- Monitoring. The shop floor control system produces a number of reports that are available on line. These reports (see Attachment 6-1) are used for control feedback, dispatching, and priority control. They describe the current status of operations on the shop floor, facilitate quick identification of any problem areas, and identify potential reasons behind these problems. The reports are simply decision-making tools. They provide the users with information to make manufacturing decisions, facilitate communication among the various elements of the production activity control system, and provide immediate and timely feedback on performance. The reports are used extensively by the foremen and dispatchers -- those held responsible for meeting the various order due dates.

  The reporting frequency tends to follow the due dates for the various departments. Reporting for the basic area is done weekly; final area reporting, like scheduling, is done daily. The reports are distributed to manufacturing supervision, other dispatchers, production planning, the production and inventory control manager, and in many cases, the plant manager. The content of these reports is summarized and reviewed at a weekly plant managers' staff meeting.

  At these weekly meetings, the progress of each department is reviewed so information becomes public knowledge. Failure to meet expected goals (as stated in standard hours to be relieved or on-time delivery) in any department is not viewed as being solely the fault of either the foreman or the dispatcher. Performance to goals is a joint responsibility.

Control/Feedback

One of the major functions of control/feedback is to identify those orders that are considered out of control. At Steelcase, an order is out of control if it is needed in the trim department for a daily completion but cannot be completed because of shortages. It is a management policy to take any action necessary to correct a trim shortage. Some typical actions might be:

- Tear down a machine or welder to put the hot job in
- Overlap operations or lot split orders
- Work through lunch periods
- Work overtime.

The prime function of the shop floor control system is to complete orders on time. In the past, this has led to calling a company president during the middle of the night in Germany or flying Steelcase personnel to North Carolina to truck back needed fabric. These actions taken by themselves are not cost effective, but they are occasionally necessary to ensure the on-time completion of an order.

In general, priority control has been the major way that the shop floor is controlled and production problems corrected. Priorities are reviewed by the production planners at the weekly scheduling meetings and communicated to the rest of the system in a priority list (Figure 6-7). Other priorities are generated from the floor when operators cannot find parts that the planning system indicates should be available.

As a rule, expediting is discouraged. Steelcase management strongly feels that expediters perpetuate the need for expediting rather than solve those conditions that give rise to the need for expediting in the first place. As a result, there are expediters in the basic area. There is only one expediter in the plant, who is responsible for expediting needed purchased parts. Other expediting is done as needed through dispatchers and planners. These persons are required to address those conditions that initially created the need for expediting. As a result, shop floor expediting is done only on an exception basis and as infrequently as possible.

The dispatcher, the foreman, and the MRP planner, initially determine the specific corrective actions to be implemented. Each controls a different aspect of the shop floor control system; the dispatcher controls priorities and reschedules, the foreman controls work center capacity and ensures adequate capacity availability, and the MRP planner determines the exact quantity that the MRP system may need in the short run. The MRP

SCHEDULE PRIORITY REPORT
521-022.0

Date Issued 7/25

G

From: P.I.C. Department No. 521 ☐ File Division ☐ Desk Division ☐ Chair Division ☐ Chrome

To: Name: Dispatcher

INSTRUCTIONS: Please manufacture the following by the Revised Required Date.

Scheduled Date	Part or Assembly Number	Description	Revised Required Date	Date Completed	Reason Code *	Remarks
8/10	43010221		7/25			weld
7/27	4540006		7/25			Irons
8/3	4541021		7/25			weld
8/3	4541022		7/25			weld

DISTRIBUTION

P. I. C.
Shop Floor Control Coordinator
Dispatcher
Supervision

* REASON CODE	
01	Inventory Adjustment by Shop Floor Control
02	Unusual Draw
03	Scrap
04	Engineering Change Notice
05	Subsidiary Order
06	Bill of Material Error
07	

Figure 6-7. -- Schedule Priority Report

planner also identifies that portion of the MRP-generated requirements that are the direct result of a customer order as compared with those resulting from the need to replenish safety stocks. If these three people cannot find an acceptable solution, the problem is referred to the shop floor control foreman. Often the problem is resolved by the time it reaches this stage. If not, then it is most often a problem involving purchased parts, and it is referred to the purchased materials superintendent.

Feedback from the shop floor control system to the planning system is done over the phone, via the VDT units, or by various reports previously discussed.

Order Disposition

When an order is completed, the dispatcher or storekeeper enters the information into the WIP database via the VDT units. This then updates the WIP on hand and closes out that particular order. The entry also informs the planning system of part order availability.

At present, how an order is closed out depends on whether it is an issue/receipt. All parts going into the hi-rises are treated as good pieces. The shop floor personnel are responsible for all scrap reporting and for ensuring that only good pieces are transferred out. As these pieces come into the warehouse, they are added to the master Steelcase locator system (MSLS). The MSLS is a generic locator system developed at Steelcase. In addition, the incoming totals are entered. During the night, the on-hand part quantities in the hi-rises are overlaid with the inventory control master (ICM) and the on hand in the warehouses becomes the ICM for the next day. The ICM number recorded every Friday becomes the number used in replanning by the MRP system.

To date, over 50 percent of all parts are handled as issue/receipts. These parts are tagged with a code, and all issues and receipts of those parts are recorded on an ongoing basis to keep the inventory records current. Eventually, all parts will be managed as issue/receipts.

A running total of the actual and expected on-hand quantities is made and variance reports based on these totals are produced. These variances are looked at twice, and the cycle counters must reconcile the differences. The most important feature of the issue/receipt system is that it puts the burden for inventory accuracy where it belongs -- on the shop floor. The numbers used in the warehouse are the same ones generated by shop floor personnel. If these people generate bad numbers, then the ICM suffers.

When the order quantity is received into the warehouse, the transaction decreases the PIC on-hand records of those parts used and increases the on-hand quantity of the part made. It also relieves the requirements against the parts used and removes the open order from the PIC records. At this point, the production activity control system has been relieved of its responsibility for the order.

Scrap and rework disposition currently is handled by the industrial engineers.

Performance Evaluation/Feedback

Performance evaluation/feedback at Steelcase is integrated into the data collection and monitoring activities of the production activity control system because foremen and dispatchers need timely information that can be used not only to improve performance but also to correct problems before they become more serious.

Department foremen are aware of the number of standard hours that their departments must relieve by week. This goal is realistic. At the end of each day, when recording the performance of the various work centers in the department, the foreman can identify those operators having difficulty meeting weekly objectives. This information can be obtained quickly by examining the balances for each work center (see Attachment 6-1). The foreman is aware that good performance is based on efficiently relieving the standard hours loaded into the department.

Another performance measure examined is the load factor, which is simply the actual hours incurred divided by the standard hours to be relieved. This ratio is useful because it simplifies the planning of actual capacity, the evaluation of efficiency, the evaluation of costs, and the identification of those work centers that are prime candidates for automation.

A load factor that exceeds one indicates that more than one hour of actual time was used to relieve one standard hour. When planning, this factor may indicate the need to schedule more hours of actual production than that indicated in the plans, or it may indicate that an unfavorable cost variance can be expected for the affected areas. It also identifies areas that are not run as efficiently as possible. Those work centers or departments with persistent and large load factors are the most likely candidates for automation. There is a great incentive present for the reduction of the load factor to a point less than or equal to 1.0. Similarly, the dispatchers are aware they are evaluated on their ability to complete the on-time delivery on the required orders. Formally, the performance of the shop floor is measured by schedule status reports.

Other Salient Features of Shop Floor Control

One of the most interesting features of the current production activity control system is its integration into the operation of the firm. First, production activity control, like the rest of the firm, makes extensive use of the MRP system. At Steelcase, the MRP system is a companywide system, not a manufacturing system. Second, there are numerous links between shop floor control and other departments. The current links, purchasing, cost accounting, engineering, quality control, production planning, payroll, maintenance, marketing, and top management, are characterized by joint decision making, and they exist to facilitate communication.

The production activity control system makes extensive use of these links. Information provided by shop floor control is often directly used by other departments (and vice versa). The establishment and maintenance of these links at Steelcase have been simplified by the presence of a common database and the use of a common planning unit (the MUC).

Third, an important feature of the production activity control system is the automated warehouse storage and retrieval system along with its computer-based, real-time update display. This system gives a true picture of WIP issues (allocation update and use) and receipts (open order disposition) at all times. It automatically ties the warehousing and production activity feedback to planning group records.

Other features of the current system include:

- Material handling, warehousing, and dispatching people are all held accountable and report to the same person. This results in better cooperation, respect, and communication, which makes for better feedback to the planning area.
- Cycle counting of parts and assemblies is done completely through their product structure.

- o Computer-based systems in the final area that handle high volumes of tedious clerical work provide manufacturing and planning with immediate and constant feedback of schedule status.

Shop Floor Control -- The Next Stage

The development of shop floor control at Steelcase is an odyssey. The current system, while good, is still not adequate. Lead times are still too long; WIP inventory still too high. To improve the system, certain changes are now being introduced.

First and foremost is the implementation of a daily dispatch list for the basic area, which will be designed with a backward scheduling technique. This development, now possible because of the recently implemented operation posting system, will provide management with the needed increase in control at the operational level. Management then can control priorities, capacities, and lead times. The development of the daily dispatch list also communicates order status to both the planning and manufacturing functions. It will make the entire shop floor control system more efficient. Management's current challenge is to develop this list without compromising the role of the human in the system.

Second, work is being done to replace the current order disposition procedure by an issue/receipt system. This system should not only simplify the maintenance of records, but it should also improve the ability of the dispatcher to identify problems quickly with shorts, priorities, and quality.

In addition, the following developments are being considered for use in the system:

- o Automated identification (e.g., bar coding)
- o Group technology (or cellular manufacturing)
- o FMS
- o JIT manufacturing (zero inventory management)
- o Manufacturing resource planning (currently well into the implementation of this system).

Shop Floor Control at Steelcase: Lessons to be Learned

Shop floor control works at Steelcase. Production activity control has given the chair plant a record of 313 of 321 schedules (weeks) at 100 percent on time (Figure 6-8). The same system helps the panel plant expand its current consecutive string of over 400 weeks at 100 percent on time. The system has also helped management to keep WIP inventory dollars down and to improve customer satisfaction, dollar returns (profits), and most of all, personnel morale.

A successful production activity control system is the result of several different factors. At Steelcase, the success of the system is based on the following:

- <u>A clear statement of the goals of the shop floor control system</u>. At the chair plant, everyone from the plant manager to the worker knows what has to be done to be successful: get a quality product out on time. There is no confusion or ambiguity. Everyone is united by one goal. An interesting result is that competition among the various departments within the plants involving on-time delivery has started. Workers are proud of their ability to meet schedules.
- <u>Consistency</u>. The shop floor control system is a consistent implementation of the Steelcase manufacturing philosophy. What management preaches regarding the role of the worker and the availability of adequate capacity is shown in the manner shop floor control is carried out. People know what is expected of them.
- <u>Adequate capacity provided up front</u>. At Steelcase, capacity is planned in advance of shop floor control; it is not an afterthought. The result is that the production activity control system does not have to be concerned about the lack of capacity. When there are shortfalls in capacity, they are minor and can be controlled by coordinating the efforts of the dispatcher, work center foreman, and the MRP planner. Having adequate capacity also simplifies dispatching, which can become a frustrating task when dispatchers know that no matter how they sequence jobs they will never have enough capacity. This is never a problem at Steelcase.
- <u>Accommodating the human</u>. At its most basic level, shop floor control is a human system. The production activity control system acknowledges this by permitting the user to introduce information

Letter of Commendation

JULY, 1983

Over the past six years, the Chair Plant has completed 313 weeks out of 321 at 100% schedule completions.

Six years of RELIABLE production is a tremendous accomplishment.

The Chair Plant Manufacturing and Staff groups have demonstrated a strong schedule - conscious posture, and are hereby commended for this outstanding record.

Vice-President, Manufacturing

Senior Vice-President, Operations

Figure 6-8. -- Letter of Commendation

regarding the order in which orders are processed. This enables the system to include information about to order grouping in the detailed assignment process. No dispatching rule can consider all the factors necessary to ensure on-time delivery. The operation of the entire shop floor control system is understood by everyone in the chair plant. This understanding encourages the user to not only accept the current system but also to use it more often.

- Providing the users with the right tools. One of the more important elements of the shop floor control system is the current reports available to foremen and dispatchers. These reports present the user with all of the information needed to identify and correct problems. It also provides visibility of upstream and downstream loads. Without this information, the ability of the dispatcher or the foreman is affected seriously, which in turn affects the overall effectiveness of the system.
- Communication. One of the major reasons for the success of the Steelcase system is that the participants are willing to communicate. This attitude encourages joint problem solving and reduces potential tension. Communication is important because dispatchers cannot force foremen to accept orders that the foremen do not feel they can complete. It is also required because foremen can bring orders forward that are similar to the ones currently in the shop if they can show the dispatchers that they have adequate capacity for the current week's requirements.
- Accountability. Everyone in the shop floor control system has tasks that he or she is held responsible for accomplishing. Each person is evaluated on the extent to which these objectives are satisfied. Accountability creates that impetus needed to ensure the successful execution of the production plans.
- Checks and balances. The system used at Steelcase has numerous checks and balances that ensure that the shop floor is executing valid plans. One of the checks is the maximum variation permitted in each week's work load. That is, each week, there is a set of capacity limits. On the high side, for example, capacity can never be increased more than 5 percent without first securing the agreement of the foreman of the affected work center. Furthermore,

the order releases authorized by the MRP planner or the order sequence issued by the dispatcher can be questioned by the foreman. This set of checks and balances creates a mutual respect among the dispatchers, foremen, and MRP planners.

ATTACHMENTS

Attachment 6-1.

1. Schedule status report is used by all basic area dispatchers to report status of dependent demand item schedule completion. This information is the feedback given to departmental supervision and the planning area.
   a. Part's standard code.
   b. Part's description.
   c. Date parts are due in stock.
   d. Amount to complete through the final operation.
   e. Delay code.
   f. Dispatchers brief description of reason for delay.
   g. Priority code.
   h. Report is weekly and issued on Wednesday morning.
   i. Standard hours late for date to stock.
2. Schedule status summary is attached to the schedule status report and distributed with it weekly.
   a. Delay codes.
   b. Priority codes.
   c. Dispatcher comments on overall department status.
   d. Percentage of standard hour completion.
3. Machine room daily capacity status is used in the machine division to measure demonstrated output and compares it to the requirements each day.
4. Machine standard hour load review is again used in the machine division to measure capacity. This is a weekly report distributed each Thursday, which the division's management uses to make short-term decisions on work force and machinery.
5. Chrome shortage report is issued by the department dispatcher daily. This is a final area department which runs to daily schedules. The report is used to expedite the parts currently needed and to preexpedite (i.e., identify parts which may be short may be short in the next planning period). It is also used to coordinate all the chroming activities within Steelcase. All plants report to one chrome planner and Steelcase uses more than one vendor for plating. The report contains the following information:
   a. Steelcase's finish code for chrome color.
   b. Inventory control master on-hand amounts.
   c. Available parts at vendor for plating.

d. Expedite and preexpedite quantities: parts in the current schedule which are short and parts needed for next day's production schedule which have not yet been received and are expected to be short.

e. Planners' and dispatchers' comments on the status.

6. Shortage list is issued for final area dispatchers to report parts needed for daily completions. This form is used by the planners and other department dispatchers.

7. Trim schedule status report is updated daily and runs continuously. It is used to monitor trims (assemblies) performance. All amounts are MUCs.

8. Daily order completion performance is a daily report that runs from week to week. It measures trim's performance through the week on orders as well as the MUCs that make up the orders.

9. Weekly schedule completion summary is a weekly report issued on Wednesdays, tracking completion percentages and units produced.

10. Order maintenance list is a daily computer-generated report which is used to edit on-line order completion transactions by the dispatchers.

11. Quality control status report is also a daily computer report which is used to follow up on containers of parts that are either on QC hold or reject.

12. Locator system transaction list is another daily report, computer generated. It is used to edit warehousing/material handling transactions and to track problems.

13. Warehouse location summary is a daily computer report printed in warehouse sequence and used for auditing warehouse locations.

14. Part number location summary is a daily computer report printed in part number sequence and used to look up part location and on-hand amounts.

15. Operation status display is a printout of an on-line display of our operation posting system. It is used to see the status of each operation of a dependent demand item in the basic area.

16. Output report is also a printout of an on-line display of a day's posted output by work center and schedule load. It is used to calculate daily output and capacity status.

17. Load report is also a printout of an on-line display. The load is the extended standard hours of each operation for each order in that schedule. It is used to calculate input.

18. Chair rack model list is a computer-printed list which prints chairs ordered by style and amount on a rack. It is used in the final area to control material flow in cut, sew, upholstery, and trim.
19. Chair label is printed for each chair ordered. This is used to track the chairs out of trim and through shipping. It is run back through the computer for MUC status calculations.

SCHEDULE STATUS REPORT

DEPARTMENT 4131

DISPATCHER Pat Dapp

HOURS WORKED 40 to 45

520-114.1 PRINTED IN USA

SCHEDULE 7-27-83 | ENDED 7-26-83

Page 1 Of 1

DATE ISSUED 7-27-83 (8)

PART / ASSEMBLY: CODE NUMBER (1)	DESCRIPTION (2)	SCHEDULE (3)	QUANTITY (4): ORDERED	INCOMPLETE	DELAY CODE (5)	REASON FOR DELAY (6)	RECOVERY DATE * (7): PROMISED: 1/S	DATE	2/S	~~RECEIVED~~: 1/6	~~DATE~~	2/6	PRIORITY CODE
4540006	Inner tube	7/20	12000	5000	1	Waiting Stock		8/2			11.9		C/0
4548053	Extension	7/20	2300	2300	6	dept. late		7/29			10.2		C/0
4411122	Stretcher	7/27	500	500	1	Waiting Stock		7/28			2.5		C/0
4540006	Inner tube	7/27	12000	12000	1	Waiting Stock		8/5			29.1		C/0
4542058	Column	7/27	2800	2800	6	Waiting grinder		7/29			6.9		B/8
4001223	Cross tube	7/27	1500	1500	1	Waiting Stock		8/2			2.5		C/0
											(63.1)		
											(9)		

SCHEDULE STATUS SUMMARY

523-007.1 PRINTED IN USA

DIVISION: Chair	DISPATCHER (1st SHIFT): Pat Sapp	DISPATCHER (2nd SHIFT): Reid Hall
OPERATION: Machine	SCHEDULE: 7-27-83 / DATE ENDED: 7-26-83	DATE ISSUED: 7-27-83
DEPARTMENT: 4131	HOURS WORKED LAST WEEK: 40 to 45	HOURS PLANNED THIS WEEK: 50
SUPERINTENDENT: Chuck Kelley	FOREMAN (1st SHIFT): Jim Watrous	FOREMAN (2nd SHIFT): Jack Steele

① ② ● Basic Processing Area ●

Schedule Delay Code: Code	Reason for Delay	Production Orders Late	Priority Condition Code*: Code	Department	Total Stock Outs
1	Material	4	A-1	Trim	
2	Tooling		A-2	Top	
3	Manpower		A-3	Chrome	
4	Schedule Overload		A-4	Upholstery	
5	Rejection		A-5	Paint	
6	Production Planning	2	B-6	Press	
7	Manufacturing Hold		B-7	Brake	
8	Schedule Revision		B-8	Weld	1
9	Others		B-9	Zinc	
			C-0	Department Late	5

COMMENTS ③

Working the grinders last Friday all day helped our completion this week, but we are still not out of trouble. We should be working them extra hours to stay on top.

④ 85% Completion

TOTAL ORDERS – DEPARTMENT LATE 6 jobs late

~~TOTAL ORDERS SCHEDULED~~ 16 jobs late last week.

*PRIORITY CONDITION CODE

A= STOCK OUT final PROCESS AREA

B= STOCK OUT basic PROCESS AREA

C= DEPARTMENT BEHIND SCHEDULE

PRINTED IN

Date: 7/19

Machine Room Daily Capacity Status

Department	4121	4125	4131	4133	4123	W-20	M-2	AEF	Div. Total
Current Load 7/20	371.1	60.0	262.8	475.9	710.1	21.5	30.8	66.4	1879.9
Backlog 7/13	230.0	7.8	119.7	96.7	191.2	21.0	66.3	109.6	645.4
Total Hrs. Req.	601.1	67.8	382.5	572.6	901.3	42.5	97.1	176.0	2525.3
Hrs. Req. w/o backlog	74.2	12.0	52.6	95.2	142.0	4.3	6.2	13.3	376.0
Hrs. Req./Day	120.2	13.6	76.7	114.5	180.3	8.5	19.4	35.2	505.1
Avg. Output/Day									
Monday Output	227.8	38.1	47.0	110.0	1651	9.3	—	17.2	588.0
Adds & Cancellations	+13.8	+3.8	—	+10.2	+52.8	—	—	—	+80.6
Balance	+ 1.0	+18.1	214.3	178.0	328.5	30.7	87.0	94.7	701.7
± Gain/Loss	+121.3	+30.0	-83.7	-28.9	-55.3	-10.7	—	-38.8	-166
Hrs. Req./Day									
Tuesday Output	219.2	49.3	67.5	124.5	199.6	10.1	15.5	19.0	660.1
Adds & Cancellations	+51.4	+8.3	+3.5	+21.5	+26.5	—	—	—	+111.2
Balance	+168.8	+59.1	150.3	75.0	155.4	20.7	71.5	75.7	152.8
± Gain/Loss									
Hrs. Req./Day									

Machine Standard Hour Load Review — Chair PIC

520-215.0 Printed in USA

ISSUE DATE 7-13-83

DEPARTMENT NUMBER	4121	4123	4125	4131	4133		TOTAL
FOREMEN Days →	Art P	Dick H.	Jim W	Jim W	Robert S.		
Nights →	Jack S	Jack H	Jack S	Jack S	Jack H		
PLANNED LOAD FOR DATE 7/27	1074.3	816.0	202.8	275.5	667.1		3035.7
STANDARD HOURS RUN AHEAD	—	—	—	—	—		—
ADJUSTED PLANNED LOAD	1074.3	816.0	203.8	275.5	667.1		3035.7
REMAINING STANDARD HOURS	601.1	901.3	67.8	382.5	572.6		2525.3
ESTIMATED STANDARD HOURS REQUIRED FOR SPECIALS	—	—	—	—	—		—
TOTAL LOAD FOR NEXT 10 DAYS	1675.4	1717.3	270.6	658.0	1239.7		5561.0
DAILY REQUIREMENT OF STANDARD HOURS	167.5	171.7	27.1	65.8	124.0		556.1
DAILY AVERAGE OF STANDARD HOURS (4 WEEKS)	212.4	165.3	48.7	55.5	118.2		600.1
STATUS AS OF ISSUE DATE	44.9	6.4	21.6	10.3	5.8		44.0
NUMBER OF DAYS X	10	10	10	10	10		10
STANDARD HOURS =	449.0	64.0	216.0	103.0	58.0		440.0
NUMBER OF DAYS =	2.1	.4	4.4	1.9	.5		7
AHEAD OR BEHIND =							

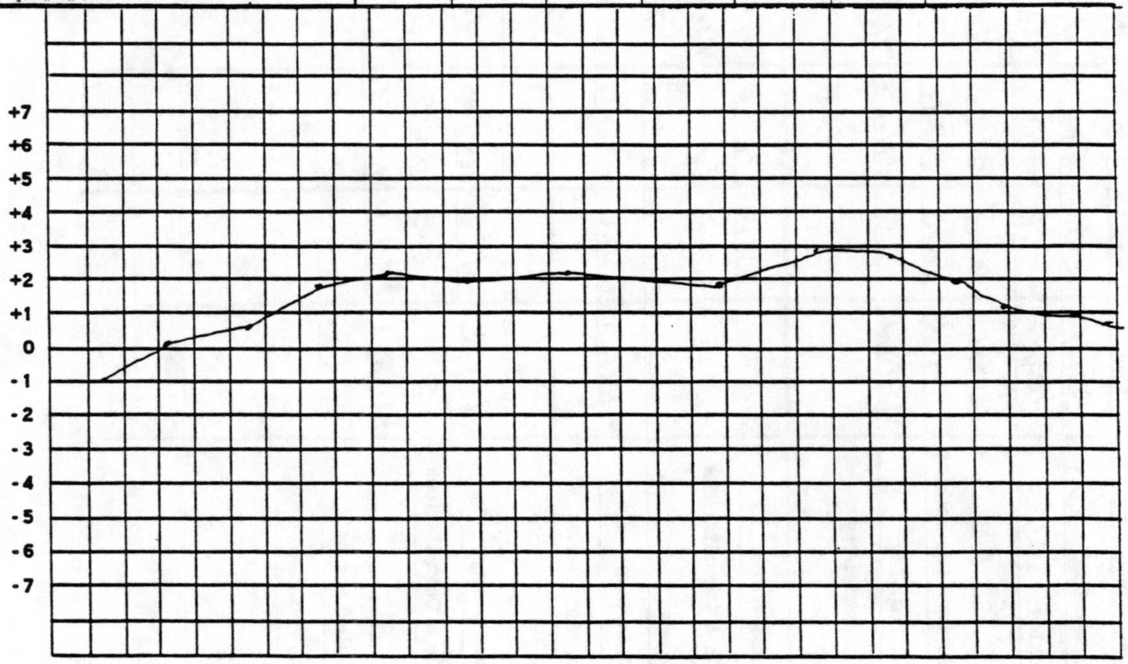

CHROME SHORTAGE REPORT

521-037.1 PRINTED IN USA

Division: ☐ Desk ☒ Chair ☐ File ☐ Panel | Schedule: 24 | Time Received: 8:00 A.M. | Page 1 Of 1

Standard Code No.	Description	Finish	Sched.	Day 1	Day 2	Day 3	Day 4	Day 5	Vendor	Promised Date	Date Received	Quantity	ICM	Raw Material At Vendor	Comments
4411606	Frame	9301	24			5		12	AC	8-3			17	60	
4411506	Frame	9301	24		13	46	90	28	AC	8-3			-330	577	
			25	174	12	26									
4632530	Ring	9350	24				6	59	VAL	8-1	8-1	36	-29	150	Call again
4548027	Arm	6602	24					38	WRI	8-4			-53	224	Need truck

* LINE IS PART OF THE WAREHOUSE SHORTAGE

SHORTAGE LIST

30-003.0

Line	Iron & Chrome	Schedule	21	Date	7-19-83
Expediter	Bonnie Higby	Supervisor	C. Harder		

Quantity	Style	Sched.	Part Late	Finish	Department	Reason Late	Promised Date	Invoice Number
8	4000540	21B	4000500	0500	4331	P/C adj	7/19	
Chrome Shortages — none reported								

TRIM SCHEDULE STATUS REPORT Ured, Benedict 523-006.0

Department: Trim | Number: 4451-2-57 | Division: Chair | Foreman: Myska-Bergaf | Prepared By: Christensen

DAILY PRODUCTION OUTPUT (Based on a (4) week moving average)

Schedule	20		21		22												Units Produced		Sched-uled Unit Balance	Units Required per Day	Hours Worked Shift	
Forecast Reqd.*	54.034		57.303		55.263																	
Production Date / Date–Day	Produced	Late	Produced	Late	Produced	Late	Produced	Late	Produced	Late	Produced	Late	Produced	Late	Produced	Late	Sched-uled	Non Sched-uled			1	2
W	9247	54077															9047		54077	11583	10	11
T	11631	40830															11631		40830	11540	10	11
F	9559	29249															9559		29219	12530	10	11
S	3208	19660															3208		19660	10929	6	0
M	10374	16452															10374		16452	11481	9	10
T	5599	6078	4663														10262		6078	11674	9	10
Total	53,555			54,055																		
____ % Completion																						
W		0	11584	52640													1584		52640	11697	9	10
T			11,106	41056													11106		41056	11893	9	10
F			8085	29950													8085		29950	13797	9	10
S			1965	21865													1965		21865	12815	5	0
M			11134	19900													11134		19900	13240	10	10
T				7510															7510			
Total																						
____ % Completion																						
W																						
T																						
F																						
S																						
M																						
T																						
Total																						
____ % Completion																						

DAILY ORDER COMPLETION PERFORMANCE

SCH.:

Prepared By: Christensen

CHAIR ORDERS REMAINING

4450		1	2	3	4	5
FORECAST		336	333	373	217	344
	M					
	T					
7-13	W	287				
7-14	TH	40+	284			
7-15	F	17	43+	332		
7-16	S	3*	10	127+	209	
7-18	M	3	8*	88	195+	
7-19	T	2	1	10*	34	207+
7-20	W	0	0	0	0*	0

CUSTOMER SERVICE

4900		1	2	3	4	5
FORECAST		57	28	86	39	74
	M					
	T					
7-13	W	0				
7-14	TH	0+	1			
7-15	F	0	0+	3		
7-16	S	0*	0	0+	3	
7-18	M	0	0*	0	3+	
7-19	T	0	0	0*	1	1+
7-20	W	0	0	0	0*	0

SHIPPING

9004		1	2	3	4	5
FORECAST		7	1	6	4	5
	M					
	T					
7-13	W	1				
7-14	TH	0+	0			
7-15	F	0	0+	2		
7-16	S	0*	0	0+	1	
7-18	M	0	0*	0	1+	
7-19	T	0	0	0*	1	1+
7-20	W	0	0	0	1+	1

+ = SCH. DAY
* = 1 DAY LATE
0 = 2 DAYS LATE
Z = 3 DAYS LATE

TRIM DATE
7-16

DAILY MUC COMPLETION

		1	2	3	4	5
FORECAST		12301	13496	11756	10172	9444
7-12	T	4663	23			
7-13	W	7338*	4300	35		
7-14	TH	167	7435*	3538	22	
7-15	F	34	673	6305*	1105	
7-16	S	0	12	837	1114*	2
7-18	M	96	59	968	7483	2692 ★
7-19	T	2	2	135	475	674
TOTAL MUC'S PRODUCED		12300	13494	11798	10199	9464
TOTAL MUC'S REMAINING		0	0	0	0	0
% ASSEMBLED ON SCHEDULE		77%	94%	91%	96%	100%
TOTAL % COMPLETED		100%	100%	100%	100%	100%

DAILY ORDER COMPLETION

		1	2	3	4	5
FORECAST		393	361	458	256	318
7-12	T	106				
7-13	W	247*	76			
7-14	TH	33	243*	123		
7-15	F	14	33	308*	44	
7-16	S	0	2	39	14+	
7-18	M	1	7	78	103	110*
7-19	T	2	1	10	35	208
TOTAL ORDERS COMPLETED		393	361	458	256	318
ORDERS REMAINING		0	0	0	0	0
% COMPLETED ON SCHEDULE		90%	88%	81%	86%	100%
TOTAL % COMPLETED		100%	100%	100%	100%	100%

WEEKLY SCHEDULE COMPLETION SUMMARY – CHAIR

530-392.0 Printed in USA

	Schedule 16		Completion % 100%		Schedule 17		Completion % 100%		Schedule 18		Completion % 100%		Schedule 19		Completion % 100%		Schedule 20		Completion % 100%		Schedule 21		Completion % 100%	
	Units Scheduled 54,124				Units Scheduled 57,676				Units Scheduled 38,562				Units Scheduled 38,242				Units. Scheduled 54,055				Units Scheduled 56,255			
	CURRENT		YEAR TO DATE		CURRENT		YEAR TO DATE		CURRENT		YEAR TO DATE		CURRENT		YEAR TO DATE		CURRENT		YEAR TO DATE		CURRENT		YEAR TO DATE	
RESPONSIBILITY	Quantity	%	Quantity	%	Quantity	%	Quantity	%	Quantity	%	Quantity	%	Quantity	%	Quantity	%	Quantity	%	Quantity	%	Quantity	%	Quantity	%
Trim																								
Upholstery																								
Paint																								
Chrome Weld																								
Weld																								
Zinc																								
Machine																								
Vendor Chrome																								
Laminate/Wood																								
Fabric																								
Cut/Sew																								
Plastic																								
Miscellaneous																								
P. I. C.																								
QC/Engineering																								
TOTAL ➡																								

4.42 CONSECUTIVE WEEKS WITH 95% OR BETTER

2.30 CONSECUTIVE WEEKS WITH 100%

PREPARED BY: Debbie Carter

5-10-29-1 DIVISION 04 O R D E R M A I N T E N A N C E L I S T 07/12/83 AT 00:32 PAGE 1

TRAN TYPE	TERM ID	CTL GRP	LOGON ID	ORDER NUMBER	ALL SEQ T	PART NUMBER STANDARD CODE	FNSH	DATE TO STOCK	QUANTITY	CUR-ORD AL-ISSD	RCV-ORD AL-RSVD	P C	WIP RCD	ALL RCD	FIRST OP /USAGE	A C D FLAGS	TRANSACTION DATE	TRANSACTION TIME
JMP	T140	HR		GR2089446	2	4001745	0000	83/07/08	17			C	4	0			83192	0816
JMP	T140	HR		GR2089448	2	4001760	0000	83/07/08	5			C	4	0			83192	0818
JMP	T140	HR		GR2089450	2	4001761	0000	83/07/08	3			C	4	0			83192	0825
JMP	T140	HR		GR2089452	2	4001785	0000	83/07/08	70			C	4	0			83192	0823
JMP	T140	HR		GR2085696	2	4001785	0000	83/07/05	22			C	4	0			83192	0828
JMP	T139	HR		GR2057064	2	4145650	0000	83/06/08	3457			C	1	0			83192	2242
JMP	T139	HR		GR7787065	2	4212520	0000	83/07/13	2910			C	5	0			83192	2243
JMP	T140	HR		GR7786705	2	4214611	0000	83/07/06	300			C	2	0			83192	0806
JMP	T140	HR		GR7788631	2	4540565	0000	83/07/13	500			C	1	0			83192	0802
JMP	T140	HR		GR2076950	2	4540762	0000	83/07/06	645			C	3	0			83192	0806
JMP	T140	HR		GR2081938	2	4541520	0000	83/07/13	500			C	2	0			83192	0803
JMP	T140	HR		GR7788673	2	45416010010	0000	83/07/13	1500			C	1	0			83192	0804
JMP	T041	HR		GR2089482	2	4542933	0000	83/07/06	3			C	3	0			83192	0949
JMP	T041	HR		GR2089484	2	4542934	0000	83/07/08	12			C	3	0			83192	0949
JMP	T041	HR		GR2089488	2	4542961	0000	83/07/08	831			C	3	0			83192	0950
JMP	T041	HR		GR2089498	2	4542969	0000	83/07/08	8			C	3	0			83192	0950
JMP	T041	HR		GR2089504	2	4542972	0000	83/07/08	342			C	3	0			83192	0950
JMP	T140	HR		GR2077000	2	4548810	0000	83/07/06	1100			C	1	0			83192	0805
JMP	T041	HR		GR2089520	2	4832601	0000	83/07/08	2			C	3	0			83192	0950
JMP	T041	HR		GR2089522	2	4832803	0000	83/07/08	2			C	3	0			83192	0952

-10-45-1 TIME 06151 QUALITY CONTROL STATUS REPORT DATE 07/22/83 PAGE 1
(OTHER THAN 01)
MFG LOC # 01 DIVISION # 04 CNTL GROUP # HR

…T NUMBER	FINISH	PALLET NUMBER	LOCATION	QUANTITY	DATE RECEIVED	QC STATUS	QC DATE	ECN NUMBER	VENDOR CODE
540761	0000	UP7131	10-25009	18	07/11/83	04		SCH 12	
210500	0009	TQ2440	04-10204	120	07/14/83	04		S 24	
210500	0000	TQ2454	49-0H	29	07/14/83	04		S 23	
210500	0000	TQ2441	04-10504	120	07/14/83	04		S 24	
210500	0000	TQ2444	03-22106	120	07/15/83	04		S 24	
210500	0000	TQ2445	03-22307	120	07/15/83	04		S 24	
210500	0000	TQ2442	03-13708	120	07/15/83	04		S 24	
210500	0000	TQ2443	03-25008	120	07/15/83	04		S 24	
210500	0000	TQ2446	06-12605	120	07/18/83	04		S 24	
210500	0000	TQ2448	49-0H	120	07/19/83	04		S 24	
210500	0050	TQ2449	03-12205	120	07/19/83	04		S 24	
210525	0000	ML9018	06-12703	2320	07/11/83	04			WILOO
210525	0000	ML9017	06-21107	1920	07/11/83	04			WILOO
210525	0000	ML9388	07-20305	1920	07/18/83	04			0000000777
210525	0000	ML9389	07-10503	2160	07/18/83	04			0000000777
210530	0000	PU0624	06-15607	114	06/16/83	08	06/27/83	S 20	
210530	0000	PU0643	06-24604	123	06/21/83	08	06/27/83	S 20	
210530	0000	PU0644	03-15504	123	06/21/83	09	06/27/83	S 20	
210530	0000	TQ2459	03-21408	120	07/13/83	04		S 24	
300510	0000	X05442	06-24306	164	07/14/83	04		S 23	
300510	0000	SR6697	03-24905	165	07/16/83	04		S 24	
300510	0000	SR6695	03-24105	165	07/16/83	04		S 24	
300510	0000	SR6698	07-23210	165	07/16/83	04		S 24	
300510	0000	SR6702	07-20203	164	07/19/83	04		S 24	
[illegible]	[illegible]	[illegible]	[illegible]	164	[illegible]	04		S 24	

LS-10-09-1 TIME 05:29 LOCATOR SYSTEM TRANSACTION LIST DATE 07/22/83 PAGE 0001

MFG LOCATION # 01 DIVISION # 04 CONTROL GROUP # HR

TRAN TYPE	DEV	PALLET NUMBER	PART NUMBER	FINISH	ORDER #	ECN/JOB NUMBER	LOCATION	QTY	QC STAT	DATE RECV	DESTINA-TION	VENDOR	PAR C	I/R F	TRANS NUMBER
ASTKU	RO3H	UP7518	2 4000590	0500			49-4E	40	01	07/21/83					83202 1046
PLNTD	RO3H	TO3636	2 4000590	0500				76							83202 1050
COMP	T140		2 4001745	0000	GR-2096260			7					C		83202 1217
COMP	T140		2 4001745	0000	GR-2094732			53					C		83202 1219
COMP	T140		2 4001765	0000	GR-2090886			1					C		83202 1247
COMP	T140		2 4001787	0000	GR-2096206			11					C		83202 1213
COMP	T140		2 4001787	0000	GR-2094738			10					C		83202 1220
COMP	T140		2 4001790	0000	GR-7791397			3					C		83202 1226
COMP	T140		2 4004953	0000	GR-2064130			100					C		83202 1250
ASTKU	RO3H	AX9414	2 4020521	0000			49-5D	125	01	07/21/83					83202 1039
PLNTC	RO3H	PU0600	2 4100500	0000			49-3B	12			4938-				83202 1547
ASTKU	RO3H	T32435	2 4100512	0000			49-2H	130	01	07/21/83					83202 1538
ASTKU	RO3H	UP7517	2 4100816	0500			49-4E	12	01	07/21/83					83202 1046
ASTKU	RO3H	T33006	2 4100816	0500			49-4E	45	01	07/21/83					83202 1046
PLNTD	RO3H	T33656	2 4100816	0500				64							83202 1050
COMP	T140		2 4101505	0000	GR-2089454			2					C		83202 1253
COMP	T140		2 4101510	0000	GR-2089456			7					C		83202 1253
COMP	T140		2 4101513	0000	GR-2085700			6					C		83202 1331
COMP	T140		2 4105530	0000	GR-2076210			31					C		83202 0947
COMP	T143		2 4105530	0000	GR-2099460			17					C		83202 1014
COMP	T141		2 4105534	0000	GR-2082464			10					C		83202 1232
COMP	T141		2 4105534	0000	GR-2090808			4					C		83202 1234
PLNTD	RO3A	QP5369	2 4121740	9201				54							83202 0551
PLNTC	T041	QP5373	2 4121740	9201			45-	230			4512-6				83202 0557
RCPT	RO3A	OR1320	2 4121740	9201			42-0	94	01	07/21/83					83202 0329
RCPT	RO3A	GP3503	2 4121740	9202			42-0	164	01	07/21/83					83202 0830
PLNTC	T041	T40C67	2 4121745	9202			45-	102			4512-8				83202 1306
COMP	T140		2 41218000030	0000	GR-7790155			100					C		83202 0957
COMP	T140		2 41218000030	0000	GR-2087052			1204					C		83202 0958
COMP	T140		2 41219000250	0000	GR-7790157			100					C		83202 0958
COMP	T140		2 41218010370	0000	GR-7780569			200					C		83202 0963

LS-10-40-1 TIME 06148 WAREHOUSE LOCATION SUMMARY DATE 07/22/83 PAGE 1

MFG LOC : 01 DIVISION : 04 CNTL GROUP : HR

LOCATION	PALLET NUMBER	PART NUMBER	FINISH	ECN NUMBER	CONT TYPE	CONTAINER QUANTITY	QC STATUS	DATE RECEIVED	DATE ISSUED	TIME ISSUED
01-10101	QP8666	2 41057120010	0000		01	80	01	06/02/83		
01-10102	QP8646	2 45059300010	0000		01	11	01	06/02/83		
01-10103	PU5638	4 897245430	6202		00	44	01	07/11/83		
01-10104	QP8647	2 45059300019	0000		01	11	01	06/02/83		
01-10105	PW9606	4 897543030	6203		00	00	01	05/31/83		
01-10106	PW9594	4 897543030	6201		00	00	01	05/31/83		
01-10107	DL3676	2 45259050010	0000		01	6	01	02/22/83		
01-10108	GO4351	4 814525050	0000		00	44	01	06/01/83		
01-10109	PW9622	4 897543030	6217		00	00	01	06/01/83		
01-10201	WL9335	4 897543030	6201	RET	00	00	01	07/12/83		
01-10202	PU5630	4 897245430	6202		00	44	01	07/11/83		
01-10203	PU5658	4 897245430	6202		00	44	01	07/11/83		
01-10204	PU5656	4 897245430	6202		00	44	01	07/11/83		
01-10205	WX5789	4 897245430	6201		00	44	01	07/20/83		
01-10206	WX5788	4 897245430	6201		00	44	01	07/20/83		
01-10207	WX5248	4 897245430	6217		00	44	01	07/20/83		
01-10208	TY0155	4 897245430	6212		00	17	01	06/13/83		
01-10209	PU5631	4 897245430	6202		00	44	01	07/11/83		
01-10301	PP1223	2 45059250010	0000		01	11	01	06/24/83		
01-10302	WX5791	4 897245430	6201		00	44	01	07/20/83		
01-10303	WX5793	4 897245430	6201		00	44	01	07/20/83		
01-10304	PU5061	4 897245430	6212		00	26	01	07/14/83		
01-10305	PT2920	4 897543030	6220		00	00	01	07/06/83		
01-10306	PU5352	4 897245430	6203		00	44	01	07/14/83		
01-10307	WX5790	4 897245430	6201		00	44	01	07/20/83		
01-10308	QP8563	2 41455200010	0000		01	80	01	06/29/83		

LS-10-35-1 PART NUMBER LOCATION SUMMARY 07/22/83 06:36 PAGE 2

MFG LOC : 01 DIVISION : 04 CNTL GROUP : HR

PART NUMBER	FINISH	LOCATION	LOAD TYPE	PALLET NUMBER	PALLET QTY	RECEIVED DATE	QC ST	QC DATE	ECN NUMBER	VENDOR	ISSUED DATE	DESCRIPTION
2 23156032	0000	09-17301	00	YI4175	100	11/10/81	01	00/00/00		0000000000		
					300							
2 2315610	0000	10-20302	01	JX7962	630	06/16/82	01					UPT ASY LEG BASE PAINTE
2 2315610	0000	10-14310	01	MX2335	500	07/22/82	01					
2 2315610	0000	09-15601	01	NT6441	600	08/11/82	01					
					1730							
2 23156102	0000	10-11308	01	PW7731	301	06/21/83	01					UPT ASY LEG BASE RAW
2 23156102	0000	08-23511	01	SR6402	563	07/14/83	01					
					864							
2 2325610	0000	10-22608	01	KT7601	125	08/16/82	01					LEG ASY (PLATE OR PAINT)
2 2325610	0000	08-13103	01	DS2711	1000	11/17/82	01					
					1125							
2 23256102	0000	08-13408	00	GM3120	52	08/11/81	01	00/00/00	BAD	0000000000		LEG ASY (RAW)
2 23256102	0000	08-23403	00	PO3020	1075	12/02/82	01					
2 23256102	0000	10-14802	00	PO3007	580	12/06/82	01					
2 23256102	0000	10-23005	00	RW5676	950	03/07/83	01					
2 23256102	0000	10-20211	00	PO3006	100	05/19/83	01					
2 23256102	0000	10-27602	00	QL9826	970	05/20/83	01					
2 23256102	0000	9621-	00	QL9858	25	05/20/83	01				07/19/83	
2 23256102	0000	10-24402	00	SP3835	1100	06/27/83	01					
2 23256102	0000	9621-	00	UY9257	580	07/05/83	01				07/07/83	
					5432							
2 24155352	0000	DISC-PIC	00	PW7479	175	06/15/83	01				07/07/83	UPT ASY LEG BASE RAW
2 24155352	0000	08-15109	00	DZ5996	623	07/06/83	01					
					798							
2 24156032	0000	09-25201	01	OZ5927	300	02/16/83	01					UPT ASY LEG BASE TEE-RAW
2 24156032	0000	10-10705	01	PW7442	255	06/29/83	01					
					555							
2 24156772	0000	10-22307	00	PG8745	883	11/08/79	01	00/00/00	RET	0000000000		LEG ASY 26 HI-RAW H/R
2 24156772	0000	09-22302	00	PG8746	878	11/09/79	01	00/00/00	RET	0000000000		
					1761							
2 4000500	0000	9621-	00	TS1696	13	05/19/83	01	06/01/83	S 16		07/08/83	CHAIR CONTROL ASSY-SWIVE
2 4000500	0000	49-3A	00	XM7323	78	07/19/83	01					
2 4000500	0000	49-3B	00	XM7325	44	07/19/83	01					
					135							
2 40005070010	0000	10-17703	01	TX1182	53	06/10/83	01					SPREADER & PLATE SUB ASY
2 40005070010	0000	10-27610	01	TX1183	61	06/10/83	01					
					114							
2 4000525	0000	10-14602	00	OG4143	148	10/27/80	01	00/00/00	RET	0000000000		
2 4000535	0000	10-21310	01	IP8822	60	09/07/82	01					

```
<==FUNCTION                    OPERATIONAL POSTING                          PS00M21
                            OPERATION STATUS DISPLAY

ORDER #: GR2088270      D.T.S: 07/27/83      ORDER QUANTITY:    7200
PART #: 3 45480011        0000   PART DESCRIPTION: ARM OVAL TUBE-RAW
    DET      OPERATION            WORK   ROUTE QTY TO  ACT HRS EXT STD REMAINING
N S ST?     DESCRIPTION          CENTER   TO:   DATE   TO DATE  HOURS  STD HOURS
0    _   CUTOFF 38 7/16 5T-4P 4133155          7200 C     0.0  17.928     0.000
0 1  _                        4133155          7200 C     0.0   0.000     0.000
2    _   DEGREASE             4133909 41231    7200 C     0.0  15.480     0.000
7    _   OPEN (2) ENDS  1T-1P 4123926          5291       0.0  19.584     5.193
8    _   BRUSH ID             4123939          4200       0.0   7.056     2.940
0    _   FORM           4T-1P 4123301 42131    3048       0.0 135.936    78.390

          TO SELECT DETAIL, KEY IN 'Y' IN DET ST? POSITION
          PRESS ENTER KEY
M)=RETURN TO MAIN MENU   (S)=RETURN TO OPERATION STATUS SELECTION
P)=PRINT SCREEN   (B)=PAGE BACKWARD   (F)=PAGE FORWARD   (X)=EXIT
2)=OPERATION DETAIL DISPLAY
      END OF OPERATIONS FOR THIS ORDER.
```

P <==FUNCTION OPERATIONAL POSTING PS00M60
OUTPUT REPORT FOR 07 / 20 / 83

WORK CENTER	LOAD DATE	STD HOURS POSTED	OVER-RUNS	UNDER-RUNS
4133386	07/27/83	6.4	0.0	0.0
4133386	08/03/83	4.6	0.0	0.0
4133903	07/20/83	0.0	0.0	0.0
4133909	07/06/83	3.3	0.0	0.4
4133909	07/13/83	0.5	0.0	0.0
4133909	07/20/83	28.3	0.0	36.2
4133909	07/27/83	34.3	0.0	14.5
4133909	08/03/83	19.6	0.0	0.0
4133948	08/03/83	8.9	0.0	0.0
**DEPT*		127.9	0.0	59.7

TO SELECT A REPORT, ENTER THE OUTPUT DATE AND PRESS ENTER.

(M)=RETURN TO MAIN MENU (1)=OUTPUT REPORT SELECTION
(P)=PRINT SCREEN (B)=PAGE BACKWARD (F)=PAGE FORWARD (X)=EXIT

<==FUNCTION OPERATIONAL POSTING PS00M50
LOAD FOR 07 / 27 / 83

WORK CENTER	STANDARD HOURS
4121109	5.9
4121113	12.8
4121117	3.0
4121152	56.1
4121153	186.9
4121156	4.9
4121157	45.9
4121224	13.8
4121225	34.4
4121226	26.1

TO SELECT A LOAD, ENTER THE LOAD DATE AND PRESS ENTER.

(M)=RETURN TO MAIN MENU (1)=LOAD DISPLAY SELECTION
(P)=PRINT SCREEN (B)=PAGE BACKWARD (F)=PAGE FORWARD (X)=EXIT

FS-02-05-1 CHAIR RACK MODEL LIST DIV 4 SHIP 24-4 PRINTED 07/27/83 PAGE 109

STD CODE	DESCRIPTION	ORDER	REFERENCE	COLORS		TOTAL	RACK
430312006	CHAIR-SWIVEL TILT-2 3/4 HARD	C24-4F31836	430-312	7111 5180	6-6203	2	79
430312006	CHAIR-SWIVEL TILT-2 3/4 HARD	C24-4F44518	430-312	7112 5273	6-6201	3	79
430312006	CHAIR-SWIVEL TILT-2 3/4 HARD	C24-4F39786	430-312	7125 5265	6-6202	26	79
450322003	CHAIR-SWIVEL TILT-2 3/16 HARD	24-4851180	430-312 S	7022 5778	6-6217 2-9201	2	79
430322003	CHAIR-SWIVEL TILT-2 3/16 HARD	24-4F41370	430-312 S	7022 5251	6-6217 2-9201	3	79

SHIP TO
A POMERANTZ DATE 08.12.83
INTERSTATE INDUST PARK
321 BENINGO BLVD
BELLMAWR NJ
08031

QTY LAB-ORD 19 SEQ- 19
F31836 01 1 OF 19
430312 DF39669
7111 5180 02-430312006
6203 CHAIR-SWIVEL
CTRU FTL TILT-2 3.4 HA
A POMERANTZ & COMPANY RD CAS

13043 24-4
DIV 4 TG 8A
C 19 RACK 78

183244021306318360100181 8
0213 CTRU
F31836
1 OF 19 430312
01 0018

SE CTRU
CH U SU
F31836
01 0213

A POMERANTZ 24-4

SHIP

24-4
DIV 4 TG 8A
RACK 78

283244021306318360100181 7
MODE-L 0213 CTRU
SCHEDULE F31836
01 0018
TOT.QTY- 19
QTY_ 1 MODL_ 430312
STD.CODE_ 02-430312006
DESC_ CHAIR-SWIVEL TILT-2 3.4
_ HARD CASTER B.SEQ_ 001
FINISH- 7111 5180
6203 SHELL

CTN- WT- 38.9
A POMERANTZ

STAGE

H 24-4
DIV 4 TG 8A
RACK 78

383244021306318360100181 6
0213 CTRU
BED-LBL 01 F31836
MUC- 1.0
01 0018
TOT.QTY- 19
QTY_ 1 MODL_ 430312
STD.CODE_ 02-430312006
DESC_ CHAIR-SWIVEL TILT-2 3.4
_ HARD CASTER B.SEQ_ 001
FINISH- 7111 5180

A POMERANTZ

TRIM

General Nature of the Firm

Twin Disc designs and manufactures advanced technological power transmission systems that are used in the off-highway construction, agriculture, marine, energy, and natural resources markets. Twin Disc has ten major product lines consisting of hydraulic torque converters; power-shift transmissions; marine transmissions; universal joints; gas-turbine starting drives; power takeoffs; electronic control systems; and mechanical, hydraulic, and pneumatic clutches.

A member of the New York Stock Exchange, Twin Disc is a well-established public company. In fiscal 1982, sales exceeded $216 million on all product lines. Currently, Twin Disc sells its products in both the domestic and international markets. To compete successfully in international markets, Twin Disc must be conscious of product quality, product price, on-time delivery, and customer service.

Domestic manufacturing facilities are located in Racine, Wisconsin (two plants), and Rockford, Illinois (one plant). The Wisconsin plants are nonunion, while the Illinois plant is organized by the United Auto Workers. Most employees are paid on an hourly basis.

Approximately 50 percent of the end items are MTO; 48 percent are manufactured to component (forecasted) stock and ATO. The remaining 2 percent are engineered and MTO. Manufacturing occurs both by product and process. An example of this is torque converters, which are manufactured in all their plants. Gears, on the other hand, are manufactured only in one plant in Racine.

The Production Process

The Organization

Figure 7-1 is the Twin Disc organizational chart. The senior vice president of manufacturing is responsible for the total manufacturing function and for the effective use of manufacturing resources. Inventory objectives and purchasing and production control activities are the responsibility of the materials manager. The production control manager is responsible for scheduling customer orders, controlling the inventory sys-

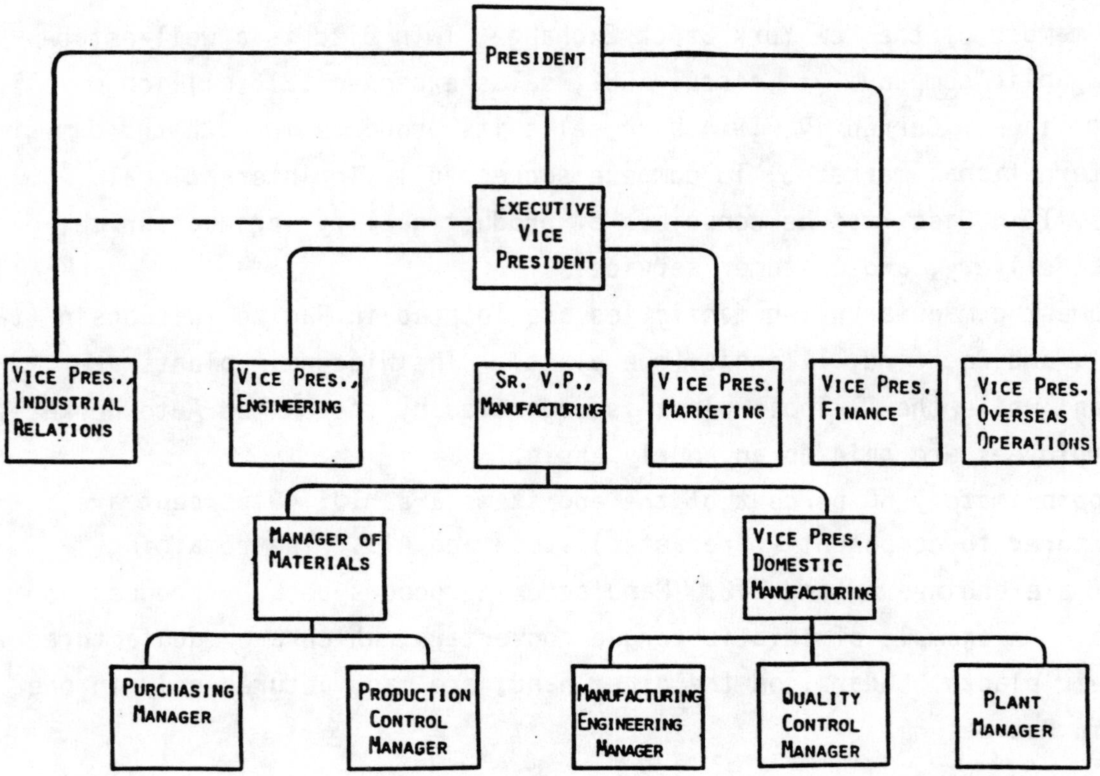

Figure 7-1. -- Organizational Chart

tem, and maintaining the integrity of the information within the manufacturing system.

The Manufactured Parts

Twin Disc has approximately 100,000 part numbers, 60,000 of which are currently active. The parts are classified into thirty-two different part families. Of the 60,000 active part numbers, 26,500 are purchased as raw material or purchased complete, and 26,000 part numbers are manufactured items with 234,000 manufacturing routed operations. The balance of the part numbers is end-item assemblies.

Part families have a varying degree of commonality. A marine transmission end item, for example, can have from 400 to 800 parts and have 60 to 80 percent commonality with other marine transmissions. In contrast, the off-highway transmissions, with 700 to 900 part numbers, may have as little as 20 percent commonality with other off-highway transmissions. Smaller products, such as clutches (with only twenty or thirty components), may have about 10 percent part commonality while other small products such as power takeoffs (with thirty to forty components) may have 30 to 90 percent commonality.

Figure 7-2 is a flowchart of the production process used at Twin Disc. Raw materials are received, verified, and released into WIP. There are 475 work centers and subcontractors available to machine gears, shafts, small and large housings, and miscellaneous small items (such as plates, pins, and spacers). Work order lot sizes range from one piece to 10,000 pieces, with 80 percent of the work orders under 100 pieces. Internal lead times range from two weeks to fourteen weeks on manufactured items.

Purchased complete items are received, verified, and placed in a finished component stockroom. Finished components are either released to the shipping department for customer service orders, or may proceed to the subassembly/assembly/test area before being released to the shipping department. A one-week lead time is allowed for the cycle time from finished component stock to finished end item ready for shipment.

End-item lot sizes vary from one to 200, with 90 percent being under 10 items. On average, less than 5 percent of all released orders have order quantity changes. Timing changes can occur daily based on changing customer or inventory requirements. On average, 140 engineering and/or BOM changes are processed each month. These changes may affect only 1 part number, or

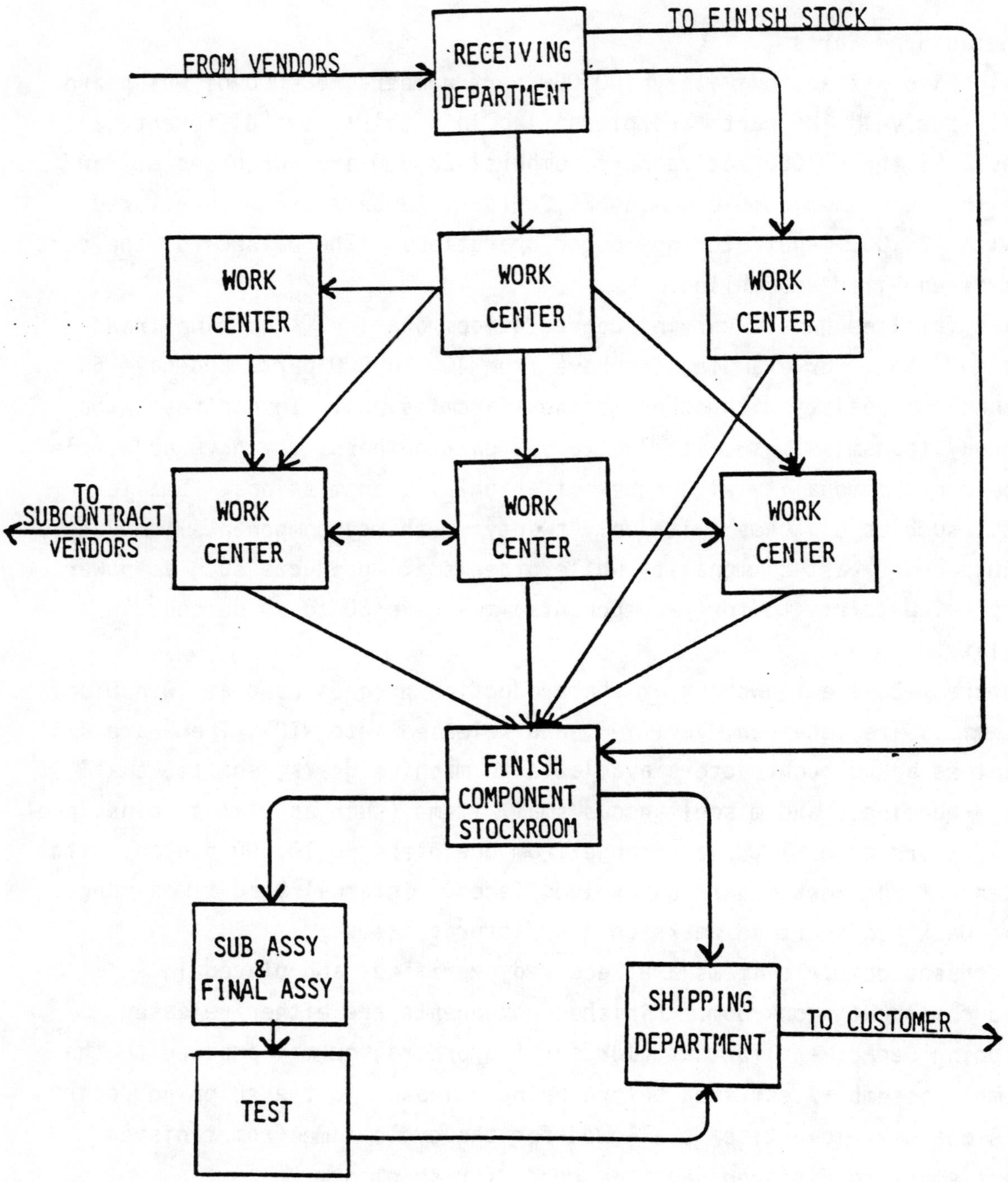

Figure 7-2. -- Production Process

they may affect over 100 part numbers, depending on the complexity of the change. The average depth of the BOM is seven levels, the maximum, nine.

Production Planning at Twin Disc

The integrated planning system used by Twin Disc (Figure 7-3) begins with current market demand and a forecast of market demand. It proceeds to manufacturing resource planning (MRP II), which includes the production plan, master schedule, material requirements planning (MRP), capacity requirements planning (CRP), shop floor management, vendor management, product shipment, and customer feedback and evaluation.

This planning process parallels manufacturing and financial planning, a unique quality that enables Twin Disc to see the manufacturing implications of planning decisions and the financial aspects of those decisions. Neither the manufacturing nor the financial aspects of a situation can dominate the planning. All of the computer systems for capacity management and shop floor management were developed internally at Twin Disc.

The completeness of the planning system is also unique. Beginning at marketing, the process cascades to manufacturing resource planning, the production plan, master schedule, MRP, CRP, shop floor management, vendor management, and evaluation and feedback from the customers. This process closes the loop from the marketplace to manufacturing and back. Completion specifications of inputs and outputs are included at each planning and execution stage.

Market Planning

The sales and marketing personnel input a market demand estimate each quarter, issuing a formal forecast in both dollars and units. The total time frame is two years. Additionally, marketing issues a five-year forecast each year by adding three extra years stated in yearly (not quarterly) projections. The forecast is reviewed by manufacturing using MRP II concepts.

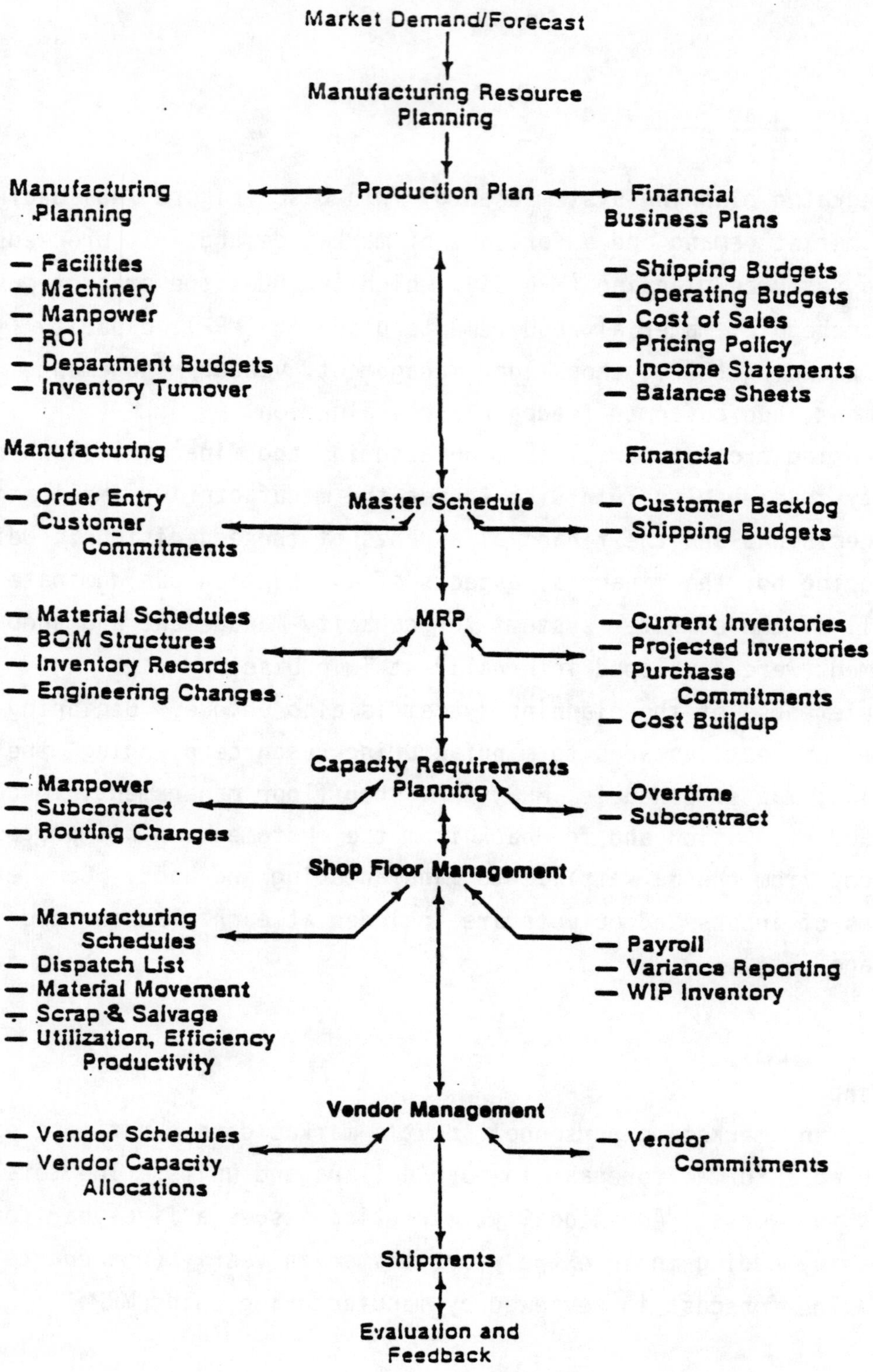

Figure 7-3. -- Integrated Planning System

The Production Plan

All capacity requirements are evaluated by an analysis of facilities, machinery, and labor force. Material requirements are verified. These analyses produce the final production plan that becomes the formal organizational plan after approval by manufacturing, marketing, and the chief executive officer.

The production plan is input to the financial and manufacturing planning systems. Financially, shipping budgets are developed that generate internal department operating budgets. Cost of sales is planned and produces the pricing policy used by Twin Disc. Profit and loss statements are formulated that include the income statements, cash flow projections, and balance sheets.

Manufacturing uses the production plan to develop facilities and machinery expenditure forecasts. These forecasts are used to produce planned return-on-investment projections. Detailed work force plans are initiated that are supported by departmental budgets. Inventory turnover goals are established that support the production and financial plans.

Long-range capacity planning is also a function of the production planning system in which the five-year forecast versus capacity (achieved output) can be analyzed to determine facilities, machinery, and work force requirements. Input/output reports are used (on an exception basis only) by department and plant (or work center) to review sold load only, planned load only, or both.

The Master Schedule

The master schedule, using information from the production plan, inputs gross requirements into the MRP system. Customer orders are entered into the master schedule within the constraints specified by the production plan. Customer commitments, in terms of acknowledged delivery dates, are established and become part of the master schedule. Although master scheduling is a daily process, monthly meetings are held by marketing and manufacturing personnel. At these meetings, the master schedule is compared with the production plan and changes are recommended to top management. The master schedule is also used to establish the current and future dollars of customer backlog, which is then compared with the shipping budgets.

The Material Requirements Plan

MRP establishes material schedules based on the committed master schedule and the forecasted production plan. Procedures to maintain BOM structures, through BOM input and verification, have been established. Inventory records are updated by a detailed transaction system which, in turn, is verified by cycle-count procedures. Engineering changes are controlled through a formal system of maintenance in the MRP system.

The master schedule drives the MRP system. Dollars of current and projected inventories are established and supported through the use of current and planned purchase commitments. Standard cost estimates are obtained through the BOM structure.

Twin Disc has used a complete net change MRP system successfully since 1965.

The Capacity Requirements Plan

At Twin Disc, management feels that capacity management is critical to the success of the entire production function. Without proper control and capacity management, the production system can become uncontrollable quickly. Management also feels that the capacity planning system, to be controllable, must be understood by the system users. This is one reason that the primary priority scheduling rule is operation due date. If capacity is managed properly, operation due date is one of the most effective priority rules available.

CRP supplies the standard hours of production, by time frame and work center, required to support the master schedule. Plant capacity is composed of and measured by standard hours of manufacturing output per week for a thirteen-week moving average. Highs and lows are discounted. Equivalent work days are used to plan for vacation absenteeism. Capacity information is used at all three planning levels -- long range during production plan development, intermediate during CRP, and short range in the sold load and dispatching systems.

MRP supplies CRP with actual shop orders and planned order releases. Overtime and subcontract schedules are formulated. Standard routing verification and changes are initiated as required. Detailed work force additions or deletions by machine center by time frame are then executed.

Capacity planning at all levels must be done thoroughly. An example of this emphasis on the complete capacity planning is found in production plan development. If all facilities are maximized and if all demands on capacity are taken into proper account (i.e., product forecast, renewal parts forecast, component forecasts for other plants and divisions, estimated hours for scrap and salvage replacement), the production plan becomes a finite capacity planning tool. Master scheduling, within the constraints of the production plan, will now not only feed the MRP system, but it will also determine the capacity and priorities reflected in the shop floor control system. Good capacity planning greatly simplifies the operation of the shop floor control system by ensuring that all plans released to the shop floor have an adequate average of planned capacity.

Shop Floor Control

Shop floor control establishes all manufacturing schedules. The dispatch list uses the MRP order need dates and operation due dates for all open shop orders. It also supplies detailed capacity information for daily and weekly control of each work center. Manufacturing tracks material movement by operation to provide current operational shop order information on the dispatch list. Scrap and salvage information are reported and used to update shop order status. Labor reporting throughout the shop floor control system provides updated efficiency, productivity, and use information, as well as accumulated actual labor for use in variance reporting against standards and for use in computing payroll costs. WIP inventory dollars are also established and controlled.

Vendor Management

The Twin Disc purchasing department supplies its vendors with realistic schedules by giving the required need dates and quantities of materials as received through the MRP system. Capacity allocation programs have been established with vendors to ensure that adequate vendor capacity is available as required. Total dollars of purchase commitments are obtained and reported. These costs are compared with the total inventory planned.

Evaluation and Feedback

Shipments to customers close the manufacturing loop by relieving requirements from the master schedule. Shipments are costed at standard.

Material and labor variances are used for sales and profit analysis.

Evaluation and feedback are continuous processes at Twin Disc. These extensively integrated systems, which use a single database, require that Twin Disc coordinate its functional requirements through the planning, execution, and control phases of the operation. A diagram of the integrated MRP, shop floor control, and financial database is shown in Figure 7-4. With this coordinated system, revisions to the plans and schedules can be accomplished efficiently. Emphasis is placed on planning and capacity evaluations because the balance of manufacturing activities evolves from these two evaluations.

Shop Floor Control

The objectives of the Twin Disc shop floor control management system are:

- To improve product quality
- To minimize WIP inventory by obtaining accurate inventory counts by operation and location
- To maximize machine and work force productivity through controlled capacity, valid priorities, and WIP accuracy
- To increase customer service by providing shorter lead times and consistent on-time delivery
- To communicate valid customer requirements, inventory objectives, and management objectives to Twin Disc employees, customers, and vendors

These objectives are accomplished by using the planning system properly, using the full capabilities offered by the current shop floor control system, and by completely reporting performance to all levels in the organization.

The shop floor control system is computerized completely and is an integral part of the computer system that supports all planning and execution activities. The system, consisting of an IBM 4341 with 3550 and 3370 disk drives, has a rated capacity of four megabits and DOS-VSE capabilities. Ninety-five percent of the programs used by the system are written in Primary Assembler, and the remaining five percent are written in Fortran. Twin Disc has CICS on-line systems in purchasing, receiving, shipping, salvage, industrial engineering, and subcontracting. There are full on-line

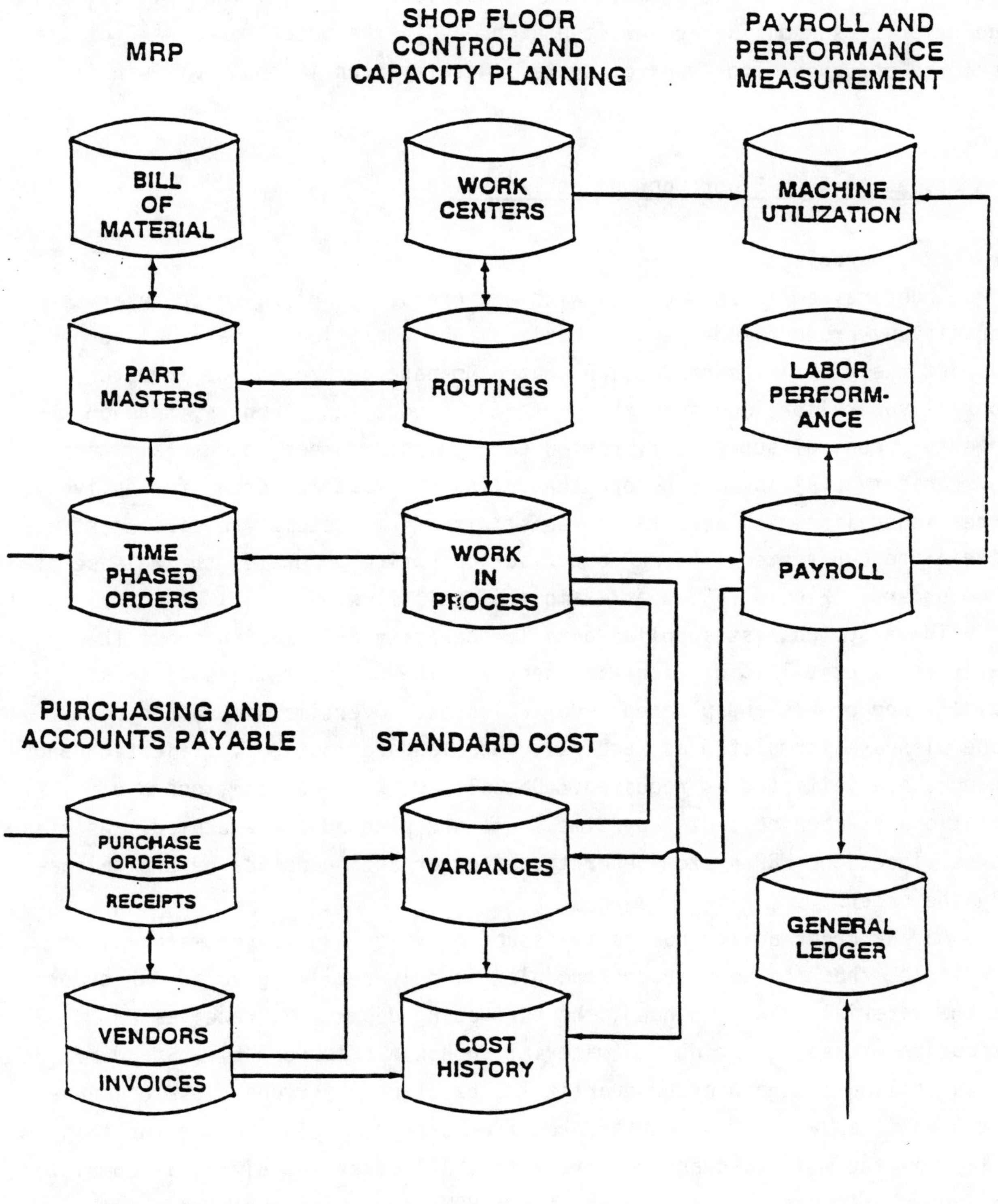

Figure 7-4. -- The Integrated Database

CRT inquiry capabilities in production control, quality control, payroll, cost accounting, and marketing.

The shop floor control system is updated in batch each evening. Salvage operations and work orders are written in an on-line real-time environment. All operation movement cards, labor cards, inventory receipts, and priority scheduling are written each day in the batch mode. All of the capacity and shop floor control systems were written in house at Twin Disc.

The Stages of Shop Floor Control at Twin Disc

Order Review/Release

Order review/release begins with the production plan, which reserves capacity by product model and authorizes the generation of material to support the plan. The production control manager, through the inventory control supervisor, monitors this system. Production planners, through the inventory control supervisor, review each customer order to ensure material and capacity availability before scheduling the customer order for delivery. Order scheduling displaces the forecast with firm customer requirements within the MRP system. An MRP order action notice generates the release of shop orders. Figure 7-5 is an example of this flow.

The dispatch list supplies detailed capacity information about the daily and weekly load of each work center. The CRP system also checks actual shop orders and planned order releases. Overtime and subcontract schedules are formulated as required, and standard routing verification and changes are initiated as required. Detailed work force additions and deletions by machine center by time frame are planned and executed. As this takes place, the MRP system generates an order action notice before releasing the order.

An MRP order action notice is issued only if lower level material is available, thus the work order scheduler is only reviewing valid MRP orders. If the material is not on hand, the purchasing department receives an exception message to bring the material in house (Figure 7-6). Standard lot sizes, called standard order quantities, exist only for one class of manufactured items -- shafts manufactured from barstock. The reason for this policy is the mill purchase requirements. All other lot sizing is completed only on the lowest purchase level of the BOM, such as for castings and

MATERIAL STATUS - PRODUCTION SCHEDULE

PART NUMBER	NAME	FORECAST QUANTITY	USED LAST YEAR	USED TO DATE	USED THIS PERIOD	YEAR TO DATE SCRAP	SAFETY STOCK	LEAD TIME	S.O.Q.	[illegible]	REQ. FREQ	CUTTING INFO.	PRINT DATE
..206002K.	BODY VALVE		1189	611	37	8							03/07/83

PLANT	BUYER	PRODUCT CODE	ORDER	CANCEL	RESCHED	EXPED	[illegible]	GET FROM MORGUE	ACTION REQUIRED: TYPE	DUE	QUANTITY	AUTHORITY	SERVICE DELIVERY THIS YEAR	SERVICE DELIVERY LAST YEAR	MORGUE QUANTITY	ALLOCATION
1		8.099					X						41	88		

WEEK	ORDER NUMBER	QUANTITY	VENDOR
0962	952A00	166	-NO-

MATERIAL COST	LABOR COST	LOT SIZE FOR STD	LOWER LEVEL OR CRITICAL PART NUMBER: PART NUMBER	QUANTITY	MODEL USED ON	SPECIAL INSTRUCTIONS
[redacted]	[redacted]	[redacted]	# 206002C	0	6F13073	B-R.O.-

	PAST DUE	03/07/3	03/14/3	03/21/3	03/28/3	04/04/3	04/11/3	04/18/3	04/25/3	05/02/3	05/09/3	05/16/3	05/23/3
REQ		80		10		12		1	10	10	10	43	29
SCHED REC		166											
AVAILABLE	ON HAND 9	95	95	85	85	73	73	72	62	52	42	-1	-30
PLND ORD								1	29	27			
								1	29	27			

	05/30/3	06/06/3	06/13/3	06/20/3	06/27/3	07/04/3	07/11/3	07/18/3	07/25/3	08/01/3	08/08/3	08/15/3	08/22/3
REQ	27				2	50	27			17	15	10	10
SCHED REC													
AVAILABLE	-57	-57	-57	-57	-59	-109	-136	-136	-136	-153	-168	-178	-188
PLND ORD	2	50	27			17	15	10	10		50		
	2	50	27			17	15	10	10		50		

	08/29/3	09/05/3	09/12/3	09/19/3	09/26/3	10/03/3	10/10/3	10/17/3	10/24/3	10/31/3	11/07/3	11/14/3	TOTALS
REQ		50											413
SCHED REC													166
AVAILABLE	-188	-238	-238	-238	-238	-238	-238	-238	-238	-238	-238	-238	-238
PLND ORD													238
													238

REQ													
SCHED REC													
AVAILABLE													
PLND ORD													

Figure 7-6. -- Material Status -- Production Schedule

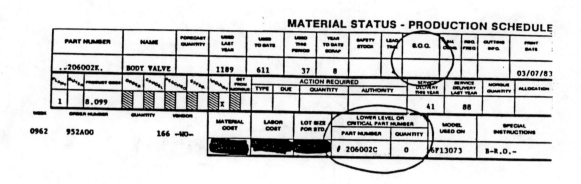

MRP INTERFACE WITH PLANNING EXECUTING AND CONTROLLING SCHEDULES ON THE SHOP FLOOR

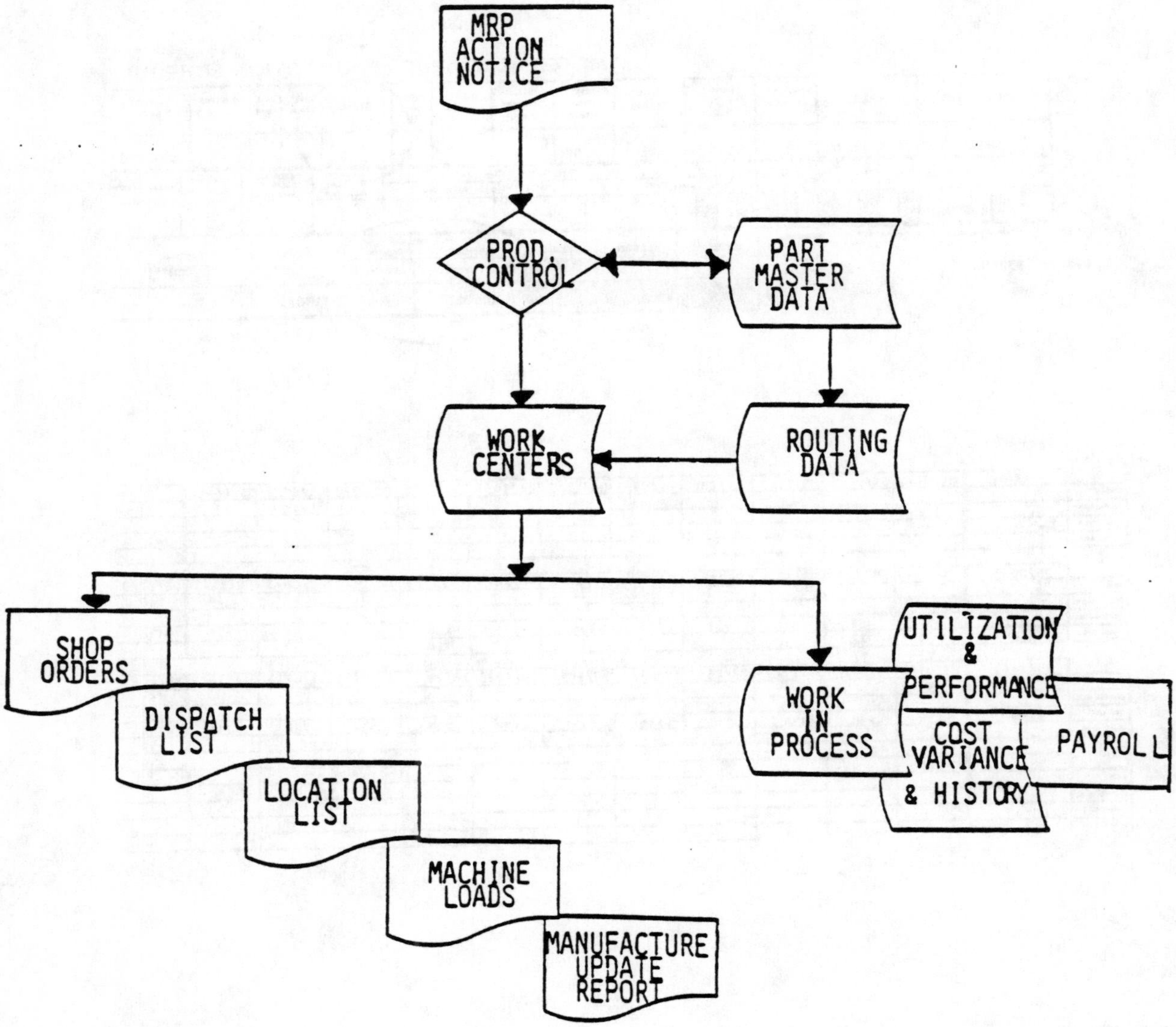

Figure 7-5. -- Flow Pattern of Shop Floor

forgings. Lot-sizing removal causes much of the nervousness experienced in the MRP, purchasing, and shop floor control systems.

If an order is to be released, the work order scheduler will duplicate a copy of the standard routing (Figure 7-7) and will rewrite the part number, quantity, and vendor name. A work order number will be assigned with the first three numbers representing the current shop week number, an alpha, and two numeric digits for identification. The work order contains the operation sequence with plant, department, work center, estimate rate coding, hours per 100, pieces per hour, special instruction sheet coding, and a brief description of the operations to be performed.

A copy of the work order is forwarded to data processing where the work order is opened but not released. A back scheduling routing is initiated that uses the MRP due dates as the last operation due date. Using queue, transportation, run, setup, and delivery time standards creates a start date for each operation, which becomes the due date for the previous operation. The calculation continues until the first operation start and due dates have been calculated.

Operation completion cards are also created and forwarded to the work order scheduler. Operation cards and the original copy of the work order go to the department foreman of the starting work center. One copy is distributed to the foreman of the receiving department. After the receiving foreman sends the materials to the foreman of the first operation, a copy is forwarded to data processing. The data processing entry will compute this as a released work order, and the system will release inventory from the bin to the WIP in the department of the first operation.

Detailed Assignment

The production foreman uses the dispatch list to perform the detailed assignment. At Twin Disc, the dispatch list is called the daily work center job schedule (Figure 7-8) and is issued daily by machine center within each department at the plant. All work orders available at a manufacturing center are ranked by earliest operation due date of each order. In the operation due date sequence of each dispatch list, all work orders available at the center are ranked as well as all work orders one previous operation away.

The due date priority is categorized into a priority of customer order (P.O. in Figure 7-8) or priority of inventory (P.I.) on the dispatch list.

IN DISC, INC.

PER NO	PART NUMBER	DESCRIPTION	PART NUMBER	WORK ORDER NO
100-1	206002K	RELIEF VALVE BODY	206002-K	952-A-00
	ROUTING DATE 04/06/81	MADE FROM/ SPEC. INSTRUCTIONS	QUANTITY 166	LOAD QTY
100-2	USED ON 6F13073	#206002-C	VENDOR NEENAH	LOAD 1 OF 1
	RANGE 1 9		HEAT NO.	

OPER. NO.	PLANT-DEPT.-CENTER	S T	HOURS/ C	PIECES/ HOUR	N S	DESCRIPTION
010	1-15-NBR					INSPECT
020	1- 6-GX		[redacted]	[redacted]	X	MILL MTG PAD
030	1- 6-ITS		[redacted]	[redacted]	X	DRILL TWO 13/32, ONE 5/16, DRILL, TAP, REAM REAM & CHAM END & SIDES & MILL TO LENGTH
040	1- 6-NB		[redacted]	[redacted]	X	DEBURR, BLAST & STAMP "K"
050	1- 6-FU		[redacted]	[redacted]	X	HONE
060	1- 6-RW					WASH & OIL
070	1-15-NBG					INSPECT

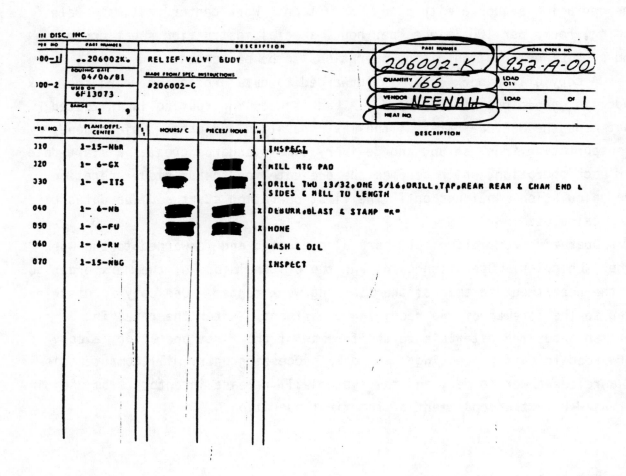

Figure 7-7. -- Standard Routing

D166078-1 DATE 03/08/83 DAILY WORK CENTER JOB SCHEDULE WEEK - 0962 DAY-TUESDAY

PLANT 01 DEPT 06 MACH. CTR ITS SHIFTS WORKED 1.0 CAPACITY 40.0

PART # NAME	W.O.	OPER# DESCRIPTION	OPER P.O.	DUE	DATE P.I.	QTY. OF OP.	QTY. COMP.	OPER HRS.	FAIL QTY +7	MRP FAIL DATE	FOREMAN COMPL. DATE	MRP DUE DATE
206002K	952A00	030	02/17/83			166		38.2	160	03/09/83	03/14/83	03/09/83
BODY VALVE		DRILL	06NB 06FU 06RW									
206796L	957A19	050	03/10/83			5		7.2	2	03/23/83		03/23/83
VALVE BODY		DRILL	06NB 06FU 06RW									
217751R	961A38	020			04/15/83	2		6.6		05/11/83		05/11/83
BODY VALVE		9ITTD	06GX 06ED 06TL 06ITS 06IA 06IM 06NB 06FU 06RW									
217751L	961A35	020			04/21/83E	3		6.9		05/18/83		05/18/83
BODY VALVE		9ITTD	06GX 06ED 06IL 06ITS 06IA 06IA 06IM 06RW 06NB 06FU 06RW									
206796P	947A85	050			00/00/00	3		6.7		00/00/00		00/00/00
BODY VALVE		DRILL	06NB 06FU 06RW									
TOTAL HOURS IN THIS MACHINE CENTER								65.6				
PARTS IN PREVIOUS WORK CENTER												
229206A	960B35	070	06IL	03/01/83	E	-5		8.5	1	03/16/83	03/20/83	03/16/83
206002B	960A23	030	06GX		04/07/83	25		11.2	7	04/20/83		04/20/83
206002C	960A24	030	06GX		04/06/83	175		46.6		04/27/83		04/27/83
TOTAL HOURS FOR THIS MACHINE CENTER IN PREVIOUS CENTERS								66.3				

Figure 7-8. -- Daily Work Center Job Schedule

This ensures that customer order work orders receive priority over safety stock or forecasted requirements work orders. The dispatch list also shows the quantity of each operation and the quantity completed. For capacity control, the report shows the operation hours required (OPER HRS.) for each operation at the work center and for each operation of parts in the previous work center, along with a subtotal of these hours. This information is used for short-term capacity planning and control on the factory floor. By comparing these hours with the work center's capacity (CAPACITY), defined as a moving average of achieved standard hours of output, a foreman can make decisions on rerouting work load, moving the work force, authorizing overtime, lot splitting, and so forth.

Additional information on the report includes pegged customer requirements (FAIL QTY+7) that is used if lot splitting is required, MRP fail date of customer need, and MRP due date of the part number. A manual input column (FOREMAN COMPL. DATE) is used by the foreman to commit to the completion of parts based on need two weeks in advance for assembly schedule purposes.

By efficiently planning and controlling capacities, the question of which order priority technique is only important in the sense that it must be valid and easily understood. This was the major reason that Twin Disc converted from the critical ratio rule to the operation due date rule in 1982. The company found that dates are understood more easily than ratios by the foreman and workers, and are definitely more transparent. Everyone understands the date of the operation and the need date of each part number.

Finally, the shop floor control system allows the foreman to make a final decision about the exact sequence in which to process the orders at the work center, provided adequate capacity is or can be made available. If capacity use is very high (i.e., approaching full use), the amount of discretion available to the foreman is reduced, and the sequence found on the dispatch list must be followed.

Data Collection/Monitoring

As operations on the work order are completed, data processing processes the operation completion card. The card updates the precise location of the work order. Labor reporting time cards report partial completions of an operation on a work order. Priority recalculation occurs each evening based on time card reporting, operation card completion reporting, and changes in work order due dates (as automatically received from the net change MRP system). All changes (additions, deletions, or operation changes) to a work order's routed information are included and may cause a change in priority calculations.

All reporting of operations on work orders updates the work order detail file, work order master file, and payroll file. This information, in turn, is used to update use and performance measures by individual, machine, and work center, along with financial cost variance and WIP file. Management reports are generated as required.

Twin Disc management believes in queue control to determine and resolve capacity constraints. The queue control philosophy states that if queues are controlled, most major work order control difficulties will be solved. Management reviews the queue of each work center in relation to the queue assigned to that work center. The queue length is also part of each operation's calculated lead time. This review allows management to reduce queue time, thus leading to decreased part manufacturing lead time and decreased inventory.

Another monitoring tool, the alternate routing notice (Figure 7-9), is introduced by the plant supervisor or production control manager to displace capacity from one work center to another, as determined through a review of the dispatch list, sold load, or CRP reports. This transaction creates WIP, shop floor control, and budget transactions.

Finally, it should be noted that Twin Disc uses one common database. Any changes originating from the shop floor control system become available to the rest of the firm. Because of the presence of a single common database, data accuracy is a constant concern. All of the production systems, including the shop floor control system, include proper edit and exception reporting to ensure that daily transactions are accurate. An example would be where the partial completion of a work order into finished stores is edited for part number, quantity, and work order number. Another example would be when the calculated lead time for a released work order is edited versus the planned manufacturing lead time in the MRP system. The reports are designed so that out-of-control or exception items can be identified and reviewed quickly to provide proper corrective action and feedback to the appropriate system.

ALTERNATE ROUTING NOTICE

t No. 206769 Work Order No. 973B68 Date 7/5/83

No. Pcs. This Order 5 No. Pcs. to be Run on this Change 5

ernate Operations To Be Completed

Code	Alternate Oper. No.	Dept.	Machine Center	Hr/C	Pcs./Hr.	E	Code	Replaces Oper. No.
AX3	020	08	BRT				DX3	020
CXA	060	08	CJ	1.72	19.5			

AX* — ADD DX* — DELETE CX* — CHANGE

* Reason Code
See Reverse Side for Code

Dept. Foreman Plant Superintendent Industrial Eng.

— 1519 Rev 5/83

1. Mach. Ctr. down for repair
2. Mach. Ctr. overload
3. Make work for Alt. Mach. Ctr.
4. Alt. Mach. small qty. less set-up cost
5. Alt. Mach. rush work order
6. Non-std. tooling
7. Tooling not available for Primary Mach.
8. Alt. Material - Mfg.
9. Alt. Material - Supplier

A. Increase Productivity
B. Mfg. Methods Change
C. Missing Operation
D. In-Process Eng. Change
E.
G.
H.

Figure 7-9. -- Alternate Routing Notice

Control/Feedback

At Twin Disc, a major emphasis of the control effort is scrap and salvage. These efforts are supported by an on-line salvage system that allows the ordering and tracking of all salvage items by operation. This system also allows the capacity requirements of the salvage to be identified and tracked.

In addition, an intermediate to long range machine load report (Figure 7-10) lists the planned hours required from the net change MRP system exploded through the standard routing file and the actual hours from the work order detail file by work center. This report allows personnel to review nine four-week buckets of load hours into the future versus the current capacity of the work center. Because salvage hours appear as a part of the actual hours, appropriate decisions to manage capacity requirements can now take place.

A scrap transaction is another major transaction that affects both the priority and capacity planning within the shop floor control system. Scrap transactions are batched together each evening for inventory and priority recalculations. Even if the scrap is questionable (i.e., it may be salvageable), a scrap ticket is generated. Twin Disc can afford to do this because the on-line salvage system allows it to salvage a part already scrapped out of inventory and credit the proper inventory, budget accounts, and shop floor control files.

On-line databases and the computer system make CRT inquiry into work order information available to the foreman. All open orders, with their current status and forward-scheduled completion dates, are available for investigation. The investigator feeds the forward-scheduled date back into the net change MRP system as the scheduled receipt for that particular part number, work order number, and quantity. (See Figure 7-11.)

Order Disposition

Because of the constant monitoring of the work order as it progresses through the various operations, order disposition is fairly straightforward. The completed work order is received into stores, the available on-hand quantity increased, and the WIP quantities decreased. The order is then closed out and evaluated by comparing actual progress against planned progress in terms of costs, labor, lead time, and level of scrap and salvage generated.

D166084 DATE 03/09/83 LONG RANGE MACHINE LOAD WEEK 0962

WORK CENTER TOTAL FOR PLANT 01 DEPT 06 WKCN ITS CAPACITY 160.0

FROM	TO	PLANNED	ACTUTAL	TOTAL
962	965	50,9	158,7	208,7
966	968	45,5	,0	45.5
969	973	93,1	,0	93,1
974	977	182,1	,0	182,1
975	981	169,9	,0	169,9
982	985	135.0	,0	135.0
986	989	116,5	,0	116,5
990	993	98,3	,0	98,3
994	996	80,6	,0	80,6

Figure 7-10. -- Long Range Load Report

PO14, 206002 K,1,952A76 IS THE NEXT WO

206002K BODY VALVE RACINE LOCATION LIST WEEK 0962 3/7/83

WO#	OPER.	OPER.DESC.	WORK CTR.	QTY.	FOREMAN	PRIORITY CODE	COMP.
952A00	030	DRILL	01-06-ITS	166	3/14/83	PO-02/17/83	962
	040	DEBURR	01-06-NB	166	3/14/83	PO-03/01/83	962
	050	HONE	01-06-FU	166	3/14/83	PO-03/04/83	964
	060	WASH	01-06-RW	166	3/14/83	PO-03/08/83	965
	070	INSPECT	01-15-NGB	166	3/14/83	PO-03/09/83	965

PAGING.......PRESS ENTER FOR NEXT PAGE OR TYPE IN NEW TRANSACTION CODE

Figure 7-11. -- Information Available to Foreman

Evaluating Twin Disc's Shop Floor Control System -- Benefits

Since the shop floor control system was introduced at Twin Disc, management has observed the following benefits:

- Improved product quality
- Controlled WIP inventory
- Improved machine use
- Improved work force efficiencies
- Increased shop productivity
- Increased on-time delivery to customers
- Reduced delivery lead time to customers.

Management strongly feels that the presence of its effective shop floor control system is one important reason for Twin Disc's continued success in an increasingly competitive marketplace. Users, including plant superintendents and foremen, believe the system is credible.

Shop Floor Control -- The Next Stage

Shop floor control is only part of Twin Disc's total integrated computer system. Therefore, if a system is improved in any area, that improvement will help manage the shop floor. The following improvements are anticipated:

- Master scheduling. More adequate forecast and consumption of firm customer orders versus the production plan forecast into MRP.
- MRP. A service forecasting system, separate from the master production system and detail pegged through all BOM levels of separate requirements (service, production, interplant, and export).
- Stockroom. Computer-used allocation, receipt, and disbursement system.

In addition, over seventy-five ranked system changes are under way, each meant to improve productivity.

The management at Twin Disc has begun the process of bringing a CAD/CAM system on line. Management has programs in place to review machining productivity processes, office automation, material handling automation, robotics, flexible manufacturing centers and flexible manufacturing systems applications, and automated identification. Management at Twin Disc is committed to productivity improvement by drawing on automation and systems development.

Shop Floor Control at Twin Disc: Lessons to be Learned

The shop floor control system at Twin Disc has been successful because of these key strengths and features:

- Twin Disc has developed a prototypical MRP II system. The system is at the leading edge of MRP II development. It includes all levels, from market planning to production planning to market feedback and evaluation, and addresses not only production concerns but also the financial aspects of decisions at every step of the process.
- The use of a single, unified database. By using a single, unified database, all key decisions at Twin Disc are made using the same, accurate information. A great deal of time and effort is spent in maintaining the integrity and validity of the unified information. But the cost of maintaining the database has been more than recovered by the increase in decision-making accuracy and effectiveness because of "better" data.
- Capacity planning is considered a key to the success of the total system. Management at Twin Disc feels that to be successful in the international marketplace, there must be sufficient production capacity in place to handle customer needs. This capacity, however, must be monitored continuously and managed to ensure that the correct orders are released to each work center and that the planning system is not overloading the production system.
- A highly automated salvage and scrap reporting system allows for efficient material recovery. Usually the scrap and salvage reporting system is a minor subsystem in the entire production system. At Twin Disc, management has realized that the cost of materials is one of the major costs of the finished goods and that it must be monitored and controlled constantly. A unique aspect of the salvage and scrap reporting system is the automated link with the total material and MRP system and with the total capacity and CRP system. This link allows for instant monitoring of material status for either good or bad material. It also enables management to evaluate the capacity effect of salvage.
- The objectives of the shop floor control system are clearly stated. With a common, well understood set of objectives, most of the communication problems concerning the purpose of the system are

circumvented easily. The availability of these objectives statement of purpose cannot be underestimated. Everyone is aware of the stated objectives of the system, and everyone works toward these common goals.

- o The important place of the communication aspects of the total production system. One of the major focuses of the shop floor control system and the total production reporting system is ease of communication. Transparency was one reason for the selection of operation due date as a priority rule. Management discovered that, while a more complex rule may be projected to be more efficient, it is the simple, easily understood rules that are most effective for the total system. Users can understand these rules, and they are able to better relate priority problems to others. Other demonstrations of Twin Disc's concern for communication shows in its use of objectives, the linking of scrap and salvage with the MRP and CRP systems, the use of a common database, and the use of responsive and timely on-line computer systems.

The shop floor control system, as well as the entire corporate planning system, shows that Twin Disc management has spent considerable time and money in developing and delivering a state-of-the-art shop floor control system. But, even with this advanced and efficient system, Twin Disc continues to improve and enhance its system. Given the overall quality of the current systems, the next step in the shop floor control odyssey should be of interest to production and operations managers.

General Nature of the Firm

Vollrath Company, headquartered in Sheboygan, Wisconsin, is a well-established, privately held firm. With annual sales of $100 million, Vollrath is an international manufacturer of stainless steel and plastic products for the food service, health care, consumer product, refrigeration, and original equipment markets. In addition, Vollrath also imports and exports related products and sells software, information network systems, and management services. The broad range of offerings is consistent with Vollrath's goal of making available a comprehensive line of products and services to its customers. Currently, these customers include firms such as Edward Don Co., McDonald's Inc., Wasserstrom, Sysco Corporation, Interstate Restaurant Supply, American Hospital, Hospital Corporation of America, Wendy's, Burger King, and Domino's Pizza.

Vollrath serves these and other customers from its manufacturing facilities in Wisconsin, Tennessee, Alabama, and Canada. It also has warehouses in New York and California.

The company is decentralized into seven major businesses: Food Services, Refrigeration, Health Care, International, Management Services, Information Services, and North Sails, Inc. Each business is a semiautonomous unit and has its own president who is responsible for that division's performance.

Regardless of which business is examined, Vollrath competes on service to the customer, cost control, and quality. Service to the customer is defined by on-time delivery (important because consistent on-time delivery enables the customer to reduce inventory investment) and quick response to customer inquiries (e.g., responses to bids). Cost control is important because Vollrath operates in a competitive market. The company has been successful in controlling costs by critically examining all of its product designs, the costs associated with each design, and by working with the various stainless steel vendors. The constant attention to these three key success factors has contributed to the recent rapid growth in market share that Vollrath has experienced. Vollrath can now be regarded as a market leader in those markets in which it competes. For example, the Food Service Division now has between 50 to 60 percent of the market share.

Because of the variety of market segments served, Vollrath is involved in all four major forms of production -- MTS, MTO, ATO, and ETO. The relative importance of each form of production is influenced by which market segment is served and which division is involved. Vollrath's Food Service and Health Care Divisions are 80 percent MTS; original equipment is both MTO and ETO.

Vollrath -- The Food Service Division

The stainless steel manufacturing plant of the Food Service Division is in Sheboygan. The plant is responsible for some 1,000 raw materials, 2,500 purchased parts, 1,800 fabricated/assembled items, and 1,900 end items. The end items are classified into fifteen families of products (e.g., restaurant pans). Commonality in these families extends to include the same size pans, various gauges of steels, or the same items arranged in various package configurations.

A typical BOM consists of three levels, although some of the fabricated items have six-level bills. End-item lot sizes vary considerably from 250 pieces per production run at one extreme to 25,000 per lot at the other. The typical end-item cycle time (i.e., cumulative lead time) is six to seven weeks. The plant is a two-shift (sixteen hour) operation; typically 75 percent of capacity is used. The machines found on the shop floor are all general purpose machines. The division employs about 450 workers, all of whom are members of the United Automobile Workers union and most (approximately 95 to 98 percent) are paid by piece rate.

The Production Process

The production process for the typical product manufactured in the stainless steel plant is described below. All raw materials are purchased in master coil widths from the mill. The first operation is to slit the material to the desired width for the manufacture of a specific product(s). Shearing, blanking, or circling of blanks is next. A draw coating solution is then applied to the blanks to prepare them for drawing operations. Singular or multiple draw operations then occur, with a brite anneal (heat treating) operation or operations between multiple draws if necessary. Trimming, spinning, beading, welding (electric or heli-arc), and punching operations are then performed to complete the manufacturing cycle. Items are washed to prepare the surfaces for inside and/or outside polishing and then sent to the assembly/packaging department for staging or packing. The route sheet for 25-20662-12 (Figure 8-1) is typical of the parts produced in this process.

Capacity is made up of either singular workstations, in the case of unique operations, or work centers consisting of machine groups when a variety of machines perform like operations. Group work (operators and helpers) is classified as one measure of capacity that depends on the number of operators. Capacity is measured in terms of demonstrated capacity, which is used to answer the question of how many hours of direct labor, on average, can be obtained on a given work center daily. Physically, capacity is measured applying input/output control to each work center. At each work center, actual capacity is compared to the demonstrated capacity.

There are three features of special interest in the production process that ultimately affect the shop floor control system. First is the presence of unique or single-use equipment. Second is the presence of reserved capacity (a common practice of the original equipment manufacturing business). Third is the extensive revision of released order specifications. About 65 percent of all released orders are subject to some form of change in terms of quantities needed, due date, or both. These changes require extensive expedite/deexpedite activities by shop floor personnel.[1]

Production Planning at Vollrath

Vollrath is currently an extensive user of a manufacturing resource planning system, the Closed Loop Accountability Management Planning System (CLAMPS). The system is top down (i.e., it begins at the top with the business plan) and consists of:

- Business planning
- Market planning

---

[1]In these situations, planners are responsible for changing the original due date to an earlier due date only after checking available downstream capacity and materials. Changes to a later date are made by the planners as dictated by master scheduling or material requirements planning.

C C	NO	ACCT NO	SPECIFICATION NO	ROUTING DATE	PLANNER	LOT SIZE	%	% SCRAP	PART DESCRIPTION	08/05/83 IN I.D. C	1. 516251	675140
	20662	2512	4223	0883	OJP	12000		5	20662 FP 6 IN 1/6 SIZE STR SIDE		PAGE	1

C	SCHEDULE DATE	OPER	DEPT	F	MACH	SETUP HRS / ACCT / BURDEN	RUN HRS / PART NO / TOOL NO	LOAD HRS / QTY W/100 / RATE	C / UM / OC	DESCRIPTION AND OPERATION / MATERIAL DESCRIPTION / RATE DESCRIPTION	
2	07/19/83	010	102	8	3158	.7	4.3	5.0		SHEAR TO 13-1/4 IN.SQ..82 FFP	
3						1060	22559	1.4211	LB	.031 13-1/4 X CL 1304 28	NC
3						1060	22561	.12707	LB	.031 13-7/16 X CL 1304 28	NC
4									1	SET UP	
4									K	OPERATOR	
2	07/21/83	020	102	2	1138	.7	13.7	14.4		CIRCLE TO 14-1/4 IN. DIA..W/FLATS	
4									1	SET UP	
4								8.20	2	OPERATOR	
2	07/22/83	030	102	3		.0	5.8	5.8		APPLY DRAW COTE - 62 PER	
4								3.48	2	OPERATOR	
4							2	3.48	3	OPERATOR HELPER	
2	07/27/83	040	102	4	1355	4.0	34.5	38.5		DRAW 1. STOP & GO, 2 MD.BUTTONS, 2 GA..W/FL	
5										INSP.EV.50 PCS.. TAND W/DRAW 2. SKID ON	
6										TABLE TO CONV.. OPER.& TRUCKER CHANGE SKID	
4									1	SET UP	
4								21.80	2	OPERATOR	
2	07/29/83	050	102	4	1907	4.0	34.5	38.5		DRAW 2. PS.GD.1 BUTTON. SET IN DIE. W/FC.	
5										INSP.EV.50 PCS.. LEAD MACH..TAND W/DRAW 1.	
6										CONV.TO TBL..TRKR.PILES DOWN TO CRT.NSTD.IN	
7										ROWS. TS 6/63. MI.=.1167	
4									1	SET UP	
4								21.80	2	OPERATOR	
2	08/02/83	055	111	1	2835	.0	14.8	14.8		CLEAN FOR ANNEAL. PL.3 PCS.EV.3 BARS. CRT.TO	
5										CRT.NSTD.ON SIDE. SET SPEED DIAL AT 45.	
6										=5.891 FT./MIN.. .0460 ACTUAL TIME/PC..	
7										1038.8 PCS./HR.AT 125%	
4									K	OPERATOR	

Figure 8-1. -- First Page of Routing Sheet

- Manufacturing planning
- Master scheduling
- MRP
- Capacity planning
- Shop floor control
- Purchasing
- Performance measurement.

All materials and capacity are planned from the master scheduling/material requirements planning system (net change MRP system), which implements the objectives stated in manufacturing planning. The manufacturing plan, formalized once a quarter, involves personnel from marketing/sales, manufacturing, engineering, master scheduling, and capacity requirements planning. All planning activities for the stainless steel plant are done entirely within the plant. The CLAMPS structure is illustrated in Figure 8-2.

The move toward the development and implementation of CLAMPS was initiated and supported by Terry Kohler, Vollrath board chairman. The project team was organized on April 1, 1979, and the new system was implemented on March 7, 1981, when the front-end planning systems were married to the existing shop floor control system.

CLAMPS is characterized by certain important features. First, CLAMPS effectively merges the operating and financial systems. All reports produced by the system can be interpreted in terms of their implications for capacity, materials, and profit. Second, CLAMPS is a well-documented, well-structured system. Everyone's duties and responsibilities are documented. The frequent meetings required by CLAMPS are scheduled one year in advance to ensure that everyone who has to be at the meeting is there. Third, CLAMPS involves top management in nearly every stage of the formal planning process.

An important aspect of CLAMPS and one central to the operation of shop floor control is the method by which capacity is planned and the resulting plans communicated. The first phase in the capacity planning process is the formulation of the production plan. One of the groups involved is marketing, which inputs information from the sales plan to manufacturing. The resulting plan is then reviewed by the division president (who always has the final say). Next, the production plan is evaluated using rough-cut requirements planning (by critical work center) to determine whether or not it is feasible. If it is not, the plan is referred back to manufacturing

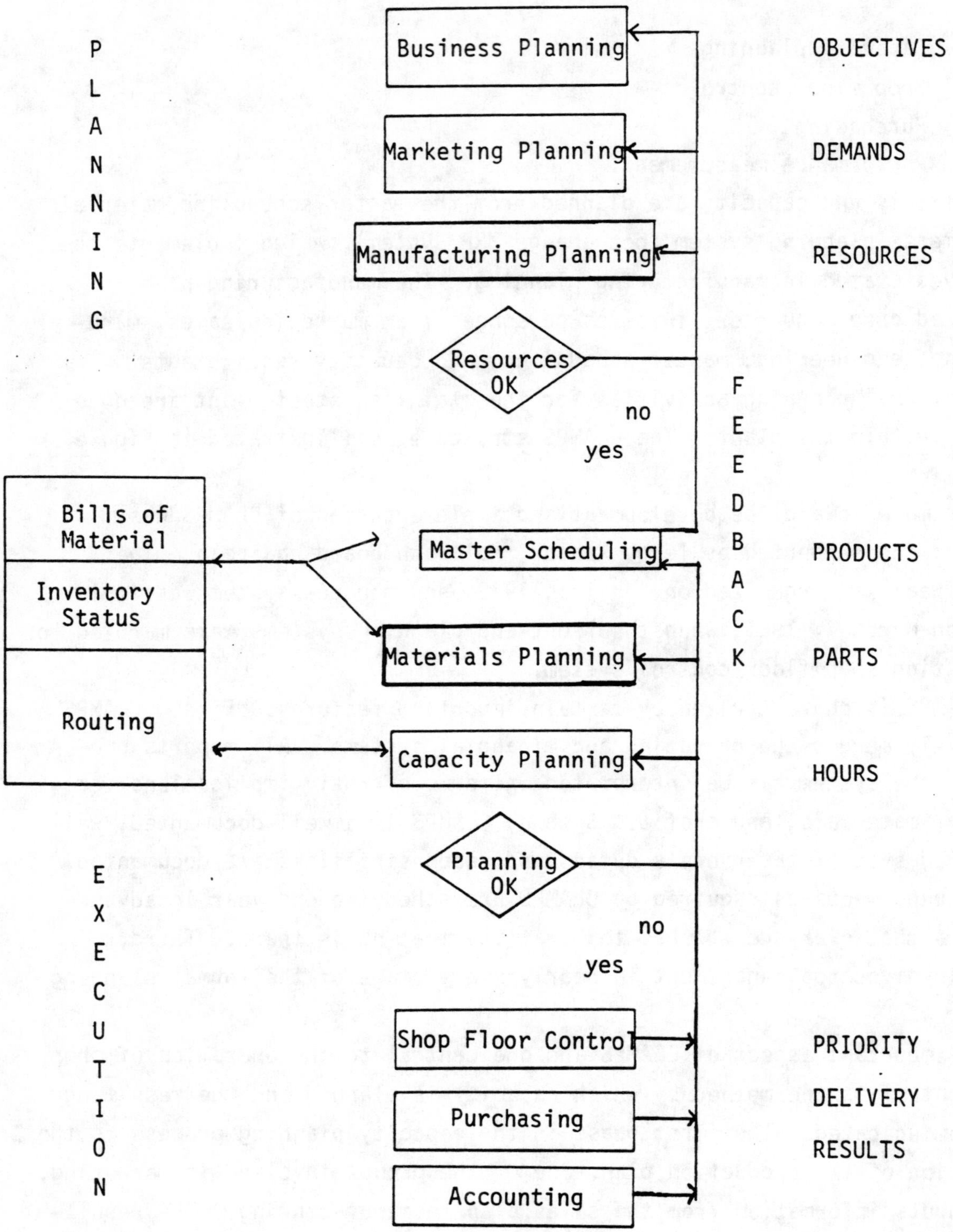

Figure 8-2. -- Vollrath's Closed Loop Accountability Management Planning System -- CLAMPS TM

for revision. If the plan is feasible, it is converted into a detailed production plan (master production schedule) that has a fifty-two week planning horizon. The key player, at this stage, is the master scheduler who is responsible for the execution of the master production schedule. The scheduler monitors incoming orders to ensure that the capacity given to the shop floor is never overbooked. If there is a huge incoming order that would exceed shop capacity, the master scheduler will not accept the order immediately but will notify manufacturing. At this stage, manufacturing, marketing, and the division president review the options. Frequently, the result is a trade-off in which the order or orders already booked in the system are rescheduled to free up the capacity needed by the incoming order.

The CLAMPS system generates and communicates planned output and capacity plans in three different ways. First, the long-range capacity plans run quarterly with the approved manufacturing plan and show the next twelve months of released, firm planned, and planned orders. Second, the short-range capacity plans run weekly and deal with the upcoming twelve weeks. The plan shows all released, planned, and firm planned orders. The third set of plans show all released orders by work center. This information is immediately communicated to the shop floor control system, and it shows ready to run hours, hours ready to run behind schedule, total hours released, total hours released behind schedule, and demonstrated capacity. All of this information is then divided by demonstrated capacity to show days of work by work center. It is subsequently accumulated by department and division. This work center load profile is updated daily.

Shop Floor Control

Of all the components of the formal planning system, the shop floor control system is the most refined and thoroughly tested system. Vollrath's current system is the latest stage in a system that has been installed since 1964. At that time, Vollrath started with IBM's 357 Shop Floor Reporting System. In 1975, that system was updated to the IBM 1030 System. The shop floor control was batch oriented until 1977 when the system was updated to IBM's 1030 System On-Line. The system was updated again in 1978 to IBM CRTs On-Line/Real-Time Labor reporting. As noted previously, the link between the shop floor control system and the formal planning system was completed on March 7, 1981. The current system was designed primarily to obtain information pertaining to current job order status and to reduce WIP.

Shop floor control at Vollrath is an integral part of the formal planning system and it plays an important role by closing the planning loop. It provides rapid feedback to the master schedule and MRP systems. Responsibility for the shop floor control systems is divided between two positions.

Scheduling of operations to meet due dates is the responsibility of each department supervisor. Overall responsibility for the shop floor control system, its logic, and any program enhancements made to the system belongs to the capacity requirements planner who reports directly to the manager of materials management (Figure 8-3). The manager's responsibilities include:

- o Assist shop production supervisors in meeting the daily/weekly production schedule
- o Communicate to all parties concerned any major shop problems that will have a negative effect on the master production schedule
- o Provide information and assistance necessary to set priorities for tool repair, machine repair/maintenance, and employee levels
- o Maintain an input/output control report of new hours added and hours completed for all defined work centers in the plant
- o Assist the vice president of operations in establishing the production plan
- o Work with the master production scheduler and shop supervisors to determine the ability to reschedule an open order, based on capacity and material.

In placing shop floor control under the capacity requirements planner, Vollrath emphasizes the critical link between capacity management and shop floor control. Good capacity management is viewed as an essential prerequisite to good shop floor control.

The shop floor control system at Vollrath is responsible for two primary structures. One is the shop floor control/feedback system, which is a data collection system that allows for on-line, real-time labor reporting of time and pieces completed for each operation performed. This system also updates load hours and pieces remaining to the operation. Second, the shop floor control system is responsible for the operation-by-operation scheduling system that calculates each operational due date (i.e., completion

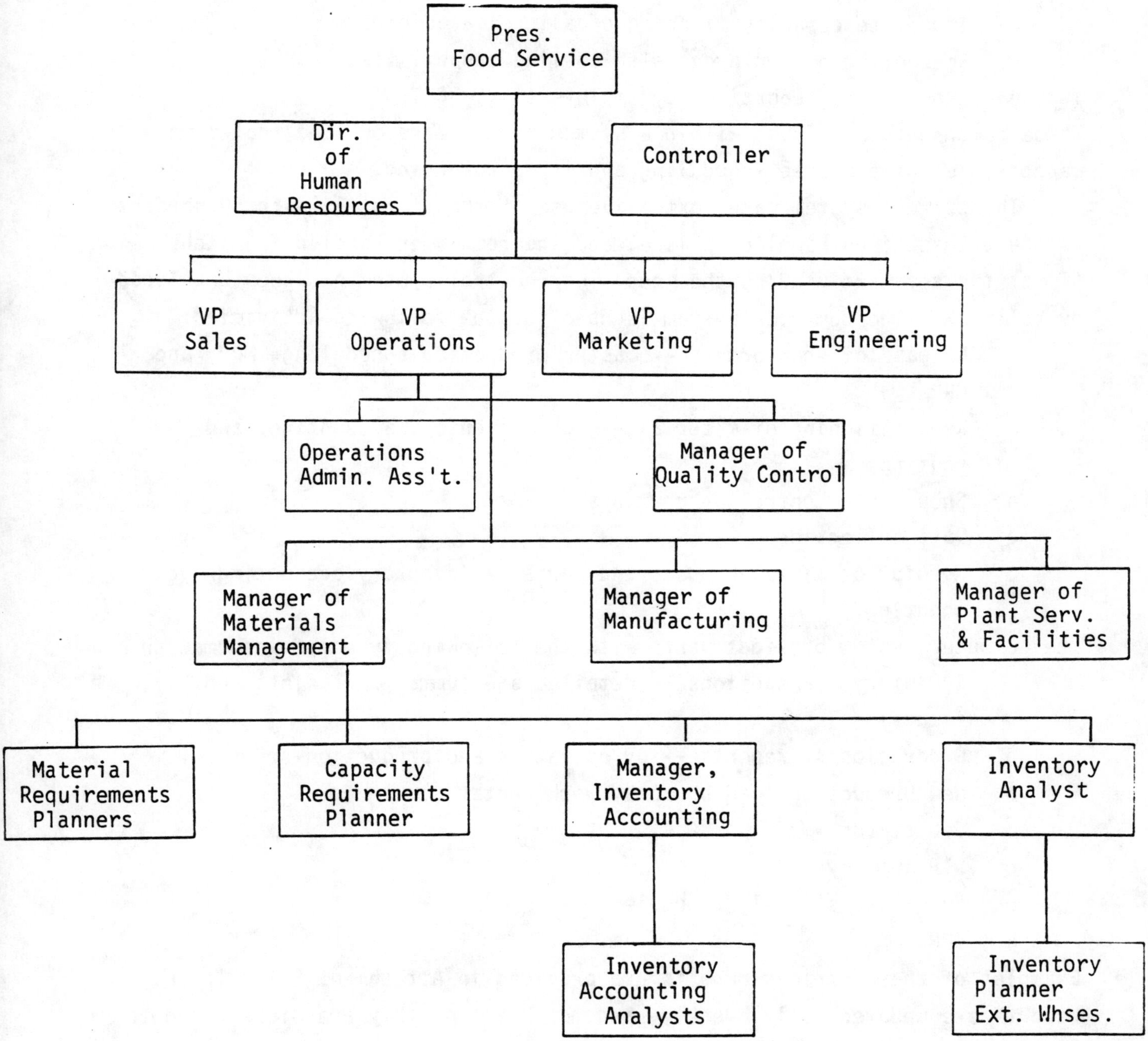

Figure 8-3. -- Organizational Chart

date), which is then offset by the completion date required by the master production schedule or MRP system.

The shop floor control system consists of four major components:

- o Daily supervisor's schedule by due date
- o Immediate capacity planning of all released orders
- o Scheduling of employees with on-line capabilities
- o Labor/piece reporting (by employees) via CRT.

These components are found within a system that offers on-line/real-time capabilities of employee scheduling and labor reporting.

The current system makes extensive use of the computer, with 80 percent of the transactions handled on line, and the remainder handled in batch. All of the software used by the shop floor control system has been developed by Vollrath. The computer system is used for the following activities:

- o Release of shop orders -- master production scheduling, MRP, and CRP
- o Requisitioning of material -- BOM, inventory accounting, and routings
- o Shop floor control -- routings
- o Data collection
- o Receipt of finished goods and parts -- inventory accounting/cycle counting.

The computer system provides users with the following types of information:

- o Inventory transactions -- detailed and summary (receipts and issues)
- o Order closing reports -- by operation and production orders
- o New production load hours by work center
- o Job status
- o WIP summary
- o Supervisors' daily schedules
- o CRP.

Examples of these various reports are provided in Attachment 8-1. These reports are updated daily, weekly, and monthly, and they are distributed to personnel in manufacturing management and materials management.

The most salient feature of Vollrath's shop floor control system, which is a result of extensive computerization, is that it operates completely on line and in real time for supervisors scheduling jobs for employees and for employees performing all labor reporting on CRTs (which immediately updates all related files pertaining to inventory and payroll). Vollrath is currently operating its stainless steel plant "electronically." The only required paper for the shop is a routing and a copy of the latest prints needed to manufacture a given product.

The Stages of Shop Floor Control at Vollrath

The shop floor control system at Vollrath reflects three key manufacturing tenets. Understanding these tenets is important because they explain the success of Vollrath's system and several of the practices observed in each shop floor control activity. These tenets are:

- Commitment to the master production schedule. Once the master production schedule has been set, it becomes the responsibility of the shop floor control system to ensure that orders are completed by the dates specified in this schedule. This is a feasible expectation for the shop floor control because the planning system has checked both the feasibility (in terms of capacity) and the consistency with corporate objectives of the master production schedule.
- Capacity. At Vollrath, the capacity decision is not delegated to the shop floor control system. Instead, the system is ensured of adequate capacity by the formal planning system. That is, the capacity plans on which shop floor control are based were approved by top management when the manufacturing plans were approved. Given adequate capacity, shop floor control can be expected to do a good job of managing its capacity.
- The prompt collection and feedback of shop floor information. The shop floor control system provides closure for the formal planning system. The information provided by the system is an essential part of this closure.

Order Review/Release

The order review/release activities of the shop floor control system mark the second stage of a planned order's life at Vollrath. During the first stage, the production/purchase orders planned by the formal planning system are reviewed by the master scheduler and firmed at planning time to reflect the cumulative lead time. Once the order is firmed, the material requirements planner firms planned orders for components and raw materials. These actions ensure the shop floor control system of adequate inventory. In the second stage (order review/release), production/purchase orders are released at their release time fence (start date). At this point, the production orders fall under the control of the shop floor control system.

Order review/release is done daily by Vollrath's shop order release system. Each day the planning database releases orders to the shop floor control database through the use of IBM's Communication-Oriented Production Information and Control System (COPICS) software advanced function material requirements planning system. Like all of the other shop floor control activities, this is done on line and in real time. The planning system passes the order information (order quantity, release date, due date, producing location, and order type) to the shop floor control system when releasing an order. An example of the order release document is provided in Figure 8-4. The process of releasing a shop order creates records in the production order database files that pertain to the operations sequence and BOM.

Before the order is released to the shop floor, it goes through a material availability check that is the responsibility of the materials requirements planner. The availability of capacity (machine and labor) is not checked at this time because it is assumed that the shop has adequate capacity with which to process the order. Any capacity problems that may be present are treated as if they can be managed. By delegating the capacity decision to the formal planning system, the operation of the shop floor control system is simplified. A check of tooling availability is not carried out because there are too many different combinations of tools required by an order (i.e., punch, die, blank holders, and so on). Checking for tooling availability, the responsibility of the shop supervisor, is done when the operation is scheduled.

Once availability is checked, the shop order release system assigns each shop order a unique production order number and calculates the due date for each operation in the order's routing. Now the order is ready to be processed.

Detailed Assignment

At Vollrath, detailed assignment refers to the process by which the shop floor control system assigns the released orders to such shop floor

```
CICS8350 RPOR AUTH:      DATA:
FN: RELS             ORDER MAINTENANCE AND RELEASE
GEO LOC: SH
ITEM NO: 1278660          STOCK POT W/COV 20 QT              DATE: 08/04/83
ORDER NO: 0917588    ORDER STATUS: F
-----                                                                  -----
DESCRIPTION                        DATA            COMMENTS
-------------------------          ----------      ---------------------------------
ORDER QUANTITY                        1,000
RELEASE DATE                       08/04/83        MUST BE VALID SHOP DATE
DUE DATE                           08/08/83        MUST BE VALID SHOP DATE
PRODUCING LOCATION                 STOCK
ORDER TYPE                         M
SHOP/PURCHASE ORDER NO.                            LOW-ORDER POSITION MUST = 0,
                                                   FOR 'M' ORDERS
KEY OPERATION                                      RELS - INDICATES BEGINNING
                                                   OPERATION
                                                   REPL - INDICATES FIRST
                                                   OPERATION TO BE AFFECTED
----- RPOR50 CHECK ORDER DATA                                          -----
FUNCTION CODES: INQU - INQUIRY (DEFAULT)          ISRT - ADD NEW PLANNED ORDER
                FIRM - FIRM A PLANNED ORDER       ISRV - ADD ORDER W COMPONENTS
                RELS - RELEASE ORDER              REPL - UPDATE ORDER
                DLET - DELETE ORDER               REPV - UPDATE ORDER W VERIFY
```

Figure 8-4. -- Order Maintenance and Release

resources as tooling, machines, labor, and material. The basic starting point for this activity is the order due date, which is established by the master production scheduling system. The system is driven by the manufacturing plan, through the use of a planning bill of material (Figure 8-5). The responsibility for setting and controlling order priorities is assigned to the divisional master scheduler. Once the order due date is set, the next step in the detailed assignment process is to integrate these priorities with Vollrath's short-term capacity management.

At Vollrath, each order priority stands alone; once the priority is set, it cannot be changed by personnel on the shop floor. Instead, it is the responsibility of plant management (production supervisor) to adjust capacity as required by the master production schedule. One of the key capacity resources that can be adjusted is labor. Labor assignment is made by using an on-line program. As a result, changes in assignments can be made as demanded by the situation.

The advantages of having an on-line, real-time shop floor control system are evident when dealing with labor assignment. Once the new assignments are entered into the computer system by the supervisor, the supervisor does not have to go to the shop to inform the employees of a new assignment. Instead, whenever the employee logs into the system via the CRT (frequently at the end of the job), the employee can identify what job is to be done next. The time lag between changing labor assignments and communicating these changes is almost eliminated as a result of this system.

The shop floor control system also controls the sequencing of rework/salvage operations, which occur every day at Vollrath. When such operations are needed for quality control reasons, it is the department supervisor's responsibility to add the required operations (with pieces and standard hours) to the standard routing sequence for that production order only. This requires introducing new information into the production order database.

Vollrath has no formal preventive maintenance or scheduled downtime system in place currently. Some of the benefits offered by a formal preventive maintenance program, however, are obtained by the capacity planning report, which helps plant management determine how critical it is to repair a broken press (once it occurs) or to schedule preventive maintenance.

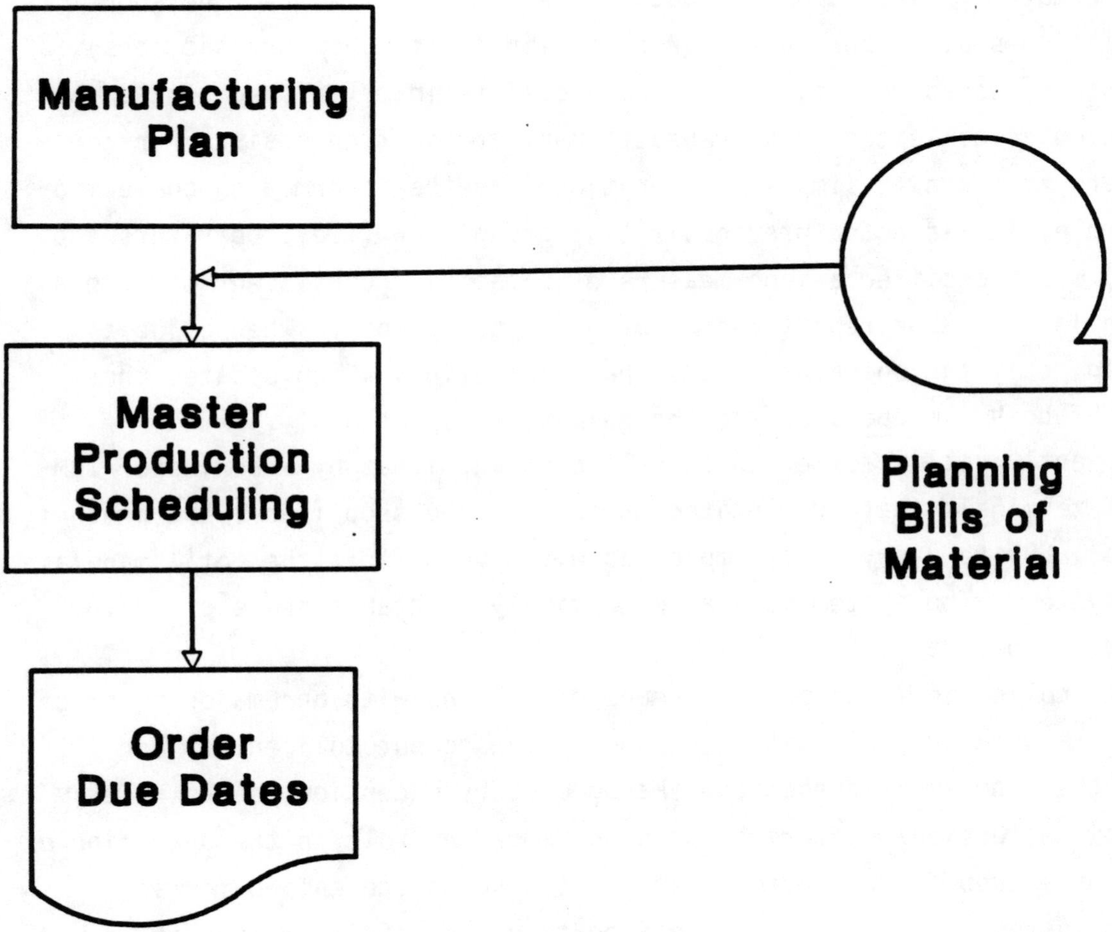

Figure 8-5. -- The Processing of Setting Due Dates Illustrated

Data Collection/Monitoring

Data collection/monitoring refers to the tasks of collecting information about:

- o The progress of the order through the shop
- o Resource status
- o Attendance reporting
- o Resource use
- o The comparison of actual to planned performance
- o Payroll, high/low earning, and pieces reported to order quantity.

This information, taken from the data collected directly from the shop floor, includes all labor (both direct and indirect labor transactions), all requisitions, scrap reporting,[2] and all receipts into finished goods. All information is collected on a transaction-by-transaction basis. Furthermore, care is taken to simplify and rationalize the information collection. For example, it was noted previously that group work (i.e., operators and helpers) was classified as one measure of capacity. Consistent with this approach is the labor report method used for group work. When a job is completed, only the operator inputs the information, which updates the records of both the operator and the helpers simultaneously.

Currently, all information is collected and input by a series of IBM 3278 CRT terminals that are located throughout the shop floor. At present, there is 1 CRT to every fifty employees with 150 CRTs in the total manufacturing system. The system is used extensively with an average of 125,000 transactions per day.

Data collection/monitoring is managed in line with one major tenet of Vollrath -- only the information needed by management to identify and correct the problem is presented. Management by exception is the rule.

Data collection/monitoring plays an important role in the operation of not only the shop floor control system but also of the entire formal planning system. To understand the importance of this activity, it is necessary to understand that the entire planning system is transaction driven. One of the key transactions that initiates changes in the database

---

[2] Scrap reporting is included in the labor reporting process and reduces the order quantities for succeeding operations. Currently scrap amounts are insignificant compared to order quantities and are not a problem.

is the data collected and input on the shop floor. Once these data are input, all of the relevant files are updated immediately. This activity is consistent with one of the major objectives of Vollrath's shop floor control system -- to provide the formal planning system with accurate and timely information from the shop floor.

Control/Feedback

Control/feedback refers to those shop floor control activities that deal with orders or resources that are considered as out of control. At Vollrath, an order is considered out of control if it was due yesterday, but it has not yet been released to the shop floor. When such an order has been identified, the shop floor control personnel must work with plant management to decide on the best date by which the order can be completed. At this point, rescheduling of order due dates is initiated by the master scheduler only after checking to see that capacity and components are available.

All changes in due dates are done manually. This feature is important to the operation of the shop floor control system because it emphasizes user accountability. The computer system could be used to determine the new due dates. In that case, however, the user might try to blame the system for any problems encountered in meeting this due date. But because the production supervisors are responsible for meeting operation due dates, they must manually examine the effects of any due date changes not only on their operations but also on downstream capacity and materials.

At Vollrath, tight control over expediting is exercised in several ways. First, there are no expediters. Second, expediting is not left up to the discretion of the plant personnel but is controlled by the master scheduler in conjunction with plant meetings. Once a week the plant supervisors meet to discuss any problems that have occurred on the floor. If there are no problems, there is no meeting. If there is a problem, then the supervisors review alternative actions. Such actions might include rescheduling a due date or leaving the due date of the problem order unchanged and relying on lead-time compression in the parent items. Third, any actions that are out of the ordinary (i.e., alternative routings or adding extra processing steps for items that need scrap and rework) must be submitted in writing (operation change record [OCR]) to the department's methods engineer, who reviews the proposed change to identify the cost implications. Again, the process of evaluating the cost implications is facilitated by the computer system. As a result, expediting is not a major factor in the operation of the system and is performed on a limited basis.

Finally, a key element of control/feedback is the relationship that exists between the production supervisors and the capacity requirements planner. The supervisor is required to communicate any problems to the planner that cannot be solved on the shop floor. These problems are then resolved jointly.

Order Disposition

Order disposition marks the final stage in the tracking process. The order has been closely monitored by the shop floor control system as it proceeded through the various stages. When the order is completed, the formal planning system (and the database) is informed of the order's availability. At this point, the order is transferred out of the shop floor control system. Any resources still assigned to the order are then released and made available immediately to other orders still on the shop floor. The cost accounting system can now determine the costs directly attributable to the completed order.

Performance Evaluation/Feedback

Vollrath evaluates the performance of the shop floor control system with two different measures: the percentage of orders released to the shop within the lead time and the percentage of orders completed on time. These two measures emphasize to the shop floor personnel the importance of certain actions. The first action is the need to minimize the number of out-of-control jobs that the shop floor control system deals with. Such jobs are disruptive to the shop floor and to the planning system. They also indicate a failure either in planning or in assuring the availability of adequate resources. If the shop floor control system is to operate effectively, such failures cannot be allowed.

The second measure, on-time delivery, reflects the basis on which Vollrath competes. Vollrath competes in the marketplace on service to the customers, cost control, and quality. On-time delivery performance links the actions of the shop floor to corporate objectives.

Other Salient Features of Shop Floor Control

The shop floor control system is well integrated into the operation of the formal planning system and has many links binding it to other functions in the firm. These links include:

- Purchasing. The planned orders for purchased items are directed to the designated buyers for actions. Receipts for the purchased parts/materials are processed by central receiving and the inventory records are updated on line and in real time. As a result, the shop floor control system and the production supervisors always know the exact moment at which needed purchased inventory becomes available.
- Cost accounting. All of the information gathered by the shop floor control system is used by cost accounting, which generates WIP values, manufacturing variance by work center, material variances from the standard BOM, and purchasing variances.
- Engineering. Engineering maintains BOM files that are current, complete, and accurate because these same files are used by manufacturing, cost accounting, and planning.
- Quality control. The shop floor control system allows edit capability to allow supervision of quality problems experienced in the past or to pass on any information regarding the quality standards of a given production order.
- Marketing. Marketing is the key to establishing necessary major changes to order due dates when conflicts arise that require a major change in the plant.
- Production planning and material control. Materials management serves as a liaison between marketing/sales and manufacturing to resolve conflicts in capacity or whatever may occur that would have an adverse effect on meeting the production schedules.
- Maintenance. The maintenance departments use the MPS and CRP to make decisions about how critical the machine repair is and when to schedule preventive maintenance.
- Top management and corporate policy and strategy. Top management is involved directly in setting realistic objectives at each step of the closed planning system.

These information-based links point to a major characteristic of the formal planning system -- the presence of a common database. One set of numbers is shared by customers, customer service representatives, planners, and plant personnel. This common database enables the shop floor control system to provide the rest of the planning system with complete and immediate feedback.

Finally, the shop floor control system, like the rest of the planning system, is an extensive user of the MRP system, which is a companywide system, not simply a manufacturing system.

Evaluating Vollrath's Shop Floor Control System -- Benefits

The major strength of the current shop floor control system is its ability to react to change quickly and to communicate any changes taken with the shop floor control system to the rest of the organization instantly. This strength combined with the one common database creates an environment that encourages people to work together as a team to satisfy the needs of not only the customers but also the company.

Furthermore, since March 7, 1981, when the closed-loop planning systems were married to the shop floor control system, the following results have been obtained:

- 14 percent improvement in use of production facilities
- 50 percent reduction in the level of WIP inventory
- 50 percent reduction in the manufacturing cumulative lead times
- Inventory accuracy as measured through cycle counting improved from 68 percent to 93 percent
- Integrity of due dates improved from 50 percent to 95 percent
- Overtime reduced even in the face of higher than anticipated sales.

In short, the shop floor control system has played a significant role in the creation of a credible and viable manufacturing planning system. It has also helped enhance Vollrath's credibility with its customers. It is now established that when Vollrath accepts an order or commits itself to a due date, the production promises will be kept. Such a situation simplifies the marketing task.

Shop Floor Control -- The Next Stage

Currently, no major developments in the shop floor control system are foreseen because most of the tools needed to be successful in the marketplace are present. Vollrath places most of its emphasis on education to ensure that the people in the firm can make the best use of the capabilities offered by the system.

Shop Floor Control at Vollrath: Lessons to be Learned

The effective and efficient shop floor control system at Vollrath is an important element of the planning system. This is not an accidental development, but one that reflects certain lessons that people at Vollrath have learned and implemented. These lessons include:

- Accountability is essential to any system. To be successful, any system must identify explicitly and simply what is expected of its personnel. The performance measurements used must be few in number, simply stated, make sense to the persons being evaluated, and relate directly to corporate objectives. The system must then measure performance against these terms. Accountability makes personnel feel responsible for their actions in the system.
- Develop a clear distinction between what the computer can do and for what the person is responsible. The computer can simplify life. It can do a good job of counting pieces and of recording changes, however, in many areas, the computer is not a substitute for the person. These areas must be identified. One such area involves any changes that affect performance evaluation, such as change of due dates. As previously noted, such changes must be done manually so that the supervisor can determine whether or not such changes are acceptable. Once accepted, the supervisor is measured on meeting these dates. By making the change process a manual one, the system ensures that the production supervisor is never able to blame the computer system for failure to meet the new due dates. Furthermore, it also ensures that the user is aware of all of the implications of a decision.
- Capacity is managed, not planned, in the shop floor control system. The shop floor control system should never be placed in the position of having to plan capacity. Better dispatching is never a substitute for good capacity planning. Instead, top management must provide the shop floor control system with adequate capacity so it can manage this capacity.

- Involve personnel. Shop floor control, as well as the entire formal planning system, requires the continuous involvement of its personnel. Such systems depend on people to formulate and implement goals. People must understand the system and its operation and must also use the system to identify and resolve any problems. People must know how to use the tools that they have been given.
- Give the person the information needed at the time needed. Information plays an important role in Vollrath's shop floor control system. It is the glue that binds the planning to the execution systems. Poor information complicates management, while accurate information simplifies management. At Vollrath, the quality of all information is ensured by the presence of one database that is shared by all and contains all of the information needed. The information is always current, complete, and accurate. Vollrath's interest in using an on-line/real-time system reflects its concern that everyone in the firm is using the latest information when making decisions. All dimensions of the information (quantity, financial, and profit) are contained in the database. This ensures that the user is always made aware of all the corporate implications of any action. Finally, the user must be given only the data needed to make decisions at the time the problem occurs. The information must be presented so the user can understand it quickly. At Vollrath, all exception reports are limited to an 8½-by-11-inch sheet. For the shop floor control system, this means that information never gets in the way of decision making.

Shop floor control is an important and integral element of the formal planning system at Vollrath. It ensures that the plans formulated in the planning system are executed successfully. Without a good shop floor control system, the firm cannot hope to achieve its objectives. The system discussed provides one example of a system that has helped one company become successful.

ATTACHMENTS

Attachment 8-1.

Shop Floor Control System Reports -- Examples

CICS8200 P=N AUTH: DATA:
FN: INQU R E V I E W T R A N S A C T I O N H I S T O R Y PAGE:
GEO LOC: SH
ITEM NO: 257711412 HANDLE D B INSET DATE: 08/11/8
EMPLOYEE: LOCATION: U/M: EA ITEM TYPE: 2 ISSCTL: 1 RECTL: 1

DATE	TC	QUANTITY	ORDER NO.	PLN QTY	PARENT ITEM NUMBER	S	JOB NO	EMP NC
		5,679			BALANCE ON HAND			
08/08/83	IM	3,435	0878183	3435	257711112	SH	1658620	0358
08/05/83	IM	1,820	0878183	1820	257711112	SH	1658620	0358
08/04/83	IM	2,315	0878183	2315	257711112	SH	1658620	0358
07/27/83	IM*		0883213		255700114	SH	1661380	0358
07/26/83	IM	60	0883213	60	255700114	SH	1661380	0358
07/22/83	IM	3,467	0878183	3467	257711112	SH	1658620	9482
07/21/83	IM	676	0878183	676	257711112	SH	1658620	9482
07/15/83	IM*		0892204		257707412	SH	1664980	0358
07/15/83	IM	50	0892204		257707412	SH	1664980	0358
07/13/83	IM*		0840105	211	257711112	SH	1641990	0358
07/13/83	IM	50	0840105	50	257711112	SH	1641990	0358
07/12/83	IM	6,610	0892204	6600	257707412	SH	1664980	0358

TO CONTINUE PRESS ENTER

PI 730 NEW PRODUCTION LOAD HOURS ADDED

DEPT F	OPERATION	LOAD HRS ADDED
101 1	BRITE ANNEAL	14.79
DEPT TOTAL		14.79
102 A	SMALL DRAW PRESSES	18.67
102 B	INTER DRAW PRESSES	23.02
102 C	LARGE DRAW PRESSES	38.94
102 D	LARGE PUNCH PRESSES	15.84
102 E	PUNCH PRESSES	23.14
102 F	HYDROFORM	8.46
102 1	SHEAR	14.15
102 2	CIRCLE	3.81
102 3	DRAW CCTE	4.97
102 6	SMALL PUNCH PRESSES	78.82
102 7	MACHINE BEND	19.52
102 8	CUT TO LENGTH	1.30
DEPT TOTAL		250.64
103 1	LATHE & QUICK TRIM	22.46
DEPT TOTAL		22.46
DIVISION TOTAL		287.89
111 1	WASH MACHINE	12.73
111 3	ELECTRO POLISH	7.61
111 4	BURNISH	3.41
111 5	DEGREASE	10.61
DEPT TOTAL		34.36
DIVISION TOTAL		34.36
125 1	POLISHING	8.93
125 2	PACK & INSPECT	45.88
125 3	DEGREASE	.15
125 6	AIR GRIND,AIR POL,SANDBL	2.87
DEPT TOTAL		57.83

ORD # 1-671780 PART# 12-78164- VEGETABLE INSET 4 1/8 QT

8,105 ORD/QTY 8,105 SHR/QTY 0 REC 147.91 L/H

REC 1 0 REC 2 REC 3

OPR	DPT/F	DESCRIPTION	PCS/OPR	PCS/RPTD	PCS/SCP	DUE/DATE	L/HR REM
010	102 8	SHEAR TO 15-3/4 IN.	8,305	8,255	50	08/10/	.88
BM	10-24559-60 PCS	13872 :	- -	PCS	:	-	- PCS
020	102 2	CIRCLE TO 15-3/4 IN	8,305	8,250	3	08/11/	.22
030	102 3	APPLY DRAW COTE - 6	8,302	8,434	0	08/12/	.00
040	102 4	DRAW 1, PS.GD.1 BUT	8,302	2,661	0	08/16/	12.67
050	102 4	DRAW 2, PS.GD.1 BUT	8,302	2,629	32	08/17/	12.67
060	102 4	DRAW 3, PS.GD.1 BUT	8,302	0	0	08/18/	23.62
070	102 4	DRAW 4, BULGE & STA	8,302	0	0	08/19/	23.92
080	102 4	TRIM & ROLL,P&R BY	8,302	0	0	08/23/	27.36
090	103 3	SPIN 2 CUTS, 4TH SP	8,302	0	0	08/30/	54.75
100	111 1	WASH MACHINE, MAX.1	8,302	0	0	09/01/	1.98
105	128 5	EMBOSS & CLEAN STAK	8,052	0	0	09/07/	13.50
110	128 2	STONE BURR & EDGE &	8,052	0	0	09/15/	35.24
120	111 1	WASH MACHINE, MAX.1	8,052	0	0	09/19/	1.95
130	128 8	SUNRAY INS.SD.,INS.	8,052	0	0	09/22/	22.15
150	129 4	BELT POL.NECK, BODY	8,052	0	0	09/28/	37.12
160	127 1	BAG & PACK 6 PER CT	8,052	0	0	10/03/	11.59
BM	25-05202-10 PCS	:	10-09060-56 PCS		:	-	- PCS

PM080531 08/09/83 WORK IN PROCESS SUMMARY BY ACCOUNT

JOB NO.	QTY	PART NO.	DUE DATE
1-671781	200	2278164	9/12/
1-673111	350	2278780	9/12/
ACCT TOTAL		22-	
1-659781	100	2483122	7/25/
1-659421	100	2488580	8/01/
1-665451	300	2480130	8/08/
1-658191	100	2489020	8/08/
1-671881	150	2485320	9/12/
1-670341	300	2495640	9/12/
ACCT TOTAL		24-	
1-672600	1,150	250308010	8/01/
1-668970	45	250375110	8/01/
1-672570	575	250064010	8/02/
1-668910	1,575	250520210	8/04/
1-669030	725	250508010	8/08/
1-666680	410	250355110	8/08/
1-662000	680	250573010	8/08/
1-672560	960	250571010	8/08/
1-672520	310	250077010	8/08/
1-672470	350	250575010	8/08/
1-672450	235	250022010	8/08/
1-672430	275	250086010	8/08/
1-672420	860	250189010	8/08/
1-671560	2,800	250565010	8/08/
1-672490	460	250061010	8/09/
1-666760	50	250462010	8/10/
1-668890	125	250022510	8/12/
1-672480	300	250061110	8/12/
1-672440	175	250065010	8/15/
1-672400	350	250109110	8/15/
1-672370	510	250461010	8/15/
1-672550	150	254069810	8/15/
1-672530	45	250373110	8/15/
1-672610	445	250183010	8/15/
1-672590	390	250126010	8/15/
1-672580	40	250247010	8/15/
1-672620	675	250027610	8/15/
1-666810	270	250067010	8/15/
1-672380	425	250149310	8/22/
ACCT TOTAL		25-10	
1-651690	565	256314011	7/19/
1-659450	4,539	256134011	8/01/
1-656180	3,621	256208011	8/02/

02 L DEPT. IIEBLE 102-8 CUT-TO-LENGTH PMC8C1CO DAILY SUPERVI. SCHEDULE RUN DATE

JOB NUMBER	PART NUMBER	ITEM DESCRIPTION	OPR NO.	OPERATION DESCRIPTION	PCS TO THIS OP	PCS REMAIN	LD HRS REMAIN	DUE DATE	RUN. OPR.
1-675140	25-20662-12	HP 6 IN 1/6 SIZE STR SIDE	010	SHEAR TO 13-1/4 IN.SQ.,82 FPM	15495	15495	5.1	07-15	R
1-675040	25-78184-12	VEGETABLE INSET 7 1/4 QT	010	SHEAR TO 18-1/4 IN. SQ.,102 FPM	7475	7475	2.9	07-29	R
1-675160	22-20662-	HOTEL PAN	010	SHEAR TO 13-1/4 IN.SQ.,82 FPM	400	400	.9	08-04	R
1-675110	25-20040-12	HP 4IN FULL SIZE ECON STD HEAV	010	SHEAR TO 20-1/4 X 26 IN.,141 FPM	2170	2170	1.4	08-05	R
1-670610	25-20243-12	HP 4 IN HALF SIZE PERFURATED	010	SHEAR TO 17-1/4 X 19-1/2 IN.-112	1200	1200	.9	08-09	R
1-672390	12-20025-	FUCD SER TRANSPORT PAN	010	SHEAR TO 16-7/8 X 24-7/8 IN.-141	4025	4025	2.0	08-12	R
1-672840	12-20023-	PERFORATED HOTEL PAN	010	SHEAR 1 CUT TO 16-7/8 X 24-7/8 1	4735	4735	2.2	08-12	R
1-675050	12-56482-	61982-78184 VEG INSET	010	SHEAR TO 18-1/4 IN.SQUARE, 102 F	200	200	.8	08-15	R
1-672120	12-20245-	FOOD TRANSPORT PAN	010	SHEAR TO 17-1/4 X 19-1/2 IN.-112	2500	2500	1.2	08-17	R
1-673110	12-78780-	BAIN MARIE POT 8 1/4 QT	010	SHEAR TO 19-1/4 IN. SQ. - 112 FP	2750	2750	1.3	08-17	R
1-670250	12-20345-	HOTEL PAN-STEP PAN	010	SHEAR TO 15 X 18 IN.-102 FPM	1200	1200	.9	08-23	R
1-669740	14-54439-	SPEC 7882 BM POT-CENTURY	010	SHEAR TO 22 IN. SQ.-123 FPM	1100	1100	.8	08-30	R

FUNCTION TOTAL $\frac{\text{TOTAL HOURS } 20}{\text{DEMONSTRATED CAPACITY } 7}$ = 3 DAYS OF WORK

• • • DEPARTMENT 127 TOTAL LOAD HOURS • • •

	1 08-08	2 08-15	3 08-22	4 08-29	5 09-05	6 09-12	7 09-19	8 09-26	9 10-03	10 10-10	11 10-17	12 10-24	PERIOD TOTALS
RELEASED RUNNING HRS.	159	23	15										198
RELEASED LOOKAHD HRS.	44	86	87	123	35	9	3	12	9	2			411
PLANNED HOURS	62	230	249	215	266	137	240	190	209	152	202	238	2392
DEMONSTRATED CAP.HRS.	50	50	50	50	50	50	50	50	50	50	50	50	600
ADJUSTMENT HOURS	14	34	27			35	35						145
WEEKLY DEM. CAPACITY	236	216	223	250	200	215	215	250 1105	250	250	250	250	2805
TOTAL LOAD HOURS	265	339	351	337	300	147	243	202 2184	217	154	202	239	3001
LOAD HOURS/CAPACITY %	112.2	156.9	157.3	134.8	150.0	68.3	113.0	80.8	86.8	61.6	80.8	95.2	106.9
CUMULATIVE RATIO %	112.2	133.6	141.4	139.6	141.5	129.7	127.4	120.9	116.8	110.8	107.9	106.7	

General Nature of the Firm

Moog of East Aurora, New York, was founded in 1951 and is a publicly held corporation and a member of the American Stock Exchange. It produces electrohydraulic servovalves, actuators, and systems for use on aircraft, missiles, robots, and machine tools. These products are sold to firms such as Rockwell International, McDonnell-Douglas, Martin, Boeing, IBM, General Electric, and Lockheed. Because of the nature of its products, Moog satisfies all of the domestic demand for its products from its production facilities in East Aurora. There are no warehouses; there are, however, manufacturing facilities located in England, Germany, France, Ireland, and Japan.

The domestic operations are organized into five major divisions: aircraft controls, missile systems, space products, industrial controls, and electronic controls. These divisions are combined into two major groups, the aerospace group consisting of the first three divisions and the industrial group consisting of the remaining two divisions. Total sales reached $166 million in 1983. Moog employs 2,250 nonunion workers, 1,950 of which belong to the aerospace group.

The aerospace business, the most important source of revenue for Moog, accounts for over 80 percent of annual dollar sales. This business is all ETO. Because aerospace programs normally exist for several years, subsequent requirements are MTO. Aerospace customers tend to be large, prime contractors (e.g., Rockwell International, Grumman, and Northrop). The specialized hydraulic systems produced for these customers are usually one of the longest lead-time items in the development cycle for aircraft and missiles. As a result, these items could have a critical impact on the ability of the contractor to deliver a quality product on time.

In contrast, the industrial business (the focus of the second group) is 65 percent MTO, 25 percent ETO, and 10 percent MTS. Industrial customers include large equipment manufacturers as well as small subcontractors. Among its industrial customers are Unimation, Cincinnati Milacron, IBM, Mertz, General Electric, Flight Safety Corporation, and Reflectone.

Regardless of the customer, Moog management feels that to compete successfully in the marketplace it must be able to:

- Deliver a quality product. Moog produces items that are used in critical areas by the customers. For example, Moog produces fifteen actuators that are used on the space shuttle to vector the engines and to control the flight surfaces. A product that is either poorly designed or poorly made can have disastrous effects. It can mean not only the destruction of an expensive plane or spacecraft but also the loss of life. The part must be right the first time that it is used. Failure in the field is not acceptable.
- Plan capacity effectively. Effective capacity planning is important to Moog at both the aggregate and the detailed levels. At the aggregate level, Moog management is concerned with ensuring both continuity and stability of employment while maintaining a high level of customer service. Consequently, anticipating changes in requirements allows management to increase capacity while maintaining the current levels of quality or to decrease capacity without creating layoffs. On the detailed level, a change in product mix can have a dramatic effect on the requirements for individual work centers. Anticipating these changes assists management in the effective purchase of tooling and in employee training.
- Control costs. The importance of cost control varies with the product, time, and division. For a well-established product (i.e., one for which there have been many past orders) or a product that Moog wishes to win, cost is important. The ability to succeed depends on the ability to keep costs low. In other instances, cost is not important and often takes a backseat to product performance.
- Deliver its products on time. Many of the products made by Moog are the longest lead-time items in the overall development cycle. Failure to deliver on time can delay an entire project. Delay of an airplane or a satellite because of a component delay would be costly to the customer and to Moog's reputation for service.

Characteristics of Moog

At Moog, the manufacture of special hydraulic controls is a job shop, batch activity. The products range in size from a 1-pound unit with 60 parts for missile fin control to a 350-pound actuator with 2,500 parts to control the space shuttle engines. BOMs are up to seven levels deep, and routings have from 5 to 150 steps, with an average of about 15.

There are approximately 400 end items produced using 10,000 manufactured and 5,000 purchased components. The amount of product commonality present is a function of whether the product is manufactured within the industrial group or within the aerospace group. There is significant commonality for 75 percent of the industrial group and very little in the aerospace product line. A generalized production flowchart is presented in Figure 9-1.

The fabrication lot sizes vary from 1 to 500 with most in the 5- to 100-unit range. Assembly lot sizes run between 1 to 25 units. The manufacturing lead times are 30 to 100 weeks. Most order changes are design or process related as opposed to quantity changes. About 2 percent of all shop orders see changes each month. The fabrication operation is approximately three times as large as the assembly and test function. Capacity is measured by work center in the fabrication area and by department in assembly and test.

Both the aerospace and industrial groups have their own machine shops. Work, however, does flow between the shops to use special capabilities and to balance capacities with requirements. In aggregate, the two shops have 690 machinists working three shifts, six days a week. Effective management of this work force is important to the success of Moog because it accounts for approximately 60 percent of direct costs.

The 550 workstations are grouped into 200 work centers spread through six buildings. Both divisions use a wide variety of machines. In general, the machine capacity can be broken down as follows:

- General purpose machines -- 48 percent of machine capacity
- Special purpose machines -- 2 percent
- Numerical control machines -- 10 percent
- Direct numerical control -- 5 percent
- Computer numerical control -- 35 percent.

Over 80 percent of all parts flow through both the general purpose and the computer numerical control machines. On average, capacity use is relatively high with machine use running at 90 percent.

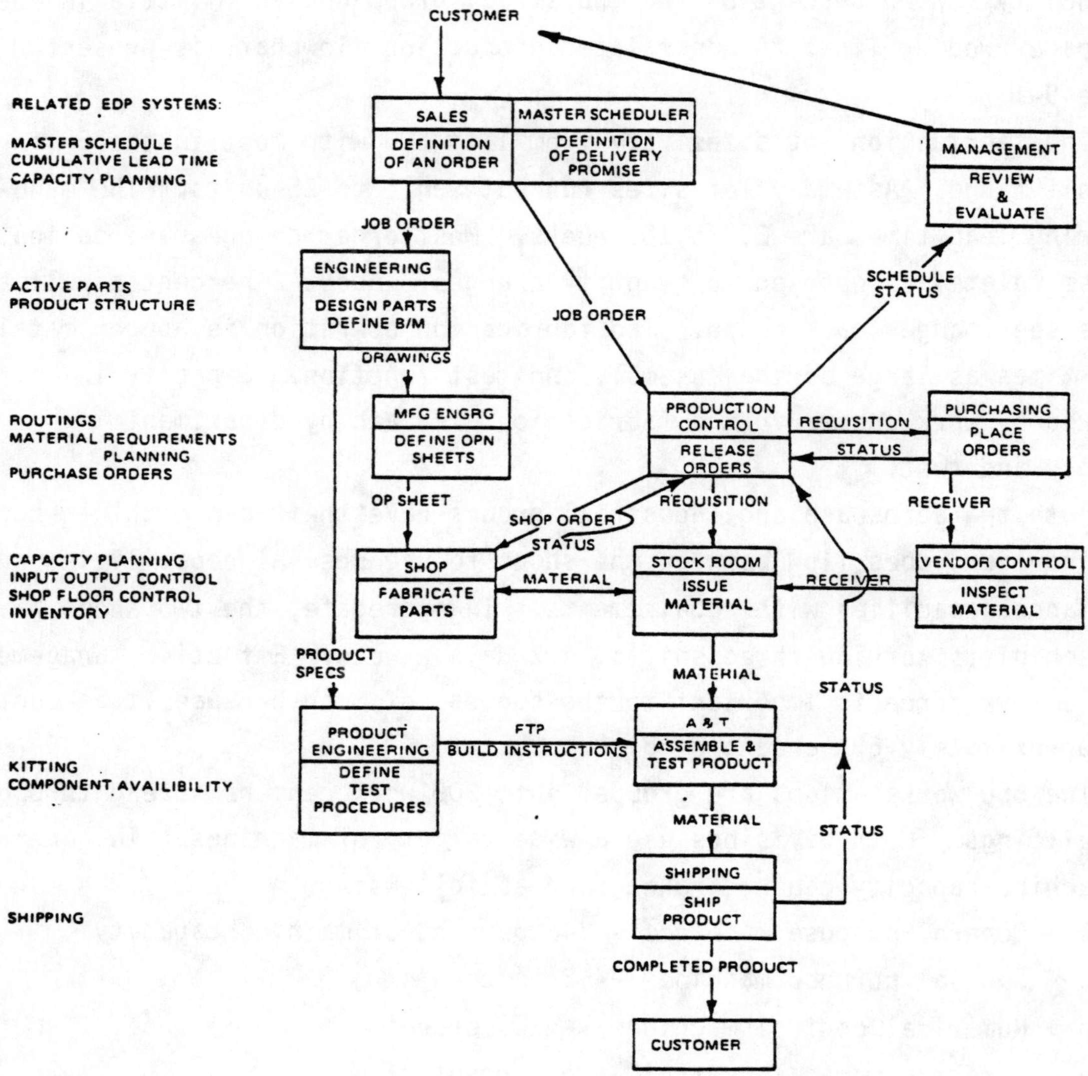

Figure 9-1. -- Production System Flowchart

The Production Process

The key characteristics of the production process that affect the shop floor control system are long routings, specialized capacities, and significant scrap and rework. These factors are important to management because they have a significant impact on the planning process. The long routings require that planning be done in advance where there are more uncertainties than in the present. The specialized capacities require similar extensive future planning as well as extensive current time-period rebalancing (i.e., ensuring that the current work load is balanced evenly across all work centers). The significant scrap and rework are disruptive factors that can be anticipated but cannot be planned by part. Consequently, management must be able to adjust priorities on the shop floor and respond to the changing situations caused by scrap and rework.

Given the large percentage of Moog's business that is ETO, the design and development of tooling are a constraining resource primarily at the front end of the job (i.e., during the initial units of production). The design and manufacture of tools are as significant in hours as is the design of the product itself. For initial units, tool manufacturing is always under pressure to meet the design release date and the required shipping date. For continuing programs, tooling is not a constraining resource for the shop floor control system.

Production Planning at Moog

The current production planning system at Moog is the latest stage in the evolution of a system first developed and implemented in the 1960s. At that time, this system included inventory control, BOM processing, machine loading, shop routings, sales master scheduling, cost accounting, and payroll. Early in the 1970s, MRP and capacity planning systems were added. In 1975, the current shop floor control system was installed. It had been written entirely by Moog personnel as a batch system. The current management planning consists of the business plan, master schedule, rough-cut capacity plan, and production plan modules. The current system is primarily a manufacturing resource planning system because it coordinates the activities of manufacturing with those of the firm.

The production planning process begins with the development of a five-year business plan. This plan is constructed annually from estimated unit sales and anticipated pricing on major programs. This level of planning is used for financial planning and sizing up the basic elements of the business.

A master production schedule is the next segment of Moog's management planning system. Covering a period of eighteen months or more, the master production schedule consists of actual and anticipated orders. Anticipated orders (or advanced material procurement authorizations [AMPA]) are placed by Moog personnel in anticipation of an actual customer order. The AMPA is released when the order falls within the cumulative lead time. It is intended to ensure that the customer will receive on-time delivery of the order when it is finally placed.

For rough-cut capacity planning purposes, the master schedule may not be filled sufficiently by firm and anticipated orders. Consequently, the master schedule will be supplemented with forecasted orders. These jobs are used for planning capacities but not for releasing material orders.

The rough-cut capacity plan is developed from this special master schedule. The unit sales forecast is exploded by capacity planning into annual work center labor requirements. This planning is done twice a year.

Using the data from the rough-cut capacity plan, as well as some judgment regarding inventories and new program start-ups, management constructs a production plan. The plan defines aggregate people requirements by department as well as major equipment purchases. This information is a major building block for the annual financial plans, capital budget, and production labor targets.

Detailed Planning

The detailed planning phase at Moog includes order promising, material planning, and assembly scheduling. The primary step in moving from the production plan to shop floor control is the material planning cycle. In this segment, the master production schedule is converted into a set of time-phased component requirements. The MRP system is regenerative and runs weekly. The output from MRP is used to:

- Plan new order releases
- Reschedule existing orders

- Suggested reschedule for purchase orders
- Automatic reschedule for fabrication orders

o Input to CRP.

There are several differences between the semiannual, rough-cut capacity planning, and the weekly capacity plan. The former incorporates forecasted orders, is not time phased, does not use beginning inventory, and does not create an ending inventory. The weekly CRP uses only planned and released shop orders, is time phased, and takes into account existing inventories.

The capacity for a work center is defined as the actual, smoothed output for that work center. Anticipated changes in staffing and equipment can be incorporated and the results displayed graphically. Based on this information, changes are made in the order release horizon and in staff scheduling.

Shop Floor Control

The current shop floor control system can trace its roots to a system that was introduced in 1975. The current system is computerized completely; the computer collects and communicates information to the users. The software was developed entirely in house and is based on ten years of experience with a homegrown machine load system as well as sections from the IBM PICS packages.

The primary objectives of Moog's shop floor control system are:

o Presenting job priorities to shop supervisors in support of job selections

o Locating jobs for shop supervision

o Presenting job status information to production control analysts and others interested in the progress of particular jobs

o Presenting information on work center status to shop supervision and production control

o Predicting normal completion dates

o Maintaining shop order quantities.

The system is used primarily to:

o Track orders through the shop

o Monitor the progress of orders against the plan

o Sequence and dispatch orders

- Facilitate short-term capacity management
- Feed back information to the planning system
- Report labor and machine efficiency.

Shop floor control at Moog is an integral part of the formal manufacturing planning system. Organizationally, shop floor control is part of Moog's materials organization; the direct formal responsibility for this system lies with the dispatch supervisor who is also responsible for all steel stores. The structure of the materials organization (as well as reporting relationships) is summarized in Figure 9-2.

Six production control analysts and eight dispatchers aid the dispatching supervisor and are part of the shop floor control system. The production control analysts can be best described as the bridge between the planning system and the shop floor. They are responsible for releasing planned orders and for changing the due dates on open orders in response to need date changes flagged by the MRP system. The dispatchers work with the movement of material on the shop floor, moving parts, doing item counts, and writing move tickets.

The Stages of Shop Floor Control at Moog

Shop floor control at Moog is built on three key manufacturing tenets. These tenets are evident in the structure and operation of the shop floor control system.

- People are crucial to the effective operation of shop floor control. There are many aspects of the actual manufacturing system that are captured adequately in the MRP-CRP-SFC simulation of that physical system (as offered by the planning system). These elements can be captured best by relying on the users and their knowledge of the system. For example, the production control analyst must anticipate, where possible, and react to changes in product design, the manufacturing process, the customer order, specifics of the shop or support department loads, and the availability of purchased components. The shop floor control system must draw on these insights wherever possible.
- Commitment to the master production schedule. The master production schedule must always be met. This is Moog's commitment to its customers. The analyst coordinates efforts to maintain the sched-

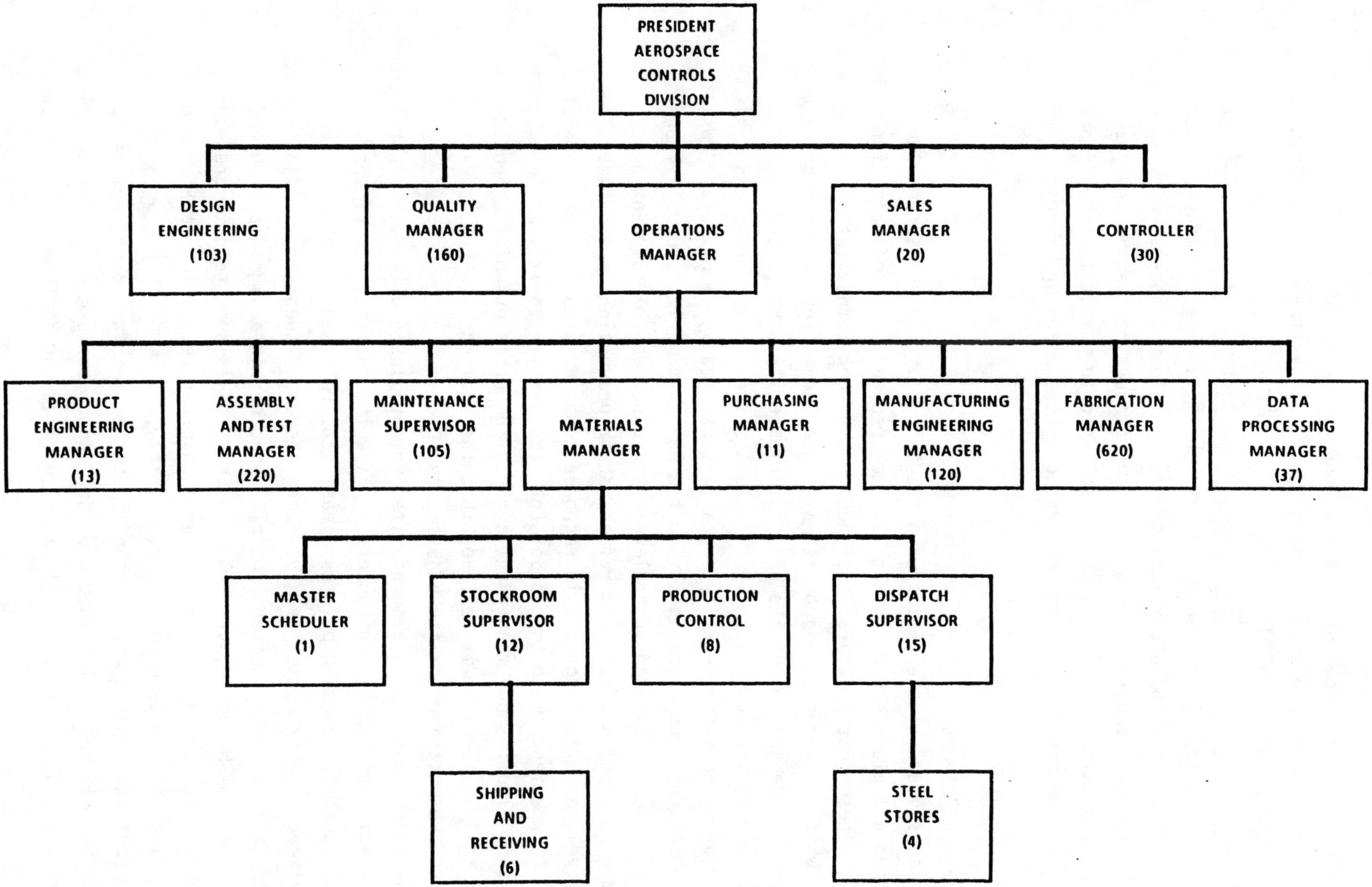

Figure 9-2. -- Materials Organization

ule. It is expected that everyone will work to minimize deviations from the schedule and to flag those changes they cannot avoid as soon as possible.

- <u>Adequate capacity and balanced loads must be ensured</u>. Management is responsible for ensuring that there is always sufficient capacity with which to complete orders. Without adequate capacity and a balanced load, the validity of any production plan is severely compromised. Finally, it is realistic to expect the shop floor to compensate for problems generated in the planning process.

Order Review/Release

Order review/release begins with the output of the MRP system, which identifies all planned orders that have matured and are candidates for order release. These jobs are first assigned a shop work authorization number (SWAN), which provides each job with a unique identifier that can be used to track and locate the job on the shop floor once it is released.

The production control analyst evaluates the planned order and typically adjusts the order quantity for an anticipated level of scrap. While this can be supported mechanically in the MRP system, it is usually done manually. The anticipated scrap levels are based on the judgment of the production control analysts and reflect their production experience. The scrap level tends to fluctuate in response to such factors as the type of job, past experience with that order (or jobs similar to it), and conditions of the shop floor. Moog management accepts the decisions of the production control analysts because it believes that the analysts are best able to arrive at the most appropriate adjustments.

The start quantity is also adjusted for available alternative parts and the allocation of limited components. While the availability of specific material is always checked before release, the released and planned loads are reviewed by work center weekly. Once the order quantity is adjusted and inventory availability checked, the planned order is assigned a SWAN and is recorded in a SWAN log (Figure 9-3). A SWAN log is sent to data processing every day. Data processing creates an open order record for each shop order by extending the standard routing by quantity.

A fabrication parts requisition is sent to manufacturing engineering. Jobs can be released to the shop and work can be performed without detailed routings, but this lack of detail makes job tracking difficult. Therefore,

SWAN	PART NUMBER	DESC (NOT PCHD)	PRNT CHNG	DUE DATE	ORDER QUANTITY	MODEL	CHRG TO	AUTHORIZATION	DEPT	MACH	DETL LOAD
124792A	A22615-001	GLAND		259	100	17-335C	O		84D		D
124800A	A22714-003	HSG		307	35	17-335C	O		72A		D
124818A	A22714-005	HSG		307	35	17-335C	O		72A		D
124826A	A44070-001	ENDCAP ASM		219	100	17-341	O		72A		D
124834A	A44361-001	BODY		265	20	17-354A	O		72A		D

Figure 9-3. -- SWAN Log

all jobs receive detailed routings except model shop work and production rework. In defining the manufacturing process, the manufacturing engineer writes a detailed process that includes tooling requirements and drawings of the part at intermediate stages of completion. Using this information, the engineer defines each routing step as any activity that requires an individual setup. Not all routing steps have standard hours applied (e.g., heat treating or outside service operations). When standard hours are applied to routing steps, the hours are defined as setup time per operation and run time per piece. Manufacturing engineering physically attaches the operation sheet and drawings to the order. When this information is returned to the production control analyst, the shop order authorization number is added to the drawings and to the operations sheet.

A drawing, an operation sheet, and a stock withdrawal form make up the shop traveler. This packet is then sent to steel stores or to the stockroom to release the necessary raw material or components.

Detailed Assignment

Released shop orders are assigned to work centers by the manually written move ticket. The dispatcher refers to the operation sheet for this assignment. If the work center and operation number specified on the move ticket do not agree with the routing, the dispatch list will use the data from the move ticket but will indicate an outside of routing condition.

All shop order due dates are set by MRP based on the master schedule. Unless the production control analyst has locked out the part number (i.e., isolated that part from the MRP system), any changes in order due dates generated by the MRP system are incorporated automatically on the shop floor. As a result, the master scheduler is in real control of order priorities. The analysts like the automatic rescheduling capabilities of the MRP system because they have confidence that most of the time the MRP system has sufficient information with which to make the right decision quickly. If there are factors outside of the system affecting the due dates, the analyst can lock the part out of the automatic reschedule.

The priority conveyed to the shop floor is a least slack time rule using the MRP-generated due dates. These priorities are generated by a rule that is similar to the critical ratio rule except that the priorities are stated in terms of "± days." A job having "+ days" priority is ahead of schedule while one with a "- days" priority is behind schedule. The reason that the priorities are expressed in this fashion is that the symbols make sense to the shop floor personnel. All priorities are updated every day and summarized in the work center daily queue list (Figure 9-4), which displays information on work orders assigned to each work center. The report shows completed operations first, followed by in-process operations, available-to-be-worked-on operations, and a limited number of scheduled but not available operations. Within each group, the work orders are in priority sequence. The report shows the status of all work orders in a given work center, and it also shows which work order should be started next. It is distributed to shop management and central dispatch. In general, the priorities found in this report are followed by shop personnel.

Another report that is often consulted by shop personnel (specifically the shop foremen) when the current work load is low is the work center look ahead report (Figure 9-5). This report indicates those shop orders that have been released to the shop, are scheduled for a given work center, but are not yet available. The foremen can see the incoming work load and prepare for high priority jobs. It also helps those jobs that can be pulled forward to the work center (especially if the work center needs work).

Preventive maintenance represents a very small proportion of the available production time and is currently not a significant factor in production scheduling. Most often it is done on the third shift or the weekend.

Data Collection/Monitoring

To provide timely information, the shop floor control system must record and process updates, changes, and additions continually. At Moog, responsibility for data collection/monitoring does not lie with any one person or group, but with the entire shop floor control system. Different individuals are responsible for collecting and recording different types of information.

Information on labor is collected from the labor cards. Time clocks are not used; the employees keep their own records. Figure 9-6 shows an example of the labor card that is completed by each employee and sent to data processing at the end of each shift. Reporting cost and payroll information on the same card avoid problems in balancing the two systems.

Another important method of recording information involves the move tickets (Figure 9-7). Whenever a job moves from one department to another,

TE PRINTED 01/24/85 JOB @5730F04 REPORT NUMBER 5732A PAGE 1
OP CALENDAR DAY NUMBER 951 WORK CENTER DAILY QUEUE LIST

RK CENTER 126-0930 DESCRIPTION CINCINNATI MTX

YS /L	SWAN	---PART NUMBER----		DESCRIPTION	LOC	DUE DTE	SCHEDULED-THIS-W/C- OPER	ST	-S/U	--RUN-	--COMING-FROM--- OPER	--W/C---	ST	HRS- AWAY	-LAST-MOVE-REPORTED- OPER	--W/C---	--QTY-	-ORDER --QTY-	WAIT DAYS
.3-	145201A	A28784	003	FRAME	ONC	999	0070	40	7.5	3.1		COMPLETED			0070	126-0343	24	24	4
7	141358A	A28784	003	FRAME	ONC	020	0140	30	1.8	24.6	SSET- 6.3 SRUN-			25.4	0070	126-0343	24	24	3
3	149823A	A28784	003	FRAME	ONC	060	0110	30	-2.2	3.3	SSET- 7.3 SRUN-			25.6	0070	126-0343	24	24	3
13-	145201A	A28784	003	FRAME	ONC	999	0140	20	6.3	25.4		AVAILABLE			0070	126-0343	24	24	4
16	149815A	A28784	003	FRAME	ONC	040	0110	20	7.3	25.6		AVAILABLE			0070	126-0343	24	24	6
30	144089A	A28784	003	FRAME	ONC	040	0140	20	6.3	23.3		AVAILABLE			0070	126-0343	22	22	0
32	126797A	A22391	001	PROFILE	ONC	010	0120	20	3.0	14.0		AVAILABLE			0120	126-0343	24	24	8
52	138727A	A22391	001	PROFILE	ONC	010	0120	20	3.0	14.0		AVAILABLE			0120	126-0343	24	24	13
18	157677A	A28784	003	FRAME	P15	060	0070	10	7.5	34.2	0060	123-0250	20	12	0040	123-0210	24	24	0

RK CENTER 126-0930 CAPACITY= 58 CRIT Q HRS= 45 TTL LOAD HRS= 194 CRIT Q DAYS= 0.8 TTL Q DAYS= 3.4

Figure 9-4. -- Work Center Daily Queue List

WORK CENTER DAILY QUEUE LIST

Legend

Days Er/La - Priority Number (Slack Time)

SWAN - Work Order Number (Shop Work Authorization Number)

Part Number - Self Explanatory

Description - Self Explanatory

Loc - Physical Location of Work Order

Due Dte - Due Date

Scheduled-this-W/C - Information on Operations to be Performed in this Work Center

Oper - Operation Number of Operation being Performed or Due to be Performed in this Work Center

St - Status Code

50 - Operation Complete

40 - Operation Complete

30 - Operation Started

20 - Operation Available to be Started

10 - Operation scheduled point not available

Su - Standard set up hours (Completed and started operations have actual hours subtracted from total set up hours)

Run - Standard Run Hours (Completed and Started Operations have Actual hours substracted from total run hours)

Coming-From - Information on Operations just prior to the Scheduled Operation

Oper - Previous Operation Number (Completed Operations show total standard set up and run hours, available operations show as available)

W/C - Previous Work Center

Hrs Away - Total Standard Hours that have to be Completed Before Work Order Arrives at this Work Center.

Figure 9-4. -- Work Center Daily Queue List (continued)

Last-Move-Reported	-	**Information from last Move Ticket Entered**
Oper	-	**Operation Number Moved to**
W/C	-	**Work Center Moved to**
Qty	-	**Quantity Moved**
Order Qty	-	**Start Quantity of Work Order**
Wait Days	-	**Number of Days the Job has been Inactive**

Total Line

Capacity	-	**Daily Demonstrated Capacity**
Crit Q Hrs.	-	**Total Standard Hours Remaining and Available of Late Jobs**
Ttl Load Hours	-	**Total Standard Hours remaining and Available of all Jobs**
Crit Q Days	-	**Critical Queue Hours/Capacity**
Ttl Q Days	-	**Total Load Hours Capacity**

Figure 9-4. -- Work Center Daily Queue List (continued)

DATE PRINTED 01/24/85

JOB @5715F04 REPORT NUMBER 5716A
SFC WORK CENTER LOOKAHEAD

W/C 120-0060 MACHINE- 0135

-SWAN--	--PART NUMBER-----	DESCRIPTION	LOC	--MOVE TICKET--- QTY	OPER	W/C	PCT CMP	-TOTAL HRS	DS	DUE DAY	DAYS E/L	MODEL NO	WAIT DAYS	----SCH THIS W/C---- OPER	S/U	RUN	TOTAL	-CUM- TOTAL
885830A	65237 002	BODY 50-414	P15	35	0060	1230320	4	389	5	710	37	050-414B	26.0	0270	5.9	17.5	23.4	23.4
889576A	72201	BODY 33	84D	40		84D	0	409	3	855	75	033-168D	4.0	0250	11.6	30.0	41.6	65.0
885830A	65237 002	BODY 50-414	P15	35	0060	1230320	4	389	5	710	37	050-414B	26.0	0340	4.9	8.6	13.5	78.5
885830A	65237 002	BODY 50-414	P15	35	0060	1230320	4	389	5	710	37	050-414B	26.0	0350	7.9	7.5	15.4	93.9
														TOTAL	30.3	63.6	93.9	

Figure 9-5. -- Work Center Look Ahead Report

COST REPORTING SECTION

Date	Empl. No.	Dept.	Employee Signature	Supervisor Signature
81583	01258	120	Ralph Jones	Andy Smith

Dept.	C/T	Model, J.O., P.N. or R.J.O.	R/N	Task	Pieces Complete	Reference	Time Hrs. Min.
120	1	739495A	N	o040	60		7:45
120	9			84			:15
							:
							:
							:
							:
							:
							:
							:
							:

204-02 **TOTAL TIME USED MUST EQUAL HOURS WORKED** 8:00

PAYROLL SECTION

ABSENT - PAID

- ____ 3 Sick
- ____ 7 Military
- ____ 8 Vacation
- ____ 6 Disability
- ____ 2 Personal
- ____ 4 Holiday
- ____ 5 Jury Duty
- ____ 0 Other ____

ABSENT - NO PAY

- ____ 1

HOURS WORKED

- 8:00 Straight Time
- ____ Overtime
- ____ Double Time

8:00 Total Hours Worked

Figure 9-6. -- Labor Card

S.W.A.N. 739495 A

Move Ticket

(DUE AT DATA PROCESSING 12:30 AM DAILY)

LOCATION 0F3

TO DEPARTMENT NO. 120

MACHINE NO. 0150

FOR OPERATION NO. 0022

AT TIME 8:35 A.M. ☒ P.M. ☐

ON DAY 81583

PIECE COUNT 60

PART NO. ________________

☐ Consider this operation complete

☐ All previous operations complete

☐ Detail Load

110-02 Rev. 4/77

Figure 9-7. -- Move Ticket

the dispatcher is responsible for moving material between departments and for record keeping. The dispatcher refers to the operation sheet for routing instructions and then records the physical location of the job, the department and the machine that are to work on the job next, the next operation number, the current piece count, and the time the job is moved.

In addition to documenting material movement, the move ticket can be used for remedial work, such as closing out one or all prior operations. That is, if an operator completes an operation but does not record it, the dispatcher can clear the remaining hours. The move ticket can be used also to request the computer to update the routing from the listed operation forward. In other words, if the routing or standard hours for a job have been changed since the issuance of a shop order, the remaining operations in the shop order's file can be updated with the new routing on request. For example, the routing change shown in Figure 9-8 could be added to any open shop order by writing a move ticket for the job and checking the detail load box.

After a shop order is issued, several changes may take place: the order may be canceled, the part description may be changed, or the model reference may be changed. The most common change is splits. Any such changes are recorded on the shop floor control sheet (Figure 9-9).

Providing for the efficient recording of information is not enough. It does not ensure the validity or accuracy of the data recorded. After all, the usefulness of any database depends on the accuracy of the information it contains. At Moog, there are several levels of data validation such as those assigned to personnel in data processing, production control, and sales. In addition, there are monthly audits of the stockroom and shop floor inventories.

One of the major features of information collection is the common corporate database. The shop floor control system shares its information with quality control, cost accounting, payroll, engineering, scrap control, purchasing, and marketing/sales. The only exception to this rule involves maintenance, which uses a different database than the one accessed by the shop floor control system.

Control/Feedback

At Moog, either a work order or a work center can become out of control. This condition most frequently is caused by unexpected high scrap

ROUTING FILE DATA SHEET

PAGE ____ OF ____

VALID TRANSACTION CODE

A – ADD ROUTING
B – ADD ROUTING OPER.
C – CHANGE OPER.
E – DELETE OPER.
M – MULTIPLE OPER.
P – PRINT
S – SAME AS

PRINT CODE (P=PRINT, N=NO PRINT; A=ACCOUNTING) 1

TRANSACTION CODE

PART NUMBER (3–20)	REV. DATE (21–26)	SAME AS RANGE P/N (27–44)
A05129	081583	

ACCOUNTING USE ONLY

REV. NO. (45–47)	NORM. RUN (48–52)	MODEL (54–62)	G P (63–64)	ENGR. (65–67)	A/S (68)	DATE REQUESTED (69–74)	BY (75–76)	CRL (77)	R I A (78–80)
		17 307B		JAG		/ /			

RAW MATERIAL DATA

DIAM.	WIDTH	LENGTH	MATERIAL (21–50)	COST (51–57)	R I B (78–80)
.	.	.			

DETAIL OPERATION DATA

T/C (2)	OPER (21–24)	ALT (25)	WORK CENTER Dept. (26–28)	WORK CENTER Machine (29–32)	DESCRIPTION (33–41)	SETUP (42–44)	TB (45)	MACHINE HOURS (46–50)	LABOR HOURS (51–55)	O.S DAYS (56–58)	CC (59)	SERVICE COST (60–64)	C/C (7–80)
1 B	111		120	0060	TURN	4.8	2		.050		2		RIC
2													
3 B	112		121	0420	GRIND	2.3			.083				
4													
5 E	110		120	0090	TURN								
6													
7													
8													
9													
10													
11													
12													
13													
14													
15													
16													
17													
18													
19													
20													
21													
22													
23													
24													
25													
26													
27													
28													
29													
30													

PREPARED BY Jim Graham DATE 8-15-83

119-28 Rev. 1080

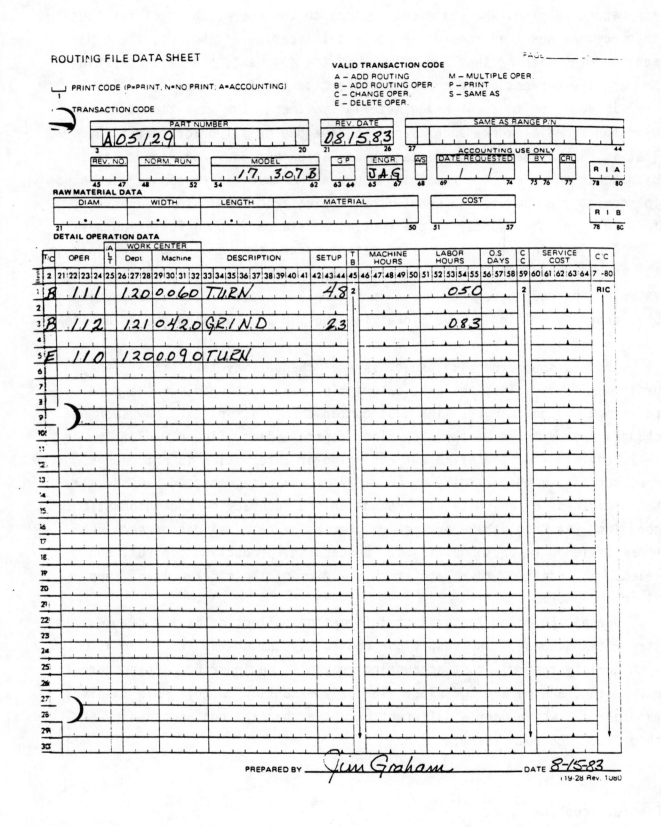

Figure 9-8. -- Routing File Data Sheet

SHOP FLOOR CONTROL CHANGE SHEET

Date: 8-15-83
By: RCS
Plant: 4

?rocessing
?o. 5611

	SWAN NO. (No. 1)	Ref. only PART NO. Not punched	CHANGE CODE (No. 2)	CHANGE INFORMATION LTR. (3)	OPER. (No.4)	QUANTITY (No. 5)	DATE (No.6)	OTHER (No.7)
1	722942F	A05129	SPLITL	J	0263	2	215	
2	732099A	A05129	SPLITL		0150	3	320	
3	119685A		ORDQTY			512		
4								
5								
6								
7								
8								
9								
10								
11								
12								
13								
16								
17								
18								
19								
20								
21								
22								
23								
24								
25								
26								
27								
28								

INSTRUCTIONS:

CHANGE DESIRED	CHANGE CODE	LENGTH	REQUIRED COLUMNS
Authorization	AUTHOR	7	'1' '2' '7'
Cancel	CANCEL	N/A	'1' '2'
Description	DESCRP	11	'1' '2' '7'
Due Date (Shop Cal.)	DUEDAY	3 (no.dec.)	'1' '2' '6'
Model Number	MODELN	9	'1' '2' '7'
Order Quantity	ORDQTY	6 (no.dec.)	'1' '2' '5'
Outside Days	OSDAYS	2 (no.dec.)	'1' '2' '4' '7'
Split	SPLITL	1 (alpha)	'1' '2' '3' '4' '5' '6'

WHITE – ORIGINATOR; PINK – DATA PROCESSING/ACCOUNTING; GOLD – PRODUCTION CONTROL

119-20 Rev. 8/77

Figure 9-9. -- Shop Floor Control Change Sheet

rates, changes to the master schedule, or a capacity bottleneck. An out-of-control situation can be identified easily within the shop floor control system.

When a work order is needed in a shorter than normal lead time, the slack time number will become negative. Every day the production control department receives a list of all negative slack time jobs in priority sequence. Several actions can be taken, initiated, and coordinated by the dispatching personnel with guidance from production control and support from shop supervision. At Moog, the dispatching personnel are responsible for bringing an out-of-control situation back under control. Moog does not use any expediters. Management at Moog believes expediters are ineffective because they treat shop floor symptoms rather than identifying and resolving those problems that gave rise to the need for expediting.

If the order can be expedited and completed within a reasonable time, it will remain as it is with its current high (negative slack time) priority. Expediting an out-of-control work order may include:

- o <u>Operation splitting</u>. That is, running the job on multiple machines for the same operation at the same time.
- o <u>Operation overlapping</u>. Allowing sequential operations to occur at the same time.
- o <u>Lot splitting</u>. Splitting the lot into small quantities that can complete each of the remaining operations much sooner.
- o <u>Solving the problem at a higher level</u>. The production control analyst can plan to make up the schedule at a higher level part number provided that there is slack available at this higher level and that the analyst cannot compress the current lead times any further.

On average, only 2 percent of all shop orders are late and require special attention.

Another type of out-of-control work order involves those with higher than anticipated levels of scrap or orders needing rework. For a scrap problem, a scrap notice is sent directly to the production control analyst who can respond by changing priorities that day. Automatic rescheduling of open shop orders would also adjust for this problem weekly.

Rework presents a different problem in that it is not clearly lost to the system. Nevertheless, the process of defining the required rework, specifying the process, and gaining government and customer approval can delay a critical part significantly. Several activities take place in response to rework. The requirements for rework operation sheets and customer approval are reflected on the dispatch list for the appropriate department. In addition, the production control analyst can resequence the open job orders to put higher priority on a shop order not in the rework cycle.[1]

An out-of-control work center can be identified by its high critical queue days. Critical queue days are calculated by dividing the hours available at that work center on orders with negative slack time by the historical daily capacity. This number appears at the bottom of the work center daily queue list and also is summarized in a weekly report. The response to this problem is typically to work overtime (including Sundays) to keep the critical jobs moving. Overtime is continued until the critical queue days indicator is back down to a reasonable level.

To facilitate the rapid and accurate flow of information between the planning and the shop floor control systems (an important part of the control/feedback activities), several reports have been developed by Moog personnel that receive regular attention. These reports are the open order status report, scheduled routing display, and shop load status report. The open order status report (Figure 9-10) displays all work orders currently released in part number sequence. This report is used to locate specific work orders on the shop floor and to review the status of all work orders for a given part number. Produced daily and containing information that is current as of midnight of the previous night, it is distributed to central dispatch, production control, and manufacturing engineering personnel.

The scheduled routing displays (Figure 9-11) are produced on CRTs when requested. This report uses specific data from the report requester for planned start date, capacity (labor relief rate), wait days between operations, previous completed operations, and lot quantity. The above data are combined with the standard routing to project the completion date for each operation. The shop load status report (Figure 9-12) is printed weekly and summarizes the work load released to the shop, as well as trends in the

---

[1]Since the 1983 conference, the process of handling rework information at Moog has been improved. Rework operations are now added to the routing of the specific shop order affected. However, the basic routing is not changed for future orders. These rework operations will change the lead-time requirements and therefore the priority of the shop order.

DATE PRINTED 01/24/85

SHOP CALENDAR DAY 951

JOB @5710F16 REPORT NUMBER 5711A
SFC DAILY OPEN ORDER STATUS REPORT
PART NUMBER SEQUENCE

ORDER NUMBER	DAYS ER/LA	--PART NUMBER-----		C-D LOC	DESCRIPTION	ORDR QUAN	---MOVE TICKET--- QUAN	OPER	DEPTW/C	PCT CMP	BALNCE HRS	-DS	-START- SCH	ACT	DUE DAY	MODEL-NO	NXT SCHEDULE OPER	DEPTW/C	WAIT DAYS
121590A	92	A28781	002	B09	BODY 26	80	42	0120	1250600	96	4	3	021	861	055	026-102B	0130	1251050	0.0
145201A	13-	A28784	003	ONC	FRAME	24	24	0070	1260930	33	453	3	906	909	999	W017-316D	0145	1230300	4.0
141358A	7	A28784	003	ONC	FRAME	24	24	0070	1260930	35	448	3	925	883	020	W017-316D	0145	1230300	3.0
149815A	16	A28784	003	ONC	FRAME	24	24	0070	1260930	21	535	3	947	930	040	W017-316D	0120	1261190	6.0
144089A	30	A28784	003	ONC	FRAME	22	22	0070	1260930	33	420	3	951	896	040	W017-316D	0145	1230300	0.0
149823A	38	A28784	003	ONC	FRAME	24	24	0070	1260930	24	511	3	967	931	060	W017-316D	0120	1230300	0.0
157677A	18	A28784	003	P15	FRAME	24	24	0040	1230250	0	672	3	967	946	060	W017-316D	0070	1260930	0.0
145219A	27	A28798	001	C07	BLANK	84	82	0080	M210420	73	20	10	965	915	994	026-219	0090	1250600	24.0

SFC OPEN ORDER STATUS REPORT
Legend

Order Number	-	Work Order Number
Days Er/La	-	Priority Number (Slack Time)
Part Number	-	Self Explanatory
C-D Loc	-	Central Dispatch Location (Physical location of work order)
Description	-	Self Explanatory
Ordr Quan	-	Start Quantity of Work Order
Move Ticket		
Quan	-	Current Quantity of Work Order
Oper	-	Current Operation Number
Dept W/C	-	Current Department and Work Center
Pct Cmp	-	Percent Complete (Standard hours completed/total standard hours)
Balance Hrs-DS	-	Balance of Standard Hours and Days Remaining to be Performed
Start Sch Act	-	Scheduled Start Day and Actual Start Day
Due Day	-	Self Explanatory
Model - No	-	Model Number (End Item Number)
Nxt Schedule		
Oper	-	Next Scheduled Operation Number
Dept W/C	-	Next Scheduled Department and Work Center
Wait Days	-	Number of Days the Job has been Inactive

Figure 9-10. -- Open Order Status Report

8-18-83

SCHEDULED ROUTING DISPLAY

Page 1

Part #A07911-001 DESCR: BODY

TYPE = MACHINED W/COMPONENTS REV DATE 8-05-83 NRQ 100

MODEL 30-263 TOTAL COMPONENT COST: LBR 23.34 MTL 2.02

QTY 100 START DATE 08-18-83 OPER 0000 QUEUE DAYS 1.0 HRS/DAY 010.0 ID 00 OD 00

DATE	OPER	W/L	DESCR	SET UP	RUN	TOTAL	CUM	O/S Days
08/18/83	0010	195-9990	INSP				.00	
08/19/83	0013	124-0690	LASER ENG	.3	4.80	5.10	5.10	
08/23/83	0015	124-0650	STAMP	.2	1.50	1.70	6.80	
08/24/83	0020	124-0600	DRILL	.5	4.30	4.80	11.60	
08/25/83	0030	124-0600	DRILL	.5	4.30	4.80	16.40	
08/26/83	0040	123-1020	EDM	.5	72.00	72.50	88.90	
09/08/83	0050	123-1020	EDM	.5	10.50	11.00	99.90	
09/09/83	0060	327-0720	CLEAN				99.90	1.0
09/12/83	0070	000-9990	PLATE				99.90	2.0
09/13/83	0080	195-9990	INSP				99.90	
TOTAL QUEUE DAYS:	7			2.5	97.4			3.0

Figure 9-11. -- Scheduled Routing Display

DATE PRINTED 12/17/84

JOB @5742G02 REPORT NUMBER 5742A
WEEKY SHOP LOAD STATUS REPORT

WORK CENTER NUMBER	WORK CENTER DESCRIPTION	TOTAL LOAD	CURRENT PERIOD INPUT	CURRENT PERIOD OUTPUT	CURRENT PERIOD CLOCK	CURRENT PERIOD O/C	SMOOTHED AVERAGE INPUT	SMOOTHED AVERAGE OUTPUT	SMOOTHED AVERAGE CLOCK	SMOOTHED AVERAGE O/C
126-0001	LABOR CHGD TO INDIRECT				630	.00			638	.00
126-0002	LABOR CHGD TO SUMRY-LOAD		300	300	304	.98	265	265	268	.98
126-0003	LABOR CHGD TO INV OPER NO				24	.00			29	.00
126-0004	LABOR CHGE TO INV MACH NO				28	.00	1	1	31	.03
126-0210	DRILL PRESS								1	.00
126-0300	BRIDGEPORT VERTICAL MILL		61	61	53	1.14	21	21	43	.48
126-0600	BENCH STATION	11	1							
126-0910	K&T 200 SERIES	13,019	1,510	713	546	1.30	600	662	627	1.05
126-0930	CINCINNATI MTX	1,892	16-	247	237	1.04	51	231	201	1.14
126-0970	MILWAUKEE-MATIC E-B	133	37	37	118	.31	13	25	51	.49
126-1190	HPZ,HPMC,CPMC,MCNC	16,784	421	1,395	1,690	.82	699	1,569	1,809	.86
126 DEPARTMENT TOTALS		31,843	2,314	2,753	3,630	.75	1,650	2,774	3,699	.74

Figure 9-12. -- Load Status Report

amounts of work released and relieved by work center. The report provides the users with visibility over current and future loads that can then be used to identify the best course of action.

Order Disposition

Given the constant tracking and monitoring that has followed the order as it proceeds through the various operations, order disposition is a relatively straightforward activity. When a shop order is moved to the stockroom, the dispatcher writes a material transfer form that is verified by the stock clerk. This form is sent on to data processing for entry into the system. The material transfer closes the shop order and adds the piece count to the stockroom inventory. At this point, the disposition of the order is complete.

Performance Evaluation/Feedback

The performance evaluation of a dispatcher covers two prime features of the job. The first aspect is the prompt movement of work throughout the shop. Under some circumstances, this prompt movement actually becomes an expediting force. The second part of the job is the correct recording of information regarding the shop order. There is a three-fold evaluation of this performance. First, are the splits, moves, and work arounds carried out promptly? This is a continuous evaluation, related to plans from the most recent parts review meeting. The second evaluation covers data errors. Move ticket errors are reported and corrected daily. The efforts are traced to and corrected by the individual dispatcher. Third is correctness of quantity and operation data. There are monthly audits of these data.

The activities of the production control analysts cover a broader range. Consequently, the evaluation of performance is less immediate and direct than the evaluation of the dispatcher. There is daily reporting of each analyst's shop orders specifying which orders are running past due. In addition, there are monthly and quarterly reviews of shipments versus the customer's schedule. There is also a monthly report of the value of slow moving inventory under each analyst's control. While each of these inputs helps evaluate the success of an analyst, the inputs do not take into account the difficulty of the program or the strength of the effort applied. It is far more difficult to achieve measurable delivery success with programs newly released from engineering than it is with mature programs. As a result, challenge, effort, and success are combined in the analyst's annual performance appraisal.

Evaluating Moog's Shop Floor Control System -- Benefits

To evaluate the effectiveness of the shop floor control system, these questions must be asked:

- o Are the shop supervisors able to understand the appropriate priorities as displayed on the dispatch lists?
- o How many jobs are not located as indicated on the dispatch lists?
- o Are the production control analysts and other interested parties able to determine the status and activity for each shop job?
- o Do the shop supervisors agree that the work center status information presented by shop floor control accurately reflects what work is available at the work center?
- o Do the predicted completion dates appropriately define what normal jobs go to stock?
- o Are the quantities and completed operation status sufficiently accurate to avoid physical inventory counts?

The current shop floor control system is regarded as successful because it does well when evaluated using these key questions. In general, Moog management is satisfied with the current system because it has met management's basic requirements for timely, understandable, and consistent information on work order priorities and status. Specifically, the system provides the following major benefits:

- o Priority control. The dispatch list provides stable and logical job priority definitions to guide the supervisors in job selection.
- o Responsiveness to schedule change. The dispatch lists implement weekly changes in the MPS.
- o Visibility of part status. The quantity, location, hours remaining, days of inactivity, and predicted completion date are available on all shop orders for decisions such as processing changes and order promising.
- o Physical inventory. Accurate quantity data eliminate the need for an annual physical inventory of the shop floor. Currently, monthly audits are sufficient.

- o <u>Scrap analysis</u>. The operation at which an item was scrapped can be readily identified, and the appropriate costs can be allocated to the scrapped part.
- o <u>Analysis of standards</u>. Operations that caused variances from standard hours can be identified and analyzed quickly.
- o <u>Location control</u>. Any shop order can be found within minutes.
- o <u>Completion predictions</u>. The standard scheduling rules are used to anticipate shipping delays.

Because the shop floor control system is an integral element of the overall manufacturing system, management has found it difficult to identify those benefits directly attributable to the shop floor control system alone. Management believes, however, that the current manufacturing system would not be as successful without the presence of an effective and integral shop floor control system.

Shop Floor Control -- The Next Stage

At present, Moog personnel are pleased with the shop floor control system. The system is not perfect, however, and actions are underway to enhance the operation. These changes will enable Moog's shop floor control system to provide more rapid information update.

Currently, the location and operation data are recorded on cards every time a shop order moves. The file, however, is updated daily from the cards. In the future, material moves will be entered into the file either through a terminal in central dispatch or from radio signal units with each dispatcher. To use this current information, the dispatch lists will appear on CRTs rather than on hard copies. Although the relief of the labor would still be done nightly in a batch mode, the dispatch lists would now indicate available work on a real-time basis.

<u>Shop Floor Control at Moog: Lessons to be Learned</u>

Moog operates in a marketplace where good planning must go hand in hand with good execution. Moog has been able to survive and grow in this marketplace because of the strength of its current shop floor control system. The system has been so successful because of certain features:

- o A shop floor control system can be expected to carry out successfully only those plans for which there is adequate material and capacity available. A key lesson and one that is always obeyed by Moog personnel is that the shop floor control system is responsible for implementing plans and for feeding information back from the shop floor. It cannot and should not be held responsible for acquiring the level of resources needed for the successful implementation of a plan. This task is the responsibility of the planning system alone. Therefore, before any plan is released to the shop floor, it is always checked to ensure that there are adequate levels of material and capacity available. Only after the plan has passed this crucial test successfully is it turned over to the shop floor control system, which can now realistically be held accountable for the successful completion of the orders.

  In the absence of such checks, the credibility of both the planning and the shop floor control system is compromised seriously. Without checking resource availability, the firm cannot have control over the actions that take place on the shop floor.
- o Keep open the information flow between the planning system and shop floor control. One of the most noteworthy features of Moog's system is that the shop floor control system is always closely linked and coordinated with the activities of the planning system. This feature is critical because it ensures that the actions that take place on the shop floor are always consistent with the objectives of the planning system. The two systems work as one. The planning system keeps the shop floor control system informed of changes in order need dates, order quantities, and product design (to name a few). In turn, the shop floor control system keeps the planning system informed of what is happening on the shop floor by reports such as the open order status report, the scheduled routing display, and the shop load status report. This free flow of information between the systems ensures that the planning system is also aware of what is happening on the shop floor and that the shop floor control system is always aware of changes taking place in planning.
- o Identify and clearly separate those activities that are to be done automatically by the computer system and those activities to be done manually by the users. The current system is computerized

extensively. This does not mean that the user has no real role in the operation of the system. Certain activities are done automatically by the system without human intervention. These include the automatic revision of open order due dates and the generation of the shop floor reports. Often these activities involve nothing more than simple bookkeeping. The users know what the computer system is doing, and they have confidence in it. There are other activities that require the experience of the user. Typical of these activities are the determination of the scrap adjustments by the production control analysts before the release of the order; preparation of the move tickets by the dispatchers; and validation of all data recorded by personnel in data processing, production control, and sales. By clearly differentiating the responsibilities, Moog has reduced confusion while enhancing the role of personnel. The users are freed from tedious bookkeeping activities so that they can use their knowledge to improve the operation of the system.

- Make the shop floor control system simple to use and to understand. To be used on an ongoing basis, any system must be simple to use and understand. This lesson is evident at Moog. The steps in the shop floor control system are well defined; the responsibilities at each stage clearly identified. Management has taken care to express operation priorities in a form clearly understandable by shop floor personnel. It is easier to understand the lateness of a job in terms of the number of days that it is behind schedule than in terms of a fraction (the way in which critical ratio rule priorities are stated). Finally, all the information is presented in a straightforward fashion with only the necessary information noted and with each report fulfilling a specific need. For example, to locate a job on the shop floor, the user would turn to the open order status report. In contrast, the anticipated completion date of a job at a specific operation can be found by using the scheduled routing display.
- Recognize the presence of certain significant manufacturing characteristics and build the shop floor control system to cope with these features. Moog deals with a production process characterized by such features as high scrap and rework and specialized capacity. These characteristics cannot be ignored if the shop floor control

system is to be effective. At Moog, definite procedures have been developed to flag out-of-control conditions based on these characteristics. Procedures have also been developed for coping with these conditions. These procedures are built into the shop floor control. As a result, the users are aware of those areas most likely to be potential problems. They also know ahead of time how to best deal with these problems. The result is a realistic system that is simple to use.

The shop floor control system is the result of an evolutionary process that began in the 1970s, and which was intended to meet manufacturing needs. The system design allows it to be flexible enough to handle reschedules, changes in routing, rework, and scrap, while at the same time preserve the necessary formality to fit within a manufacturing resource planning environment. The continuous fine-tuning of the shop floor control system has resulted in a system that can now satisfy manufacturing's needs quickly and efficiently.

General Nature of the Firm

Miles Laboratories, headquartered in Elkhart, Indiana, is a leading international manufacturer and marketer of pharmaceutical and biological products, diagnostic agents and instruments, hospital supplies, animal health care products, household scouring products, and insect repellants. Miles Laboratories reported total sales of $1.2 billion in 1984 resulting in total operating profits of $60.2 million and total assets of $977 million. The major operating divisions are pharmaceutical products, Cutter Division, professional products, biotechnology products, Consumer Healthcare Division, and household products.

The pharmaceutical products division is responsible for manufacturing and marketing ethical pharmaceutical drugs such as antiinfectives, cardiovascular drugs, dermatologicals, allergens, and chemotherapeutics. The division consists of three major operating units, Miles Pharmaceuticals, Hollister-Stier, and Dome/Hollister-Stier. The Cutter Division is a major manufacturer of supplies for the hospital and veterinary markets. The professional products division, consisting of Ames and Miles Scientific, produces a broad range of chemical reagent and microbiological test systems in addition to electronic medical instruments used in disease detection and monitoring. It also manufactures and markets tissue processing products for histology/pathology laboratories, disposable plastic labware, and a line of biologicals for researchers. The biotechnology products division supplies ingredients, services, and processing to the food and beverage industry. The two operating units are Biotech Products, which produces and sells citric acid and enzymes, and Marschall Products, which manufactures agricultural products such as cheese starters. The Consumer Healthcare Division produces and sells a line of over-the-counter proprietary medicines and vitamin supplements. The sixth division is household products, which manufactures and sells household scouring products and insect repellants.

These six divisions employ some 12,000 employees. Production takes place at fifteen facilities throughout the United States.

Overall, production is divided between MTS (the most important category) and MTO (typically for promotions) with some ATO products (for promotions). Miles Laboratories serves a diverse market, and management believes that it competes on quality, assurance of quality (adequate documentation and batch control), service to the customer, and cost control. Because of the nature of its products and their use, Miles Laboratories must ensure that its products are of a high level of quality consistently. Quality assurance is concerned with tracking, controlling, and monitoring the progress and quality of products passing through the system. Miles must be able to demonstrate to both its customers and such government agencies as the Food and Drug Administration that it has taken the appropriate steps to ensure a quality product. Service to the customer is defined by on-time delivery, quick response to customer orders, and competitive moves. As market competitiveness increases, cost control becomes more important for success.

Miles Laboratories is a wholly owned subsidiary of Bayer Aktiengesellschaft (Bayer Ag) of West Germany. Bayer Ag, a worldwide manufacturer of pharmaceutical and chemical products with annual sales of over $18 billion, employs over 174,000 people.

The Consumer Healthcare Division

The Consumer Healthcare Division (CHD) manufactures mass-produced products including vitamin supplements, cough and cold remedies, topical antiseptics, and effervescent analgesics. Among the brand names are Alka-Seltzer (r), Alka-Seltzer Plus (r), Flintstones (tm) Chewable Vitamins, One-a-Day (r) Vitamins, and Bactine (r). CHD is considered a product leader in the vitamin and mineral supplements and effervescent analgesics markets. The division, along with its manufacturing facility, is located in Elkhart.

The CHD products are marketed to over 7,000 different accounts including Kroger, Safeway, Revco, and A&P. CHD's sales force services most of its accounts directly. All customer deliveries are made from one of seven public warehouses located across the country or the two company warehouses in Elkhart and West Haven, Connecticut. In addition to the domestic commercial accounts, the CHD also manufactures and ships items to Canada.

CHD operates in a competitive market with cost control and manufacturing flexibility as key considerations. The need for cost control is self-evident. Manufacturing flexibility is required because CHD must be able to respond quickly to actions taken in the marketplace.

CHD produces twenty-three different product families. Before these products are packaged, they are measured in terms of thousands of pieces produced. The number of products to be controlled increases dramatically because of packaging. CHD is responsible for 65 different package sizes, 150 variations, and between 250 to 300 stock keeping units (SKUs). The major difference between a package size and a variation lies in whether the package is for open stock (MTS) or for promotion (MTO or ATO).

Packaging for open stock requires no promotional markings (special graphics) on the package. It is the type of package the company produces daily. In contrast, a promotional package is a limited item. CHD typically runs between nine to twelve promotional cycles per year, and it generally involves many different package sizes (each with its own graphics). A promotion can be regional or national and can take a number of forms:

- A coupon redeemable on future purchases
- Bonus tablets
- A cents off offer on the current purchase
- A free product offer in the package.

Each promotion requires a different type of packaging and frequently, both types of packaging (open stock and promotional) are run at the same time.

Expertise in forcasting sales demand is important for CHD. Product demand must be forecasted in terms of two key manufacturing attributes, the quantity to be produced and the type of packaging required. Forecasting quantities by product lines is straightforward. The future demand for a given product line is affected by product type (i.e., whether the product is new or is well established), the state of the economy, promotions, and the seasonality of demand. Forecasting the demand for such products as Alka-Seltzer is relatively easy because demand is constant through the year. Demand forecasting for other products such as Alka-Seltzer Plus and One-a-Day Vitamins is more difficult because demand is far more seasonal. (The demand for Alka-Seltzer Plus, a cold remedy, tends to be greatest during February, March, and April.)

The real challenge is forecasting individual SKU needs. Promotional activities within CHD and potential marketplace actions, combined with the consumer nature of CHD's products account for the extreme volatility of sales demand.

CHD's manufacturing facilities are divided into three major operations, bulk vitamins, Alka-Seltzer, and packaging. These operations are worked by union employees and operate primarily on two shifts (sixteen hours), five days a week. On average, capacity use is high and generally exceeds 80 percent. A third shift is used mainly for setups, machine repairs, preventive maintenance, and cleaning. The process deals with approximately 2,000 different part numbers. Some of the products are manufactured at the West Haven plant.

Like the other divisions of Miles Laboratories, CHD operates in a highly regulated manufacturing environment. Quality assurance is important, and the government requires documentation of both the manufacturing process and material use. Management must be able to identify a product in terms of its production batch and material lots used.

Quality assurance monitors the flow of raw materials from the receiving docks to the shop floor. No material can be used by production until it has been approved by quality assurance.

The Production Process

All production takes place in the Elkhart and West Haven plants (with most done in Elkhart). The production process is characterized by several features. First, the production process is more like repetitive than discrete batch (job shop) manufacturing. Volume is high. Each product follows a straight line routing from the withdrawal and weighing of raw materials to the completion and inventory of the finished tablets. The stages of this process typically include such operations as central weighing, mixing, kiln drying, sizing, final mix, press, film coat, inspect, and WIP inventory. These processes take place in the bulk manufacturing department (Figure 10-1). At any point in time, each line can produce only one product to prevent cross contamination. For most products except Alka-Seltzer, more than one product is made per line so the setup costs are relatively high. For example, they vary from one-half to two days. All setups, as a rule, are done on off shifts. A typical finished goods batch has a thirty-two hour run time (i.e., four out of ten weekly shifts) and a four-week cumulative lead time.

The only exception to this flow is Alka-Seltzer. Because of its high volume and constant sales, the Alka-Seltzer lines are set up to run from raw material to final product packaging. The lines dedicated to its production are started up on Monday morning and shut down on Friday night.

The production of each product requires a set of master formula cards, which are essentially the BOMs. The cards tell operational personnel what and how much inventory to requisition. On average, for each end product,

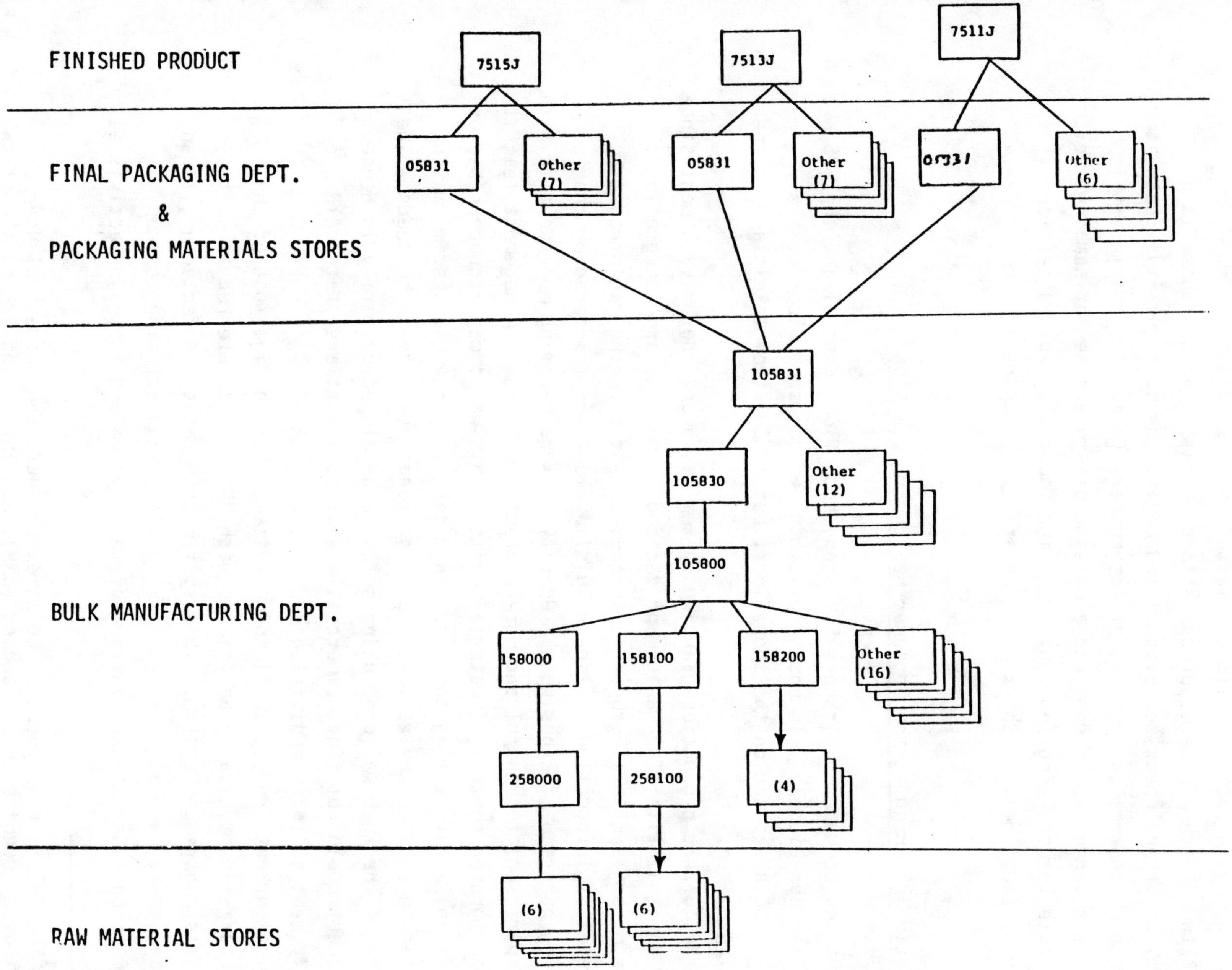

Figure 10-1. -- Product Flowchart

eight unique BOMs are needed. In Figure 10-1, part numbers 105831, 105830, and 158200 would each have its own master formula card.

Between each of the major operations in this process, there is a quality assurance check to validate and monitor product quality. Each item produced is controlled by a set of lot numbers (e.g., for raw materials, there is a vendor lot number and a Miles cross-reference lot number), which facilitate lot tracking and control. Tight control, rapid detection of problems, and timely feedback of information are important.

Production Planning at the Consumer Healthcare Division

At the Consumer Healthcare Division, shop floor control and the MPS are tied together closely. In most firms, many of the shop floor control activities take place on the shop floor, but at CHD they take place in the planning system.

The current production planning system has been under development since 1977. At that time, CHD management decided to move toward integrating all of the major functional groups in an environment offering rapid and timely retrieval of information on line. This movement was triggered by the changing nature of the business. Operations were becoming more complex with more operations to control and more products to manage. Management felt it needed improved control of material costs. This was a major concern because significant manufacturing costs are in materials. The old system, which operated in a batch environment, could no longer satisfy these needs. The closing of the loop was done using software developed primarily in house. Management could not find commercially available software that could adequately meet all of the division's needs.

The current production planning system, while having most of the characteristics typically associated with MRP II, is referred to as the materials management system. This system integrates manufacturing, finance, top management, and accounting; it also links manufacturing to the distribution system.[1] An overview of this system and its major activities

---

[1]The CHD is considered to be an experienced and successful user of distribution requirements planning (DRP). It introduced DRP at almost the same time that it began the move to close the loop.

are provided in Figure 10-2. The module labeled production activity control is more commonly and accurately referred to as production and labor reporting by division personnel.

The production planning system plays a critical role in the effective operation of CHD. One of the major management objectives is to maintain level employment combined with full employment for its existing work force. This is a difficult task to achieve in a marketing environment characterized by extremely volatile consumer demand. Management uses the production planning process to level employment. Annual planning is done once a year, and period planning is done monthly or weekly, if necessary.

Annual Planning

Annual planning is an important activity at CHD because it helps management answer four important questions:

- o Does CHD have the human resources to meet its production needs?
- o Does CHD have enough material and capacity to satisfy production requirements for the upcoming year?
- o Can CHD acquire enough of those resources to satisfy next year's needs?
- o How much will it cost CHD to satisfy next year's production plan?

The major output of this process is the annual master plan, which is an approximate production plan developed for each product code and major production operations. It is the authorization by which the division acquires the necessary inputs for the upcoming year and establishes capacity constraints that the division cannot violate. The annual master plan sets the standards for costs, inventory (the inventory plan), and production. These standards are then used to evaluate performance in the upcoming year. In short, the annual master plan becomes top management's handle on the division.

Annual planning is done in June and begins with the formulation of the annual sales forecast (Figure 10-2), which is derived by top management representatives from sales, marketing, and finance, and is based on customer and market data. The forecast is then evaluated to determine if it is compatible with the overall performance objectives set for the division by top management. These objectives are usually stated in terms of desired profit levels. If it is, it is passed on to the materials management system. The forecast is broken down and restated in several forms:

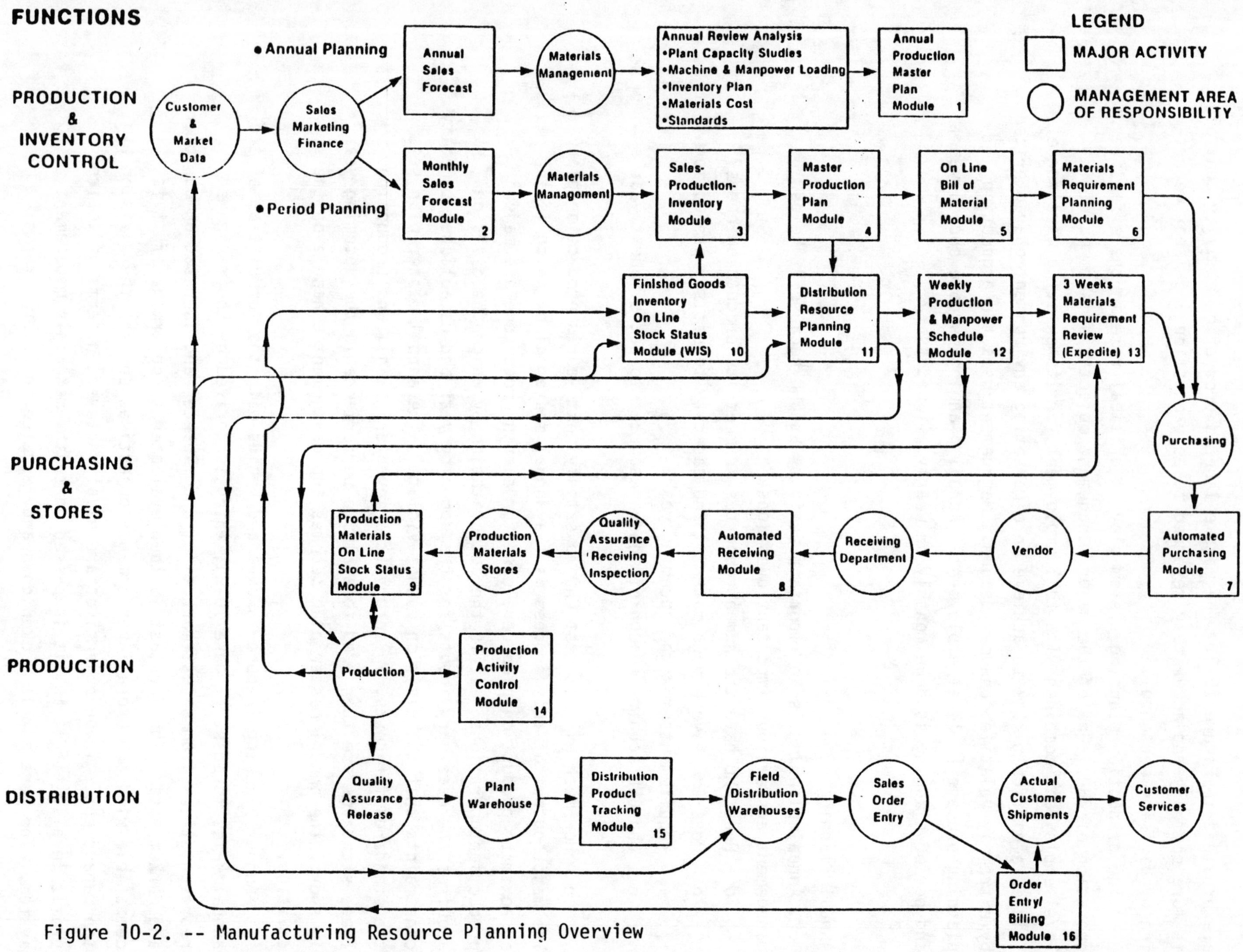

Figure 10-2. -- Manufacturing Resource Planning Overview

- Plant capacity studies
- Machine and work force loadings (the monthly implications of the annual sales forecast on the demand for machinery and workers)
- Inventory plan (by month and product type)
- Material costs
- Standards.

These analyses are done primarily by personnel from materials management. Once a plan has been formulated that is feasible and acceptable to top management, finance, sales, and manufacturing, it becomes the annual master plan.

Period Planning

Annual planning sets the standards and authorizes the requisition of needed resources. Period planning is the way management reacts to the realities of implementing the plan. It is a monthly or a weekly (when necessary) activity that updates operations achieving current marketplace needs. Corrective actions are necessary in light of the high volatility of demand faced by CHD and usually take advantage of production flexibility. Examples of corrective actions used by management include:

- Internal work force transfers
- Use of a third shift for changeovers
- Overtime and extra capacity.

Period planning begins with the monthly sales forecast, which projects sales out over the next twelve months on a rolling basis. Unlike the annual sales forecast, the monthly sales forecast is far more detailed and deals with all major product variations. It reflects revised projected sales.

Materials management uses the sales forecast for the sales/production/inventory (SPI) review. The revised sales figures are examined to identify their effect on production and inventory. This review is done by product type (i.e., A, B, or C class product) and the minimums and maximums set for each product. The minimums and maximums are only guidelines; they can be exceeded in the case of expected variation or the introduction of new packages.

The SPI is the major device used by materials management to get back on plan. In the short term (i.e., one month minimum), materials management attempts to minimize changes to the schedule because of material and work force commitments. Schedule flexibility is also influenced by such marketing considerations as advertising commitments. As a result, the relationship between the firmness of the schedule and the month being scheduled can be expressed as follows:

- o The first month, 95 percent of the schedule is firm
- o The second month, 75 percent of the schedule is firm
- o The third month, 50 percent of the schedule is firm
- o The fourth month and beyond, the schedule is completely free to change.

Most of the deviation encountered in the SPI come from actual sales variations. The SPI is the responsibility of three finished goods planners who represent nutritional bulk tablets, nutritional packaging, and medicinal products.

After the SPI has been evaluated and acceptable changes incorporated, it is then broken down by week and by both finished goods and WIP. This breakdown results in the creation of the master production plan (MPP), which is the master production schedule at CHD. This plan is linked to both the warehouses (by a DRP system) and the MRP module.

Currently, the MPP (Figure 10-3) is formulated manually using a Gantt chart. This plan sets the production schedule for the next nine months, determines the exact manner in which CHD will use its available capacity, and decides the exact order in which the products are to be manufactured. Once set, this sequence is not changed frequently. This production sequence determines the order in which components are to be processed.

If the MPP must be changed, then the changes are always evaluated for feasibility from both capacity and material perspectives. No plan that is infeasible is ever passed down to the shop floor.

While the MPP can be viewed as a capacity plan, the plans generated by the MRP system are essentially material plans. Once a month or on demand, the MRP system determines the material requirements for the next nine months. All purchases of materials and packaging are made on the basis of these plans and are done completely on line by the automated purchasing module.

When using the MRP system, a new set of planners enters the manufacturing planning process. These are the material planners, whose responsibilities are divided into chemical material components and packaging material for nutritional and medicinal products. These planners are vital to the operation of the shop floor control system.

PART NUMBER	U/M	LINE	WK NO	DATE	QTY	WK NO	DATE	QTY	WK NO	DATE	QTY	WK NO	DATE	QTY	WK NO	DATE	QTY
*************** DEPT. 60 40 01 02				COMP & BOTTLING													
130400	MPC	00.00	45	NOV05	55600	46	NOV12	35900	47	NOV19	20940	48	NOV26	39900	49	DEC03	39900
MIXTURE			50	DEC10	34900	51	DEC17	34900	52	DEC24		01	DEC31		02	JAN07	34900
			03	JAN14	34900	04	JAN21	34900	05	JAN28	34900	06	FEB04	34900	07	FEB11	24555
			08	FEB18	19640	09	FEB25	24555	10	MAR04	24555	11	MAR11	24555	12	MAR18	34900
			13	MAR25	34900	14	APR01			APR85	86734		MAY85	109408		JUN85	54308
				JUL85	67611												
000133	MPC	00.00	45	NOV05	55600	46	NOV12	35900	47	NOV19	20940	48	NOV26	39900	49	DEC03	39900
FIN GRAN			50	DEC10	34900	51	DEC17	34900	52	DEC24		01	DEC31		02	JAN07	34900
			03	JAN14	34900	04	JAN21	34900	05	JAN28	34900	06	FEB04	34900	07	FEB11	24555
			08	FEB18	19640	09	FEB25	24555	10	MAR04	24555	11	MAR11	24555	12	MAR18	34900
			13	MAR25	34900	14	APR01			APR85	86734		MAY85	109408		JUN85	54308
				JUL85	67611												
193199	DOZ	2.1	45	NOV05	41075	46	NOV12	24000	47	NOV19	24000	48	NOV26	40000	49	DEC03	40000
26 FILL CAP			50	DEC10	40000	51	DEC17	40000	52	DEC24		01	DEC31		02	JAN07	40000
			03	JAN14	40000	04	JAN21	40000	05	JAN28	40000	06	FEB04	40000	07	FEB11	
			08	FEB18		09	FEB25		10	MAR04		11	MAR11		12	MAR18	40000
			13	MAR25	40000	14	APR01			APR85	120000		MAY85	176000		JUN85	
				JUL85	64000												
193499	DOZ	2.2	45	NOV05		46	NOV12		47	NOV19		48	NOV26		49	DEC03	
8 FILL CAP			50	DEC10		51	DEC17		52	DEC24		01	DEC31		02	JAN07	
			03	JAN14		04	JAN21		05	JAN28		06	FEB04		07	FEB11	27500
			08	FEB18	22000	09	FEB25	27500	10	MAR04		11	MAR11	27500	12	MAR18	
			13	MAR25		14	APR01			APR85			MAY85			JUN85	82500
				JUL85													
*************** DEPT. 60 40 01 04 A/S FOILING																	
4012A	DOZ	4.4	45	NOV05		46	NOV12		47	NOV19	3000	48	NOV26	19200	49	DEC03	16000
36 SHIPPER			50	DEC10		51	DEC17		52	DEC24		01	DEC31		02	JAN07	
			03	JAN14		04	JAN21		05	JAN28		06	FEB04		07	FEB11	
			08	FEB18		09	FEB25		10	MAR04		11	MAR11		12	MAR18	
			13	MAR25		14	APR01			APR85	51200		MAY85	48000		JUN85	
				JUL85	33600												
4012M	DOZ	4.4	45	NOV05	27200	46	NOV12	18500	47	NOV19	4000	48	NOV26		49	DEC03	
36 CPN BOOK			50	DEC10		51	DEC17		52	DEC24		01	DEC31		02	JAN07	
			03	JAN14		04	JAN21		05	JAN28		06	FEB04		07	FEB11	
			08	FEB18		09	FEB25		10	MAR04		11	MAR11		12	MAR18	
			13	MAR25		14	APR01			APR85			MAY85			JUN85	
				JUL85													
4012P	DOZ	4.4	45	NOV05		46	NOV12		47	NOV19		48	NOV26		49	DEC03	
36 CPN OFFER			50	DEC10		51	DEC17		52	DEC24		01	DEC31		02	JAN07	

Figure 10-3. -- Master Production Plan

Another manufacturing plan is the weekly production and manpower schedule (WPMS), which is very detailed and covers a one-week production period. It is computer generated every Friday morning and is distributed to planners (both finished goods and material), and quality assurance, plant, sales/distribution/marketing, and warehouse personnel. Using their knowledge of the products and their lead times, these people examine the detailed plan to identify any potential production surprises (i.e., conditions that may prevent the successful implementation of the production plans). Such problems, when they do occur, are frequently the result of quality assurance or shop floor difficulties. Any such surprises are corrected by issuing an updated schedule (see Control Feedback section). Figure 10-4 is an example of the WPMS, and Figure 10-5 summarizes the process of formulating this plan.

Closely linked to the WPMS is the three-week material requirements review (more commonly referred to as the JIT sheet, Figure 10-6). The JIT sheet is primarily a materials exception report. Distributed every Friday, it reflects information received during the week since the printing of the WPMS. The JIT sheet is reviewed on Friday by the JIT committee, which is made up of quality assurance, production warehousing, and material and production planners.

The JIT sheet is the final check before the plans are released to the shop floor for execution. It is also the way production planning personnel can rank the actions of quality assurance. The JIT sheet identifies those materials that are needed next week for production but that have not yet cleared quality assurance or that have not yet been received. It also identifies the times the various materials are needed by the shop floor. Once the plan has passed through this state, it is turned over to the shop floor for execution.

The formulation of the MPP and the generation of the material plans by the MRP system mark the starting point for the shop floor control system. The production planning system and the shop floor control system have merged.

Shop Floor Control

The current shop floor control system can trace its roots back to the old batch control system first implemented in 1969. The development of this

REPORT CMI002A7
PROGRAM CMF002A7 LVL (060) [redacted]

PAGE 4
WEEK OF 08/06/84
ORIGINAL SCHEDULE

TO: G.E. KNOLL DEPT NO 09 61 400120 DEPT NAME VITAMIN TABLETS

PRODUCT CODE	DESCRIPTION	U/M	LN/ST	:	DAILY SCHEDULED PRODUCTION MON 187	TUE 188	WED 189	THU 190	FRI 191	SAT 192	TOTAL WEEKS PRODUCTION	TOTAL SCHEDULED MFG RUN DATE	QUANITY
258100	MV+M VIT BASE RF	MPC	00.00	1	1,950	1,950	1,950	1,950	1,950		19,500	177-203	68,250
			COMTS				*3						
				2	1,950	1,950	1,950	1,950	1,950				
158100	MV+M FIN VIT BASE RF	MPC	00.00	2	3,900	3,800	3,900	3,900	3,990		19,590	178-205	68,250
258000	MV+M MIN BASE RF	MPC	00.00	1	2,025	2,025	2,025	2,025	2,025		10,125	173-202	70,200
158000	MV+M FIN MIN BASE RF	MPC	00.00	1	2,025	2,025	2,025	2,025	2,025		10,125	175-203	70,200
105800	MIN FIN GRAN RF K	MPC	00.00	1				2,800	2,800		16,800	185-208	67,200
				2	2,800	2,800	2,800		2,800				
			COMTS				*4						
			BAT #					217-220	221-228				

SCHEDULED MANPOWER REQUIRED		MON	TUE	WED	THU	FRI	SAT
	1ST SHIFT	L OH 20	L H 20	L H 20	L H 20	L H 20	L H
	2ND SHIFT	L H 19	L H 19	L H 19	L H 19	L H 19	L H
	3RD SHIFT	L H	L H	L H	L H	L H	L H

SPECIAL INSTRUCTIONS:

1 - MTN645 (MPE - WARNER JENKINS - ORANGE LAKE FILM COAT)
2 - MIN644-3 (MPE - HOFFMAN LAROCHE- CAL PAN) 1 MIX
3 - PENDING RELEASE OF 9159MR (NICACINAMIDE)
4 - PENDING RELEASE OF 9802MR (PREGEL STARCH)
5 - PENDING AVAILABILITY OF MANPOWER

PREPARED BY

W.J. KEYSER

P.I.C PLANNER

APPROVED BY

G.E. KNOLL

PRODUCTION SUPERVISOR

FORM NO. 9981

Figure 10-4. -- Weekly Production and Manpower Schedule

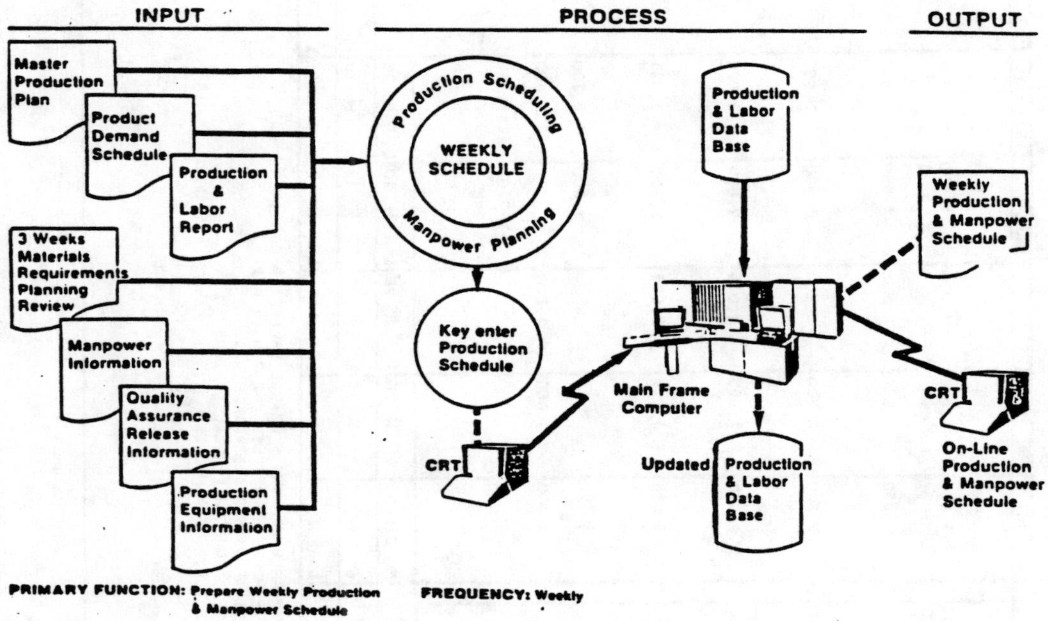

Figure 10-5. -- Weekly Production and Manpower Scheduling

ELKHART PRODUCTION MATERIALS

JIT Committee

0.	DESCRIPTION	VENDOR	P.O.# - LOT #	DATE REQUIRED IN PRODUCTION	UNITS REQUIRED	STATUS	
f May 13							
	Max Form 30 Insert		MD046055	5/16		Awaiting QA release	5
	Max Form 30 IC Carton	Garber	46993JC64	5/16	50,000 pcs	To arrive 5/15/	
	Ferrous Fumarate		MR093055	5/13		Awaiting QA release	5
	Cal Carb 90%		MR071055	5/13		Awaiting QA release	5
	Yellow Film Coat	Colorcon	52064JK64	5/14	805 kg	Due 5/10	
	Lido HCL		MR121045	5/15		Awaiting QA release	4
	Cal Pan		MR003055	5/15		Awaiting QA release	5
	Povidone		MR069055	5/16		Awaiting QA release	5
f May 20							
	Vit A&D_3		MR009055	5/20		Awaiting QA release	5
	B_{12}		MR027055	5/20		Awaiting QA release	5
	Silica Gel		MR088055	5/20		Awaiting QA release	5
	Cupric Sulfate		MR046074	5/21		Awaiting QA release	5
	Startch Pregel		MR094055	5/21		Awaiting QA release	5
	Mag Hydrox		MR092055	5/22		Awaiting QA release	5
	Zinc Sulf	TGD	52083JK64	5/24	850 kg	Due 5/7	

Figure 10-6. -- JIT Sheet

system has been the result of both major periodic enhancements and continuous fine-tuning of these changes. The major enhancements have resulted from two factors:

- o <u>Regular reviews</u>. Every five years, all programs developed and used in CHD are reviewed and revised. Management believes that five years is the average useful life for any system. After this period, most systems are essentially obsolete and must be replaced or undergo major revisions.
- o <u>Changing nature of the business</u>. At CHD, the shop floor control system supports the overall business activities of the division. As these activities change, the shop floor control system must change. Since 1969, the business has become more complex, dynamic, and competitive. These changes have placed a premium on timely and accurate information and tight cost control -- requirements incorporated into subsequent major revisions of the shop floor control system.

The fine-tuning of the system is ongoing and demonstrates the close relationship that exists between the users of the shop floor control system and Management Information Systems data processing. As the users identify their needs, these needs are related to data processing which, in turn, develops the appropriate software. The major concern of the data processing department is to develop software that will be used effectively by people on the floor. The latest fine-tuning of the shop floor control system software occurred in 1983.

Like the other components, the shop floor control system is completely computerized. All transactions are handled in an on-line, real-time environment. All of the information required by the users is available on line and all revisions to the database are done in real time. Miles uses two IBM mainframe computers for all operations.

The current shop floor control system, an integral element of the entire manufacturing planning process, closes the loop between the shop floor with its responsibility for implementing the manufacturing plans and production planning. The shop floor control system provides the planning system with the following information daily, monthly, and yearly for each work center:

- o Job priorities
- o Production quantity reporting for MRP and accounting
- o Order status pertaining to WIP and by batch/lot number control

- o Labor reporting for accounting and work force planning.

Unlike shop floor control systems found in discrete batch manufacturing (job shops) settings, the shop floor control system at CHD delegates a great deal of its decision making to the planning system. This delegation reflects a basic reality of production at Miles -- most of the production uncertainty is encountered at the planning stage, not on the shop floor. The factors frequently requiring decision making on the shop floor (queuing and the need to decide which order to process next) are almost nonexistent in this division.

Responsibility for shop floor control is divided between the planners and the plant foreman. The planners are responsible for ensuring that all production plans passed to the shop floor are feasible, that is, that there is adequate capacity, work force, and material available for the released plans. The plant foremen are responsible for:

- o Achieving the scheduling
- o Requisitioning the necessary materials from stores when needed
- o Reporting on the progress of the orders daily
- o The <u>immediate</u> reporting of any problems that can affect order progress to the planners
- o Returning to the warehouse all unused materials upon completion of the process or the order.

These two groups, through their continuous interaction, bear the major responsibility for the successful operation of the shop floor control system.

<u>The Stages of Shop Floor Control at CHD</u>

The shop floor control system at CHD is based on these important tenets:

- o <u>People, not computers, are crucial to the successful operation of the shop floor control system</u>. At first glance, given the extensive use of the computer, it would seem that the human plays a small role in the operation of the system. This is not the case. The computer-based system, viewed simply as a sophisticated bookkeeping system, simplifies the task of managing information and of updating the appropriate records. It helps in tracking orders and lots for quality assurance. The computer system portrays the production environment at a given point in time. It does not make decisions. Either the planner or foreman is held responsible for identifying problems in advance and for correcting those potential problems, relying on knowledge of the product and its lead times. The shop floor control system is structured to make the greatest use of people.

- Capacity, work force, and material availability are responsibilities of the planning system and not the shop floor control system. There is one rule of shop floor control that is never violated -- no order is to be released to the shop floor unless adequate capacity, work force, and material have been planned and their availability verified.
- Material use must always be tightly monitored and controlled by the shop floor control system. Materials are the single most important cost component encountered during the manufacturing process. In many instances, materials account for over 60 percent of total manufacturing costs. Good control of this component can make the difference between acceptable rates of return and unacceptable rates of return. As a result, the entire shop floor control system focuses heavily on the withdrawal, use, and return of materials.
- The reporting form used by the shop floor control system is consistent with the requirements and forms used by quality assurance. CHD operates in a regulated industry. Quality assurance must be able to track an order by date of manufacture, batch number, and the batch numbers of the material components used. These information requirements are incorporated into the data collection capabilities of the shop floor control system. Lot control is essential.
- All feedback must be done promptly and accurately. CHD deals with very large batches. Problems must be identified quickly; costs must be tracked and controlled closely. These concerns place a heavy premium on timely and accurate feedback from the shop floor.

Order Review/Release

The order review/release activities are concerned with passing on to the shop floor and the foreman orders for which there is adequate capacity, workers, and material available. These feasibility tests are done in the planning system. The availability of capacity and work force is assessed when the order is entered into the MPP. Evaluation of material availability is done on review of a BOM explosion of the WPMS and in the JIT committee.

Packaging materials are received one week in advance of their need while chemical raw materials are received two weeks in advance. These materials must clear quality assurance and be available for use on the Monday of the week in which they are needed. Providing this assurance is the major responsibility of the JIT committee.

Once successfully passed through the MPP, WPMS, and the JIT committee, the order can be released to the shop floor. Planning has guaranteed the foremen that they will have the necessary capacity, workers, and materials required to complete the order. Starting on Friday, the foremen can withdraw material and begin processing the order. All authorizations for material withdrawal and all routings are contained in the computer system. There is no need for a traveler to accompany the order.

Detailed Assignment

The detailed assignment activities of shop floor control are concerned with:

- o Scheduling of orders for the floor
- o Control and coordination of the activities of quality assurance
- o Preventive maintenance.

These activities are achieved without dispatching and are executed primarily during the planning phase and not on the shop floor.

The scheduling of orders is first done in the MPP and more detailed scheduling is done during the formulation of the WPMS. At this time, the exact sequence in which the orders are to be released to the floor for processing is determined by the planners and reflects such considerations as:

- o Work force affected by the order sequence
- o Need for the specific finished goods
- o Back-order status.

The JIT committee controls the actions of quality assurance, which is made aware of those materials it must release for the upcoming week and the exact order in which these materials are needed. Once the order is released to the shop floor, it is given an order due date. All orders are sequenced by earliest due date. The plant foremen are responsible for meeting all order due dates and have previously signed off on the WPMS. Therefore, they have committed themselves to achieve the schedule.

Preventive maintenance is not formally dispatched at CHD. Instead, most preventive maintenance and changeovers are done on off-shifts and are scheduled by production.

Data Collection/Monitoring

Data collection/monitoring is one of the most important shop floor control activities carried out by shop foremen at CHD. The collected information forms the basis on which problems are identified and performance evaluated, and ensures the continuous validity of both the database and the entire planning system.

Daily, each shop foreman records:

- o The orders being processed (by batch/lot number control)
- o The total number of units produced by shift
- o The total number of units rejected by shift
- o The total number of hours worked
- o The reasons for any problems encountered on the shop floor.

This information, entered by each foreman into one of the thirty-five terminals located on all plant floors or in the warehouses, makes up the production and labor report, which is updated daily. At the end of each day, a batch job is run and reports for the various departments produced. All information entered into the database by the foreman is reviewed by cost accounting and the finished goods planners. Any input errors identified by these two groups are corrected quickly so the level of data accuracy in the CHD is high. For example, in 1983, data accuracy by part and by location was 99.98 percent.

Data accuracy is critical to both the shop floor control system and the entire manufacturing planning system. The CHD operates in a highly regulated industry characterized by high quality standards and the requirement for extensive, accurate, and complete documentation. Furthermore, high data accuracy is also required by the CHD's reliance on a common corporate database, which integrates quality assurance, cost accounting, materials management, purchasing, marketing, manufacturing, and distribution.

Control/Feedback

The identification of out-of-control orders depends on a joint review by the plant foremen and production planners. Typically, these orders are behind schedule or are experiencing production problems such as machine breakdown or product problems. Once an out-of-control order has been identified, the conditions underlying it must be solved immediately. Controlling such orders is the responsibility of the foremen and the finished goods planners. Out-of-control orders are brought back under control by working overtime, running extra shifts, or working on weekends. The MPP is updated by correcting a major shop floor problem.

An important feature of the control/feedback activities is the total absence of expediters. Expediters are not used because the weekly WPMS serves this function. To management, expediters treat shop floor symptoms, not the causes of shop floor problems.

Nearly all of the control/feedback activities center on one critical report -- the production and labor report, which relates the amount of production and labor for each production department by scheduling code daily and cumulatively. In addition, it also compares actual-to-scheduled production and actual-to-standard labor. The labor is calculated in hours and dollars. A daily and month-to-date efficiency performance factor and scheduled completion percentage are calculated on the production and labor report to analyze operating effectiveness and related quality assurance information. At the end of every month, a month-end and year-to-date production and labor report (Figure 10-7) is generated from the daily reports reflecting the same information. The process by which this report is formulated is diagrammed in Figure 10-8.

The production and labor report, distributed to cost accounting, production and inventory control, manufacturing, and industrial engineering, focuses attention on cost control, performance to schedule, lot traceability, work force, quality, and effective use of material and capacity. The report enables everyone to follow the progress of orders on the shop floor and to identify problem orders. It links the shop floor to the rest of the organization and highlights the performance of operations. Because the report emphasizes variances (both positive and negative) daily, foremen can assess their operating performance. Using information contained in the production and labor report, any user can further query the database to identify the conditions surrounding the negative variances generated for a specific schedule.

DEPT: ALKA–SELTZER
PACKAGING

DATE: 01/23

PRODUCTION AND DIRECT LABOR REPORT

DEPT	S	DAY	CODE NUMBER	PROD/DESC	U/M	DIR/HRS	SCHED/PD	ACTUAL/PD	CPL%	STD $	ACT $	$ VAR	DAILY EFF
400102	1	007	4007D	A/S 8 O/S	DOZ	39.00	7,600	7,126	93.8	213.78	228.97	15.19–	93.4
400102	1	008	4007D	A/S 8 O/S	DOZ	39.00	7,600	4,850	63.8	145.50	228.97	83.47–	63.5
400102	1	009	4007D	A/S 8 O/S	DOZ	39.00	7,600	7,638	100.5	229.14	228.97	.17	100.1
400102	1	010	4007D	A/S 8 O/S	DOZ	39.00	7,600	7,648	100.6	229.44	228.97	.47	100.2
400102	1	011	4007D	A/S 8 O/S	DOZ	30.20	7,600	7,544	99.3	226.32	228.97	2.65–	98.8
400102	1	013	4007D	A/S 8 O/S	DOZ	39.00	7,600	8,261	108.7	247.83	228.97	18.86	108.2
400102	1	014	4007D	A/S 8 O/S	DOZ	39.00	7,600	8,547	112.5	256.41	228.97	27.44	112.0
400102	1	015	4007D	A/S 8 O/S	DOZ	39.00	7,600	8,097	106.5	242.91	228.97	13.94	106.1
400102	1	016	4007D	A/S 8 O/S	DOZ	39.00	7,600	7,890	103.8	236.70	228.97	7.73	103.4
400102	1	017	4007D	A/S 8 O/S	DOZ	39.00	7,600	5,506	72.4	165.18	177.30	12.12–	93.2
Totals						DIR/HRS	SCHED/PD	ACTUAL/PD	CPL%	STD $	ACT$	$VAR	MTD/EFF
						381.20	76,000	73,107	96.2	2,193	2,238	44.82–	98.0
								BAL/DUE					
								2,893					

Figure 10-7. -- Production and Direct Labor Report

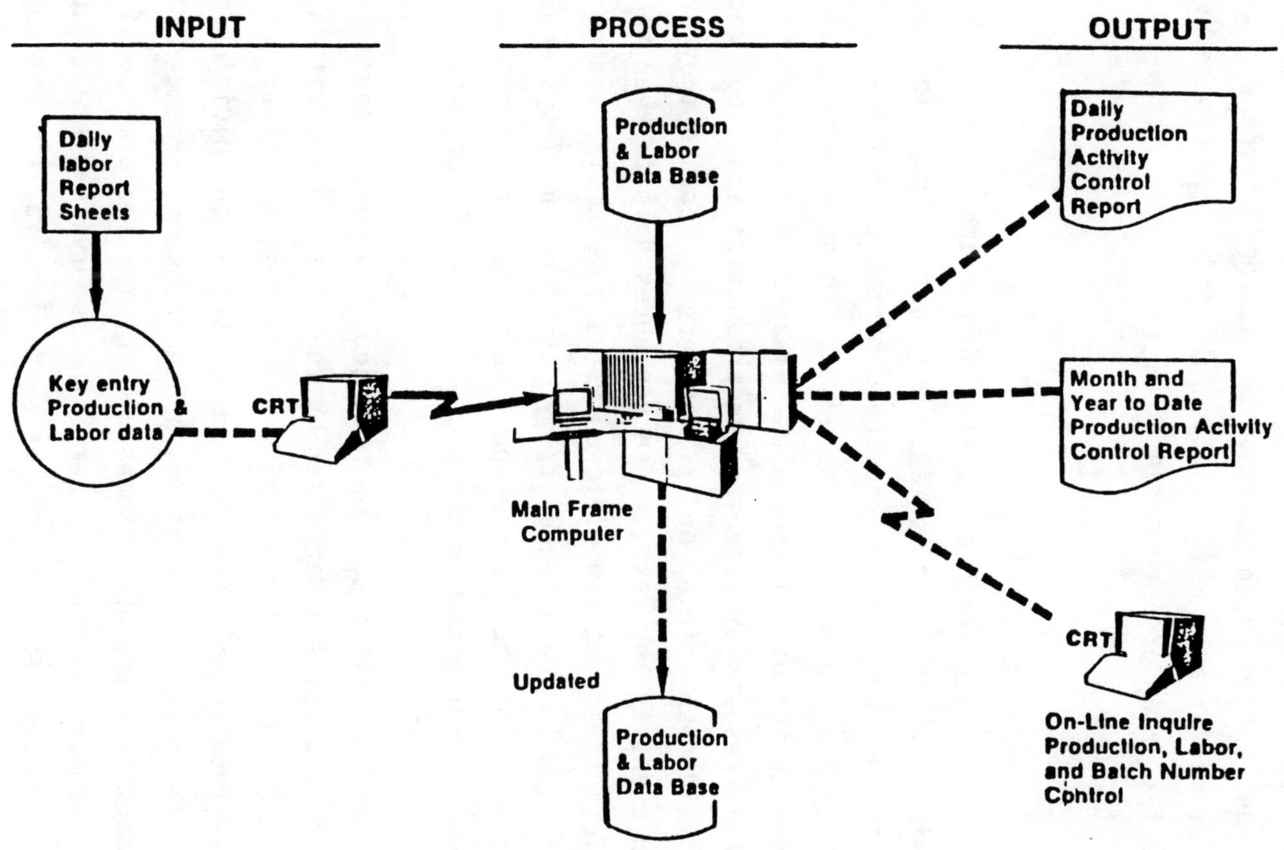

Figure 10-8. -- Production Activity Control Reporting

Order Disposition

Because the progress of the order has been tracked and reported by the shop floor control system, the process of closing out the shop order is simple. When the order is completed, it is closed out to the warehouse. The open order is reduced by the amount completed, and the finished goods planners are notified of the order's availability. Any material requisitioned for the order but not used must now be returned to the warehouse (otherwise a negative variance may result). The order can now be evaluated in terms of actual-to-standard performance.

Performance Evaluation/Feedback

Performance evaluation/feedback is straightforward, timely, and always reflects the basis on which CHD competes. This set of shop floor control activities affects the shop foremen and the department managers. The shop foremen, since they have approved the schedule, are held responsible for the successful implementation of all schedules released to them and are evaluated using the daily results provided by the production and labor report. The foremen are held responsible for all variances. Because they are stated in terms of both quantity and cost, these variances help to keep the foremen aware of the relationship between efficiency (as an example) and cost.

Because the reports are produced daily, the foremen always know how they are performing. They have ample opportunity to correct problems before their performance, as reflected in the production and labor report, deteriorates further.

All the foremen know that to do a good job they must produce each batch on time within the quality standards set by the division and within the capacity, material, and work force limits represented by the production standards. These requirements are the same ones that the division must achieve if it is to compete successfully in the consumer products market.

The department managers are responsible for the performance of all work centers and the foremen assigned to them. The supervisors are evaluated using the production and labor report, as summarized for the entire department. The performance of the managers is measured by the reported variance, and the managers tend to monitor the performance of all operations under their control. CHD has ensured that these two management groups work together closely to implement the plans released to them.

Evaluating CHD's Shop Floor Control System -- Benefits

Because the shop floor control system is an integral element of the overall production planning system, it is difficult to identify those benefits attributable to the shop floor control system alone. As part of the current production planning system, however, shop floor control has contributed to the following qualitative and quantitative improvements:

- Rapid and timely identification of operation problems. In CHD, production problems can become serious very quickly. Production runs are large in quantity but short in time (taking less than a week to complete), and problems can be costly. The current system has given management good control over the manufacturing process by providing rapid and timely information from the shop floor. When a problem does occur, it quickly becomes visible to management. Management knows what the problem is, what the options are, and how to correct the problem. Thus, production is rarely stopped.
- Better material control. Effective material control is important to CHD management because it accounts for approximately 65 percent of the total manufacturing costs. Problems in material use can affect cost and operating profits adversely. Since the introduction of the shop floor control system and the production planning system, material control has been improved. Management is always aware of how material is being used on the shop floor. For example, in 1983, total material adjustment was about .00561 percent of total use (Figure 10-9).
- Improved inventory turns. Another indication of material control is an increase in inventory turns, which indicates that the production system can support growing sales with an inventory base that has grown less than sales. As indicated in Figure 10-10, inventory turns have more than doubled since 1974 (from 4.3 in 1974 to 9.1 in 1983).
- Improved customer service levels. Since the introduction of the system, consumer service has improved. Currently, 95 percent of all products are shipped within forty-eight hours. Consolidation shipments are done within seventy-two hours.
- Improved cooperation. Another benefit of the system has been the development of better and closer relationships between the shop floor and other functional groups (specifically quality assurance and cost accounting). In the case of quality assurance, the

Production Materials
Physical Inventory Control

Material Usage	**$35,600,000**
Total Inventory Adjustment	**$2,000**
Percent of Usage	**.00561%**

Figure 10-9.

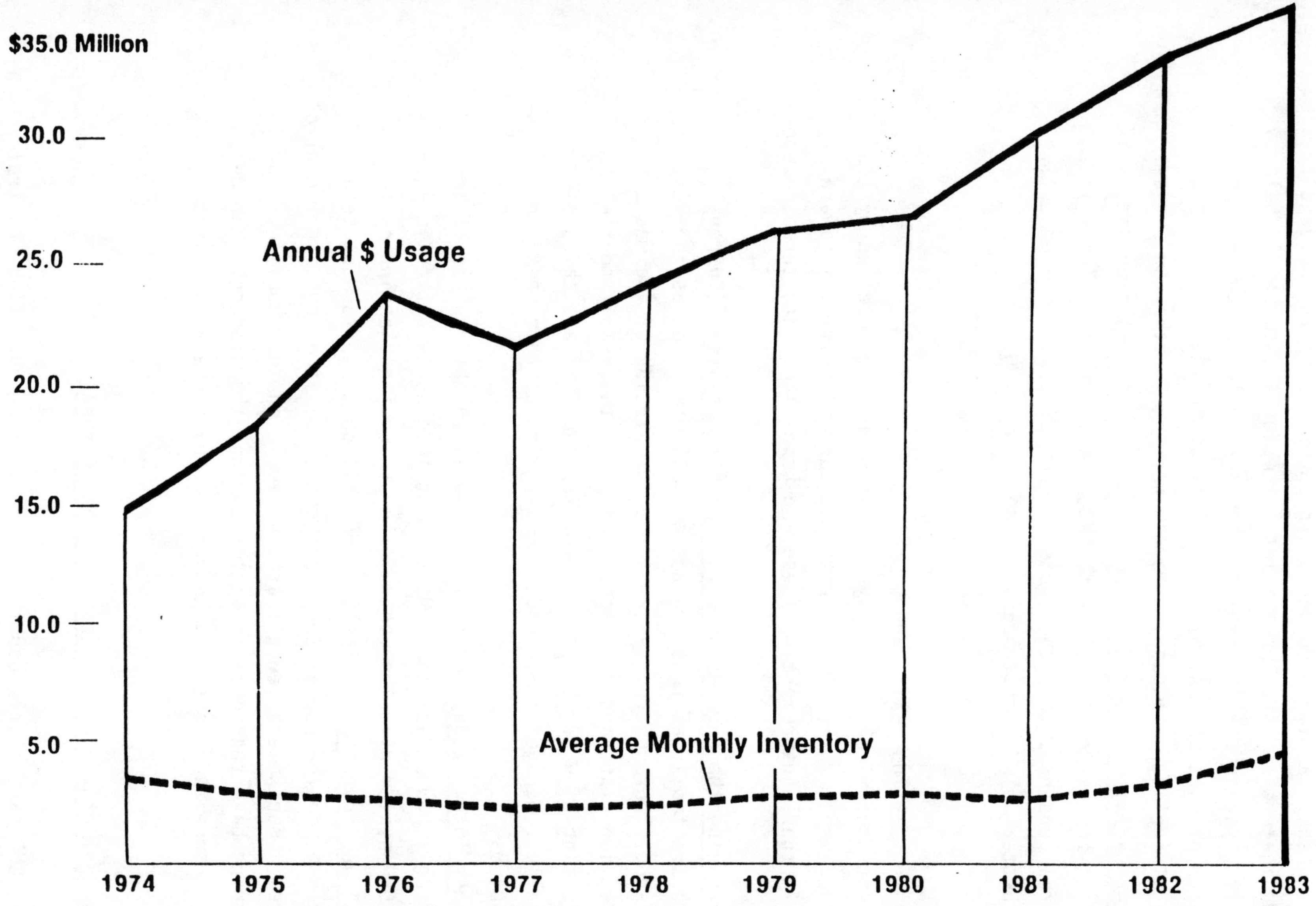

Annual $ Usage	15.0	18.7	24.2	22.1	24.7	26.9	27.5	30.9	35.3	35.6
Average $ Monthly Inventory	3.7	3.1	2.8	2.4	2.7	3.1	3.2	3.0	3.2	3.9
Turnover Rates	4.3	6.1	8.6	9.1	9.3	8.8	8.6	10.4	11.0	9.1

Turnover Goal 1984 — 10.0

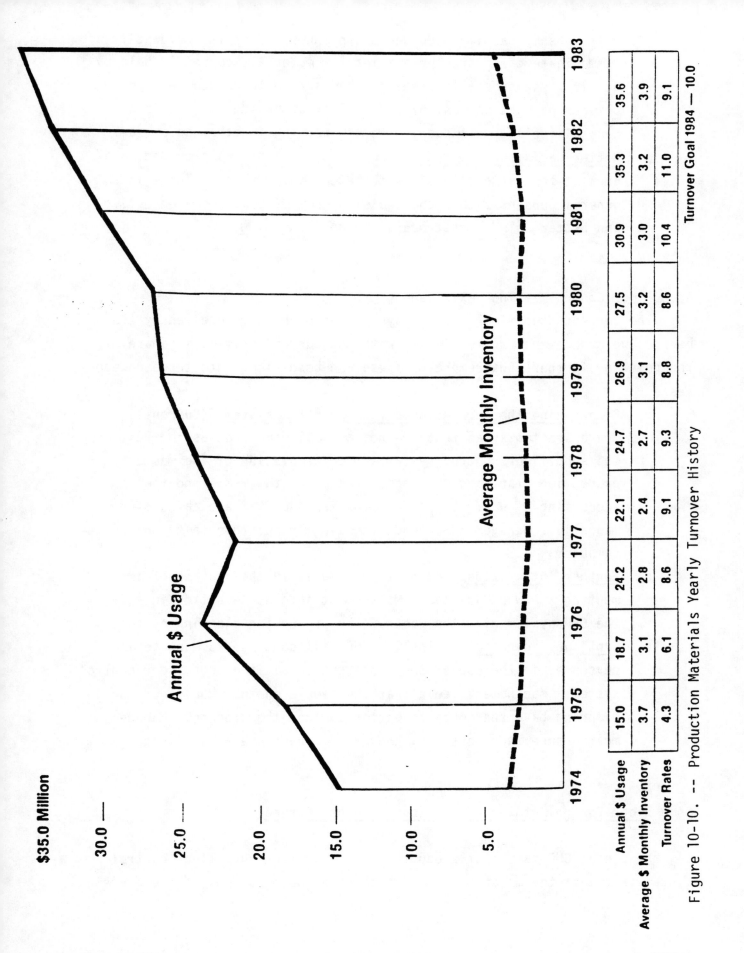

Figure 10-10. -- Production Materials Yearly Turnover History

relationship has improved because planners are able to identify and communicate their true priorities for materials currently held by quality assurance. This ability has served to reduce tension between production control and quality assurance. There is a general feeling that people are now working together as a team.

- Better decisions are made. Shop floor control has provided managers at the various levels with better information. There is a general consensus that the decisions now made are more effective and better able to meet operating goals.

Shop Floor Control -- The Next Stage

The current shop floor control system has been well received by the users, and management, while pleased with the current system, is aware of the need for further enhancements. These can be divided into three categories:

- Fine-tuning the current shop floor control system. Currently, there are two areas that are not as well developed as the rest of the shop floor control system: the formulation of the master production plan (and its associated plan, the WPMS) and the accounting of WIP. Currently, the MPP and WPMS are calculated manually. Management intends to have more of this task done by the computer.
- Further integration. At present, CHD is in the process of implementing a new DRP system. Management intends to better integrate the DRP system with the rest of the production planning system.
- Continued education. Finally, CHD will continue to educate its personnel in the use of the tools present in the shop floor control system. Management feels that the people on the shop floor and in planning have the tools to better control the process. Management must ensure that personnel know how to best use these tools.

Shop Floor Control at the CHD: Lessons to be Learned

People at CHD have little doubt that the current shop floor control system is one of the major reasons for the continued success of the division in a competitive and dynamic market. The features of the system responsible for this success are:

- <u>Acknowledgment that people are essential to a successful shop floor control system</u>. The shop floor control system has been designed to make the most efficient use of a critical resource -- a person's knowledge of the various intricacies of the system. The current system is extensively computerized with many of the mundane bookkeeping transactions taken over by the system. The system tracks and collects information that is then made available to the user. The user can evaluate the availability of resources, assess the feasibility of releasing a given order to the shop floor, identify when an order is going out of control, and determine what corrective actions to take. As is evident from the discussion of the MPP and the WPMS, it is the person that gives the entire system the flexibility required by CHD to compete effectively in its volatile market.
- <u>A shop floor control system that is simple to use and understand</u>. The system, while complex in computer structure, has been designed to be simple to use and understand. The system has a distinct formal structure, which is time phased. For example, every Friday, the JIT committee meets to decide how to handle those orders that have not yet cleared quality assurance or receiving. The foremen know what order they are responsible for and when these orders are to be completed.

  Each user is given access to the information needed. The data are presented in a form that the user can quickly use and understand. For example, the JIT sheet shows the users what materials are needed next week and have not been released by quality assurance.

  Finally, each user is evaluated on the basis of a small number of well-defined, clearly understood, and meaningful performance criteria. For the shop foremen and department managers, these criteria are contained in the production labor report. The measures reflect the basis on which CHD competes (cost, quality, on-time delivery). There is no confusion over what each person has to do well to be successful.

- <u>User efficiency emphasized, not data processing efficiency</u>. The software used in CHD's shop floor control system has been designed to encourage its use by people on the shop floor. The software has been developed with extensive interaction between the users and the data processing department. Often, data processing efficiency has suffered, but this tradeoff has been accepted by both management and data processing. The goal of any software system is to support the user, not data processing.
- <u>The planning system always ensures the presence of adequate material and capacity availability</u>. At CHD, the shop floor control system is responsible for implementing and executing plans released to it by the planning system. The shop floor control system can do so only by drawing on resources available to it. If the system does not have adequate capacity or material, then it cannot be expected to carry out the plans. At every stage in the planning process (i.e., at the formulation of the annual production plan, MPS, and WPMS), an explicit evaluation of the capacity and material availability is made.
- <u>The presence of a common database</u>. One of the key features of the shop floor control system at CHD and a strength of the entire production planning system is the common database. There is only one set of files, and it is centrally located, always accurate, and readily accessible. The database contains all of the information, financial and operating, needed to manage the firm. Such a database greatly simplifies the operation of the shop floor control system as well as improving its reaction speed. All of the information gathered by the shop floor control system immediately becomes available to the rest of the firm. Accounting, for example, can quickly assess the state of operations on the shop floor. The common database strengthens the ties that bind shop floor control to the rest of the firm.
- <u>Rapid, accurate, and timely feedback always provided</u>. The final lesson that can be learned from studying shop floor control at CHD is the importance of timely and accurate feedback. This feedback is bidirectional -- from the shop floor to planning and back. By providing such information problems can be identified and corrected quickly. This information increases the visibility of performance on the shop floor. Feedback not only provides raw data, it also

acts as a motivational force to encourage shop floor personnel to be in line with their planned objectives.

Shop floor control at CHD plays an important role in the continued success of this business unit. It is an integral and effective component of the total production planning system because it was designed to be so.

General Nature of the Firm

The Consolidated Diesel Company (CDC) of Whitakers, North Carolina, manufacturers diesel engines in the 45- to 250-horsepower range. These engines are designed for automotive applications, off-road use (i.e., in construction and agriculture), marine applications, and stationary power. Currently, the product lines consist of two families of engines. Family I is intended for low-horsepower applications and consists of four- and six-cylinder engines. Family II is designed for high-horsepower applications and consists of only one product line, the Big Six cylinder engine. CDC plans to add a three-cylinder engine to the product lines in the future. With the exception of the three-cylinder engine, all engines are available in naturally aspirated, turbocharged, and turbocharged aftercooled models. Of these three types of diesel engines, the four-cylinder engines are the most important product for CDC, accounting for 70 percent of all production. The six-cylinder accounts for 27 percent of the production, and the Big Six cylinder engine accounts for 3 percent. CDC is mainly an ATO operation, although the options that make up the various applications are frequently not stockable. For example, producing a turbocharged engine is not simply a matter of putting a turbo on the engine. It also requires different pistons, rings, fuel pump, and so on. CDC offers over 900 different options. At present, all of CDC's output is consumed by two firms, the Cummins Engine Company and J. I. Case Tractor.

Located outside of Whitakers (approximately 50 miles from Raleigh), CDC's production facilities consist of a 1.1 million-square-foot factory. This plant, opened in 1983, has sufficient capacity to meet CDC's anticipated needs into the early 1990s.

CDC is a newcomer in its market, having produced its first diesel engine July 1, 1983. CDC's competitors in the low-horsepower diesel market include well-known and well-established names like Mercedes, Perkins, Isuzu, Caterpillar, John Deere, and General Motors. There is a surplus of productive capacity among these companyies and a tendency for some of the major customers to be their own suppliers. For example, General Motors, a major consumer of such diesels, is also a supplier. While customer requirements vary (from the need for high-volume, low-cost, high-quality standard diesels to low-volume diesels fitted with various options), it is generally agreed that success in this market depends on the ability of the firm to:

- <u>Maintain and control costs</u>. For most customers, the diesel engine is one of the most expensive components. Because the products using the components (e.g., tractors) are sold to other industrial users, the manufacturer is under pressure to keep costs under control. There may not be an opportunity to pass higher costs on to customers. In the case of those customers who are their own suppliers, lower cost becomes a major argument used to win contracts. Firms like CDC must be able to supply the same engine produced by the customer at a lower cost. In some cases, the cost differential must be significant.
- <u>Deliver a quality product</u>. Diesel engines are expected to stand up to the demands placed on them in the field. Failure in the field is expensive. Not only must the engine be repaired, but the downtime that results from the engine breakdown may also be expensive. A diesel that has a reputation for unreliability will not be purchased. Finally, CDC must compete with firms that have well-established reputations for quality and durability.
- <u>Design and deliver fuel-efficient engines</u>. In a market where fuel efficiency is a key consideration for the buyer, the attractiveness of any diesel engine is influenced greatly by its full efficiency.
- <u>Deliver its products on time</u>. The diesel engines produced by CDC are used as components in trucks and tractors. Failure to deliver on time can delay the completion of these trucks and result in the build up of very expensive WIP.
- <u>Reduce lead time</u>. Not only must a firm deliver on time, it must also try to reduce its lead time to the customer. Reduced lead time helps to decrease costs and increase flexibility. It also helps to differentiate a supplier from its competitors.
- <u>Provide rapid option flexibility</u>. For some customers, the exact configuration of the engine is not known until very shortly before they need the engine. As a result, such customers require that their suppliers be able to accommodate different production configurations in a short lead time (sometimes as short as a week or less).

To compete in this market and to compensate for its late entry, CDC management sees that success relies on its ability to carry out the above factors better than everyone else. To do so, CDC developed a firm that is unique in both its market and the industry as a whole. CDC is:

- A joint partnership between two major firms in the diesel industry
- Organized into teams that are responsible not only for managing the manufacturing process but also for controlling nonmanufacturing areas (e.g., budgets)
- Committed to CIM on the shop floor
- Committed to the development of a JIT manufacturing system.

Of these four factors, the last three are elements that management hopes to use in its attempt to capture market share in a highly competitive and overcapacitated industry.

These four factors influence nearly every aspect of CDC corporate life. They have a significant effect on the structuring, development, and operation of the shop floor control system.

Consolidated Diesel -- A Corporate History

CDC is a partnership between the Cummins Engine Company and J. I. Case Tractor, with each owning 50 percent of the business. Cummins, a publicly held company, is the managing partner and directs overall operations at CDC. The vice president for international business at Cummins is also responsible for CDC. J. I. Case is privately held by the Tenneco Corporation.

CDC is the result of two parties with distinct and important needs that neither had the resources to meet alone. In 1976, Cummins engineers designed a low-horsepower diesel engine. Cummins is a leader in the high-horsepower diesel segment of the market (with 50 to 60 percent of the market), but it offered no products in the low-horsepower end of the spectrum. By producing such an engine, management felt that Cummins' market position would be improved because it could offer its customers a complete product line. Cummins did have enough capital available at the time to build the facilities and tooling needed for engine production, and Case needed a new tractor engine for equipment that it produced for the agricultural and construction industries. So in 1979, Cummins and Case formed an equal partnership. A facility was constructed on a site already owned by Cummins. The Whitakers site, at that time, consisted of a renovated 250,000-square-foot plant that had been converted from an old textile mill. A new, modern plant opened on this site in 1983.

From the outset, the partnership had intended CDC to be the only plant it would own (but the engine design could be produced by other plants owned by Cummins or other partnerships). CDC is a manufacturing concern only and does not have engineering or marketing departments. These services are provided by other partners.

Case and Cummins are CDC's only customers, with allocations for product divided equally. Case uses its allocation for installation in its products (primarily tractors) whereas Cummins sells its units to a worldwide market that includes automotive OEMs, private fleets, stationary power companies, and other tractor companies. Currently, Case's demand for engines is well defined while Cummins is trying to develop a market share for its products.

The total yearly volumes have been set by contract between the two partners as have the processes to negotiate transfer of allocation. The partners must always provide CDC with a yearly forecast of needs each month. Within this twelve-month forecast, the first three months are frozen by volume (and mix by type of cylinder). By contract, there must be firm planned orders for the first five weeks. The contract provides for a predictable demand on CDC's output rate.

CDC's responsibility to its owners is straightforward -- to produce diesel engines of the highest quality on time and cost efficiently. CDC is relying on its unique organizational structure, its highly efficient manufacturing process, and its commitment to JIT manufacturing.

Organizational Structure

Like other aspects of CDC, the organizational structure is unique. From the outset, the intent of this structure was to encourage overall flexibility while ensuring the presence of good integration and coordination between CDC and its two customer/owners. These objectives were achieved by a four-level structure. At the first level is the partnership committee, which is the general overall governing body of CDC consisting of three vice presidents from Case and three vice presidents from Cummins. Cummins has been designated as the managing partner with one of its vice presidents directly responsible for CDC. The partnership committee reviews CDC's progress and develops the production plan.

Under the partnership committee is the general manager who is responsible for the day-to-day operations at CDC. Under the general manager are the directors. Under the directors are the managers. Finally, under the managers is everyone else. The organizational structure for CDC is summarized in Figure 11-1.

An interesting feature of this last level of the structure is that not only do most of the employees fall into this level, but more importantly, this level spans a large salary range. Unlike many other structures, earnings at CDC do not reflect seniority; they reflect the level of skill acquisitions. The more skills that the employee acquires, the higher that employee's earning. This emphasis on skill acquisition is consistent with management's goal of developing and maintaining a flexible work force.

In addition, the CDC structure is unusual because it has no marketing or engineering departments. There is no need for a marketing function because CDC sells to only Case and Cummins. The engineering function is redundant because all of the product designs are developed by the engineering staff at Cummins.

The Team Concept in Action

Consolidated Diesel is team oriented from the general manager to the employee working on the shop floor. The team manages the various operations. At the top is the company operating team consisting of the general manager and the directors who are responsible for setting the production plan. Activities on the shop floor are managed by various teams. Some teams are involved in manufacturing while other teams manage assembly and test.

Each team consists of twenty-five employees (technicians). Of these technicians, fifteen are involved directly in operations on the shop floor. The success or failure of CDC lies with these teams. Although there are managers who work with these teams, their role is primarily advisory. They provide advice to the team members, but they do not have the authority to implement changes on their own because changes must come through the team.

Each team is responsible for all aspects of business in its area. For example, each team is responsible for:

- <u>On-time performance</u>.
- <u>Inventory accuracy</u>. Each team is responsible for managing its own inventory. It must take the inventory from the receiving dock, record it, and move it to the appropriate location.
- <u>Budget management</u>. Each team is given a budget within which it must work. The budget must be met if the team is to be successful. This requirement has placed an additional burden on management

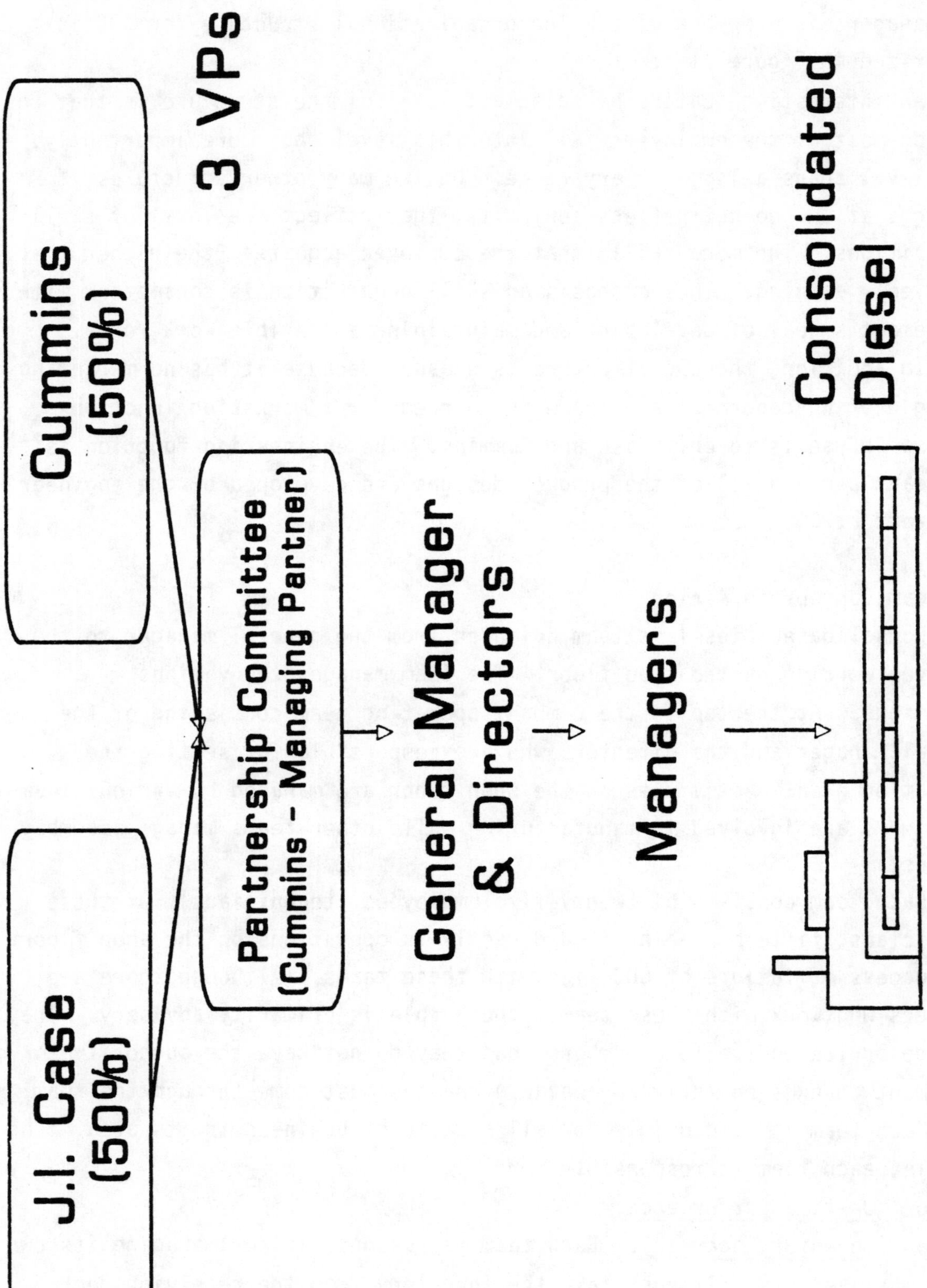

Figure 11-1. -- Organizational Structure

A2C112223 DATA DATE 07/11/85 — CONSOLIDATED DIESEL CO. — 07/11/85 PAGE 1

REQUESTOR ID AGS — INDENTED BILL OF MATERIAL — A174035 — PAGE

OPTIONS- EFFECTIVITY 4 DATE

PARENT ITEM NUMBER	ITEM DESCRIPTION	ITM TYP	ITM CLS	ITEM STAT	UM	ENG REV	MFG REV	DEM CTL	ISS CTL	DSGN SRCE	DWG NUMBER	DWG SIZE
A174035	CONSTRUCTION6BT 59	1	K	2	EA	00	00	1	1			

LEVEL ..:..5....10....15	FIND NO	COMPONENT ITEM NUMBER	ITEM DESCRIPTION	ITM CLS	QTY TYP	QTY	UM	COMP TYP/U	-PCT- CP	-PCT- SC	DEM CTL	ISS CTL	EFFECT	REV LVL	ECO NUMBER
1	COI	AP 9013	DATAPLATE (CASE)	F	1	1	EA	5	00	00	1	1	IN07/02/85	00	C-07015
2	AP	S-2280	SCREW,DRIVE	B	1	2	EA	1	00	00	1	1	IN08/06/84	00	A50065
													OUT06/03/85	01	855-226.
2	AP	3907690	DATAPLATE (J I CASE)	B	1	1	EA	1	00	00	1	1	IN08/06/84	00	A50066
2	111	3900812	SCREW,DRIVE	B	1	2	EA	1	00	00	1	1	IN06/03/85	01	855-226
1	COI	BP 9003	BASE PARTS, NO CONT.	F	1	1	EA	5	00	00	1	1	IN07/02/85	00	C-07015
1	COI	BP 9702	COVER,FRONT GEAR	F	1	1	EA	5	00	00	1	1	IN07/02/85	00	C-07015
2	104	3900629	SCREW,HEXAGON HEAD (FLG)	B	1	16	EA	1	00	00	1	1	IN04/01/83	00	825-351
2	104	3900633	SCREW,HEXAGON HEAD (FLG)	B	1	11	EA	1	00	00	1	1	IN04/01/83	00	825-351
2	104	3902364	GASKET,GR HSG(OBS AC50093	B	1	1	EA	1	00	00	1	1	IN04/01/83	00	825-351
													OUT01/02/85	08	AC50093
2	104	3902369	GASKET,GEAR COVER (OBS)	B	1	1	EA	1	00	00	1	1	IN04/01/83	00	825-351
													OUT05/18/83	02	835-104
2	104	3902830	SCREW,ROUND HEAD CAP	B	1	2	EA	1	00	00	1	1	IN04/01/83	00	825-351
													OUT02/14/86	09	855-215
2	104	3903276	HOUSING,GEAR (OBS 835-460	B	1	1	EA	1	00	00	1	1	IN04/01/83	00	825-351
													OUT10/24/83	06	835-460
2	104	3903463	CAP,FRONT COVER	B	1	1	EA	1	00	00	1	1	IN04/01/83	00	825-351
2	104	3903475	SEAL,RECTANGULAR RING	B	1	1	EA	1	00	00	1	1	IN04/01/83	00	825-351
2	104	3903653	COVER,GEAR ASSEMBLY	B	1	1	EA	5	00	00	1	1	IN04/01/83	00	825-351
3	104	3900709	SEAL,OIL	B	1	1	EA	1	00	00	1	1	IN10/29/82	00	825-288
3	104	3903794	COVER,GEAR	B	1	1	EA	1	00	00	1	1	IN10/29/82	00	825-288
2	104	3903923	HOUSING,TIMING(OBS835-226	B	1	1	EA	1	00	00	1	1	IN04/01/83	00	825-351
													OUT04/01/83	01	825-384
2	104	3903924	PIN,TIMING	B	1	1	EA	1	00	00	1	1	IN04/01/83	00	825-351
													OUT04/01/83	01	825-384
2	104	3903925	RING,INTERNAL RETAINING	B	1	1	EA	1	00	00	1	1	IN04/01/83	00	825-351
													OUT04/01/83	01	825-384
2	104	3903926	GASKET,CAP (OBS 835-406)	B	1	1	EA	1	00	00	1	1	IN04/01/83	00	825-351
													OUT11/02/83	05	835-406
2	104	3903927	SEAL,O RING	B	1	1	EA	1	00	00	1	1	IN04/01/83	00	825-351
													OUT04/01/83	01	825-384
2	104	3904179	HOUSING,TIMING PIN	1	1	1	EA	5	00	00	1	1	IN04/01/83	01	825-384
													OUT03/01/84	04	835-226
3	104	3903923	HOUSING,TIMING(OBS835-226	B	1	1	EA	1	00	00	1	1	IN04/01/83	00	825-384
3	104	3903924	PIN,TIMING	B	1	1	EA	1	00	00	1	1	IN04/01/83	00	825-384
3	104	3903925	RING,INTERNAL RETAINING	B	1	1	EA	1	00	00	1	1	IN04/01/83	00	825-384
3	104	3903927	SEAL,O RING	B	1	1	EA	1	00	00	1	1	IN04/01/83	00	825-384
2	104	3904492	GASKET,GEAR COVER	B	1	1	EA	1	00	00	1	1	IN05/18/83	02	835-104
													OUT06/01/83	03	AC50015
2	104	3904961	HOUSING,TIMING PIN (ASSY)	1	1	1	EA	5	00	00	1	1	IN03/01/84	04	835-226
													OUT03/12/84	07	835-511

Figure 11-2. -- Bill of Material

because it had to teach the technicians about finance and budget management.

- o <u>Variance analysis</u>. Any variances that arise in the team areas must be justified by the team.
- o <u>Attendance goals</u>.
- o <u>Number of rejects attributable to the team</u>.
- o <u>Line balancing</u>.
- o <u>Factor analysis</u>. Factor analysis, a continuous evaluation of the processes and tasks taking place in each team area, is done to identify more efficient or effective methods.
- o <u>Group discipline</u>. Each team is evaluated on the performance of the group as a whole. As a result, the members must manage discipline within the team. This task entails identifying problem workers and structuring appropriate corrective actions. Under some conditions, the team is responsible for terminating problem workers.

This approach to operations management on the shop floor has been chosen because management feels that the shop employees are best able to control the shop floor. They know what is going on from moment to moment and can recognize problems as they occur.

<u>The Production Process</u>

The key characteristics of the production process that significantly affect the shop floor control system are:

- o Extensive commonality in engines/high option flexibility
- o Continuous low-batch production
- o Limited storage.

The design of the diesel engine manufactured at CDC is relatively simple, and there is a high degree of commonality among the three major engine types manufactured. The only real difference in components between a four- or six-cylinder diesel engine is length. The Family II diesel engine is a stand-alone unit that shares a number of the same components with other models. The four-cylinder engine uses some 500 purchased parts, and the small six engines require only an additional fifteen parts.

The major complicating factor is the number of options. While Case tractors have only forty-five applications for this engine, Cummins sells to a world of application needs. To develop a strong foothold in the marketplace,

Cummins has been pressured from prospective customers to increase the amount of option flexibility.

Each increment of horsepower requires different options, each different transmission requires a different flywheel housing and flywheel, and each frame needs a different oil pan. Many of the options involve different fuel pumps. This is an expensive option because fuel pumps must be purchased from an overseas supplier.

Such flexibility can complicate the planning production process so management has structured the BOM in a modular format. Each option and its associated hardware has its own bill. The end-item bill is compiled and structured only after a customer order is received. The typical BOM at this point is four levels deep (Figure 11-2).

The Production Process Described

From the outset, the production process was designed to be simple. Production at CDC is divided between the manufacturing and the assembly/test (A/T) areas and the four major work centers of test, block, head, and rods. The manufacturing area produces the only three major items manufactured at CDC -- blocks, heads, and connecting rods. All other items are supplied by outside vendors.

In the manufacturing area, production involves large batches. Initially, the average batch size was 2,400 units. This has been dropping steadily to 1,000 units -- a direct result of setup reduction activities.

One major feature of production in the manufacturing area involves line changeover. Presently, it takes one day to change the line over physically; however, because of WIP stored in the line, it takes six to eight days for throughput to change (that is, for the new items to replace the old items within the line and to work themselves through the process). The problem of changeovers affects the block line. There is no problem in the rod line because the same rod is used by every product manufactured at CDC. Changeovers limit the ability of the manufacturing area to accommodate rapids changes in block types needed. It is also this changeover problem that accounts for the need to produce in large batches.

All of the items required for the assembly of the engine are brought together in the A/T area, which drives the entire production process (both planning and execution). All purchasing and manufacturing activities are coordinated to satisfy the activities and needs of the A/T area.

A/T begins with line set. During line set, the engines are set (fixed) on the assembly line. Line set is important because it determines the exact sequence in which the engines are to be assembled. Once set onto the line, the sequence is seldom changed (and then only in case of quality problems or manufacturing emergencies). It is in A/T that the exact configuration for each order is built up. As the order progresses through the various assembly stages, the various options are added to the engine. The production and option information for each engine is communicated by:

- o <u>A CDC engine history data tag</u>. A tag is assigned to each engine that is line set. This tag identifies the engine by a part identification number (PIN). The PIN and MFG (manufacturing) numbers are designed to be machine readable. The PIN identifies each engine uniquely and is used on the shop floor when tracking and reporting. In contrast, the MFG number identifies each part in terms of the customer order to which that part belongs. While the PIN is unique, the MFG number is not. Parts belonging to the same customer order batch have the same MFG number.
- o <u>The computer system</u>. Monitors, placed at various locations along the assembly line in the A/T department, are the links that connect the worker with the computer and its BOM.

A small amount of WIP links the manufacturing and A/T departments. For some items, there is no more than two hours of inventory in this storage area.

CDC was designed so it has no capacity problems in the short term. CDC can manufacture 150,000 engines and 50,000 kits per year (a kit is a matched set of block, heads, and rods). At full capacity, the production process employs some 1,000 technicians. At this level of capacity, management does not expect any capacity constraints until 1992. At that time, it is expected that CDC will be constrained in the machining area (specifically the rod line that has lead time of two years).

Labor is a more immediate concern. At present, CDC employs some 300 technicians. Technicians cannot be added or dropped quickly. Given the high technology environment present and the unique team approach in place, all production people in the plant must go through a seven-month full-time training program. Every new employee must also pass through an intensive selection process before being hired. The total lead time for adding new labor is nine to ten months so effective production planning becomes a necessity. Significant volume changes must be identified at the production planning stage and controlled to prevent unacceptable changes in labor demand levels.

CIM at CDC

From the outset, production was designed with two key considerations in mind:

- o <u>To provide enough capacity for long-term growth</u>. CDC was to have enough capacity so that its growth would not be limited by this factor.
- o <u>To provide a sophisticated and integrated manufacturing process</u>. To produce a diesel engine meeting the criteria previously described in this chapter required the use of the most advanced diesel manufacturing procedures. Furthermore, by providing such procedures, CDC gained an important competitive advantage.

Cummins and Case invested heavily in CIM. Its presence is evident in nearly all production. The engine blocks, for example, are manufactured on a line that, because of extensive computer control, requires a minimum of human intervention when it is operating. The blocks are produced in a straight line flow in a system that has benefited extensively from the use of transfer line technology. In the A/T department, rods are fitted together by a computer-driven system that can distinguish between the long and short rods and that can make extremely fine adjustments in the resulting assemblies.

CIM is also evident in testing activities. Many tests and measures required on the line are so fine and precise that technicians cannot do them consistently and adequately. For example, the degree of accuracy required to inspect the pistons is often beyond the capabilities of technicians working with standard testing procedures. Engines, when completed, are tested on a computerized test bed. The computer monitors various aspects of the engine's performance and identifies those areas that are below standard. By using such procedures, CDC management has been able to reduce the testing time required while increasing the overall quality level of the engines coming off the end of the line.

The entire manufacturing database as well as the flow of information from the shop floor to the database and back are managed through the computer. Order/engine information is recorded using optical character recognition. Computer monitors are positioned at various locations on the assembly line and are used to inform the technicians of the options that go on a specific engine at their workstation.

As a result of the extensive use of CIM in production and testing, the entire manufacturing and assembly process at CDC is considered to be one of the most advanced and integrated in the entire diesel manufacturing industry.

Production Planning at Consolidated Diesel

The production planning process includes many of the components of a manufacturing resource planning system. The primary modules of this system are the production plan, the master schedule, the final assembly schedule, material requirements planning, and shop floor control. The entire production planning system tries to avoid any late shipments. An order, if built early, can always be preshipped. A late order is generally not acceptable.

Production planning and master scheduling. Production planning and master production scheduling are closely related activities. The production plan sets the overall parameters (e.g., plant loading, capacity use, production rates). The master production schedule drives the MRP system and provides the major vehicle for option planning.

Production planning starts with the partnership contract, which establishes the annual production planning volumes for the period 1983 to 1993. Each partner is required to provide CDC with a twelve-month forecast of future cylinder needs (e.g., 400 four cylinders in December, 200 six cylinders in December, and 50 Family II cylinders in December). Every month, these forecasts must be rolled and updated.

The quantities provided by the partners are added together, along with quantities allocated to reliability testing and preproduction (i.e., equipment shakedown and new model introduction). The resulting sum is tested against the contract to assess compliance and to evaluate the degree of variability. The conflicts are identified and resolved by the partnership committee.

Within three months of production, each partner must provide a forecast that is frozen by volume (the partners are allowed to change mix by cylinder levels). Thirty days out, the partners are required to give CDC firm planned orders.

These requirements impose different levels of constraints on the two partners. For Case, the production requirements are met easily because it has a well-developed need that CDC engines satisfy. Case can fix its demand with certainty six months out. Cummins management, on the other hand, is attempting to build market share in a very competitive market. As a result, management is under constant pressure to offer more options and to allow its customers the luxury of delaying placement of orders until the latest possible moment. These factors make it difficult for Cummins to fix its volume requirements three months out and its actual orders thirty days out.

The demands identified and evaluated during production planning are loaded into the master production schedule where planning bills reside. The master production schedule provides a forecast of demand at the option level as well as planning data at the component level.

Requiring the partners to provide a weekly forecast of options three months out aids the master schedule. At two months, a 10 percent change in the option forecast is acceptable but aspiration (which affects carburetor demand) must be locked in. At one month, firm orders must be provided with expected ship dates. These orders must be within 10 percent of the previous month's forecast.

Once a month, the CDC directors and the general manager meet to plan production using the data described in the preceding paragraphs. Any conflicts created by the forecast or the creation of orders that cannot be resolved at the plant level are sent to the partnership committee.

MRP. MRP is used primarily for material and purchasing control. Component planning during the entire process is controlled by the MRP system. CDC uses a regenerative MRP system with a weekly cycle. The output generated by the MRP system is shared with vendors and provides the major coordinating mechanism.

Capacity planning. The lack of any formal capacity planning module is noticeable. CDC currently operates under a condition of excess capacity. In general, all plans are evaluated in terms of their effect on labor capacity use. Management at every level of the planning process is aware of the importance of maintaining level loads on the shop floor.

Final assembly scheduling (FAS). The FAS plays a crucial role in the operation of the planning system because it drives the assembly line in the A/T area. The FAS also marks the transition area between the manufacturing planning system and shop floor control.

FAS development begins with weekly meetings held by the operations groups. At these meetings, the resource managers establish weekly goals for their areas (based on orders contained in the MPS), review the feasibility of these goals in light of material availability, and analyze any quality problems.

The FAS for each day is generated at a daily meeting of the operations group. The sequence of orders to be run (line set) is based on weekly goals plus inputs from the customer service group.

The FAS marks the beginning of the shop floor control system. It is at the FAS stage that management identifies which orders are to be released to the shop floor and in what order. Management also identifies any problem orders (those for which there are not enough parts). These orders are held off the shop floor until the necessary parts become available.

The Move to JIT Manufacturing

CDC is considered a true JIT manufacturer. Everyone works toward the goal of developing a system in which the engines completed at the end of the day are generated by orders received that day. When the production plans for CDC were drawn up, management did not intend to build a JIT facility. In 1979, only a few people in North America were even aware of JIT. CDC was designed to be a continuous, low-batch production system with several significant design features:

- Limited space for WIP on the line and between departments
- The development of a product design offering relatively few options and intended to be built efficiently on an assembly line
- Rapid changeover of lines (especially in the rod areas).

When the plant was designed, these and other features were introduced to maintain consistency with the continuous, low-batch production theme. When management learned about JIT, it noted that many of these features were consistent with the JIT approach. JIT has offered CDC an effective and appropriate method for competing in the marketplace.

To make JIT work at CDC, management has taken a number of different approaches:

- <u>The development and maintenance of a flexible work force</u>. Organizing the shop floor into teams and providing financial rewards for skill acquisition by technicians are measures intended to produce a worker that can work at almost any job on the shop floor.
- <u>Quality control at the source</u>. Every technician is responsible for his or her own quality on the line.

- Continuous review and reevaluation of the production process. Management has instituted the factor control program, which is carried out on company time. The technicians review and analyze actual operations. It is up to the technicians who are most familiar with operations on the shop floor to identify the most efficient methods for carrying out all operations.
- Setup reduction Setups, especially those in the manufacturing area, have been simplified and reduced.

Purchasing has played a significant role in JIT development. Several policies have been introduced to reduce purchasing inventory and lead times while maintaining on-time delivery.

- Working with fewer suppliers. In general, a diesel engine manufacturer deals with over 500 different suppliers. CDC deals with only 100. By reducing the number of suppliers, purchasing feels that it can develop the type of close relationship between buyers and vendors required by JIT manufacturing.
- The supplier quality assurance program. To reduce the problem of faulty vendor-supplied components arriving at CDC, purchasing inspects at the source. Vendors who are able to satisfy quality standards consistently are certified, which eliminates inspection at the source and at CDC. Shipments received from a certified vendor are assumed to be defect free. Over 50 percent of the vendors are certified.
- Reduced demand variability for the vendor. Purchasing attempts to provide its vendors with sufficient stability in orders over time. For example, purchasing will not change any order for the next three months by more than 5 percent and any order for the next four months by more than 10 percent. As a result, when compared to CDC and its customers, the vendors are subject to far less variability in demand.

Much of the current success results from the unique combination of factors present in CDC's environment: a stable demand at the MPS level, worker flexibility, reliable vendors, continuous low-batch production, and adequate capacity. Management noted that JIT does not replace MRP -- instead the two work closely together. MRP provides visibility over future needs, it does not provide adequate detailed scheduling. JIT facilitates effective detailed scheduling, it does not provide the visibility needed by production planners and vendors.

The entire production system can be best described as a system in transition. Management must always work at balancing long-term objectives with the achievement of short-term successes.

Shop Floor Control

The primary responsibility of the shop floor control system is to facilitate the management of activities on the shop floor. This is not a straightforward task because it involves working with a production system with elements of small batch (job shop) manufacturing, repetitive manufacturing, and JIT principles. Management's challenge has been to develop a shop floor control system that will work in this setting by adapting to the changes introduced by these various elements.

The shop floor control system is computerized and used primarily to collect information and communicate it to the users. The manufacturing system is run on two systems -- one for material control and the other for shop floor control. Material control, carried out using a software package purchased from the Comserv Corporation, contains modules including BOMs, material control, purchasing, standard costing, and master production scheduling. This system was implemented as purchased with no modifications. The Comserv package runs on an IBM 4341 mainframe.

The shop floor control system, the Assembly Information Management System (AIMS), was developed to CDC's specifications by Texas Instruments. AIMS resides on a dual host Texas Instruments 990/12 computer. The interface between these two computer systems was written internally. The two packages work closely together on an ongoing basis. The Comserv package provides AIMS with BOM, order detail, and order due date information. AIMS provides the Comserv package with inventory issue information.

These two systems provide CDC with a comprehensive manufacturing system characterized by on-line data collection capabilities. Some data are collected on line automatically while other data are entered manually. All inventory-related transactions and some database records are processed in real time. The balance is deferred for batch processing. Nearly all of the reports are available on a real-time basis. The computer system acts as the primary interface between the technicians on the shop floor and the manufacturing database.

The computer system, like the other components of the manufacturing system, has been designed to support the activities of the technicians on the shop floor. The system provides the users with continuous access to needed information; it also relieves the users of any transaction requiring bookkeeping. The computer system has a limited amount of decision-making capability.

The primary objectives of CDC's shop floor control system are:

- Providing timely feedback for operations personnel
- Tracking orders (even down to the PIN level)
- Presenting information on department status to teams at various levels within the firm
- Facilitating communications both among operating teams and between the shop floor and the planning system
- Providing a basis for factor analysis
- Identifying potential problems on the shop floor.

Organizationally, shop floor control is decentralized. No one person is responsible -- instead, each of the various operations teams is responsible, an approach consistent with the organizational design structure. The teams are aided by three production controllers whose major responsibility is to take physical inventory weekly and to track orders on the shop floor.

The Stages of Shop Floor Control at CDC

Shop floor control at CDC is built on three major manufacturing tenets. These tenets are:

- People are crucial to the effective operation of shop floor control. The production system operation is most effective when the people on the shop floor are given the tools and the authority to correct problems as soon as they occur. As a result, the shop floor control system must support, on an ongoing basis, the activities of the people working on the floor. It must also relieve the shop floor personnel of the responsibility for such time-consuming clerical activities as bookkeeping, data collection and recording, and data reconciliation. The shop floor control system should also flag those events requiring intervention.

- o <u>The shop floor control system must always be consistent with the intent and long-term objectives of management</u>. CDC is in transition. It is moving toward a system characterized by low lead times, high and consistent quality, tightly controlled cost, and the ability to satisfy orders received that day. In the short term, the shop floor control system must help management meet its objective of on-time delivery of quality products to meet customers' needs. These short-term successes cannot come at the expense of long-term objectives.
- o <u>To be truly effective, the shop floor control system must be flexible and responsive</u>. Events can change quickly on the shop floor. The shop floor control system must be able to keep pace with these changes. Problems must be identified and acted on when they occur, and user requests reacted to quickly.

This shop floor control system brings together the elements found in shop floor control systems operating in job shop settings and in repetitive manufacturing environments.

Order Review/Release

Order review/release begins with the generation of the manufacturing order. CDC uses a monthly order horizon that is rolled over into weekly buckets. Each manufacturing order is based on the due date and can be randomly based on customer demand. When an order matures (i.e., reaches its planned release date), a series of checks is begun automatically. The system must first verify that all the material required by the order is present. A key rule of order review/release is that an order is never released or line set unless all of the required parts are available. At this point, the list of released orders is downloaded to AIMS. AIMS is responsible for the final engine assembly schedule, which is based on the order due dates and other considerations, some of which are identified in the daily meeting of assembly and manufacturing managers. The managers discuss such issues as material availability, actual customer needs (identified daily by the customer service group), and quality problems. The meeting is also the vehicle by which A/T managers learn of the status in manufacturing and vice versa, as measured in terms of inventory levels and production (i.e., what is currently being produced on the lines). Management has found that face-to-face communication is more responsive to change and provides more timely information than the corresponding computer reports.

The managers also discuss other constraints on the number of engines line set sequentially that require a specific option that has a long installation time. A final important factor is the need to improve efficiency by grouping engines. While it is possible to line set the engines randomly, the managers attempt to group orders together into minimum assembly batches of ten engines. Using this information, AIMS develops the final engine assembly schedule.

At the same time, the AIMS is downloaded from the IBM computer proliferated parts list for each manufacturing order. This allows the display of option parts at the station where that particular component is installed. This process eliminates the need for a BOM or manufacturing list to travel with each engine.

The implementation of the final engine assembly schedule involves line setting each engine. Each engine is assigned an engine serial number (ESN), used to track the engine through the manufacturing process. This number, recorded on the CDC engine history data tag, is attached directly to the engine. Information such as build dates, notes specific to the engine, and the component parts' serial numbers, is recorded on this tag.

Because of low-capacity use levels, capacity is not a major issue when line setting. Once the engine has been line set and given its ESN, it can proceed.

The order review/release procedure is somewhat different for manufacturing. The block, head, and rod lines are driven completely by the MPS. The routing for each part is a fixed process along the transfer lines and the tooling requirements. As a result, detailed routings are not generated. The major concern, when releasing work to the manufacturing department, is the block line. While the rod and head lines are capable of meeting the assembly needs without downtime for tooling changes, the block line needs one day for the actual changeover and six to eight days for the old work to make its way out of the line. As a result, the block line schedules downtime based on the MPS.

Detailed Assignment

Detailed assignment is relatively straightforward. All orders are given a due date, which is based either directly on the customer order (in the case of engines) or on a derived due date using MRP logic. All dispatching is based on these due dates. The exact order in which engines are processed, however, is determined by the order in which they are line set. Under certain conditions, the sequence established during line setting can be changed. These changes are most often introduced as a result of production problems (i.e., an engine is removed to correct a problem encountered during assembly) or to respond to an urgent customer request for a specific order to be moved up.

Preventive maintenance is ongoing. All technicians working on the shop floor are responsible for doing routine maintenance on their equipment (e.g., oiling, cleanup). Any potential equipment problems are reported and corrected before the machines can break down and cause production disruptions.

Data Collection/Monitoring

Of the major shop floor control activities, data collection/monitoring is the most automated and is managed as an integral element of the AIMS program.

Because the assembly of engines can be done randomly, there may be as many as ten to fifteen different orders on the assembly line in any one lot at any given time. The computer system must be able to track and identify the order to which any given engine might belong. The system also collects data for entry in the engine history database. These data must be collected by serial number for each engine, updated as the engine passes through its various operations. The data collected includes not only material-related information (e.g., serial number of components used), but also related information such as critical torque data on each engine built. These detailed data are used for inventory record keeping. More importantly, the data are used for warranty and quality control purposes.

The computer system also provides for material issue as an engine moves from one team's build station to the next. It tracks engine status as the engine goes from team to team, during major repair, and while it is in test. All data are collected on line and in real time.

The computer system itself is responsible for collecting certain data. This situation occurs when the computer takes over the monitoring function. For example, the computer monitors all critical torques on the engine, including main bearing caps, head bolts, and connecting rod cap screws. While monitoring the torque, the computer system records this information into the database automatically. This arrangement offers several important advantages. First, the possibility of an error in the data recording as the reading is transcribed into the manufacturing database by the technician is reduced. Second, the computer is capable of recording information precisely. Third, the technician is free to do other more productive work.

Other data are manually entered. All inventory-related transactions, as well as some database records, are processed in real time. The balance is deferred for batch processing over night.

The computer system also generates all the reports (Attachment 11-1) used by managers in the system, including:

- Line set sequence list report. The list of current day's engines to build
- Backlog report. List of the current day's scheduled but unbuilt engines
- Engines built. List of engines built on the current day
- Engines skidded. List of engines skidded and ready for delivery in the current day
- Engines scrapped. The list of engines scrapped in the current day
- Line set sequence list dump. A list of the exact order in which the various parts have been line set in A/T.
- Station contents. List of current PIN and pallet numbers at each team's station
- Line set engine location. List of current team, station, and pallet number for each PIN known to the system
- Engine history. Print out of all information stored in engine history record
- Production performance. Number of accepts, rejects, and reject rate for each team's station
- Reject analysis. Top ten reject codes in the order of number of occurrences
- Repair history. List of all repairs performed on a particular engine PIN
- Master display parts list. Print out of the master list display parts.

All except the backlog report are available on a real-time basis.

The critical role played by the computer system in data collection is not accidental. CDC operates in a high-volume, multiple-option environment -- one in which an extensive amount of detailed data are collected and recorded. The computer is necessary for survival. It also offers management a means of freeing shop floor personnel from some of the more mundane data collection and recording activities. It is management's intent to computerize as much of the business as the technology allows. For shop floor control purposes, all records are on the computer database, including the forecast, order entry data, the master schedule, the final assembly schedule, detailed inventory records, and shipping activities.

Some decision-making capabilities are vested in the computer, the most notable being the line set sequence. The computer also aids decision making at the lowest level by providing visual displays at those assembly stations where there is a proliferation of parts. At these work centers, the technicians access the computer by entering the ESN. The computer system brings up the components needed for that specific engine. As a result, the computer system has eliminated the need for a hard-copy BOM to accompany the engine. It has provided a means for the immediate updating of material requirements as modifications are introduced into the manufacturing database.

Monitoring is jointly undertaken by both the computer system and the technicians on the shop floor. Every person working on the assembly line is responsible for his/her own quality control. As a result, technicians are required to monitor all engines passing through their workstations. Engine monitoring is done using:

- o Visual inspection
- o Inspection by fit
- o Inspection using the new engine build standards
- o Inspection using the new engine test standards.

If a problem involving an engine is identified, the technicians are required to take the appropriate corrective actions. They are also required to monitor the status of their equipment and workstations and perform preventive maintenance. In general, the responsibility for quality and monitoring has been placed at the lowest and most appropriate level -- with the technicians on the shop floor.

The machining area has a different set of technology to track its scheduled management and production rate. The block line has a master control system that monitors each machine in the transfer line to determine downtime, production rates, and tool change requirements. In addition, the management in the block line has developed a report (Figure 11-3) to facilitate monitoring. This report, developed to run on Lotus 1-2-3 using an IBM PC, summarizes the status of every machine and production order processed during a given week. Any variances in performance, a strong indicator of a

FILE NAME: DAILY PRODUCTION FOR FAMILY I

MACH NUMBER	BLOCK SIZE (3, 4,) (OR 6)	START TIME OF MACH	TOTAL NUM PARTS RAN	TOTAL NUM SCRAP PARTS	TOTAL NUM DISC PARTS	TOTAL NUM GOOD PARTS	DISCREPANT IN YELLOWBOX 4	6	TOTAL PARTS IN MACH	PARTS AHEAD OF MACH	ACTUAL MACH RUN TIME	MACH STATUS AT DAYSEND	VARIANCES -REASONS THAT MACHINE WILL NOT START THE NEXT MORNING AT 7:00
QUALIF	4		607	0	0	607	0	0	0	0		O.K.	301 DAYS 306 NIGHTS
BROACH	4		660	0	0	660	0	0	0	0		O.K.	338 DAYS 322 NIGHTS
MACH 1	4		649	0	0	649	0	0	0	0		O.K.	350 DAYS 299 NIGHTS
MACH 2	4		611	0	0	611	0	0	0	0		O.K.	310 DAYS 301 NIGHTS
MACH 3	4		587	0	0	587	0	0	0	0		O.K.	275 DAYS 312 NIGHTS
MACH 4	4		560	0	0	560	0	0	31	54		O.K.	250 DAYS 310 NIGHTS
MACH 5	4		578	0	0	578	0	0	19	35		O.K.	268 DAYS 310 NIGHTS
MACH 6	4		547	0	0	547	0	0	11	35		O.K.	265 DAYS 282 NIGHTS
MACH 7	4		467	0	1	466	0	0	35	52		O.K.	219 DAYS 247 NIGHTS
MACH 8	4		425	0	18	408	0	0	25	52		O.K.	193 DAYS 215 NIGHTS
MACH 10	4		375	2	2	371	0	0	0	0		O.K.	169 DAYS 202 NIGHTS

Figure 11-3. -- Monitoring Report

FILE NAME:

DAILY PRODUCTION FOR
FAMILY I

MACH NUMBER	BLOCK SIZE (3, 4,) (OR 6)	START TIME OF MACH	TOTAL NUM PARTS RAN	TOTAL NUM SCRAP PARTS	TOTAL NUM DISC PARTS	TOTAL NUM GOOD PARTS	DISCREPANT IN YELLOWBOX 4	DISCREPANT IN YELLOWBOX 6	TOTAL PARTS IN MACH	PARTS AHEAD OF MACH	ACTUAL MACH RUN TIME	MACH STATUS AT DAYSEND	VARIANCES -REASONS THAT MACHINE WILL NOT START THE NEXT MORNING AT 7:00
MACH 11	4		435	1	1	433	0	0	2	2		O.K.	203 DAYS-INCLUDE 1 REWORK IN TOTL 230 NIGHT-INCLDS 4 REWORK IN TOTL
MACH 12	4		512	0	0	512	0	0	0	0		O.K.	241 DAYS 271 NIGHTS
MACH 13	4		600	0	0	600	0	0	0	0		O.K.	285 DAYS 315 NIGHTS
MACH 14	4		581	0	0	581	0	0	1	6		O.K.	290 DAYS 291 NIGHTS
MACH 16	4		485	32	50	403	0	0	0	0		O.K.	206 DAYS 197 NIGHTS
TOTAL				35	72		0	0			)		SALVAGE REPORT: NO REPORT TURNED IN.

USE THIS SPACE BELOW TO LIST ANY REOCCURRING VARIANCES THERE MIGHT BE:

Figure 11-3. -- Monitoring Report (continued)

TO : DIST-RESOURCE
DIST-OPS
FROM: L.L. GRIFFIN
SUBJECT: PRODUCTION 2/20 & 2/21

BLOCK PRODUCTION 4 CYL 529 INPUT QUALIFIER 4 CYL. 668
C SERIES 6 CYL 21

FINISHED INVENTORY 4 CYL 973 6 CYL 1480 C 66

MACHINE DOWNTIME:
2/20 BROACH DOWN APPROX. 12 HRS QUALITY PROBLEM PAN RAIL; LOOSE DETAILS IN FIXTURE.

2/21 BROACH DOWN APPROX. 5 HRS. QUALITY PROBLEM PAN RAIL; LOOSE DETAILS IN FIXTURE.
MACH. 13 DOWN APPROX. 1 1/2 HRS. MECHANICAL PROBLEM
WASHER DOWN APPROX. 3 HRS PUMP MOTOR

****

FINISHED INVENTORY BANK 4 CYL 1525 6 CYL 1630
ACTUAL 4 CYL 923 6 CYL. 1400

****

DARLINGTON PLAN TO SHIP 254 6 CYL. WK 2/23

THIS IS THE CURRENT PRODUCTION STATUS AND PLAN

*** 6 (C) CYLINDER ***		23-Jun	24-Jun	25-Jun	26-Jun	27-Jun	28-Jun	29-Jun
BEGINNING INV	PLAN	61	65	69	73	21	25	25
	ACTUAL	16	16	29	26	21	21	NA
A/T CONSUMPTION	PLAN	12	12	12	12	12	0	0
	ACTUAL	0	0	3	0	0	0	0
SVC CONSUMPTION	PLAN	0	0	0	0	0	0	0
	ACTUAL	0	12	0	28	0	0	0
CONSUMPTION-CUMM	PLAN	358	370	382	394	406	406	406
	ACTUAL	241	253	256	284	284	NA	NA
PRODUCTION-DAILY	PLAN	16	16	16	16	16	0	0
	ACTUAL	0	25	0	28	0	0	0
PRODUCTION-CUMM	PLAN	320	336	352	368	384	384	384
	ACTUAL	153	178	178	206	206	NA	NA
COUNT ADJUSTMENTS		0	0	0	-5	0	0	0
ENDING INV	PLAN	65	69	73	77	25	25	25
	ACTUAL	16	29	26	21	21	NA	NA
OVER/(UNDER) LINESET-CUM		-117	-117	-126	-110	-122	NA	NA
OVER/(UNDER) PRODUCT-CUM		-167	-158	-174	-162	-178	NA	NA

Figure 11-3. -- Monitoring Report (continued)

potential problem, are explained in the variance column of the report. This type of detailed monitoring greatly simplifies the control/feedback activities in the machining department.

The head line has a similar system for monitoring its production problem. CDC's operating philosophy allows each machine line to be managed as one work center. This eliminates the need to do detailed tracking of the WIP inventory in the machining areas.

Control/Feedback

The control/feedback stage at CDC consists of three related activities: resolution of short-term problems, long-term correction of shop floor problems and continued enhancement of the production process, and the maintenance of information flows.

The resolution of short-term problems deals with missed due dates, quality problems identified during testing, scrap, and failure to complete operations during the standard cycle time. Each problem is handled differently.

- Missed due dates. The AIMS system not only performs a line sequencing function but also allows everyone, from a technician to the plant manager, to monitor the assembly, particularly if there is a hot order to ship. If for some reason a due date is missed, AIMS corrects itself by scheduling all backlogged orders first. It also creates a backlog report so that management can review it and decide what corrective action (e.g., scheduled overtime, major and minor report work) needs to take place.

  The due date of the manufacturing order, and subsequently the customer acknowledgment of the ship date, are the driving factors in both the AIMS and the material system. At CDC, the point of control for meeting the schedule is at the lowest level possible. Technicians expedite parts if their team is short of material and assembly materials resources readjust the line set sequence if priorities need realignment. The person who has the most knowledge about a particular situation has the ability to exert the most control when a variance occurs.
- Quality problems identified during testing. Every engine that is assembled must be tested. During testing, problems are identified that range from a loose hose coupling to a defective component. In

the past, the testing personnel repaired the problem. This practice was discontinued because it was found that the testing personnel became extremely familiar with the construction of diesel engines while the assembly personnel were ignorant of many of the problems encountered during test.

Currently, testing personnel pull any engine off the line that fails to meet quality standards. The problem is identified on a tag, and the engine is sent back to the responsible team. The team then corrects the problem and sends the repaired engine back to the testing area within the day. This approach works because it provides immediate feedback.

- Scrap. Every manufacturing and assembly process generates some form of scrap or rework. The shop floor control system handles these problems differently for machining than for assembly. In machining, all scrap is removed from inventory. When a machining line scraps out a part, it is done at either rough stock value or finished stock value, depending on what point in the process the part was scrapped.

  In assembly, there are basically two types of scrap -- a scrap component and a scrap engine. Individual components are removed from inventory by the technicians in the team working on the component. This is a manual process. If a complete engine is scrapped, the good components are reverse issued manually, and the ESN is scrapped out from the engine history database. This results in an engine missing from the total demand generated by the MPS. It is CDC's position that it is acceptable to ship the customer order short and to generate a new manufacturing order to replace the lost engine. The customer is given a new promise date for the missing engine.

These actions, adequate to preserve CDC's capability to deliver a low-cost, high-quality engine on time, form only one half of an adequate control mechanism. The other half involves the long-term resolution of these problems and the continued enhancement of the system. This second half is accomplished by factor analysis, which is a formalized process managed by the technicians themselves and involves a continuous evaluation of both the process and the various tasks. Factor analysis is a responsibility of each team and is done on company time. To prevent any disruption in the production process, management replaces the technicians on the line during this time period.

The shop floor control system places a high priority on maintaining a regular information flow between the shop floor and the rest of the firm. Face-to-face interaction is more effective than the computer report and allows for rapid reaction to problems on the shop floor. Communication between test and the various teams takes place continuously. There is also regular communication between the manager determining the line set sequence and the machining department.

Order Disposition

Order disposition, which closes the manufacturing loop at CDC, requires the issuing of individual components to the manufacturing order and the receipt of the manufacturing order into finished goods inventory. In machining, the manufacturing order is received automatically and inventory charged off when enough parts leave the end of the machining line to satisfy that particular order In A/T, AIMS automatically issues each component to the manufacturing order at the end of each team. This allows each team to maintain inventory integrity with only its own WIP representing outstanding issues. Accordingly, AIMS receives the engine into finished goods inventory after the engine has been painted and upfitted. This nightly process occurs in a batch mode, which allows the next morning's inventory account to be as accurate as possible.

Performance Evaluation/Feedback

Performance evaluation/feedback at CDC is simple, straightforward, and helps to create a self-regulating system. Formal evaluation is done by the team, and every team knows its responsibilities. Each team is responsible for such areas as conformance to budget, quality, delivery to schedule, and inventory accuracy. Performance is monitored continuously with this information readily available to every member of the team. As a result, there is no confusion over what has to be done well for the team to succeed. If the group is having difficulties meeting its performance objectives, it can ask for assistance from management either within operations or from other functional areas such as accounting.

While management evaluates team performance, it does not tend to get involved in evaluating individual performance. That responsibility is left up to the group. This feature has resulted in a self-regulating system. The group identifies those individuals whose performance on the line is hurting group performance. Everyone in the group continuously monitors the day-to-day work of those individuals. While these individuals can hide their problems from management, they cannot hide from the group.

It is also the group that determines the necessary corrective action. In some cases, this may be nothing more than a reminder. In other cases, the group can recommend that the individual be put on a corrective action program, in which the individual has sixty days to improve performance before termination. In this program, the management and group members work with the problem worker to help that person meet the expected standards. In extreme cases, the group can recommend that the worker's employment be terminated or the employee transferred out of the group. In this entire process, management is called in as needed.

Evaluating CDC's Shop Floor Control System -- Benefits

Currently, CDC is built on a manufacturing system that is in transition. As a result, it is very difficult to assess the benefits directly attributable to the presence of the shop floor control system. It is management's position that the major returns to be obtained from the current system will occur as capacity use increases. The current system accommodates and controls future growth on the shop floor.

Important benefits that have been realized are:

- Better control over the shop floor. The shop floor control system has provided both management and technicians with the needed level of control over activities on the shop floor. Problems are identified quickly, and the response of the system is rapid. There is almost no expediting.
- Better decisions. In talking with technicians, it is evident that they are using the shop floor control system to solve problems. They are using the information provided to make decisions.
- More time for decision making. One of the most immediate benefits of the current system is that it has provided the technicians with

more time for problem solving. This time has been freed up by automating data collection and some of the simple decision making processes.

Shop Floor Control at CDC -- The Next Stage

The shop floor control system is in transition. It is moving toward the long-term goal of encouraging and supporting true JIT production on the shop floor. While the basic structure of the current shop floor control system is acceptable and recognized as being effective, there are several future modifications needed to ensure the continued effectiveness of the system:

- Introduction of statistical process control. Technicians working on the shop floor can identify problems once they have occurred. However, this is not enough. By introducing statistical process control (SPC), the technicians will be given the tools to identify and correct potential problems before they can affect production.
- Improved ability to cope with a changing market. The production process at CDC was designed initially for a product with few options. However, to compete in an increasingly competitive marketplace, product flexibility resulting from the availability of numerous options is becoming increasingly more important. The challenge for CDC is to provide such flexibility without jeopardizing the strengths of the current system and without relying on excess inventory throughout the system. These requirements have forced management and personnel at CDC to look for different answers.

  One problem facing the technician is parts proliferation. As more options are demanded, more components are needed. For example, CDC must currently deal with over fifty different types of dipsticks (as compared to the some twenty-five different types needed when the plant first started). These dipsticks are stocked on the assembly line. Management, however, is investigating the possibilities of placing a machine near the line to make the dipsticks as needed.

  Another problem results from different option requirements. Often these requirements create different engines that must be assembled on the line. Management is investigating the possibility of working with the partners to redesign the engine so that the options can be fitted at the last stage in the line. Each engine assembled up to that point will be the same. In all of these activities, technicians play an integral part. In the case of the dipstick problem, the solution was proposed by the technicians.

- Reducing setup in the manufacturing department. The flexibility of the manufacturing department has been impaired by setups. As pointed out previously, it takes one day to change the line over but eight days to work the old inventory through the system. This problem is now being addressed by the technicians in the manufacturing department.
- Improved management of scrap, rework, and salvage. Current procedures for dealing with these three types of orders are crude. Scrap is costed out at either the raw material level or the finished cost level. Rework and salvage create situations in which material is pulled off the line (and out of AIMS) only to reappear later on. Control over rework and salvage is not as strong as it should be. In part, this is a problem with AIMS. Management is currently working on correcting this problem.
- Continued education training. The technicians working on the shop floor must be made aware of the capabilities and tools offered by the shop floor control system if this system is to be used to its fullest extent. This requires more training and education. Training is not a one-time activity. As changes are made in the system and as new uses of the system are discovered, the users must be educated.

In general, management is pleased with the current system. The system does achieve its objectives. However, everyone at CDC is aware of the need to fine-tune this system continually. Shop floor control that is adequate for today may not be adequate tomorrow.

Shop Floor Control Consolidated Diesel: Lessons to be Learned

CDC is a young company that is trying to succeed in a competitive market by offering its customers the highest quality engine at the lowest possible cost. To achieve this objective, CDC has turned to a marriage of CIM and JIT. The plant, for example, was built with state-of-the-art technology and with proven suppliers and techniques. The system makes extensive use of large "advanced" production recording and monitoring equipment and material handling devices such as bar-coded reading of specific components, electrified monorails for major subassembly handling, VDT displays instead of hard-copy BOM, and computer-managed data collection. The manufacturing system was built to eliminate all forms of manufacturing waste. To this end, CDC has placed the decision-making power in the hands of the people best able to make such decisions. Frequently, these people have been the technicians working on the shop floor.

Shop floor control at CDC has become an integral element of the total system. Management realizes that without an effective, well thought out and well-structured shop floor control system the critical link between planning and the shop floor is threatened. A successful shop floor control system must reflect these traits:

- Build a system to support the activities of the key decision makers. At CDC, it is recognized that most of the critical problems are best resolved by the technician working on the shop floor. The shop floor control system has been structured to support and emphasize the role of this person. The computer system, for example, has been built to provide the technician with timely access to needed information. The system also frees the technician to spend more time in problem solving by reducing the time required for data collection and recording. Finally, the system makes the technician aware of potential problems.
- Ensure immediacy of feedback. If the system is to work well, people should know how they are performing at any time. Providing such immediate feedback is one of the responsibilities of shop floor control. Immediacy of feedback is accomplished by making errors visible quickly. This lesson is best demonstrated by the current testing procedures. If a problem is uncovered during testing, the team responsible for the problem is identified and the engine is returned to that team at once. The team is then responsible for correcting the problem and returning the engine to test before the end of the shift. Such immediacy prevents technicians from continually repeating the same error. It also encourages quality production. Management learned that immediacy of feedback is often provided by face-to-face communication.

- Build and maintain discipline on the shop floor. If the shop floor control system is to be effective, it must be used. This requires user discipline. The user must record all information at the time that information is generated, otherwise errors are introduced into the manufacturing database. Users must use the shop floor control system for problem solving and follow the procedures set down in shop floor control. Without discipline, management's handle on the shop floor is weakened.

  Discipline is built in two ways. First, the users must be educated about the procedures and capabilities of the shop floor control system. Second, management must be prepared to fine-tune the shop floor control system. The system must keep pace as user needs change.
- Keep shop floor control simple. The shop floor control system can only be effective to the extent that it is used. While training is important, it does not, by itself, lead to increased use. If shop floor control is to be used regularly, then it must be easy to understand. It must not complicate operations on the shop floor. This principle can be seen in different aspects of the CDC shop floor control system. During testing, for example, when an engine fails to meet quality standards, it is returned to the responsible team. The problem is identified, and the team repairs the engine within that shift. This process is simple to use and understand; there are no needless report forms complicating this process.
- Have clear, concise, uncluttered statement of goals. If people working on the shop floor are to meet or exceed their objectives, they must be first informed of these goals, which are concise and few in number. At any point when the worker is on the line, he or she should be able to tell anyone what has to be done at that moment for the system to work. At CDC, for example, all workers know that they are responsible on the line for completing their tasks within the time standard and for quality (in the engines produced, parts used, and the maintenance of the work area). Along with the need for a clear statement of goals, there is a corresponding need for ensuring that these goals are always being met. At CDC, this aspect has been achieved by relying on group pressure to ensure compliance.

- Maintain a balance between long-term objectives and short-term success. From the outset, it should be recognized that the move toward any system as complex and different as that being built at CDC cannot be done overnight. Instead, this move consists of a series of short-term actions. One major problem encountered at CDC is frustration. Everyone knows what must be done and how much more there is to do. Working toward the successful implementation of JIT manufacturing also requires that the long-term development of the production system not be compromised by the need for short-term successes. An example of this problem can be seen in the area of parts proliferation. The pressure to compete effectively in an increasingly more competitive marketplace has meant a growth in the number of options offered. These options potentially threaten the inventory reductions currently underway.
- Recognize the priority of development. CDC implemented three new systems almost simultaneously -- a new production process, a new manufacturing planning and control system, and a new method of organizing the work force and managing the employees (i.e., the team method). Introducing these systems has proven to be a major source of corporate stress and frustration. It is now generally agreed that there is a distinct sequence for implementing these developments. The first step should always be to implement and debug the manufacturing planning and control system. This system provides the structure into which the other two systems fall. It also provides management with the means of effectively guiding the implementation of the other systems and for directing them. Finally, if the planning and control system is not present before beginning the implementation of the production process, it will not be developed during implementation. The reason is that once you begin implementing the production process, you come under continued pressure to get output out the door. This pressure makes any development of the control system seem secondary in nature.

Can CIM be merged successfully with JIT manufacturing in North America? Based on the experiences of CDC, the answer is an emphatic yes. However, any success obtained depends on having the appropriate supporting shop floor control system in place. Without the structure offered by systems such as shop floor control, any success achieved is a result of chance.

ATTACHMENTS

4.10.2.1 LINE SET REPORT. THE LINE SET REPORT PROVIDES INFORMATION ABOUT ENGINES THAT WERE LINE SET AND NOT COMPLETED FOR THE CURRENT DAY. THE REPORT IS AN ORDERED LIST OF INDIVIDUAL ENGINES AND THEIR CORRESPONDING MANUFACTURING ORDER NUMBER AND ENGINE CINFIGURATION.

OUTPUT FORMAT OF THE LINE SET SEQUENCE LIST REPORT APPEARS AS:

01/82 CONSOLIDATED DIESEL - WHITAKERS PLANT CPU - 1
00:36 AIMS - LINE SET REPORT
PAGE XXX

MFG ORDER	PIN	ENG CONFIG PART #	DUE DATE	DEST ID	LINE SET SEQ/ITEM #
00250628	00850620	XXXXXXX	XX/XX/XX	DDDDDDD	XXXXXXXXXX
00250628	00850621	XXXXXXX	XX/XX/XX	DDDDDDD	XXXXXXXXXX
00250628	00850624	XXXXXXX	XX/XX/XX	DDDDDDD	XXXXXXXXXX
00250628	00850625	XXXXXXX	XX/XX/XX	DDDDDDD	XXXXXXXXXX
00250629	00850634	XXXXXXX	XX/XX/XX	DDDDDDD	XXXXXXXXXX
00250629	00850636	XXXXXXX	XX/XX/XX	DDDDDDD	XXXXXXXXXX
00250629	00850637	XXXXXXX	XX/XX/XX	DDDDDDD	XXXXXXXXXX
00250629	00850638	XXXXXXX	XX/XX/XX	DDDDDDD	XXXXXXXXXX
00250741	00850060	XXXXXXX	XX/XX/XX	DDDDDDD	XXXXXXXXXX
00250741	00860061	XXXXXXX	XX/XX/XX	DDDDDDD	XXXXXXXXXX
00250741	00860062	XXXXXXX	XX/XX/XX	DDDDDDD	XXXXXXXXXX
00250741	00860063	XXXXXXX	XX/XX/XX	DDDDDDD	XXXXXXXXXX
00250741	00860066	XXXXXXX	XX/XX/XX	DDDDDDD	XXXXXXXXXX
00250741	00860067	XXXXXXX	XX/XX/XX	DDDDDDD	XXXXXXXXXX
00250745	00860505	XXXXXXX	XX/XX/XX	DDDDDDD	XXXXXXXXXX
00250745	00860506	XXXXXXX	XX/XX/XX	DDDDDDD	XXXXXXXXXX
00250745	00860508	XXXXXXX	XX/XX/XX	DDDDDDD	XXXXXXXXXX
00250745	00860509	XXXXXXX	XX/XX/XX	DDDDDDD	XXXXXXXXXX
00250745	00860511	XXXXXXX	XX/XX/XX	DDDDDDD	XXXXXXXXXX
00250745	00860512	XXXXXXX	XX/XX/XX	DDDDDDD	XXXXXXXXXX
00250747	00860545	XXXXXXX	XX/XX/XX	DDDDDDD	XXXXXXXXXX
00250747	00860546	XXXXXXX	XX/XX/XX	DDDDDDD	XXXXXXXXXX
00250747	00860547	XXXXXXX	XX/XX/XX	DDDDDDD	XXXXXXXXXX
00250747	00860550	XXXXXXX	XX/XX/XX	DDDDDDD	XXXXXXXXXX
00250747	00860551	XXXXXXX	XX/XX/XX	DDDDDDD	XXXXXXXXXX

TOTAL ENGINES LINE SET 0025

Line Set Report

4.10.2.3 ENGINES BUILT REPORT. THIS REPORT GIVES A LIST OF BUIL ENGINES THAT HAVE EXITED TEAM 7 ON THE CURRENT DAY. THIS REPORT I ORDERED BY MANUFACTURING ORDER AND LISTS THE PIN, MODEL ID, ENGIN CONFIGURATION PART #, AND DUE DATE OF EACH ENGINE.

```
11/18/83          CONSOLIDATED DIESEL - WHITAKERS PLANT          CPU - 3
15:32:30              AIMS - ENGINES BUILT REPORT
                                                                 PAGE  XXX
```

MFG ORDER	PIN	ENG CONFIG PART #	DUE DATE	DEST ID	LINE SET SEG/ITEM #
00250628	00850620	XXXXXXX	XX/XX/XX	DDDDDDD	XXXXXXXXX
00250628	00850621	XXXXXXX	XX/XX/XX	DDDDDDD	XXXXXXXXX
00250628	00850622	XXXXXXX	XX/XX/XX	DDDDDDD	XXXXXXXXX
00250628	00850623	XXXXXXX	XX/XX/XX	DDDDDDD	XXXXXXXXX
00250628	00850624	XXXXXXX	XX/XX/XX	DDDDDDD	XXXXXXXXX
00250628	00850625	XXXXXXX	XX/XX/XX	DDDDDDD	XXXXXXXXX
00250629	00850634	XXXXXXX	XX/XX/XX	DDDDDDD	XXXXXXXXX
00250629	00850636	XXXXXXX	XX/XX/XX	DDDDDDD	XXXXXXXXX
00250629	00850637	XXXXXXX	XX/XX/XX	DDDDDDD	XXXXXXXXX
00250629	00850638	XXXXXXX	XX/XX/XX	DDDDDDD	XXXXXXXXX
00250741	00850060	XXXXXXX	XX/XX/XX	DDDDDDD	XXXXXXXXX
00250741	00860061	XXXXXXX	XX/XX/XX	DDDDDDD	XXXXXXXXX
00250741	00860062	XXXXXXX	XX/XX/XX	DDDDDDD	XXXXXXXXX
00250741	00860063	XXXXXXX	XX/XX/XX	DDDDDDD	XXXXXXXXX
00250741	00860066	XXXXXXX	XX/XX/XX	DDDDDDD	XXXXXXXXX
00250741	00860067	XXXXXXX	XX/XX/XX	DDDDDDD	XXXXXXXXX
00250745	00860505	XXXXXXX	XX/XX/XX	DDDDDDD	XXXXXXXXX
00250745	00860506	XXXXXXX	XX/XX/XX	DDDDDDD	XXXXXXXXX
00250745	00860508	XXXXXXX	XX/XX/XX	DDDDDDD	XXXXXXXXX
00250745	00860509	XXXXXXX	XX/XX/XX	DDDDDDD	XXXXXXXXX
00250745	00860511	XXXXXXX	XX/XX/XX	DDDDDDD	XXXXXXXXX
00250745	00860512	XXXXXXX	XX/XX/XX	DDDDDDD	XXXXXXXXX
00250747	00860545	XXXXXXX	XX/XX/XX	DDDDDDD	XXXXXXXXX
00250747	00860546	XXXXXXX	XX/XX/XX	DDDDDDD	XXXXXXXXX
00250747	00860547	XXXXXXX	XX/XX/XX	DDDDDDD	XXXXXXXXX
00250747	00860550	XXXXXXX	XX/XX/XX	DDDDDDD	XXXXXXXXX
00250747	00860551	XXXXXXX	XX/XX/XX	DDDDDDD	XXXXXXXXX

TOTAL ENGINES BUILT 0027

Engines Built Report

4.10.2.4 ENGINES SKIDDED REPORT. THE FOLLOWING REPORT GIVES A LIST OF ALL ENGINES SKIDDED FOR THE CURRENT DAY. IT IS ORGANIZED BY MANUFACTURING ORDER AND LISTS THE PIN, MODEL ID, ENGINE CONFIGURATION PART #, AND DUE DATE FOR EACH ENGINE SKIDDED.

11/18/83 CONSOLIDATED DIESEL - WHITAKERS PLANT CPU - 3
15:32:30 AIMS - ENGINES SKIDDED REPORT
PAGE 1

MFG ORDER	PIN	ENG CONFIG PART #	DUE DATE	DEST ID	LINE SET SEQ/ITEM #
00250628	00850620	XXXXXXX	XX/XX/XX	DDDDDDD	XXXXXXXXX
00250628	00850621	XXXXXXX	XX/XX/XX	DDDDDDD	XXXXXXXXX
00250628	00850622	XXXXXXX	XX/XX/XX	DDDDDDD	XXXXXXXXX
00250628	00850623	XXXXXXX	XX/XX/XX	DDDDDDD	XXXXXXXXX
00250628	00850624	XXXXXXX	XX/XX/XX	DDDDDDD	XXXXXXXXX
00250628	00850625	XXXXXXX	XX/XX/XX	DDDDDDD	XXXXXXXXX
00250629	00850634	XXXXXXX	XX/XX/XX	DDDDDDD	XXXXXXXXX
00250629	00850636	XXXXXXX	XX/XX/XX	DDDDDDD	XXXXXXXXX
00250629	00850637	XXXXXXX	XX/XX/XX	DDDDDDD	XXXXXXXXX
00250629	00850638	XXXXXXX	XX/XX/XX	DDDDDDD	XXXXXXXXX
00250741	00850060	XXXXXXX	XX/XX/XX	DDDDDDD	XXXXXXXXX
00250741	00860061	XXXXXXX	XX/XX/XX	DDDDDDD	XXXXXXXXX
00250741	00860062	XXXXXXX	XX/XX/XX	DDDDDDD	XXXXXXXXX
00250741	00860063	XXXXXXX	XX/XX/XX	DDDDDDD	XXXXXXXXX
00250741	00860066	XXXXXXX	XX/XX/XX	DDDDDDD	XXXXXXXXX
00250741	00860067	XXXXXXX	XX/XX/XX	DDDDDDD	XXXXXXXXX
00250745	00860505	XXXXXXX	XX/XX/XX	DDDDDDD	XXXXXXXXX
00250745	00860506	XXXXXXX	XX/XX/XX	DDDDDDD	XXXXXXXXX
00250745	00860508	XXXXXXX	XX/XX/XX	DDDDDDD	XXXXXXXXX
00250745	00860509	XXXXXXX	XX/XX/XX	DDDDDDD	XXXXXXXXX
00250745	00860511	XXXXXXX	XX/XX/XX	DDDDDDD	XXXXXXXXX
00250745	00860512	XXXXXXX	XX/XX/XX	DDDDDDD	XXXXXXXXX
00250747	00860545	XXXXXXX	XX/XX/XX	DDDDDDD	XXXXXXXXX
00250747	00860546	XXXXXXX	XX/XX/XX	DDDDDDD	XXXXXXXXX
00250747	00860547	XXXXXXX	XX/XX/XX	DDDDDDD	XXXXXXXXX
00250747	00860550	XXXXXXX	XX/XX/XX	DDDDDDD	XXXXXXXXX
00250747	00860551	XXXXXXX	XX/XX/XX	DDDDDDD	XXXXXXXXX

COUNT OF SKIDDED ENGINES 0027

Engines Skidded Report

4.10.2.5 ENGINES SCRAPPED REPORT. THIS REPORT GIVES A LIST OF A ENGINES SCRAPPED FOR THE CURRENT DAY AND THE REASONS WHY THEY WE SCRAPPED. THE REPORT GIVES THE MANUFACTURING ORDER NUMBER AND THE P OF THE ENGINES SCRAPPED. AN ENGINE WILL BE SCRAPPED WHEN THE BLOCK IRREPARABLE OR WHEN THE REPAIR IS NOT ECONOMICALLY FEASIBLE.

11/18/83 CONSOLIDATED DIESEL - WHITAKERS PLANT CPU - 1
15:32:30 AIMS - ENGINES SCRAPPED REPORT
PAGE 1

FRAME: SHIFT 1 ON 11/18/83 - PARTIAL

MFG ORDER	PIN	ENG CONFIG PART #	LINE SET SEG/ITEM #	CODE / REASON
00250629	00850621	XXXXXXX	XXXXXXXXXX	X02 CRACKED BLOCK
00250629	00850635	XXXXXXX	XXXXXXXXXX	X05 SCORED BORES
00250740	00860053	XXXXXXX	XXXXXXXXXX	X09 WARPED BLOCK
00250745	00860507	XXXXXXX	XXXXXXXXXX	X01 UNDER SIZED JOURNALS
00250748	00860545	XXXXXXX	XXXXXXXXXX	X07 BLEW UP IN HOT TEST

COUNT OF SCRAPPED 5

EXAMPLE 4-11 ENGINE SCRAPPED REPORT

Engines Scrapped Report

07/16/85 CONSOLIDATED DIESEL - WHITAKERS PLANT CPU - 1
11:15:15 AIMS - LINE SET SEQUENCE LIST DUMP

PAGE 1

SORTED BY: ENG CONFIG

MFG ORDER	PIN	LINE SET SEQ/ITEM #	ENG CONFIG PART #	START DATE	MODEL ID	SUB FLAGS	STAT
MFG0701383	44134598	8506270153	32383	4/28/85	6B 59		TW
MFG70318384	44133845	8506190003	32384	2/14/85	6BT 59		TW
MFG0715384	44134748	8507010199	32384	5/ 7/85	6BT 59		UP
	44134749	8507010200	32384	5/ 7/85	6BT 59		UP
	44134752	8507010203	32384	5/ 7/85	6BT 59		UP
	44134756	8507010207	32384	5/ 7/85	6BT 59		UP
MFG0729384		8507160213	32384	5/17/85	6BT 59		H
MFG0805384		8507160214	32384	5/17/85	6BT 59		H
		8507160215	32384	5/17/85	6BT 59		H
		8507160216	32384	5/17/85	6BT 59		H
		8507160217	32384	5/17/85	6BT 59		H
		8507160218	32384	5/17/85	6BT 59		H
		8507160219	32384	5/17/85	6BT 59		H
MFG0722424	44135126	8507080166	32424	5/ 7/85	6BT 59		UP
	44135127	8507080167	32424	5/ 7/85	6BT 59		PA
MFG0701449	44134431	8506250304	32449	4/28/85	4B 39		UP
	44135055	8507050103	32449	4/28/85	4B 39		UP
MFG0715449	44135200	8507080306	32449	5/ 7/85	4B 39		UP
MFG0729449	44135419	8507120113	32449	5/ 7/85	4B 39		T7
	44135420	8507120114	32449	5/ 7/85	4B 39		T7
	44135421	8507120115	32449	5/ 7/85	4B 39		T7
	44135422	8507120116	32449	5/ 7/85	4B 39		T7
	44135423	8507120117	32449	5/ 7/85	4B 39		T7
	44135424	8507120118	32449	5/ 7/85	4B 39		T7
	44135425	8507120119	32449	5/ 7/85	4B 39		T7
	44135426	8507120120	32449	5/ 7/85	4B 39		T7
	44135427	8507120121	32449	5/ 7/85	4B 39		T7
	44135428	8507120122	32449	5/ 7/85	4B 39		T7
	44135429	8507120123	32449	5/ 7/85	4B 39		T6
	44135430	8507120124	32449	5/ 7/85	4B 39		T6
	44135431	8507120125	32449	5/ 7/85	4B 39		T6
	44135432	8507120126	32449	5/ 7/85	4B 39		T6
	44135433	8507120127	32449	5/ 7/85	4B 39		T6
MFG0715449		8507160090	32449	5/ 7/85	4B 39		H
MFG0701450	44134830	8507020111	32450	4/28/85	4BT 39		W5
MFG0715450	44135146	8507080186	32450	5/ 7/85	4BT 39		PA
	44135147	8507080187	32450	5/ 7/85	4BT 39		R6
	44135149	8507080189	32450	5/ 7/85	4BT 39		PA
MFG0805450	44135482	8507150062	32450	5/ 7/85	4BT 39		T4

Line Set Sequence List Dump

4.10.2.7 STATION CONTENTS REPORT. THIS REPORT PROVIDES A LISTING THE ENGINE CURRENTLY LOCATED AT EACH TEAMS STATION. THIS INCLUDES PIN AND PALLET NUMBER.

OUTPUT FORMAT APPEARS AS FOLLOWS:

```
 8/15/82        CONSOLIDATED DIESEL - WHITAKERS PLANT            CPU -
 15:32:30         AIMS - STATION CONTENTS REPORT
                                                                PAGE   1

                                                   LINE SET
TEAM#   STATION#     PALLET#      PIN            SEG/ITEM #     MFG ORDER
-----   --------     -------    --------        ----------     ---------

  1        1           XXX      XXXXXXXX        XXXXXXXXXX      00250659
  .        .            .          .                .               .
  .        .            .          .                .               .
  1       22            .          .                .           00250700
  2        0           XXX      XXXXXXXX        XXXXXXXXXX      00250701
  .        .            .          .                .               .
  .        .            .          .                .               .
  2       11            .          .                .           00250720
  3        0           XXX      XXXXXXXX        XXXXXXXXXX      00250720
  .        .            .          .                .               .
  .        .            .          .                .               .
  3       14            .          .                .           00250727
  4        0           XXX      XXXXXXXX        XXXXXXXXXX      0025073
  .        .            .          .                .               .
  .        .            .          .                .               .
  4       15            .          .                .           0025073
  5        0           XXX      XXXXXXXX        XXXXXXXXXX      0025074
  .        .            .          .                .               .
  .        .            .          .                .               .
  5       11            .          .                .           0025074
  6        0           XXX      XXXXXXXX        XXXXXXXXXX      0025074
  .        .            .          .                .               .
  .        .            .          .                .               .
  6        9            .          .                .           0025075
  7        0           XXX      XXXXXXXX        XXXXXXXXXX      0025075
  .        .            .          .                .               .
  .        .            .          .                .               .
  7       11           XXX      XXXXXXXX            .           0025075
```

Station Contents Report

4.10.2.8 LINE SET ENGINE LOCATION REPORT. THIS REPORT PROVIDES LISTING OF THE LOCATION OF EVERY ENGINE CURRENTLY KNOWN TO THE SYSTEM THIS LOCATION INFORMATION INCLUDES PIN, CURRENT TEAM AND STATION (I DEFINED), PALLET NUMBER, PALLET NUMBER, MANUFACTURING ORDER, AN STATUS.

OUTPUT FORMAT APPEARS AS FOLLOWS:

```
 8/15/82       CONSOLIDATED DIESEL - WHITAKERS PLANT          CPU - 1
15:32:30        AIMS - LINE SET ENGINE LOCATION REPORT
                                                              PAGE   1

   PIN       TEAM#      STATION#     PALLET#    MFG ORDER    STATUS
 --------    -----      --------     -------    ---------    ------

 XXXXXXXX      X           XX          XXX      00250833       L
 XXXXXXXX      X           XX          XXX      00250833       L
 XXXXXXXX      X           XX          XXX      00250834       L
 XXXXXXXX      X           XX          XXX      00250834       R
 XXXXXXXX      X           XX          XXX      00250834       H
 XXXXXXXX      X           XX          XXX      00250835       S
     .         .           .            .           .
     .         .           .            .           .
     .         .           .            .           .
 XXXXXXXX      X           XX          XXX      00250885       R
 XXXXXXXX      X           XX          XXX      00250887       S
 XXXXXXXX      X           XX          XXX      00250888       L


          "L" = LINE SET          "S" = SHIPPED (FUTURE)
          "R" = REPAIR            "H" = HOT TEST
```

Line Set Engine Location Report

4.10.2.9 ENGINE HISTORY REPORT. THIS REPORT PROVIDES A "FULL PRINT OUT" OF THE CURRENT CONTENTS OF THE ENGINE HISTORY RECORD. THI INCLUDES ALL THE SPECIAL PART SERIAL NUMBERS WHICH HAVE BEEN ENTERE BY THE OPERATOR (CAMSHAFT, CRANKSHAFT, FUEL PUMP, AND TURBO CHARGER) CURRENT STATUS, AND ALL ACCUMULATED ANALOG DATA ON TORQUES AND ANGLES THE SIZE OF THIS REPORT WILL VARY DEPENDING ON HOW FAR INTO THE BUIL SCHEDULE THE SPECIFIED PIN IS AT THE TIME OF REPORT GENERATIO (OUTPUT).

OUTPUT FORMAT APPEARS AS FOLLOWS, FOR A COMPLETELY BUILT ENGINE:

Engine History Report

```
8/15/82         CONSOLIDATED DIESEL - WHITAKERS PLANT         CPU - 1
15:32:30           AIMS - ENGINE HISTORY REPORT
                                                              PAGE   1

 PIN: XXXXXXXX   MFG ORDER: 0025078    TEAM: X    STATION: XX
 PALLET: XXX     MODEL ID: XXXXXXX   ENG CONFIG PART #: XXXXXXX
                    BORE GRADE: A  D  A  A  D  A

      CAMSHAFT S/N: XXXXXXXXXX      CRANKSHAFT S/N: XXXXXXXXXX
     FUEL PUMP S/N: XXXXXXXXXX   TURBO CHARGER S/N: XXXXXXXXXX

TEAM: 1  ENTER: YYMMDDHHMM          EXIT: YYMMDDHHMM

                          STATION: 13/14

     TORQUE:   XXX.X   XXX.X   XXX.X   XXX.X   XXX.X   XXX.X   XXX.X
               XXX.X   XXX.X   XXX.X   XXX.X   XXX.X   XXX.X   XXX.X
     ANGLE:    XXX.X   XXX.X   XXX.X   XXX.X   XXX.X   XXX.X   XXX.X
               XXX.X   XXX.X   XXX.X   XXX.X   XXX.X   XXX.X   XXX.X

                          STATION: 17

  IN-PROCESS:  XXX.X   XXX.X

TEAM: 2  ENTER: YYMMDDHHMM          EXIT: YYMMDDHHMM

               STATION: 6          STATION: 7          STATION: 8

     TORQUE:   XXX.X   XXX.X     XXX.X   XXX.X     XXX.X   XXX.X
     ANGLE:    XXX.X   XXX.X     XXX.X   XXX.X     XXX.X   XXX.X

                          STATION: 10

  IN-PROCESS:  XXX.X

TEAM: 3  ENTER: YYMMDDHHMM          EXIT: YYMMDDHHMM

                          STATION: 5

     TORQUE:   XXX.X   XXX.X   XXX.X   XXX.X   XXX.X   XXX.X
               XXX.X   XXX.X   XXX.X   XXX.X   XXX.X   XXX.X
               XXX.X   XXX.X   XXX.X   XXX.X   XXX.X   XXX.X

                          STATION: 6

     TORQUE:   XXX.X   XXX.X   XXX.X   XXX.X   XXX.X   XXX.X
               XXX.X   XXX.X   XXX.X   XXX.X   XXX.X   XXX.X
               XXX.X   XXX.X   XXX.X   XXX.X   XXX.X   XXX.X
               XXX.X   XXX.X   XXX.X   XXX.X   XXX.X   XXX.X
```

Engine History Report (continued)

```
8/15/82        CONSOLIDATED DIESEL - WHITAKERS PLANT          CPU - 1
15:32:30          AIMS - ENGINE HISTORY REPORT
                                                              PAGE   2
 PIN: XXXXXXXX   MFG ORDER: 0025078     TEAM: X    STATION: XX
 PALLET: XXX     MODEL ID: XXXXXXX   ENG CONFIG PART #: XXXXXXX
                   BORE GRADE: A  D  A  A  D  A

     CAMSHAFT S/N: XXXXXXXXXX        CRANKSHAFT S/N: XXXXXXXXXX
    FUEL PUMP S/N: XXXXXXXXXX    TURBO CHARGER S/N: XXXXXXXXXX

TEAM: 4  ENTER: YYMMDDHHMM          EXIT: YYMMDDHHMM

                           STATION: 9/10

    TORQUE:   XXX.X  XXX.X  XXX.X  XXX.X  XXX.X  XXX.X  XXX.X
              XXX.X  XXX.X  XXX.X  XXX.X  XXX.X  XXX.X
              XXX.X  XXX.X  XXX.X  XXX.X  XXX.X  XXX.X  XXX.X
              XXX.X  XXX.X  XXX.X  XXX.X  XXX.X  XXX.X
    ANGLE:    XXX.X  XXX.X  XXX.X  XXX.X  XXX.X  XXX.X  XXX.X
              XXX.X  XXX.X  XXX.X  XXX.X  XXX.X  XXX.X
              XXX.X  XXX.X  XXX.X  XXX.X  XXX.X  XXX.X  XXX.X
              XXX.X  XXX.X  XXX.X  XXX.X  XXX.X  XXX.X
TEAM: 5  ENTER: YYMMDDHHMM          EXIT: YYMMDDHHMM

                           STATION: 11/12

    TORQUE:   XXX.X  XXX.X  XXX.X  XXX.X  XXX.X  XXX.X
              XXX.X  XXX.X  XXX.X  XXX.X  XXX.X  XXX.X
```

Engine History Report (continued)

8/15/82 CONSOLIDATED DIESEL - WHITAKERS PLANT CPU - 1
15:32:30 AIMS - PRODUCTION PERFORMANCE REPORT
PAGE 2

TEAM: 1-7 OR ALL
FRAME: SHIFT 1 ON 8/15/82 - PARTIAL

TEAM#	STATION#	ACCEPT COUNTS	REJECT COUNTS	REJECT RATE
5	0	XXXXX	XXXXX	XXX.X
.	.	.	.	.
5	11	.	.	.
**** TEAM # 5 SUMMARY ****		XXXXX	XXXXX	XXX.X
6	0	XXXXX	XXXXX	XXX.X
.	.	.	.	.
6	9	.	.	.
**** TEAM # 6 SUMMARY ****		XXXXX	XXXXX	XXX.X
7	0	XXXXX	XXXXX	XXX.X
.	.	.	.	.
7	11	.	.	.
**** TEAM # 7 SUMMARY ****		XXXXX	XXXXX	XXX.X

Production Performance Report

4.10.2.11 TOP TEN REJECT REPORT. THIS REPORT PROVIDES A LISTING OF THE TEN (10) REJECT CODES WHICH OCCURED MOST FREQUENTLY. THE TEN REJECT CODES ABE LISTED IN DECREASING ORDER ACCORDING TO NUMBER OF OCCURENCES. THIS REPORT ALSO SUMMARIZES THE TOTAL COUNT OF ALL REJECTS, THE TOTAL FOR THE TOP TEN, AND THE PERCENTAGE OF TOTAL REJECT OCCURENCES THE TOP TEN REPRESENTS.

OUTPUT FORMAT APPEARS AS FOLLOWS:

```
 8/15/82        CONSOLIDATED DIESEL - WHITAKERS PLANT           CPU - 2
15:51:51             AIMS - TOP TEN REJECT REPORT
                                                                PAGE   1

      TEAM:  1-7 OR ALL
      TIME:  HOUR  2 OF SHIFT  1 ON 8/15/82

      REJECT                                      TOTAL     % OF
      CODE    DESCRIPTION                         REJECT     PROD
      ------  -------------------------           ------    -----

       XXX    AAAAAAAAAAAAAAAAAAAAAAAAA            XXXX     XXX.X
       XXX    AAAAAAAAAAAAAAAAAAAAAAAAA            XXXX     XXX.X
        .             .                             .         .
        .             .                             .         .
       XXX    AAAAAAAAAAAAAAAAAAAAAAAAA            XXXX     XXX.X
       XXX    AAAAAAAAAAAAAAAAAAAAAAAAA            XXXX     XXX.X
                                                  ------    -----
                                      TOTAL  =   XXXXX     XXX.X

       GRAND TOTAL REJECT CODES =     XXXXX
       TOP TEN REJECT CODES     =     XXXXX
       TOP TEN REJECT CODES ARE:  69.7 % OF TOTAL REJECT CODES
```

Top Ten Reject Report

11/18/83 CONSOLIDATED DIESEL - WHITAKERS PLANT CPU - 3
15:32:30 AIMS - DISPLAY PARTS MASTER LIST REPORT
PAGE 1

TEAM	STATION	P/N	DESCRIPTION
X	XX	390002501	STANDARD PUMP
		390002507	HD WATER PUMP
		390002510	3" HOSE PUMP
		390002520	LH WATER PUMP
X	XX	390003000	3 CYL BALANCER
		390003005	4 CYL BALANCER
		390003007	6 CYL BALANCER
		390003015	6 CYL II BALANCER
X	XX	390004501	DRY SEAL
		390004502	WET SEAL
X	XX	390005001	STANDARD 3 CYL PAN
		390005002	SHALLOW 3 CYL PAN
		390005003	DEEP FRONT 3 PAN
		390005004	DEEP REAR 3 PAN
		390005005	HIGH CAP. 3 PAN
		390005011	STANDARD 4 CYL PAN
X	XX	390005023	DEEP FRONT 6 PAN
		390005024	DEEP REAR 6 PAN
		390005025	HIGH CAP. 6 PAN
		390005031	STANDARD 6II CYL PAN
		390005032	SHALLOW 6II CYL PAN
		390005033	DEEP FRONT 6II PAN
X	XX	390005034	DEEP REAR 6II PAN
		390005035	HIGH CAP. 6II PAN
X	XX	390457321	STANDARD HOUSING
		390453542	11" HOUSING
		390452814	14" HOUSING
		390559921	SPICER HOUSING
		390978231	MARINE HOUSING
X	XX	390014001	6 DEG. TUBE
		390014002	14 DEG. TUBE
		390014005	SHORT TUBE
		390014007	LONG TUBE
X	XX	390557321	HYDRAULIC CLUTCH
		390553542	11" CLUTCH
		390632814	14" CLUTCH
		390989921	SPICER CLUTCH
		390998231	MARINE CLUTCH

Display Parts Master List Report

CHAPTER 12: GENERAL ELECTRIC CONTROL DIVISION

General Nature of the Firm

General Electric (GE) of Erie, Pennsylvania, is the home for the Transportation Systems Business Operation (TSBO), which produces finished diesel locomotives and provides control and propulsion equipment to a very diverse market that includes transit, off-highway vehicles, and drilling equipment original equipment manufacturers. Its products are used for both land and marine applications. TSBO also provides replacement and spare parts for these same markets.

TSBO is noteworthy for several reasons. First, it provides an excellent example of how one American firm became competitive in spite of facilities which were mostly completed between 1911 and 1917. Management took the existing outmoded facilities and made them viable. This turnaround has occurred partially as a result of an investment in new technology and management's ability to master the fundamentals of manufacturing. The first major successful implementation of a large-scale flexible manufacturing system (FMS) was at TSBO. Management learned to formulate good plans and implement them on the shop floor.

Second, TSBO competes in markets that are competitive and diverse. For example, in the transit and locomotive markets, TSBO must concern itself with issues of cost and quality. In contrast, achieving success in the spare parts business is much more difficult to achieve.

The spare parts business requires that TSBO be prepared to provide component stocks for any vehicle (transit or locomotive) produced in a twenty-year span. This is not an easy requirement to meet given the extensive amount of technological change that has occurred in the last twenty years (especially in the area of electronics). This is also a [illegible] volatile market in which it is difficult to predict the changes in de[illegible] Orders often arrive without prior warning, and TSBO must be prepared [illegible] these orders around quickly.

TSBO competes in both the domestic and international marketpl[illegible] competes against competitors located in the United States, Canada[illegible] Japan. Its markets include such countries as Mexico, Australia, [illegible] Recently, for example, TSBO received a contract to supply locom[illegible] People's Republic of China (currently considered to be the lar[illegible] locomotive market in the world).

TSBO is organized into four major divisions: locomotive fabrication and assembly, propulsion equipment manufacturing, engine manufacturing, and control equipment manufacturing. These divisions employ some 7,800 workers (down from past levels of 15,000). This case study focuses primarily on the control equipment division.

The Control Equipment Division

Control manufacturing produces a complete line of electromechanical controls. These products must handle large electrical currents and high voltages, operate in a high shock/vibration environment, and survive across a broad range of temperature variations. The components used in the product range from the simplest fabrication to the most sophisticated microelectronic circuit. The production process uses about 1,400 different raw materials in conjunction with 30,000 purchased parts to produce about 30,000 components
d assemblies going into 10,000 finished products. Because of the diversity
mponent requirements, control manufacturing draws on many different
turing processes.

rol manufacturing services four major categories of customers:

omotive
it
hway
newal part operations (TRPO).

erent. The locomotive market, for example, is fairly
the sales (mainly gear boxes) are built around a core
omponents. The typical BOM for this market is
st, transit is a more difficult market because
ith little standardization. Of the four
difficult to manage is TRPO.

refurbishing of existing equipment. As
equipment for longer periods of time,
d maintenance has increased. This

wo reasons. First is techno-
st be prepared to rebuild
old. Over this time period, a
and manufacturing have occurred.
d by a twenty-year-old locomotive may

no longer be available. Control manufacturing must resolve these problems by relying either on an extensive stock of inventory or by product redesign.

The second problem created by this market segment is high system shock. Equipment is brought in for rebuilding for two reasons -- the equipment broke down and has to be rebuilt before it can work properly, or it has been brought in as part of a large rebuilding program. In either case, control manufacturing is often given little warning. When the equipment arrives, management is pressured to get the equipment back into operation as soon as possible. TRPO tends to place significant demands on capacity, and loads fluctuate rapidly over time.

The Production Process

Control manufacturing is primarily a job shop involved in ETO and MTO production. Currently, ETO production is 50 percent; MTO, 40 percent, and MTS, 10 percent. Any MTS production occurs at the lower levels of the product structure. At these levels, there is some degree of low-level commonality so lot sizes tend to be larger in the machining and subassembly area and smaller at the top-level assembly areas. The product structure is typically six to eight levels in depth, and the standard lead time averages about twenty-six weeks. A flow diagram of the control manufacturing process is shown in Figure 12-1.

Control manufacturing is divided into five work units and a model shop area. All production takes place in one or more of these work units:

Unit I -- machine shop. This area deals mainly with punched parts, formed parts, small subassemblies, and a plating operation. In addition, it includes the resistor assembly area.

Unit II -- machine shop. This area deals with numerical control machining, milling, drilling, and various turning operations.

Unit III -- final assembly. This area covers final assembly, the wire harness, and heavy devices.

Unit IV -- fabrication. This area deals mainly with sheet metal parts and welding. It also has a wood shop area.

Unit V -- subassembly and device. This area produces panels, electronic cards, small electronic modules, coil winding, and benching molding.

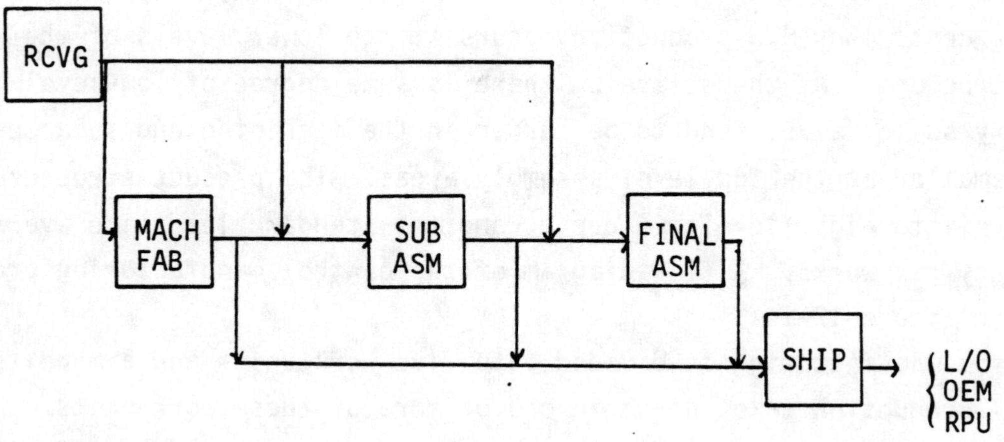

Figure 12-1. -- Control Manufacturing Process Flow

Model shop. This area produces three types of products. The first type consists of renewal parts, direct shippers, and contributing items that cannot be produced economically or by piecework in the factory. The second type is engineering prototypes for test and development, and the third type is field modifications with compressed build cycles.

Production Planning at General Electric

The current system is the result of a series of changes started in 1978. Before that time, control manufacturing used a classic order and expedite system. All ordering was traceable and front end loaded. The mechanized information about WIP was a dispatch system that printed massive reports weekly. Location information was based on extracting operations claimed from the timekeeping system. Information on the dispatch reports was usually two or three weeks old. By the time production control people obtained copies of the dispatching runs, it was necessary to find out if the orders that were short at assembly had ever started. This information was then processed by an army of expediters who would go out and put the missing parts through the shop.

By 1978, management in control manufacturing recognized that its current system was no longer adequate. The costs created by an increasing ratio of indirect to direct labor-hours caused by a high level of expediting were too high. Production forecasts indicated that, unless something was done soon, capacity would be pressed to the limit. Third, production control had difficulty with large orders. The system could not locate these orders nor could it track the assigned material. It also could not track tooling and offered little or no visibility. Everyone knew that control manufacturing was effectively being driven by the informal system. The final factor that caused management to act was the early retirement of several people who knew the details of how to run the system.

A team was formed, which consisted of the materials manager, production control manager, and representatives from the manufacturing systems, operations (i.e., the shop floor), and the MIS system. This team met during Christmas 1979 to determine what should be done to upgrade the total materials ordering and materials information system. The team decided that a closed-loop MRP system (called a baseline system at GE) was needed. The baseline system implementation was to be completed during 1982.

Teams were formed to design and implement the various pieces of the baseline system: master scheduling, MRP, BOM, inventory, shop floor control, and CRP. Management felt the problems the business had in responding to master schedule changes and the communication of proper priorities to all areas of the business could be best accomplished with this type of system.

The first four components of the baseline systems (MPS, MRP, BOM, and inventory) were implemented by 1982. Shop floor control was in place by early 1984. Rough-cut capacity planning is being done at the MPS stage, and there are some day-to-day capacity planning reports generated by the shop floor control system.

Of the five components in place, shop floor control was the most difficult to implement.

Production Planning in Control Manufacturing

The production planning system structure is influenced by the product and production characteristics of control manufacturing. Control manufacturing is primarily a piecework shop, lot size is set at the time of release by MRP, and direct labor-hours are used for capacity measurement.

In spite of the relatively long average lead time, GE often accepts orders within less than normal lead time so the production planning system must deal with both firm and forecasted orders. This concern is evident in the master scheduling activities.

Master Scheduling

Management coordinates the overall activities of the various functional groups by master scheduling. There is only one master scheduling process for the four areas, and the same master schedule is used for the four major product lines (transit, renewal parts, off-highway vehicle, and locomotive). In the first stage, management generates the master production program schedule (MPPS); the MPS, formulated in the second stage, is a more detailed disaggregation of the manufacturing requirements identified in the MPPS.

The MPPS formulation begins with marketing programs. Based on contacts with potential customers, marketing has identified potential orders (or programs). Information about these orders is recorded using proposal requisition, which is reviewed by a screening team headed by marketing and consisting of representatives from cost accounting, engineering, finance, and manufacturing. The screening team identifies those proposals that are suitable for GE. The team applies a series of questions to the proposals:

- o Do we want the contract?
- o Do we have the level of resources (capacity) required by the contract?
- o Are we willing to invest the necessary resources to get and successfully fulfill the contract?
- o What are our probabilities of winning the contract?

At this stage, the capacity implications of the contract are identified using a rough-cut capacity planning procedure. The real problem with evaluating capacity implications, however, lies in determining when the capacity impact will occur.

When a proposal is approved by the screening team, it is distributed and becomes a work indicator. At this point, it is entered into the MPPS (Figure 12-2), which brings the order in on schedule, and plans and coordinates the design, manufacturing, and shipping activities. Stated in terms of the products to be shipped (this does vary by the type of customer), the MPPS identifies the responsibilities and timing for each of the accepted marketing programs. The MPPS covers a thirteen-month time horizon and consists of both accepted (firm) orders and orders that marketing feels GE has a good chance of winning.

Once an initial version of the MPPS has been formed, it is reviewed regularly every month with top management and a committee, consisting of representatives from engineering, manufacturing, and marketing. This review identifies and resolves problems in the MPPS and smoothes out production. Top management, in conjunction with manufacturing, determines what level of production is for sales and the level for roll. Roll is building to inventory with the intent of either buffering or leveling employment. Past actions are also reviewed at this meeting. The finalization of the MPPS marks the starting point for the second stage of the master scheduling process -- the setting of the MPS.

In contrast to the MPPS, which deals with engineering, manufacturing, and shipping activities, the MPS is a manufacturing document consisting of shippable level items. These items are manufactured for both internal and external customers.

The MPS is formulated and reviewed weekly by representatives from engineering, customer service (this group represents GE's commitment to the customer), marketing (the sellers), warranty (the interface between manu-

APPROVED HWO PRELIMINARY

PROGRAM (SHIPPABLE DEVICES)

MASTER PRODUCTION PROGRAM SCHEDULE

Ⓥ FINAL A.N OR VALIDATED DWGS
△ MASTER SCHED. RELEASE
Ⓢ SHIP DATE, SALES, BY AIR WITH QUANT. PER PRELIM. MARKETING SCHEDULE 6-7-85
Ⓢ SURFACE SHIP REQ'MT

YEAR 1985/86

PAGE 1 OF 4

BY

DATE

REV.

Weeks: JUNE 22 23 24 25 26 | JULY 27 28 29 | AUG 32 33 34 35 | SEPT 36 37 38 39 | OCT 40 41 42 43 44 | NOV 45 46 47 48 | DEC 49 50 51 52 | JAN 1 2 3 4 5 | FEB 6 7 8 9 | MAR 10 11 12 13 14 | APR 15 16 17 18 | MAY 19 20 21 22 23 24

	RESP
SURGE RES (VAL) (20)	
BUILD PLAN	
SHUNT RES (VAL) (25)	
BUILD PLAN	
MAIN KNIFE SW (VAL) (23)	
BUILD PLAN	
MAIN FUSE (VAL) (19)	
BUILD PLAN	
BUS FUSE (VAL) (20)	
BUILD PLAN	
TERMINALS (VAL) (18)	
BUILD PLAN	
INSUL BOLT (VAL) (10)	
BUILD PLAN	
ROOF RES (VAL) (24)	
BUILD PLAN	
ROOF RES (VAL) (24)	
BUILD PLAN	
GROUND SW (VAL) (24)	
BUILD PLAN	
TRANS'F (VAL)	
BUILD PLAN	
MAG VALVE (VAL) (18)	
BUILD PLAN	
PROP. SWITCH (VAL)	
BUILD PLAN	
CHANGEOVES SW (VAL)	
BUILD PLAN	
SPEED SEN. (VAL)	
BUILD PLAN	
CONTROLLER (VAL)	
BUILD PLAN	

Figure 12-2. -- Master Production Program Schedule

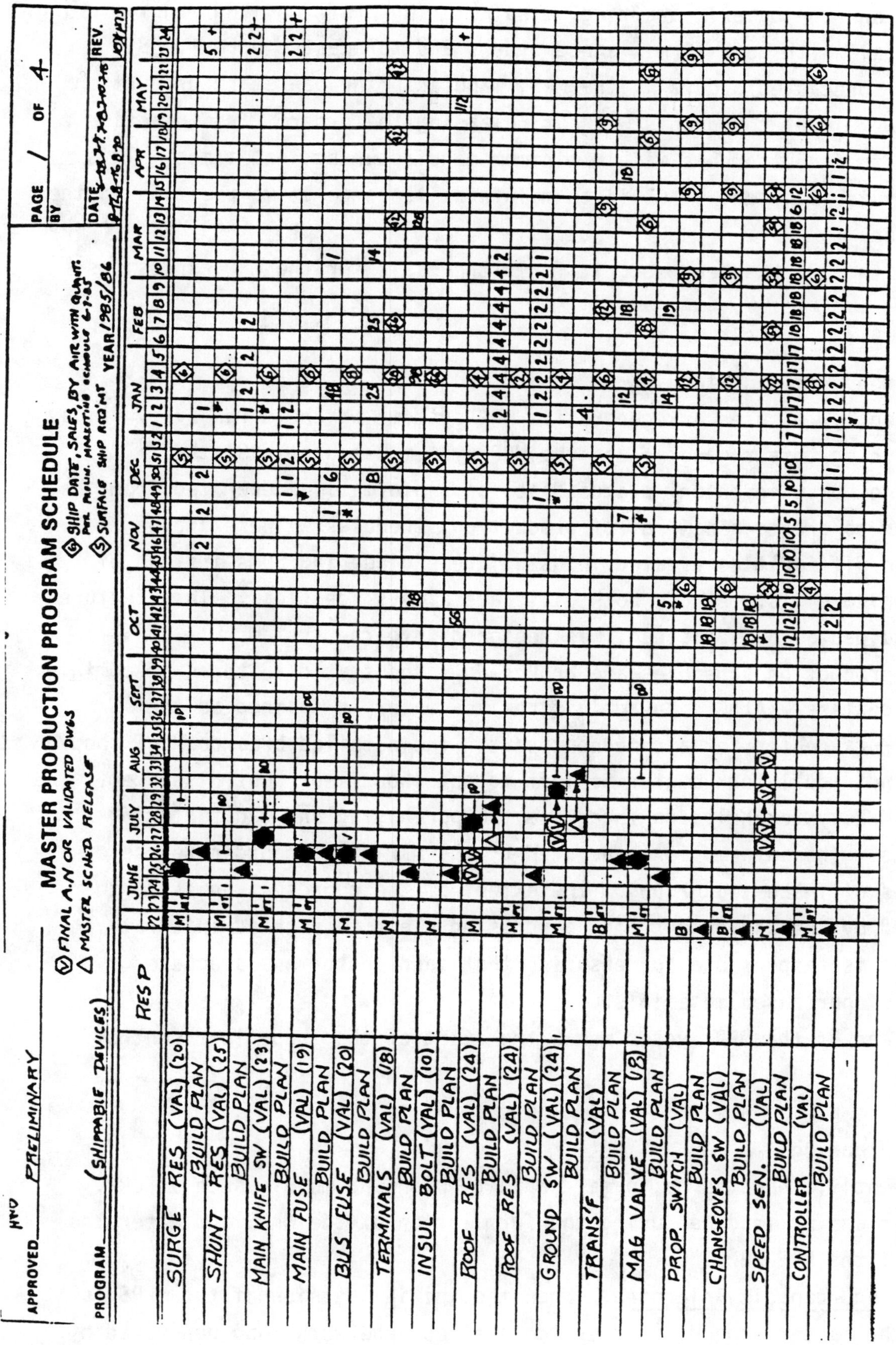

Figure 12-2. -- Master Production Program Schedule (continued)

facturing and the buyer), drafting, manufacturing drafting, and manufacturing. The MPS deals with both firm planned orders and forecasted orders. By including forecasted orders in the MPS, manufacturing can start production on the lower level components without releasing the order. This practice allows GE to accept orders within minimum manufacturing lead times. This capability is important if GE is to maintain its competitive position in the marketplace.

Once the MPS has been set, it forms the basis for the MRP explosions.

Material Requirements Planning

Currently, GE uses a regenerative MRP system, which is run every Friday night. During this regeneration, the MRP system uses the MPS, the engineering BOMs, inventory status data, and information generated from the shop floor to create a new set of production schedules. There are no production difficulties created in using the engineering BOMs instead of manufacturing bills. At GE, both bills are always identical. This feature is not accidental but, instead, was designed into the system.

The production schedules are broken down and stated in terms of administrative centers. At GE, an administrative center is defined as the starting work center for a component/part. The detailed breakdown of shop load by individual work center is left to the shop floor control system.

The MRP system helps to integrate the purchasing and manufacturing activities. The information generated by the MRP helps coordinate the activities of these two groups. The extent of the coordination is further emphasized by the assignment of a purchasing clerk to each administrative center who is responsible for ensuring that each center has adequate supplies of purchased materials.

The end of the MRP system marks the start of the shop floor control system.

Capacity Planning

Currently, there is no formal capacity planning module such as CRP. Capacity planning is done during the formulation of the MPPS and after the receipt of the MRP runs.

<u>MPPS and capacity planning</u>. When the initial version of the MPPS is formed, the master scheduler tries to level out the work load generated by the programs. This initial version of the MPPS is then passed to the top

management committee members who make a rough-cut capacity plan. Any major load problems are resolved and a modified form of the schedule is passed on to the shop foremen who, in turn, do a more detailed rough-cut capacity plan. The foremen do not deal with the MPPS, but they do work with a report that forecasts and summarizes labor requirements (the major resource of interest) by area. This report, the labor forecast summary report, converts the MPPS into labor requirements by administrative work center. The foremen review this report.

The foremen try to identify any capacity shortfall present in the MPPS, and they examine the effect of the MPPS on shop work balance. They consider:

- o The effects of new hires and the learning rates of the workers
- o Failure rates
- o Bid out rates
- o Months to bid out.

This evaluation is done monthly. After marketing submits the MPPS, the foremen have two weeks to identify the capacity effects.

Capacity problems identified during this first review are brought out in a load meeting. Acceptable solutions are also identified. The revised schedule is turned over to the master scheduler, and the schedule is booked. This set of capacity reviews is rough because of the uncertainty surrounding the acceptance of the programs and the timing of order arrivals.

MRP and capacity planning. Capacity planning is next done by the shop floor control system and is based on the MRP output. Monthly, the shop foremen take the output of the MRP system and break down the load by work center. They also establish the capacity availability by work center. The capacity levels reflect absenteeism, operator efficiency, and operator skill.

The foremen evaluate both load and capacity availability in terms of total labor and total labor dollars. These measures (especially total labor) are useful because they provide a common unit of measurement and act as an adequate measure of effective daily capacity.[1]

---

[1]Currently, management is trying to change the focus away from total labor to other measures more consistent with the MRP goals. The MRP system, after all, measures contributions to shippable output.

The foremen typically work with a minimum window of six months. The work load consists of three major components:

- o Load generated by the MRP reports.
- o Backlog that exists because foremen can elect to either roll or backlog work. Backlog is an attempt to smooth out the work load.
- o Short cycle work primarily due to TRPO orders.

The three components are summed and entered into a microcomputer (running Lotus 1-2-3). The selection of which line to use when evaluating work load is a function of the current work load composition. If there is a great deal of TRPO work in the system, the foremen use the line consisting of MRP+BKLG+SC. Otherwise, they look at either the MRP+BKLG or MRP lines. When comparing these lines with the capacity available, foremen can identify any capacity problems.

When faced by an overbooked work center, the foreman has a number of options available. These include:

- o Hire (either temporary or permanent)
- o Farm out (either internal or external)
- o Replan the work to another workstation
- o Move the work in
- o Overtime (not a preferred option)
- o Reassign hourly people (depends on the flexibility of the work force)
- o Test the MRP requirements
- o Revise the MPS (a last option).

Within the minimum six-month visibility, the foreman has excellent visibility (in terms of work load certainty) for the first three months. As a result, the foreman always has three months advance notice, which provides enough warning for most of the adjustments.

These capacity plans are made before the plan hits the shop floor. This capacity planning activity identifies a region in which there is little distinction between the shop floor control system and the production planning system.

Challenges for Control Manufacturing

In spite of many accomplishments, the current production planning system is in transition. The ultimate form taken by this system will depend on how management copes with certain key manufacturing challenges. These challenges are:

- <u>Better management of product diversity</u>. Product diversity is currently a major source of manufacturing problems. The problems created by product diversity are expected to increase. This trend can complicate manufacturing by increasing the difficulties present in product design, inventory management, and production planning and scheduling. GE must be able to better manage such diversity if it is to compete in a marketplace sensitive to cost, lead time, and quality.
- <u>Better management of space</u>. For GE, the construction of new facilities is both time-consuming and expensive. As GE expands, management must be able to accommodate the changes by better managing the space available in the current facilities.
- <u>Control and reduce the number of parts in the system</u>. It is a manufacturing fact of life that the markets in which GE competes require a large diversity of parts and components, thus requiring a large investment in both money and space. They also complicate the tracking process. The challenge is to improve the control of these parts and to reduce inventory investments. One method of achieving these goals is by redesigning parts to reduce the number of parts in the system without affecting the diversity of functions offered by the parts.
- <u>Meeting the challenge of the "factory of the future."</u> Management invested in modern technology resulting in the installation of one of the first fully operational FMS in North America. Now management must decide how to integrate this technology with the current manufacturing system and how to use the capabilities FMS offers.
- <u>Coping with a market that has been softer than anticipated</u>. When GE started developing its manufacturing system in the late 1970s, the market was expected to grow. This growth has not materialized. Product demand has fluctuated greatly.
- <u>Better control and reduction of lead times</u>. More and more often, customers want their products within less than normal lead times. The challenge for the manufacturing system is to reduce manufacturing lead times at every stage of the process.

To cope with these and other manufacturing challenges, GE management recognizes that good planning, no matter how well done, is not enough. To be successful, GE must gain control over the execution of plans, which is afforded by effective shop floor control.

Shop Floor Control

As designed and implemented in control manufacturing, shop floor control is an important and highly integrated component of the manufacturing system. It is directly responsible for controlling the execution side of the system. Preparation for shop floor control began in 1980; a test bed implementation was completed in the second quarter, 1982; and full-scale implementation was begun in late 1982. By 1984, the implementation was complete.

Like other components of the manufacturing system, the current shop floor control system is not simply a modification of the system that existed before 1982. The shop floor control system had to be rebuilt from the ground up. The new system is a result of this rebuilding.

Current System Background

In 1980, a shop floor control implementation team was formed, which consisted of people with key day-to-day production responsibilities and a full-time project manager. The team was charged with developing a shop floor control system that could serve as a model for the other areas of the Erie plant.

The team formulated a set of system specifications that required development of a model. After extensive conversations with other companies, consultants, and software vendors such as IBM, Honeywell, and Burroughs, the team found that there was no real model of shop floor control. The team developed a system framework that served as the model for the new system (Figure 12-3). The model was compared against day-to-day problems and what-if testing was done against the model.

The team tried to involve the users in the implementation process so the shop floor personnel, in many cases, became the real designers of the system. They identified the features needed in the system and defined the

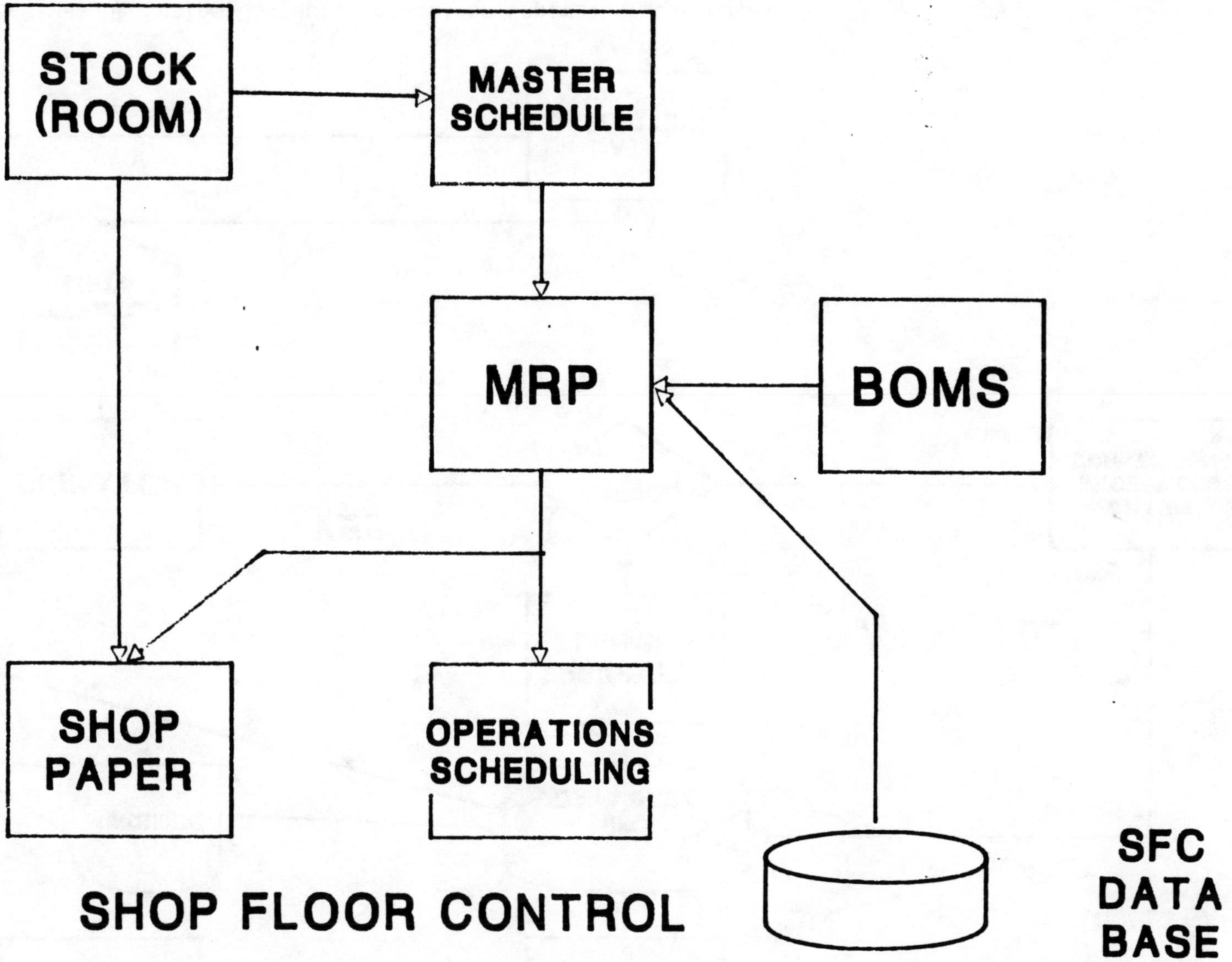

Figure 12-3. -- GE System Concept

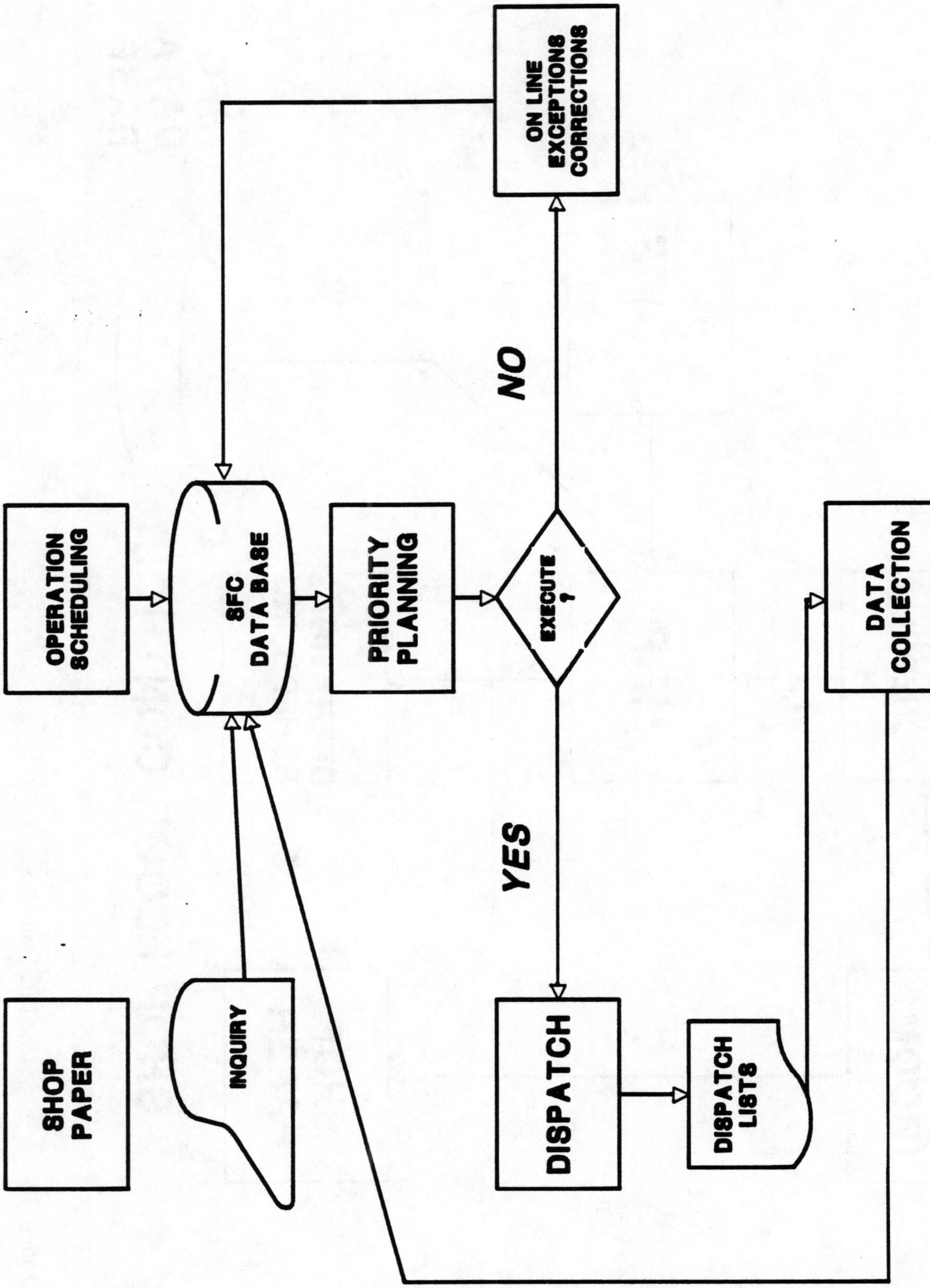

Figure 12-3. -- GE System Concept: Shop Floor Control (continued)

structure, format, and content of the reports produced. They also identified the location of the terminals.

Critical functionality was defined using the model. The primary function of the new system was to give users real-time status and priorities. Control manufacturing seemed to get the job done. The only problem was that no one, under the old system, knew which job needed to be done. The new system had to be able to flag jobs that were in trouble and be able to tell technicians that could fix the problem that their services were needed.

The team members agreed that events happened rapidly in control manufacturing, but they could not agree on whether a batch or on-line system was needed. To evaluate the need for an on-line system, the batch dispatch system was modified to look like the shop floor control model. The old timekeeping interface was replaced by feedback cards input nightly into the system. Several new types of reports designed to generate workstation dispatch lists were created. A prioritizing scheme that closely approximated the team's notion of what was wanted was developed. In the second quarter of 1982, these changes were introduced in the form of a test bed shop floor control system.

Each morning a dispatch list was distributed; nightly, feedback cards were collected and processed. The results of the test bed were very encouraging. The test demonstrated the inadequacy of a batch system and the urgent need for an on-line system and proved that a dispatch list could work if it could be kept up-to-date. Because there was no exception reporting capability, the test bed proved that jobs in trouble had to be taken off the active dispatch list and placed in the proper hands for problem resolution. The shop floor control system is easy for a user to understand and personnel who work with the system daily could accept and work with the new concept and system much more easily than could middle and upper management.

One of the major problems that the project team faced was identifying a shop floor control software package that was compatible with the balance of the baseline system and that provided the required functionality. The package had to run on a Honeywell computer system. This was not a small requirement since GE uses a variety of different computer systems. Moving a package from a system such as DEC VAX to a Honeywell would require a complete rewriting of the package. The team selected GE-developed software from Aerospace Electronics of Utica, New York. This package was developed on a Honeywell system and was used primarily for the database design. The shop floor control software was written in house.

The final event that influenced the development of shop floor control was the annexation of control manufacturing by the locomotive operation.

Overview of the Current Shop Floor Control System

The shop floor control system is part of the overall production control organization. In addition to shop floor control, production control consists of four other groups (Figure 12-4).

The program production control group looks at the business from the top level down. It is responsible for starting the final assembly operations and for communicating how the overall position schedule is affecting the business. Job starts are responsible for getting piecepart and subassembly jobs on the floor on time. Material support is responsible for the operation of the inventory system and associated stockrooms. It is also responsible for support services such as shipping, receiving, and transportation.

Shop floor control has responsibility for system maintenance and the day-to-day shop floor production control activities. Direct responsibility for the system lies with the manager who supervises those responsible for the major production units within control manufacturing. They are:

- Units I & IV (machine shop and fabrication)
- Unit II (machine shop)
- Unit III (final assembly)
- Unit V (subassembly and device)
- System administration.

The responsibility for the operation and maintenance of the shop floor control system lies with all users. Management expects that all areas of the business will use and respond to the information and measurements made available from the shop floor control system.

In general, the shop floor control system:

- Provides location and status information for all work released and in process
- Calculates the priority of all WIP based on due date
- Generates daily dispatch lists by workstation and sorts in priority sequence
- Collects all data necessary to support the daily generation of information that supports this system

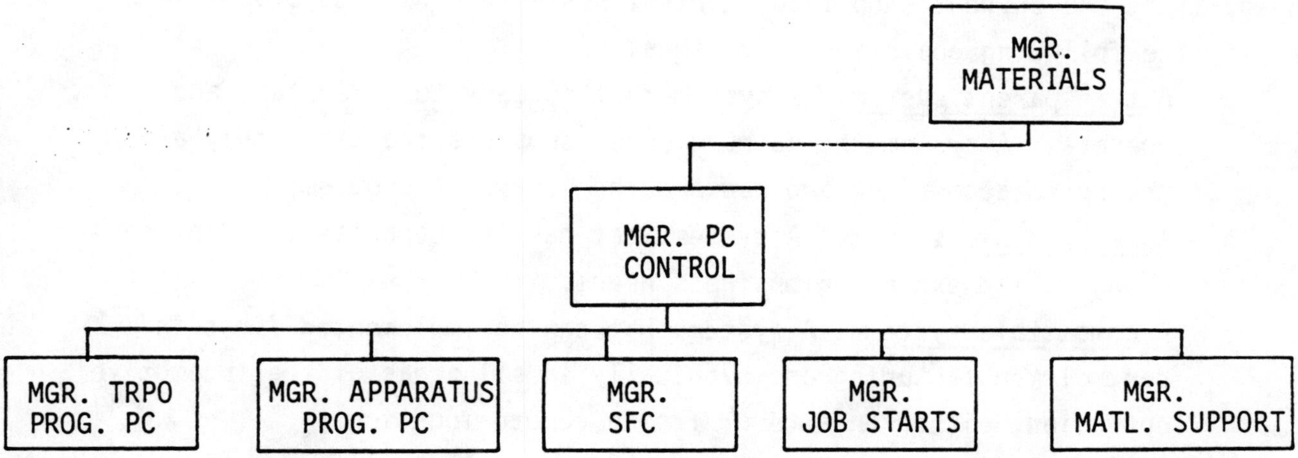

Figure 12-4. -- Production Control Organization

- o Collects feedback on orders not proceeding according to plan and communicates the information to the responsible organization through exception reports
- o Provides performance statistics
- o Validates quantity of parts from operation to operation
- o Accepts and responds to inquiries about all orders within the control of shop floor control
- o Documents general necessary shop information.

In addition, the current shop floor control system has been developed to satisfy the following goals and objectives:

- o A transparent system. A system that is easy to understand and operate. A system the users can see supports the tasks they are trying to accomplish and can see the source of problems.
- o An expandable system. A system that has the capacity to adapt to changing and expanding business needs.
- o A compatible system. A system that can be implemented first in control manufacturing and eventually in all areas of the locomotive operation, either on-site or from a remote location.
- o A flexible system. A system that has the flexibility to accept both batch and on-line inputs and provides both batch and on-line outputs.

Shop floor control at GE is seen as a dynamic system that controls shop floor activities now and accommodates the production requirements of the future.

The Stages of Shop Floor Control in Control Manufacturing

Shop floor control in control manufacturing is built on four major manufacturing tenets. These tenets have influenced both the design and operation of the shop floor control system. They are:

- o Effective systems are simple systems. Any system should perform its functions in the most direct, simple, and uncomplicated fashion. Whenever someone complicates the operation and requirements of a system, no matter what the intentions are, the result is increased confusion, reduced use, and a tendency to fall back on informal procedures. These results run counter to the intention of

GE management -- developing a system that everyone will readily understand, accept, and use consistently.

- <u>People are crucial to the effective operation of shop floor control</u>. Production system operation is more effective when people on the shop floor are given the tools and the authority to correct problems as they are flagged. The system must allow personnel to focus on problem resolution by relieving them of the responsibility of bookkeeping and data reconciliation. The shop floor control system should provide a vehicle for drawing on the insights and job-related knowledge of shop floor employees. In short, the shop floor control system must support the activities of the people working on the shop floor on an ongoing basis.
- <u>Focus must be maintained on the central task of meeting the schedules</u>. Once the order is released to the shop floor, all of the activities must be directed to meeting the time commitments of the schedule. One method of achieving this objective is to ensure that all shop floor personnel are aware of the schedule status of any job on the floor. Late jobs must always be highlighted and those that are currently inactive must be kept moving. Shop floor control supports the schedule.
- <u>Emphasize the need for continued discipline on the shop floor</u>. Shop floor control is only effective as long as it is used as it is intended to be used. There must be discipline in the system, however, it will be present only as long as the system makes clear the need for such discipline and reinforces this need during operation.

Order Review/Release

The process of releasing an order to the shop floor begins with the output generated by the MRP system. MRP generates a set of shop books that is available before the start date of the job. These books contain the key production information for each job: drawing number, order number, quantity, and due date. The books are picked up by shop production control and taken to the production control office.

To be able to track an order mechanically, the shop floor control system must go against the planning file and extract routing, as well as setup and run times for each operation. With this information, shop floor control uses stored scheduling rules to establish due dates for each operation. This activity is performed in the operation scheduling component of the system. The schedule is then stored in the shop floor control database.

Before the order is released, the priority of the order is established. This activity, done by the priority planning component of shop floor control, establishes a priority number for each operation by comparing the time remaining to completion with the work remaining to completion. The result is a slack number that shows the number of days that the job is currently ahead of (+) or behind (-) schedule. This calculation is done before the job is released because it is not unusual for MRP to release a job to the shop floor within minimum manufacturing lead times. Such jobs must be flagged from the outset.

To this point, order review/release has been primarily generating the various components of order documentation. The next test, execution testing, determines if the job is ready for labor input and execution testing checks various status codes that identify a job's availability. Most of these tests are concerned with material availability. If there is not enough material available, there are two choices. The first is not to release the order and to treat it as an exception. Or, the order quantity is adjusted to be consistent with the level of material available.

If all the tests are passed and the due date for starting the job has been reached, the necessary shop documentation is generated. A message also is transmitted automatically to the stockroom to start material accumulation. When accumulation is completed, the stockroom informs the shop floor control system, and the job is considered released to the shop floor.

The current process, while an improvement over the old procedure, is still not considered a complete order review/release process. Missing is the evaluation of the capacity impact of the order at the point of release. There is no formal leveling of the shop load. The shop floor control system is subjected to floods of orders as a result of MRP releases. This is one area that management wants to improve.

The order review/release activities are under the direct control of the production control supervisors. It is their responsibility to control the flow of work from the MRP system to the shop floor and make any necessary modifications in order quantities.

Detailed Assignment

The detailed assignment activities manage three types of dispatching: orders, tooling, and maintenance.

The dispatching of orders is straightforward and concerned primarily with active jobs, which are ready to be processed at a given work center. The order has:

- o Adequate material
- o A work center with an operator
- o No problems due to quality, engineering, or shop support (machine down, tool and die repairs and replacement, and tool modification and repair).

The dispatching process for orders begins with the assignment of an operation priority.

Each order, active or inactive, is assigned a priority number based on the slack. This priority is indicated in terms of the number of days that the order is behind or ahead of schedule. The priority, while calculated automatically by the shop floor control system, can be modified manually by the dispatcher when necessary. The priority order is important because it forms the basis on which all orders are ranked. The current priority scheme has been readily accepted by shop floor personnel and makes the urgency of any given order clear to them. It is this clarity that leads the designers of the shop floor control system to choose this priority rule over the CRR, which does not generate clear, meaningful priorities for shop floor personnel.

There is a second criterion frequently used in dispatching. This is the number of days that an order is inactive (denoted as IA in all shop floor control reports and forms). This criterion tracks the number of work center days since the order was done primarily by the operator at each work center. This ensures that all orders keep moving. The shop floor control system tries to ensure that no order experiences a large number of inactive days. If it does, it is moved up in priority.

At each work center, the operator begins by reviewing the daily dispatch list (Figure 12-5), which is printed daily and made available to the operator by an on-line CRT. The list contains all of the jobs assigned to the work center for that given day. All jobs are ranked in terms of the SLAC priority. Typically, the work indicated in the dispatching list is broken into two components: work currently in queue at the work center and all of the other jobs that are in the carousel waiting to be dispatched to

TRANS NO 6GR010 — SHOP FLOOR CONTROL — DAILY DISPATCH LIST — WORK STA 0719 ACTIVE JOBS — 06/18/85 12:09

SLAC	BOOK	OPER QTY	REPORT QTY	DRAWING	DESC	LOC	CURRENT STA	CURRENT OPR	PREVIOUS STA	PREVIOUS OPR	DAYS I/A
55-	721826	1129	1124 (*)	6700392G1	CONTACT	719	0719	005	0831	001	8
17-	721829	1500	1500	8860749G1	FINGER		0719	020	0831	001	5
17-	721824	2300	2300	8807882G1	CONTACT	M/S	0719	005	0831	001	21
13-	723746	1500	1500	8860749G1	FINGER		0719	020	0831	001	5
12-	722518	2300	2300	8807882G1	CONTACT	M/S	0719	005	0831	001	21
12-	723694	1610	1610	6700549G1	CONT ASM		0719	010	0721	005	3
12-	722519	2300	2300	8807882G1	CONTACT	M/S	0719	005	0831	001	21
7-	725056	2300	2300	8807882G1	CONTACT		0719	005	0831	001	8
7-	725057	2300	2300	8807882G1	CONTACT		0719	005	0831	001	8
6-	723556	2500	2500	9964601G2	BOX ASM		0719	025	0160	020	1
5-	725063	1000	1000	8867935G1	FRAME ASM		0719	005	0831	001	12
5-	724915	28	28	41D757119G2	BASE		0719	030	0168	015	7

-----------------------------------HOLD UP JOBS-----------------------------------

CODE	04	25	42	30 (**)
NO	21	1	1	1

TOTAL JOBS 21

(**) In addition to the 21 jobs active, there are 24 jobs inactive on hold up codes

1. Input 010,work station & press new line or enter key
   Example: 010,0719

   Output is about 10-13 lines of data and then a summary

2. Input 010,work station & number of lines wanted, press new line or enter key
   Example: 010,0719017

   Output is 17 lines of data & then a summary as in 1 above

3. Input 010,work station & ALL, press new line or enter key
   Example: 010,0719ALL

   Output is all items active for the work station & total plus summary of inactive jobs

4. If it is a dispatch coded operation (central dispatching in 42-7 only) the 01 status means that the job is in the carousel waiting to be dispatched to the work station.

5. The (*) means the job is on multiple hold up codes at that operation/work station.

Figure 12-5. -- Daily Dispatch List

the work center. Typically, operators begin with the job at the top of the dispatching list and work their way down. The operator has some flexibility when combining jobs to improve efficiency by taking advantage of continuous setups.

The format of the daily dispatch list provides the operator with focus. The operator knows what has to be completed during the day. The list also only shows the operators those orders on which they work. There is no confusion resulting from the operator trying to sort the active from the inactive jobs because the computer system has already completed this task.

The high frequency of orders with negative slack should be interpreted carefully. Frequently, negative slack indicates a late release order, a partial release, or a split lot. In the latter two cases, the orders are given the same due date as the original order.

In addition to the daily dispatch list, the operator can obtain information from the shop floor control system about:

- o Daily dispatch list of inactive jobs
- o Jobs at the workstation
- o Direct labor-hour load generated by job on the dispatch list for a given work center
- o Work coming to the work center.

This information is provided through the inquiry reports generated on line by the shop floor control system. The operator always has the information that is needed.

In contrast, the dispatching of tooling is the direct responsibility of the foreman who is responsible for the storage, use, and maintenance of all tooling.

Preventive maintenance is a regularly scheduled activity and is managed by the preventive maintenance department. The department tracks the status of equipment and identifies the times at which a work center (machine) is to be taken down. The actual scheduling of maintenance is done jointly between the foreman and preventive maintenance. This interaction ensures that preventive maintenance does not interfere with production.

Data Collection/Monitoring

Data collection/monitoring can be considered one of the strong points of GE's shop floor control system. The MRP system updates records weekly during each regeneration so the continuous updating of records is done by the data collection/monitoring activities of the shop floor control system.

The data collection segment of this activity is done on line or in batch. The on-line mode is used for inquiry, data entry, and data modification; the batch mode is used for generating detailed summaries. Of the two, most of the data collection activity takes place on line.

Data collection is an ongoing activity. The entire shop floor has been prepared for this activity with every work center in control manufacturing described in terms of area code, foreman code, and dispatcher code. These terms help locate the work center and identify responsibility for the work center.

All of the production activities of the operator are entered into the computer system. These activities include recording information on quantity completion (either full or partial), location change, or holdup of any order. Each type of transaction has its own special on-line entry (Figure 12-6), which has a set of required and option fields. In addition, extensive error checking and reporting exists. For example, to enter a quantity completion successfully, the operator must ensure that the pay number is consistent with the operator number and that the book number is correct. These features have been added to ensure that correct data always pass to the shop floor control database.

In addition, there is a set of restricted (or limited) feedback transactions that can be used for data collection and/or modification (Figure 12-7a). Access to these transactions is restricted to certain personnel within the shop floor control system. These transactions are used to modify basic characteristics of the order or inventory status. Supplementing these transactions is a set used only by shop floor control office personnel (Figures 12-7b).

The entire data collection system is supported by comprehensive inquiry reports, which are available either on line (Figure 12-8) or in batch mode (Figure 12-9), and provides shop floor personnel with a thorough view of activities taking place on the shop floor. The reports also form a basis for the control/feedback activities.

In designing the data collection system used by shop floor control, emphasis was placed on having the users accept the system. For example, there are currently 120 CRTs and twelve card readers in control manufacturing. The location of these terminals was determined by user input. There is extensive interaction between the system administrator for the shop floor

GENERAL SFC FEEDBACK TRANSACTIONS

TRANSACTION NUMBER		DESCRIPTION	FUNCTION
903	(F1)	FULL QTY FEED-BACK	COMPLETES FULL OPERATION QTY AT AN OPERATION (REPORT QTY=OPR QTY).
904	(F6)	TRANSFER FEED-BACK	ACKNOWLEDGES RECEIPT OF MATERIAL AT A XST CODED OPERATION.
** 906	(F8)	HOLD-UP CODE F/B	CREATES, MODIFIES OR DELETES HOLD-UP CODES. CREATES DATA FOR LOCATION FIELD INSERTS A REPAIR OPERATION.
933	(F2)	PARTIAL QTY F/B	COMPLETES A PARTIAL QTY AT AN OPERATION (PARTIAL QTY CANNOT EXCEED THE REPORT QTY AT THAT OPERATION).
934	(F3)	LOCATION CHANGE F/B	ENTERS A MATERIAL LOCATION OTHER THAN THE WORK STATION. OTHER USES EXIST AS NO EDIT IS MADE FOR THIS FIELD.
* 975		PARTIAL QTY F/B - MRP	COMPLETES AS TRANSACTION 933 EXCEPT IT ALSO FEEDS BACK COMPLETED DATA TO MRP FOR 'A' & 'C' CODED OPERATIONS.
* 976		FULL QTY F/B - MRP	COMPLETES AS TRANSACTION 903 EXCEPT IT ALSO FEEDSBACK COMPLETED DATA TO MRP FOR 'A' & 'C' CODED OPERATIONS.

NOTE: ALL INPUT IS VIA A CRT OR CARD READER.

* ALSO FEEDS BACK ALLOCATIONS & COMPLETIONS TO MRP.

** EXCEPT H/U 31 AND 32 MUST USE 978.

Figure 12-6. -- Feedback Transactions

'LIMITED' SFC FEEDBACK TRANSACTIONS

TRANSACTION NUMBER	DESCRIPTION	FUNCTION
901	ESTABLISHES, MODIFIES OR DELETES BOOK RECORDS	Used by SFC office and receiving to delete invalid data inputed to SFC. Other SFC functions as necessary.
913	CANCELLATION FEEDBACK	Used by stockroom to 'cancel' unstarted jobs as indicated by the hold-up code 31 report
935	BOOK QTY ADJUST	Used by the job starts to cut-back unstarted jobs. F/B to MRP necessary.
966	MANUAL BOOK LOAD	Loads a record to the SFC system. Used by Shop Operations for loading IR's & MCN's to SFC. Additional SFC office uses.
967	MANUAL JOB RESTART	Restructures status of the job to show all 'unstarted' at operation 001 or the first operation
974	PURCHASED ITEM LOAD	Loads a record to the SFC system. Use by Receiving for purchased receipts & loading IR's to the system. Additio SFC office uses.
978	INV CONTROL CANCELLATIONS	Adds, modifies, or deletes hold-up codes 31 and 32 in addition to all oth
980	MODIFY SLACK	Used to make a temporary or a permanen slack change instantly.
981	HOLD-UP CODE FEEDBACK	Used to put all jobs at a given work station on a specific hold up code, remove the hold-up code or modify the code.
984	DISPATCH FEEDBACK	Used to dispatch a job coded D. Centra dispatching.

Figure 12-7a. -- Limited Feedback Transactions

TRANSACTION NUMBER	DESCRIPTION	FUNCTION
902	OPERATIONAL MAINTENANCE	Creates, modifies, & deletes any operational record
905 (F5)	FALLOUT QTY FEEDBACK	Reduces the operation qty by the amount input as a result of scrap IR's & RLRR's
909	PHYSICAL INVENTORY	Loads physical inventory results for each in-process operation to the SFC data base
916	DELETED RECORDS	Lists all deletes for the week
918/919	SELECTIVE BOOK/OPERATION	Establishes, modifies, or deletes operation and book records
920	PAY NUMBER MAINTENANCE	Creates, modifies, or deletes the access & password for an individual by pay number
922	STOCKROOM PARAMETERS	Used to select the start date (slack) to be used for duspatching each stockroom
929	REPORT PARAMETER SELECTION	Establishes the parameters for selected reports
961	HOLD-UP CODE MASTER MAINTEN-ANCE	Creates, modifies or deletes hold-up. Adds a repair operation
962	WORK STATION MAINTENANCE	Creates, modifies or deletes various portions of the WS/WC tables
963	WORK CENTER MAINTENANCE	Creates, modifies or deletes various portions of the WS/WC tables

Figure 12-7b. -- Transactions Used Only by SFC Office

INQUIRY	DESCRIPTION	FUNCTION
008	BOOK INQUIRY	Provides detailed data concerning the job
009	DRAWING NUMBER INQUIRY	Lists all orders on SFC of that drawing number. Provides status information.
010	DAILY DISPATCH ACTIVE	Lists in slac sequence all status 01 jobs at the work station requested. Also indicates all inactive jobs under the hold-up codes
011	DAILY DISPATCH INACTIVE	Lists in slac sequence all jobs with a status other than 01. Reason code of the job is inactive is indicated.
012	JOBS AT WORK STATION	Lists jobs actually dispatched to the work station. Central dispatching.
017	WORK STATION/WORK CENTER LIST	Provides a listing of all work stations and their work centers and responsibilit areas. Also work center to station lis:
018	WORK STATION LOAD INQUIRY	Shows direct labor hours for jobs on the dispatch list for a work station
020	WORK COMING TO WORK STATION	Shows all work 1 operation away from the work station input
023	WORK CENTER LOAD INQUIRY	Shows direct labor hours for jobs on the dispatch list for a work center
039	HOLD-UP CODE LIST INQUIRY	Lists in slac order all jobs on a specific hold-up code
040	WORK CENTER DISPATCH LIST (ACTIVE)	Shows all active jobs available by work center requested
041	WORK CENTER DISPATCH LIST (INACTIVE)	Shows all jobs with hold-up codes by work center requested
042	JOBS AT WORK STATION	Lists jobs actually dispatched to the work center. Central dispatching.
089	PAY NUMBER INQUIRY	Controlled by access code - lists authorized transactions for a pay numbe
090	DAILY DISPATCH LIST	Similar to 010, indicates jobs at a wor station & also indicates data from the REQ FIELD & the ORDER NOTE FIELD.

Figure 12-8. -- Inquiry Reports

CURRENTLY AVAILABLE

INQUIRY NUMBER	DESCRIPTION	FUNCTION
0021	UPDATE ERRORS	VARIOUS ERRORS FROM MRP TO SFC LOAD
0117	CANCELLATION & RESCHEDULE STATS	STATISTICAL LISTING OF NUMBER OF JOBS CANCELLED/RESCHEDULED BY AREA
0120	CANCELLATION & RESCHEDULE ERRORS	LISTING OF ERRORS AS A RESULT OF CANCELLATION/RESCHEDULE ATTEMPTS BY MRP
0124	SLACK DISTRIBUTION	LISTS CUMULATIVE % INPROCESS BY SLACK & PERCENT
0126	TOOL CONTROL EXCEPTION REPORT	
0128	CLONE LISTING	PROVIDES A LIST OF SFC 'CLONES'
0138	DATA COLLECTION STATS	LISTS ALL TRANSACTIONS BY NUMBER FOR A GIVEN TIME FRAME ALSO LISTS ERRORS & THE PERCENTAGE OF ERRORS
0151	TOP PRIORITY ORDERS	IDENTIFIES ALL OR PART OF THE JOBS LOCAT WITHIN AN AREA THAT ARE THE HIGHEST PRIORITY FOR THAT AREA
0152	TOP INACTIVE ORDERS	IDENTIFIES ALL OR PART OF THE JOBS LOCAT WITHIN AN AREA THAT HAVE THE GREATEST AMOUNT OF DAYS INACTIVE
0153	DAYS INACTIVE DISTRIBUTION	LISTS IN SLACK SEQUENCE THE NUMBER OF JOBS INACTIVE FOR A GIVEN RANGE OF DAYS
0202	MISCELLANEOUS FILE MAINTENANCE	LISTS NUMBER OF JOBS CANCELLED, LISTS JOBS OVER 90 DAYS INACTIVE & VARIOUS PAY NUMBER TYPE ERRORS
0292	WORK STATION MOVE ERRORS	WHEN A 6GM929 TRANSACTION HAS BEEN INPUT REFERENCING REPORT 0292, THE OUTPUT PROVIDES DATA RELATED TO THAT TRANSACTION
0295	FEEDBACK CODE ADD (TO ADD A 'F' TO ALL WORK STATIONS/BOOKS ON SFC)	WHEN A 6GM929 TRANSACTION HAS BEEN INPUT REFERENCING REPORT 0295 THE OUTPUT PROVIDES DATA RELATED TO THAT TRANSACTION
0300	MRP F/B FILE LOAD	DUMP OF 099 DAILY COMPLETES
0301	MRP F/B CODE EXCEPTION REPORT	CHECKS FOR MRP ORDER NUMBER 'N'

Figure 12-9. -- Batch Reports

control system and the users, which is a result of training that takes place three times a week (at the beginning, intermediate, and advanced levels). The training meetings provide feedback for potential modifications of the current system. In addition, the system administrator reviews all suggestions provided by the users for improving the system. When a suggestion is accepted, the user is drawn into the modification process. It is widely recognized and accepted in system administration that the needs of the users are always changing as the users become more familiar with the system, its capabilities, and their needs.

There are several indications that the current data collection system is widely accepted by shop floor personnel. In 1985, there were between 22,000 and 25,000 updating transactions per week. In addition, 175,000 inquiry transactions were entered weekly. Since 1983, there have been over 400 changes to data collection and to the transactions used by this system. All of these changes have come from the users.

Factors complicating the data collection activities in control manufacturing are the lack of a common database and the presence of several different computer systems. The shop floor control system is only one component and currently operates on a Honeywell system. The shop floor control database must interact with both MADTRAN (the control manufacturing material support system for stockrooms) and HISAM (the purchasing receiving system). These other systems have their own databases and operate on different computers located in different cities. This situation is the result of how control manufacturing computer use evolved over time.

Like data collection, monitoring is an ongoing activity. Every shop floor employee must monitor all activities taking place on the shop floor. This includes not only orders but also the shop floor resources (employees, machine, tooling, and inventory). When a problem is identified, the first action is to flag the problem by a holdup transaction (Figure 12-10), which reports the presence and location of a holdup. The type of holdup is described by an assigned code (Figure 12-11). The creation of the holdup report is the first major step in control/feedback.

Control/Feedback

Control/feedback focuses on two types of problems: late orders and orders with quality problems. Each is managed differently; however, in each case, the control/feedback activities of shop floor control have been

```
TRANS NO 6GM906              SHOP FLOOR CONTROL
                            HOLD UP CODE FEEDBACK

          PAY NO           __R__ PASSWORD __R__

          FUNCTION         R                  (C=CREATE, M=MODIFY, D=DELETE)

          BOOK NUMBER      __R___

          OPERATION NO     R__

          HOLD UP CODE     R

          QUANTITY         ______ If qty left blank, SFC assumes the full qty at the operat:
                                  held up
          DAYS             _*_    * Leave blank

          REASON           __________

          LOCATION         __________

          ADD REPAIR OPER      _  If 'Y' or yes, reason must start with IR, MC, OR or BL
                                  and location must start with a valid repair work station
                                  per a SFC file of authorized work stations
```

R = required input

A. TO OBTAIN THIS PROMPT:

1. On CRT key in 906 & new line or enter key -or-
2. On CRT, press the F8 key (the darker colored key located on the upper right side of the keyboard)
3. On wall mounted card reader press the shift key & while holding down press the ST code key then release both

B. See CBL 7.151 for additional details on hold up codes

C. SPECIAL NOTES:

Use C (CREATE) in the function field when the hold up code currently does not exist on the operation record. You may transmit after completing the hold up code field, but depending upon the code, additional data may be neede

Use M (MODIFY) in the function field when the hold up code currently exists o the operation record but you need to change data in the qty, days, reason or location fields

Use D (DELETE) in the function field if you want a hold up code currently existing on the operation record to be removed. You may transmit after the hold up field has been completed. (Data on the location filed will not be removed as a result of this input - see transaction 934).

Figure 12-10. -- Holdup Transaction

SPECIAL EDITS

Repair work station will not be inserted if:

1. The operation already has a hold-up code indicated.
2. IR, MC, BL, or OR are not the first two characters of the reason field.
3. The hold up code input is not on the SFC file of authorized "repair" hold up codes. Currently 03, 04 and 07.
4. The work station input in the first 4 spaces of the location field is not an authorized repair work station per the SFC file.
5. Material is "upstream" of the operation you are attempting to insert the repair option.
6. The operation number just prior to the operation with the rejected material is equal to the current operation minus one.
7. The repair work station is not in the first 4 positions of the location field.

NOTE: All data input in the reason field will move to the location field upon successful completion of the repair insertion option.

If the hold up code was successfully transacted the message will read: TRANS COMPLETE - REPAIR OPER ADDED

If the repair insertion defaulted the message will read: TRANS COMPLETE - HU CODE ADDED

Figure 12-10. -- Holdup Transaction (continued)

HOLD-UP CODES

SHOP OPERATIONS		DEFAULT VALUE (DAYS)	DISPOSITION PRIMARY	RESPONSIBILITY FOLLOWUP
02	NO OPERATOR	2	FOREMAN	UNIT MANAGER
* 03	ON MCN (MATERIAL CORRECTION NOTICE)	5	FOREMAN	UNIT MANAGER
* 04	ON IR (INSPECTION REJECTION)	5	FOREMAN	UNIT MANAGER
05	LOST BOOK (JOB IN PROCESS)	2	FOREMAN	P/C SUPVR
06	LOST, ILLEGIBLE, OR INCORRECT DRAWING	2	FOREMAN	P/C SUPVR
07	REJECTIONS - BLDG. 42-7	5	FOREMAN	UNIT MANAGER
MATERIALS				
21	NO BOOK (NOT STARTED)	5	MTL ORDER	JOB STARTS
* 22	RAW MATERIAL SHORTAGE (NOT STARTED)	10	JOB STARTS	PURCHASING
23	WRONG MATERIAL (WRONG ITEM IN ACCUM, RAW MTL)	2	STOCKROOM	JOB STARTS
24	SUBSTITUTE MATERIAL (NNED DEVIATION NOTICE)	5	JOB STARTS	SUPVR JOB STARTS
25	ASSEMBLY SHORT PARTS (JOB STARTS RELEASED COMPLETE)	10	P/C SUPVR	SFC MANAGER
26	ASSEMBLY SHORT PARTS (JOB STARTS RELEASED INCOMPLETE)	10	JOB STARTS	MGR JOB STARTS
* 27	MATERIAL ON RLRR	5	P/C SUPVR	MGR SFC
28	RELEASE FOR SAC (18-12)	2	S/R DATA BASE	STOCKROOM MGR
29	RELEASE FOR SAC (18-15)	2	" " " ADM	STOCKROOM MGR
* 30	POTENTIAL IN-PROCESS CANCELLATION	666	INVENTORY CTL	ORDERING
* 31	POTENTIAL CANCEL (NOT STARTED) (I.C. ONLY)	666	ORDERING MECH	ORDERING MECH
* 32	CANCELLED JOBS	999	ORDERING MECH	ORDERING MECH
33	974 LOAD ERRORS - RECEIVING	2	RECEIVING CLERK	DATA BASE ADM
34	SURPRISE SHORTAGE IN STOCKROOM (IR PRODUCED FOR MISSING ITEM)	10	STOCKROOM	STOCKROOM MGR
35	RELEASE FOR SAC (18-10)	2	S/R DATA BASE ADM	STOCKROOM MGR
36	SAC IN TROUBLE	4	STOCKKEEPER	STOCKROOM SUPVR
37	PRE-ACCUMULATED	4	JOB STARTS	MGR JOB STARTS
* 38	MATERIAL CAN'T BE LOCATED AT INSPECTION	5	P/C SUPVR	INSP SUPVR
39	POTENTIAL I/P CANCELLATION DUE TO A/N	5	AN SPEC	AN MGR
	DOUBLE ALPHAS JOB NOT STARTED			
MANUFACTURING ENGINEERING				
41	NO PLANNING / PLANNING INCORRECT	3	PLANNING	SUPVR
42	NO METHOD / METHOD INCORRECT	5	METHODS	SUPVR
43	FIXTURES	5	METHODS	SUPVR
44	N/C TAPE (ERROR, AN, BROKEN)	5	METHODS	SUPVR
45	N/C SET-UP SHEET (WRONG, LOST, AN)	5	METHODS	SUPVR
46	PLANNING & DRAWING DO NOT AGREE	5	PLANNING	SUPVR
47	NEED I.E. DEVELOPMENT	5	METHODS	SUPVR
48	MATERIAL RECEIVED INCOMPLETE & NEEDS VOUCHERS	2	PLANNING	SUPVR
49	PRODUCIBILITY	5	METHODS	SUPVR
82	NO TOOLS	3	TOOL CRIB	SUPVR
83	NEED SHOP SUPPLIES	3	TOOL CRIB	SUPVR
ENGINEERING				
50	1ST ARTICLE - NO Q/C PLANNING RECORD	5	Q/C ENGR	ENGR
51	PRODUCT SOFTWARE UNAVAILABLE	5	ENGR	MANAGER
52	TEST SOFTWARE UNAVAILABLE	5	ENGR	MANAGER
QUALITY CONTROL				
61	NO INSPECTION PLAN	5	SUPVR INSP	MGR Q/C
62	NEED ENGINEERING INTERPRETATION	5	SYPVR INSP	MGR Q/C
63	NO TEST AVAILABLE	5	SUPVR INSP	MGR Q/C
64	NEED IR DISPOSITION	5	SUPVR INSP	MGR Q/C
SHOP SUPPORT				
81	MACHINE DOWN	3	MAINTENANCE SUPERVISOR	
* 84	TOOL & DIE REPAIRS & REPLACEMENT	3	MODEL SHOP	SUPVR
85	TOOL MODIFICATION & REPAIR	5	MODEL SHOP	SUPVR

* SPECIFIC DATA INPUT NECESSARY IN THE REASON & LOCATION FIELDS

Figure 12-11. -- Codes

designed to make the problem visible and to provide a quick resolution of the problem.

Late orders. All orders flowing through control manufacturing can be assigned to one of three categories:

- Red jobs. These are orders that are forty plus days behind schedule. These jobs are considered the most critical by the shop floor control system.
- Orange jobs. These are orders that are twenty plus days behind schedule.
- Remainder. All other orders on the shop floor.

The major concern of dispatchers, supervisors, and shop foremen is to reduce the number of red and orange jobs.

These jobs are flagged by the shop floor control system in several ways. First, the late orders are always reported at the top of all dispatch lists. Second, any user can request three batch reports (Figure 12-12) that focus on late orders:

- Top priority orders. This report identifies all or part of the jobs located within an area that have the highest priority for that area. (See Figure 12-12a as an example.)
- Top inactive orders. A list identifying all or part of the jobs located within a given area that have the greatest number of days inactive (Figure 12-12b).
- Days inactive distribution. This report lists in slack sequence the number of jobs inactive for a given range of days (Figure 12-12c).

Each report focuses on different aspects of lateness. In general, a job with negative slack is not considered a problem. The key to managing such a job successfully is not to let the job remain inactive. Jobs that are late should never be allowed to stay inactive for one or more days. As a result, when a red job is identified, everyone on the shop floor focuses on the inactive days indicator. Dispatchers and operators work to reduce the number of days inactive of all red jobs.

Orders with quality problems. The shop floor control system must deal with three types of problem orders. These are:

- Scrap. Scrap describes any item that cannot be made to meet the specifications.

ᴬNS NO 6GR016 — SHOP FLOOR CONTROL — 09/06/84 06:48

ↃRT ODC0151 — TOP PRIORITY

FOR AREA 06

SLAC	ST	BOOK	ORDER QTY	REPORT QTY	DRAWING NUMBER	DESC LOC	CURRENT WORK STA	CURRENT OPR NO	PREVIOUS WORK STA	PREVIOUS OPR NO	DAYS I/A
213-	30	632469	12	12	41R997693G1	HARNESS DLC	0302	005	0807	001	30
197-		EB8137	56	56	41B566565G1		0347	002	0805	001	24
137-		637415	4000	3000	41A257901P6	NAME PLATE OK	0343	005	0807	001	9
137-		637407	4000	3000	41A257901P12	NAME PLATE OK	0343	005	0807	001	9
132-		637414	4000	3500	41A257901P6	NAME PLATE OK	0343	005	0807	001	9
132-		637406	4000	2800	41A257901P12	NAME PLATE OK	0343	005	0807	001	9
127-		637405	4000	3000	41A257901P12	NAME PLATE	0343	005	0807	001	9
122-		662501	20000	10000	41A274679G2	PIN TO PIN OK	0321	005	0807	001	4
121-		104393	12	12	185V837P1	IND PL	0341	020	0160	019	1
116-	30	643467	50	50	41A255325P3	NAMEPLATE DLC	0342	005	0807	001	94
101-		645034	50	50	41A278832P1	NAMEPLATE	0342	005	0807	001	81
1-		669124	10	10	41A322010AUG102	WIRES OK	0345	010	0302	005	13
91-		647586	10	10	41A278832P1	NAMEPLATE	0342	005	0807	001	72
86-		669120	6	6	41A322010BCG100	WIRE LIST OK	0345	020	0302	015	13
77-		669126	9	9	41A322010AUG101	WIRES	0345	010	0302	005	13

A. TO OBTAIN THIS PROMPT:

1. INPUT 016,0151,06 & NEW LINE OR ENTER KEY (AUX AFTER IF YOU WANT IT PRINTED)
   OUTPUT: TOP JOBS IN DECLINING ORDER

2. A MAXIMUM OF FIVE AREA CODES CAN BE INPUT AT ONE TIME
   EXAMPLE: 016,0151,02,03,04,05,06

Figure 12-12a. -- Top Priority Orders

TRANS NO 6GR016 SHOP FLOOR CONTROL 09/06/84 06:30
REPORT ODC0152 TOP DAYS INACTIVE
FOR AREA 06

SLAC	ST	BOOK	ORDER QTY	REPORT QTY	DRAWING NUMBER	DESC LOC	CURRENT WORK STA	CURRENT OPR NO	PREVIOUS WORK STA	PREVIOUS OPR NO	DAYS I/A
116-	30	643467	50	50	41A255325P3	NAMEPLATE	0342	005	0807	001	94
						DLC					
101-		645034	50	50	41A278832P1	NAMEPLATE	0342	005	0807	001	81
91-		647586	10	10	41A278832P1	NAMEPLATE	0342	005	0807	001	72
41-		655998	22	22	41A322010CCG100	WIRE LIST	0345	015	0302	010	50
22-		640877	1	1	41R997621G1	HARNESS	0304	078	0347	075	47
64-		654235	10	10	41D750860P5	STOP ASM	0341	005	0807	001	47
64-		654234	10	10	41D750860P5	STOP ASM	0341	005	0807	001	47
64-		654233	10	10	41D750860P5	STOP ASM	0341	005	0807	001	47
64-		654231	10	10	41D750860P5	STOP ASM	0341	005	0807	001	47
64-		654230	10	10	41D750860P5	STOP ASM	0341	005	0807	001	47
66-	47	661210	2	2	41R955076G2	WIRES	0344	005	0807	001	41
						DLC					
[illegible]-	47	661209	2	2	41R955076G1	WIRES	0344	005	0807	001	41

A. TO OBTAIN THIS REPORT:

1. INPUT 016,0152,06 & NEW LINE OR ENTER KEY (AUX AFTER IF YOU WANT IT PRINTED)
   OUTPUT: TOP INACTIVE ORDERS IN DECLINING DAYS INACTIVE ORDER
2. A MAXIMUM OF 5 AREA CODES CAN BE INPUT AT ONE TIME
   EXAMPLE: 016,0152,02,03,04,05,06

Figure 12-12b. -- Top Inactive Orders

TRANS NO 6GM968 SHOP FLOOR CONTROL 08/09/85
REPORT ODC0153 DAYS INACTIVE DISTRIBUTION
SUMMARY

SLAC	1	2	3	4	5	6-10	11-15	16-20	21-25	>25
>+91	2	0	4	1	0	18	12	8	2	12
+90	0	0	0	0	0	1	0	1	0	2
+80	0	0	0	0	0	1	0	0	0	1
+70	1	0	0	0	0	0	1	1	1	3
+60	0	0	0	0	0	0	0	0	1	2
+50	1	2	0	0	0	1	1	3	0	1
+40	0	3	0	0	1	2	1	3	0	12
+30	5	2	2	2	0	15	5	11	1	26
+20	21	9	8	2	2	182	13	19	12	26
+10	388	196	127	18	47	1541	138	201	32	65
-10	115	114	129	26	41	224	248	446	185	110
-20	247	88	112	51	40	172	37	96	220	172
-30	195	106	45	33	49	139	99	88	125	525
-40	176	94	36	54	38	83	52	43	55	406
-50	89	49	34	30	23	45	24	21	18	244
-60	65	39	11	23	10	37	13	14	11	417
70	43	20	28	14	4	24	15	10	17	153
-80	24	11	5	9	6	17	17	5	3	39
-90	18	7	6	2	2	13	5	2	2	30
<-91	51	24	31	28	8	55	22	12	12	65
TOTAL	1441	764	578	293	271	2570	703	984	697	2311

A. **TO OBTAIN THIS REPORT:**

1. **Input 016,0153,*** & new line or enter key**

   Output: Days inactive distribution

2. **A maximum of five area codes can be input at one time**

   Example: 016,0153,02,03,04,05,06

Figure 12-12c. -- Days Inactive Distribution

- o *Rework*. This is any item that can be made to the drawing specifications after the application of additional labor or a change in routings.
- o *Repair*. A repair item can be made functional, but it cannot meet all of the specifications of the drawing.

These problem orders are made by a system that is administered by quality control and that is a joint effort between quality control and shop floor control.

The system developed to correct and manage these problem orders is primarily a financial system in which quality control acts as an independent auditor. A budget for scrap, rework, and repair is established at the start of each fiscal year for control manufacturing. The budget is divided up by shop area and foremen. Each foreman is responsible for managing a portion of the budget. The foremen's performance evaluations are based partially on their ability to manage their allotted segment of the budget.

The budget also affects capacity planning. It gets loaded into the capacity plan so that a portion of the capacity, in labor-hours, is set aside for rework and repair. (No capacity is provided for scrap.) By budgeting for capacity, there is enough capacity for both the normal work and for rework and repair. There are few capacity conflicts.

The control/feedback procedure for problem orders has three objectives. First, the procedure allocates the cost and is responsible for both the initial problem and its correction. Second, it identifies the cause of the problem. Finally, the procedure tries to prevent the recurrence of the problem. To satisfy the objectives, the control procedures embody two major premises:

- o *A defect is a treasure*. A defect, when it occurs, gives shop floor personnel the opportunity to learn about a potential problem on the floor. Any procedure must obtain as much information about the defect as possible.
- o *All defects must be resolved quickly*. Once a defect is identified, it must be resolved within twenty-four hours. Quick disposition of the defect makes people more aware of it.

The first step in the control/feedback activities for problem orders is problem detection. A defect is typically flagged by an inspector who fills out a defective material report (DMR) (see Figure 12-13) and a defective tag is attached to the rejected item (Figure 12-14). A holdup code is then assigned. A copy of the DMR is sent to the quality control office where a

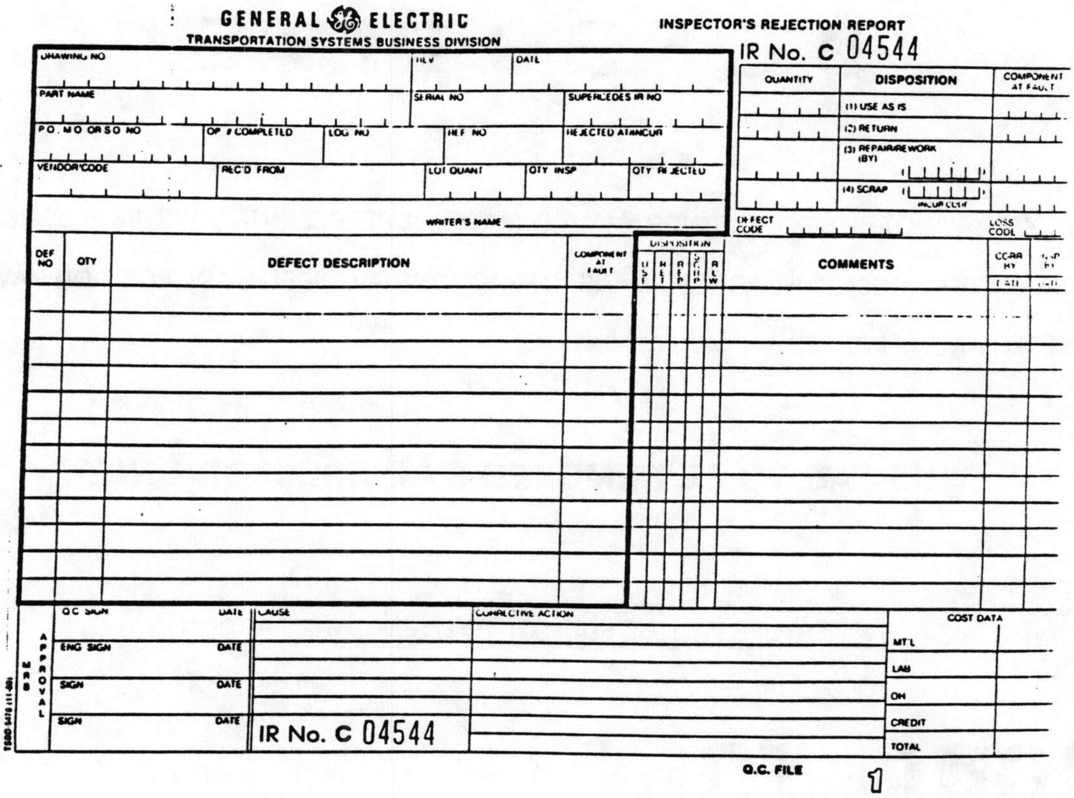

GENERAL ELECTRIC
TRANSPORTATION SYSTEMS BUSINESS DIVISION

INSPECTOR'S REJECTION REPORT
IR No. C 04544

DRAWING NO | REV | DATE
PART NAME | SERIAL NO | SUPERCEDES IR NO
P.O. MO OR SO NO | OP # COMPLETED | LOG NO | REF NO | REJECTED AT/ANCUR
VENDOR CODE | REC'D FROM | LOT QUANT | QTY INSP | QTY REJECTED
WRITER'S NAME

QUANTITY	DISPOSITION	COMPONENT AT FAULT
	(1) USE AS IS	
	(2) RETURN	
	(3) REPAIR/REWORK (BY)	
	(4) SCRAP	

DEFECT CODE | LOSS CODE

DEF NO	QTY	DEFECT DESCRIPTION	COMPONENT AT FAULT	DISPOSITION USE	RET	REP	SCRP	RW	COMMENTS	CORR BY	DATE

MRB APPROVAL
QC SIGN | DATE
ENG SIGN | DATE
SIGN | DATE
SIGN | DATE
CAUSE
CORRECTIVE ACTION
COST DATA: MT'L | LAB | OH | CREDIT | TOTAL

IR No. C 04544

Q.C. FILE 1

Figure 12-13. -- Rejection Report

DEFECTIVE

THIS IR TAG MAY NOT BE REMOVED, NOR MAY ANY MATERIAL REPRESENTED BY THIS IR BE RELEASED FOR USE UNTIL DISPOSITION HAS BEEN MADE, AND ACTIONS REQUIRED BY DISPOSITION HAVE BEEN COMPLETED AND APPROVED.

THIS TAG TO BE REMOVED BY INSPECTOR ONLY

VIOLATORS WILL BE SUBJECT TO DISCIPLINARY ACTION.

MOVE TO ______________________

Figure 12-14. -- Defective Tag

file on the defect is opened on the computer system. The data on the problem order are keypunched into the system and are referenced by the drawing number. Another copy of the report is sent to the members of the material review board (MRB).

The MRB brings together representatives from quality control, engineering, purchasing, and manufacturing. It is also organized by shop area (with a different MRB responsible for each shop area). The MRB meets daily and is responsible for deciding on DMR disposition. In the case of a manufactured item, the MRB can decide whether to scrap, rework, or use the item as is. For purchased parts, the MRB can return the items to the vendor. While most dispositions are resolved jointly, the decision to use defect items as is can only by authorized by engineering. The MRB must dispose of all DMRs received within twenty-four hours.

If the MRB decides to scrap an item, this action is carried out automatically. The cost of the scrap is charged against the budget and the cost burden assigned to the area responsible. Scrap costs are broken down and recorded by scrap material and scrap labor.

In the case of rework, the assignment of costs depends on how the rework is carried out. If the rework is done by someone other than the responsible operator, then there is a charge against the budget. This charge can be avoided by having the responsible operator do the rework. The operator, however, does not receive any pay for the doing of the rework. Operators do receive information about problems for which they are responsible.

In the case of repair, the foreman responsible has to pay someone to carry out the repair. Before payment is made, the foreman must receive a DMR number from the MRB. The cost information comes back as a labor ticket and is charged against the budget.

When dealing with either rework or repair, the MRB is responsible for disposition while the shop floor control system must schedule the work. When scheduling rework and repair, the due dates for the affected items are not changed. As a result, such orders frequently proceed through the shop with negative slack.

This procedure puts pressure on the foremen to control the levels of scrap, rework, and repair. This pressure comes from two sources. First, is the budget. Poor control over scrap, rework, and repair results in unfavorable variances and poorer evaluations. Second, rework and repair operations are considered part of indirect labor. Another measure on which foremen are evaluated is the percentage of indirect to direct labor. As the level of rework and repair increases, the percentage of direct to indirect labor also increases.

When the DMR has been disposed, it comes back through the quality control system where it is closed out. To be closed out, a quality control inspector must examine the part and approve of the close out.

The steps to this point have only dealt with allocation of cost and responsibility. The other two objectives (problem identification and resolution) are realized as a result of the follow-up actions.

Follow-up begins with the generation of the DMR summaries printed weekly. Quarterly, all actions against the various drawing numbers are summarized and printed out by drawing number. More detailed information on a specific DMR is available on request.

These reports are sent to each shop area's loss committee, which brings together the foreman for that area and representatives from quality control, engineering, methods and planning, and tooling. Meeting weekly, the committee examines DMR losses, identifies the cause of important losses, and proposes and begins implementation of long-term solutions.

The committee focuses primarily on a loss that generates over $200 in costs. Otherwise, the committee focuses on the top ten cost items. For each loss identified, the committee must determine whether the loss is due to a persistent problem or simply a one-shot problem. For persistent problems, the committee must arrive at a solution and commit funds to the implementation of the solution.

These steps have given shop personnel effective control over problems occurring on the shop floor.

Order Disposition

Order disposition is straightforward. Before the shop floor control system can relieve itself of responsibility for an order, it must first close out the order. To be closed out, all items of an order must be accounted for. That is, the completed items and those items that fell out (due to scrap, rework, or repair) must equal the order quantity initially released to the floor. All fallouts must be explained by a fallout report. The explanations can be either descriptive or a holdup code. Once all of the items of an order have been accounted for and any fallouts explained, the shop floor control system can relieve itself of the order.

Performance Feedback and Evaluation

The shop floor control system attempts to build an environment in which people can correct problems and in which cooperation, not conflict, is emphasized. A contributing factor is the method developed for performance feedback and evaluation. All information on performance (of a work center or shop area, for example) is readily available. In most cases, the information is obtained within twenty-four hours. The only exception is the weekly summary of DMRs.

The structure of the shop floor control system encourages cooperation. The foremen, for example, are responsible for a block of workstations. They are responsible for detailed labor scheduling, labor standards, tooling issues, and detailed execution of the production schedules. To do well, they must work closely with the operators and the dispatchers. They must also work closely with the production control supervisors who are responsible for scheduling the shop (work loads) and for the general labor schedules. Their decisions have important impacts on the foremen. In turn, the actions of the foremen affect the supervisors who are trying to carry out the schedule. The shop floor control system encourages people to recognize the presence and importance of the interdependent tasks and positions.

Evaluating General Electric's Shop Floor Control System -- Benefits

GE's control manufacturing area has been working on its shop floor control system since 1982. In that time, the development of this system has generated several important benefits (both quantitative and qualitative). The most significant are:

- Reduced inventory levels. Overall, inventory levels have fallen appreciably.
- Decrease in the number of late order releases. In a late order release, an order is released to the shop floor even when it is known that the order cannot hope to make its due date. Late order releases are indicative of problems in the overall manufacturing system. Since the introduction of shop floor control, the control area has been able to reduce late order releases by 67 percent. This result reflects an increasing awareness of the order/review release role.

- Improved stockroom accuracy. Overall, the stockroom accuracy at the control area has increased by over 80 percent. Employees are now aware of the relationship between information accuracy (and its need) and shop floor performance. Furthermore, the accuracy requirements are now far more stringent than they have ever been.
- Reduction in shop orders on the shop floor. No longer are orders automatically released to the shop floor where they increase shop floor congestion. The flow of orders to the shop floor is tightly controlled.
- Reduced staffing requirements. By improving the operation of the shop floor control system, GE management has been able to do more with less. Productivity per employee has increased.
- Improved control over physical inventory. Before the development of the current shop floor control system, a complete physical inventory count would take three days and a complete shutdown of the facilities. Now, shop floor personnel can do a complete physical inventory count in one afternoon with little advance preparation.
- Improved housekeeping. The overall cleanliness of facilities at GE has increased. Inventory is never left in the aisles. All machines and work centers are constantly maintained and kept clear of debris. All tooling is returned to the tool storage areas on completion. Shop floor personnel are now aware of the importance of order and discipline.
- Improved rescheduling capabilities. Management is able to reschedule orders over night. All priorities used on the floor always reflect actual needs.
- Improved application of material. More of the material used in the system is traceable. There are no longer as many unnecessary allocations.
- Improved morale. Morale has never been as high as it is now. One reason is that shop floor personnel feel good about the tools that they have been given. They feel that the shop floor control system is now helping them meet their objectives.

One of the strongest indications of the importance of the current shop floor control system to the people in the control area comes from the strong feeling that no one wants to return to the way shop floor was managed in the past. The emphasis is now on improving the current system and making what they have even better.

Shop Floor Control at General Electric -- The Next Stage

Currently, GE has finished implementing its shop floor control system within the control area. In general, everyone within the control area is pleased with the operation of this system. In the future, management has planned the following activities involving shop floor control:

- Extension of the current shop floor control system to other manufacturing areas of the Erie plant. The shop floor control system installed in the control area was intended as a prototype for the other areas.
- Improvement in the capacity planning capabilities of the manufacturing system. Management is attempting to enhance the capacity planning capabilities of the managers' operation on the shop floor. This direction involves the development and refinement of better capacity models using the IBM PC and such programs as Lotus 1-2-3.
- Revision/fine-tuning of the computer reporting system. One area that is continuously undergoing revision is the computer system. Management personnel responsible for this system work closely with the users. Based on feedback received from the shop floor, they revise features of the computer system. These revisions take many forms: addition of new reports or data screens, deletion of current reports or screens, or changes in the format of the current screens. These revisions are intended to make the system easier to use and more useful to shop floor personnel. The computer system, in its design and form, is dynamic. As the needs and capabilities of the users change, so must the computer system.
- Training of shop floor personnel and upper level management. Control area management is working on training the shop floor personnel better. This training is necessary to ensure that the users on the shop floor can use the full capabilities offered by the current system. In addition, management must also work on making its top management aware of the current state of the shop floor control system, which can offer top management the capacity to monitor and control operations on the shop floor. These

capabilities are important because they enable top management to develop better plans. Training enables personnel from the control area to make top management aware of the crucial link that exists between capacity and material planning and the resulting effectiveness of the shop floor control system.

Shop Floor Control at General Electric: Lessons to be Learned

The current shop floor control system has played an important role in the revitalization of the GE facilities in Erie. It is an integral element of the modernized manufacturing system. When reviewing the events surrounding the implementation and development of its shop floor control system, there are several lessons that should be noted:

- Do it fast. Any implementation of shop floor control should be done within a short time frame. It should never take more than eighteen months. If the implementation takes too long, people start to lose interest, and it is difficult to hold the implementation group together for longer than eighteen months. The implementation of shop floor control in the control area took three years.
- Develop a sense of ownership. The development of an effective shop floor control will only occur when personnel see that system as being their system. When this occurs, they will do everything in their power to make the system work. They will incorporate into the system modifications drawn from their experiences and insights. They will also use the system. Ownership occurs when the users are given responsibility for making the system. An example is found in the approach taken concerning placement of terminals on the shop floor. The users identified the locations where the terminals should be placed. Often, these terminals are hidden from sight, however, they are used because they are convenient.
- Always use a test bed. Before implementing the shop floor control system in all areas, first prove the worth of the system in a limited setting. This approach gives management the opportunity to observe the operation of the new system in action, and gives management the chance to correct any problems with the system uncovered in the operation.

- <u>Maintain the three keys to effective shop floor control: transparency, K.I.S.S., and validity</u>. These three keys form the basis for developing an effective system that is always used. To maintain these three keys requires that the developers of the system be responsive to the user. It also requires that the system provides users with rapid and accurate access to data contained within the manufacturing database.
- <u>The computer should never be the constraint</u>. The computer should never hold up system development. There should never be any question about computer power or concerns about the ability of the computer or the costs of using the computer. Within the shop floor control system, the involvement of the user should be seen as an "A" item while the computer should be viewed as either a "C" class or, at best, a "B" class item.
- <u>Ensure education of upper management</u>. In the shop floor control implementation process, there is a tendency to focus on shop floor personnel and to ignore upper level management. This tendency must always be fought if the system is to be effective. Upper level management must be kept aware of changes taking place on the shop floor. These changes often significantly affect the planning process. In addition, as the shop floor control system evolves, it places new demands on the planning system (such as better capacity planning). When these changes occur, management must be ready to change the planning process to keep pace.
- <u>Build the key shop floor control relationships early</u>. No shop floor control system can operate or should operate in isolation. The practices used on the shop floor and the information generated by the system should reflect inputs from other key functions within the firm. The developers of the shop floor control system should work at building the necessary bridges between themselves and the other key functional areas. These bridges should be built early in the implementation process when these groups have a chance to affect the features and structures of the new shop floor control system. Specifically, management should work at building the necessary link between the new shop floor control system and:
    - Cost accounting and finance
    - Manufacturing engineering

- Quality assurance (this relationship can influence the structure of the data collection activities)
    - Purchasing
    - Engineering
    - Marketing.

- o <u>Recognize the importance of formalized capacity planning</u>. Formal capacity planning should be present from the outset. Without it, effective shop floor control is difficult to achieve. This is one lesson that personnel in the control area have learned through experience. The success achieved in the control area, in the absence of such capacity planning, has occurred because of shop floor personnel initiative and microcomputer availability. These successes, however, are due to short-term, stopgap measures. The shop floor control system still needs formalized capacity planning.
- o <u>Understand the importance of order review/release</u>. The key to preventing and managing the "Monday morning flood" is a well-structured order review/release mechanism. GE management has given attention to the problem of controlling the release of orders to the shop floor. It has found that managing this flow is far more important than the best dispatching system.
- o <u>Understand and emphasize the importance of discipline</u>. A major factor underlying any effective shop floor control system is the compliance of shop floor personnel with the requirements of the system. The user must be willing to always follow the procedures laid down in the shop floor control system. The user must always function within the boundaries of the system. Such behavior cannot occur without discipline.
- o <u>Never underestimate the difficulties of changing an existing system</u>. It is easier to implement a shop floor control system in a setting where there was no previous system. As the management of the control area discovered when attempting to change an existing system, there are numerous hidden land mines. There are three obstacles that require special attention. The first is the database. Changing the database is difficult because people are reluctant to change past procedures. They are not willing to disregard what are essentially hidden sunk costs. The second area consists of the past procedures used on the shop floor. People are not willing to abandon something that is known and familiar (even

if these procedures are not effective) in favor of a set of new and unknown procedures. Users must be convinced that the costs of using the old procedures are greater than any costs that can be met when applying the new system. This is a long-term, difficult task. Finally, there is the problem of management. Like the user, management must be weaned away from the old system to the new. Often, managers are more reluctant to change than shop floor personnel.

Control area management of the Erie plant is proud of the changes that have come about in the manufacturing system. An outmoded facility has been transformed into an efficient facility that can compete successfully in today's industrial environment. A key element of this transformation has been the shop floor control system, which harnesses the power offered by modern computers and other new manufacturing technology.

CHAPTER 13: JOY MACHINERY COMPANY: DIVISION OF JOY MANUFACTURING COMPANY

General Nature of the Firm

The Joy Manufacturing Company, Inc., of Pittsburgh, Pennsylvania, is a public firm that first started selling and trading shares in 1919. Since that time, Joy has grown into a successful business organized into six major business segments:

- Mining machinery and equipment
- Air machinery
- Petroleum equipment and products
- Air pollution control equipment
- General products
- Ore processing equipment.

These six business segments are assigned to one of two divisions. The first division, Joy Industrial Equipment Company, is responsible for the manufacturing and sales of process equipment, general products, petroleum equipment, and environmental systems (air pollution control equipment). The second division, Joy Machinery Company, is responsible for mining and construction equipment, industrial compressors, and coal machinery. The structure of the Joy Manufacturing Company is summarized in Figure 13-1.

Franklin Operations, the Joy Machinery Company

The Franklin, Pennsylvania, operations of the Joy Machinery Company (Joy-Franklin) is the world's leading manufacturer of underground mining equipment. Its principal products are continuous miners; shuttle cars; shearing machines for longwall mining; and conventional mining equipment, including cutters, loaders, and drills. Joy-Franklin's major customers are domestic and international underground coal mining companies.

Joy-Franklin's manufacturing business is mostly ATO, although its chain products operation is both ATO (to support capital equipment manufacturing) and MTS (for support of the aftermarket).

In addition to its major production facilities located in the United States, the Joy Machinery Company also has manufacturing facilities in Australia and South Africa.

Joy Machinery Company

- Mining and Construction Group
- Industrial Compressor Group
- Coal Machinery Group
  - Coal Machinery Division
    - Franklin Operations
      - Machine Shop
      - Fabrication Shop
      - Assembly Shop
      - Chain Plant Operations

Joy Industrial Equipment Company

- Process Equipment Group
- General Products Group
- Petroleum Equipment Group
- Environmental Systems Group

Figure 13-1. -- Joy Manufacturing Company, Inc.

Production Process

The principal manufacturing processes at Joy-Franklin are machining, fabrication, subassembly, and final assembly. The flow of material (Figure 13-2) can be described as follows:

- o Purchased parts are used in the subassembly and final assembly processes. Some of the purchased hardware items, however, are consumed in the fabrication process.
- o Bar stock and castings are used in the machining process and are then used in the subassembly and final assembly processes.
- o Steel plate goes through the burn, cut up, and preparation areas before going to welding, matching, and/or final fit-up welding. All this takes place before final assembly. (Some items that are fabricated and machined also go to subassembly before final assembly.)

An organizational chart for Joy-Franklin is shown in Figure 13-3. The machine, fabrication, and assembly shops are all separate plants. Manufacturing capacity is distributed approximately as follows:

- o Machining -- 35 percent
- o Fabrication -- 25 percent
- o Subassembly -- 10 percent
- o Final assembly -- 30 percent.

All capacities are measured and reported in standard hours.

Joy-Franklin is a union shop. The work force in all areas except final assembly is paid on an incentive basis.

Production Planning at Joy-Franklin

Joy-Franklin currently manages its organization using an MRP II philosophy. Business planning and sales planning provide inputs into the production planning process. A production planning meeting, chaired by the vice president of operations, is held monthly and includes representatives from marketing, sales, engineering, manufacturing, and materials. Here, the results of the past month are reviewed, and the participants review the production plan for the next eighteen months and make any changes, if and when required, to reflect changes in market conditions.

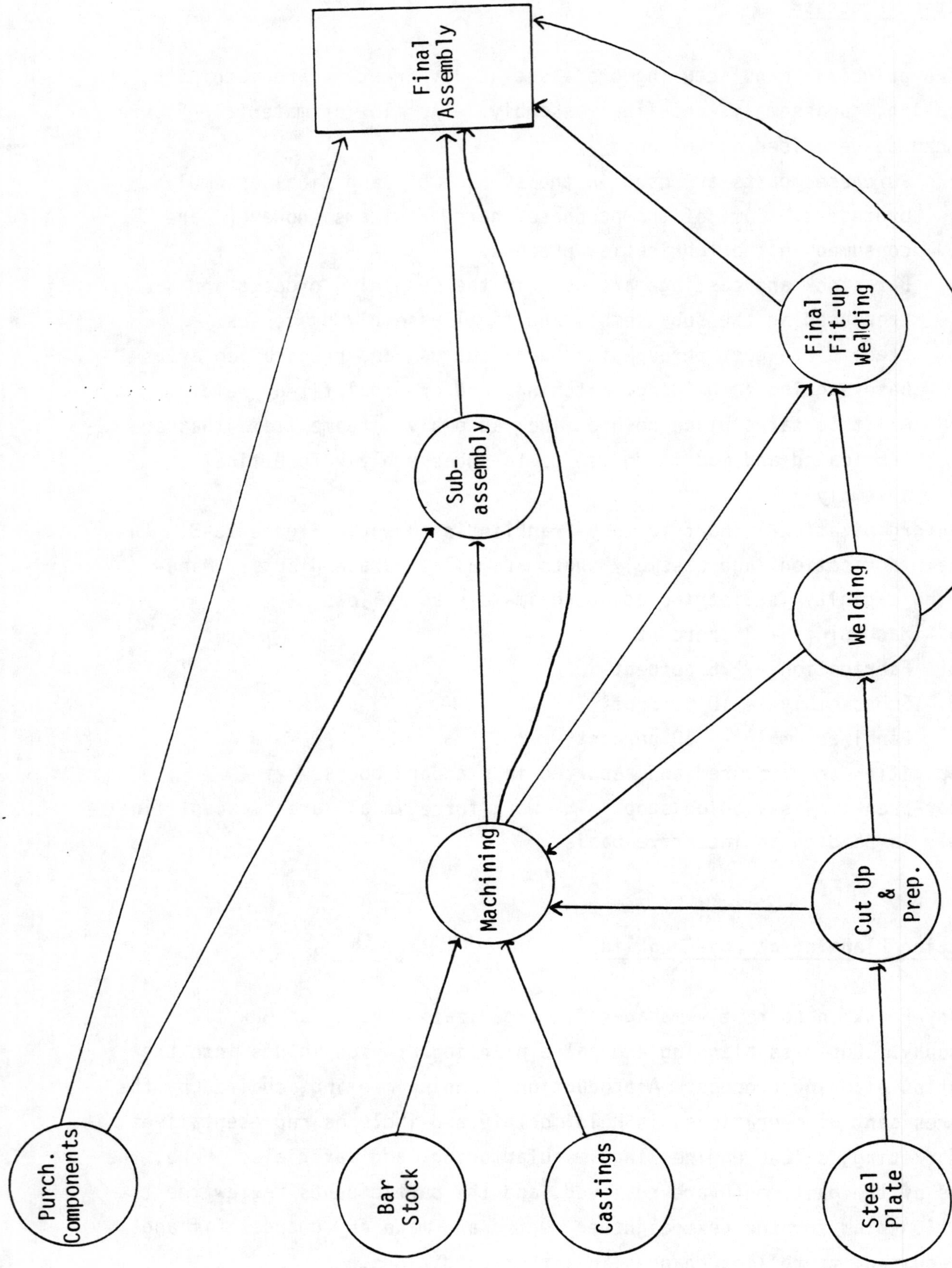

Figure 13-2. -- Material Flow

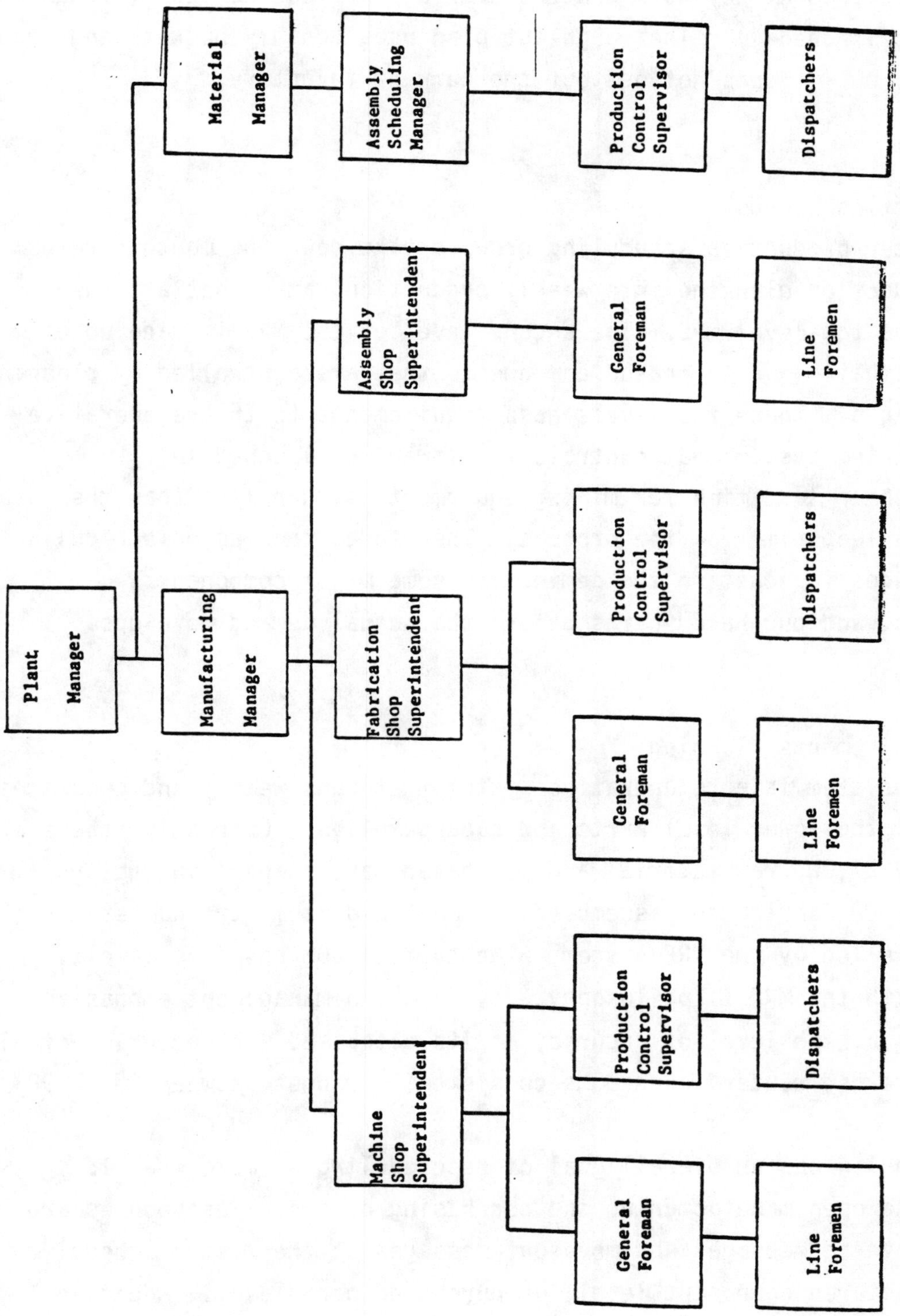

Figure 13-3. -- Organizational Chart

Rough-cut capacity for key work centers is also planned at this meeting. Twelve product families are used as the basis for constructing the production plan and the rough-cut capacity plan. The rough-cut plan looks at the project load at key work centers over a five-year horizon (it can go out ten years if needed). The rough-cut plan uses monthly buckets and lead time offsets, but it does not net out the current inventory.

Master Production Scheduling

The master production scheduling group breaks down the monthly rates found in production planning into weekly production rates that are then considered the top-level MPS. The second level of the MPS is made up of major subassemblies and purchased components that are controlled by planning bill percentages. These two levels pass requirements to the regenerative material planning system that controls the lower level schedules.

The customer lead time for mining equipment is much less than the total manufacturing lead time for the product. Therefore, the master scheduling process includes forecasting the demand for some major components, subassemblies, and purchased parts before the actual demand develops.

Material Requirements Planning

The MRP system is a regenerative system that runs weekly and generates schedules for the lower level parts and subassemblies. Currently, there are approximately 27,000 raw material and purchased part numbers in the system and about 85,000 fabricated, assembled, or machined item part numbers that must be controlled by the MRP system. The typical BOM has five levels. Consistent with the MRP II philosophy, Joy-Franklin management emphasizes and maintains a high level of accuracy in its database. The accuracy of all inventory records, routers, and BOMs consistently ranges between 95 to 98 percent.

Joy-Franklin has an overall goal of rescheduling no more than 15 percent of the open manufacturing and purchasing orders. Reschedules are defined as move-in messages and move-out messages at the master schedule level, manufactured component level, or purchased part level. Additional changes occur in order quantity adjustments (i.e., order quantity increases or decreases) and order cancellations.

Capacity Requirements Planning

Released and planned orders (using standard routings) are used to generate weekly capacity requirements plans for each work center fifty-two weeks into the future. A weekly capacity meeting, chaired by the plant manager and attended by representatives from machining, fabrication, assembly, and materials, is held to discuss capacity actions affecting manufacturing. At this meeting, capacity for order availability is evaluated and capacity availability is matched to capacity demands (as represented by the released and planned orders). This meeting ensures that there is always adequate capacity available in each week to meet the production demands placed on the shop floor. Finally, load leveling, based on the weekly capacity requirements plan, is executed at this meeting.

The effectiveness of shop floor control is linked directly to the effectiveness of the CRP process. Any capacity problems are to be identified and solved at this stage of the planning process. They are not to be passed down to the shop floor for solution. As a result, the shop floor control system does not have to evaluate the availability of capacity. Adequate capacity can be assumed to exist because of the work of the capacity planning process.

In general, the shop floor control system and the CRP system work closely together.

Implementation History

The current manufacturing planning system at Joy-Franklin is the latest stage in a process that began in 1973 with the first attempt to implement MRP. The production and material planning systems were implemented in the following sequence:

- Material requirements planning -- 1973
- Shop floor control -- 1976
- Purchasing system -- 1976
- Resource requirements planning -- 1981
- Production planning/master production scheduling -- 1981
- Material requirements planning (revised) -- 1981
- Capacity requirements planning -- 1982
- Shop floor control (revised) -- 1982.

All of the software needed to support these systems was developed in house.

Shop Floor Control

The current shop floor control system was implemented in 1982 and is an enhanced version of the 1976 system. The earlier system, which provided order tracking capabilities, was not enough by itself. Any shop floor control system, to be useful to Joy-Franklin, had to control priorities and maintain valid due dates on the shop floor. This awareness led to the development and use of the current system.

The primary objectives of Joy-Franklin's current shop floor control system are:

- To support the activities of all personnel involved in the operation of the shop floor control system
- To facilitate communication among the various groups working on the shop floor
- To present job priorities to dispatchers in support of job selections
- To locate and track jobs for shop personnel
- To present job status information to any person interested in the progress of a particular job
- To present information on work center status to dispatchers and others
- To facilitate the identification of potential problems on the shop floor.

The shop floor control system is currently used to:

- Track orders through the shop
- Monitor the progress of orders against the plan
- Sequence and dispatch orders
- Feed back information to the planning system
- Report labor and machine efficiency.

The shop floor control system supports all areas of manufacturing except final assembly.

The current shop floor control system is 100 percent computer based. All software used in support of the system has been developed in house. The inputs used by the current shop floor control system and the CRP system are CP10 change capacity and input output values and CP11 mass change input output values. Figure 13-4 lists the principal outputs from these systems. The overlap noted in these figures (especially the output reports) serves to

The system outputs are as follows:

INQUIRIES		REFERENCE
CP20	Capacity Requirements Plan Detail	Figure 6
SF50	SFC Part Number Inquiry	Figure 7
SF51	SFC Nonstock Status	Figure 8
SF52	SFC Order Status	Figure 9
SF53	SFC Operation Detail	Figure 10
SF54	SFC Facility Detail and I/O Report	Figure 11
SF55	SFC Dispatch List	Figure 12
SF56	SFC Order Detail	Figure 13
SF57	SFC Router Format Inquiry	Figure 14
SF58	SFC Operation Dates Inquiry	Figure 15

BATCH REPORTS	REFERENCE
Dispatch Lists	Figure 16
Interrupt Report	Figure 17
Capacity Requirements Plan	Figure 18
Input Output Report	Figure 19

Figure 13-4.-- System Outputs

reinforce the observation that at Joy-Franklin the capacity plan and shop floor control are linked closely and continuously.

The shop floor control system has been designed to improve the decision-making capabilities of all shop floor personnel and to be consistent with the operation of the formal manufacturing system. Shop personnel are informed of their responsibilities by a formal policy statement (Figure 13-5).

The Stages of Shop Floor Control at Joy-Franklin

The way the shop floor control system is structured and operated reflects several important management philosophies. These philosophies are:

- Management is committed to using all aspects of the MRP II system to manage the business. Shop floor control is integrated into the manufacturing planning system. Information generated on the shop floor is made available to the manufacturing planning system.
- Data accuracy is maintained to facilitate valid decision making when using the system.
- All shops are expected to provide on-time delivery performance. To support this, all work centers maintain an on-schedule position. Any action that violates or compromises the on-schedule position of any work center is not allowed.
- Shop schedules are expected to be valid. This includes the schedule of each operation of a shop order.

Order Review/Release

Order review/release begins with the identification of a matured planned order by the MRP system. When a net requirement comes within the ordering horizon for a part, a planned order is signaled for release by the MRP system. The ordering horizon is the sum of the manufacturing lead time, the order review and processing time, and the material picking time. At this time, the manufacturing system establishes an order due date, and the order is backscheduled from the order due date through each of the operations specified on the router to establish operation start dates for

PAGE 1	SDM/70 GENERAL DOCUMENTATION FORM	PROJECT NUMBER	IS2044
		DATE	11/1/82 REV
		PAGE	12

PHASE	SYSTEM TITLE	SFC/CRP	DOCUMENT PART	I: Management Guide
	TASK NUMBER	-	DOCUMENT SECTION	1.0 System Summary

Shop Floor Control Policy

1. The purpose of Shop Floor Control is to communicate the schedules to the shop and control the execution of the shop schedules to the operation due dates. On time completion of each operation insures on time completion of each shop order. The foreman can schedule the work in any sequence provided operation due dates can still be met. The sequence will be established based on the following items:

   - Schedule dates
   - Economics (i.e., combining set ups, nesting, etc.)
   - Machine capability
   - Tooling availability
   - Downstream workcenters
   - Operator skills

2. At times, actual shop conditions will dictate a change from the standard routing. This could be alternate workcenters, a different sequence of operations, or additional operations. Changed routings will be updated in the SFC system as they occur.

3. Factory work orders and R-orders will have special routings prepared and they will be set up in the SFC system. Progress will be tracked against these special orders.

4. If rework operations cannot be completed on the same calendar day, a rework router will be set up in the SFC system.

5. Outlined below are the basic SFC responsibilities for the Franklin (CPO) plants:

   Plant Manager (or Manager of Chain Products Operations) - Monitor the execution of all manufacturing plans.

   Manufacturing Manager - Monitor the execution of all manufacturing plans within his plant.

   Superintendent - Insure that 95% of all shop orders within his departments are completed in full order quantity by due date. Insure that his departments maintain 95% SFC reporting accuracy. Insure that no more than one week of capacity is past due at any workcenter within his departments. Provide feedback to the Manufacturing Manager for exceptions to these guidelines.

Figure 13-5. -- Policy Statement

PAGE 2	SDM/70 GENERAL DOCUMENTATION FORM	PROJECT NUMBER	IS2044		
		DATE	11/1/82	REV	
		PAGE	13		

PHASE	SYSTEM TITLE	SFC/CRP	DOCUMENT PART	I: Management Guide
	TASK NUMBER		DOCUMENT SECTION	1.0 System Summary

Supervisor, Production Control (or Shop Scheduler, CPO) - Provide for timely, accurate SFC reporting. Maintain valid shop schedules by providing feedback to Material Control whenever order due dates cannot be met. Negotiate valid operation schedules with Material Control for less than lead time order releases and order reschedules whenever the schedule changes are outside established guidelines.

General Foreman (or Lead Foreman, CPO) - Insure on-time completion of shop schedules for workcenters on his assigned shift. Provide feedback to the Superintendent and the Supervisor of Production Control when these schedules will not be met. Insure that the SFC Procedures are followed.

Line Foreman - Insure on-time completion of shop schedules for all assigned workcenters. Provide feedback to the shift General Foreman when these schedules will not be met. Insure that the SFC Procedures are followed.

Material Control - Insure that valid operation schedule dates are established for all shop orders released to less than full leadtime and all order reschedules. This requires negotiation with the Supervisor of Production Control whenever schedule changes are outside of established guidelines.

Figure 13-5. -- Policy Statement (continued)

all operations. The planning system also sets up the order in the shop floor control system.

Before the order can be released to the floor, it must be approved for release by one of the material planning analysts. When reviewing the orders, they apply two checks: the availability of material and the presence in the routing of any operations that may have been backscheduled past due. Before the order is released, the necessary components must be available and each operation must have a valid schedule (i.e., one in which there are no past due operations).

Material availability is checked by a material availability inquiry (Figure 13-6) that is entered through a CRT. The inquiry identifies any material shortages. Schedule validity is checked by calling up a display report (Figure 13-7) that provides the schedule for each operation of a shop order. Past due conditions, which are often created by short lead-time orders, can be eliminated by changing the order quantity, the order due date, or by compressing the lead time. The lead time can be compressed using an on-line transaction (Figure 13-8) to modify the move and/or queue times for the order and reschedule it. This can be done by simulation until the desired results are achieved. At this point, the system can be updated with the new schedule. A similar process is used to reschedule open orders. Shop personnel can compress the queue time up to 25 percent on their own initiative, but a compression of more than 25 percent must be first cleared with production control. The goal at Joy-Franklin is to not compress the queue time on more than 5 percent of the orders and not to reschedule more than 5 percent of the open orders. The underlying message of these two goals is clear: Lead-time compression and reschedule are to be used as infrequently as possible. Adequate lead time and capacity must come from the planning system; they are not to be obtained on the shop floor by rescheduling and compressing lead times.

A capacity check is not done when the order is released because it is assumed that capacity problems have been resolved in the weekly capacity meetings.

When an order is authorized for release, the material planning analyst reserves (allocates) the necessary material components, authorizes their picking, and generates the shop paper (traveler). Materials management assembles the order packet, which includes copies of the router and the part drawing, sends the packet to the shop, and updates the order status accordingly. At this time, a measurement is done to see if the order has

```
MM38,00535068 0046,999999,8452,18;
IC173A  V477        ORDER MATERIAL AVAILABILITY          07/27/84   11:13:39  PAGE   1
                          QTY    REQD                                        QTY
COMPONENT PRT   DESC     SHORT   DATE   SOURC   SRC ORD   SLL          REQD   PARENT PART
01567370 0012   RAIL        18   8447   1       NO ORDER   3            18    01566875 1380
01567370 0012   RAIL        18   8447   1       NO ORDER   3            18    01566875 1381
01567617        HOLD        36   8449   4173    NO ORDER   6            36    00535068 0046
END OF DATA
```

Figure 13-6. -- Material Availability Inquiry

```
SF58,383928;
PC003     V477        SFC OPERATION DATES INQUIRY          07/27/84   11:17:14   PAGE    1
                              R                              ORDER      QTY    ORDER   ORD  S
 PART NUMBER     ORDER NO     T   DESCRIPTION                  QTY      DUE     DUE     ST  C
00534461 0008    383928       A   CASE        WELD CORE BR      1         1 09/28/84   U   N
CONTROL                   S   START   DUE       MOVE C    QUEUE C    SETUP     PROD    HOURS
NUMBER    OPER W/C DP     T   DATE    DATE      DAYS F     DAYS F    HOURS    HOURS    RMAIN
5201371    05  000 04     U   08094 08094      2.000      0.000      0.000    0.000      0.0
5201389    10  520 SH     U   08144 08144      0.083      1.000      0.000    0.000      0.0
5201397    20  511 SH     U   08164 08174      0.083      2.000      2.000    7.500      9.5
5201405    30  506 SH     U   08234 09054      0.083      4.000      6.000  121.000    127.0
5201413    40  513 SH     U   09074 09104      0.083      2.000      0.500    4.500      5.0
5201421    50  515 SH     U   09124 09124      0.083      2.000      0.000    0.000      0.0
5201439    60  521 SH     U   09134 09134      0.083      1.000      0.000    0.000      0.0
5201447    70  515 SH     U   09174 09174      2.000      2.000      0.000    0.000      0.0
5201454    90  A20 04     U   09244 09244      0.167      3.000      0.141    1.390      1.5
5201462   100  000 30     U   09244 09244      0.167      0.000      0.000    0.000      0.0
5201470   110  A20 04     U   09244 09254      0.000      0.000      0.141    9.134      9.3
5201488   120  027 04     U   09274 09274      0.167      2.000      0.141    0.340      0.5
5201496   130  000 30     U   09274 09274      1.000      0.000      0.000    0.000      0.0
* TOTAL                                        5.999     19.000      8.923  143.864    152.8

SFC007M TRANSACTION COMPLETE
```

Figure 13-7. -- Operation Dates Inquiry

PC101-01 TIME 01:05 SHOP FLOOR CONTROL DISPATCH LIST DATE 07/30/84 PAGE 24

WORK CENTER 013 HG-1,2,3,4 PLANT 1 DEPARTMENT 04

TOTAL JOBS COMING

PART NUMBER	ORDER NUMBER	ORDER DUE MMDDY	*** CURRENT OPERATION *** ORDER QTY	OPER NO	S T	W/C	OPER DUE MMDDY	QTY IN QUEUE	QTY IN TRANS	*** NEXT OPERATION *** OPER NO	S T	OPER START MMDDY	OPER DUE MMDDY	*** HOURS COMING	COMMENTS
01567465 0081	407830 Z	08154	3	10	A	013	07304	3	0	20	0	08014	08014	.1	
64534 6	412195 Z	08084	8	10	D	011	C8014	8	0	20	0	08024	08024	.1	00801111 ROUNCS 3/8 DIA
65137	411714	08104	158	10	D	010	C8014	158	0	15	C	08024	08024	2.4	STRAP C0801111 ROUNDS 3/8 DIA
01066178 0002	410117 Z	08064	2	10	A	011	C8014	2	0	20	0	08024	08024	.0	00803335 FLAT 1-1/2 X 2
01069090 0522	414252	08104	1	10	D	011	08014	1	0	20	C	08024	08024	.1	BOSS
01189808 0141	415216	08104	20	10	A	013	08C14	20	0	20	C	08024	C8024	.5	ARM SUB CONTRACT
01563770 1526	413815 Z	08084	1	10	D	013	08C14	1	0	20	0	08024	08024	.0	
01565024 0003	413199 Z	08064	6	10	D	011	07314	6	0	20	0	08024	08024	.0	00811619 PLATE 3/4 IN A283D
01565107 0682	413213 Z	08094	1	10	A	011	08C14	1	0	20	0	08024	08024	.0	00811619 PLATE 3/4 IN A283D
01565204 0174	413256 Z	08064	4	10	D	011	08014	4	0	20	0	08024	08024	.0	00811619 PLATE 3/4 IN A283D
01565422 0099	414369 Z	08024	2	10	D	011	08014	2	0	20	0	08024	08024	.0	00803265 FLAT 1 X 1
01566189 0156	400705 Z	08024	1	10	D	011	07314	1	0	20	0	08024	08024	.0	00803100 FLAT 1/2 X 2
01566189 0157	400705 Z	08024	1	10	D	C11	08014	1	0	20	0	08024	08024	.0	00803100 FLAT 1/2 X 2
01566308 1097	412224 Z	08C24	6	10	A	011	08014	6	0	20	0	08024	08024	.1	008C1111 ROUNCS 3/8 DIA
01566322 0190	R77922	08104	1	10	A	013	C8014	1	0	15	0	08024	08024	.0	
01566326 0730	397626 Z	08174	1	10	D	013	08014	1	0	20	0	08024	08024	.1	
01566326 0825	R78264	08024	2	10	D	014	08014	2	0	20	0	08024	08024	.0	PLATE
01566493 0388	413269 Z	08074	12	10	A	014	C8014	12	0	20	0	08024	08024	.3	
01566493 0399	413269 Z	08074	2	10	A	014	08C14	2	0	20	0	08024	08024	.1	
01566840 0493	413232 Z	C8074	2	10	D	011	07314	2	0	20	C	08024	08024	.0	C0811619 PLATE 3/4 IN A283D
01566840 0494	413232 Z	08074	1	10	D	011	08014	1	0	20	0	08024	08024	.0	00811619 PLATE 3/4 IN A283D
01566840 1019	413264 Z	08094	1	10	A	013	08014	1	0	20	0	08024	08024	.0	
01566860 2308	414369 Z	08024	1	10	D	014	08014	1	0	20	0	08024	08024	.0	
01566860 2592	414369 Z	08024	2	10	D	013	07314	2	0	20	C	08024	C8024	.0	
01566860 2593	414369 Z	08024	2	10	C	013	08C14	2	0	20	0	08024	08024	.0	
01566860 2648	414369 Z	08024	1	10	D	013	08014	1	0	20	0	08024	08024	.0	
01566860 5654	413267 Z	08064	20	10	A	C14	08014	20	0	20	0	08024	C8024	.3	
01566860 6978	413652	08104	1	10	A	014	03014	1	0	20	0	08024	C8024	.1	PANEL
01566860 8148	409016 Z	08084	6	10	A	013	C8C14	6	0	20	0	08024	08024	.3	
01567314 0706	R77900 Z	08024	2	30	A	019	08014	2	0	40	0	08024	08024	.1	
01189990 0001	406035	08244	14	10	D	014	C8C14	14	0	20	0	08024	08064	5.1	FLANGE
63386 2	408279 Z	08064	3	30	D	025	C8024	3	0	40	0	08064	08064	.1	
01065554 0038	401312	08174	12	10	A	010	08024	12	0	20	0	08064	08064	.2	BRACKET 01564383 1004 CSTG 6088/200 EST
01065762 0004	415058	08104	50	10	A	010	C8C24	50	0	20	C	08064	C8064	.4	BAR

Figure 13-8. -- Dispatch List

been released to the shop with adequate lead time (i.e., the actual order review time is compared with the planned order review time).

Warehouse personnel pick the required component parts, send them to the appropriate shop department, and update the inventory records on line using a CRT. Any discrepancies between the planned and actual pick quantities are also recorded.

Detailed Assignment

Joy-Franklin uses a centralized dispatching approach with dispatching offices located throughout the shop floor. Order status updating is done by funneling all paperwork to the appropriate shop dispatch office. Only the dispatcher can update order status information in the database; the foremen and operators do not enter any data.

When the order packet for a new order arrives in the shop dispatch office, the dispatcher notes its arrival on the order status record on line using a CRT. After the component parts arrive in the shop, they are located in a WIP warehouse. The dispatcher again uses the CRT to indicate when the material arrived, where it is located, and any discrepancies between the planned number of parts and the number of parts actually delivered.

Orders to be worked on are selected from the dispatch list (Figure 13-8) by the dispatcher. This list identifies jobs in queue, jobs coming, and jobs interrupted. The jobs in queue are those that are assigned to each work center, have been sent to a work center, or are available when the shop has both the paperwork and the material. After an order has been selected, the system is updated and the order packet and material are sent to the work center. At this point, the job is considered dispatched.

The dispatch list is the major tool for communicating order priorities to the shop. The operation start date defines the priority. Foremen can select the exact sequence in which they want to work jobs that have been dispatched, but above all, they know that they must meet the due dates.

While a hard copy of the dispatch list is printed daily, information is always accessible by CRT and is being updated on a real-time basis continuously.

Data Collection/Monitoring

After the work has been completed at a work center, the order count is verified, the material is sent to a WIP warehouse, and the order packet is sent to the dispatch office. The dispatcher uses the information provided in the order packet to update the operations completed on the order status record. An order may go through several operations before the shop packet is returned and the part is put into inventory. In this case, a move ticket is completed after each operation and is sent to the dispatch office so that the order status can be updated. If an order is completed but not moved, this information is also reported to keep the input/output report current.

The status of a work center can be determined by reviewing the following reports:

- <u>Dispatch list</u> (Figure 13-8). The dispatch list comes out in three parts: Jobs in queue, sequenced by operation start date, are jobs that have been dispatched to the work center or are available; jobs coming are jobs at preceding work centers; jobs interrupted are jobs delayed because of machine breakdown or because they have been put on hold for any reason (e.g., a customer order cancellation). The dispatch list is updated in real time as orders are completed.
- <u>Capacity requirements plan</u> (Figure 13-9). This report provides a window into the future for each work center. It shows scheduled input as well as the planned output for each work center. The CRP report shows the weekly and cumulative load on each work center. The routine report has a twenty-six week horizon and an extended version is available with an additional twenty-six weeks of visibility. The CRP report shows any work on subcontract or any hours on hold separately. Copies of the CRP reports go to the master scheduler and to the work centers. Summary reports are also available to the plant managers and supervisors.
- <u>Input/output report</u> (Figure 13-10). This report provides a snapshot of the past. It also provides an analysis of actual versus planned queues. Work completed in one work center automatically generates input to the next work center if it is in the same plant. If not, a materials received transaction is issued from the work center in the next plant when the work arrives. The input/output reports are available on line. The input/output report helps identify bottlenecked work centers and shows a planned queue based directly on the CRP reports and the actual queue at the

CP01d-01 TIME 05:04:09

CAPACITY REQUIREMENTS PLAN

WORK CENTER 236 TTL-8,7 DISP. CENTER 00711 TAPE TURRET DEPT 11 PLT 2 MANNING 2 A

		P.DUE	(44)	(45)	(46)	(47)	(48)	(49)	(50)	(51)	(52)	(01)	(02)	(03)
	FISCAL WEEK / WEEK ENDING (MMDDY)		08034	08104	08174	08244	08314	09074	09144	09214	09284	10054	10124	10194
1	HOURS (RELEASED ORDERS)	97	22	23	84	85	34	17	29	3	34	47	7	0
2	HOURS (PLANNED ORDERS)	0	0	0	0	19	0	17	26	41	70	33	20	52
3	SCHEDULED HOURS (1+2)	97	22	28	88	104	34	34	55	45	104	80	28	52
4	PLANNED OUTPUT	0	64	64	64	64	64	64	64	64	64	64	64	64
5	OVER/UNDERLOAD (3-4)	97	41-	35-	24	40	29-	29-	8-	18-	40	16	35-	11
6	CUMUL SCHEDULED HOURS	97	120	149	235	341	376	410	466	511	616	697	725	777
7	CUMUL PLANNED OUTPUT	0	64	128	192	256	320	384	448	512	576	640	704	768
8	CUMULOVER/UNDERLOAD (6-7)	97	56	20	44	85	56	26	18	0	40	57	21	9
9	SUBCONTRACT RELIEF	56	0	0	0	0	0	0	0	0	0	0	0	0
10	HOURS ON HOLD	0	0	0	0	0	0	0	0	0	0	0	0	0

		(05)	(06)	(07)	(08)	(09)	(10)	(11)	(12)	(13)	(14)	(15)	(16)
	FISCAL WEEK / WEEK ENDING (MMDDY)	11024	11094	11164	11234	11304	12074	12144	12214	12284	01045	01115	01185
1	HOURS (RELEASED ORDERS)	0	0	0	0	0	0	0	0	0	0	0	0
2	HOURS (PLANNED ORDERS)	16	64	105	53	46	99	72	88	0	30	62	69
3	SCHEDULED HOURS (1+2)	16	64	105	53	46	99	72	88	0	30	62	69
4	PLANNED OUTPUT	64	64	64	64	64	64	64	64	64	64	64	64
5	OVER/UNDERLOAD (3-4)	48-	0	41	10-	17-	35	8	24	64-	33-	1-	5
6	CUMUL SCHEDULED HOURS	854	918	1023	1076	1123	1222	1294	1382	1382	1413	1475	1544
7	CUMUL PLANNED OUTPUT	896	960	1024	1088	1152	1216	1280	1344	1408	1472	1536	1600
8	CUMULOVER/UNDERLOAD (6-7)	41-	41-	0	11-	28-	6	14	38	25-	59-	60-	55-
9	SUBCONTRACT RELIEF	0	4	0	0	0	0	0	0	0	0	0	7
10	HOURS ON HOLD	0	0	0	0	0	0	0	0	0	0	0	0

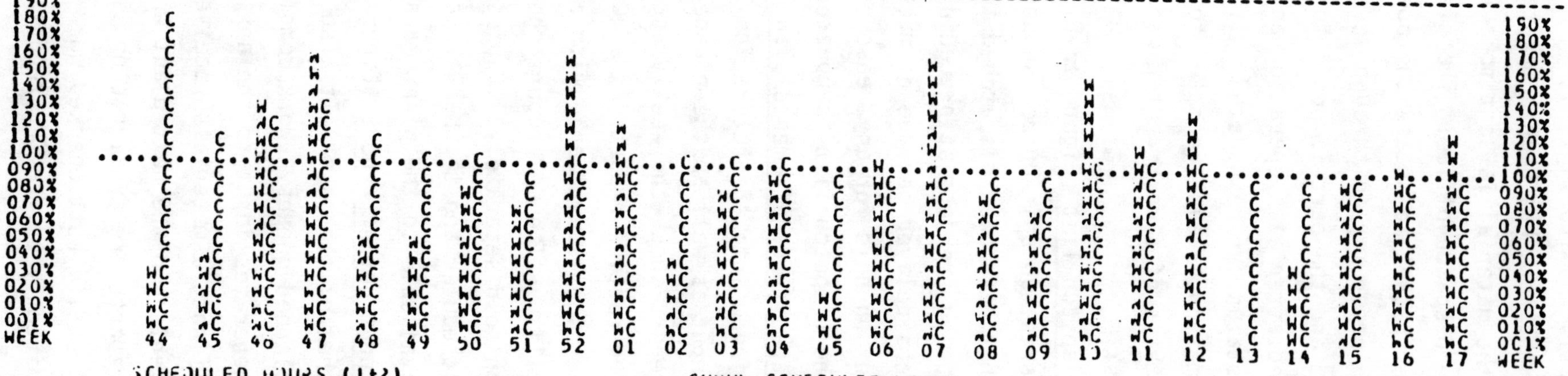

W = SCHEDULED HOURS (1+2) / PLANNED OUTPUT

C = CUMUL SCHEDULED HOURS / CUMUL PLANNED OUTPUT

Figure 13-9. -- Capacity Requirements Plan

CP031-01 TIME 01:52 INPUT/OUTPUT REPORT DATE 07/30/84 PAGE

WORK CENTER 172 BG84-1 WEEK ENDING 08034 DEPT 11 PLANT 2

# MACH	HR/DAY	HR RATIO	STD-IN	STD-OT	MANNING	RPT GP	DISPATCH CENTER	DISP CTR DESCRIPTI
1	16	0.90	29	64	2	20	00211	BLANCHARD GRINDER

INPUT

FISCAL WEEK	36	37	38	39	40	41	42	43
WEEK ENDING (MMDDY)	06084	06154	06224	06294	07064	07134	07204	07274
PLANNED INPUT	31	31	31	31	31	31	31	29
ACTUAL INPUT	35	52	67	48	5	40	64	36
DEVIATION	4	21	36	17	26-	9	33	7
CUMUL DEVIATION	4	25	61	78	52	61	94	101

TOLERANCE PERCENT 50% TOLERANCE STD HRS 123

OUTPUT

PLANNED OUTPUT	32	32	32	32	32	32	32	64
ACTUAL OUTPUT	24	43	33	14	2	30	41	30
DEVIATION	8-	11	6	18-	30-	2-	9	34-
CUMUL DEVIATION	8-	3	9	9-	39-	41-	32-	66-

TOLERANCE PERCENT 50% TOLERANCE STD HRS 144

INPUT/OUTPUT PLANS

FISCAL WEEK	44	45	46	47	48	49	50	51	52	01	02	03
WEEK ENDING (MMDDY)	08034	08104	08174	08244	08314	09074	09144	09214	09284	10054	10124	10194
PLANNED INPUT	29	29	29	29	29	29	29	29	29	29	29	29
PLANNED OUTPUT	64	64	64	64	64	64	64	64	64	64	64	64

FISCAL WEEK	05	06	07	08	09	10	11	0	13	14	15	16
WEEK ENDING (MMDDY)	11024	11094	11164	11234	11304	12074	12144	12214	12284	01045	01115	01185
PLANNED INPUT	29	29	29	29	29	29	29	29	29	29	29	29
PLANNED OUTPUT	64	64	64	64	64	64	64	64	64	64	64	64

PLANNED QUEUE DAYS	1
TOTAL QUEUE DAYS	2
CURRENT QUEUE DAYS	2
AVERAGE WEEKLY O/P	27

* OUT OF TOLER

Figure 13-10. -- Input/output Report

work center. A tolerance for the deviation between planned performance and actual has been established previously by management. When the tolerance is exceeded, that work center is discussed at the weekly capacity meeting.

A current queue field has been added to the input/output report showing that portion of the actual queue that still has a current demand on it. This feature was added after a sharp downturn in business caused the cancellation of many customer orders. As a result, the shop personnel can ready those orders with current demand and process them before the other orders.

Labor efficiency, productivity, and use are tracked in a separate system that is tied to the labor reporting system.

Control/Feedback

At Joy-Franklin, an out-of-control order is one that is not completed on schedule. Late orders are flagged by the shop floor control system in a number of ways. Any work not completed on schedule ends up on the top of the dispatch list with the highest priority. It is also identified by the planning system during the weekly regeneration and are flagged as an exception. All past due hours are reflected in the capacity requirements plan reports.

The assembly scheduling manager chairs a morning production meeting, at which jobs not on schedule are discussed and plans developed to get them back on schedule. The flow of jobs between plants is also coordinated at this meeting, so the manager is aware of problems that could affect the on-time shipment of customer orders.

Order Disposition

Completed orders are sent to the finished parts warehouse. The receiving personnel perform an order receipt transaction that closes the order out of both the planning system and the shop floor control system. The receiving system directs the material either to the finished parts warehouse or routes it onto the assembly floor.

Certain items produced by the structural shop or by a subassembly area are not sent to the warehouse but directly to the assembly floor. In these cases, a batch transaction is used that closes out the shop order and shows the items as disbursed to a specific machine.

Scrap or rework can be reported to the shop floor control system. The system has the capability to set up special rework operations and return to any step in the router.

Performance Evaluation/Feedback

The input/output report measures performance to plan in the shop. Plans for input and output hours are developed for each work center based on the CRP. When the cumulative deviation on input or output exceeds a predefined tolerance, the work center is reviewed for possible capacity actions and to identify the reasons for the problems. The actions taken are consistent with the cause of the problem. A persistent problem is treated differently than a short-term problem.

Interfaces with the Rest of the Firm

The shop floor control system, linked to other areas of the firm in many ways, interfaces with the MRP system. First, the orders signaled for release by MRP are added automatically to the shop floor control system. Orders can be rescheduled or split, and order quantities can be adjusted. Interface logic keeps the two systems in concert. Finally, when the planning system processes an order completion, the order is deleted from both systems.

Shop floor control is also tied directly to industrial engineering by the routings. If routing changes are made after a shop order is created, the shop floor control system can be updated accordingly.

Inspection times have been set up on the routings for inspection work centers. Shop floor reporting is done for these operations. As a result, the inspection work centers can use all the standard shop floor control tools.

The need for subcontracting creates an interface with purchasing. Orders or selected operations to be subcontracted are coded by purchasing personnel.

To date, there are no direct interfaces with engineering, marketing, maintenance, or accounting. Labor reporting is done separately from shop floor reporting.

Evaluating Joy-Franklin's Shop Floor Control System -- Benefits

Joy-Franklin personnel (management and shop floor) are pleased with the shop floor control system. This satisfaction reflects the many strengths that are built into the current system. Most notable are:

- The shop floor control system is a complete set of tools. It contains all the standard features and provides detailed information on each order and work center. The system can also provide summary information for higher level management.
- The shop floor control system is completely interactive. All updating is done on line using CRT terminals. Special features found in the system include on-line dispatch lists, input/output reports, and CRP reports. It is also possible to modify all back-scheduling parameters and simulate or update new operation schedule dates.
- The shop floor control system has the ability to store an unlimited number of comments about each order. This helps eliminate the need to keep unstructured information in handwritten scheduling with a realistic view of the actual impact of the reschedules.
- The shop floor control system has allowed the reduction of manufacturing lead times. Reduced lead times have made it possible to reduce WIP inventory while providing improved customer delivery service. The emphasis on a scheduling environment and an excellent set of tools have caused old problems to surface and be solved. For example, for one major item, the calculated lead time was thirty-five weeks. A detailed analysis revealed that 8 percent of the lead time was for setup and production while 80 percent was taken up sitting in queue and 12 percent was move time. The lead-time calculation on this item was reduced to three weeks, and the shop currently produces this item within the required three-week lead time. Although all examples are not as dramatic as this one, the overall impact of lead-time reduction in the shop has been significant.
- The shop floor control system allows better control of the business. With the shop floor control system and the MRP II philosophy in place, it was possible to manage the business through a severe economic downturn effectively.

A challenging test of the shop floor control system recently developed during a union strike at Joy-Franklin. Rather than shut down production completely, management elected to try to meet customer orders by using a network of repair and refurbishing centers that it had established across the nation. These shops were experienced in tearing down, refurbishing, and reassembling problems, and could execute almost all of the manufacturing processes that routinely occurred in the shops at Franklin. Each center was identified as a work center in the shop floor control system and managed together as a factory. The geographical dispersion caused obvious logistics problems, but the shop floor control system was able to cope with the factory spread across the country. Output was maintained.

Shop Floor Control -- The Next Stage

A project is currently underway to extend the shop floor control system to the final assembly area. Final assembly was not addressed in the current system because of its highly variable and complex nature. Other new system features will include the capability to handle variable final assembly routings and operations that take place simultaneously and the identification of the components needed for each operation.

Other possible enhancements include merging labor reporting with shop floor control reporting (thus moving one step closer to a complete MRP II system) and the use of automated identification (e.g., bar coding).

Shop Floor Control at Joy-Franklin: Lessons to be Learned

The shop floor control system at Joy-Franklin has been tailored over a number of years to meet the needs of manufacturing and material. The design of the system allows the shop floor control system to be flexible enough to handle reschedules, changes in routings, temporary work centers, rework, and so on. At the same time, the current system has preserved the necessary formality needed to fit in with an MRP II philosophy. In many ways, shop floor control at Joy-Franklin is a classic and successful implementation.

When studying shop floor control at Joy-Franklin, several factors can be identified that account for the system's success.

- Effective capacity planning is a prerequisite to effective shop floor control. At Joy-Franklin, capacity planning is tied closely to shop floor control. This relationship is important because the shop floor control system depends on the CRP system to identify and resolve, in advance, any capacity problems on the shop floor. It is well known at Joy-Franklin that no order will be released to shop floor control without adequate capacity. Shop floor control never evaluates capacity availability before releasing a job to the shop floor because it is assumed that the capacity requirements planning system has done its job well. Without adequate capacity, the shop floor control system cannot hope to implement successfully the orders released to it by the MRP system.

The need for capacity management is ongoing. As soon as capacity problems become apparent on the shop floor, this information must be passed back to CRP. Shop floor control and CRP work together to resolve these problems.

- <u>Clear guidelines must be established for shop personnel</u>. Management recognizes that the key ingredient in a shop floor control system is the user. The user, not the computer system, must make decisions. To simplify the work of the user, management has put in place a number of guidelines, which identify the responsibilities of shop personnel. They have also identified certain objectives that must be satisfied. Foremen, for example, know that they can process jobs in a different order to improve efficiency (e.g., to take advantage of similarities in setup) as long as due dates are not compromised. These guidelines also identify the amount of flexibility in decision making that the shop personnel have. Material planning analysts, for example, know that they can compress queue times up to 25 percent. Any queue time compression beyond 25 percent must involve production control. By having clear guidelines, everyone involved in the shop floor control system knows what he or she can or cannot do. Everyone also knows the objectives for which they are responsible. Confusion is reduced. Accountability becomes an integral feature of the system because shop personnel can now be evaluated on their achievement of their objectives.
- <u>The actions of shop personnel must be supported with the appropriate set of tools</u>. Every day, the people involved in the operation of the shop floor control system are required to make decisions and take action. The system must support these decision-making activities with an appropriate set of tools. In the case

of Joy-Franklin, the tools available to the user consist of reports and a simulation (what if) capability. These tools enable the user to identify what is actually taking place as well as what would take place if certain actions were taken. The users are now able to identify, in advance, the impact of their actions.

- Accurate information is a prerequisite to good decisions made by shop floor personnel. The shop floor control system is built on the extensive use of on-line systems. Such systems provide the users with the capability to update information contained in the database quickly. Such systems also provide the users with rapid access to all necessary information. Users always make their decisions based on conditions as they currently exist on the shop floor, not as they existed a day or a week ago. In addition, the shop floor control system has controls for data accuracy. One of the most obvious controls is the dispatcher who can enter data taken from the shop floor. Dispatchers are responsible for ensuring the accuracy of all information entered.
- The shop floor control system must identify problems as soon as they occur. Problems should be identified not hidden. At Joy-Franklin, a problem order is one that is slipping behind its schedule. The shop floor control system has been designed to bring such problem orders to the top. They appear at the top of the dispatch list. Such orders are also flagged by both the MRP and the CRP systems. As a result, attention is focused on these problems, which then must be resolved because the systems will not let the users ignore them. Because these problems are identified early, the solutions are often easy and less costly.

The shop floor control system at Joy-Franklin provides a good example of a system that is able to satisfy manufacturing needs on time and cost effectively. It is a system that has provided nearly all of the conditions necessary for improved decision making on the shop floor.

CHAPTER 14: FMC CORPORATION: ORDNANCE DIVISION

General Nature of the Firm

FMC Corporation is an international producer of agricultural chemicals, industrial chemicals, defense equipment, construction equipment, material handling equipment, and petroleum and food processing equipment. The company was formed in 1884 by John Bean who designed and manufactured orchard sprayers. The company's early growth was in the food machinery area. Diversification into chemical and other machining areas increased FMC's value to the nearly $4 billion of today.

FMC is publicly held with corporate headquarters in Chicago. It operates more than 131 manufacturing and mining facilities in twenty-nine states and fourteen foreign countries, and employs approximately 39,000 people worldwide. FMC is divided into nine business groups, which are further divided into operating divisions. These groups and divisions operate as autonomous business units.

FMC has been an important developer and manufacturer of defense equipment for the U.S. Armed Forces since World War II. For the past two decades, FMC has been the sole U.S. manufacturer of the M113 family of tracked personnel carriers for the U.S. Army and a principal supplier to the armed forces of forty other nations. The corporation's newest defense product, the Bradley Fighting Vehicle, is now being supplied to the U.S. Army.

The Bradley vehicle is manufactured by the FMC Ordnance Division in San Jose, California. Vehicle fabrication, assembly, and testing take place at the San Jose facility. Approximately one-third of the vehicle's welded and machined component parts are, or will be, produced by a satellite plant located in Aiken, South Carolina.

Customer demand for the Bradley vehicle is secured through annual production contracts with the U.S. Army. The contract requirement creates the independent demand for the San Jose assembly master production schedule. Using an MRP-based manufacturing system, San Jose generates component requirements. Requirements for the Aiken plant end-item parts are submitted as independent demands to be master scheduled by Aiken. The plant operates as an autonomous facility with a customer-supplier relationship with San Jose. Although the vehicle demand is very stable (due to annual contracts), the Aiken plant demand is more volatile because of variances caused by spare parts orders, San Jose scrap, shrinkage, and assembly schedule changes.

The Production Process

The Aiken plant began production of high tolerance fabricated machined and welded component parts in July 1982. Conceptual planning for the plant began in late 1980 and focused on incorporating state-of-the-art equipment, organizational philosophies, and manufacturing systems. Features of the Aiken plant include:

- Plant equipment of the latest design, including twenty computer numerical controlled machines
- Automated manufacturing systems, including closed-loop MRP, installed and operational from start-up
- Entire plant operates in a participative management style -- all employees are organized into teams designed to have the tools and authority to take responsibility for team performance
- Commitment to training -- all production team members participate in over 150 hours of specialized FMC training, including MRP and shop floor control.

The FMC Aiken plant currently manufactures 500 parts, of which approximately 200 are end-item parts. There are 200 raw material and purchased part numbers. In approximately two years, the plant will reach capacity with approximately 2,000 component parts, of which 500 will be end items; purchased parts will grow to 400.

Production processes include machining or forming aluminum castings, forgings, extrusions, plate and sheet, and welding component parts. A typical BOM is composed of two to three levels. The typical cumulative manufacturing lead time for end items is approximately three weeks. Lot sizes are lot for lot, generally one-month quantities or the quantity ordered by the customer.

The FMC Aiken plant operates under a comprehensive integrated manufacturing system, of which the shop floor control system is one part. This system was developed by Martin Marietta under the name MAS II and was modified extensively by FMC to add on-line capability and to handle government contract reporting requirements. Components of this system include:

- o Master production scheduling
- o MRP
- o Engineering change control
- o Purchasing
- o Work order generation and priority planning
- o Shop floor control
- o Input/output control
- o Capacity planning.

The Aiken plant was started and continues to operate exclusively under this system. There are no informal systems that supplant the formal system. Because the manufacturing system is integrated, relevant information from one component of the system is communicated and taken into account in other components.

Shop Floor Control

Shop floor control is the responsibility of the production control team. This team was in place before plant start-up and was heavily involved in system installations. It is currently responsible for:

- o Analyzing capacity
- o Analyzing input/output
- o Managing critical ratio priorities for all work centers
- o Determining daily work center schedules
- o Ensuring on-schedule work order performance
- o Determining production control policies such as efficiency, utilization, queue time, and so forth
- o Reporting and monitoring variances of actual daily production versus work center daily production rate commitments

The manufacturing system operates in an on-line batch mode. Critical information such as work order operation status is maintained on line. Shop floor control information updates, monitoring, and analysis are performed within the computer-based system. No manual systems are used to process shop floor control data.

Key shop floor control functions performed by the system are:

- o Generating and releasing work orders
- o Calculating critical ratio priorities of work orders and generating work center schedules daily
- o Maintaining work order operation status (on line)
- o Recording actual versus standard labor and reporting efficiency and utilization statistics daily
- o Providing work order closure reconciliation analysis daily
- o Reporting input/output results weekly
- o Reporting labor and machine capacity monthly.

Unique features of the Aiken computerized system stem from the way the system is used rather than software design. For example, inventory stores accuracy is 96 percent, and work order status transaction accuracy is 98 percent. All functions (materials, manufacturing, and engineering) rely on the same set of data generated from the system, and plant management decisions and performance measurements are based on system information.

Stages of Shop Floor Control at FMC

Order Review/Release

Work order release at FMC Aiken is triggered by the MRP. The release is not automatic; it is first reviewed by an analyst. At the time of release (once a day), the physical work order packet is delivered to production control and the work center schedule is updated automatically.

At the time of work order release, the following data are given to production control: work order start and due date, operating routing, expected completion date, standard hours and scheduling factors (expected efficiency and utilization), drawing configuration, and raw material requirements.

Material availability is checked before release. Initial tooling, numerical control tapes, and so forth, are confirmed before introduction of new parts, after which availability is assumed. Capacity availability is reviewed and adjusted at a higher level, thus at the time of release infinite capacity is assumed.

Detailed Assignment

Order priorities are established by critical ratios calculated by the system. Through the use of the daily work center schedule, which displays the relative priority of all work orders for a specific work center, the production control scheduler and the production team manager (shop foreman) decide the daily production schedule. This decision process is performed each morning, taking into account such factors as tooling availability, equipment downtime, and work center backlog.

The primary criteria for work order assignment is the relative priority of the order as determined by the CRR. Both the scheduler and production team manager share the same objective of scheduling work to ensure on-schedule completion. Unresolved disagreements on the planned schedule are rare.

Detailed assignment of work orders determined by the scheduler and team manager is not overridden by higher plant management. The detailed schedule is well communicated, and everyone from the plant manager to the operator works from the same production plan.

In addition to determining the detailed schedule each morning, a daily output commitment is also made. Typically, production team members (operators) will participate in the output commitment. The commitments are communicated to each production team and variances are reported the next morning.

Data Collection/Monitoring

Labor hours and actual quantities are reported on each employee's labor card, and the system is updated daily. Upon completion of an operation, a final quantity count is reported on line by the scheduler and work order status is updated. Although available daily, labor efficiency and utilization are reported weekly. Input/output results are reported weekly, and capacity is reported monthly. Computerized shop floor data collection has also been implemented.

Control/Feedback

Behind-schedule orders are identified when their system-calculated expected due date falls beyond the required due date. This situation is first identified in the daily meeting between the scheduler and production team manager. The number of orders behind schedule is one measure of how well the scheduler and the team manager are performing.

Behind-schedule orders automatically become candidates for overtime work, advancing partial quantities, and shrinking final inspection and shipping lead times as appropriate.

Expediting is discouraged and does not play an important part in the production process. Only 5 percent of open work orders are expected to receive specific expediting activity. The Aiken plant does not use hot lists or rush tags. The work center schedule priority alone determines work order expediting.

Work orders behind schedule due to work center or labor bottlenecks are dealt with through input/output and capacity reporting. Semimonthly production plan review meetings with various plant department heads address discrepancies in capacity and production problems that cause variance with the plant production plan.

Order Disposition

As a work order's final operation is completed and parts are received into stores, the system order status is updated on line. The manufacturing system then triggers an order closure summary report, which is reviewed for accuracy. Count discrepancies are reconciled. An on-line transaction releases work center resources as each operation is completed.

Scrap and rework are critical problem areas for the Aiken plant. Because of the start-up mode and the workers' relative inexperience with parts and the manufacturing processes, scrap and rework are at relatively high levels. Rejected parts are identified as a separate status in the inventory system. The disposition status of the rejected parts is maintained on line by the system. Rework orders are created and scheduled in the same way as a standard work order.

Measuring Effectiveness

The effectiveness of the shop floor control system and overall shop performance are measured in a variety of ways: on-schedule shipping performance, on-schedule work order performance, average priority of work orders at critical work centers, effectiveness of balancing input/output, daily output commitments versus actual performance, adherence to production plan and effectiveness of balancing capacity with load, labor and machine efficiency and use against standard, and count and transaction accuracy.

Evaluating FMC's Shop Floor Control System -- Benefits

Major system characteristics include:

- o Manufacturing system in place before plant became active
- o Shop floor control system part of an integrated computerized manufacturing system
- o No informal systems compete against the formal manufacturing system
- o A single production plan from capacity to detailed work center assignments developed, communicated, and monitored
- o A high level of system accuracy
- o Extensive training and operator participation
- o A high degree of credibility throughout the organization.

Shop Floor Control -- The Next Stage

The shop floor control functions and system will continue to develop and change as the plant moves from a start-up mode to a more stable mode of operation. The effects of this transition should strengthen the system as Aiken becomes more experienced with its capability and fine-tunes its performance.

An FMS for machining selected group of castings and forgings has been installed in Aiken. Assimilation of the advanced scheduling capabilities of the FMS into the existing shop floor control system presents management with a new challenge.

Through the use of group technology methods, manufacturing cells within Aiken have been identified. The first cell was created in December 1983. Since then, more cells have been implemented. The process of implementing manufacturing cells is still going on.

Incorporating JIT manufacturing or zero inventory techniques in Aiken, with its traditional manufacturing layout and high setup times, will be a difficult task. Aiken is committed to reducing setup time, manufacturing lead time, and inventory. To date, manufacturing lead time and work center queue time have been managed very tightly, purchase part lot sizes have been reduced, and a program to reduce setup times has been initiated. These actions plus the incorporation of the FMS and the cells should position the plant for the introduction of JIT manufacturing techniques.

General Nature of the Firm

Wright Line is a subsidiary of Barry Wright Corporation, Worchester, Massachusetts. It produces and markets documentation handling systems, including specialized filing cabinets, workstations, work surfaces, filing devices, and accessories for use in automated office applications such as data processing, telecommunications, and micrographics. Wright Line fills a unique niche in information processing markets by providing systems for the filing, retrieval, accessing, and protection of a wide variety of information media including computer printouts, documents, magnetic tapes, disk packs, microfilm, and punched cards.

The company was founded in 1934 when E. Stanley Wright began manufacturing card files and guides for punched cards used with IBM's "machine accounting" system. Since then, the company has grown steadily to approximately 1,000 employees and $80 million in annual sales.

Wright Line products can be segmented into three broad categories: steel, plastics, and resale. Approximately 60 percent of the products are MTS, and 40 percent are MTO. Wright Line does ETO and MTO for large specialized applications.

Steel products are primarily produced at the sheet metal fabrication facility in Worchester. This facility processed about 12 million pounds of sheet stock in 1982.

The Production Process

Figures 15-1 and 15-2 show the operations flow and plant layout of the sheet metal facility. Steel is received into the shear department from a steel mill or warehouse and is handled with a traveling overhead crane. Raw steel is split and sheared into proper dimensions called blanks. After the blanking operation, material is stacked on pallets to be moved to the press department.

The press department punches and notches the blanks to produce the desired shapes, holes, or patterns. After all press operations are complete, the material is routed to the brake/forming department.

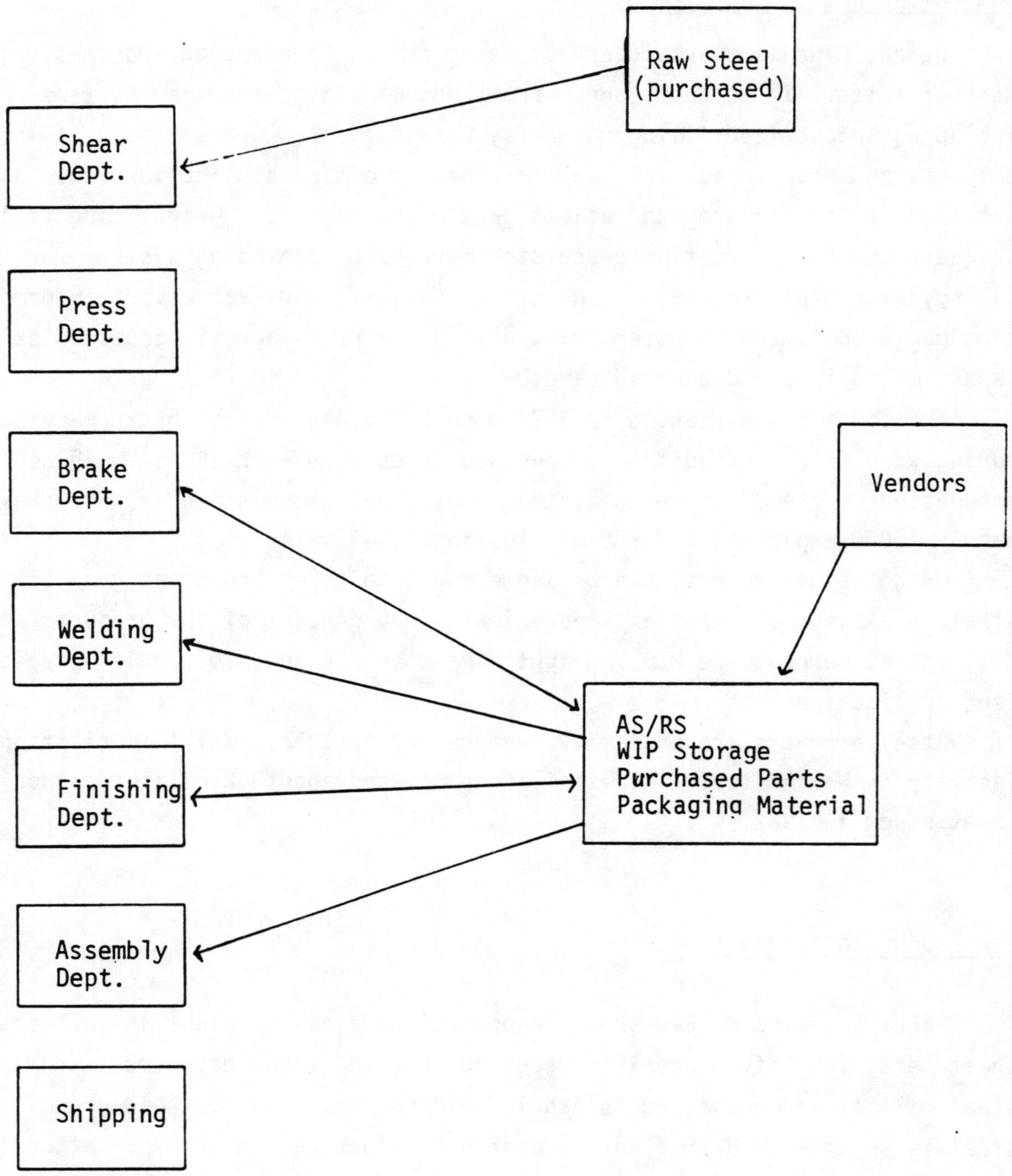

Figure 15-1. -- Sheet Metal Operations Flow

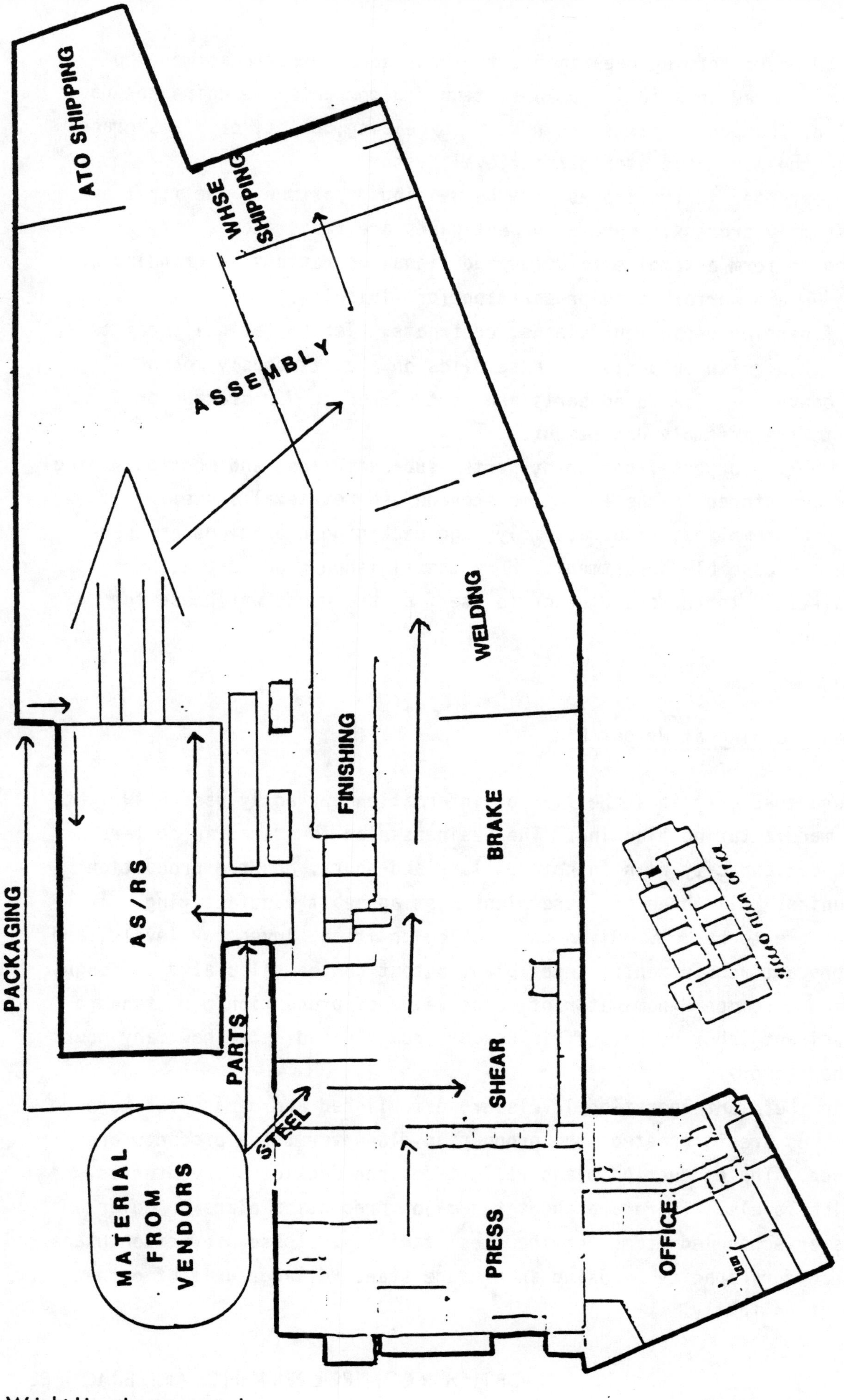

Figure 15-2. -- Sheet Metal Operations Plant Layout

In the brake/forming department, the punched blanks are formed, roll formed, and hemmed in a series of operations to complete the component part fabrication. Component parts are routed to welding, paint, or WIP storage located in the automatic storage/retrieval system.

The next step in the process is the welding department, the first step in the assembly process. Here component parts are resistance (spot) or gas-welded to form assemblies. Often additional operations -- grinding or deburring -- are performed in preparation for finishing.

The finishing department cleans, pretreats, electrostatically paints, and bakes the finish on parts and assemblies on a continuously moving overhead conveyor. Completed parts are sent either to WIP storage or directly to the assembly department.

All work in process, component parts, subassemblies, and most packaging materials are stored in the automatic storage and retrieval system.

All subassemblies, final assembly, and packaging operations are performed in the assembly department. Here the finished goods are either shipped directly to the customer or to the finished goods warehouse for distribution.

Production Planning at Wright Line

Figure 15-3 describes the flow of information currently used at Wright Line for manufacturing planning. The business plan is stated in dollars, the rough-cut capacity plan in both dollars and hours, and the production plan in units. All three of these plans must agree if manufacturing objectives are to be met. Given the backlog position, inventory levels, and dollar forecast requirements, total plant output can be calculated in rough terms using a common denominator of sales value of production per standard hours of direct labor output. This concept roughly indicates how many hours to run the factory.

After the plant operating levels are established and demand for major product lines are forecasted, the production plans for these products are established. The production plans reflect desired backlogs, inventories, and service levels. There are about ten major production plans to cover 1,500 master scheduled items for the steel facility. These production plans are checked for capacity by using an average standard labor unit of output per production family.

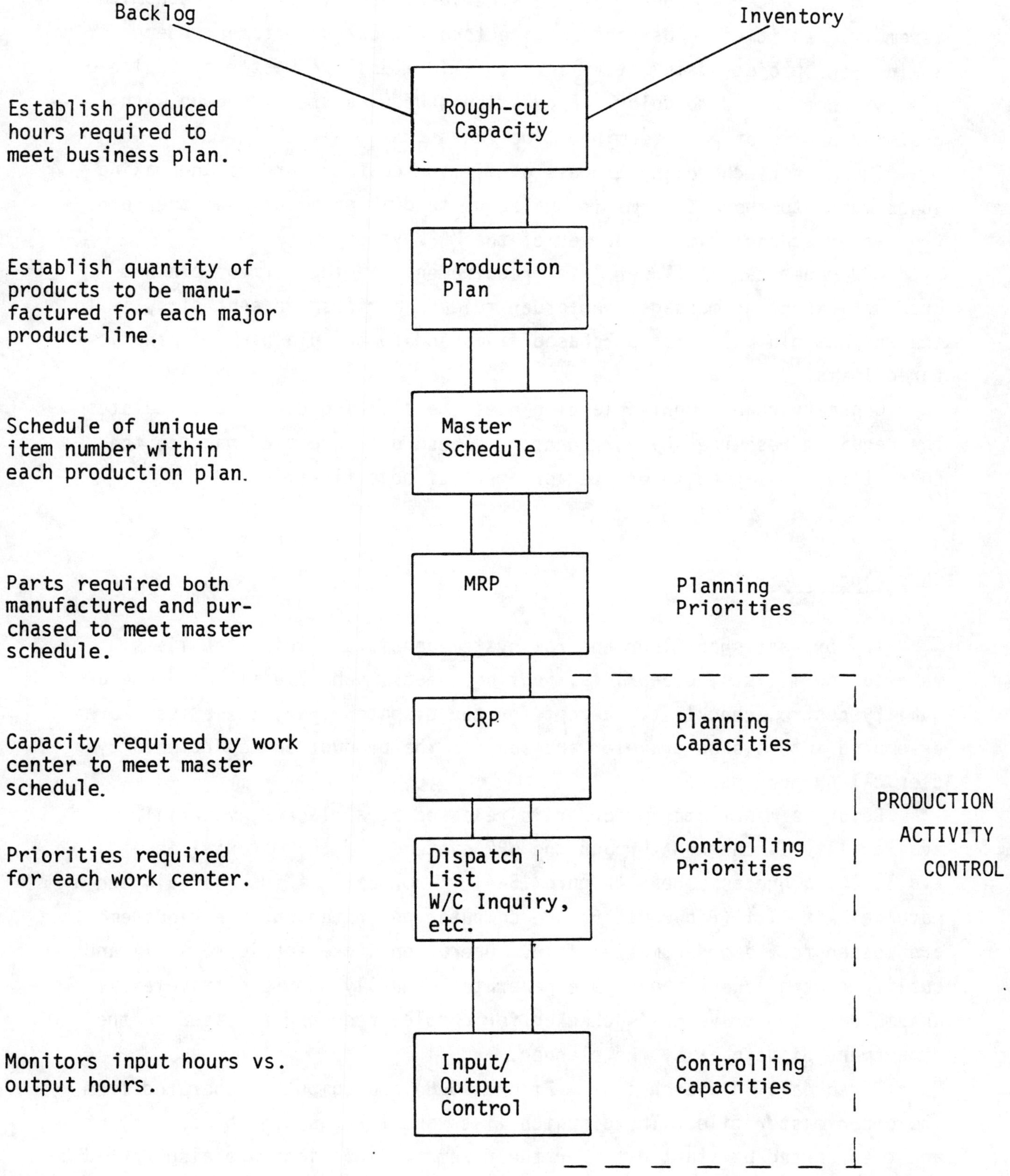

Figure 15-3. -- Manufacturing Planning System Forecast (Tactical Plan)

Once manufacturing and marketing agree on the production plans, each MTS item is master scheduled at the stockkeeping unit level in economic assembly quantities. Customer service then allocates customer orders against the projected inventory levels. ATO items are master scheduled by item without regard to color. Production schedules are firmed up with customer orders at predetermined time fences.

The master scheduling process of firming customer orders and making adjustments to the MTS items is analogous to driving a car down the road -- the master schedule is the driver of the MRP system.

MRP generates all lower level requirements in the form of planned orders. Exception messages and order release notices are sent directly to the responsible buyer for purchased items and to the planner for manufactured items.

Capacity requirements planning uses the planning data and calculates the required resources by work center. These data are tied back to the current business plan to ensure agreement of objectives.

Shop Floor Control

The present shop floor control system consists of dispatch lists, material pull lists, blueprints, routing sheets, schedule tickets, and a quality control checklist. Except for the dispatch list, these items are assembled into a shop traveler and sent to the production departments by a clerical support person.

Before a manufacturing order is released by a planner, material availability is checked through the MRP system. If the material is available, a process sheet (Figure 15-4), labor cards (Figure 15-5), and a material kit list (Figure 15-6) are computer generated and the requirements are posted to the order master file. Operation tickets (Figure 15-7) and quality control check sheets are generated manually when the traveler is assembled. The traveler is checked for completeness and released to the department dispatcher by the planner.

Three daily dispatch lists (Figure 15-8) are computer generated from the order master file. The dispatch lists are first sorted by department and then sorted by start date for the foremen. The lists are also sorted by

REPORT NO.- MFG023
ORDER-NO.-A195-059580 000203 WRIGHT LINE INC.
QTY SCHEDULED 20 PAGE 1 08/11/83

XXXXXXXXXXXXXXXX
X 59580 X
XXXXXXXXXXXXXXXX

D-R-A-W-I-N-G SHOP PROCESS SHEET

SIZE	NUMBER	REV
C	059580	A

WELD B-LEG LH 22.5

M A T E R I A L R E Q U I R E M E N T S

BLANK SIZE/RAW MAT. SIZE THICK	WIDTH	LENGTH	TYPE	E	QUANTITY	PART NUMBER	DESCRIPTION	QTY/ UNIT	UNIT MEAS	ST CD	PI
									A		6 4
			2		1.000	10019	UPPER LEG PLATE				
			1		1.000	29973	LEG PLATE WELD				
			1		1.000	32804	LEG FILLER WELD 25"				
.000	.000	.000	3		.002	58069	PAINT-1622 BLACK				
			2		1.000	59576	LEG LH 22.5				

OPER NO.	DEPT NO.	WORK CENTER NUMBER	CURRENT STD.HRS.	LN NO	S Q	OPERATION DESCRIPTION	NO. MEN	NO. HITS	INC. CODE	LABOR CODE	ENG INT	AUDIT DATE	CHANGES
010	14	11140001417		1	1	SU OPER 15 LINE JOB	01		2	02	-		
				1	2	14-6283							
				10	1	99914- F-6283-							
015	14	11140001417	.019100	1	1	POS & WELD FILLER	02	20	1	01	-		
				1	2	POS & WELD LEG PLATES							
020	14	11140001480		1	1	MOVE TO EDP SYSTEM	01		2	05	-		
025	15	11150001515		1	1	HANG ON RACK PAINT	04		2	01	-		
				1	2	INSPECT							
030	20	11200002030		1	1	MOVE TO STOCKROOM	01		2	05	-		

Figure 15-4. -- Shop Process Sheet

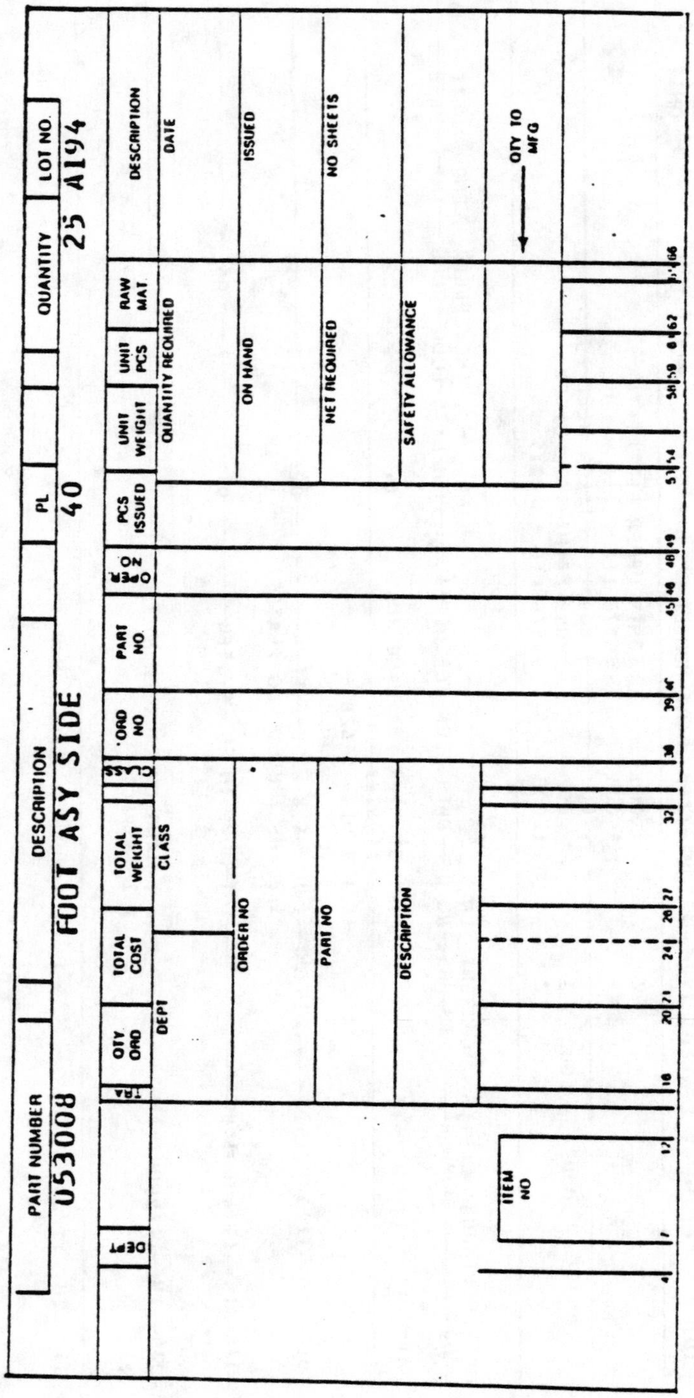

Figure 15-5. -- Labor Ticket

27-00-A REL 1.07.1 BATCH 509 M R P MANUFACTURING ORDER RUN DATE 08/10
AS OF 08/08/83 - 192 WRIGHT LINE INC

MANUFACTURING ORDER

KIT PULL LIST FOR 000000053008 FOOT ASY SIDE BAR B/M REV ORDER NUMBER 530

COMMENTS	LOCATION	BAL IN LOCATION	BALANCE ON HAND	MK BY	PART DESCRIPTION	PART NUMBER	UNIT OF MEASURE	TOTAL REQUIRED	ACT ISSU
	ASRS	252	252	2	FOOT 18-PLATED	000000052986	EACH	25	
	ASRS	17,850	17,850	2	END CAP MR FOOT	000000053005	EACH	50	

Figure 15-6. -- Material Kit List

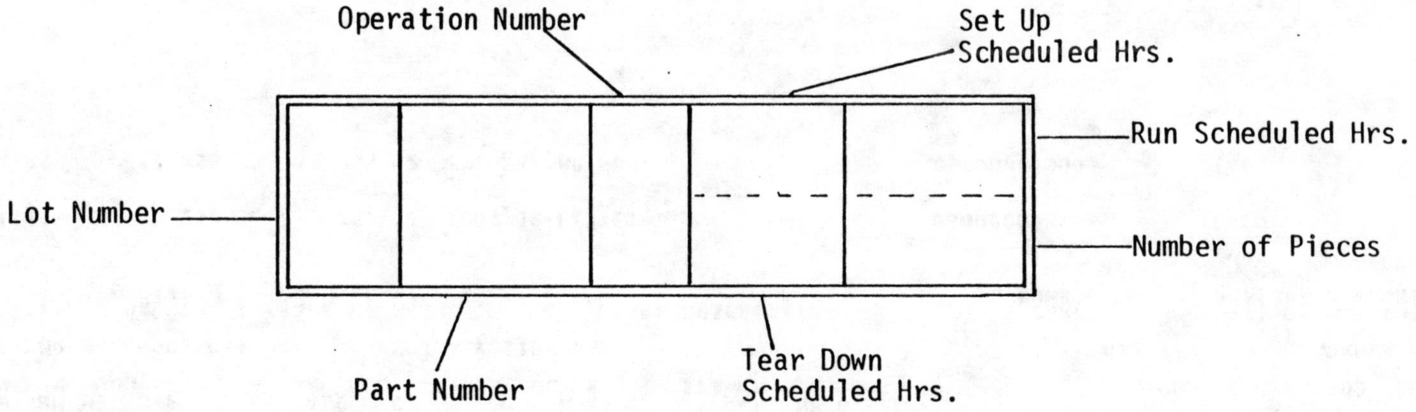

Figure 15-7. -- Operation Ticket

REPORT-NO: MF6006

DEPARTMENT-NO: D11

WRIGHT LINE INC.

*** DAILY DISPATCH REPORT ***

*** DISPATCHER ***

ITEM NUMBER	STRT/FIN DEPT	DESCRIPTION	ORDER QUANTITY	ORDER BALANCE	ORDER NUMBER	START-DATE	DUE-DATE	LEAD TIME	BUY PLN	STA CDE	O D
57174	D11/D11	HEX SHAFT MKS 29899	3000	3000	57174A183	07/12/83-183	08/02/83-188	5	AAA	CUW	*
55863	D10/D11	RETAINER MKS 55576	605	605	55863A178	07/12/83-183	08/04/83-190	7	BBB	CUW	*
56464	D11/D11	PANEL LOCK MKS 56465	5500	5500	56464A187	07/15/83-186	08/05/83-191	5	EEE	CUW	*
59030	D11/D11	MINIEDGE TRIM	900		59030A174	07/15/83-186	08/05/83-191	5	CCC	CFR	*
8961	D11/D11	SIDE PANEL 1360-0360	525	525	8961A169	07/01/83-177	08/08/83-192	15	EEE	CUW	*
53918	D10/D11	FRONT HANGING FRAME	36	36	PLAN/ORDER	07/01/83-177	08/08/83-192	15	AAA	PLN	*
56306	D11/D11	SUPPORT HANGER BAR	3	3	PLAN/ORDER	08/01/83-187	08/08/83-192	5	CCC	PLN	*
60431	D11/D11	SIDE FRAME FRONT RH-	350	350	60431A178	07/15/83-186	08/08/83-192	6	CCC	HFM	*
60432	D11/D11	SIDE FRAME FRONT LH-	350	350	60432A178	07/15/83-186	08/08/83-192	6	CCC	HFM	*
60432	D11/D11	SIDE FRAME FRONT LH-	196	196	PLAN/ORDER	07/15/83-186	08/08/83-192	6	CCC	PLN	*
60433	D11/D11	SIDE FRAME REAR RH	370	370	60433A178	08/01/83-187	08/08/83-192	5	CCC	HFM	*
60434	D11/D11	SIDE FRAME REAR LH	370	370	60434A178	08/01/83-187	08/08/83-192	5	CCC	HFM	*
59450	D10/D11	SIDE LEFT HAND	36	36	PLAN/ORDER	07/05/83-178	08/09/83-193	15	AAA	PLN	*
60307	D11/D11	CROSS SUPPORT TILT	150	150	60307A169	08/02/83-188	08/09/83-193	5	CCC	CUW	*
9880	D11/D11	TOP TRACK MULTI PURP	3060	3060	9880A182	07/13/83-184	08/10/83-194	10	AAA	CUW	*
10152	D11/D11	BACK PANEL 30 X 30	200		10152A187	08/01/83-187	08/10/83-194	7	BBB	CUW	*
55558	D10/D11	GUIDE R/O FORMS SHEL	575	575	55558A178	08/01/83-187	08/10/83-194	7	BBB	CUW	*
60431	D11/D11	SIDE FRAME FRONT RH-	275	275	PLAN/ORDER	08/02/83-188	08/10/83-194	6	CCC	PLN	*
10056	D10/D11	BACK PLATE	7	7	PLAN/ORDER	08/02/83-188	08/11/83-195	7	AAA	PLN	*
55332	D11/D11	SIDE RIGHT R/O SHELF	3273		55332A182	08/02/83-188	08/11/83-195	7	AAA	CUW	*
55333	D11/D11	SIDE LEFT R/O SHELF	3446	172	55333A182	08/02/83-188	08/11/83-195	7	AAA	CUW	*
59893	D11/D11	BOTTOM PLATE,SWIVEL-	21	21	PLAN/ORDER	07/12/83-183	08/11/83-195	12	CCC	PLN	*
57178	D11/D11	HANGER BAR MKS 53508	300	300	57178A193	08/05/83-191	08/12/83-196	5	AAA	HFM	
57676	D11/D11	MOUNTING PLATE ASY	199	10	57676A182	03/09/83-193	08/12/83-196	3	AAA	CUW	
59025	D11/D11	TOP-CPS L/U - 53150	500		59025A178	07/15/83-186	08/12/83-196	10	EEE	CUW	
59366	D11/D11	BOTTOM CROSS BRACE 6	25	25	59366A192	08/05/83-191	08/12/83-196	5	CCC	CUW	
60467	D11/D11	HANDLE ASSEMBLY	460	460	60467A159	08/05/83-191	08/12/83-196	5	CCC	HFM	

Figure 15-8. -- Dispatch List

due date for the dispatcher and sorted by planner identification number for planners to monitor orders for which they are responsible. There are about 1,500 manufacturing orders in the file at any time.

Information Flow

When the planner releases the manufacturing order, the traveler goes to the shop floor and is placed in queue by start date by work center in the department. When an operation is complete in a work center, the next job in queue is entered onto the schedule board. At this time, material is issued to the order from a stocking location. It is the foremen's responsibility to complete jobs as scheduled, while using their expertise to combine job setups whenever possible.

Incentive labor cards are filled out and turned in by direct labor personnel. When all operations are complete, the traveler is turned into the dispatcher and the order is closed out.

The labor data from the incentive labor cards are accumulated daily through payroll and are compiled weekly and tracked on an output report by department.

The current shop floor control system is informal and difficult to administer, but it is flexible, and provides priority direction and backlog reporting by department. The system lacks true work center priority planning, input analysis, rework planning, scrap reporting, and operational tracking. There is no formal feedback to the other systems.

Shop Floor to be Implemented by October 1983

To correct the inadequacies of the current shop floor control system, a project team was formed to implement a system that would provide managers with complete shop floor status by operation and more accurate capacity reporting of orders in process. The project team recommended that the closed-loop approach be continued and that a shop floor file be added to the present software package (Figure 15-9).

After the addition of a shop floor file, when an order is released it will be posted to the order master file, and the operations required will be posted to the shop floor file. This addition will allow a new level of control by operation.

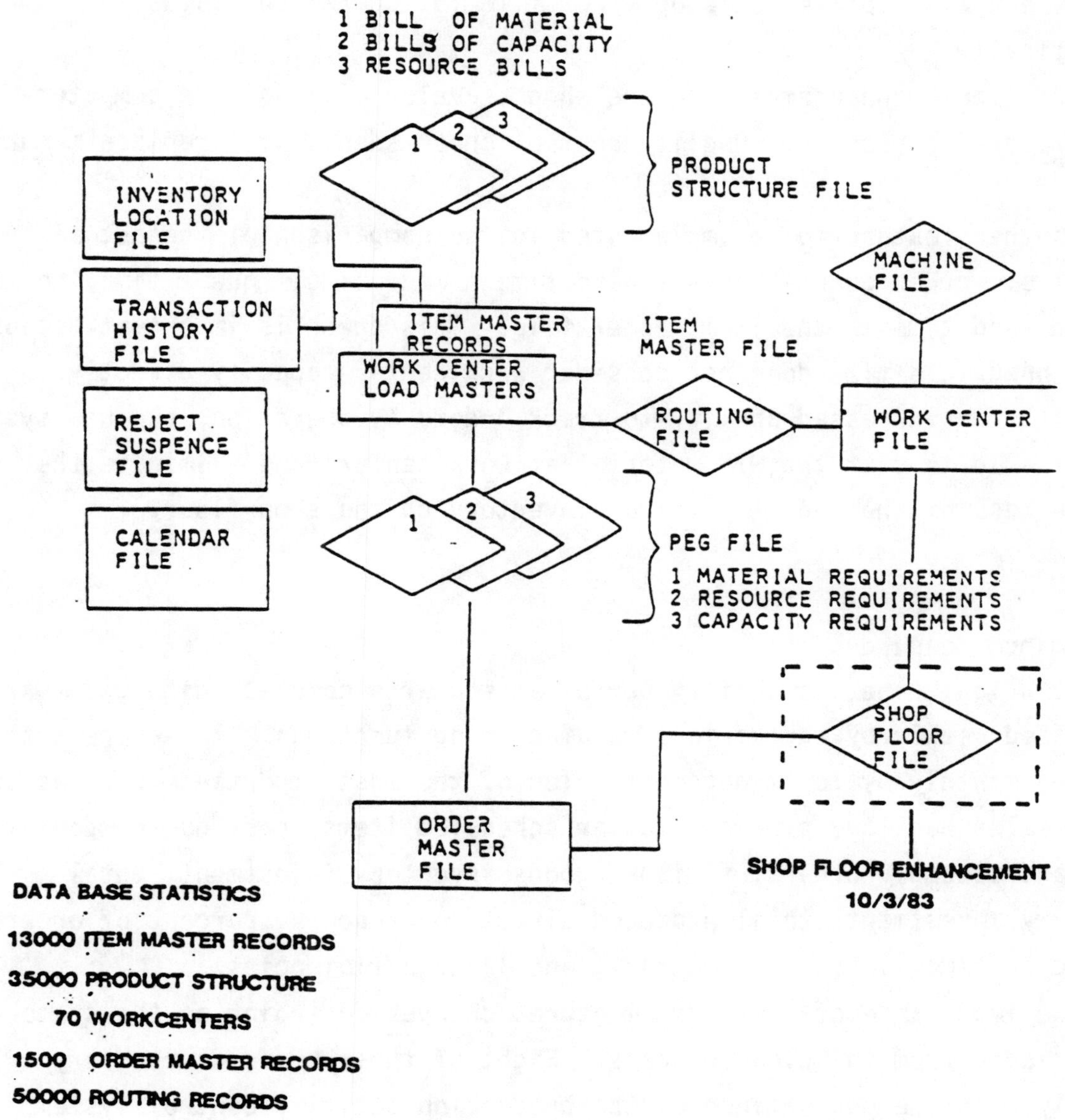
1 BILL OF MATERIAL
2 BILLS OF CAPACITY
3 RESOURCE BILLS
PRODUCT STRUCTURE FILE
INVENTORY LOCATION FILE
TRANSACTION HISTORY FILE
ITEM MASTER RECORDS
ITEM MASTER FILE
WORK CENTER LOAD MASTERS
MACHINE FILE
ROUTING FILE
WORK CENTER FILE
REJECT SUSPENCE FILE
CALENDAR FILE
PEG FILE
1 MATERIAL REQUIREMENTS
2 RESOURCE REQUIREMENTS
3 CAPACITY REQUIREMENTS
SHOP FLOOR FILE
ORDER MASTER FILE
SHOP FLOOR ENHANCEMENT
10/3/83
DATA BASE STATISTICS
13000 ITEM MASTER RECORDS
35000 PRODUCT STRUCTURE
70 WORKCENTERS
1500 ORDER MASTER RECORDS
50000 ROUTING RECORDS

Figure 15-9. -- Shop Floor Enhancement

A new dispatch list, with job priority by work center rather than by department, will be generated. Work center input and output analysis and an audit trail by operation will be available. This will do away with the impossible task of keeping order priorities up to date on the schedule boards. This enhancement will allow reporting scrap by operation and daily backlog by work center and department. Labor reporting under this enhancement will update the shop floor file for operation status automatically.

Additional enhancements to the shop traveler will include computer-generated scrap reports. Quality control check sheets will replace manual forms.

Another feature to be implemented is the comparison of the actual lead time (i.e., order quantity x standard time + move time + queue time) to the planned lead time in the item master file. This check is important because the planned lead time does not consider work center capacity directly.

With the increased ability to track orders by operation, the new system will be able to cost the WIP material at work centers and eliminate the tedious task of the annual physical inventory on the shop floor.

Performance Measures

At Wright Line, some fifty performance charts complete with goals are maintained weekly by the various manufacturing functions. These are also reviewed monthly by top management. Ten of the most important measures are: sales, sales backlog, past due master scheduled items, past due component parts and assembly orders, finished goods inventory investment, total inventory investment, total produced direct labor-hours, percent of orders shipped on time, inventory accuracy, and labor efficiencies.

The importance of these ten measures changes depending on the state of the variance from the planned goals. Eight of these ten measures vary directly with the performance of the production activity control system. If Wright Line performs well on the above ten measures, then it performs well on profit.

In the future, Wright Line foresees a continual effort to upgrade its manufacturing systems to keep pace with such technological advances as flexible automation, on-line data collection, and communications linking minicomputer-controlled work centers and the formal planning system.

Manufacturing personnel advocate the acquisition of highly productive, yet flexible, production systems. While these systems may be geared to a specific product family, individual pieces of equipment would also be used to produce other items. This raises a question of whether to treat such a system as one work center or the separate pieces of equipment in the system as work centers that are to be grouped by a series of routings. Put another way, should the system plan priorities for the flexible system or for each piece of equipment within the system?

Because the new work centers for flexible automation are controlled by minicomputers, many equipment vendors offer an option to tie planning data into the work center queue for maximum efficiency and material use. This would eliminate the need for shop travelers for the work centers.

To effectively use the new system, on-line data collection will be needed. Batch processing with a twenty-four hour turnaround will no longer be adequate to handle all the detail in the new system.

Wright Line has enjoyed steady growth in recent years. The company realizes its continued growth depends on the quality of its products and the service it provides to its customers. Management understands the need and advocates the use of efficient tools to manage and increase productivity. Shop floor control plays an integral role in achieving these objectives.

The Ingersoll Milling Machine Company (Ingersoll Milling) of Rockford, Illinois, is currently recognized as one of the foremost implementers of CIM systems in the United States. In 1982, Ingersoll Milling received the LEAD[1] award from the Computer and Automated Systems Association of the Society of Manufacturing Engineering (CASA/SME), in recognition of the time and effort that management at Ingersoll Milling has spent making CIM a corporate way of life.

To everyone at Ingersoll, CIM is the glue that binds all aspects of the firm together. CIM not only links the various departments of Ingersoll Milling, it also ties corporate strategy directly to the activities of the shop floor. What is done on the shop floor is strategic in that it plays a critical role in the day-to-day implementation of corporate objectives.

Since receiving the LEAD award, Ingersoll Milling has evolved beyond CIM. Ingersoll is currently at a stage in the evolution of computer-based systems that management describes by the term, computer-integrated flexible manufacturing (CIFM).

General Nature of the Firm

Ingersoll Milling is a major part of the Ingersoll Company. The Ingersoll Company is a privately held company with annual sales of approximately $250 million. The company of four operating entities includes (Figure 16-1):

- o The Ingersoll Milling Machine Company -- the American-based special machinery builder
- o Ingersoll Cutting Tool Company -- the American-based cutting tool company

[1]LEAD stands for Leadership and Excellence in the Application and Development of computer-integrated manufacturing. This award is presented annually to a single company in the world that CASA/SME considers to be the best example of how to incorporate an "innovative, leading edge" CIM program into its operation.

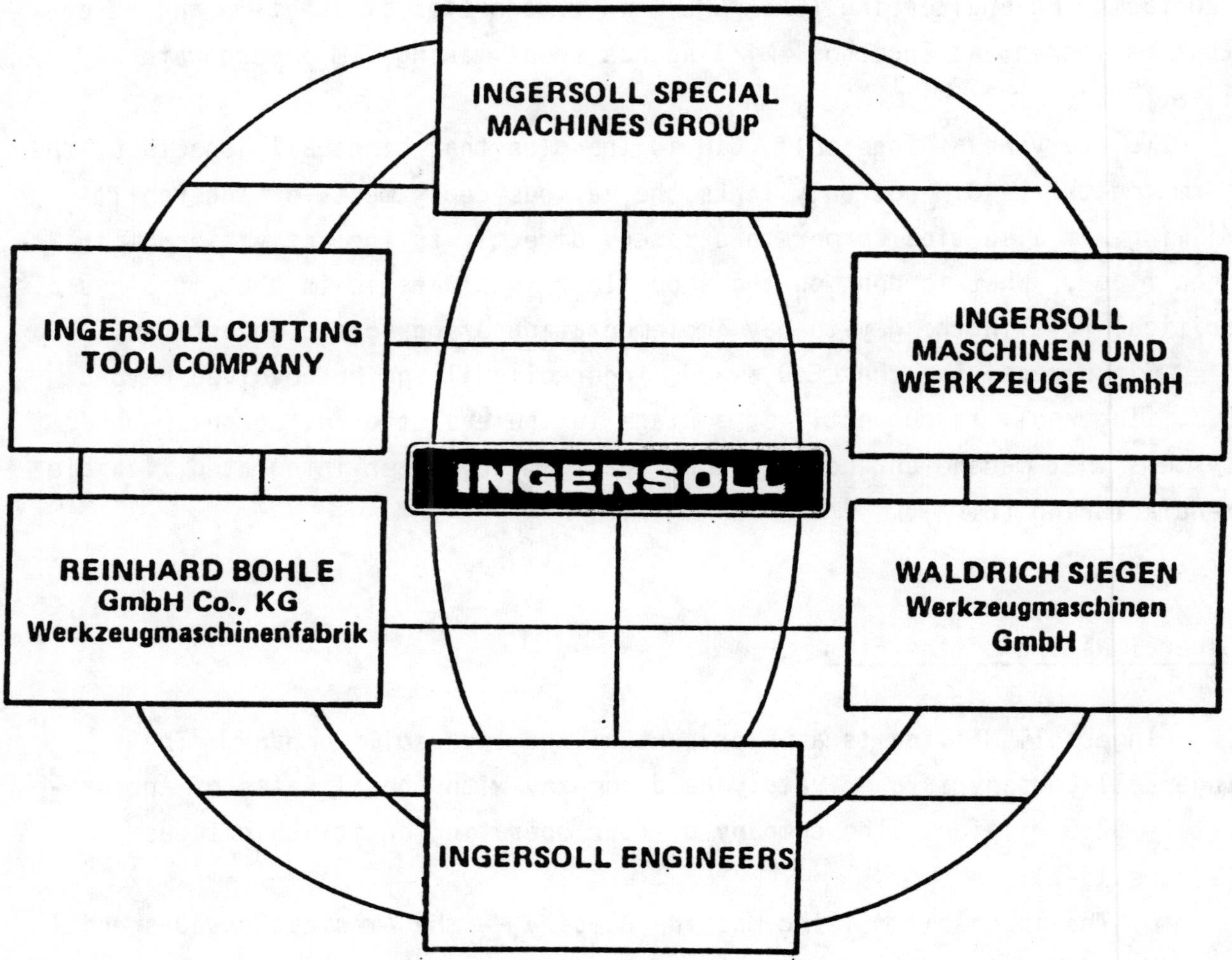

Rockford, Illinois
Rugby, England
Dusseldorf, Germany
Annecy, France

Figure 16-1. -- Operations

- o Ingersoll Maschinen Und Werkzeuge GmbH -- the German-based manufacturing company building machinery and cutting tools with its subsidiaries, Waldrich-Siegen and Bohle
- o Ingersoll Engineering Incorporated -- the multinational consulting company with offices in four countries.

Ingersoll Milling accounts for between 40 to 45 percent of total sales. Ingersoll Maschinen Und Werkzeuge GmbH is a close second.

Ingersoll Milling is primarily an ETO firm that produces heavy special machinery systems. The systems range from transfer lines and rail mills to stand-alone numerical control machines. These systems are built for a wide range of manufacturing settings, running from job shops to flow shops. Its customers include such firms as General Motors, General Dynamics, Grumman, Lockheed, and Boeing.

Within the industry, Ingersoll Milling is considered to be the "Cadillac." Its customers pay a premium for a package that consists of both engineering and manufacturing capabilities. Customers expect and receive the on-time delivery of specialized equipment that is extensively engineered and of extremely high quality.

The only exception to this position involves the production of systems that have never been built before and draw on new engineering designs and features. These systems are so technologically advanced that there is a real question of whether they can be built. Under such conditions, the customer understands that the due dates established are tentative. The dates can be moved out if any problems (typically engineering) are encountered. Failure to meet the due date on these products is acceptable. However, failure to meet the due date on the other products manufactured by Ingersoll Milling is not acceptable. As a result, Ingersoll Milling has a reputation within the industry of producing systems that continually push out the technical frontier.

The Production Process

Ingersoll Milling is located on one site in Rockford. It employs some 1,800 nonunion workers. The workers are evenly divided between the light shop, which produces items measuring up to 1-meter cube in size, and the heavy shop, which produces all larger size orders. Both shops consist of fabrication and assembly/test areas.

All employees are treated as salaried personnel. In each shop, the division between production and nonproduction labor is approximately equal with routing designers considered part of production.

Because Ingersoll Milling is primarily an ETO firm, it faces certain unique production problems:

- Very small lot sizes. Lot sizes cannot be applied realistically. In a typical year, Ingersoll Milling produces approximately 25,000 different parts. Of these, over 70 percent are built in lots of one. Few of the production lots go beyond two pieces.
- Little repetition of production. A great deal of what is built at Ingersoll Milling will never be built again. Of the 25,000 parts produced in a typical year, about 50 percent will never be made again.
- Importance of design learning as compared to production learning. In many traditional production systems, the managers of these manufacturing systems tend to make extensive use of the detailed insights of their shop floor personnel. They rely on shop floor personnel to improve efficiency by taking advantage of similarities in setups or processing. Management, however, does not have this luxury. Because of the unique and changing nature of the product mix, workers are always at the first stages of the learning curve. The only learning that does take place is in the design stages of order processing and design. There is a strong tendency to reuse engineering extensively. Designs done for past jobs are frequently called up and used in new jobs.
- Extensive engineering. All of the products manufactured by Ingersoll Milling are extensively engineered. The average engineering cycle is typically five months or greater, and engineering costs account for between 5 to 15 percent of the selling price. When design engineering is combined with numerical control programming, the result is that for every half hour of production, approximately fourteen hours of engineering are required. Engineering is critical because it is held responsible for ensuring that parts are made right the first time.
- Long cumulative lead times. The total lead time for an order often exceeds twelve to eighteen months. For a typical product, the lead time is fifteen months. This lead time is divided into the following segments: five months are spent in engineering, six weeks

in process routing, sixteen weeks in build, sixteen weeks in assembly/test, and ten weeks for customer changes and revision and engineering cleanup.

The total lead time varies depending on the type of order received. For example, if the order has never been built before, the lead time allowance is longer.

- Frequent design changes. The design of any given product can be altered at any point in the production process. It can change even after manufacturing on the order has started. These design changes can come from either engineering or from the customer. In spite of these changes, manufacturing is still expected to complete the order on time.
- No manufacturing standards. Ingersoll Milling uses no standards because of the unique nature of the products made and the processes used. Instead, estimates provided by engineering are used. Because of the lack of standards, capacity planning is difficult and has a strong subjective character.

Given these unique production problems, management has been forced to use alternative approaches to the production process. These moves have been undertaken to maintain and enhance the firm's competitive position in the industry. The latest of these approaches, in use since 1983, is CIFM.

CIFM Background

CIFM can be best described as a marriage between CIM and flexible manufacturing systems (FMS). CIFM is the sixth and latest stage in an evolutionary process that can be described as follows:

- The use of numerically controlled machines in the 1950s. This marked the beginning of CAM at Ingersoll Milling.
- The use of CAD from the moment it was practical.
- The use of computer graphics as a method of accelerating CAD and building a solid foundation for CAM. The introduction of computer graphics was the key element in integrating CAD/CAM.
- The rewriting of all company information system application software programs to facilitate the installation of a companywide database information system. This was the beginning of the integrated management and business information system.

- o The implementation of a $20 million FMS to replace the light machine shop. The light machine shop manufactures prismatic parts, 1-meter cube or smaller. When combined with the previous four stages, this stage gave rise to the CIFM system.

Each of the stages has contributed significantly to the development of CIFM. The CAD/CAM system has been important because of its inherent value to the customer in creating products with superior performance, features, and uptime. Furthermore, the CAD/CAM system has helped management deliver such products at lower costs and consistently on time. CAD/CAM has also been of significant importance to the suppliers. Other benefits attributed to the presence of CAD/CAM include: shorter development cycles, improved quality, lower inventory, reduced costs, and better control over setups.

This last benefit is of special interest. Under CAD/CAM, setups are designed when the part is designed. The part design can be modified to improve setup performance. In addition, the best method for the setup can be identified and evaluated before the order hits the shop floor. This control over the setup makes it easier to produce the part right the first time, which is a requirement for Ingersoll Milling's success in the market.

The integrated management and business information system has ensured that the activities of manufacturing are always integrated and coordinated with the activities of other functions within the firm. It also ensures that the actions taken by manufacturing and engineering are always consistent with corporate objectives.

The single corporate database eliminates many of the obstacles to cooperation. There is no question of which numbers are right or wrong. Everyone knows where to find information. Ingersoll Milling currently has the world's largest database in terms of the span of integrated business functions operating under one database. The center for the common corporate database is the BOM.

In combining the single database, the integrated management and business information system, and the CAD/CAM system with the FMS, management has created a single fully integrated monolithic system. This system covers all aspects of manufacturing from the formulation of the master schedule to execution in the shop, to job cost and management reports.

The Role of the CAD/CAM Computer Graphics System in CIFM

Computer graphics is part of nearly every aspect of the manufacturing and design process. It is used extensively in presale negotiations to ensure that the product and its requirements, as envisioned by the customer, correspond to the product being designed by the engineers at Ingersoll Milling. It is used during the design stage to develop and evaluate the product design. A computer simulation model of the proposed design is built and its operation dynamically simulated. During this simulation, any problems (e.g., two parts or cutting surfaces colliding due to inadequate clearances) are identified and corrected before the product is released to process routing and the shop floor.

Finally, computer graphics provides the major link between engineering and numerical control programming. The designs created by the engineers and captured in the computer graphics are passed on to numerical control programmers. During numerical control programming, the programmer can rotate the part on the computer screen and evaluate the effects of the proposed routings before the order is released. Any problems with routings due to product design can be referred back to the engineer by the numerical control programmer. Computer graphics helps management attain its objective of building the part right the first time.

Flexible Manufacturing Systems

The move toward the extensive use of FMS began in 1983. Ultimately, management intends to replace 90 percent of the conventional light machine shop equipment with FMS.

One of the objectives of implementing FMS is to enable management to increase overall manufacturing capacity while reducing the amount of floor space needed for production facilities. Ingersoll Milling is a growing company located in an area where physical expansion is no longer possible. The only economical method of accommodating the growth in sales is through the better use of current production floor space.

The technology of FMS did not precede the structure. FMS is a technological response to a set of problems facing management at Ingersoll Milling. These problems were both well defined and well understood before management went searching for a solution. FMS is the appropriate response to the problem.

Currently, FMS consists of five Bohle-Ingersoll machining centers and two Lablond-Makino machining centers. The Bohle-Ingersoll centers have eliminated seventeen older machines. Due to a management policy that forces shop personnel to justify the continued use of any equipment that is at least five years old, the machines replaced were still relatively new. Even the equipment that was replaced was, when compared to equipment located in other manufacturing firms, more productive.

The major difference between the Bohle-Ingersoll and Lablond-Makino centers lies in the size of parts produced. The Bohle-Ingersoll centers process parts that cannot be easily lifted by a worker and require some form of mechanized material handling system. In contrast, the Lablond-Makino centers process parts that are transported easily by the worker.

In the next implementation phase, six new FMS will be introduced. These will eliminate twenty-three older machines.

Each FMS at Ingersoll Milling is organized around six basic resources that must be allocated and controlled by that system: parts, pallets, fixtures (including setup), storage (via automated storage and retrieval systems), transportation (automated guided vehicle systems, robots), and machines (cutting, deburring, washing, measuring). These six resources are managed continuously and in a real-time environment. For example, the FMS software always monitors the status of all tools in terms of wear, use, state, and location.

FMS deals not only with the control and monitoring of equipment and tooling but also with setups and the setup process. The setup procedures used in the FMS cover both the production of the part and the setup of the fixtures.

In converting to FMS, management has attempted to achieve certain key objectives, the most important of which are a reduction in manufacturing lead time, improved product quality, reduced direct labor requirements on the shop floor, and better coordination with the computerized planning and design system. To date, these objectives have been achieved by a system that is highly automated, extremely flexible, and adapts well to change.

FMS is not only an area of production, it is also a laboratory for the management of Ingersoll Milling. As management operates its FMS, it learns how to take advantage of the capabilities offered by this system and about the limitations and problems present. These lessons are then passed on to those customers who purchase FMS from Ingersoll Milling.

Production Planning at Ingersoll Milling

The production planning system, part of the integrated management and business information system, is designed to support all of the planning and production activities necessary to process a customer order. In structure, the production planning system is similar to MRP II. The major modules of this system are:

- Master schedule
- Engineering design
  - Assembly and piece part drawing
  - BOMs
- Production planning and control
- Inventory control
- Purchasing and accounts payable
- Routing and process planning
- Numerical control programming and post processing
- Flexible machining system
- Assembly
- Job cost and management reports

Except for the flexible machining system, these modules are important because they provide the structure required by a system such as CIFM. This structure is necessary to make CIFM a corporate system rather than an engineering system.

The steps in the production planning process follow the order process closely. Each step in the production planning process supports an appropriate major step in the order process.

Production Planning and the Order Process

At Ingersoll Milling, the order process consists of a number of distinct steps. The early steps are characterized by an emphasis on planning and extensive involvement by top management. Good planning at these stages greatly simplifies execution on the shop floor.

Preorder activities. The order process begins with the initial issuing of the bid and the receipt of engineering's initial designs and cost estimates. During these early stages, the computer is used extensively. For example, during the preliminary design stages, all drawings are done using the computer-based CAD/CAM system. By using the computer, the engineers can ensure that their designs are consistent with the customer's needs. The preliminary design is saved in the computer and becomes the basis for the final design if Ingersoll Milling receives the order.

Getting the design done right at this stage is important because the estimates generated at this point define the work loads that will be placed on the manufacturing (i.e., light, heavy, and assembly areas) and engineering departments. These estimates are used to manage capacity once the order has been placed.

Immediate actions on receipt of the order. If the bid submitted by Ingersoll Milling is accepted by the customer, the agreed on delivery date is put into the master schedule the day the order is received. At the same time, the accounting department registers the order as an order received. The contracts department is advised. The order is assigned a five digit serial number used to track the order through the various stages of the process.

The contracts departments prepares an acknowledgment to the customer on the same day, confirming the customer delivery date. The contracts department is part of Ingersoll Milling's performance planning activity, which provides project management from the time the order is received until the completed order is turned over to production in the customer's plant.

Initial loading of the master schedule. The master schedule enters four key dates into the master schedule system: the shipping date, the engineering completion date, the machine shop completion date, and the purchase completion date. These dates drive the detailed scheduling done within the individual functions.

The master schedule (Figure 16-2) is a computer record that contains and controls all dates in the company related to that job. Each order has its own master schedule record. It directly drives the engineering, purchasing, and manufacturing systems. It also simplifies the rescheduling of a job, no matter how many component parts are in process. Rescheduling a job requires one action -- changing one demand date via a computer terminal. This transaction is subject to careful security checks; only the vice president of manufacturing can change a date in the master schedule.

Generation of BOMs. Once the receipt of the order has been acknowledged and the order entered into the master schedule, the drawing is returned to engineering. In engineering, the design is cleaned up and refined and the appropriate BOMs generated. Again, the computer is used extensively.

GT201OT MANUFACTURING MASTER SCHEDULE INQUIRY 03-28-84
MAIN MACHINES AND REBUILDS PAGE 1

PARENT SHOP ORDER : 25789 FISHER/KALAMAZOO

SERIAL RANGE : 25789 THRU 25789
ADDITIONAL SERIALS :

MACHINE ERECTION : 10-05-84 CUSTOMER DEMONSTRATION : 11-30-84
POWER ON : 10-08-84 MACHINE SHIP : 11-30-84

ROUP	MECH ENG	CNTRL ENG	ROUGH MATL	FAB TAPES	FAB	MACH RTGS	MACH TAPES	M.W. FINSH	PURCH	SOFT WARE	TOOLS	SUB-ASSY
000	PARENT DATES											
TART :	09-30	11-01	03-12	03-12	04-09	03-19	03-19	04-16	02-12	12-01	03-01	08-06
STOP :	01-27	05-01	04-09	04-09	06-18	04-16	04-16	08-10	08-10	06-01	10-05	09-06
COMP :												
001	BEDS/TABLES											
TART :	09-30	11-01	03-12	03-12	04-09	03-19	03-19	04-16	02-12			08-06
STOP :	02-01	05-01	04-09	04-09	06-18	04-16	04-16	08-06	08-06			09-06
COMP :												
002	HEAD											
TART :	09-30	11-01	03-12	03-12	04-09	03-19	03-19	04-16	02-12			08-06
STOP :	01-09	05-01	04-09	04-09	06-18	04-16	04-16	08-08	08-08			09-06
COMP :												
003	RAIL											
TART :	09-30	11-01	03-12	03-12	04-09	03-19	03-19	04-16	02-12			08-17
STOP :	01-27	05-01	04-09	04-09	06-18	04-16	04-16	08-17	08-17			09-06
COMP :												

PF1 - PRIOR PAGE PF3 - PARENT SUMMARY CLEAR - INQUIRY MENU
PF2 - NEXT PAGE PA2 - RETURN TO C.I.C.S.

Figure 16-2. -- Master Schedule

The computer aids the engineers by doing the complex design calculations and finite element, stability, and strength analyses. The results are described by a geometric model that is stored in the computer. This model is used to produce the necessary assembly and piece part drawings (done using the CAD/CAM system). These drawings form the basis for the BOMs.

Next, the engineers start with the assembly layout drawings and dissect them to make the individual part details. The geometric models for these parts in the computer are used extensively in the numerical control programming for the machining and coordinating index measuring machines.

Each part and subassembly is identified by a unique attribute. This attribute is attached to its identification number on the main assembly layout drawing in the computer graphics files. This number tells the computer to down load the information automatically to the alphanumeric database. This then automatically becomes the BOM for the job. It also controls the design integrity of the product from then on.

Structuring of the BOM is primarily the responsibility of engineering, but other departments are also involved. Purchasing, for example, establishes a long lead-time report, updated monthly, which helps the engineers identify the parts that will require early release. By having engineering release individual items on a working bill, purchasing can place long lead-time items on order before the final BOM is released.

Within the engineering cycle are the functions of design, detail, and check. The checked geometric model and the checked BOM are released to the manufacturing function at the time engineering is complete.

The completed BOM and checked geometric models are available to both the upstream and downstream planning functions. Before leaving this discussion, it should be noted that the BOMs generated by engineering consist primarily of A and B (i.e., high dollar volume) class items. Any fast moving, commonly used C items (i.e., low dollar volume) are omitted. These items are controlled by ensuring that there is always enough inventory on hand. The cost of this policy is minimal, yet the simplifications that result are significant.

Material and capacity planning. The finalized BOM is returned to the master schedule. Here, the master schedule and the BOM are used together to develop gross requirements by area (purchasing, manufacturing, and inventory supplies). They are also used to develop a set of dated net requirements. These requirements are placed on purchasing, in the case of all items to be bought, and manufacturing, for all items internally manufactured. Purchases account for between 40 and 50 percent of the total cost of the job, with manufacturing providing the most of the balance of the costs. Stockroom supplies account for very little of the cost.

Top management, including the CEO, meets once a week to evaluate the capacity implications of the master schedule. Management assesses the capacity implications using the capacity estimates generated in the preorder stage. The purpose of the evaluation is twofold: to ensure that there is adequate capacity for the order and to level the work load.

Management evaluates capacity impact for the shop as a whole. Using information provided by engineering, management evaluates the load, comparing the load generated by all orders (current and planned) against the capacity available. Load is measured using two indicators: parts and operations. A fully loaded shop consists of 250,000 operations and 25,000 parts. Management is careful not to exceed these limits in any given time period. Finally, if there are imbalances in work load, management can level work by bringing work forward (i.e., releasing it early).

If capacity is clearly insufficient, management can approve subcontracting. Planning in advance for subcontracting enables management to better control this activity: Subcontracting budgets can be drawn up, shop floor personnel can be warned of the upcoming need for subcontracting, and subcontractors can be evaluated for performance to budget and due date.

Programming. The geometric models and BOMs are used by the numerical control programming and quality control departments to generate the required tapes and processing information. Numerical control programs are prepared in the numerical control programming department using both graphics and other languages. In generating these tapes, the programmers use the computer to make sure that the programs do not cause collisions (two parts or surfaces striking each other). The operation times from these programs are fed back and added to the routing for machine stop load planning. This planning is done far in advance of the release of the order to the shop floor.

The quality numerical control (QNC) programming for the quality control inspection machine is done either by the QNC programmer writing a program in advance, or by the inspector directing a minicomputer through the necessary steps to inspect the first part. If there are subsequent parts, they are inspected automatically by playing back either of these programs. All inspection times and steps are provided to routing for use in shop loading.

Process routing. The final stage in the production planning process is process routing. This stage is the crossover point between the planning process and shop floor control; it marks the last stage of the planning process and the first stage of shop floor control.

This stage is the responsibility of the routing department. The personnel from this department take the processing and setup time information generated by the numerical control programming and quality control departments and convert these data into detailed routings for each order. They are responsible for finding the best combination of machines and operations for any given part.

Personnel from the routing department are aided extensively by the computer. For example, during the routing process, personnel draw on the group technology code inquiry report (Figure 16-3), based on a group technology coding scheme internal to Ingersoll Milling. The codes help the users identify parts that can be treated in the same manner (i.e., routed through the same machines and parts). Past experience with parts having the same group technology code can also be used in identifying the routing. Once the order has gone through process routing, it is released automatically to the shop floor for processing.

Production Planning and CIFM

At Ingersoll Milling, the production planning process is tightly structured and highly integrated. It provides the framework for CIFM. This structure assures management that every new stage in technology introduced on the shop floor is consistent with the overall corporate objectives and is needed by the firm to maintain or enhance its current competitive position. As a result, technology has become a solution to a specific well-defined problem rather than an answer looking for a problem.

The importance of this integrated planning process cannot be overstated. It must be in place before the advent of technology. Without such a process, management can quickly lose control over any new technology introduced.

Shop Floor Control

The shop floor control system provides management with the needed control over the execution side of operations at Ingersoll Milling. This

```
ɩT202OT        MASTER ROUTING GROUP TECHNOLOGY CODE INQUIRY          03-28-84
                                                                     PAGE 001

                   INQUIRY CRITEREA : A1AA    00 0

                                         S                                     LAST
GT CODE       PART NUMBER        VER  T DESCRIPTION            CREATED   BY   USED

A1AAAA002     SK-022883-01            A KEY                    02-28-83  DS  02-28-83
A1AAAA002     SK-030783-03            A KEY                    03-07-83  DS  03-07-83
A1AAAA002     11038574100             A SPINDLE NUT KEY        11-30-83  RB  11-30-83
A1AAAA002     11915864100             A TIT KEY                08-02-83  BH  08-02-83
A1AAAA002     12245704100             A SHOE FOR ECCENTRIC     09-15-83  DS  09-15-83
A1AAAA002     12583284200             A STOP KEY               10-13-82  RB  01-25-84
A1AAAA002     20299844503             A RETAINER CLIP          01-04-83  RB  01-04-83
A1AAAA002     20333444200             A PLATE                  08-26-82  MW  08-26-82
A1AAAA002     20428784200             A ENCODER CLAMP          05-24-83  BH  05-25-83
A1AAAA002     20457364300             A SHOE LEFT & RIGHT      02-22-84  MH  02-22-84
A1AAAA002     20472904300             W DRIVE KEY              01-05-84  DS  01-18-84
A1AAAA002     20473294900             A KEY                    12-22-83  DS  12-23-83
A1AAAA002     20481034900             A LOCATING KEY           12-28-83  DS  12-29-83
A1AAAA002     25450120103             A DOG CLAMP              08-30-83  DS  08-30-83
A1AAAA002     25464630263             A SHIM                   12-21-82  BH  12-21-82
A1AAAA002     25486280413             A SHIM                   02-21-83  BH  02-21-83
A1AAAA002     25511060133             A KEY                    08-25-82  BH  08-25-82
A1AAAA002     25525690583             A SPACER                 08-09-82  BH  08-10-82
A1AAAA002     25543060093             A KEY                    09-01-82  DS  03-24-83
A1AAAA002     25564370443             A SPINDLE KEY            01-13-83  BH  01-14-83
A1AAAA002     25568100363             A SHIM                   09-20-82  BH  09-22-82
A1AAAA002     25667350149             A KEY                    08-30-83  BH  08-30-83
A1AAAA002     25670350059             A KEY                    08-26-83  BH  08-26-83
A1AAAA002     25742420199             A KEY                    02-17-84  BH  02-20-84
A1AAAA002     87500100053             A MOTOR COUP. KEY        06-13-83  BH  02-08-84
A1AAAA002     87500100093             A RACK SHIM              06-13-83  BH  02-20-84
A1AAAA002     99003464301             A KEY                    08-26-83  DS  08-26-83
A1AAAA002     99015004300             A DRIVE KEY              11-03-82  DS  07-20-83
A1AAAA002     99015354302             A KEY                    10-27-83  DS  11-17-83

  ENTER - BUILD INQUIRY        PF1 - PAGE BACKWARD         PF3 - ROUTING INQUIRY
  CLEAR - RETURN TO MENU       PF2 - PAGE FORWARD          PF4 - ROUTING MAKE FROM

                   PF3 AND PF4 REQUIRE A CURSOR SELECTION
```

Figure 16-3. -- Group Technology Code Inquiry Report

control is crucial because management often relies on the shop floor to compensate for any increases incurred in engineering time. If a customer demands a redesign, it may increase the lead time required by engineering. The due date, however, is seldom changed. The burden is on the shop floor to pick up the slack and to meet the due date. To do so requires an effective shop floor control system.

The current shop floor control system has been in place since 1980. It is supported by a computer software system designed completely in house. Currently, the system is extensively computerized, with 75 percent of all transactions managed by the computer and the remaining 25 percent manually completed. The shop floor control system is one of the responsibilities of the production control manager (Figure 16-4). In addition to shop floor control, the production control manager is responsible for planning and material handling. The production control manager reports directly to the vice president of manufacturing.

The production control manager is supported by a production control department consisting of fifteen employees and is assisted by three superintendents and five production supervisors. The supervisors are responsible for all production activities in their areas. Their tasks include making out performance evaluations, correcting personnel problems, and explaining the performance of their departments.

The supervisors must work closely with the various foremen. There are twenty foremen who manage the operations of the various work centers in both the heavy and light shop. These foremen also manage, on a day-to-day basis, the 273 operators in these two departments.

Currently, the primary objectives of the shop floor control system reflect those factors seen as essential for the firm's success. That is, shop floor control is held responsible for:

- Ensuring on-time delivery
- Maintaining and increasing the flexibility of the process to accommodate changes in product design at any point in the process
- Decreasing the level of WIP
- Decreasing the level of scrap
- Decreasing material costs
- Decreasing labor costs
- Tracking orders throughout the process
- Reporting on the status and location of all orders

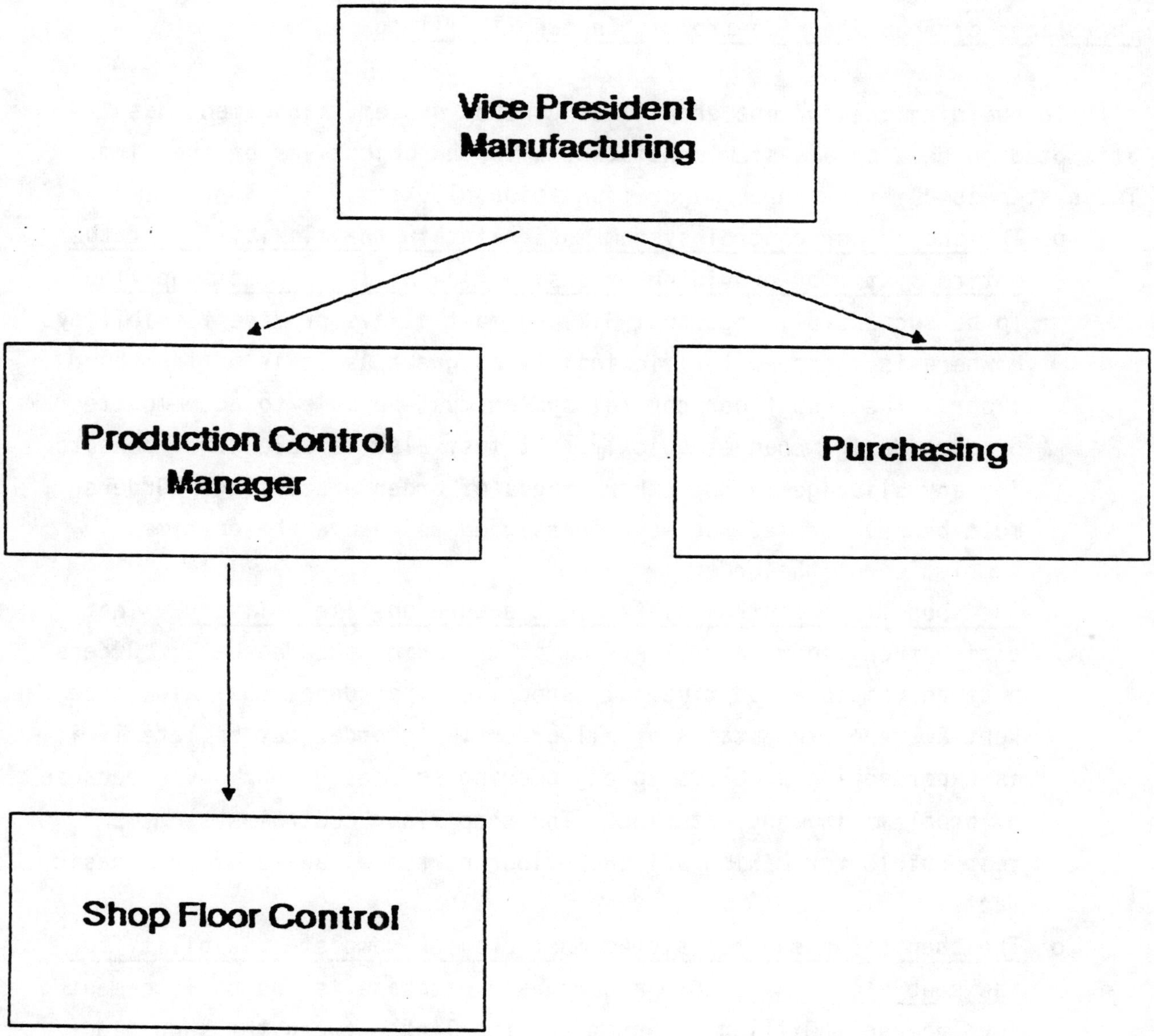

Figure 16-4. -- Shop Floor Control Reporting Relationships

- o Reporting on the status and location of tooling
- o Providing data for quality control.

Management places a heavy emphasis on the first two objectives and on the tracking and reporting activities of shop floor control.

The Stages of Shop Floor Control at Ingersoll Milling

In building the current shop floor control system, management has attempted to develop a system consistent with the objectives of the firm. The system is built on three major foundation blocks:

- o The shop floor control system must maintain the flexibility of the entire system by providing extensive flexibility on the shop floor. To be successful, Ingersoll Milling must always provide flexibility. Nowhere is the need for flexibility as great as it is on the shop floor. The shop floor control system must be able to accommodate product design changes quickly. It must also be able to compensate for any slippage in the other stages of order processing. Orders must be rescheduled and work reassigned to ensure the on-time completion of the order.
- o The shop floor control system must ensure on-time delivery. The entire shop floor control system is driven by the due date. Orders must be completed on time; all shop floor personnel must always be kept aware of the status of all orders. An order may be late if it is experiencing problems in engineering and design but never because of problems in manufacturing. The shop floor control system is responsible for making all shop floor personnel aware of this basic fact.
- o The shop floor control system must provide complete visibility for the shop floor. The common corporate database is the basic cement for Ingersoll Milling's system and the link between the shop floor and the rest of the firm. It is the responsibility of the shop floor control system to maintain this link. Information captured on the shop floor must be entered into the database on time and accurately. The shop floor control system must provide for early identification of any problems encountered on the shop floor and report these problems to the rest of the firm by using the database. These actions ensure that the rest of the firm is always aware of

what is taking place on the shop floor. The result is a shop floor that is highly visible to the entire firm.

Order Review/Release

The extensive overlap between the planning and execution sides of the manufacturing process may be illustrated by the implementation and execution of the order review/release activities. Order review/release is responsible for managing the flow of orders from engineering release to shop floor release. As such, it influences planning activities such as the generation of BOMs and routing. Order review/release is responsible for identifying and resolving any bottlenecks in the planning system that may jeopardize the on-time completion of the order.

One such bottleneck is engineering. The engineering release date marks that point in time when the order is available to manufacturing. Postponing this date means that there is less time to complete the order. As a result, the production control manager constantly monitors this date. The office of the production control manager is next to the office of the engineering manager; this arrangement encourages a constant interaction.

Once an order is released by engineering, the order review/release stage of shop floor control is responsible for generating the appropriate documentation. This task is done within the routing department, which establishes the best route for any order, identifies any special tooling requirements, brings together the necessary tapes for the parts programs, and ensures that the necessary material is ordered. The routing department is aided in these tasks by I-CAPP (Ingersoll Computer Aided Production Planning), a program available on Ingersoll Milling's computer system.

One of the major products of the routing department is the shop packet. The shop packet contains an order sheet (Figure 16-5) describing all the operation steps in the routing. Each step is bar coded. The packet also contains a manuscript of the numerical control tape programs, part prints (i.e., blueprints), computer-generated graphics, and reporting cards (Figure 16-6).

In general, routing and the production of the shop packet are done quickly. They are activities scheduled to an extent by both the manufacturing manager and the production control manager. Once the routing has been completed and is available to the shop floor, the release of the routing is indicated by the production routing release report (Figure 16-7).

25742-41

BOEING COMMERCIAL AIRPLANE CO.

5742-41-031-9 | 184870 QTY 1
LOT NO

TS 1
A

BALL NUT ANCHOR BRKT

CODE 010 RTD BY DS GT D4FEEC552 DATE 03-23-84

TEM#	PCS	TYPE	SHAPE	LENGTH	THK/ID/DIA	WIDTH/OD	WALL/WEB THK	PREP
01	1	MS	■	10.750	7.000	8.000		

			EMP. NO	DATE
010	4083	TORCH CUT COMP LEAVE STK FOR FINISH AS SHOWN TORCH CUT TO LOWER R.H. VIEW		
020	9900	INSPECT		
030	9821	STRESS RELIEVE (H.T. DEPT)		
040	1221 N/C	BOHLE 1ST SET-UP PLACE PART SIDE (6) DOWN-SIDE (3) TOWARDS PALLET SIDE (3) XXXXXXXXXXXXXXXXXXXXXXXXXXXXXX (1) RUFF MILL SIDE (1)-LV. .12 STK. (2) RUFF MILL SIDE (2)-LV. .12 STK. RUFF MILL STEP ON SIDE (2) LV. .12 STK. ON (125) FIN. SURFACE		
050	1221 N/C	BOHLE 2ND SET-UP PLACE PART SIDE (6) DOWN-SIDE (1) TOWARDS PALLET SIDE (3) XXXXXXXXXXXXXXXXXXXXXXXXXXXXXX (1) MILL SIDE (3) COMP. (2) FIN. MILL SIDE (4) FIN. MILL STEP ON SIDE (4)		
060	1221 N/C	BOHLE 3RD SET-UP PLACE PART SIDE (1) DOWN-SIDE (5) TOWARDS PALLET SIDE (3) XXXXXXXXXXXXXXXXXXXXXXXXXXXXXX (1) MILL SIDE (6) COMP.		

Figure 16-5. -- Order Sheet

PART NUMBER	QUANTITY	SHOP ORDER	DW. NUM.	LOT NUM.	OPER.	SEQ.
20495774900	6	26423-67		246969		

COST CENTER	EMPLOYEE NUM
MACHINE NUM	WEIGHT
DATE	
TIME IN	
TIME OUT	

JOB CARD

THE INGERSOLL MILLING MACHINE CO

BE SURE TO CHECK ONE

OPERATION COMPLETED ☐

OPERATION NOT COMPLETED ☐

FOREMAN ______________________

REV 9/82 PRYOR 59659

Figure 16-6. -- Job Card

```
MRT305UD                MACHINE DIVISION I-CAPP SYSTEM                 03-28-84
                         PRODUCTION ROUTING RELEASE

                BOM LOCKOUT ERROR - USE PF12 TO SET OVERRIDE

           PART NUMBER : 25742410319     VERSION :         PURGE CODE : _

             DW NUMBER : _____   FROM : 000 THRU : 999   ORIGINAL LOT : 00000
             PRIME S/O : 2574240

               SHOP            BOM    ORDERED     M.W.     HEADING CODE : _
              ORDER    QTY     QTY      QTY       DATE     PRINT IT NOW : N
                                                                   RUSH : N
             2574240   001     000      000     05-18-84    VALID HEADING CODES
             _______   000     000      000     00-00-00
             _______   000     000      000     00-00-00      1 = "REPAIR"
             _______   000     000      000     00-00-00      2 = "BREAKDN"
             _______   000     000      000     00-00-00      3 = "WELDMENT"
             _______   000     000      000     00-00-00      4 = "PREMACH"
             _______   000     000      000     00-00-00      5 = "INT BKDN"
             _______   000     000      000     00-00-00
             _______   000     000      000     00-00-00
             _______   000     000      000     00-00-00
             _______   000     000      000     00-00-00
             _______   000     000      000     00-00-00
             _______   000     000      000     00-00-00
             _______   000     000      000     00-00-00
             _______   000     000      000     00-00-00
             _______   000     000      000     00-00-00
             _______   000     000      000     00-00-00
             _______   000     000      000     00-00-00
             _______   000     000      000     00-00-00
             _______   000     000      000     00-00-00
             _______   000     000      000     00-00-00
             _______   000     000      000     00-00-00
             _______   000     000      000     00-00-00
             _______   000     000      000     00-00-00
             _______   000     000      000     00-00-00
             _______   000     000      000     00-00-00
             _______   000     000      000     00-00-00
             _______   000     000      000     00-00-00
             _______   000     000      000     00-00-00
             _______   000     000      000     00-00-00
```

Figure 16-7. -- Production Routing Release Report

The production routing release report is a summary and shows the major characteristics of each job (e.g., degree of urgency, department to which the part has been released, order quantity).

The last step in the order review/release process is determining when to release the order. An order can be released at any time once its routing has been completed and as long as there is adequate material for the order. In practice, however, orders are released only when there is capacity available. The production control manager tries to keep all excess work off the shop floor by limiting the release of orders to the shop floor. Management believes that too much work on the shop floor not only increases manufacturing lead times but, more importantly, also causes confusion. Confusion is the enemy of on-time delivery.

Detailed Assignment

The shop floor control system schedules three types of work flows on the shop floor. These are orders going to non-FMS work centers, orders going to FMS work centers, and preventive maintenance. Each type of work flow is managed differently.

Scheduling non-FMS work centers. All parts routed to the non-FMS work centers are scheduled using the latest start date priority rule. In determining the latest start date for each order arriving at a work center, schedulers use a pessimistic approach; each part is assumed to take one day per operation, and transit between operations is assumed to take one day.

The work order priorities are summarized on a dispatch list (Figure 16-8), which is generated for each work center once a day. This list, current as of 11 p.m. the previous night, identifies all parts that have been released to the work center and the status of these orders. That is, it identifies whether the numerical control tapes for the order are available or the part is being held up.

Shop operators have some discretion in deciding the order in which to run the parts. Orders can be rearranged to improve efficiency by taking advantage of commonalities in setup, components, or processing. The operators work under one constraint -- they must meet due dates. They can do so if they begin processing the part no later than its latest start date.

Scheduling FMS work centers. The computer system plays a role in scheduling orders through the FMS work centers by establishing the order sequence. This sequence explicitly considers such factors as tooling,

10155 READY TO RUN DISPATCH LIST 03/28/84 = 2411 PAGE 1

FOR OPERATION 1224-MAKINO M/C

T MBER		SHOP ORD OR SW #	PART NUMBER	OP SEQ	S T	QUE	DESCRIPTION	QTY	LSD		MACH WRK
9233	#	25763-38	20481034900	030	W	19	LOCATING KEY	32	2392		03/16/84
2976		25775-38	20474214900	040	A	12	PIVOT SHAFT(E	2	2393		04/16/84
		69432 -									
3551		25714-09	84009001114	020	A	121	BRG BLOCK (CE	36	2402		04/13/84
5300		25714-09	84009001314	020	A	105	BRG BLOCK (UP	36	2402		04/13/84
6523	#	25719-30	20465864300	020	A	46	TAKE-UP BLOCK	3	2404		04/09/84
3548		25714-09	84009000814	030	W		BRG BLOCK	36	2404		04/13/84
77054	#	25719-30	20465824300	020	A	48	ANCHOR BLOCK	3	2406		04/09/84
77051	#	25719-30	20465954300	020	A	48	TAKE-UP BLOCK	3	2406		04/09/84
72646		25714-10	84001000214	010	A	130	COVER	22	2406		04/13/84
77053	#	25719-30	20465784300	020	A	48	BLOCK	3	2408		04/09/84
77055	#	25719-30	20465834300	020	A	48	ANCHOR BLOCK	3	2408		04/09/84
77052	#	25719-30	20465914300	020	A	48	TAKE-UP BLOCK	3	2408		04/09/84
32971		25745-62	25745620149	100	A	6	W DISPENSER H	24	2409		04/12/84
78261		25746-10	25746100029	080	P	16	W DIE MOUNTIN	9	2410		04/19/84
34568		25749-10	25749100049	020	A	3	SPACER	1	2410		04/19/84
		69684 – defective work ticket #									
79490	#	25775-24	20477264900	150	A	27	COUPLING HALF	4	2410		04/30/84
34424		58042-84	99029564900	030	W	2	ADAPTER	15	2413		04/27/84
30135		25747-10	25747100069	020	W	32	AXLE	3	2414		04/19/84
30136		25747-10	25747100089	020	P	33	DRAG ARM	12	2414		04/19/84
30841	#	25763-69	20479234900	060	W	28	CARTRIDGE (EC	8	2414		04/30/84
31108		25747-10	25747100279	020	A	6	HOOK BRACKET	3	2416		04/19/84
33671	#	25763-31	25672310049	030	W	-	SIDE PLATE (A	8	2416		04/23/84
32772	#	25763-31	20479104900	080	A	15	W BRG. SUPPOR	4	2418		04/23/84
78539	#	25775-24	20477254900	040	A	38	COUPLING HALF	5	2419		04/30/84
32845	#	25763-09	25525090153	020	A	2	T-HANDLE	8	2420		04/23/84
33069	#	25775-09	20477974400	100	A	17	W R.H. COLUMN	2	2423		04/30/84
31207	#	25775-30	25450300343	020	A	37	WIPER BRKT	40	2423		04/30/84
32751	#	25775-29	20470454900	030	W	3	W LH IN.SPACE	5	2425		04/30/84
34269		25742-40	25742400359	020	P	3	ROLLER MTG. P	4	2425		05/18/84
33712		25742-11	20460874300	020	A	11	RH BLOWOFF BR	2	2427		05/18/84
33711		25742-11	20460884300	020	A	11	LH BLOWOFF BR	2	2427		05/18/84
33951		25742-40	25742400189	020	P	3	LINER	20	2427		05/18/84
34059		25742-40	25742400199	020	P	2	LINER	20	2427		05/18/84
33621		25767-38	20473804400	050	A		SPINDLE ORIEN	1	2427	+	06/22/84
		69556									
31799		25769-38	20473804400	050	P	8	SPINDLE ORIEN	1	2427	+	06/22/84
		69027									
32788	#	25717-36	25717360059	010	P	25	GROUND INSUL.	4	2429		05/16/84

- MULTIPLE LOT WITH PRIME SHOP ORDER DISPLAYED
A - N/C TAPE AVAILABLE
D - # DNC # TAPE AVAILABLE
+ - EXCEEDS 12 WEEK LIMIT

Figure 16-8. -- Dispatch List

fixture and machine availability, and order due dates. Once set, this sequence is implemented directly on the shop floor. There is no intervention by the operator.

In addition, the computer system also sequences machine setups. Setup planning is done up front during the planning and design of the part or order. Program tapes and manuscripts are also prepared for setups. The computer indicates when to begin the setup so the order is available for the work center when the work center finishes with the current order. At the appropriate time, the computer flags the operator to begin setup.

As a part is set up on the setup stands, the computer notifies the tool room operator what tools are required. The automatic-guided vehicles move the pallet containing the fixtured part to the incoming table of each machine.

In the pallet setup area, the parts are mounted in fixtures on specific pallets that are identified to the computer. From this point on, only the pallets are tracked and dispatched. There are five setup stands in the FMS area. Each one uses modular fixture components. When the part is set up completely, the operator identifies the pallet and signals the cell computer that the part is ready to be entered into the system. The cart then picks up the pallet at the setup stands automatically and delivers it to the machine.

The FMS work centers are a laboratory for Ingersoll Milling. The dispatching procedures currently implemented are undergoing continual revision. Eventually, management intends to develop a set of computer software programs that will identify that sequence of orders that simultaneously maximizes tooling and fixture use, machine utilization, and on-time deliveries.

Preventive maintenance. All preventive maintenance activities are scheduled at two levels. The first level, minor preventive maintenance (accuracy checks, machine cleanups, oiling, and minor equipment adjustments), is done regularly. At the second level (the maintenance of all important major equipment assets), the scheduling of equipment maintenance is managed formally by using the preventive maintenance program, which schedules, in advance, the equipment downtime and required level of maintenance.

Data Collection/Monitoring

Data collection/monitoring is a critical shop floor control activity. This stage provides Ingersoll Milling with that needed visibility over the shop floor. This stage is well developed.

All monitoring and data collection are done on an ongoing basis. The data generated are recorded on a transaction-by-transaction basis. Information is recorded in one of three forms (depending on where in the production process the transaction takes place). In the weld and fabrication shops, all data are collected and entered by foremen on CRTs located on the shop floor. In the other departments, information is gathered and recorded using either prepunched cards or operator key punched cards. The information is recorded and collected at the end of every shift by the foremen. The prepunched cards are read using card readers. The operator-punched cards are entered by key punch operators (not shop floor personnel).

Currently, there are 260 CRTs and card readers at Ingersoll Milling that are used continuously. On a typical day, there are between 2,500 and 3,000 transactions recorded using these input devices.

In addition, management has implemented an extensive set of error checking/data validation routines in the computer system to prevent bad data from getting into the corporate database. These routines rely on the operator to double punch all data to ensure that the data entered are correct. In addition, the computer system flags and reports potential data errors such as reported transactions with invalid part numbers, invalid employee numbers, and invalid job tickets. A list of these errors is produced after three days and is turned over to the foremen who must resolve the errors at once.

Monitoring, like data collection, is a continuous activity. All parts are checked against specifications as they proceed through the various operations of the routing. This checking is done in two modes: visual and computer-aided inspection. Operators visually check parts as they complete them using the part drawings and geometric graphics that accompany the order in the order packet. These items set forth the specifications that must be followed.

Parts are also checked using a quality control inspection machine, which provides a level of quality and inspection far in excess of that provided by visual inspection. It ensures that the parts are able to satisfy all important performance specifications. This machine is driven by

QNC program tapes produced by the quality control department. These tapes are part of the shop packet. This testing also marks the first stage in the control/feedback activities of Ingersoll Milling's shop floor control system.

The monitoring activities are done somewhat differently in the FMS areas. Here, the computer automatically carries out all of the monitoring activities. The monitoring system, for example, tracks the use of each tool, as well as the current state and location of each tool. In addition, there is an inspection station associated with the FMS work area. This station consists of two Zeiss Mauser coordinate measuring machines. These operate under full direct numerical control when evaluating each part produced in the FMS area.

The information generated by either the data collection or monitoring activities is entered into the common corporate database. Here, the information generated by the shop floor is shared with the entire firm -- departments such as quality control, cost accounting, payroll, maintenance, engineering, scrap control, purchasing, and marketing/sales. This feature underlines the soundness of the common corporate database and the contributions of the shop floor control system to this database.

Control/Feedback

Given the dynamic nature of operations at Ingersoll Milling, control/feedback is a critical feature of the shop floor control system. Control/feedback is responsible for managing all changes that take place on the shop floor and for ensuring that the rest of the firm is kept aware of the status of orders released to the shop floor.

One of the major responsibilities of control/feedback involves bringing back out-of-control problem orders. An order can become a problem order for one of three reasons: the order has been released to the shop floor late, the order has undergone changes in the design BOM since it was released, or one or more of the parts required by the order failed to pass a quality inspection. Each of these problem orders is handled somewhat differently by the shop floor control system.

Late orders. Typically, the planning process tries to provide the shop floor with about fifteen weeks in which to complete the order. This lead time allowance is usually regarded as more than adequate. However, the shop floor frequently does not get all of this fifteen weeks. Orders are often released late from the engineering system. The problem for the shop floor control system is that it must meet its due dates even if the order is received late. Typically, late releases are not a major problem.

Late releases do become a major problem if the order is due within six weeks and production has not yet started. At this point, the production control department looks at the order. If the order is one month out from the due date, it is then reviewed by the supervisors. If the order has not yet started any of its operations, an expediter is assigned to the order. It is the expediter's responsibility to follow the order through the shop and to ensure that the operators are aware of the importance of the job.

Excessive expediting is not a major problem at Ingersoll Milling. On average, only 5 percent of the parts flowing through the shop require any form of expediting because manufacturing continually interacts with engineering to ensure that the order is not released to the shop floor too late. Typically, late releases are associated with either an engineered product (i.e., one never designed or built before) or an extensively engineered product.

Engineering changes. An order is rarely completed without undergoing at least one change in its BOM. On average, every year there are 15,000 engineering changes to the BOMs. Because of the large volume of changes combined with the differing levels of complexity associated with these various changes, Ingersoll Milling has developed a comprehensive system for managing engineering change notices.

In general, once an engineering change has been approved, the corporate database is updated immediately. Every night, changes to the BOMs are entered and run. Within twenty-four hours the shop floor control system is working with the revised BOM. Depending on the complexity of the revisions, new shop order packets may be issued to the shop floor. Engineering changes in the BOM do not result in changes in the order due date.

Scrap, salvage, and rework. Because of the emphasis on quality, quality rejects tend to be high. On average, between 10 to 20 percent of all parts on the shop floor are flagged for defective work. This flagging is typically done during the inspection by the inspector. Once an item has been flagged, the inspector must fill out a defective work report (Figure 16-9). The report identifies the part number, quantity rejected, the reasons for the rejection, the nature of the disposition (rework, scrap, or accepted), and any corrective actions taken.

DEFECTIVE WORK REPORT

90789

PART NUMBER	MATERIAL CODE	MONTH DAY YEAR	PART NAME

INSP. CODE	QTY. RECEIVED	QTY. REJECTED	SHOP ORDER	LOT NUMBER	OTHER SHOP ORDERS

OPERATION AND SEQUENCE DEFECT OCCURRED	COST CENTER	EMPLOYEE NO.	SHIFT	PARTY RESPONSIBLE	INSPECTOR/ORIGINATOR
LAST OPERATION AND SEQUENCE COMPLETED	**COST CENTER**	**EMPLOYEE NO.**	**SHIFT**	**PARTY RESPONSIBLE**	**INSPECTION FOREMAN**

PURCHASE ORDER NUMBER	VENDOR NAME

DISPOSITION

REWORK ☐ SCRAP ☐ ACCEPTED ☐

QUALITY ____________________

ENGINEERING ____________________

REASON FOR REJECTION

FEATURE	DRAWING SPECIFICATIONS	ACTUAL	DEVIATION	QUANTITY DEFECTIVE	REMARKS	ENG DISPOSITION FIX	ENG DISPOSITION OK

CORRECTIVE ACTION

SCRAPPED QUANTITY REJECTED RESTARTED IN THE SHOP	ASSEMBLY REQUIRED DATE
DATE PER	

OPERATION NUMBER	REMARKS	EMPLOYEE NUMBER	DATE COMPLETED

9900 DELIVER TO INSPECTION DMINISTRATIVE COPY 90789

Figure 16-9. -- Defective Work Report

The next step in the control process is the disposition of the problem part. If the item is obviously scrap, then it is immediately disposed of at the work center. The record of the disposal is entered into the corporate database. Otherwise, the problem part is taken to a central location for disposition.

At the central location, the problem part can be either reworked or accepted. Acceptance can be done only by an engineer. If the part is reworked, the appropriate modifications to the routing are entered on the defective work report. Any rework must pass through an inspection before it can be accepted.

One of the final tasks of disposition is to identify the responsible party, most often a shop floor employee. A copy of the report is sent to the responsible party. It is then up to the employee to take the appropriate corrective actions.

Copies of the report are also sent to the originator and to administration where it is entered into the file. Another copy of the report accompanies the defective part.

Other comments. The management of problem orders is not entirely reactive. Certain types of orders have a higher probability of resulting in high levels of scrap or rework (e.g., parts that have very tight tolerances, use special metals, or require special handling). Manufacturing people review the routings of all parts before they are released and try to identify such parts from the routings. A warning is then issued to the shop floor, cautioning shop floor personnel to take special care when processing these parts. The intent of this warning is to prevent problems by flagging such orders in advance.

Feedback. The computer system that supports shop floor control produces a large number of reports, the most important of which are:

- The production lot summary. This report identifies all shop orders that belong to a given production lot. It also summarizes the number of hours of work posted against the order and the current status of the production lot (Figure 16-10).
- Shop order routed part inquiry. This inquiry report identifies all of the part numbers required for a given shop order, the number of operations per part number, the status of the part numbers (C for completed, W for WIP), and the last operation (Figure 16-11). On the first page is a detailed report on all the parts. The second

PRODUCTION LOT SUMMARY

LOT NUMBER : 184870

STATUS : W WORK IN PROCESS

TYPE : S SINGLE

BOM QTY : 1
TOTAL QTY : 1

PRIME S/O : 25742-41

VALID HOURS POSTED : 0000.0
ADDITIONAL HOURS POSTED : 0000.0

TOTAL HOURS POSTED : 0000.0

LOT NUMBER SHOP ORDER LIST :

SHOP ORDER	QTY	HOURS	SHOP ORDER	QTY	HOURS
25742-41	1	0.0			

DEPRESS THE CLEAR KEY TO RETURN TO PRODUCTION LOT DISPLAY

Figure 16-10. -- Production Lot Summary

MRT603OT SHOP ORDER ROUTED PART INQUIRY - ALL ITEMS 03-28-84
PAGE 001

SHOP ORDER : 2574241

	S/O DASH	PART NUMBER	SW #	**** LOT **** NUMBER	ST	TYP	DESCRIPTION	TOT QTY	TOTAL OPERS	LAST OPER
?	41	25742410029		184478	W	S	MOTOR CARRIER	1	14	0
?	41	25742410039		184165	W	S	RETAINER	1	11	0
?	41	25742410049		184496	W	S	W TORQUE TUBE	1	18	0
?	41	25742410059		184072	W	S	SPACER	2	9	20
?	41	25742410069		184276	W	S	BALL NUT ANCHOR BRKT	2	12	0
?	41	25742410079		184307	W	S	SHIM	2	7	10
?	41	25742410089		184315	W	M	WAY (RAM)	6	21	0
?	41	25742410099		184250	W	S	REAR BRG CART.	1	16	0
?	41	25742410109		183332	W	S	ADAPTER RING	1	8	0
?	41	25742410139		184197	W	S	CONNECTOR ADAPTOR	1	7	20
?	41	25742410149		183233	W	S	CONN. ADAPTER	3	10	20
?	41	25742410159		184274	W	S	ADAPTOR	1	11	0
?	41	25742410169		184310	W	S	ADAPTOR COVER	1	11	0
?	41	25742410189		184352	W	S	DUST COLL. TUBE	1	3	0
?	41	25742410199		183472	W	S	BRG. RETAINER	1	14	0
?	41	25742410209		184181	W	S	TUBE STABILIZER	1	8	20
?	41	25742410269		183504	W	S	W L.S. SUPPORT BRKT	1	16	80
?	41	25742410279		183509	W	S	W L.S. SUPPORT	1	16	70
?	41	25742410289		183881	W	S	L.S. DOG	1	8	10
?	41	25742410299		184198	W	S	CONNECTOR ADAPTER	1	7	20
?	41	25742410309		184311	W	S	W L.S. SUPPORT	1	6	0
?	41	25742410319		184870	W	S	BALL NUT ANCHOR BRKT	1	14	0
?	41	90111774111		183466	C	S	SPACER	2	5	30
?	41	90400074100		183505	W	S	PLUG	3	2	0

CLEAR - INQUIRY MENU PF1 - PRIOR PAGE
CURSOR SEL - ROUTED LOT INQUIRY PF2 - NEXT PAGE

Figure 16-11. -- Shop Order Routed Part Inquiry

```
MRT6030T      SHOP ORDER ROUTED PART INQUIRY - ALL ITEMS            03-28-84
                                                                    PAGE 002

                        SHOP ORDER : 2574241

   S/O                               **** LOT ****                     TOT TOTAL LAST
   DASH PART NUMBER          SW #   NUMBER ST TYP DESCRIPTION          QTY OPERS OPER


                      TOTAL                COMPLETED              SHORT
   PARTS                37                     2                     35
   ROUTINGS             24                     1                     23
   OPERATIONS          254                    32                    222




               CLEAR - INQUIRY MENU                 PF1 - PRIOR PAGE
          CURSOR SEL - ROUTED LOT INQUIRY           PF2 - NEXT PAGE
```

Figure 16-11. -- Shop Order Routed Part Inquiry (continued)

page provides a quick snapshot of the status of all the parts needed for a given shop order.

- Routed part where-used inquiry. This report is essentially a peg report, identifying the parents for a given part number (Figure 16-12).

The purpose of these reports is to provide the user with complete and timely visibility over the shop floor and its activities. At any point in time, the user can locate a given shop order, either in total (all part numbers) or in part (for a given part number). They are available, either through the CRTs or in hard copy, to the entire firm.

Order Disposition

The last stage of shop floor control is quite complex at Ingersoll Milling. It embodies all of the activities required from the point the product is assembled initially until that product is tested, accepted, and set up in the customer's own facilities. Order disposition starts with the assembly production control shortage report (Figure 16-13).

When the manufacturing and purchasing systems complete their functions, they deliver all required parts to the assembly stores area. At that time, the BOM is checked to ensure that all the parts specified by the bill are available. Any missing parts are recorded on the assembly production control shortage report. A printed report is prepared for each machine on the assembly floor and is available by 7:00 a.m. everyday. An instantaneous update of the report can be obtained at any time from any computer terminal.

The assembly operation begins on or about the date the machine work is complete. Some subassemblies are begun before the machine work has been completed on other parts (specifically, parts that require less time to assemble).

As the machine is erected on the assembly floor, the contracts department may bring the customer in to observe the machine and its progress. This gives the customer the opportunity to review progress and become more familiar with the machine. After the assembly people finish the construction work and the electrical people turn the power on, the machine is ready for testing.

After testing is complete, the customer comes to Rockford for the final runoff of the machine. The machine cuts samples of the metal parts the customer expects to produce on the machine. The finished piece is sent to

```
MRT606OT                ROUTED PART WHERE-USED INQUIRY              03-28-84
                                                                    PAGE 001

                 PART NUMBER : 25742410319
         PART NUMBER      SHOP ORD SW #    LOT #  TYPE STATUS QTY  PRME S/O

       ? 25742410319      25742-41         184870   S    W      1



INQUIRY MODE :

       ENTER - SPECIFIC PART NUMBER INQUIRY
         PF3 - DISPLAY ALL OCCURRENCES THAT MATCH FIRST 11 CHARACTERS
DISPLAY MODE :

         PF1 - PAGE BACKWARD
         PF2 - PAGE FORWARD
         TO VIEW A SPECIFIC ROUTING LOT :
              USE THE CURSOR SELECT KEY TO INDICATE ROUTING TO DISPLAY
              AND DEPRESS THE "ENTER" KEY

                     CLEAR - RETURN TO INQUIRY MENU
```

Figure 16-12. -- Routed Part Where-used Inquiry

APC2010T ASSEMBLY PRODUCTION CONTROL SHORTAGE INQUIRY 03-28-8·
PAGE 00·

SHOP ORDER/SERIAL : 2574241

INGERSOLL PART NUMBER	ENG QTY	RECD QTY	PART CODE	WIR/ ENOC	DEBIT MEMO	PO NUMBER	REQUEST DATE	PROMISE DATE	COMPLETE DATE	FOI MA:
92441283000	4	0	B/P			50437-23	05-18-84	04-01-84		
580							UNION*LENZ*100-6-6 TUBE			
92441513000	4	0	B/P			50437-23	05-18-84	04-01-84		
580							FITTING*LENZ*100-8			
93515583000	6	4	B/P			50432-23	05-18-84	04-01-84	02-24-84	
580							COUPLING*HANSON*3100 "QUICK D:			
94430273000	2	0	B/P	45430			03-13-84	05-18-84		
460							CONNECTOR*CANNON*MS3106 F-16 V			
							** BOM OLD QTY WAS 3			
							PURCHASED MATERIAL NOT ORDEREI			
94431533000	1	0	B/P	45430			03-13-84	05-18-84		
460							CONNECTOR*CANNON*MS-3106F-10S			
							** BOM PART ADD **			
							PURCHASED MATERIAL NOT ORDEREI			
94431543000	1	0	B/P	45430			03-13-84	05-18-84		
460							CONNECTOR*CANNON*MS-3106F-28-1			
							** BOM PART ADD **			
							PURCHASED MATERIAL NOT ORDEREI			
96172143005	1	0	B/P			20422-21	05-18-84	04-06-84		
320							BEARING*INA*NA-4852 NEEDLE			
96172443000	1	0	B/P			20289-21	05-18-84	03-30-84		
300							BEARING*TIM*JXR637050 CROSSED			

PF1 - PAGE BACKWARD PF3 - FIRST PAGE
PF2 - PAGE FORWARD PF4 - LAST PAGE CLEAR - RETURN TO CICS

Figure 16-13. -- Assembly Production Control Shortage Report

quality control where a high accuracy coordinate measuring inspection machine measures the actual geometry of the part. This information is fed back to the computer where the exact measurements for the part have been stored previously. Based on a comparison of the actual with the standards, adjustments are calculated and implemented. By having the computer calculate and implement the adjustments, Ingersoll Milling can assure its customers that the adjustments are always made right the first time.

The computer-directed inspection machines are also used to check the accuracy of the parts made in the FMS area before being sent to the assembly floor. The result is that the main floor is a real production assembly floor rather than a cut and trial fit department.

A representative of Ingersoll Milling's field service organization is present during the final stages of the machine's runoff. The assigned service person is also present during the reerection of the machine on the customer's floor. He stays with the machine while it is being disassembled, boxed, and packed so that he will know where every part has gone. This makes the erection of the machine at the customer's plant much easier.

The shipping organization works closely with the customer's traffic department during the last few weeks of the assembly to establish a plan for packing and shipping the job properly. A typical job will go on several trucks or railroad cars, and can go to as many as forty or fifty trucks, depending on the size.

The order disposition stage ends once the job has been packaged and has left Ingersoll Milling's shipping dock. There is no need to identify and resolve any unexplained variances; this has been done at every stage of the production process.

Performance Evaluation/Feedback

Performance evaluation and feedback of the shop floor control system is coordinated and integrated with the performance planning system at Ingersoll Milling. This system is used to manage and coordinate work flow from the date of the order until the machine is in full production in the customer's plant. Performance planning consists of three modules:

- <u>Manufacturing planning</u>. This is a joint effort between engineering and manufacturing for maximizing producibility.
- <u>Assembly planning</u>. In this module, the detailed schedules for assembly are developed. The resources required are also specified.

- o Installation planning. This module is used to develop the plan for receiving and installing the machine in the customer's plant. Also identifies the resources required.

Each of these modules identifies objectives and performance measures. The performance measures are identified in terms of time standards (i.e., how well were due dates met?) and cost standards (i.e., how well did actual costs compare against budgeted costs?). Cost standards are based on the budgets generated during the early stages of the order process in such categories as total engineering cost, total purchase cost, total fabrication cost, machine shop cost, assembly cost, and the grand total. Performance is tracked continuously. Feedback can be obtained at any one of the computer terminals.

At each level of the shop floor control system, the responsible shop floor personnel are evaluated in terms of a limited number of well understood and readily available measures. Operators are evaluated on meeting due dates and the quality level of their production. Similarly, supervisors' evaluations reflect the performance of their departments.

Continuous performance measurement and evaluation offers shop floor personnel adequate warning of problems. It provides the personnel with adequate time to correct problems. It also creates an environment in which there are no surprises.

Observations on Shop Floor Control in an CIFM Setting

Having the latest technology on the shop floor is quite commonplace at Ingersoll Milling. However, while the introduction of CIFM has changed the processes used in production, it has not altered the structure of shop floor control. When the technology of CIFM is stripped away, a traditional shop floor control system is left. The introduction of CIFM takes the existing manufacturing structure and improves the capabilities offered by this structure. It makes a system such as shop floor control more effective (i.e., in less time and with fewer resources).

Evaluating Ingersoll Milling's Shop Floor Control System -- Benefits

Assessing the benefits of shop floor control to the overall operation of the CIFM system is not an easy task. In general, the CIFM system has proven to be very successful in practice. Since its implementation in 1983, the system has created the following benefits for Ingersoll Milling:

- 5 to 20 percent reduction in personnel costs
- 15 to 30 percent reduction in engineering design costs
- 30 to 60 percent reduction in overall lead time
- 30 to 60 percent reduction in WIP levels
- 40 to 70 percent gain in overall production
- 20 to 300 percent gain in capital equipment operating time
- 200 to 500 percent product quality gain
- 300 to 3500 percent gains in engineering productivity.

But without an effective shop floor control system, it is unlikely that CIFM would have had such a significant impact on operations at Ingersoll Milling.

There have been certain benefits observed at Ingersoll Milling that can be attributed directly to the presence of its shop floor control system. The most important of these benefits include:

- A significant reduction in confusion on the shop floor. The shop floor control system is an important communication vehicle. It tells the people working on the shop floor what has to be done and when. It recognizes key or critical operations and warns of potential problems. As a result, there is now an absolute minimum of confusion on the shop floor.
- Significantly improved on-time delivery performance. Statistics on performance to due date are confounded by the engineered products (machines never built before and incorporating state-of-the-art features that are seldom completed on time). When these orders are excluded, the overall performance of the shop floor is improved significantly. In general, the manufacturing process is able to complete most of its production at levels of 100 percent on-time completion. This success is due in large part to the presence of shop floor control.
- Significant improvements in product quality.
- Significant reduction in WIP levels.
- Significant reduction in overhead costs and better control of these costs. In the dynamic environment in which Ingersoll Milling must operate, large production control staffs are common. This, however, is not the case. The entire production process is managed by a staff of fifteen people. The current shop floor control system has enabled the people operating on the shop floor to do more with less.

Clearly, shop floor control has played a critical role in the success of Ingersoll Milling.

Shop Floor Control -- The Next Stage

The next stage in shop floor control is linked closely to the movement towards increased use of FMS. As these systems become more prevalent, more and more aspects of the shop floor control system are expected to be managed directly by the computer. Functions such as dispatching, monitoring, and data collection are expected to be carried out automatically by the computer. In the case of dispatching, as an example, the computer will produce a dispatch list the operator will follow exactly. This list will be efficient since it will be based on such considerations as tooling availability and location, machine capacity available, and amount of due date slack. As the computer system takes over these functions, it will free planners to spend more time planning and correcting problems as they occur.

Aside from this trend, the next step for the shop floor control is continued fine-tuning. Management wants to make the current system even better.

<u>Shop Floor Control at Ingersoll Milling: Lessons to be Learned</u>

Shop floor control works at Ingersoll Milling. It is one of the foundations on which CIFM is built. The current system also illustrates dramatically what has to be done to make any new technology such as FMS a corporate weapon rather than a manufacturing concern. The success of the current system is based on several important factors:

- <u>Plan completely then execute the plan well</u>. Shop floor control, as the name suggests, manages operations once they are released by the planning system. The number of problems this system has is determined by the quality of planning (both product and process). The planning system must recognize that it is responsible for removing any surprises. The part must be designed correctly the first time. To do otherwise puts the burden on the shop floor, which is the wrong place to correct such problems. Similarly, if there are any uncertainties in the process, these uncertainties must be addressed and resolved by the planning system. In short, good planning is an important prerequisite to an effective shop floor control system.

- Know the capabilities of the equipment and stay within them. One of the starting points for an effective shop floor control system is an assessment of the shop floor and its equipment. Those responsible for shop floor control must be able to ensure that all plans and orders released to the shop floor are within the capabilities of the equipment. With such consistency, success on the shop floor is more readily attained and the overall level of frustration much lower.
- Maintain the capabilities of the equipment at a constant level. Preventive maintenance of all equipment must be an integral element of the shop floor control system. Planning for maintenance must be done in advance and never ignored. The purpose of any piece of equipment is to produce parts that can keep tolerances. If preventive maintenance is not done, then the shop floor control system must recognize the presence of a form of uncertainty: the amount of capacity available. In addition, poorly maintained equipment results in higher levels of scrap, salvage, and rework, all requiring more documentation and attention. Well-maintained equipment simplifies the operation of the shop floor control system.
- Integrate the shop floor control system with the operations of the rest of the firm. Shop floor control is not a stand-alone system. It must work closely with the rest of the firm on an ongoing basis. The shop floor control system must be kept aware of changes in engineering designs, routings, and due dates. In turn, it must keep the rest of the firm informed about the status and location of all orders. The shop floor control system works best when the two systems (planning and execution) work closely together.
- Capacity must be planned and managed in advance of the order. Shop floor control is a capacity manager, not a capacity procurer. Any changes in capacity should be identified in advance and planned for. Capacity should never be a short-term reaction to changes in order flows. The importance of capacity is clearly evident at Ingersoll Milling. All capacity planning and broad shop loading is done by top management far in advance of the actual release of the order to the shop floor.
- Identify and focus on the bottlenecks. Not all work centers in the shop and not all shop floor control activities are equally

important. There will always be one or more activities or operations that are more critical than others. These critical operations form bottlenecks; they also determine the effectiveness of the entire shop floor control system. For shop floor control to be effective, these must be identified in advance. Management attention should be directed towards managing these bottlenecks. At Ingersoll Milling, one of the major bottlenecks is the engineering release date. Management works closely with engineering to ensure that the timing of the order release provides adequate lead time for the shop floor.

- Setups should be planned, managed, and controlled. Setups can be a source of uncertainty and a potential hindrance to effective shop floor control if they are left uncontrolled. It is never known whether the current setups are the most efficient or correctly done. Problems in the process can often be traced to problems in the setup. To bring the setups under control, management is now moving the planning of setups from the shop floor to the planning system. This is most evident at FMS work centers.
- Keep the shop floor control system simple to use and understand. Because changes take place rapidly, management needs a complex and comprehensive system. Complexity, however, tends to hinder widespread acceptance and use of the shop floor control system. Making the system simple to use and understand encourages shop floor personnel to use the system. This concern for simplicity is reflected in such areas as data collection and monitoring (e.g., the design of input forms). The result is an improved sense of discipline combined with the presence of an effective system.

It is difficult to overstate the importance of shop floor control to the Ingersoll Milling management. This system helps management fulfill its promise to the customer: the delivery of a well-engineered and well-built product, available to the customer by the promised due date. No firm can hope to satisfy this promise without the capabilities offered by an effective shop floor control system. Such a system must be built on the considerations and issues raised in this study.

General Nature of the Firm

Aladdin Industries, with corporate headquarters in Nashville, Tennessee, is a diversified, privately owned company with operations in more than twenty countries. For seventy-five years, Aladdin has been committed to:

- Research and development
- Innovative marketing
- Continual improvement of products and services.

Aladdin manufactures all of the products for the American market and a high percentage of goods for export at its production facilities in Nashville. In addition, licensees located throughout the world manufacture products or assemble U.S. parts into products intended for their individual markets.

Aladdin is organized into three major product divisions: the consumer business unit, the energy business unit, and the institutional business unit. The principal products of the consumer business unit are Stanley steel thermos bottles, glass-lined thermos bottles, foam-insulated thermos bottles, Pump-a-Drink and Pump-a-Jug, insulated chests, decorated children's lunch kits, adult lunch bags, and food storage jars. The energy business unit manufactures a wide range of heat producing products such as kerosene mantle lamps, kerosene round-wick lamps, electric conversion kits, and kerosene heaters. The institutional business unit provides food service systems for hospitals, airlines, and prisons. This unit also markets insulated commuter tumblers.

Manufacturing for all three product divisions is consolidated under the Aladdin Products and Service Unit in Nashville. This unit also manages product engineering, maintenance, purchasing, distribution and materials planning, and control. There is a fourth division, the International Division, which is responsible for dealing with all of Aladdin's international customers and affiliates.

Aladdin uses two major distribution networks to get its products to the customer. The first is mass merchandising. Aladdin distributes its products through large retailers, such as K-Mart and Wal-Mart, and through hardware stores (both chain and independent units). Distribution for the institutional business unit is managed through individual service contracts negotiated with hospitals, airlines, and prisons.

In an effort to reach a larger market, Aladdin recently implemented some new marketing and distribution programs. One marketing strategy, for example, uses sports figures to help sell new, higher priced products distributed through upscale department stores. Aladdin has also changed its distribution channels by distributing some of its traditional products through convenience outlets.

The products provided by the three main business units serve different markets and compete on different dimensions. For example, the competition for consumer goods centers primarily around price and convenience. In contrast, hospitals, airlines, and institutions are more interested in durability and contribution to their costs-per-meal. Kerosene heaters depend on cost-effectiveness when competing as an alternative form of heating.

Overall, Aladdin serves a broad range of customers through a variety of distribution networks. The customers and distribution networks have their own special demands -- demands that manufacturing and materials must meet if Aladdin is to maintain and expand its market position.

The Production Process

Although essentially a MTO supplier, Aladdin does engage in a large amount of decoration-to-order. For school lunch kits, standard twenty-four-pack assortments are offered. A significant amount of this business is sort-to-order, accomplished by holding school kits in nearly finished form without final packaging until firm orders are received. On receipt of the firm order, the kits are completed, packaged, and sent out to the customer.

Aladdin's product technology is focused on thermal transfer/nontransfer and kerosene heating and lighting.

Aladdin, a union shop, uses a variety of manufacturing processes. The major elements of the process include metal forming, welding, plastic injection molding, plastic intrusion, plastic bonding, glass forming and welding, and plastic decoration. All of these are combined in a high-volume, high-speed production process that lies on the border between high-volume discrete batch manufacturing and repetitive manufacturing.

While the diversity of manufacturing technologies and different production rates have kept some operations separate, manufacturing at Aladdin, in general, has not been segregated into functional work centers. Instead, products are generally produced in self-contained production lines, following many of the principles of group technology.

Flow diagrams for the principal product lines are shown in Figure 17-1: Diagram A describes the general flow of consumer goods; B, the general flow of Stanley metal bottles; C, the general flow of food servers and disposable dishes; D, the general flow of the kerosene lamp assembly; and E, the purchase of finished goods.

Aladdin's production process uses 1,316 raw materials, 85 purchased parts, 1,585 fabricated or assembled parts, 2,500 manufactured finished, and 999 purchased finished goods. On average, BOMs run between four to six levels with few being more than ten levels. Lot sizes throughout the manufacturing processes are very large, usually more than 1,000 units.

Production Planning at Aladdin

The current production planning system was introduced in 1979. In that year, Aladdin began implementation of the Arista MRP package. Aladdin sent nine senior staff and seventeen middle management employees to Oliver Wight courses. Videotape courses were used to educate all manufacturing and support personnel and union officers. Internal courses for union employees were conducted with up to twenty-four hours of total education given before the changeover to the new MRP system.

MRP implementation was originally justified on the basis of traditional reductions in inventory and improved stock turns. Even before the MRP system was fully implemented, it allowed Aladdin management not only to control business during a recession but to post two consecutive banner years. Once implemented, Aladdin achieved its payback on the MRP system within two years.

Aladdin has modified the Arista package. Installed modules include:

- o Inventory records control
- o Manufacturing standards
- o Master production schedule
- o Material requirements planning
- o Shop floor control.

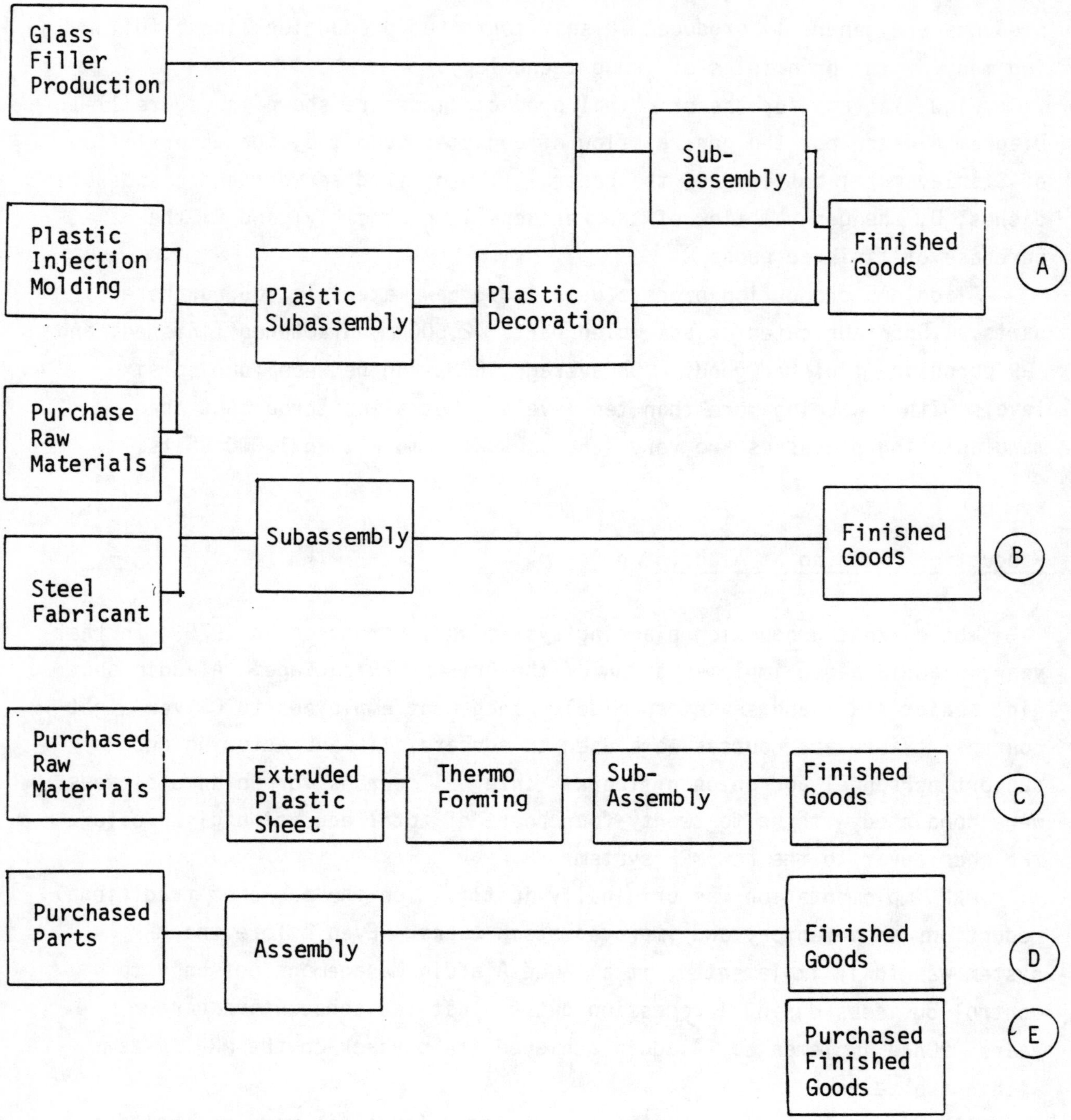

Figure 17-1. -- Production Flow Diagram

Capacity requirements planning was not implemented, nor is it scheduled to be installed. Rough-cut capacity planning is done within the MPS module. This entire production planning system (Figure 17-2) is referred to as Leading Aladdin Management Planning (LAMP).

Business Planning

Business planning at Aladdin is formal and occurs on a regular and ongoing basis. Each month, corporate management meets with the general managers from each business unit and their key assistants. The business unit performance is reviewed and business plans are either revised or reformulated.

Master Production Scheduling

Using the business plan and a rough-cut capacity plan, master scheduling produces a two-tier master production schedule. Because of relatively shallow BOMs and the speed of production, the MPS is also a valid assembly schedule for some products such as thermos bottles. Furthermore, because each thermos bottle has one glass vacuum filler, part planning for glass fillers is scheduled directly from the MPS. Six sizes of glass fillers are run on four production lines indicating nearly continuous production on large weekly orders.

Capacity is generally constrained by machinery and tooling. Labor, on the other hand, is flexible and is not viewed as a major capacity constraint.

The master scheduling process accomplishes a number of important objectives. It generates an MPS for six four-week periods, firms the schedule with balanced labor and capacity at a three-week time fence, and drives requirements to the MRP system over the entire horizon.

Throughout the process, the availability of capacity and tooling is reviewed by master scheduling using rough-cut capacity planning. This review is a prerequisite to the release of the order to the shop floor control system. Material and labor availability are verified by production planning through MRP and shop floor control reports.

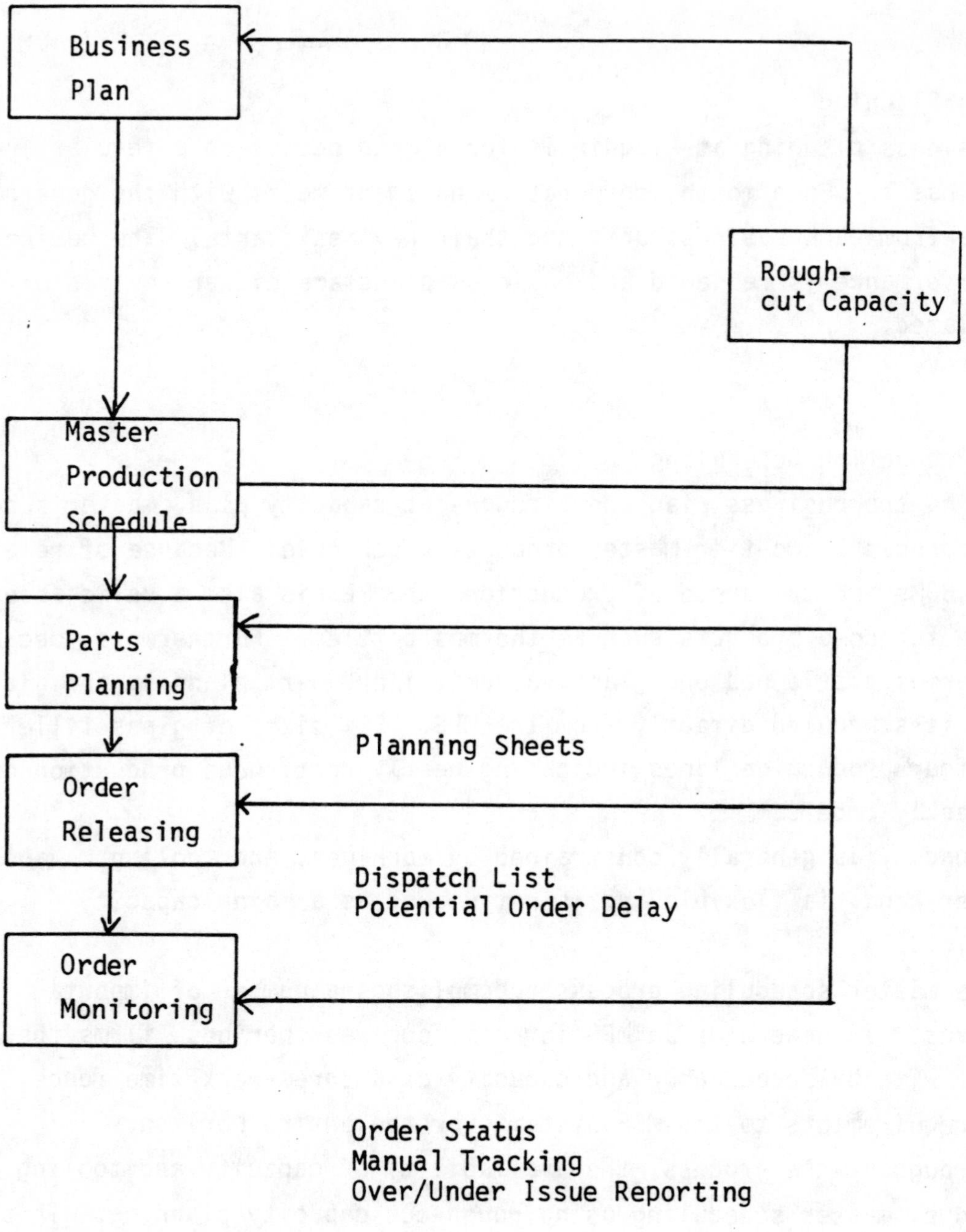

Figure 17-2. -- Production Planning Process

Material Requirements Planning

Production planning supervises overall production by:

- o Organizing firm orders given in weekly time buckets from the MPS
- o Ordering assembly orders into a daily sequence
- o Releasing orders to the shop floor.

The key element in scheduling (and an element present in the preceding three activities) is the order due date. Plastics injection modeling, lower level assemblies, and decoration are also scheduled and managed by production planning, which coordinates priorities, communicates with the shop foremen, monitors performance, and verbally reports problems to master scheduling. A continuous cycle of planning and replanning takes place.

Data entry and order maintenance are done in nightly batches. Planning sheets are regenerated on Monday mornings and net change planning sheets are produced during the remainder of the week. These sheets are generated by an MRP system, which is run in a regenerative mode over the weekend and in a net change mode during the week.

Shop orders can be released to parts planners nightly for distribution at daily meetings with the production personnel. The list of orders is usually issued on Thursday morning and covers all of the orders to be run during the following week.

Orders are released on request from the parts planners. These hard-copy shop orders give information on:

- o Order number
- o Part number to be produced
- o Component part numbers
- o Quantities to be used
- o Quantity of the end items to be completed
- o Start date
- o Order due date
- o Priority within the due date.

The planned dispatch list is reviewed daily and supplemental order changes are released as orders are modified.

Production activity dramatically outruns batch reporting at Aladdin, and it will continue to do so even with the next anticipated change: on-line batch input. Even real-time, on-line reporting would not completely resolve the lag from production to planning.

Parts planners depend on planning sheets (Figure 17-3), a dispatch list (Figure 17-4 and Figure 17-4a), and a potential order delay report (Figure

MATERIAL REQUIREMENTS PLANNING SHEET

1	Time Buckets	. Weekly for one overdue period and 31 weeks
2	Single Level Pegging	
3	Scheduled Receipts	
4	Requirements	. Order numbers assigned manually or system generated (Plan)
5	Net Available	. Net available equals on-hand plus scheduled receipts minus requirements plus safety stock.
6	On Hand	
7	Scheduled Receipts	
8	Requirements	
9	Safety Stock	
10	Total Requirements	. Total of firm order requirements excluding planned requirements
11	Location/On-Hand	. Quantities and location of balances not included in available inventory.

. The MPS Order JX33172 for 9000 includes 4500 of the Quart Blue Stripe jacket.

. Total of JX33172 (4500) and JX32873 (1500) equal 6000 required in bucket 7/18/83 as 8.

. These 6000 have blown through to the next level for the Quart Ivory jacket. (Part Number 02 51532) as a planned order for 1571.

. Calculation

```
 6000 required
-4499 on hand
 1501
1.050 shrink
 1571
```

Figure 17-3. -- Planning Sheet

Aladdin MATERIAL REQUIREMENTS PLAN — ALADDIN CONSUMER PRODUCTS DIVISION — PLANNER X — DATE 07/01/83 PAGE 1604

PART NUMBER	BASIC DESCRIPTION						U/M CONV FACT	PRIME STOCK LOC				SUBSTITUTE PART NUMBER								
02 51527	QT BLUE STRIPE JKT	76	M	C	EA			MULTIPLES		N	3		L	.045		0	F	0	0	

6> 4499		61100 10>	61100	PRD OQ	1		1	NONE <9		0	08/26/82	
										0		0.000

SETUP COST													
0.00	0.00	1.00	0.00	1.00	0.00	1.00	0.1105	0.0405	0.0000	0.0818	0.0193	0.1105	0.0405

ORDER — 1 — ACTION MESSAGES — INV. CTL. MRP — SPECIAL INSTRUCTIONS — L — 0 — 12/09/82

WEEK	OVERDUE	07/04/3	07/11/3	07/18/3	07/25/3	08/01/3	08/08/3	08/15/3	08/22/3	08/29/3	09/05/3	09/12/3	09/19/3	09/26/3	10/03/3	10/10/3
	0	0	0	0	0	0	0	0	0	0	0	0	0	0	0	0
REQUIREMENTS	0	0	0	6000 <8	0	0	500	11000	0	0	0	6500	2500	850	6500	4000
SCHEDULED RECEIPT	0	0	0	7> 0	0	0	0	0	0	0	0	0	0	0	0	0
AVAILABLE	5> 4499	4499	4499	*-1501	-1501	-1501	*-2001	*-13001	-13001	-13001	-13001	*-19501	*-22001	*-22851	*-29351	*-33351
PLANNED ORD REL	0	0	0	1571	0	0	523	11518	0	0	0	6806	2617	890	6806	4188
WEEK	10/17/3	10/24/3	10/31/3	11/07/3	11/14/3	11/21/3	11/28/3	12/05/3	12/12/3	12/19/3	12/26/3	01/02/4	01/09/4	01/16/4	01/23/4	01/30/4
	0	0	0	0	0	0	0	0	0	0	0	0	0	0	0	0
REQUIREMENTS	8000	0	0	3500	11500	0	250	0	0	238	2182	4459	5686	5735	5735	5621
SCHEDULED RECEIPT	0	0	0	0	0	0	0	0	0	0	0	0	0	0	0	0
AVAILABLE	*-41351	-41351	-41351	*-44851	*-56351	-56351	*-56601	-56601	-56601	*-56839	*-59021	*-63480	*-69166	*-74901	*-80636	*-86257
PLANNED ORD REL	8376	0	0	3664	12041	0	261	0	0	249	2284	4669	5953	6005	6005	5885
WEEK	02/06/74	03/05/74	04/09/74	05/07/74	06/04/74	07/02/74	08/06/74	09/03/74	10/01/74	10/29/74	11/26/74	12/24/74	01/21/75	02/18/75	03/18/75	04/15/75
	0	0	0	0	0	0	0	0	0	0	0	0	0	0	0	0
REQUIREMENTS	20436	20470	16695	1028	1443	0	0	0	0	0	0	0	0	0	0	0
SCHEDULED RECEIPT	0	0	0	0	0	0	0	0	0	0	0	0	0	0	0	0
AVAILABLE	*-106693	*-127163	*-143858	*-144886	*-146329	-146329	-146329	-146329	-146329	-146329	-146329	-146329	-146329	-146329	-146329	-146329
PLANNED ORD REL	21396	21433	17479	1075	1508	0	0	0	0	0	0	0	0	0	0	0

SCHEDULED RECEIPTS <3 — REQUIREMENTS <4

REQUIRED DATE	REQUIRED QUANTITY	REFERENCE NUMBER	ORDER NUMBER	LEVEL	REQUIRED DATE	REQUIRED QUANTITY	REFERENCE NUMBER	ORDER NUMBER
07/18	4500	02 15504 <	JX33172 <2	RP	12/26	865	02 15504	PLAN
07/18	1500	02 31506	JX32873	RP	12/26	681	02 41242	PLAN
08/08	500	02 31506	JX33710	RP	12/26	636	02 15502	PLAN
08/15	11000	02 15504	JX32523	RP	01/02	675	02 15502	PLAN
09/12	6000	02 15504	JX32868	RP	01/02	2875	02 15504	PLAN
09/12	500	02 31506	JX33406	RP	01/02	909	02 41242	PLAN
09/19	2500	02 15504	JX33173	RP	01/09	900	02 15502	PLAN
09/26	850	02 31506	JX33711	RP	01/09	64	02 31506	PLAN
10/03	6500	02 15504	JX33174	RP	01/09	909	02 41242	PLAN
10/10	4000	02 15504	JX33887	RP	01/09	3813	02 15504	PLAN
10/17	7500	02 15504	JX33400	RP	01/16	3813	02 15504	PLAN
10/17	500	02 31506	JX33712	RP	01/16	113	02 31506	PLAN
11/07	3500	02 15504	JX33401	RP	01/16	900	02 15502	PLAN
11/14	11500	02 15504	JX33704	RP	01/16	909	02 41242	PLAN
11/28	250	02 31506	JX33713	RP	01/23	900	02 15502	PLAN
12/19	238	02 41242	PLAN		01/23	909	02 41242	PLAN

11 — LOC/ON-HAND QUARAN 0 SCRAP 2470 100 0 101 0 246 -3228 251 0 500

Figure 17-3. -- Planning Sheet (continued)

PLANNED SHOP DISPATCH LIST

This report is currently being revised almost completely because it is overly sophisticated for the environment and because the lag of data limits its usefulness as an operating tool for the foremen.

Sorting Priority:

1 Department

2 Work Center

3 Tool Number

4 Start Date of the Order

5 Priority (Time remaining over time remaining on the order

6 Horizon

- Specified by Production Planning at three weeks.
- Report is issued daily
- The Shop Dispatch List shows only the week horizon and is given to production supervisors for their use.

7 Order Number

8 Order Status

- 5 = Some production reported
  4 = released, no production reported.
- Orders are dropped when they achieve Status 6, closed order status.

Figure 17-4. -- Planned Shop Dispatch List

477-25 ALADDIN CONSUMER PRODUCTS DIVISION PLANNED SHOP DISPATCH LIST PRINTED 05/15/83 PAGE 30

WORK CENTER 246010300 PRINTED JACKETS FOR PERIOD 06/15/83 TO 09/04/83

PART NUMBER	ORDER NUMBER	SET-UP HOURS	REMAIN. ORD.QTY	-OPERATION- RTO	ACT#	CRW	SCHEDULER MESSAGE	PRIORTY	S T	SCHEDULED DATES START	COMPLETE	PR ST	OPERATION DESCRIPTION	SCHD. HOURS	MAN HOURS
TOOL NUMBER QUART															
02 51350	XW8C801	2.000	29500	001	7145	003	PRINT QT R	7.00	4	08/21/83	08/22/83		QT RED PLAID PRT JKT	22.0	66.0
02 51531	XW8C805	2.000	10000	001	7145	003	PRINT QT R	7.00	4	08/22/83	08/22/83		QT RED STRIPE PTD JK	8.8	26.4
02 51862	XW81516	2.000	900	001	7145	003	PRINT QT R	7.00	4	08/22/83	08/22/83		QT RED VANGUARD JKT	2.6	7.8
02 51338	XW81501	2.000	1500	001	7145	003	PRINT QT R	14.00	4	08/29/83	08/29/83		QT WOODGRAN PRTD JKT	3.0	9.0
02 51350	XW81502	2.000	5300	001	7145	003	PRINT QT R	14.00	4	08/29/83	08/29/83		QT RED PLAID PRT JKT	5.6	16.8
02 51548	XW81508	2.000	2000	001	7145	003	PRINT QT R	14.00	4	08/29/83	08/29/83		QT RED KON TIKI PRT	3.4	10.2
													TOOL NUMBER TOTAL HOURS	83.9	251.7
TOOL NUMBER X-4															
02 52513	XW72624	2.000	7000	001	7145	003	PRINT X-4	7.00-	4	08/08/83	08/08/83		CIRCUS TIME PRT JKT	5.9	17.7
02 10115	JX39921	.000	7000	001	7146	003	PRINT X-4	6.00-	4	08/09/83	08/09/83		SPORT RACER X4 J/LNR	.0	.0
02 10116	JX39922	.000	7000	001	7145	003	PRINT X-4	6.00-	4	08/09/83	08/09/83		CIRCUS TIME X4 J/LNR	.0	.0
02 51442	XW8C102	2.000	4750	001	7145	003	PRINT X-4	1.00	4	08/16/83	08/16/83		X-4 SUPERMN PRTD JKT	4.6	13.8
02 51478	XW8C104	2.000	5250	001	7145	003	PRINT X-4	1.00	4	08/16/83	08/16/83		X4 TOMEJERRY PRTD JK	4.9	14.7
02 51464	XW81101	2.000	3750	001	7146	003	PRINT X-4	1.00	4	08/16/83	08/16/83		X4 H HOBBIE FS PRT JK	4.1	12.3
02 51822	XW80121	2.000	1700	001	7146	003	PRINT X-4	2.00	4	08/17/83	08/17/83		X4 STRWBERRY PRT JKT	2.9	8.7
02 51830	XW8C122	2.000	2000	001	7146	003	PRINT X-4	2.00	4	08/17/83	08/17/83		X4 RAINBOW PRT JKT	3.1	9.3
													TOOL NUMBER TOTAL HOURS	25.5	76.5
TOOL NUMBER 1/2 PINT															
02 51623	XW81509	2.000	2750	001	7143	003	PRINT HP J	14.00	4	08/29/83	08/29/83		HP RED STRIPE JKT	3.6	10.8
02 51624	XW81510	2.000	3000	001	7143	003	PRINT HP J	14.00	4	08/29/83	08/29/83		HP BLUE STRIPE JKT	3.7	11.1
02 52384	XW81519	2.000	2000	001	7143	003	PRINT HP J	14.00	4	08/29/83	08/29/83		HP BOOTS PRT JKT BLU	3.2	9.6
02 52087	XW81520	2.000	2050	001	7143	003	PRINT HP J	14.00	4	08/29/83	08/29/83		HP BOOTS PRT JKT BEG	3.2	9.6
02 52936	XW81521	2.000	5750	001	7143	003	PRINT HP J	14.00	4	08/29/83	08/29/83		HP BURLAP PRT JACKET	5.3	15.9
													TOOL NUMBER TOTAL HOURS	19.0	57.0
													WORK CENTER TOTAL HOURS	280.7	842.1

Figure 17-4. -- Planned Shop Dispatch List (continued)

Similar to Planned Shop Dispatch List

477-28 ALADDIN CONSUMER PRODUCTS DIVISION — SHOP DISPATCH LIST — PRINTED 08/15/83 PAGE 27

WORK CENTER 246010300 PRINTED JACKETS — FOR PERIOD 08/15/83 TO 08/21/83

PART NUMBER	ORDER NUMBER	SET-UP HOURS	REMAIN. ORD. QTY	-OPERATION- GRP # SEQ	SCHEDULER MESSAGE	PRIORTY	S T	SCHEDULED DATES START	COMPLETE	PR ST	OPERATION DESCRIPTION	SCHD. HOURS	MAN HOURS
TOOL NUMBER PINT REG													
02 51717	XW71805	2.000	133	001 7141 003		13.00-	5	08/02/83	08/02/83		PT RED MURPHY PRTD	2.1	6.3
02 51529	XW72605	2.000	110	001 7141 003		7.00-	5	08/08/83	08/08/83		PT RED STRIPE PRT JK	2.1	6.3
02 51525	XW72603	2.000	2991	001 7141 003		7.00-	5	08/08/83	08/08/83		PT BLU STRIP PRT JKT	3.7	11.1
02 52088	XW72623	2.000	63	001 7141 003		6.00-	5	08/09/83	08/09/83		PT BOOTS PRT JKT BEG	2.0	6.0
02 51713	XW80118	2.000	1067	001 7141 003		.00	5	08/15/83	08/15/83		PT RED PLAID PRTD JK	2.6	7.8
02 51529	XW80107	2.000	2920	001 7141 003		.00	5	08/15/83	08/15/83		PT RED STRIPE PRT JK	3.7	11.1
02 51525	XW80105	2.000	4000	001 7141 003		.00	4	08/15/83	08/15/83		PT BLU STRIP PRT JKT	4.3	12.9
02 51713	XW80806	2.000	20000	001 7141 003		4.00	4	08/19/83	08/19/83		PT RED PLAID PRTD JK	13.6	40.8
											TOOL NUMBER TOTAL HOURS	34.1	102.3
TOOL NUMBER PT W/M													
02 51904	XW80809	2.000	500	001 7143 003		1.00	4	08/16/83	08/16/83		PTWM TAN/BG GRAP PJK	2.3	6.9
02 51534	XW80115	2.000	9000	001 7143 003		1.00	4	08/16/83	08/16/83		PT WM GRAPHIC PRT JK	7.2	21.6
02 51805	XW80120	2.000	10000	001 7143 003		2.00	4	08/17/83	08/17/83		PTWM BESTBUY PRT JKT	7.8	23.4
											TOOL NUMBER TOTAL HOURS	17.3	51.9
TOOL NUMBER QUART													
02 51527	XW72604	2.000	132	001 7145 003		14.00-	5	08/01/83	08/01/83		QT BLUE STRIPE JKT	2.1	6.3
02 51350	XW80101	2.000	7240	001 7145 003		2.00	5	08/17/83	08/17/83		QT RED PLAID PRT JKT	6.9	20.7
02 51531	XW80111	2.000	3000	001 7145 003		5.00-	4	08/10/83	08/10/83		QT RED STRIPE PTD JK	4.0	12.0
02 51531	XTERESA	2.000	10	001 7145 003		4.00-	4	08/11/83	08/11/83		QT RED STRIPE PTD JK	2.0	6.0
02 51527	XTERESA	2.000	10	001 7145 003		4.00-	4	08/11/83	08/11/83		QT BLUE STRIPE JKT	2.0	6.0
02 51867	XW80124	2.000	1050	001 7145 003		2.00	4	08/17/83	08/17/83		QT TEMPRITE PRTD JKT	2.7	8.1
02 51866	XW80123	2.000	850	001 7145 003		2.00	4	08/17/83	08/17/83		QT MURPHY PRTD JKT	2.6	7.8
02 51527	XW80106	2.000	3800	001 7145 003		3.00	4	08/18/83	08/18/83		QT BLUE STRIPE JKT	4.6	13.8
02 51531	XW80112	2.000	1250	001 7145 003		3.00	4	08/18/83	08/18/83		QT RED STRIPE PTD JK	2.8	8.4
02 51527	XW80803	2.000	10000	001 7145 003		4.00	4	08/19/83	08/19/83		QT BLUE STRIPE JKT	8.8	26.4
02 51350	XW80801	2.000	29500	001 7145 003		7.00	4	08/21/83	08/22/83		QT RED PLAID PRT JKT	22.0	66.0
											TOOL NUMBER TOTAL HOURS	60.5	181.5
TOOL NUMBER X-4													
02 52513	XW72624	2.000	7000	001 7145 003		7.00-	4	08/08/83	08/08/83		CIRCUS TIME PRT JKT	5.9	17.7
02 10116	JX39922	.000	7000	001 7146 003		6.00-	4	08/09/83	08/09/83		CIRCUS TIME X4 J/LNR	.0	.0
02 10115	JX39921	.000	7000	001 7146 003		6.00-	4	08/09/83	08/09/83		SPORT RACER X4 J/LNR	.0	.0
02 51464	XW81101	2.000	3750	001 7146 003		1.00	4	08/16/83	08/16/83		X4 H HOBBIE FS PRTJK	4.1	12.3
02 51442	XW80102	2.000	4750	001 7146 003		1.00	4	08/16/83	08/16/83		X-4 SUPERMN PRTD JKT	4.6	13.8
02 51478	XW80104	2.000	5250	001 7146 003		1.00	4	08/16/83	08/16/83		X4 TOMEJERRY PRTD JK	4.9	14.7
02 51833	XW80122	2.000	2000	001 7145 003		2.00	4	08/17/83	08/17/83		X4 RAINBOW PRT JKT	3.1	9.3
02 51822	XW80121	2.000	1700	001 7146 003		2.00	4	08/17/83	08/17/83		X4 STRWBERRY PRT JKT	2.9	8.7
											TOOL NUMBER TOTAL HOURS	25.5	76.5
											WORK CENTER TOTAL HOURS	137.4	412.2

Figure 17-4a. -- Shop Dispatch List

POTENTIAL ORDER DELAY

This report is used by Production Planners to verify material availability.

1	Order Horizon	
2	Order Number	
3	Parent Part Number	
4	Component Part Numbers	. Only components required for the order with due date within current lead time and not enough on-hand
5	Item Type	. Manufactured
6	Planner Code	. An individual Production Planner
7	Buyer Code	. F if bulk issue stock retained on the shop floor
8	Requirements Status	. R = Required P = Phantom
9	Open Orders	. For the component
10	Shop Order or Purchase Order	
11	Type and Status	
12	Open Order Quantity	
13	Balance Remaining	
14	Due Date	
15	Required Date	. For the component
16	On Hand Balance	
17	Required Quantity	. For pegged orders
18	Time Bucket	
19	Suggested Action	

Figure 17-5. -- Order Delay Report

```
436-83  ALADDIN CONSUMER PRODUCTS DIVISION                         POTENTIAL ORDER DELAY REPORT              PRINTED 08/10/83 PAGE   23
        HRZN(1)=08/11/83 HRZN(2)=08/15/83 HRZN(3)=08/19/83
                                                               * * * * * * * * * * * * O P E N   O R D E R S * * * * * * * * * * * * *
                                                               ORDER/NBR LOT VENDOR TS ORD/QTY BAL/DUE DUE/DATE NEED/DATE HRZN MESSAGE
                                              T P B R    DATE    BALANCE        QTY * *REQUIREMENTS* * *
ORDER NBR   LOT ASSEMBLY NBR    PART NUMBER   T L Y S REQUIRED UN HAND          REQ HRZN(1) HRZN(2) HRZN(3) DESCRIPTION
JX12345       02 10105                                   19123             18200    P6    1500      100 08/02/83 08/01/83  *     FOLLOWUP PD
JX12361       02 10104          02 77903      P B   R 08/01/83           0    150    1340        0       0 LARGE POLYBAG
                                                        19123             18200    P6    1500      100 08/02/83 08/01/83  *     FOLLOWUP PD
JX12500       02 10101          02 77900      P B   R 08/03/83          -2    167     500        0       0 SHIPPER-PLAS JKTS
                                02 77903      P B   R 08/03/83           3    167    1340        0       0 LARGE POLYBAG
                                                        19123             19200    P6    1500      100 08/02/83 08/01/83  *     FOLLOWUP PD
JX12501       02 10102          02 77900      P B   R 08/03/83          -2    333     500        0       0 SHIPPER-PLAS JKTS
                                02 77903      P B   R 08/03/83           3    333    1340        0       0 LARGE POLYBAG
                                                        19123             18200    P6    1500      100 08/02/83 08/01/83  *     FOLLOWUP PD
                                02 77904      P B   R 08/03/83        1154    667    1167        0       0 PAD-JKT CTN DIC JPAN
JX12502       02 10103          02 77903      P B   R 08/05/83           3    167    1340        0       0 LARGE POLYBAG
                                                        19123             18200    P6    1500      100 08/02/83 08/01/83  *     FOLLOWUP PD
JX31024       02 15104          02 72140      P B   R 07/29/83           3   3800    5800        0       0 AD BAND HP GRAPHIC
                                                        19153             12025    P4   35000    35000 08/19/83 07/29/83  *     RESCH IN PD
JX32405       02 15104          02 72140      P B   R 08/10/83           3   2800    5800        0       0 AD BAND HP GRAPHIC
                                                        19153             12025    P4   35000    35000 08/19/83 07/29/83  *     RESCH IN PD
JX32491       02 12312          02 72914      P B   P 08/02/83           3    315     315        0    4000 AD BAND PT PLAID K-M
                                                        19103             12025    P4   35000    35000 08/19/83 08/02/83  *     RESCH IN PD
JX32523       02 15504          02 51527      M X   R 06/18/83       -3225   3500       0        0    3500 QT BLUE STRIPE JKT
                                                        XM72604                SHOP    M5    8500      132 08/01/83 08/10/83  *     FOLLOWUP
                                                        XM90113                SHOP    M5    3000      560 08/10/83 08/10/83  *     FOLLOWUP
                                                        XTERESA                SHOP    M4      10       10 08/11/83 08/10/83  *     RESCH IN
                                                        XM80106                SHOP    M4    3500     3500 08/15/83 08/10/83  *     RESCH IN
                                                        XM90803                SHOP    M4   10000    10000 08/22/83 08/18/83  ***   RESCH IN
                                02 51531      M X   R 06/18/83        2621   3500       0        0    3500 QT RED STRIPE PTD JK
                                                        XM80111                SHOP    M4    3300     3000 08/10/83 08/18/83  ***   FOLLOWUP
                                02 53072      M Z   R 08/18/83       21656   3500     782    18200    5200 QT RED CUP
                                                        Z080304                SHOP    M4   70023    70023 08/17/83 08/18/83  ***   FOLLOWUP
                                02 53493      M Z   R 08/18/83        1468   3500       3        0    3500 QT REG BLUE CUP
```

Figure 17-5. -- Order Delay Report (continued)

17-5) to control the shop floor. Additional reports including over and under issue reports, error reports, operation detail reports, part status reports, and order status reports assist in this job.

Given a feasible schedule (a major responsibility of the entire production planning process), parts planners communicate the plan to the shop by shop orders and dispatch lists. Parts planners also monitor the accomplishment of the schedule, replan (when and if necessary), and feed information back to master scheduling on an ongoing basis.

Audit control reports to the production control manager as do the parts planners and the stores-receiving managers. Audit control batches input, coordinates control cards for the LAMP processing run, and reconciles errors. It also coordinates the stockroom cycle counting programs.

Purchasing also uses planning sheets from the MRP module. Purchases of finished goods are also linked via the network to the master schedule. The purchasing department plans material acquisitions to due dates.

Shop Floor Control

The task of controlling the shop floor is complicated by two important aspects of Aladdin's business:

- High-volume production. Production is closest to the repetitive environment in terms of its characteristics. All production takes place in large volumes and at high speeds. As a result, the shop floor control system must be able to identify problems as soon as they occur, and it must be able to react quickly to these problems. Failure to do so can result in a sizable loss of production on the shop floor.
- High seasonal demand. The demand for many of Aladdin's products is seasonal. There is as much as a 50 percent swing in end-item requirements with high production building steeply from January through July and then dropping off to a low at the end of August.

Injection molding of parts is dramatically affected by seasonality and by the multiple combinations of over fifty colors and seventy-two mold inserts for various end items. As an adaptation of the MRP system, Aladdin has taken a unique approach to planning the load on the thirty-two mold machines.

Molds have been added to BOMs (Figure 17-6), and each part, regardless of color or mold insert, is linked to the mold. By this method, the MRP module provides the ability to group parts mechanically, allows scheduling that reduces major mold changes, and identifies color and insert changes.

This method has allowed the leveling for seasonality to be accomplished in matched set of parts, which in 1982 meant a savings of $245,000. It has also provided a manual ability to accomplish rough-cut capacity planning for this area. The predictability factor has been about 96 percent to date.

Only about 5 percent of released orders are changed significantly when released to the shop floor. Production or machine problems, inventory errors, schedule errors, or management decisions are among the reasons for change.

Assembly departments can move from order to order and nearly always meet their schedule by week's end. They rarely incur labor penalties as a result. Orders are set up and stock drawn four to six hours in advance of starting time, thus allowing crews to leave a problem, move to another order on another line, and return later to finish the first order.

The Stages of Shop Floor Control at Aladdin

Detailed Assignment

More control of the daily schedule is being assumed by manufacturing personnel. Order quantities are being produced closer to the scheduled quantities that have a tolerance of plus or minus 3 percent. The high volume and speed allow some measure of flexibility in quantity produced. Aladdin management believes that precision beyond this range is unnecessary because labor incentive rates and labor productivity must also be considered in the scheduling process.

Planning values are dynamic within a gradual pattern of change. They are reviewed continuously as the schedule is planned and replanned. However, planning values are stable enough that they create no real difficulties for master scheduling or production planning.

Scheduled downtime for maintenance is negotiated by manufacturing departments and production planning at daily schedule meetings and communicated to master scheduling for inclusion in the production plan. Information for shop activity such as issues, receipts, and production is assimilated into the replanning of priorities.

INDENTED BILL OF MATERIAL

1 Part Number	. 02 15504
2 Item Type	. Manufactured
3 Item Status	. Currently in production
4 Point of Usage	. Department 246
5 Structure Type	
6 Current ECN	. 8/18/82
7 Item Type of Component	. Manufactured
8 Item Status of Component	. Current
9 Component - Level 1	. 02 51531 Quart Red Stripe Printed Jacket
10 Component - Level 2	. 02 51532 Quart Ivory Jacket (On Printed Jacket)
11 Component - Level 3	. 02 58010 Natural Polypropylene
12 Mold Required to Produce Part	. 02 M19554 Quart Jacket Mold
13 Total Hour	. A planning part number which gives hours required to produce one part as a sub-level to the mold 12. It is used to sum hours for each mold by time bucket.
14 500-Ton Hour	. A planning part number which gives hours required to produce one part for smoothing the work center load.
15 X-3 Printer	. A planning part number which gives hours required to decorate one jacket.
16 Total Hours Print	. A planning part number which gives hours required to decorate by size for smoothing the work-center load.

Figure 17-6. -- Indented Bill of Material

Feedback/Control

The summary plan execution measurements report contains summaries for each planner code within each division (business unit) and a summary of all activities for the business unit. Divided into sections, the summary reports on purchase orders, shop orders, an analysis of shop orders added or changed, and an analysis of shop orders completed out of quantity tolerance.

The general management summary reports on:

- Master schedule plan to actual performance
- Customer service
- Forecast accuracy
- Shipping performance
- Productivity
- Open order coverage
- Purchase order accuracy
- Error message summary
- Average lead time
- Freight premiums
- Inventory variances
- Purchase commitments
- Order completion accuracy
- Purchase order coverage
- Inventory accuracy
- BOM accuracy
- Routing accuracy
- Negative inventory balances
- Document control
- Procedural accuracy
- Computer reliability.

Shop Floor Control -- The Next Stage

The next steps in the development of Aladdin's management planning and control system might well be called control for shop floor. Continuing refinements in computer operations, systems, forecasting, financial control, payroll, labor reporting, and distribution will all lend themselves to smoother, more stable production requirements and production performance.

Perhaps the most significant improvement for shop floor control will be realized when the systems group creates a single database from the disparate array of inventory reporting and order processing systems remaining from the divisional consolidations of 1981. When complete, the present reports will be produced as they are now if desired by the business units, but processing will be shortened by the elimination of cross-reading and synchronization of separate files.

The development and installation of distribution requirements planning (DRP) will lend further control to the business plan and improve customer service. A locator system to replace the one-bucket category of finished goods now in the planning system will come with DRP. Consolidation and consistent storage reporting will improve the production planner's ability to use the potential order delay report in short-term scheduling.

Direct labor reporting can be accomplished over the next few years, most likely in two steps. A modern system will be installed that will first be served by on-line batching of data input and eventually by real-time input from the shop floor.

All business units either use or will use the available-to-promise reports offered by the planning system. These reports directly link planned and actual units from the planning system in place or previous generation reports devised locally.

Process improvements and reorganization of production lines have further simplified the production process and will add more reliability and flexibility to performance-to-schedule.

Aladdin will be involved in the APICS repetitive manufacturing studies effort. JIT manufacturing has long been a hallmark of production at Aladdin, but new techniques in changeover time reductions and process revisions will be the next big area of emphasis in manufacturing operations.

The use of robotics is coupled with shop floor improvements. For two years, Aladdin has moved a robot throughout the plant in test situations during actual production activity and is now ready for the first permanent installation of a robot on the shop floor.

Like many other companies, Aladdin is required to label goods for large customers with machine readable bar coding. Aladdin is installing equipment to produce labels and to position itself for further future internal use.

Aladdin will also add an integrated accounts payable, purchasing, receiving, and quality assurance subsystem within a few months. An outgrowth of this subsystem will be vendor certification, which will further enhance the overall reliablity of raw material delivery and quality to production planning.

The production planning system is part of a closed-loop management planning and control system. It uses the outputs of the system to:

- o Set a realistic business plan
- o Schedule production
- o Control the shop floor
- o Provide management with performance information.

Still under development, this system seeks to integrate information in all aspects of the business for control.

WHY SHOP FLOOR CONTROL?

Manufacturing success can only occur when good planning is complemented by the effective execution of the plans on the shop floor. Planning and execution must always be kept in balance. Without the balance, one side will always act as the limiting factor and constrain the overall effectiveness of the manufacturing system.

Most manufacturing managers are familiar with the structure and operation of such material planning systems as MRP, and aware of many of the principles and practices that underlie effective master production scheduling. Most managers are now well aware of the importance of good planning, but the current knowledge of shop floor control is not as complete. Few are able to provide an answer to the question of what has to be done to develop an effective shop floor control system. This question is central to this study.

The answer to this question comes from two sources, shop floor control literature and leading edge firms. The development, structure, and operation of thirteen leading edge systems have been examined. The firms presented differ in terms of size, markets served, nature of ownership, and products manufactured, but they have had common experiences with shop floor control, including:

- <u>Shop floor control is an important element in the overall success of the firms</u>. Each firm examined in this report is a market leader -- a state due, in part, to an effective shop floor control system, which closes the critical gap between the planning system and the shop floor.
- <u>Shop floor control is more than either dispatching or data collection</u>. Shop floor control embodies a large number of activities, beginning with order review release and ending with order disposition. Order dispatching and data collection are just two of these activities. Often these activities were not as critical as might be imagined.
- <u>Shop floor control is not a task that can be done overnight</u>. The development of an effective shop floor control system, like the development of an effective planning system, takes time, effort,

and resources. All of the shop floor control systems examined in this study were developed over a period of years.

- It must always be consistent with and supportive of overall corporate objectives. Management in every firm had a clear idea of what it had to do well on the shop floor for the firm as a whole to achieve its objectives. These ideas were built into the resulting shop floor control system.
- It is never a substitute for planning. To management, there was always a clear distinction between what the planning system and the shop floor control system do. The planning system obtained the resources to be used by the shop floor control system and generated the plans to be implemented on the shop floor. The shop floor control system carried out these plans using the available level of resources. Deficiencies in planning (e.g., insufficient resources) could never be resolved on the shop floor.
- It makes the best use of all of its resources. Shop floor control uses four resources (machine capacity, tooling, material, and work force). Of these resources, it is the human who is most often critical to the successful operation of this system.
- Development is a never-ending task. Shop floor control systems (especially effective ones) are constantly undergoing change. At times, these changes reflect refinements introduced as a result of users becoming better acquainted with the system and better able to identify their requirements and expectations of the system. In other instances, these changes are a result of the introduction and use of new planning procedures, new methods for solving production problems, or physical changes in the production process.

SUMMARY

This study has not limited itself to a review of the experiences of the thirteen leading edge firms. It has attempted to recast these experiences using a format that is based on a unified and integrative framework for shop floor control. This study has tried to:

- Develop a better definition of shop floor control
- Develop a better understanding of what shop floor control is by creating and presenting an integrative model of this system
- Describe the techniques and procedures that are being used actively by firms at the leading edge of the development and implementation of shop floor control systems
- Identify those elements and practices that are common to the systems of the participating firms and that characterize effective shop floor control
- Identify and define those terms and concepts important to developing a clear understanding of shop floor control.

Currently, shop floor control is a source of frustration to many managers and has become a manufacturing millstone. The time, money, and effort that management has spent on improving its manufacturing planning capabilities seem wasted by the inability to carry out these same plans on the shop floor successfully. As demonstrated by the thirteen representative firms in this book, it does not have to be so. Shop floor control can be made into a manufacturing strength and can be an important corporate weapon -- a method of differentiating a firm from its competition in a competitive marketplace.

By studying the experiences of the leading edge systems, this book has identified those basics of shop floor control that must be mastered and used to develop an effective system. Whether shop floor control remains a manufacturing millstone or becomes a corporate weapon depends on how these basics are used.

BIBLIOGRAPHY

Berry, W. L.; Vollmann, T. E.; and Whybark, D. Clay. Master Production Scheduling: Principles and Practices. Washington, D.C.: American Production and Inventry Control Society, 1979.

Browne, J.; Boon, J. E.; and Davies, B. J. "Job Shop Control." International Journal of Production Research 19 (1981):633-643.

Bruhn, G. L. "Shop Floor Control? You Can't Control If You Don't Know..." In American Production and Inventory Control Society 22nd Annual Conference Proceedings, pp. 175-176. St. Louis: October 1979.

Butts, J. T. "Controlling the Shop Floor." Manufacturing and Engineering 3 (1980).

Fogarty, D. W., and Hoffmann, T. R. Production and Inventory Management. Cincinnati: South-Western Publishing, 1983.

Groover, M. P. Automation, Production Systems, and Computer-Aided Manufacturing. Englewood Cliffs, N.J.: Prentice-Hall, 1980.

Gue, F. S. "Input/Output Control in the Job Shop." In American Production and Inventory Control Society 18th Annual Conference Proceedings, pp. 58-72. San Diego: October 1975.

Hall, R. W. Zero Inventories. Homewood, Ill.: Dow Jones-Irwin, 1983.

IBM. "Engineering and Production." Communications Oriented Production Information and Control System. White Plains, N.Y.: IBM Technical Publications Department, 1972.

IBM. "Manufacturing Activity Planning." Communications Oriented Production Information and Control System. White Plains, N.Y.: IBM Technical Publications Department, 1972.

Irastorza, J. C., and Deane, R. H. "Starve the Shop -- Reduce Work-in-Process." Production and Inventory Management 17 (1976):20-25.

Janson, R. L. "Production Control -- Shape Up or Ship Out." In American Production and Inventory Control Society 15th Annual Conference Proceedings, pp. 378-383. Toronto: October 1972.

Levulis, R. J. "Group Technology Strategies in the U.S." In Spring Annual Conference Proceedings - AIIE. Atlanta: 1980.

Meck, R. A., Jr. "Maximizing the Full Benefits of Shop Floor Control." In American Production and Inventory Control Society 18th Annual Conference Proceedings, pp. 80-84. San Diego: October 1975.

Melynk, S. A., and Carter, P. L. "Viewing Kanban as an (S.Q.) System: Developing New Insights into a Japanese Method of Production and Inventory Control." In Management by Japanese Systems, edited by S. M. Lee and G. Schwendiman. New York: Praeger Publishers, 1982.

Melnyk, S. A.; Carter, P. L.; Dilts, D. M.; and Lyth, D. M. "The Principles and Practices of Shop Floor Control: The First Phase." APICS Research Report. Submitted to the APICS Educational and Research Foundation, March 1984.

Melnyk, S. A.; Carter, P. L.; Dilts, D. M.; and Lyth, D. M. Shop Floor Control. Homewood, Ill.: Dow Jones-Irwin, 1985.

Melnyk, S. A.; Gonzalez, R. F.; and Anderson, S. T. "Manufacturing Resource Planning: Preliminary Insights into a New Corporate Way of Life." APICS Research Report. Submitted to the APICS Educational and Research Foundation, June 1983.

Milwaukee APICS Chapter. Shop Floor Control: APICS Training Aid. American Production and Inventory Society, 1972.

Monks, J. G. Operations Management/Theory and Problems. New York: McGraw-Hill, 1982.

Nellemann, D. O. "Closing the Shop Floor Control Financial Loop." In American Production and Inventory Control Society 23rd Annual Conference Proceedings, Los Angeles: October 1980.

Nicholson, T. A. J., and Pullen, R. D. "A Practical Control System for Optimizing Production Schedules." International Journal of Production Research 16 (1978):219-227.

Orlicky, J. A. Material Requirements Planning. New York: McGraw-Hill, 1975.

Sherrill, R. C. "Hot Lists to Queue Lists." In American Production and Inventory Control Society 20th Annual Conference Proceedings, pp. 428-433. Washington, D.C.: November 1977.

Wallace, T. F. APICS Dictionary. 4th ed. Washington, D.C., American Production and Inventory Control Society, 1980.

Appendix B

PREPARATION FOR THE CONFERENCE: THE QUESTIONNAIRE AND REQUIREMENTS FOR PARTICIPATION

The following two documents were used in preparation for the conference. The first is the questionnaire that was administered to all of the firms identified as being leading users of shop floor control. The second lists the requirements that every participating firm had to satisfy as a condition for attending the conference.

SHOP FLOOR CONTROL STUDY:

QUESTIONNAIRE

Instructions to the Respondent:

This questionnaire is part of a study being conducted by a team from the College of Business at Michigan State University in conjunction with the American Production and Inventory Control Society. This questionnaire has been constructed to help us better understand your firm and its Shop Floor Control system. The questionnaire is being distributed only to firms with "leading edge" Shop Floor Control systems.

Please note that the responses to this questionnaire should be based on the experiences of that plant in your firm which you feel has the best developed Shop Floor Control system. If yours is a multi-plant firm, please restrict yourself to only one plant. Also note that the responses should refer to the Shop Floor Control system as it currently exists.

We would like you to complete and return the questionnaire within two weeks of receipt. Please use the enclosed envelope to return the questionnaire.

Thank your for taking the time to complete this questionnaire.

Phillip L. Carter

David M. Dilts

Steven A. Melnyk

SHOP FLOOR CONTROL STUDY:

QUESTIONNAIRE

1. Please fill in your name: ______________________________

2. Position in the company: ______________________________
(Questions 1 and 2 are asked for identification purposes only)

3. Please identify the plant that you have selected for this questionnaire? (This should be the one with the best developed Shop Floor Control system).

____

____

4. The following are modules which could be found in production and inventory control system. Please rate the degree to which the activities encompassed by these modules are under the control of the plant. Use the following scale when rating:

0 ---------- 1 ---------- 2 ---------- 3 ----------4 ---------- 5

0	1	3	5
Not Done Currently	Done wholly by the plant	50% in plant 50% out-of-plant	100% Done Outside of Plant

a)	Production Planning	0	1	2	3	4	5
b)	Master Production Scheduling:	0	1	2	3	4	5
c)	Resource Requirements Planning:	0	1	2	3	4	5
d)	Rough Cut Capacity Planning:	0	1	2	3	4	5
e)	Parts Inventory Control:	0	1	2	3	4	5
f)	Capacity Requirements Planning:	0	1	2	3	4	5
g)	Shop Floor Control:	0	1	2	3	4	5

5. If you are not using Material Requirements Planning (MRP), briefly describe the system that you are currently using:

____

____

____

____

____

6. How long have you been using the current material and priority planning system described in Questions 5: ____________ year(s)

7. What is the <u>current estimated machine utilization</u> in the plant (as observed over the past month)? ____

8. a) What is the <u>average</u> estimated machine utilization for the plant (based on your past experiences of the long term utilization)?

____

b) If you run more than one (1) shift, then indicate the number of total hours per day that the plant is <u>typically operated</u>?: ____

Shop Floor Control Survey

9. In the following question, you are asked to evaluate plant capacity. In the first part, you are asked to describe the composition of plant capacity by identifying how much of plant capacity belongs to a particular process. In the second part you are asked to describe the extent to which your parts typically flow through each type of process.

Types of Processes	% of Capacity:	% of Parts:
a) General purpose (GP) machines:	________%	________%
b) Numerical Control (NC) Machines:	________%	________%
c) Direct Numerical Control (DNC) Machines:	________%	________%
d) Computer Numerical Control (CNC) Machines:	________%	________%
e) FMS (Flexible Manufacturing Systems):	________%	________%
f) Machining & Assembly Robots:	________%	________%
g) Special Purpose Machines with Interchangeable Fixtures:	________%	________%
h) Special Purpose Machines with Dedicated (Fixed) Fixtures:	________%	________%
i) Other:	________%	________%

If other, please describe briefly:

____

____

10. What percentage of your production falls into the following categories:

Engineer to Order: _____% Make to Order: _____%
Assemble to Order: _____% Make to Stock: _____%

Shop Floor Control Survey

11. Which of the following phrases best describes the frequency with which released shop orders are modified due to engineering changes:

Check One:

Never -- No changes are allowed: ____
Rarely -- Once in a great while: ____
Sometimes: ____
Frequently: ____
Almost always: ____

12. How frequently are customer requested changes to a shop order allowed, once the order has been released for production:

Check One:

Never/Not applicable: ____
Rarely -- Once in a great while: ____
Sometimes: ____
Frequently: ____
Almost always: ____

13. Which of the following statements best describes the average size of an order for a typical finished product. If more than one phrase applies, then check the appropriate phrase(s) and indicate the percentage of orders so affected:

Each run is extremely small, consisting one or two items: ____ ____%
Each run is small in size: ____ ____%
Each run is large in size: ____ ____%
Production is continuous; once a machine is set up, we keep running the product through it: ____ ____%

14. How much run time (i.e., setup + run time) is required for the average shop order identified in Question 13?

(Please answer in hours): ________________________________

Shop Floor Control Survey

15. Which of the following statements best describes the average size of a shop order for a typical part/component. If more than one phrase applies, then check the appropriate phrases and indicate the percentage of orders so affected:

Each run is extremely small, consisting one or two items:	____	____%
Each run is small in size:	____	____%
Each run is large in size:	____	____%
Production is continuous; once a machine is set up, we keep running the product through it:	____	____%

16. How much time (i.e., setup + run time) is required for the average shop order identified in Question 15:

(Please answer in hours): ______________________________

17. What is the typical cumulative manufacturing lead time from raw material to finished product (i.e., net of purchasing lead time) for a typical finished product:

____

18. a) How many different raw materials and/or purchased parts does the current system control?

____

b) How many fabricated or assembled parts and components does the current production system control?

____

c) How many finished products or modular Bills of Material do you have? (Please identify whether finished products or modular bills)

____

19. What is the depth (i.e., number of levels) of a typical Bill of Materials in your plant?:

____

20. Sketch or provide an organizational chart of the material function for the plant. Indicate in this chart:

1) where the Shop Floor Control function is currently located;
2) to whom Shop Floor Control reports; and,
3) to whom does the material function reports:

21. a) Who in this chart is responsible for the Shop Floor Control Function (Please indicate on chart):

____

b) What is his/her title: __________________________________

c) For what other major tasks is this person responsible: __________

____

____

22. How long has the plant been working on the development and use of the current Shop Floor Control system: ____________________ (years)

23. Please choose that statement that best describes the degree to which your current Shop Floor Control system is computer driven?:

The system is completely manual: ___

The system is about 75% manual with the rest being handled by the computer: ___

The system is about 50% manual and 50% computerized: ___

The system is about 25% manual and 75% computerized: ___

The system is completely computerized: ___

24. Check that statement which best describes the development of your current Shop Floor Control system's software:

The computer software was designed completely in-house: ___

The computer software currently in use is an unmodified standard package obtained from an outside vendor/supplier. ___

The computer software was developed by taking a standard package and then extensively modifying it in-house. ___

The software is a result of taking a standard package and adding to this package in-house designed components. ___

The current system was designed specifically for the firm by an outside software developer: ___

Other (Please briefly describe): ______________________________ ___

____

Unknown: ___

Shop Floor Control Survey

25. If a standard package was used, please identify the package, source and year of installation:

____

____

26. The following are several activities which may be found in a Shop Floor Control system. Rate each activity with respect to its importance in your plant. Use the following scale in rating these activities:

1	2	3	4	5
Not done/ Not important	Little importance	Some importance	Important	Crucial

a)	Tracking of orders through the shop:	1 2 3 4 5
b)	Monitoring progress against plan:	1 2 3 4 5
c)	Order Sequencing and Dispatching:	1 2 3 4 5
d)	Short Term Capacity Management: (i.e., within the cumulative lead time)	1 2 3 4. 5
e)	Feedback of information to planning systems:	1 2 3 4 5
f)	Expediting:	1 2 3 4 5
g)	Reporting labor and/or machine efficiency:	1 2 3 4 5
h)	Scrap and rework reporting:	1 2 3 4 5
i)	Material Availability Checking:	1 2 3 4 5

Shop Floor Control Survey

27. For which of the following objectives has your Shop Floor Control system provided the greatest benefit. Use the following scale for this question:

1 -------- 2 --------- 3 --------- 4 ---------- 5

Little/No Benefit	Some Benefit	Greatest Benefit

a) Maximize equipment utilization:	1 2 3 4 5
b) Maximize worker utilization:	1 2 3 4 5
c) Ensure the on-time delivery of all orders:	1 2 3 4 5
d) Ensure flexibility of system to accommodate changes:	1 2 3 4 5
e) Reduce Work-in-process inventory:	1 2 3 4 5
h) Reduce scrap/improve output quality:	1 2 3 4 5
g) Maintain accurate set of records and standards:	1 2 3 4 5
h) Reduce and control Material Costs:	1 2 3 4 5
i) Reduce and control Labor Costs:	1 2 3 4 5

28. What is the primary method by which you prioritize orders as they pass through the various work centers:.

	Check One:
First-come-first-served:	____
Shortest Processing Time:	____
Critical Ratio Rule:	____
Least Slack:	____
Order Due-Date:	____
Operation Due-Date:	____
By similarity of setups:	____
Other:	____

If Other, please describe: ______________________________

____

Shop Floor Control Survey

29. Under <u>normal conditions</u>, how often do you update priorities:

Weekly:___ Daily: ____ At the end/start of each shift: ____
1/2 Day: ____ Hourly: ____ As Needed: ____ Never: ____

30. Who (by position) is responsible for setting and controlling priorities:

____

31. How are the shop order due-dates determined:

____

____

____

32. How is the information pertaining to shop order status and other similar attributes currently collected? (check one):

Computer Terminals: ___ Cards: ___ Pencil & Paper: ___ Voice: ___
Bar Code Readers: ___ It is not: ___ Other: ___

For Other, please describe: ______________________________

33. Under <u>normal circumstances</u>, how frequently do you collect information pertaining to the status of a shop order? (check one):

Never: ____ Upon Completion of each operation: ___
Upon Completion of order: ____ When needed: ____
Periodically: _____ If periodically, how often: ______________

Shop Floor Control Survey

34. a) How frequently do you update the status of orders which are behind schedule and require special attention?:

Weekly:___ Daily:___ At the end/start of each shift:___
1/2 Day:___ Hourly:___ As Needed:___ Never:___

b) What percentage of orders are typically behind schedule require special attention?:

_______________%

35. If an order is late then rate each of the following with respect to its frequency as a cause of the lateness. Use the following scale:

1 ----------- 2 ----------- 3 ------------ 4 ----------- 5
Never/Rarely a cause — Some of the time — Very Frequently

a)	Lack of Material:	1 2 3 4 5
b)	Tooling breakdown/unavailability:	1 2 3 4 5
c)	Lack of machine capacity:	1 2 3 4 5
d)	Lack of labor capacity:	1 2 3 4 5
e)	Engineering change:	1 2 3 4 5
f)	Quality problems:	1 2 3 4 5
g)	Schedule Revisions:	1 2 3 4 5
h)	Other:	1 2 3 4 5

If other, please describe: ____________________________________

____

36. Using the same scale as in Question 35, rate each of the following remedial actions with respect to the frequency of use in your plant:

a)	Rescheduling the order:	1 2 3 4 5
b)	Split lots:	1 2 3 4 5
c)	Overtime:	1 2 3 4 5
d)	Subcontracting:	1 2 3 4 5
e)	Substitute other materials or parts:	1 2 3 4 5
h)	Do nothing:	1 2 3 4 5
f)	Temporary labor:	1 2 3 4 5
g)	Alternative routings:	1 2 3 4 5

37 a) Do you currently have any shop personnel who are typically assigned to follow up on late shop orders or who guide the late shop orders through the various stages:

Yes: ____ No: ____ Uncertain: ____

b) If yes, how many such personnel do you have: ____________________

Shop Floor Control Survey

38. Rate the following phrases regarding the involvement of your shop floor personnel in the setting and executing of shop plans using the following scale:

1 ---------- 2 ----------- 3 ------------ 4 ---------- 5

Of little or No importance	Somewhat Important	Extremely Important

a) The shop floor personnel have to review the plans before they are released to the floor for execution: 1 2 3 4 5

b) The shop floor personnel have to be held responsible for executing the plans: 1 2 3 4 5

c) The plans given to the shop personnel must never exceed existing or demonstrated capacity: 1 2 3 4 5

d) Agreement to the plans to be carried out on the shop floor by those responsible for execution is an essential requirement: 1 2 3 4 5

e) The shop personnel must have input into the plan and the system before the plan is released to the floor: 1 2 3 4 5

39. Please rate both the current and the anticipated future impact of the following procedures to your shop floor control system. Rate using the following scale:

0 ——— 1 ———— 2 ———— 3 ———— 4 ———— 5

0	1	2	3	4	5
N/A	Little or No Impact	Limited Impact	Noticeable Impact	Important Impact	Crucial to system

Advance:	Current	Future:
Group Technology:	0 1 2 3 4 5	0 1 2 3 4 5
Computer Aided Manufacturing (CAM):	0 1 2 3 4 5	0 1 2 3 4 5
Flexible Manufacturing Systems:	0 1 2 3 4 5	0 1 2 3 4 5
Kanban/Just-in-Time:	0 1 2 3 4 5	0 1 2 3 4 5
Manufacturing Resource Planning:	0 1 2 3 4 5	0 1 2 3 4 5
Input/Output Control:	0 1 2 3 4 5	0 1 2 3 4 5
Bar Coding/Optical Scanning:	0 1 2 3 4 5	0 1 2 3 4 5
Magnetic Coding:	0 1 2 3 4 5	0 1 2 3 4 5
OPT:	0 1 2 3 4 5	0 1 2 3 4 5
Flow Management:	0 1 2 3 4 5	0 1 2 3 4 5
Preventive Maintenance:	0 1 2 3 4 5	0 1 2 3 4 5
Material Requirements Planning (MRP):	0 1 2 3 4 5	0 1 2 3 4 5

Shop Floor Control Survey

40. To what extent does your plant's Shop Floor Control system and the following systems share the same data (i.e., access a common data base). Use the following scale in answering:

1 --------------- 2 ------------- 3 ------------ 4 ----------- 5

The two systems have completely different data bases	The two systems share some but not all the same data	Both use the same data base

The Shop Floor Control System and Quality Control:	1 2 3 4 5
The Shop Floor Control System and Cost Accounting:	1 2 3 4 5
The Shop Floor Control System and Payroll:	1 2 3 4 5
The Shop Floor Control System and Maintenance:	1 2 3 4 5
The Shop Floor Control System and Engineering:	1 2 3 4 5
The Shop Floor Control System and Scrap Control:	1 2 3 4 5
The Shop Floor Control System and Purchasing:	1 2 3 4 5
The Shop Floor Control System and Marketing/Scales:	1 2 3 4 5

41 a) Do you anticipate any changes to the current system in the near future?

Yes: ___ No: ___ Unsure: ___

b) If yes, please describe the most significant of these changes in the following space.

____

____

____

____

____

____

42. Are there any features of your current Shop Floor Control System which make it unique?

____

____

____

____

____

____

Thank You for Your Time and Effort

PLEASE PUT THE COMPLETED QUESTIONNAIRE IN THE ENVELOPE
AND RETURN WITHIN TWO WEEKS.

Shop Floor Control Survey

REQUIREMENTS FOR PARTICIPATION

All the companies invited to participate in the conference are required to meet several initial conditions. These include:

1. To complete and return the shop floor control questionnaire by no later than June 21, 1983.

2. To be presented at the conference by a key manager knowledgeable with the firm's shop floor control system (either as it is used or under development).

3. To submit a written presentation describing the shop floor control system (details of the presentation format to follow) by no later than August 15.

4. To agree to publication of the written presentation in the final conference report.

LIST OF CONFERENCE PARTICIPANTS BY FIRM

The following list contains the names of all of the participating managers, grouped by firm, who attended the 1983 conference on leading edge shop floor control held at Michigan State University, August 28-31, 1983.

Aladdin Industries, Inc., Nashville, Tennessee. Ken Jorgensen, vice president of operations, steering committee member; Dick Brannan; and Ken Miner.

Bently-Nevada Ltd., Minden, Nevada. David Biggs.

Consolidated Diesel Corporation, Whitakers, North Carolina. Bob Seger and and Mary Sue Rogers.

FMC Corporation, Aiken, South Carolina. John Gremp.

General Electric Company, Erie, Pennsylvania. Michael Hicky.

Ingersoll Engineering, Rockford, Illinois. Dick Smith.

Joy Manufacturing Company, Franklin, Pennsylvania. Richard Russell and Rodney Morris.

Miles Laboratories, Consumer Products Group, Elkhart, Indiana. Jack Durben and Jim B. Satterfield.

Moog, Inc., East Aurora, New York. Richard Sherrill, David Moore, and Michael Winewicz.

Steelcase, Inc., Grand Rapids, Michigan. Jim Austhof, representing Larry Barton as steering committee member, and Ron Heys.

Twin Disc, Inc., Racine, Wisconsin. Michael Hablewitz, steering committee member, and William Williams.

The Vollrath Corporation, Sheboygan, Wisconsin. Wally Gartman.

Wright Line, Inc., Worchester, Massachusetts. Paul E. Moran.

Appendix D

GLOSSARY OF SHOP FLOOR CONTROL TERMINOLOGY [1]

Automated Identification. A broad term used to describe any information gathering procedure in which information is encoded in a form that can be transmitted and recorded using an electronic device. There are four major automated identification procedures: bar coding, optical character recognition, magnetic strips, and voice recording. See Bar Code; Optical Character Recognition; Magnetic Strips.

Automation. The technology concerned with the application of complex mechanical, electrical, electronic, and computer-based systems in the operation and control of production. This technology includes: automatic machine tools for processing parts; automatic material handling systems; automatic assembly machines; continuous-flow processes; feedback control systems; computer process control systems; computerized systems for data collection, planning, and decision making to support manufacturing activities (Groover, 1980, pp. 3-4).

Backward Scheduling. A form of scheduling which begins with the order due date and proceeds backward through the various required operations to arrive at the latest start date for the order. See Scheduling.

Bar Code. An array of rectangular bar and spaces arranged in a predetermined pattern to represent characters for machine reading.

Breakdown Maintenance. See Maintenance, Breakdown.

CAD. See Computer-Aided Design.

CAM. See Computer-Aided Manufacturing.

CAPP. See Computer-Aided Production Planning.

Capacity. The capability of a facility to process a work load in a given period of time. Typically, the work load processed is measured in terms of an aggregate unit of measurement such as standard hours.

Capacity Control. The process of measuring production output and comparing it with the level of planned output, as indicated by a formal capacity planning system such as capacity requirements planning, determining if the variance exceeds preestablished limits and taking the appropriate corrective action to get back to plan if the limits are exceeded (APICS Dictionary, 1980, p. 4). Typically the adjustments are by short-term changes in capacity. See Capacity Requirements Planning.

---

[1] From S. A. Melynk et al., Shop Floor Control. (Homewood, Ill.: Dow Jones-Irwin, 1985.)

Capacity Evaluation. A part of the order release activity in shop floor control. During capacity evaluation, the capacity required by the shop order is compared against the capacity available in the system. If the available capacity is inadequate, then the release of the order may be delayed until the required capacity becomes available. See Order Release.

Capacity Planning. See Capacity Requirements Planning.

Capacity Requirements Planning. The function of establishing, measuring, and adjusting limits or levels of capacity that are consistent with a production plan. The term capacity requirements planning in this context is the process of determining how much labor and machine resources are required to accomplish the tasks of production (APICS Dictionary, 1980, p. 4). Also referred to as CRP.

Capacity Utilization. See Utilization.

Cellular Layout. As contrasted to the functional layout, a physical rearrangement of the shop floor in which the various machines are grouped into manufacturing cells. A physical implementation of Cellular Manufacturing. See Functional Layout; Manufacturing Cells; Cellular Manufacturing.

Cellular Manufacturing. An approach to the production of parts in which each part is assigned to a specific group of machines for production. The machines assigned to the cell are restricted to the production of a limited number of parts, typically a part family. The grouping can be limited to the planning stage alone (with the assigned machines being physically located in functional work centers) or it can be physically implemented on the shop floor. Cellular manufacturing is most frequently a result of the application of Group Technology. See Group Technology; Part Family.

CIM. See Computer-Integrated Manufacturing.

Closed-Loop Material Requirements Planning. A system built around material requirements planning that includes the additional production oriented planning functions of production planning, master production scheduling, and capacity requirements planning. Once the planning phase is complete and the plans have been accepted as realistic and attainable, the execution function (and shop floor control) comes into play. The term, closed loop, implies that each of these elements is included in the overall system and that there is feedback from each lower level of the system to the higher levels in order to ensure that the plans are kept valid at all times (APICS Dictionary, 1980, p. 5). Also referred to as Closed-Loop MRP. See Material Requirements Planning.

Closed-Loop MRP. See Closed-Loop Material Requirements Planning.

Computer-Aided Design. Any design activity that involves the use of the computer in order to facilitate the creation of new engineering designs and the modification of existing designs (Groover, 1980, p. 262).

Computer-Aided Manufacturing. The effective utilization of computer in the management, control, and operation of the manufacturing facility through either direct or indirect computer interface with the physical and human resources of the firm.

Computer-Aided Production Planning. The use of a computer in the automatic generation of a process plan or route sheet for the manufacturing of a given part. The development of these plans takes advantage of standard manufacturing operation sequences that are stored in a computer. These sequences are developed as a result of the implementation of parts coding and classification system. Most frequently found in systems using group technology. Also called CAPP. See Group Technology.

Computer-Integrated Manufacturing. A manufacturing process in which the computer is used to facilitate the operation of the various functional areas and also to unify these areas. The major means by which this unification takes place is information. For example, typical of computer-integrated manufacturing is the introduction of a companywide common database.

Continuous Manufacturing. A major classification of production involving the high volume production of a nondiscrete item (e.g., petroleum) in a process characterized by a sequence of operations common to most items, short lead times, and very small queues.

Control. Within the context of shop floor control, control is part of the fourth major phase. Control involves the short-term adjustment of the shop floor capacity to compensate for any difficulties being experienced by the out-of-control order (i.e., a shop order with actual progress not sufficiently close to the planned progress). Also referred to in the context of the shop floor control framework as capacity control.

Control/Feedback. The fourth major phase of shop floor control. This phase involves those actions undertaken by management at the various levels of the firm in controlling out-of-control shop orders.

CPM. See Critical Path Management.

Critical Path Management. A network planning technique used in scheduling and controlling the various activities of a project. Critical path management shows the sequence of each activity in addition to its associated time. This enables management to determine the latest and earliest start date for each activity, the latest and earliest finish date for each activity, and the critical path for the entire project. The critical path identifies those elements that actually constrain the total time for the project. The project's minimum completion time is determined by the critical path. See Project Evaluation and Review Technique.

Critical Ratio Rule. The critical ratio rule is a priority rule that determines an order's priority by dividing the time remaining to the order due date by the expected remaining processing time. The remaining processing time may or may not include an allowance for queue time. The result is a ratio. Typically, ratios of less than 1.0 indicate orders behind schedule; ratios greater than 1.0 indicate orders ahead of schedule; and a ratio of 1.0 indicates that the order is on schedule. See Dispatching Rule.

CRP. See Capacity Requirements Planning.

CRR. See Critical Ratio Rule.

Customer Service Level. A measure of the availability of items to the customer.

Database, Manufacturing. See Manufacturing Database.

Data Collection/Monitoring. The third major phase of shop floor control. This phase consists of all the activities involving the collection of all information pertaining to the actual progress of shop orders as they move through the various stages of their routing and the comparison of this information against standards. The purpose of the comparison is to identify orders that may require intervention by the shop floor personnel.

Dependent Priority. Recognizes that the priority of an order depends on the availability, or lack of availability, or some other inventory item(s) at the time of order completion (Orlicky, 1975, pp. 146-147). Dependent priority is broken down into two categories, horizontal dependency and vertical dependency. See Horizontal Dependency and Vertical Dependency.

Detailed Assignment. The second major stage of shop floor control. Detailed assignment consists of those activities that formally match the supply of shop floor resources (labor, machines, inventory, and tools) to the demands placed on these resources. The demands come from competing orders, scheduled preventive maintenance, and scheduled downtime. The assignments are stated in terms that identify which resources are to be assigned; the quantity of resources to be assigned; the time at which the resources are to be assigned; the location from which the resources are to be drawn; and the priority in which the various competing demands are to gain access to the appropriate resources. See Maintenance, Preventive.

Discrete Batch Manufacturing. A classification of production processes that involves the production of discrete units in small batches. Each batch does not necessarily follow the same sequence of operations (as contrasted with continuous or repetitive manufacturing). Lead time tends to be relatively long due to large queues. Also referred to as job shop manufacturing.

Dispatch List. A listing of manufacturing orders in priority sequence according to the dispatching rules. The dispatch list is usually communicated to the manufacturing floor via hard copy or CRT display and contains detailed information on priority, location, quantity, and the capacity requirements of the manufacturing order by operation. Dispatch lists are normally generated daily and oriented by work center (APICS Dictionary, 1980, pp. 8-9). See Dispatching Rule.

Dispatcher. A shop floor employee responsible for determining the sequence in which orders are to be processed through the various work centers.

Dispatching. The selection and sequencing of jobs to be run at individual work centers and the authorization or assignment of work to be done (APICS Dictionary, 1980, p. 8).

Dispatching Rule. The logic or predetermined set of steps used when assigning priorities to jobs waiting at a given work center (APICS Dictionary, 1980, p. 8).

Due Date. The latest time at which an order is to complete a prespecified set of actions and be made available to the planning system for subsequent actions. The due date can be stated as either an operation or order due date. See Operation Due Date; Order Due Date.

Earliest Due Date. A dispatching rule that sequences orders waiting in a queue according to order due date. The job with the lowest order due date is given the highest priority, while the job with the highest order due date is given the lowest priority in that queue. See Dispatching Rule; Order Due Date.

Earliest Operation Due Date. A dispatching rule that sequences orders waiting in a queue according to operation due date. The job with the lowest operation due date is assigned the highest priority, while the job with the highest operation due date is given the lowest priority in that queue. See Dispatching Rule; Operation Due Date.

EDD. See Earliest Due Date.

EODD. See Earliest Operation Due Date.

Exception Reporting. A formal reporting produced by the shop floor control system that relates information concerning shop floor difficulties to the managers responsible for resolving the problems. Produced during the control/feedback phase of shop floor control. See Control/Feedback.

Expediting. All the activities that are undertaken by shop floor personnel to ensure that critically needed parts and orders are available in time to meet delivery commitments. The most significant expediting activities include: interoperation time reduction, overlapping and operation splitting, lot splitting, and temporary augmentation of shop floor capacity.

Feedback. An activity of the control/feedback stage of shop floor control. Feedback is the process of relating information regarding the progress of shop orders (with special emphasis on those considered to be out-of-control) to the planning system. The planning system may choose to evaluate alternatives to correct current problems. Frequently, the corrective actions introduced affect either the demands placed on the shop floor or the demand for the problem orders. See Control/Feedback.

FCFS. See First-Come-First-Served.

FIFO. See First-In-First Out.

Finite Loading. Putting an amount of work into a department or work center that is equal to or less than its capacity in any period.

First-Come-First-Served. A dispatching rule that sequences jobs in the same order as they arrive. See First-In-First-Out; Dispatching Rule.

First-In-First-Out. See First-Come-First-Served.

Flexible Manufacturing System. An automated job shop in which the various processing centers are linked by an automated material handling and storage system. The resulting linked production system is under central computer control. Also referred to as computerized manufacturing systems.

Forward Scheduling. A form of scheduling that begins with a known start date for the first operation and proceeds from this operation until the last required operation. The earliest completion date for the order can be determined by forward scheduling. See Scheduling.

Functional Layout. A physical arrangement of the shop floor in which the various machines are grouped together based on the similarity of the function performed. A contrast to the Cellular Layout. See Cellular Layout.

Gateway Work Center. Typically, a gateway work center is one through which most of the orders released to the shop floor must begin.

Group Technology. A systematic methodology where component similarity is used to form part families, plan common production processes, and establish manufacturing cells so that economic benefits are achieved (Levulis, 1980, p. 67).

Horizontal Dependency. A type of dependent priority. Horizontal dependency is the realization that the priority of any component order is affected by the progress of the other components needed in the parent assembly. Should one or more of these component orders not be available (due to such problems as excessive scrap or machine breakdown), then the priority of the other orders should be altered because they will not be needed on the original due date. See Dependent Priority.

Infinite Loading. Determining the amount of work that has to be performed in a work center regardless of the capacity available to perform this work. Used to determine the match with capacity demands and capacity availability. See Capacity Requirements Planning.

Input/Output Control. A technique for capacity control where actual output from a work center is compared with the planned output developed by a formal capacity planning system such as capacity requirements planning. The input is also monitored to see if it corresponds with plans (APICS Dictionary, 1980, p. 13). Input/output control enables the user to identify if the production problems being experienced at a certain work center are the result of problems in processing (capacity imbalances), in the rate of order input, or both.

Input/Output Planning. A capacity planning technique that plans input and output to a plant or department with differences between input and output affecting work-in-process inventory and lead time (Fogarty and Hoffmann, 1983, p. 681).

Interactive Scheduling. A form of scheduling in which the order of jobs released or processed is determined in an iterative fashion involving the user and the computer. Typically, the user defines an initial schedule and feeds this schedule to the computer. The computer then determines the effects of this schedule and may suggest alternatives. Based on this feedback, the user formulates and inputs another schedule. This process continues until an acceptable schedule has been identified.

Intermittent Production. See Discrete Batch Manufacturing.

Interoperation Time. The time interval between the completion of one operation and the start of the next operation. Typically, interoperation time is the sum of queue time, preparation time, postoperation time, wait time, and transport time (IBM, 1972, p. 22).

Interoperation Time Reduction. A form of expediting that concentrates on reducing the amount of time that a critical order spends in interoperation time (i.e., waiting in queues or waiting for transportation to take it to the next operation). See Expediting.

Job. See Shop Order.

Job Shop Control. Another term for Shop Floor Control. See Shop Floor Control.

Job Shop Manufacturing. See Discrete Batch Manufacturing.

Just-in-Time. A comprehensive system of production and inventory control that attempts to reduce the level of inventory within the production system to its lowest possible level by identifying and attacking all of those factors that cause such inventory to exist.

Kanban. The name given to the Japanese method of production and inventory first developed and used at Toyota of Japan. Kanban has three distinct meanings. First, it is the system of control cards (e.g., conveyance or withdrawal kanbans). Second, it is used to describe the day-to-day system of production and inventory control. Finally, it describes the entire production and inventory control system in use at Japanese firms such as Toyota (Hall, 1981). Of these three meanings, the second is the one most commonly used. That is, kanban denotes a system designed for the day-to-day on-floor control of production and inventory. In controlling these activities, kanban relies on a series of control triggers typically in the form of cards (Melnyk and Carter, 1982, p. 168). It is the predecessor of just-in-time manufacturing. See Just-in-Time.

Lead Time, Manufacturing. See Manufacturing Lead Time.

Line Balancing. Reassigning and redesigning work done on an assembly line to make the work cycle times at all stations approximately equal (Hall, 1983, p. 19).

Load. The amount of scheduled work ahead of a manufacturing facility, usually expressed in terms of hours of work or units of production.

Load Leveling. The procedure of shifting operations or order releases to smooth the demands placed on the work force and machinery capacities of the shop floor over part or all of the relevant planning horizon.

Lot Size. The quantity of a specific item that is ordered from either the plant or the vendor. Also referred to as an order quantity.

Lot Sizing. The process of determining the lot sizes. Frequently involves the use of a lot sizing technique such as lot-for-lot or the economic order quantity.

Lot Splitting. A form of expediting in which the critical order is broken up into several smaller lots. A sufficient quantity is then pushed ahead to satisfy the upcoming delivery requirements while the remainder is allowed to proceed normally (IBM, 1972, p. 34). See Expediting.

Machine Cell. Another term for manufacturing cell. See Manufacturing Cell.

Magnetic Strip. A form of automated identification. A relatively new procedure, the magnetic strip consists of magnetic stripes and characters that can be read using hand-held wands or slot readers. The major advantage of magnetic strips is that information can be encoded at much higher density than with either bar coding or optical characters. See Automatic Identification.

Maintenance, Breakdown. Emergency maintenance, including diagnosis of the problem and repair of a machine or facility after a malfunction has occurred (IBM, 1972, p. 13). A form of maintenance distinct from preventive maintenance. See Maintenance, Preventive.

Maintenance, Preventive. Maintenance work that is done regularly at intervals. Included in preventive maintenance are such operations as lubrication and inspection, and major jobs like the overhaul of a press (IBM, 1972, p. 13). It describes any maintenance that is not triggered by the breakdown of the machine or facility.

Manufacturing Activity Planning. Another term for Shop Floor Control. See Shop Floor Control.

Manufacturing Cell. The manufacturing cell consists of all the machines required for the production of a part family. The manufacturing cell, most often the result of group technology, can be found in a range of configurations. In its simplest form, the manufacturing cell can consist of only one machine. At the other end of the spectrum, a manufacturing cell can consist of a group of machines connected by a conveyor system. See Group Technology.

Manufacturing Database. A set of files (usually implemented on a computer system) that contain information of use to the manufacturing system. This set of files can be centrally located or, alternatively, it can be dispersed with each function controlling those files of direct interest to it.

Manufacturing Data Sheet. See Route Sheet.

Manufacturing Lead Time. The interval from the time that an order is released from the planning system to the execution system until the time the order is completed and sent to inventory.

Manufacturing Order. See Shop Order.

Manufacturing Resource Planning. A method for the effective planning of all the resources of a manufacturing company. Ideally, it addresses operational planning in units, financial planning in dollars, and has a simulation capability to answer what-if questions. It is made up of a variety of functions, linked together: business planning, production planning, capacity requirements planning, and the execution systems for capacity and priority. Outputs from these systems would be integrated with financial reports, such as the business plan, purchase commitment report, shipping budget, inventory projections, etc. Manufacturing resource planning is a direct outgrowth and extension of material requirements planning (APICS Dictionary, 1980, p. 16). Also referred to as MRP II.

MAP. See Shop Floor Control.

Master Production Schedule. The master production schedule is a statement of what the company expects to manufacture expressed in specific configurations, quantities, and dates. The master schedule drives a formal material and priority planning system such as material requirements planning. The master production schedule should not be confused with a sales forecast that represents a statement of demand. The master production scheduler takes forecast plus other important considerations (backlog, availability of material, availability of capacity, management policy, and goals, etc.) into account before determining the best master production schedule (Berry, Vollmann, and Whybark, 1979, p. 180). It influences the operation of the shop floor control system because it determines both the total demand for capacity and the ultimate production priorities. Also referred to as the Master Schedule.

Master Schedule. See Master Production Schedule.

Material Checking. A major activity of the order release phase of shop floor control. Material checking is the checking of the inventory status and records of those components required by a shop order to ensure that the inventory will be available in sufficient quantity at the necessary time. Material checking determines whether component inventory will hinder the progress of the order through the shop. See Order Release.

Material Requirements Planning. A system that uses bills of material, inventory, planned lead times, open order data, and master production schedule information to calculate requirements for materials. It makes recommendations to release replenishment orders for material. Because it is time phased, it makes recommendations to reschedule open orders when due dates and need dates are not in phase. Originally seen as merely a better way to order inventory, today it is thought of primarily as a scheduling technique, that is, a method for establishing and maintaining valid due dates on orders (APICS Dictionary, 1980, p. 18).

MICLASS Classification System. A parts classification and coding system frequently found in group technology implementations. The term MICLASS stands for the Metal Institute Classification System. MICLASS uses a classification number of between twelve to thirty digits, where the first twelve digits are a universal code and the other eighteen digits can be used to code data specific to the firm. Unlike other classifications systems (e.g., Opitz), MICLASS allows interactive coding of parts.

MPS. See Master Production Schedule.

MRP. See Material Requirements Planning.

MRP II. See Manufacturing Resource Planning.

MS. See Master Production Schedule.

Need Date. The date when net requirements become positive. That is, the combined coverage of on-hand inventory plus scheduled receipts for that period are not sufficient to cover the gross requirements generated by that component's parents.

Operation Due Date. The latest date by which a job is to be completed at a given work center.

Operation List. See Route Sheet.

Operation Splitting. A method of expediting orders in which the critical order is performed in parallel on two or more machines or in two or more workstations. Usually requires the assignment of more personnel to the critical order. See Expediting.

Operations Sequence. See Routing.

Opitz Classification System. A parts classification and coding system found in group technology implementations.

Optical Character Recognition. A form of automated identification. Optical character recognition uses codes that can be read by both humans and mechanical readers such as light pens or point-of-sale terminals. See Automated Identification.

Order. See Shop Order.

Order Batching. The temporary combining of orders to take advantage of commonalities in setup or components or to better use certain production capacity (e.g., combining orders at a heat treat operation because the furnace has the capacity to accommodate more than one order).

Order Completion. The process of closing out or disposing of an order. See Order Disposition.

Order Disposition. The fifth and final phase of shop floor control. This phase describes all of the activities that the shop floor control system must complete to relieve itself of responsibility for a shop order. Part of this phase is the release of those shop floor resources assigned to but no longer needed by the shop order. On the completion of order disposition, the shop order can go into either inventory or scrap.

Order Documentation. One of the activities undertaken during the order release phase of shop floor control. Order documentation provides the shop order with that information that is needed by the shop floor to ensure the successful completion of the shop order. Typically, the information assigned by order documentation includes: order identification, routings, time standards, material requirements, tooling requirements, and due dates (either operation or order). See Order Release; Order Due Date; Operation Due Date.

Order Due Date. The latest time by which a job is to be completed on the shop floor and made available to fulfill subsequent delivery commitments.

Order Overlapping. See Overlapping.

Order Release. See Order Review/Release.

Order Review/Release. The first major phase of shop floor control. The order release phase consists of those activities that must take place before an order released by the formal planning system can be allowed to enter the shop floor. The major activities of order release are: order documentation, material checking, capacity evaluation, and load leveling. See Load Leveling; Order Documentation.

Order Sequencing/Dispatching. The process of determining by a prespecified set of decision-rules the order in which a facility is to process a number of different shop orders. When processing these orders, order sequencing/dispatching is also responsible for the corresponding assignment of workers, tooling, and materials to the selected jobs. The order of resource assignment is consistent with a predetermined set of goals that the shop floor control system attempts to satisfy (e.g., meeting due dates, reducing maximum lateness of orders).

Out of Control. A term used to describe a shop order with an actual level of progress which, when compared with a standard, exceeds preestablished limits. Shop orders identified as being out of control are the objects of corrective actions taken by management.

Overlapping. A method of expediting a critical job in which the next required operation is allowed to begin before the previous operation of the entire lot has been completed (IBM, 1972, pp. 27-28). See Expediting.

PAC. See Shop Floor Control.

Part Family. A collection of parts that are similar either because of geometric shape and size or because similar processing steps are required in their manufacture. The parts within a family are different, but their similarities are great enough to merit their identification as members of the part family. (Groover, 1981, p. 539).

PERT. See Project Evaluation and Review Technique.

Preparation Time. Time during which the order is delayed before processing. Typically, preparation time is expressed as a percentage of the operation duration (i.e., setup time plus run time) (IBM, Glossary, 1972, p. 16). Preparation time is caused by some preparatory operation not in the routing, such as cleaning, heating, marking out, etc. It is a component of manufacturing lead time. See Manufacturing Lead Time.

Preventive Maintenance. See Maintenance, Preventive.

Priority. In a general sense, priority refers to the relative importance of jobs, that is, which jobs should be worked on and when (Fogarty and Hoffmann, 1983, p. 693).

Priority, Dependent. See Dependent Priority.

Priority Integrity. Ensuring that the order priorities assigned actually reflect what must (as based on the master production schedule) and can be produced (based on capacity availability) (Orlicky, 1975, p. 146).

Priority Rule. See Dispatching Rule.

Priority Validity. Maintaining the alignment between the due date and the indicated need date. In MRP, priority validity is considered a mechanical issue (Orlicky, 1975, p. 146).

Process Routing. See Routing.

Production Activity Control. See Shop Floor Control.

Project. A major category of production. A project involves the production of a unique product or service that requires the coordination of large amounts of resources that either have never before been organized into a single processor are infrequently brought together. Examples of project manufacturing include: construction of a transfer line, development of a prototype, and construction of ship. Most frequently managed by means of either PERT or CPM. See Critical Path Method; Project Evaluation and Review Technique.

Project Evaluation and Review Technique. A project planning technique similar to the critical path method, which additionally includes a range of time estimates for the completion of each activity in the network. The range of estimates typically consists of a pessimistic, most likely, and optimistic time for each activity. These estimates are then used in calculating the most likely completion time for the project along the critical path. See Critical Path Method.

Pull System. 1. As applied in the context of shop floor control, a system responsible for getting the right parts completed at the time of actual need. Examples of pull systems include expediting. 2. The production of items only as demanded for use or to replace those taken for use (Hall, 1983, p. 20).

Push System. 1. As applied in the context of shop floor control, a push system is one that launches orders onto the shop floor for completion. 2. The production of items at the time required by a given schedule planned in advance (Hall, 1983, p. 20).

Queue. A waiting line of jobs available to go through an operation (i.e., process or work center) in the shop. See Queue Time.

Queue Time. The amount of time that a job waits at a work center before it can gain control of the work center (i.e., until setup for the job has begun). In many production systems, queue time is the largest component of manufacturing lead time. See Manufacturing Lead Time.

Repetitive Manufacturing. A classification of production involving the high volume production of a discrete item that is either standard in form or made from standard options (e.g., automobiles) in a process with a sequence of operations common to most items, short lead times, and very small queues.

Rescheduling. The changing of order or operation due dates, usually as a result of their being out of phase with when they are needed (Fogarty and Hoffmann, 1983, p. 696).

Rework. That portion of a shop order that must go through additional steps in order to correct problems encountered on the shop floor. In rework, unlike salvage or scrap, the affected items of the order do not change identity.

Robot. When used in an industrial setting, a robot is a general purpose, programmable machine possessing certain anthropomorphic characteristics. It is most typically used for parts handling tasks but can also be used in conjunction with a variety of manufacturing processes. The robot can be programmed to carry out a sequence of mechanical movements. It will perform that sequence over and over again until reprogrammed (Groover, 1980, p. 247).

Robotics. The study of the application of robots in industrial settings to solve manufacturing problems.

Route Sheet. A document that specifies the operations on a part and the sequence of operations, with alternate operations and routings wherever feasible. Other processing specifications that can be included on a route sheet are the material required (kind and quantity), machine tolerances, the tools, jigs and fixtures required, and the time allowance for each operation. Also referred to as a process chart, operation list, operation sheet, operation chart, and manufacturing data sheet (APICS Dictionary, 1980, p. 24).

Routing. Also called operations sequence or process routing. A routing is a list of the steps required to complete the manufacture of a product. A routing describes what operation has to be done next, where (i.e., department and work center), by whom, and how much time is allowed for setup and run, and for total elapsed time until the next operation can start.

Safety Capacity. That portion of the total capacity of the shop, as measured in terms of tooling, work force, and machine time, that is not used or allocated to production on average. The purpose of safety capacity is to enable the shop floor control system to deal with unexpected changes either in the level of demand (e.g., increases in demand) or capacity (e.g., decreases resulting from such factors as worker illness).

Salvage. That portion of a shop order that can no longer be completed in that form specified when the order was released. That is, a portion of the order has experienced some difficulties during processing. These difficulties affect the final form taken by those parts. The affected portion can be processed into finished items of a different form. These completed items can be subsequently used by the production system. An example of salvage is a blemished 60-inch bolt of cloth that can be recut into an unblemished 48-inch bolt of cloth.

Scheduling. 1. The sequencing or dispatching activity plus the determination of the lot size and the allocation of resources to complete the job. 2. The process of setting operation start dates and completion dates (i.e., due dates) for each job released to the shop floor. The purpose of assigning these dates is to indicate the operating constraints within which the order must operate if it is to be completed by its order due date. Scheduling can take the form of either forward scheduling or backward scheduling. See Forward Scheduling; Backward Scheduling.

Scheduling, Backward. See Backward Scheduling.

Scheduling, Forward. See Forward Scheduling.

Scheduling, Interactive. See Interactive Scheduling.

Scrap. Any portion of a shop order that is no longer usable by the manufacturing system.

Sequencing. Determining the order in which a manufacturing facility (e.g., work center) is to process a number of different jobs in order to achieve certain objectives (APICS Dictionary, 1980, p. 25).

Setup Time. The time required to prepare a machine or facility so that an order can be processed. Setup time is one of the major components of manufacturing lead time. The setup time can be either a standard or an actual. In the case of a standard, setup time is the allowance provided in which the machine or facility is to be set up. In the actual setup times, this is the time actually consumed by the machine setup. In contrast to the standard setup time, the actual setup time is only known after the completion of the setup.

Shop Floor Control. A major subsystem within the manufacturing system. Shop floor control is that group of activities directly responsible for managing the transformation of planned orders (i.e., orders released to the shop floor by the planning system) into a set of outputs that conform to some set of prespecified evaluation criteria. Shop floor control governs the very short term detailed planning, execution, and monitoring activities needed to control the flow of an order from the moment that it is released until the order is filled and its disposition completed. The shop floor control system is responsible for making the detailed and final allocation of labor, machine capacity, tooling, and materials to the various competing orders. It collects data on the activities taking place on the shop floor involving the progress of various orders and the status of resources and makes this information available to the planning system. Shop floor control consists of five major sets of activities: order release, detailed assignment, data collection/monitoring, control/feedback, and order disposition. Also referred to as manufacturing activity planning (MAP), production activity control (PAC), and job shop control. See Order Release; Detailed Assignment; Data Collection/Monitoring; Control/Feedback; Order Disposition.

Shop Floor Resources. Those resources that the shop floor control uses to manage the transformation of a shop order or job from the point that it is released to the shop floor by the formal planning system until it is completed or can no longer be processed. Typically, there are four major types of shop floor resources: inventory, tooling, work force, and machinery capacity.

Shop Load. See Load.

Shop Loading. The process of scheduling work into a manufacturing facility. See Load.

Shop Order. The entity that is controlled by the shop floor control system as it moves through the various stages on the shop. Typically a shop order is an authorization issued by the planning system to the execution system for the manufacture of a certain quantity of a certain part to be available by no later than the due date. Also called a job, manufacturing order, or order.

Shop Packet. A set of paperwork that travels with the order and may include routings, blueprints, material requisitions, move tickets, time tickets, etc. See Traveler.

Shortest Operation Time. See Shortest Processing Time.

Shortest Processing Time. A dispatching rule that sequences orders at a work center according to their processing times (setup plus total variable processing time) in that work center. Orders with the shortest processing times have the highest priorities. See Dispatching Rule.

SIT. Shortest imminent (processing) time. See Shortest Processing Time.

Slack. The difference in time between the order due date and the time at which the order is expected to be completed. Frequently, slack is used as a measure of the degree of urgency associated with an order. It is also used by many due-date-based dispatching rules such as critical ratio rule and the least slack per remaining operations.

Slack Per Remaining Operation. A dispatching rule that lets the priority of a job be equal to its slack (due date minus time now = remaining processing time) divided by the number of remaining operations. See Dispatching Rule; Slack.

SOT. Shortest operation time. See Shortest Processing Time.

SPT. See Shortest Processing Time.

Staging. The physical withdrawal and assembly (kitting) of the component material to ensure its availability. Frequently done before the release of the shop order at the time that material is checked. The purpose of staging is to identify any material shortages before the order is released.

Standard Processing Time. See Standard Time.

Standard Setup Time. See Standard Time.

Standard Time. 1. The time that should be needed to set up a given machine or assembly operation (also referred to as standard setup time). 2. The time that should be required to run one part/assembly/end product through that operation (also referred to as standard processing time). (Fogarty and Hoffmann, 1983, p. 701).

Stockless Production. See Just-in-Time.

Tooling. Equipment and special fixtures such as dies that are used during the setup of a machine or assembly operation. One of the four major shop resources (the others being labor, machine capacity, and inventory). See Tools.

Tooling Requirements. A determination of the tooling required to complete the setup on a machine or process.

Tools. Items (wrenches, for example) used during a setup procedure but which are not attached to the machine during setup or considered part of the machine (Hall, 1983, p. 21).

Transport Time. The time required to transport parts between two work centers. Frequently transport time can be found in the form of a table (matrix). Transport time is a component of manufacturing lead time (IBM, Glossary, 1972, p. 22). It can refer to either a standard value (used in the move time standards) or an actual value.

Traveler. A copy of the manufacturing order that actually moves with the work through the shop. See Shop Packet.

Validity. See Priority Validity.

Vertical Dependency. A type of dependent priority. Vertical dependency is the realization that the priority of a component order is directly dependent on the availability of an item or items on a higher level in the product structure (Orlicky, 1975, p. 174). See Dependent Priority.

Voice Recognition. A form of automated identification by which the employee directly inputs information into the computer by voice. See Automated Identification.

Wait Time. The time spent by orders on the shop floor waiting for transportation. A component of manufacturing lead time, wait time can refer to either a standard value (i.e., a predetermined time allowance) or an actual value (i.e., the recorded time that the order actually spends waiting for transportation).

WIP. See Work in Process.

Work Center. A production facility consisting of one or more people and/or machines that can be considered as one unit for the purposes of capacity requirements planning and detailed assignment (Fogarty and Hoffmann, 1983, p. 705). See Capacity Requirements Planning; Detailed Assignment.

Work in Process. Items in various stages of completion throughout the plant including raw material that has been released and finished material awaiting final inspection or shipment to a customer (Fogarty and Hoffmann, 1983, p. 705). Included in work-in-process inventories are: raw material in stock, semifinished component parts in stock, finished component parts in stock, subassemblies in stock, component parts in process, and subassemblies in process (Orlicky, 1975, p. 17).

Utilization. The percentage of time a machine, work center, line, or facility is not down due to equipment failure, lack of material, lack of work, or lack of an operator (Fogarty and Hoffmann, 1983, p. 704).

Zero Inventory. See Just-in-Time.